INTRODUCTION TO MANAGEMENT ACCOUNTING

Charles T. Horngren Series in Accounting
Charles T. Horngren, Consulting Editor

Auditing: An Integrated Approach, 7/E
Arens/Loebbecke

Financial Statement Analysis, 2/E
Foster

Government and Nonprofit Accounting: Theory & Practice, 6/E
Freeman/Shoulders

Financial Accounting, 3/E
Harrison/Horngren

Cases in Financial Reporting, 2/E
Hirst/McAnally

Cost Accounting: A Managerial Emphasis, 9/E
Horngren/Foster/Datar

Accounting, 4/E
Horngren/Harrison/Bamber

Introduction to Financial Accounting, 7/E
Horngren/Sundem/Elliott

Introduction to Management Accounting, 11/E
Horngren/Sundem/Stratton

INTRODUCTION TO MANAGEMENT ACCOUNTING

Eleventh Edition

CHAPTERS 1-15

CHARLES T. HORNGREN
Stanford University

GARY L. SUNDEM
University of Washington—Seattle

WILLIAM O. STRATTON
University of Southern Colorado

 PRENTICE HALL, *Upper Saddle River, New Jersey 07458*

Executive Editor: Deborah Hoffman Emry
Development Editor: David Cohen
Editorial Assistant: Jane Avery
Assistant Editor: Natacha St. Hill Moore
Editor-in-Chief: P.J. Boardman
Executive Marketing Manager: Beth Toland
Production Editor: Marc Oliver
Project Manager: Susan Rifkin
Managing Editor: Bruce Kaplan
Manufacturing Supervisor: Paul Smolenski
Manufacturing Manager: Vincent Scelta
Designer: Jill Little
Design Manager: Patricia Smythe
Photo Research Supervisor: Melinda Lee Reo
Image Permission Supervisor: Kay Dellosa
Photo Researcher: Teri Stratford
Cover Design: Lorraine Castellano
Cover Photo: UNIPHOTO Stock Photography, Washington, D.C.
Composition: Carlisle Communications, Ltd.

Credits and acknowledgments for materials borrowed from other sources and reproduced, with permission, in this textbook appear on page xix.

 Copyright ©1999, 1996, 1993, 1990, 1987 by Prentice-Hall, Inc.
A Simon & Schuster Company
Upper Saddle River, New Jersey 07458

All rights reserved. No part of this book may be reproduced, in any form or by any means, without written permission from the Publisher.

ISBN 0-13-986654-X

Prentice-Hall International (UK) Limited, *London*
Prentice-Hall of Australia Pty. Limited, *Sydney*
Prentice-Hall Canada, Inc., *Toronto*
Prentice-Hall Hispanoamericana, S.A., *Mexico*
Prentice-Hall of India Private Limited, *New Delhi*
Prentice-Hall of Japan, Inc., *Tokyo*
Simon & Schuster Asia Pte. Ltd., *Singapore*
Editora Prentice-Hall do Brasil, Ltda., *Rio de Janeiro*

Printed in the United States of America

10 9 8 7 6 5 4 3

To Joan, Chelsea, Erik, Marissa,
Liz, Garth, Jens,
Norma, Gina, Adam, and Nisha

Charles T. Horngren   (center) is the Edmund W. Littlefield Professor of Accounting, Emeritus, at Stanford University. A graduate of Marquette University, he received his MBA from Harvard University and his Ph.D. from the University of Chicago. He is also the recipient of honorary doctorates from Marquette University and DePaul University.

A Certified Public Accountant, Horngren served on the Accounting Principles Board for six years, the Financial Accounting Standards Board Advisory Council for five years, and the Council of the American Institute of Certified Public Accountants for three years. For six years, he served as a trustee of the Financial Accounting Foundation, which oversees the Financial Accounting Standards Board and the Government Accounting Standards Board.

Horngren is a member of the Accounting Hall of Fame.

A member of the American Accounting Association, Horngren has been its President and its Director of Research. He received its first annual Outstanding Accounting Educator Award.

The California Certified Public Accountants Foundation gave Horngren its Faculty Excellence Award and its Distinguished Professor Award. He is the first person to have received both awards.

The American Institute of Certified Public Accountants presented its first Outstanding Educator Award to Horngren.

Horngren was named Accountant of the Year, Education, by the national professional accounting fraternity, Beta Alpha Psi.

Professor Horngren is also a member of the Institute of Management Accountants, where he has received its Distinguished Service Award. He was a member of the Institute's Board of Regents, which administers the Certified Management Accountant examinations.

Horngren is the author of other accounting books published by Prentice-Hall: *Cost Accounting: A Managerial Emphasis*, Ninth Edition, 1997 (with George Foster and Srikant Datar); *Introduction to Financial Accounting*, Seventh Edition, 1999 (with Gary L. Sundem and John A. Elliott); *Accounting*, Fourth Edition, 1999 (with Walter T. Harrison, Jr., and Linda Bamber); and *Financial Accounting,* Third Edition, 1999 (with Walter T. Harrison, Jr.).

Horngren is the Consulting Editor for the Charles T. Horngren Series in Accounting.

Gary L. Sundem   (left) is the Julius A. Roller Professor of Accounting and Co-Chair of the Department of Accounting at the University of Washington, Seattle. He received his B.A. degree from Carleton College and his MBA and Ph.D. degrees from Stanford University.

Professor Sundem was the 1992-93 President of the American Accounting Association. He was Executive Director of the Accounting Education Change Commission, 1989-91, and served as Editor of *The Accounting Review*, 1982-86.

A member of the Institute of Management Accountants, Sundem is past president of the Seattle chapter. He has served on IMA's national Board of Directors, the Committee on Academic Relations, and the Research Committee.

Professor Sundem has numerous publications in accounting and finance journals including *Issues in Accounting Education, The Accounting Review, Journal of Accounting Research*, and *The Journal of Finance*. He was selected as the Outstanding Accounting Educator by the American Accounting Association in 1998 and by the Washington Society of CPAs in 1987. He has made more than 150 presentations at universities in the United States and abroad.

William O. Stratton   (right) is Professor of Accounting at the University of Southern Colorado. He received B.S. degrees from Florida State University and Pennsylvania State University, his MBA from Boston University, and his Ph.D. from the Claremont Graduate School.

A Certified Management Accountant, Stratton has lectured extensively at management accounting conferences in North America and Europe. He has developed and delivered professional workshops on activity-based management and performance achievement to manufacturing and service organizations throughout the United States and South America. In 1993, Professor Stratton was awarded the Boeing Competition prize for classroom innovation.

Stratton has numerous publications in accounting and international business journals including *Management Accounting, Decision Sciences, IIE Transactions*, and *Synergie*.

BRIEF CONTENTS

Preface xxiii

FOCUS ON DECISION MAKING
PART ONE

1 Managerial Accounting and the Business Organization   2
2 Introduction to Cost Behavior and Cost-Volume Relationships   38
3 Measurement of Cost Behavior   80
4 Cost Management Systems and Activity-Based Costing   122
5 Relevant Information and Decision Making: Marketing Decisions   164
6 Relevant Information and Decision Making: Production Decisions   212

ACCOUNTING FOR PLANNING AND CONTROL
PART TWO

7 The Master Budget   248
8 Flexible Budgets and Variance Analysis   286
9 Management Control Systems and Responsibility Accounting   326
10 Management Control in Decentralized Organizations   364

CAPITAL BUDGETING
PART THREE

11 Capital Budgeting   404

PRODUCT COSTING
PART FOUR

12 Cost Allocation and Activity-Based Costing   452
13 Job-Costing Systems   498

14   Process-Costing Systems   534

15   Overhead Application: Variable and Absorption Costing   568

APPENDIX A   A1

APPENDIX B   A6

GLOSSARY   G1

INDEX   I1

CONTENTS

Preface xxiii

PART ONE   FOCUS ON DECISION MAKING

1   Managerial Accounting and the Business
     Organization   2
     Chapter Opener: The Marmon Group, Inc.   3
     Accounting and Decision Making   4
     Management Accounting in Service and Nonprofit
       Organizations   8
     Cost-Benefit and Behavioral Considerations   9
     The Management Process and Accounting   9
     Planning and Control for Product Life Cycles and the
       Value Chain   12
     Accounting's Position in the Organization   16
     Career Opportunities in Managerial Accounting   20
     Adaptation to Change   21
     Importance of Ethical Conduct   23
     Ethics at General Motors   25
     Highlights to Remember   26
     Accounting Vocabulary   27
     Fundamental Assignment Material   28
     Additional Assignment Material   30
     Business First   34
     Collaborative Learning Exercise   36

2   Introduction to Cost Behavior and Cost-Volume
        Relationships   38
    Chapter Opener: Boeing Company   39
    Activities, Costs, and Cost Drivers   40
    Comparison of Variable and Fixed Costs   41
    Cost-Volume-Profit Analysis   44
    Break-Even in the Auto Industry   46
    Additional Uses of Cost-Volume Analysis   54
    Lowering the Break-Even Point   56
    Nonprofit Application   56
    Highlights to Remember   58
    Appendix 2A: Sales-Mix Analysis   59
    Appendix 2B: Impact of Income Taxes   60
    Accounting Vocabulary   61
    Fundamental Assignment Material   62
    Additional Assignment Material   64
    Business First   73
    Collaborative Learning Exercise   78

3   Measurement of Cost Behavior   80
    Chapter Opener: America West   81
    Cost Drivers and Cost Behavior   82
    Management Influence on Cost Behavior   85
    Cost Functions   87
    Activity Analysis at Hughes Aircraft Company   90
    Methods of Measuring Cost Functions   91
    Highlights to Remember   100
    Measuring Cost Behavior at Hewlett-Packard   100
    Appendix 3: Use and Interpretation of Least-Squared
        Regression   101
    Accounting Vocabulary   105
    Fundamental Assignment Material   105
    Additional Assignment Material   107
    Business First   113
    Collaborative Learning Exercise   120

4   Cost Management Systems and Activity-Based
    Costing   122

Chapter Opener: AT&T   123
Classifications of Costs   125
Cost Accounting for Financial Reporting   128
Cost Behavior and Income Statements   132
Activity-Based Costing   136
Contribution Approach and Activity-Based Costing   137
Illustration of Activity-Based Costing   137
Cost-Management Systems   144
Identifying Activities, Resources, and Cost Drivers in the
    Health Care Industry   145
Highlights to Remember   147
Accounting Vocabulary   148
Fundamental Assignment Material   148
Additional Assignment Material   151
Business First   162
Collaborative Learning Exercise   162

5   Relevant Information and Decision Making:
    Marketing Decisions   164

Chapter Opener: The Grand Canyon Railway   165
The Concept of Relevance   166
The Special Sales Order   169
Deletion or Addition of Products, Services, or
    Departments   173
Optimal Use of Limited Resources   176
Pricing Decisions   177
General Influences on Pricing in Practice   180
Role of Costs in Pricing Decisions   181
Target Costing   186
Target Costing, ABC, and Service Companies   189
Highlights to Remember   191
Accounting Vocabulary   192
Fundamental Assignment Material   192
Additional Assignment Material   196
Business First   203
Collaborative Learning Exercise   211

6   Relevant Information and Decision Making:
        Production Decisions   212
    Chapter Opener: Starbucks Coffee Company   213
    Opportunity, Outlay, and Differential Costs   214
    Make-or-Buy Decisions   216
    Joint Product Costs   218
    An Example of Make-or-Buy: Outsourcing   218
    Irrelevance of Past Costs   220
    Sunk Costs and Government Contracts   223
    Irrelevance of Future Costs That Will Not Differ   223
    Beware of Unit Costs   224
    Conflicts Between Decision Making and Performance
        Evaluation   224
    Highlights to Remember   228
    Accounting Vocabulary   228
    Fundamental Assignment Material   229
    Additional Assignment Material   232
    Business First   244
    Collaborative Learning Exercise   246

PART TWO   ACCOUNTING FOR PLANNING AND CONTROL

7   The Master Budget   248
    Chapter Opener: Ritz-Carlton   249
    Budgets and the Organization   250
    Preparing the Master Budget   254
    Photon Sees the Light   255
    The Budgeting Process at Daihatsu   261
    Difficulties of Sales Forecasting   262
    Getting Employees to Accept the Budget   263
    Financial Planning Models   264
    Activity-Based Budgeting   264
    Highlights to Remember   268
    Appendix 7: Use of Spreadsheets for Budgeting   269
    Accounting Vocabulary   272
    Fundamental Assignment Material   272

Additional Assignment Material   274
Business First   279
Collaborative Learning Exercise 285

8   Flexible Budgets and Variance Analysis   286
    Chapter Opener: McDonalds   287
    Flexible Budgets: Bridge Between Static Budgets and
        Actual Results   288
    Isolating the Causes of Variances   293
    Caterpillar Tracks Multiple Cost Systems Through Master
        Budget   296
    Flexible-Budget Variances in Detail   299
    Overhead Variances   303
    General Approach   303
    Highlights to Remember   305
    Accounting Vocabulary   308
    Fundamental Assignment Material   308
    Additional Assignment Material   311
    Business First   315
    Collaborative Learning Exercise   323

9   Management Control Systems and Responsibility
        Accounting   326
    Chapter Opener: Foundation Health Systems, Inc.   327
    Management Control Systems   328
    Designing Management Control Systems   330
    Controllability and Measurement of Financial
        Performance   336
    Nonfinancial Measures of Performance   339
    Poor Quality Nearly Short-Circuits Electronics
        Company   340
    Measuring the Cost of Quality   343
    Nissan Captures Top Productivity Rating 4 Years
        Running   345
    Management Control Systems, Service, Government, and
        Nonprofit Organizations   346
    Future of Management Control Systems   347
    Highlights to Remember   348
    Accounting Vocabulary   350
    Fundamental Assignment Material   350

Additional Assignment Material   354
Business First   356
Collaborative Learning Exercise   362

10   Management Control in Decentralized
        Organizations   364
      Chapter Opener: Nike   365
      Centralization Versus Decentralization   366
      Decentralization in the 1990's   367
      Transfer Pricing   368
      Activity-Based Costing and Transfer Pricing   370
      Performance Measures and Management Control   375
      Measures and Profitability   378
      A Closer Look at Invested Capital   382
      Keys to Successful Management Control Systems   385
      Highlights to Remember   386
      Accounting Vocabulary   388
      Fundamental Assignment Material   388
      Additional Assignment Material   392
      Business First   399
      Collaborative Learning Exercise   402

PART THREE   CAPITAL BUDGETING

11   Capital Budgeting   404
      Chapter Opener: Deer Valley Lodge   405
      Capital Budgeting for Programs or Projects   406
      Discounted-Cash-Flow Models   406
      Sensitivity Analysis and Risk Assessment
         in DCF Models   410
      The NPV Comparison of Two Projects   411
      Income Taxes and Capital Budgeting   415
      Confusion About Depreciation   423
      Capital Budgeting and Inflation   423
      Other Models for Analyzing Long-Range Decisions   426
      Performance Evaluation   428
      Highlights to Remember   429
      Accounting Vocabulary   430
      Fundamental Assignment Material   430

Additional Assignment Material   434
Business First   445
Collaborative Learning Exercises   449
Solutions to Exercise in Compound Interest,
Problem 11-A1   450

PART FOUR PRODUCT COSTING

12   Cost Allocation and Activity-Based Costing   452

Chapter Opener: Dell Computer Corporation   453
Cost Allocation in General   454
Allocation of Service Department Costs   456
Allocation of Costs to Final Cost Objects   463
Activity-Based Costing   464
Activity-Based Costing at Hewlett-Packard   473
Allocation of Joint Costs and By-Product Costs   474
Highlights to Remember   478
Accounting Vocabulary   479
Fundamental Assignment Material   479
Additional Assignment Material   483
Business First   490
Collaborative Learning Exercise   496

13   Job-Costing Systems   498

Chapter Opener: Dell Computer Corporation   499
Distinction Between Job Costing and Process Costing   500
Illustration of Job Costing   501
Accounting for Factory Overhead   504
Illustration of Overhead Application   505
Simplifying Product Costing at Harley-Davidson   506
Problems of Overhead Application   508
Activity-Based Costing/Management in a Job-Costing
   Environment   511

Product Costing in Service and Nonprofit
  Organizations   513
Highlights to Remember   516
Accounting Vocabulary   517
Fundamental Assignment Material   517
Additional Assignment Material   520
Business First   525
Collaborative Learning Exercise   533

14   Process-Costing Systems   534
Chapter Opener: Nally and Gibson Georgetown, Inc.   535
Process Costing Basics   536
Application of Process Costing   539
Physical Units and Equivalent Units (Steps 1 and 2)   540
Calculation of Product Costs (Steps 3 to 5)   541
Effects of Beginning Inventories   543
Weighted-Average Method   544
First-In, First-Out Method   544
Process Costing in a JIT System: Backflush Costing   549
Highlights to Remember   552
Appendix 14: Hybrid Systems-Operation Costing   553
Accounting Vocabulary   555
Fundamental Assignment Material   555
Additional Assignment Material   558
Business First   562
Collaborative Learning Exercise   566

15   Overhead Application: Variable and Absorption
      Costing   568
Chapter Opener: L.A. Darling Store Fixtures   569
Variable Versus Absorption Costing   570
Variable Costing at Northern Telecom   575
Fixed Overhead and Absorption Costs of Product   575
Effect of Other Variances   582
Highlights to Remember   586

Appendix 15: Comparisons of Production-Volume
    Variance with Other Variances   587
Accounting Vocabulary   589
Fundamental Assignment Material   589
Additional Assignment Material   591
Business First   598
Collaborative Learning Exercises   606

APPENDIX A   A1
APPENDIX B   A6
GLOSSARY   G1
INDEX   I1

PHOTO CREDITS

Chapter 1.   Page 2—Jim Smith photo, Courtesy Marmon Group, Inc.; Steel pipe photo, Courtesy Marmon/Keystone Corporation.; Union Tank Car photo, Courtesy Union Tank Car Company; Appliance store photo, Courtesy Marmon Group, Inc.; Sterling Crane photo, Courtesy Merle Prosofsky Photography, Ltd.

Chapter 2.   Page 38—Boeing photo, Courtesy Boeing Commercial Airplane Group.

Chapter 3.   Page 80—America West photo, Courtesy Rick Rickman/Matrix International.

Chapter 4.   Page 122—AT&T photo, Property of AT&T Archives. Reprinted with permission of AT&T.

Chapter 5.   Page 164—Grand Canyon Railway photo, Courtesy Peggy Pavlich/Grand Canyon Railway.

Chapter 6.   Page 212—Starbucks photo, Courtesy Mark Richards/PhotoEdit.

Chapter 7.   Page 248—Ritz-Carlton photo, Courtesy The Ritz-Carlton.

Chapter 8.   Page 286—McDonald's photo, Courtesy Terry Vine/Tony Stone Images.

Chapter 9.   Page 326—Doctor-girl photo, Courtesy QualMed Health Care.

Chapter 10.   Page 364—Niketown photo, Courtesy Ullmann/Monkmeyer Press.

Chapter 11.   Page 404—Skier photo, Courtesy Deer Valley Resort.

Chapter 12.   Page 452—Kevin Rollins photo, Courtesy Mark Phillips/Dell Computers/AP/Wide World Photos.

Chapter 13.   Page 498—Dell workers photo, Courtesy Bob Daemmrich Photo, Inc.

Chapter 14.   Page 534—Nally & Gibson mine photo, Courtesy Gordon Morioka/Simon & Schuster/PH College.

Chapter 15.   Page 568—Best Buy store photo, Courtesy Spencer Grant/PhotoEdit.

PREFACE

"Managers have to understand how their decisions affect costs if they want to make good decisions."

Introduction to Management Accounting, 11/E, takes the view that managers make important economic decisions. We want students to view management accounting as an essential tool that enhances managers' abilities to make good economic decisions. *IMA,* 11/E, describes the concepts and techniques that managers and accountants use to produce information for decision making. Because understanding concepts is more important than memorizing techniques, this book introduces the concepts together with the techniques. From the first chapter, students are encouraged to think about why techniques are used, not to blindly apply the techniques. We hope that students will thus be able to learn both the *theory* and *practice* of management accounting. Understanding today's accounting practice, though, goes beyond mere concepts and techniques. To illustrate real-world practice and to highlight how management accounting helps managers understand the potential impacts of their decisions, the concepts and techniques in this book are presented in the context of real decisions. Two of the authors were members of the Accounting Education Change Commission (AECC) and recommendations of the AECC have been implemented throughout the text.

This book attempts a balanced, flexible approach. It deals as much with nonprofit, retail, wholesale, selling, and administrative situations as it does with manufacturing. It focuses broadly on planning and control decisions, not on product costing for inventory valuation and income determination.

OUR PHILOSOPHY

Introduce the simple concepts and principles early, revisit them at more complex levels as students gain understanding, and provide appropriate real-company examples at every stage.

Just as managerial accounting builds on financial accounting, the concepts within managerial accounting build on one another as they are used to facilitate managerial decision making. Once students have fully grasped the more basic concepts, they can then build on what they have learned and progress on to more complex topics. Students begin their understanding of managerial decision making by asking, "How will my decisions affect the costs and revenues of the organization?" and then progress to more complex questions: What is the most appropriate cost management system for the company? What products should we produce? What do our budget variances mean? As students absorb the simpler concepts and techniques of management accounting and move on to the more complex, they will become more comfortable with, and more adept at, using those concepts and techniques to make business decisions.

Our goals have been to choose relevant subject matter and to present it clearly and accessibly, using many examples drawn from actual companies. *IMA*, 11/E, stresses the understanding of concepts, yet makes them concrete with profuse illustrations.

WHO SHOULD USE THIS BOOK?

Introduction to Management Accounting, 11/E, is primarily for students who have had one or two terms of basic accounting. It is also appropriate for continuing educational programs of varying lengths in which the students have had no formal training in accounting. The four financial accounting chapters (Chapters 16-19) make the book especially appropriate for short courses introducing managers to accounting because both financial and management accounting can be presented from a user's perspective without requiring two textbooks.

This text is oriented to managers who use management accounting reports, not accountants. Managers should understand the basics of management accounting, and this book shows how management accounting will be useful to them. However, *IMA*, 11/E, also pays ample attention to the needs of potential accountants and provides them with an understanding of how the reports they produce will be used by decision makers. In focusing on accounting within the context of the overall managerial function, this text covers important topics that all business students should study and demonstrates how accounting bolsters and fits into the broader scheme of today's business environment.

IMPORTANT CHANGES TO THIS EDITION

- **Two Versions of This Text Now Available.** *Introduction to Management Accounting,* 11/E, is available with chapters 16-19, which provide a financial accounting introduction or review, or without the financial chapters for those instructors wanting only coverage of the core management accounting chapters.
- **Expansion of Modern Management Accounting Topics** Management accounting is changing to meet the needs of today's dynamic business environment. This textbook is also changing to recognize new concepts and techniques. Topics that have been added or expanded in this edition include activity-based management, value-chain analysis, target costing, balanced scorecard, and economic value added.
- **"Business First" Focus Provides Stronger Link to Real World Practice** Understanding business and then applying accounting within a decision-making context continues to be *IMA*'s unifying framework. Each chapter opens with a real company vignette showing "what accounting is" in today's business world. "On Location!" video segments, custom created for this text, reinforce and expand upon each vignette. *IMA*, 11/E, stresses accounting's relevance to business operations by presenting business concepts first, so accounting can be taught within this context. Each chapter includes a comprehensive "capstone" learning objective that links major chapter topics. "Business First" assignments in every chapter revisit the company used in the chapter opening vignette. The PHLIP Web site provides hotlinks to each company's Web site.

- **Take It to the Web!** A huge assortment of financial information is available on the Web—a resource *IMA*, 11/E, utilizes. The PHLIP (Prentice Hall Learning on the Internet Partnership) Web site guides students through many sites and links that make accounting realistic and accessible. The PHLIP Web site also contains links to many of the other companies featured as text examples. For instructors, we provide a passcode protected resource area where instructors can download key supplements.

- **Collaborative Learning Exercises** For those instructors trying to facilitate group learning, each chapter now includes a collaborative learning exercise. Each of these exercises has been specifically designed to promote classroom and student interaction through research, role playing, and other popular learning techniques.

- **Enhanced Accessibility** Students learn best if a text appeals to them. Accordingly, *IMA*, 11/e, has adopted a more open, attractive four-color design. Also, the text's art and photo programs have been improved and expanded, and, perhaps most importantly, the writing style of the text has been simplified and tightened to provide a more student-friendly presentation.

RETAINED FEATURES

- **Introduction to Management Accounting,** 11/E, is part of a matched set of texts that enables any instructor to teach a full year of financial and management accounting. You can pair this text with *Introduction to Financial Accounting,* 7/E, also available in a new edition, by Horngren, Sundem, and Elliott. Both texts share authors, chapter organization, pedagogy, commitment to emphasizing accounting's importance in business decisions, and depth and breadth of available problem material. The newest editions of each text have been designed to work together as seamlessly as possible.

- Boxed material, highlighting real-world issues, has been expanded and revised.

- As in every edition, *Introduction to Management Accounting,* 11/E, continues to offer the best problem sets available—both in quality and quantity. Problem material in this edition has been updated and expanded and relies extensively on actual business situations.

SUPPLEMENTS FOR INSTRUCTORS

INSTRUCTOR'S RESOURCE MANUAL BY SCOTT YETMAR, DRAKE UNIVERSITY. This supplement contains the following elements: chapter overview, chapter outlines organized by objectives, teaching tips, chapter quizzes, transparency masters derived from textbook exhibits, suggested readings and a Video Guide that carefully integrates the videos into classroom lectures. Also included are Collaborative Learning Techniques based on selected end-of-chapter assignments.

SOLUTIONS MANUAL AND TRANSPARENCIES BY TEXT AUTHORS. Solutions are provided for all the end-of-chapter assignments. The Solutions Manual is also available in acetate form and on disk to adopters. A list of check figures provides key amounts for all numerical exercises, problems, and cases.

TEST ITEM FILE BY MARVIN BOUILLON, IOWA STATE UNIVERSITY. The Test Item File contains more than 2200 test items. Each chapter includes multiple choice, true/false, comprehensive problems, short-answer problems, and critical thinking questions. Each test item is tied to the corresponding learning objective and has an assigned difficulty level.

PRENTICE HALL CUSTOM TEST, BY ENGINEERING SOFTWARE ASSOCIATES (ESA), INC. This computerized Test Item File is an easy-to-use computerized testing program available on 3.5″ diskettes. Instructors can create exams, evaluate, and track student results. The PH Custom Test also provides on-line testing capabilities. Test material is drawn from the Test Item File.

ON LOCATION! VIDEO LIBRARY BY BEVERLY AMER, NORTHERN ARIZONA UNIVERSITY. Video segments created for this book contain all the fast-paced and engaging qualities of TV while focusing on the successful accounting activities of the real-world companies highlighted in each chapter's opening vignettes. A Video Guide in the Instructor's Resource Manual carefully integrates the videos into your classroom lectures.

PH PROFESSOR: A CLASSROOM PRESENTATION ON POWERPOINT BY CARROLL BUCK, UNIVERSITY OF NEVADA, RENO. Available for each chapter of the text, this computerized supplement provides the instructor with an interactive presentation. It is not necessary to have PowerPoint in order to run the presentation. However, having PowerPoint will provide instructors with the flexibility to add slides or modify existing ones to meet course needs.

POWER NOTES BY CARROLL BUCK, UNIVERSITY OF NEVADA, RENO. Power Notes are reproductions of PowerPoint slides with additional space for taking notes. Power Notes allow students to focus their attention on class lectures and take down additional explanations and examples given by the instructor. This efficient note-taking supplement is also a great tool for studying!

ACTIVITIES IN MANAGEMENT ACCOUNTING BY MARTHA DORAN OF SAN DIEGO STATE UNIVERSITY. This workbook contains interactive learning assignments designed to help students see beyond the technical aspects of accounting through active learning. In addition, these group activities fulfill the AECC recommendations by providing students with the chance to practice and improve their writing, speaking, and reasoning skills. An Instructor's Manual provides an overview of each activity, highlights important content and process objectives, and provides step-by-step instructions for running each activity.

FOR THE STUDENTS

STUDY GUIDE BY FRANK SELTO, UNIVERSITY OF COLORADO, BOULDER.   The Study Guide provides overviews, study tips, and chapter reviews formatted for easy note-taking, and self-tests including a variety of test questions and problems to help students prepare for examinations. Full solutions with explanations are included.

NEW IMPROVED SPREADSHEET TEMPLATES BY ALBERT FISHER, COMMUNITY COLLEGE OF SOUTHERN NEVADA.   Templates are available for selected exercises and problems that are identified in the text by a spreadsheet icon. The documentation includes short tutorials on how to use Excel and Lotus 1–2–3 as well as step-by-step instructions for completing each template. We've enhanced our spreadsheet templates by adding more problems and increasing the difficulty level. Students are now provided with the opportunity to enter more formulas to solve problems. Solutions are available on disk to the instructor upon adoption of the text.

CAREER PATHS IN ACCOUNTING-CD-ROM (WINNER OF THE NEW MEDIA INVISION GOLD AWARD IN EDUCATION!)   Alone or with the text, this CD-ROM provides students with a dynamic, interactive job-searching tool. Included are workshops in career planning, resume writing, and interviewing skills. Students can learn the latest market trends and facts as well as the skills required to get the right job. In addition, the CD-ROM provides the student with salary information, video clips describing specific jobs, and profiles of practitioners in the field.

NEW!! MEDIA SUPPORT FOR BOTH INSTRUCTORS AND STUDENTS

PHLIP (PRENTICE HALL LEARNING ON THE INTERNET PARTNERSHIP).   Offers a content rich Web site to support both professors and students. **Visit the site at www.prenhall.com/phlip.**
- New bi-monthly updates are integrated into specific chapters of the text.
- Internet resources are linked to a wide variety of sites to enhance and expand the texts' coverage of select topics.
- Companion Web site (On-line Study Guide) capabilities allow students to test their knowledge of chapter learning objectives.

ACKNOWLEDGMENTS

We have received ideas, assistance, miscellaneous critiques, and assorted assignment material in conversations and by mail from many students, professors, and business leaders. Each has our gratitude, but the complete list is too long to enumerate here.

The following professors supplied helpful comments and reviews of the previous edition or drafts of this edition: Mark E. Bettini, University of California, Berkeley; Brian Boscaljon, Calvin College; Kenneth M. Boze, University of Alaska, Anchorage; Akhilesh Chandra, North Carolina Agricultural and Technical State University; William D. J. Cotton, State University of New York at Geneseo; Thomas Hoar, Houston Community College; Manu Kaiama, University of Hawaii at Manoa; John B. MacArthur, University of North Florida; John N. McKenna, Pace University; Noel McKeon, Florida Community College at Jacksonville; Douglas Sharp, Wichita State University; Gregory Sinclair, California State University, Hayward; Raymond L. Slager, Calvin College; and James E. Williamson, San Diego State University.

The Chapters 4 and 12 illustrations of activity-based costing and the Chapter 9 illustration of a management control system are based (in part) on cases developed by Sapling Corporation. Derek Sandison of Sapling provided useful suggestions for these illustrations.

Barbara Pearson skillfully produced the solutions manual, and Anya Chaliotis, Karren Hills, Gillian Montford, Debra Moore, Demitri Semonov, and Marianne Bradford provided help in proofing.

And, finally our thanks to P.J. Boardman, Deborah Hoffman Emry, Annie Todd, Natacha St. Hill Moore, Jane Avery, Beth Toland, Bob Prokop, Christopher Smerillo, Marc Oliver, Paul Smolenski, Vincent Scelta, Richard Bretan, Pat Smythe, Jill Little, Susan Rifkin, and Bruce Kaplan at Prentice Hall.

Comments from readers are welcome.

Charles T. Horngren
Gary L. Sundem
William O. Stratton

Introduction to Management Accounting

INTRODUCTION TO
MANAGEMENT ACCOUNTING

MANAGERIAL ACCOUNTING & THE BUSINESS ORGANIZATION

Jim Smith, Director of Cost Management at The Marmon Group, works closely with management accountants at more than 60 member companies to design management accounting systems for services such as crane rentals, and manufacturing such as steel and aluminum pipe, tank cars, and store display fixtures.

Learning Objectives

When you have finished studying this chapter, you should be able to

1   Describe the major users of accounting information.

2   Explain the cost-benefit and behavioral issues involved in designing an
    accounting system.

3   Explain the role of budgets and performance reports in planning and control.

4   Discuss the role accountants play in the company's value-chain functions.

5   Contrast the functions of controllers and treasurers.

6   Identify current trends in management accounting.

7   Explain a management accountant's ethical responsibilities.

8   **Understand how managerial accounting is used in companies.***

The Marmon Group, Inc. embodies nearly all of the reasons why management accounting is a vital and growing function in today's leading companies. The Marmon Group, Inc., headquartered in Chicago, is an international association of more than 60 manufacturing, distribution, and service companies with annual revenues in excess of $6 billion. Because operations are in many different countries with thousands of diverse products and services (such as worker's gloves, water coolers, railroad tank cars, and credit services for banks), management accounting information takes on a more meaningful role.

What exactly is the role of management accountants at Marmon? According to Jim Smith, Marmon's Director of Cost Management, "The role of the management accountant is changing dramatically in most of our companies." In the past, Marmon's management accountants were basically clerical workers who spent most of their time analyzing monthly cost variances. Now, however, Marmon's management accountants work closely with operating and sales managers, providing cost information in a format that makes sense to those managers. Says Smith, "In the past few years the management accountant has become much more of a financial and business strategy adviser to senior management. Operating and sales managers are demanding meaningful cost information, and management accountants are helping them see how their actions affect costs and the bottom line."

Management accountants have become more important to Marmon, according to Smith, because recessions and foreign competition over the past ten years have awakened the understanding in most managers that costs must be managed. Knowing

---

The last learning objective in each chapter is an overall objective. It stresses the importance of understanding the material covered throughout the chapter, therefore it is not identified at a specific point in the text.

what a product truly costs or the cost of servicing a particular customer has become essential to Marmon's profitability.

"To help manage costs," says Smith, "accountants and managers are shying away from using one cost, often the cost used for financial reporting purposes, as the only important cost." Instead they are now using costs calculated for the decision at hand. "Depending on the decision, any of the cost methods described in this book are relevant." According to Smith, this is a very positive change, "since it allows and, in fact, requires the management accountant to understand all of the functions in a business and how each one adds value to the product or service."

Just as the case at the Marmon Group companies illustrated, managerial accounting can help managers in all types of organizations answer vital questions. Consider questions raised in the following situations:

- Boeing engineers have prepared manufacturing specifications for a new airplane, the 747-X. There are three possible ways to organize the assembly of the plane. Which is the most cost-effective approach?

- A product manager at Kellogg's is designing a new marketing plan for Frosted Flakes. Market research predicts that distributing free samples in the mail will increase annual sales by 4%. How will the cost of the free samples (including the cost of distributing them) compare with the profits from the added sales?

- University National Bank offers free checking to customers who keep a minimum balance of $600 in their account. How much does it cost the bank to provide this free service?

- Kitsap County Special Olympics holds a series of athletic events for disabled youth. How much money must be raised in the group's annual fund drive to support its planned activities?

- Chez Bonaparte is a dinner-only restaurant located in a middle-class neighborhood. The proprietor is considering opening for lunch. To be competitive, the average lunch must be priced about $7, and about 40 patrons can be served. Can the restaurant produce a lunch that meets its quality standards at an average cost of less than $7?

- The Monroe County School District is negotiating with the teachers' union. Among the issues are teachers' salaries, class size, and number of extracurricular activities offered. The union and the district have each made several proposals. How much will each of the various proposals cost? If class size were to increase by one student per class, what would be the added cost, and would these costs differ for elementary, junior high, and high school levels?

In answering these and a wide variety of other questions, managers turn to management accountants for information. In this chapter, we consider the purposes and roles of accounting and accountants in different types of organizations as well as some of the trends and challenges faced by accountants today.

ACCOUNTING AND DECISION MAKING

The basic purpose of accounting information is helping someone make decisions. That "someone" may be a company president, a production manager, a hospital or school administrator, an investor—the list could go on and on. Regardless of who is making the decision, the understanding of accounting information allows for a more informed, and better, decision.

USERS OF ACCOUNTING INFORMATION

In general, users of accounting information fall into three categories.

Objective 1
Describe the major users of accounting information.

1. Internal managers who use the information for short-term planning and controlling routine operations.
2. Internal managers who use the information for making nonroutine decisions (for example, investing in equipment, pricing products and services, choosing which products to emphasize or de-emphasize) and formulating overall policies and long-range plans.
3. External parties, such as investors and government authorities, who use the information for making decisions about the company.

Both internal parties (managers) and external parties use accounting information, but the ways in which they use it differ. Therefore, the types of accounting information they demand may also differ. *Management accounting* refers to accounting information developed for managers within an organization. In other words, **management accounting** is the process of identifying, measuring, accumulating, analyzing, preparing, interpreting, and communicating information that helps managers fulfill organizational objectives. In contrast, **financial accounting** refers to accounting information developed for the use of external parties such as stockholders, suppliers, banks, and government regulatory agencies.[1] The major differences between management accounting and financial accounting are listed in Exhibit 1-1. Despite these differences, most organizations prefer a general-purpose accounting system that meets the needs of all three types of users.

What are the needs or uses? Good accounting information helps an organization achieve its goals and objectives by helping to answer three types of questions.

1. *Scorecard questions:* Am I doing well or poorly? **Scorekeeping** is the accumulation and classification of data. This aspect of accounting enables both internal and external parties to evaluate organizational performance.
2. *Attention-directing questions:* Which problems should I look into? **Attention directing** means reporting and interpreting information that helps managers to focus on operating problems, imperfections, inefficiencies, and opportunities. Attention directing is commonly associated with current planning and control, and with the analysis and investigation of recurring *routine* internal accounting reports.
3. *Problem-solving questions:* Of the several ways of doing a job, which is the best? The **problem-solving** aspect of accounting quantifies the likely results of possible courses of action and often recommends the best course to follow.

The scorecard and attention-directing uses of information are closely related. The same information may serve a scorecard function for a manager and an attention-directing function for the manager's superior. For example, many accounting systems provide performance reports in which actual results of decisions and activities are compared with previously determined plans. By pinpointing where actual results differ from plans, such performance reports can show managers how they are doing and show the managers' superiors where to take action.

In contrast, problem-solving information may be used in long-range planning and in making special, nonrecurring decisions, such as whether to make or buy parts, replace

management accounting
The process of identifying, measuring, accumulating, analyzing, preparing, interpreting, and communicating information that helps managers fulfill organizational objectives.

financial accounting The field of accounting that develops information for external decision makers such as stockholders, suppliers, banks, and government regulatory agencies.

scorekeeping The accumulation and classification of data.

attention directing Reporting and interpreting information that helps managers to focus on operating problems, imperfections, inefficiencies, and opportunities.

problem solving The aspect of accounting that quantifies the likely results of possible courses of action and often recommends the best course of action to follow.

---

[1]*For a book-length presentation of the subject, see Charles T. Horngren, Gary L. Sundem, and John A. Elliott,* Introduction to Financial Accounting *(Upper Saddle River, NJ: Prentice Hall, 1999), the companion to this textbook.*

	Management Accounting	**Financial Accounting**
Primary users	Organization managers at various levels.	Outside parties such as investors and government agencies but also organization managers.
Freedom of choice	No constraints other than costs in relation to benefits of improved management decisions.	Constrained by generally accepted accounting principles (GAAP).
Behavioral implications	Concern about how measurements and reports will influence managers' daily behavior.	Concern about how to measure and communicate economic phenomena. Behavioral considerations are secondary, although executive compensation based on reported results may have behavioral impacts.
Time focus	Future orientation: formal use of budgets as well as historical records. Example:19X9 budget versus 19X9 actual performance.	Past orientation: historical evaluation. Example: 19X9 actual performance versus 19X8 actual performance.
Time span	Flexible, varying from hourly to 10 to 15 years.	Less flexible; usually 1 year or 1 quarter.
Reports	Detailed reports: concern about details of parts of the entity, products, departments, territories, etc.	Summary reports: concern primarily with entity as a whole.
Delineation of activities	Field is less sharply defined. Heavier use of economics, decision sciences, and behavioral sciences.	Field is more sharply defined. Lighter use of related disciplines.

equipment, or add or drop a product. These decisions often require expert advice from specialists such as industrial engineers, budgetary accountants, and statisticians.

ACCOUNTING SYSTEMS

accounting system A formal mechanism for gathering, organizing, and communicating information about an organization's activities.

An **accounting system** is a formal mechanism for gathering, organizing, and communicating information about an organization's activities. Using one accounting system for both financial and management purposes sometimes creates problems. External forces (for example, income tax authorities and regulatory bodies such as the U.S. Securities and Exchange Commission and the California Health Facility Commission) often limit management's choices of accounting methods for external reports. Many organizations develop systems primarily to satisfy legal requirements imposed by external parties. These systems often neglect the needs of internal users.

generally accepted accounting principles (GAAP) Broad concepts or guidelines and detailed practices, including all conventions, rules, and procedures that together make up accepted accounting practice at a given time.

Consider the annual financial reports by public corporations. These reports must adhere to a set of standards known as **generally accepted accounting principles (GAAP).** GAAP includes broad concepts or guidelines and detailed practices, including all conventions, rules, and procedures, that together make up accepted accounting practice at a given time. However, internal accounting reports need not be restricted by GAAP. For instance, GAAP requires that organizations account for their assets (economic resources) according to their historical cost. For its own management purpose, however, an organization can account for its economic resources on the basis of their *current values,* as measured by estimates of replacement costs. No outside agency can prohibit such accounting. Managers can create whatever kind of internal accounting system they want—provided they are willing to pay the cost of developing and operating the system.

Of course, satisfying internal demands for information (as well as external demands) means that organizations may have to keep more than one set of records. At least in the United States, there is nothing immoral or unethical about having simultaneous sets of books—but they are expensive. Because external financial reports are required by authorities, many organizations do not choose to invest in a separate system for internal management purposes. Managers are thus forced to use information designed to meet external users' needs instead of information designed for their specific decisions.

EFFECTS OF GOVERNMENT REGULATION

Even when management is willing to pay for a separate internal accounting system, that system may be affected by government regulation. The reason is that government agencies have legal power to order into evidence any internal document that they deem necessary.

Universities and defense contractors, for example, must allocate costs to government contracts in specified ways or risk government's refusal to pay. For example, in a widely publicized case in the early 1990s, Stanford University and several other prominent universities were denied reimbursement for certain costs that the government deemed inappropriate.

The **Foreign Corrupt Practices Act** is a U.S. law forbidding bribery and other corrupt practices. This law also requires that accounting records be maintained in reasonable detail and accuracy, and that an appropriate system of internal accounting controls be maintained. The title is misleading because the act's provisions apply to all publicly held companies, even if they conduct no business outside the United States.

The greatest impact of the act on accounting systems stems from the requirement that management must document the adequacy of internal accounting controls. As a result, many companies have greatly increased their internal auditing staffs and have elevated the status of such staffs. Often the internal audit staff reports directly to the president, sometimes even to the board of directors.

Internal auditors help review and evaluate systems to help minimize errors, fraud, and waste. More important, many internal auditing staffs have a primary responsibility for conducting management audits. A **management audit** is a review to determine whether the policies and procedures specified by top management have been implemented. Management audits are not confined to profit-seeking organizations. The General Accounting Office (GAO) of the U.S. government conducts these audits on a massive scale. Most states also have audit agencies that audit departments of the state government. Some also audit municipalities and other local government organizations.

The overall impact of government regulation is very controversial. Many managers insist that the extra costs of compliance far exceed any possible benefits. One benefit, however, is that operating managers, now more than ever, must become more intimately familiar with their accounting systems. The resulting changes in the systems sometimes provide stronger controls and more informative reports.

Foreign Corrupt Practices Act U.S. law forbidding bribery and other corrupt practices, and requiring that accounting records be maintained in reasonable detail and accuracy, and that an appropriate system of internal accounting controls be maintained.

management audit A review to determine whether the policies and procedures specified by top management have been implemented.

SUMMARY PROBLEM FOR YOUR REVIEW

Try to solve this problem before examining the solution that follows.

PROBLEM

The scorekeeping, attention-directing, and problem-solving duties of the accountant have been described in this chapter. The accountant's usefulness to management is said to be directly influenced by how good an attention director and problem solver he or she is.

Evaluate this contention by specifically relating the accountant's duties to the duties of operating management.

SOLUTION

Operating managers may have to be good scorekeepers, but their major duties are to concentrate on the day-to-day problems that most need attention, to make longer-range plans, and to arrive at special decisions. Accordingly, because managers are concerned mainly with attention directing and problem solving, they will obtain the most benefit from the alert internal accountant who is a useful attention director and problem solver.

MANAGEMENT ACCOUNTING IN SERVICE AND NONPROFIT ORGANIZATIONS

The basic ideas of management accounting were developed in manufacturing organizations. These ideas, however, have evolved so that they apply to all types of organizations including service organizations. Service organizations, for our purposes, are all organizations other than manufacturers, wholesalers, and retailers. That is, they are organizations that do not make or sell tangible goods. Public accounting firms, law firms, management consultants, real estate firms, transportation companies, banks, insurance companies, and hotels are profit-seeking service organizations.

Almost all nonprofit organizations, such as hospitals, schools, libraries, museums, and government agencies, are also service organizations. Managers and accountants in nonprofit organizations have much in common with their counterparts in profit-seeking organizations. There is money to be raised and spent. There are budgets to be prepared and control systems to be designed and implemented. There is an obligation to use resources wisely. If used intelligently, accounting contributes to efficient operations and helps nonprofit organizations achieve their objectives.

The characteristics of both profit-seeking and nonprofit service organizations include the following:

1. *Labor is intensive:* The highest proportion of expenses in schools and law firms are wages, salaries, and payroll-related costs, not the costs relating to the use of machinery, equipment, and physical facilities.
2. *Output is usually difficult to define:* The output of a university might be defined as the number of degrees granted, but many critics would maintain that the real output is "what is contained in the students' brains." Therefore, measuring output is often considered impossible.
3. *Major inputs and outputs cannot be stored:* An empty airline seat cannot be saved for a later flight, and a hotel's available labor force and rooms are either used or unused as each day occurs.

Simplicity is the watchword for installation of systems in service industries and nonprofit organizations. In fact, many professionals such as physicians, professors, or government officials resist even filling out a time card. In fact, simplicity is a fine watchword for the design of any accounting system. Complexity tends to generate costs of gathering and interpreting data that often exceed prospective benefits. Concern for simplicity is sometimes expressed as *KISS* (which means "keep it simple, stupid").

In addition to simplicity, managers should keep two other ideas in mind when designing accounting systems: (1) cost-benefit balances and (2) behavioral implications.

The **cost-benefit balance**—weighing estimated costs against probable benefits—is the primary consideration in choosing among accounting systems and methods. Therefore, we will refer again and again to cost-benefit considerations throughout this book. For now, consider accounting systems to be economic goods—like office supplies or labor—available at various costs. Which system does a manager want to buy? A simple file drawer for amassing receipts and canceled checks? An elaborate budgeting system based on computerized models of the organization and its subunits? Or something in between?

The answer depends on the buyer's perceptions of the expected benefits in relation to the costs. For example, a hospital administrator may consider installing a TECHNICON computerized system for controlling hospital operations. Users of such a system need only enter a piece of information once and the system automatically incorporates it into financial records, medical records, and so forth. Such a system is highly efficient and is subject to few errors, but it costs $14 million. Is the TECHNICON system a good buy? That depends on its expected benefit. If its value to the hospital is greater than $14 million, then it is a good buy. If not, the administrator should consider another accounting system.

The value of a loaf of bread may exceed a cost of 50 cents a loaf, but it may not exceed a cost of $5 per loaf. Similarly, a particular accounting system may be a wise investment if its cost is sufficiently small. Like a consumer who switches from bread to potatoes if the cost of bread is too high, managers seek other sources of information if accounting systems are too expensive. In many organizations it may be more economical to gather some kinds of data by one-shot special efforts than by a ponderous system that repetitively gathers rarely used data.

In addition to the costs and benefits of an accounting system, the buyer of such a system should also consider **behavioral implications,** that is, the system's effect on the behavior (decisions) of managers. The system must provide accurate, timely budgets and performance reports in a form useful to managers. If managers do not use accounting reports, the reports create no benefits.

Management accounting reports affect employees' feelings and behavior. Consider a performance report that is used to evaluate the operations under the responsibility of a particular manager. If the report unfairly attributes excessive costs to the operation, the manager may lose confidence in the system and not let it influence future decisions. In contrast, a system that managers believe in and trust can be a major influence on their decisions and actions.

In a nutshell, management accounting can best be understood as a balance between costs and benefits of accounting information coupled with an awareness of the importance of behavioral effects. Even more than financial accounting, management accounting spills over into related disciplines, such as economics, the decision sciences, and the behavioral sciences.

> **cost-benefit balance**
> Weighing estimated costs against probable benefits, the primary consideration in choosing among accounting systems and methods.

> **Objective 2**
> Explain the cost-benefit and behavioral issues involved in designing an accounting system

> **behavioral implications**
> The accounting system's effect on the behavior (decisions) of managers.

THE MANAGEMENT PROCESS AND ACCOUNTING

Regardless of the type of organization, managers benefit when accounting provides information that helps them plan and control the organization's operations.

THE NATURE OF PLANNING AND CONTROLLING

The management process is a series of activities in a cycle of planning and control. **Decision making**—the purposeful choice from among a set of alternative courses of action designed to achieve some objective—is the core of the management process. Decisions

> **decision making** The purposeful choice from among a set of alternative courses of action designed to achieve some objective.

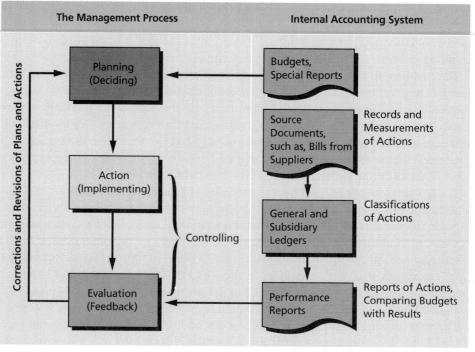

Exhibit 1-2

Accounting Framework for Planning and Control

range from the routine (making daily production schedules) to the nonroutine (launching a new product line).

Decisions within an organization are often divided into two types: (1) planning decisions and (2) control decisions. In practice, planning and control are so intertwined that it seems artificial to separate them. In studying management, however, it is useful to concentrate on either the planning phase or the control phase to simplify the analysis.

The left side of Exhibit 1-2 demonstrates the planning and control cycle of current operations. Planning (the top box) refers to setting objectives and outlining how they will be attained. Thus planning provides the answers to two questions: What is desired? When and how is it to be accomplished? In contrast, controlling (the two boxes labeled "Action" and "Evaluation") refers to *implementing* plans and *using feedback* to attain objectives. Feedback is crucial to the cycle of planning and control. Planning determines action, action generates feedback, and feedback influences further planning. Timely, systematic reports provided by the internal accounting system are the chief source of useful feedback. None of this cycle would be possible without accounting.

MANAGEMENT BY EXCEPTION

The right side of Exhibit 1-2 shows that accounting formalizes *plans* by expressing them as budgets. A **budget** is a quantitative expression of a plan of action. It is also an aid to coordinating and implementing the plan. Budgets are the chief devices for compelling and disciplining management planning. Without budgets, planning may not get the front-and-center focus that it usually deserves.

Accounting formalizes control as **performance reports** (the last box), which provide feedback by comparing results with plans and by highlighting **variances,** which are deviations from plans. The accounting system records, measures, and classifies actions in order to produce performance reports.

Exhibit 1-3 shows a simple performance report for a law firm. Performance reports are used to judge decisions and the productivity of organizational units and managers. By

Objective 3
Explain the role of budgets and performance reports in planning and control.

budget A quantitative expression of a plan of action, and an aid to coordinating and implementing the plan.

performance reports Feedback provided by comparing results with plans and by highlighting variances.

variances Deviations from plans.

Exhibit 1-3

Performance Report

	Budgeted Amounts	Actual Amounts	Deviations or Variances	Explanation
Revenue from fees	xxx	xxx	xx	—
Various expenses	xxx	xxx	xx	—
Net income	xxx	xxx	xx	—

comparing actual results to budgets, performance reports motivate managers to achieve the budgeted objectives.

Performance reports spur investigation of exceptions—items for which actual amounts differ significantly from budgeted amounts. Operations are then made to conform with the plans, or the plans are revised. This is often called **management by exception,** which means concentrating on areas that deviate from the plan and ignoring areas that are presumed to be running smoothly. Thus the management-by-exception approach frees managers from needless concern with those phases of operations that are adhering to plans. However, well-conceived plans should incorporate enough discretion or flexibility so that the manager may feel free to pursue any unforeseen opportunities. In other words, control should not be a straightjacket. When unfolding events call for actions not specifically authorized in the plan, managers should be able to take these actions.

management by exception
Concentrating on areas that deviate from the plan and ignoring areas that are presumed to be running smoothly.

ILLUSTRATION OF BUDGETS AND PERFORMANCE REPORTS

Suppose the Casaverde Company manufactures and sells electric fans. Consider the department that assembles the fans. Workers assemble the parts and install the motor largely by hand. They then inspect each fan before transferring it to the packaging and shipping department. The present sales forecast has led managers to plan a production schedule of 10,000 fans for the coming month. The assembly department budget in Exhibit 1-4 shows cost classifications.

The operating plan for the department, in the form of a department budget for the coming month, is prepared in conferences attended by the department manager, the manager's supervisor, and an accountant. They scrutinize each of the costs subject to the manager's control. They often use the average amount of the cost for the past few months as a guide, especially if past performance has been good. However, the budget is a *forecast* of costs for the projected level of production activity. Hence, conference members must predict each cost in light of trends, price changes, alterations in product mix and characteristics, production meth-

Exhibit 1-4

Casaverde Company
Assembly Department Budget for the Month Ended March 31, 19X9

Production activity	10,000 fans
Material (detailed by type: metal stampings, motors, and so on)	$ 68,000
Assembly labor (detailed by job classification, number of workers, and so on)	43,000
Other labor (managers, inspectors)	12,000
Utilities, maintenance, and so on	7,500
Supplies (small tools, lubricants, and so on)	2,500
Total	$133,000

Exhibit 1-5

Casaverde Company
Assembly Department Performance Report for the Month Ended March 31, 19X9

	Budget	Actual	Variance
Production activity in units	10,000	9,860	140 U
Material (detailed by type: metal stampings, motors, and so on)	$ 68,000	$ 69,000	$1,000 U
Assembly labor (detailed by job classification, number of workers, and so on)	43,000	44,300	1,300 U
Other labor (managers, inspectors)	12,000	11,200	800 F
Utilities, maintenance, and so on	7,500	7,400	100 F
Supplies (small tools, lubricants, and so on)	2,500	2,600	100 U
Total	$133,000	$134,500	$1,500 U

U = Unfavorable—actual exceeds budget
F = Favorable—actual is less than budget

ods, and changes in the level of production activity from month to month. Only then can they formulate the budget that becomes the manager's target for the month.

As actual factory costs are incurred, Casaverde's accounting system collects them and classifies them by department. At the end of the month (or weekly, or even daily, for such key items as materials or assembly labor), the accounting department prepares an assembly department performance report. Exhibit 1-5 is a simplified report. In practice, this report may be very detailed and contain explanations of variances from the budget.

Department heads and their superiors use the performance report to help appraise how effectively and efficiently the department is operating. Their focus is on the variances—the deviations from the budget. Casaverde's assembly department performance report (Exhibit 1-5) shows that although the department produced 140 fewer fans than planned, material costs were $1,000 over budget, and assembly labor was $1,300 over budget. By investigating such variances, managers may find better ways of doing things.

Notice that although budgets aid planning and performance reports aid control, it is not accountants but other managers and their subordinates who evaluate accounting reports and actually plan and control operations. Accounting assists the managerial planning and control functions by providing prompt measurements of actions and by systematically pinpointing trouble spots.

PLANNING AND CONTROL FOR PRODUCT LIFE CYCLES AND THE VALUE CHAIN

product life cycle The various stages through which a product passes, from conception and development through introduction into the market through maturation and, finally, withdrawal from the market.

Many management decisions relate to a single good or service, or to a group of related products. To effectively plan for and control production of such goods or services, accountants and other managers must consider the product's life cycle. **Product life cycle** refers to the various stages through which a product passes, from conception and development through introduction into the market through maturation and, finally, withdrawal from the market. At each stage, managers face differing costs and potential returns. Exhibit 1-6 shows a typical product life cycle.

Product life cycles range from a few months (for fashion clothing or faddish toys) to many years (for automobiles or refrigerators). Some products, such as many computer software packages, have long development stages and relatively short market lives. Others, such as Boeing 777 airplanes, have market lives many times longer than their development stage.

In the planning process, managers must recognize revenues and costs over the entire life cycle—however long or short. Accounting needs to track actual costs and revenues

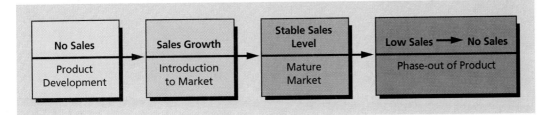

Exhibit 1-6

Typical Product Life Cycle

throughout the life cycle, too. Periodic comparisons between planned costs and revenues and actual costs and revenues allow managers to assess the current profitability of a product, determine its current product life-cycle stage, and make any needed changes in strategy.

For example, suppose a pharmaceutical company is developing a new drug to reduce high blood pressure. The budget for the product should plan for costs without revenues in the product development stage. Most of the revenues come in the introduction and mature-market stages, and a pricing strategy should recognize the need for revenues to cover both development and phase-out costs as well as the direct costs of producing the drug. During phase-out, costs of producing the drug must be balanced with both the revenue generated and the need to keep the drug on the market for those who have come to rely on it.

THE VALUE CHAIN

How does a company actually create the goods or services that it sells? Whether we are making donuts in a shopping mall or making $50 million airplanes, all organizations try to create goods or services that are valued by its customers. The **value chain** is the set of business functions that add value to the products or services of an organization. As shown in Exhibit 1-7, these functions are as follows:

value chain The set of business functions that add value to the products or services of an organization.

- Research and development—the generation of, and experimentation with, ideas related to new products, services, or processes.
- Design of products, services, or processes—the detail and engineering of products.
- Production—the coordination and assembly of resources to produce a product or deliver a service.
- Marketing—the manner by which individuals or groups learn about the value and features of products or services (for example, advertising).
- Distribution—the mechanism by which a company delivers products or services to the customer.
- Customer service—the support activities provided to the customer.

Not all of these functions are of equal importance to the success of a company. Senior management must decide which of these functions enables the company to gain and maintain a competitive edge. For example, Dell Computers (see page 453 for a more detailed company profile) considers the design function a critical success factor. The features designed into Dell's computers create higher quality. In addition, the design of efficient processes used to make and deliver computers lowers costs and speeds up delivery to its customers. Of course, Dell also performs the other value-chain functions, but it concentrates on being the best process designer in the computer market.

Accountants play a key role in all value-chain functions. Providing estimated revenue and cost data during the research and development and design stages (especially the design stage) of the value chain enables managers and engineers to reduce the life-cycle costs of products or services more than in any other value-chain function. Using computer-based planning software, accountants can give managers rapid feedback on ideas for cost

Objective 4
Discuss the role accountants play in the company's value-chain functions

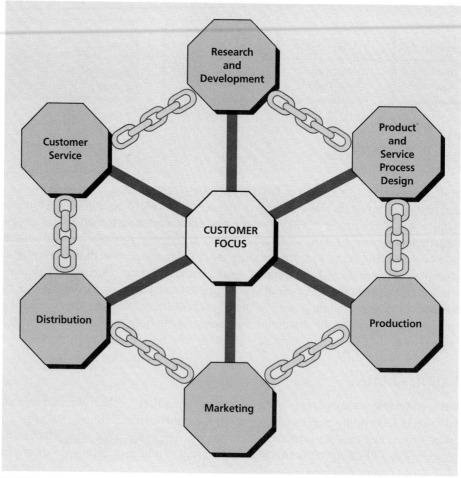

Exhibit 1-7

The Value Chain of Business Functions

reductions long before the company must make a commitment to purchase expensive equipment. Then, during the production stage, accountants help track the effects of continuous improvement programs. Accountants also play a central role in cost planning and control through the use of budgets and performance reporting, as described in the previous section. Marketing decisions have a significant impact on sales but the cost of promotional programs is also significant. Accountants analyze the trade-off between increased costs and revenues. Distributing products or services to customers is a complex function. Should a company sell its products directly to a chain of retail stores, or should it sell to a wholesaler? What transportation system should be used—trucks or trains? What are the costs of each alternative? Finally, accountants provide cost data for customer service activities, such as warranty and repair costs and the costs of goods returned. As you can see, cost management is very important throughout the value chain.

Note that customer focus is at the center of Exhibit 1-7. Successful businesses never lose sight of the importance of maintaining a focus on the needs of its customers. For example, consider the comments of the following business leaders.

> *Customers, by the choices they make, grant companies a future or condemn them to extinction. We will continuously strive to achieve total customer satisfaction. . . . We will seek to truly understand the complexity of our customers' needs, not push our own ideas or technology.*
> **Philip Condit, Chairman and Chief Executive Officer, Boeing Company**

Improving comparable sales in the competitive U.S. market means selling more food. So, our emphasis is on increasing customer visits. In the U.S., we'll do that by concentrating on our customers: re-energizing and focusing our marketing efforts, being aggressive in providing maximum price value, continuing to improve service in our restaurants and enhancing food taste.

**Mike Conley, Executive Vice President and
Chief Financial Officer, McDonald's Corporation**

The value chain and the concepts of adding value and focusing on the customer are extremely important to companies, and they are becoming more so every day. Accountants must focus on the values created compared to the costs incurred in each link of the value chain. Therefore, we will return to the value chain and use it as a focus for discussion throughout the book.

SUMMARY PROBLEM FOR YOUR REVIEW

Try to solve this problem before looking at the solution that follows.

PROBLEM

Starbucks Coffee Company is the leading roaster and retailer of specialty coffee in North America, with annual sales revenue of more than $1 billion. For each of the following activities, indicate the value-chain function that is being performed.

   a. Process engineers investigate methods to reduce the time to roast coffee beans and to better preserve their flavor.

   b. A direct-to-your-home mail-order system is established to sell custom coffees.

   c. Arabica coffee beans are purchased and transported to company processing plants.

   d. Focus groups investigate the feasibility to a new line of Frappuccino drinks.

   e. A hot line is established for mail-order customers to call with comments on the quality and speed of delivery.

   f. Each company-owned retail store provides information to customers about the processes used to make its coffee products.

SOLUTION

   a. *Design.* Both the design of products and, as here, design of production processes are part of the design function.

   b. *Distribution.* This provides an additional way to deliver products to customers.

   c. *Production.* The purchase price of beans and transportation (or freight-in) costs are part of product costs incurred during the production function.

   d. *Research and development.* These costs (mostly wages) are incurred prior to management's final decision to design and produce a new product.

   e. *Customer service.* These costs include all expenditures made after the product has been delivered to the customer; in this case, Starbucks obtains feedback on the quality and speed of delivery.

   f. *Marketing.* These costs are for activities that enhance the existing or potential customers' awareness and opinion of the product.

To assist other managers in the decision making vital to an organization's success, most companies (and many nonprofit organizations and government agencies) employ a variety of accounting personnel with various types of authority and responsibility.

LINE AND STAFF AUTHORITY

line authority Authority exerted downward over subordinates.

The organization chart in Exhibit 1-8 shows how a typical manufacturing company divides responsibilities. Notice the distinction between line and staff authority. **Line authority** is authority exerted downward over subordinates. **Staff authority** is authority to advise but not command. It may be exerted downward, laterally, or upward.

staff authority Authority to advise but not command. It may be exerted downward, laterally, or upward.

Most organizations specify certain activities as their basic mission. Most missions involve the production and sale of goods or services. All subunits of the organization that are directly responsible for conducting these basic activities are called line departments. The others are called staff departments because their principal task is to support or service the line departments. Thus staff activities are indirectly related to the basic activities of the organization. Exhibit 1-8 shows a series of factory-service departments that perform staff functions supporting the line functions carried on by the production departments.

controller (comptroller) The top accounting officer of an organization. The term comptroller is used primarily in government organizations.

The top accounting officer of an organization is often called the **controller** or, especially in a government organization, a **comptroller.** This executive, like virtually everyone in an accounting function, fills a staff role, whereas sales and production executives and their subordinates fill line roles. The accounting department does not exercise direct authority over line departments. Rather, the accounting department provides other managers with specialized services including advice and help in budgeting, analyzing variances, pricing, and making special decisions.

Exhibit 1-9 shows how a controller's department may be organized. In particular, note the distinctions among the scorekeeping, attention-directing, and problem-solving roles of various personnel. Unless some internal accountants are given the last two roles as their primary responsibilities, the scorekeeping tasks tend to dominate and the system becomes less responsive to management's decision making.

THE CONTROLLER

The controller position varies in stature and duties from company to company. In some firms the controller is confined to compiling data, primarily for external reporting purposes. In others, such as General Electric, the controller is a key executive who aids managerial planning and control throughout the company's subdivisions. In most firms controllers have a status somewhere between these two extremes. For example, their opinions on the tax implications of certain management decisions may be carefully weighed, yet their opinions on other aspects of these decisions may not be sought. In many organizations (such as the Marmon Group companies), controllers have a growing role as internal "consultants," helping managers gather relevant information for their decisions.

Although controllers (or comptrollers) have a staff role, they are generally empowered by the firm's president to approve, install, and oversee the organization's accounting system to ensure uniform accounting and reporting methods. In theory, the controller proposes these systems and methods to the president, who approves and orders compliance with them on the part of line personnel (thus preserving the "staff" advisory role of accounting). In practice, however, controllers usually directly specify how production records should be kept or how time records should be completed. The controller holds delegated authority from top-line management over such matters.

Exhibit 1-8

Partial Organization Chart of a Manufacturing Company

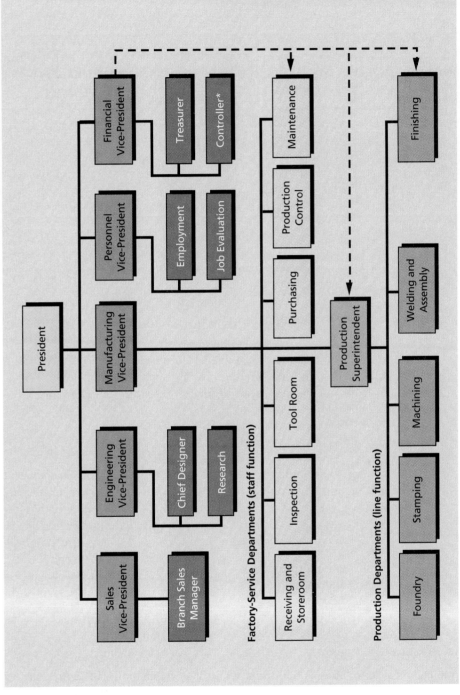

*For detailed organization of a controller's department, see Exhibit 1-9. Dashed line represents staff authority of the finance staff to advise those in manufacturing operations.

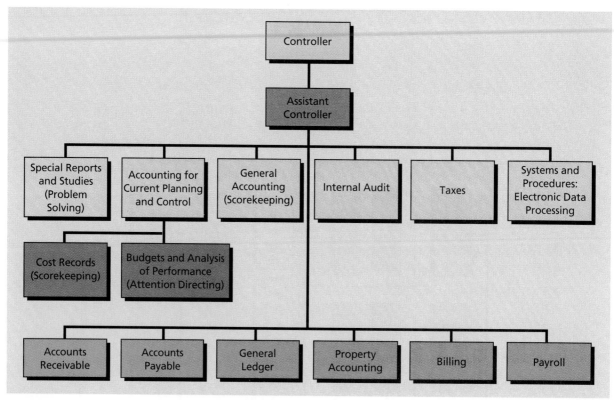

Exhibit 1-9

Organization Chart of a Controller's Department

In theory, then, controllers have no line authority except over the accounting department. Yet, by reporting and interpreting relevant data, controllers do exert a force or influence that leads management toward logical decisions that are consistent with the organization's objectives.

DISTINCTIONS BETWEEN CONTROLLER AND TREASURER

Many people confuse the offices of controller and treasurer. The Financial Executives Institute, an association of corporate treasurers and controllers, distinguishes their functions as follows:

<table>
<tr><td>Objective 5
Contrast the functions of controllers and treasurers.</td><td>

CONTROLLERSHIP
1. Planning for control
2. Reporting and interpreting
3. Evaluating and consulting
4. Tax administration
5. Government reporting
6. Protection of assets
7. Economic appraisal

</td><td>

TREASURERSHIP
1. Provision of capital
2. Investor relations
3. Short-term financing
4. Banking and custody
5. Credits and collections
6. Investments
7. Risk management (insurance)

</td></tr>
</table>

Management accounting is the primary means of implementing the first three functions of controllership.

The treasurer is concerned mainly with the company's financial matters, the controller with operating matters. The exact division of accounting and financial duties varies from company to company. In a small organization, the same person might be both treasurer and controller.

SUMMARY PROBLEM FOR YOUR REVIEW

PROBLEM

Using the organization charts in this chapter (Exhibits 1-8 and 1-9), answer the following questions:

1. Which of the following have line authority over the machining manager: maintenance manager, manufacturing vice-president, production superintendent, purchasing agent, scorekeeper, personnel vice-president, president, chief budgetary accountant, chief internal auditor?

2. What is the general role of service departments in an organization? How are they distinguished from operating or production departments?

3. Does the controller have line or staff authority over the cost accountants? Over the accounts receivable clerks?

4. What is probably the major duty (scorekeeping, attention directing, or problem solving) of the following:

Payroll clerk	Cost analyst
Accounts receivable clerk	Head of internal auditing
Cost record clerk	Head of special reports and studies
Head of general accounting	Head of accounting for planning
Head of taxes	and control
Budgetary accountant	Controller

SOLUTION

1. The only executives having line authority over the machining manager are the president, the manufacturing vice-president, and the production superintendent.

2. A typical company's major purpose is to produce and sell goods or services. Unless a department is directly concerned with producing or selling, it is called a service or staff department. Service departments exist only to help the production and sales departments with their major tasks: the efficient production and sale of goods or services.

3. The controller has line authority over all members of his or her own department, all those shown in the controller's organization chart (Exhibit 1-9, p. 18).

4. The major duty of the first five—through the head of taxes—is typically scorekeeping. Attention directing is probably the major duty of the next three. Problem solving is probably the primary duty of the head of special reports and studies. The head of accounting for planning and control and the controller should be concerned with all three duties: scorekeeping, attention directing, and problem solving. However, there is a perpetual danger that day-to-day pressures will emphasize scorekeeping. Therefore accountants and managers should constantly see that attention directing and problem solving are also stressed. Otherwise the major management benefits of an accounting system may be lost.

The many types and levels of accounting personnel found in the typical organization mean that there are broad opportunities awaiting those who master the accounting discipline.

CERTIFIED MANAGEMENT ACCOUNTANT

Certified Public Accountant (CPA) In the United States, an accountant earns this designation by a combination of education, qualifying experience, and the passing of a two-day written national examination.

Certified Management Accountant (CMA) The management accountant's counterpart to the CPA.

Institute of Management Accountants (IMA) The largest U.S. professional organization of accountants whose major interest is management accounting.

When accounting is mentioned, most people think first of independent auditors who reassure the public about the reliability of the financial information supplied by company managers. These external auditors are called certified public accountants in the United States and chartered accountants in many other English-speaking nations. In the United States, an accountant earns the designation of **Certified Public Accountant (CPA)** by a combination of education, qualifying experience, and the passing of a two-day written national examination. The major U.S. professional association in the private sector that regulates the quality of outside auditors is the American Institute of Certified Public Accountants (AICPA).

In recent years, increased interest in and demand for management accounting has led to development of the **Certified Management Accountant (CMA)** designation, the internal accountant's counterpart to the CPA. The **Institute of Management Accountants (IMA),** oversees the CMA program and is the largest U.S. professional organization of accountants whose major interest is management accounting.

The highlight of the CMA program is a two-day qualifying examination in four parts: (1) economics, finance, and management; (2) financial accounting and reporting; (3) management reporting, analysis, and behavioral issues; and (4) decision analysis and information systems.[2] The CMA designation is recognized as the management accounting equivalent to the CPA.

TRAINING FOR TOP MANAGEMENT POSITIONS

In addition to preparing you for a position in an accounting department, studying accounting—and working as a management accountant—can prepare you for the very highest levels of management. Accounting deals with all facets of an organization, no matter how complex, so it provides an excellent opportunity to gain broad knowledge. Accounting must embrace all management functions, including purchasing, manufacturing, wholesaling, retailing, and a variety of marketing and transportation activities. Senior accountants or controllers in a corporation are sometimes picked as production or marketing executives. Why? Because they may have impressed other executives as having acquired general management skills. A number of recent surveys have indicated that more chief executive officers began their careers in an accounting position than in any other area, including marketing, production, and engineering.

For example, former controllers have risen to the top of such mammoth companies as Pepsico and Pfizer. According to *Business Week,* controllers

are now getting involved with the operating side of the company, where they give advice and influence production, marketing, and investment decisions as well as corporate planning. Moreover, many controllers who have not made it to the top have won ready access to top management. . . . Probably the main reason the controller is getting the ear of top management these days is that he or she is virtually the only person familiar with all the working parts of the company.

---

[2]*Information can be obtained from the IMA, 10 Paragon Drive, Montvale, NJ 07645.*

The growing interest in management accounting also stems from its ability to help managers adapt to change. The one constant in the world of business is change. Today's economic decisions differ from those of 10 years ago. As decisions change, demands for information change. *Accountants must adapt their systems to the changes in management practices and technology.* A system that produces valuable information in one setting may be valueless in another.

Accountants have not always been responsive to the need to change. A decade ago many managers complained about the irrelevance of accounting information. Why? Because their decision environment had changed but accounting systems had not. However, most progressive companies have now changed their accounting systems to recognize the realities of today's complex, technical, and global business environment. Instead of being irrelevant, accountants in such companies are adding more value than ever. For example, *Management Accounting* (September 1994) reported on a Champion International Corporation paper mill that made major changes in its accounting system. By working with managers to produce the information considered relevant for their decisions, accountants became regarded as "business partners." Previously, managers had considered accountants to be a "financial police department." Instead of merely pointing out problems, the accountants became part of the solution.

CURRENT TRENDS

Three major factors are causing changes in management accounting today:

1. Shift from a manufacturing-based to a service-based economy
2. Increased global competition
3. Advances in technology

Each of these factors will affect your study of management accounting.

Objective 6
Identify current trends in management accounting.

The service sector now accounts for almost 80% of the employment in the United States. Service industries are becoming increasingly competitive, and their use of accounting information is growing. Basic accounting principles are applied to service organizations throughout this book.

Global competition has increased in recent years as many international barriers to trade, such as tariffs and duties, have been lowered. In addition, there has been a worldwide trend toward deregulation. The result has been a shift in the balance of economic power in the world. Nowhere has this been more evident than in the United States. To regain their competitive edge, many U.S. companies are redesigning their accounting systems to provide more accurate and timely information about the cost of activities, products, or services. To be competitive, managers must understand the effects of their decisions on costs, and accountants must help managers predict such effects.

By far the most dominant influence on management accounting over the past decade has been technological change. This change has affected both the production and the use of accounting information. The increasing capabilities and decreasing cost of computers, especially personal computers (PCs), has changed how accountants gather, store, manipulate, and report data. Most accounting systems, even small ones, are automated. In addition, computers enable managers to access data directly and to generate their own reports and analyses in many cases. By using spreadsheet software and graphics packages, managers can use accounting information directly in their decision process. Thus, all managers need a better understanding of accounting information now than they may have needed in the past. In addition, accountants need to create databases that can be readily understood by managers.

Technological change has also dramatically changed the manufacturing environment for many companies, causing changes in how accounting information is used. Manufacturing processes are increasingly automated. Automated manufacturing processes make extensive use of robots and other computer-controlled equipment and less use of human labor for direct production activities. Many early accounting systems were designed primarily to measure and report the cost of labor. Why? Because human labor was the largest cost in the production of many products and services. Clearly, such systems are not appropriate in automated environments. Accountants in such settings have had to change their systems to produce information for decisions about how to acquire and use materials and automated equipment efficiently.

JUST-IN-TIME PHILOSOPHY AND COMPUTER-INTEGRATED MANUFACTURING

Changes in technology have produced changes in management philosophy. The most important recent change leading to increased efficiency in American factories has been the adoption of a **just-in-time (JIT) philosophy.** The essence of the philosophy is to eliminate waste. Managers try to (1) reduce the time that products spend in the production process and (2) eliminate the time that products spend on activities that do not add value (such as inspection and waiting time).

Process time can be reduced by redesigning and simplifying the production process. Companies can use *computer-aided design (CAD)* to design products that can be manufactured efficiently. Even small changes in design often lead to large manufacturing cost savings. Companies can also use *computer-aided manufacturing (CAM),* in which computers direct and control production equipment. CAM often leads to a smoother, more efficient flow of production with fewer delays.

Systems that use CAD and CAM together with robots and computer-controlled machines are called **computer-integrated manufacturing (CIM) systems.** Companies that install a full CIM system use very little labor. Robots and computer-controlled machines perform the routine jobs that were previously done by assembly-line workers. In addition, well-designed systems provide great flexibility because design changes require alterations only in computer programs, not retraining of an entire work force.

Time spent on activities that do not add value to the product can be eliminated or reduced by focusing on quality, improving plant layout, and cross-training workers. Achieving zero production defects ("doing it right the first time") reduces inspection time and eliminates rework time. One midwestern factory saved production time by redesigning its plant layout so that the distance products traveled from one operation to the next during production was reduced from 1,384 feet to 350 feet. Another company reduced setup time on a machine from 45 minutes to 1 minute by storing the required tools nearby and training the machine operator to do the setup. A British company reduced the time to manufacture a vacuum pump from 3 weeks to 6 minutes by switching from long assembly lines to manufacturing cells that accomplish the entire process in quick succession.

Originally, JIT referred only to an inventory system that minimized inventories by arranging for materials and subcomponents to arrive just as they were needed and for goods to be made just in time to be shipped to customers—no sooner and no later. But JIT has become the cornerstone of a broad management philosophy. It originated in Japanese companies such as Toyota and Kawasaki, and now has been adopted by many large U.S. companies including Hewlett-Packard and Xerox. Many small firms have also embraced JIT.

just-in-time (JIT) philosophy A philosophy to eliminate waste by reducing the time products spend in the production process and eliminating the time products spend on activities that do not add value.

computer-integrated manufacturing (CIM) systems Systems that use computer-aided design and computer-aided manufacturing, together with robots and computer-controlled machines.

IMPLICATIONS FOR THE STUDY OF MANAGEMENT ACCOUNTING

As you read the remainder of this book, remember that accounting systems change as the world changes. The techniques presented in this book are being applied in real organizations today. Tomorrow may be different, however. *To adapt to changes, you must understand why the techniques are being used, not just how they are used. We urge you to resist the temptation simply to memorize rules and techniques.* Instead, develop your understanding of the underlying concepts and principles. These will continue to be useful in developing and understanding new techniques for changing environments.

IMPORTANCE OF ETHICAL CONDUCT

Although accounting systems may change, the need for accountants to adhere to high ethical standards of professional conduct has never been greater.

STANDARDS OF ETHICAL CONDUCT

Public opinion surveys consistently rank accountants high in terms of their professional ethics. CPAs and CMAs adhere to codes of conduct regarding competence, confidentiality, integrity, and objectivity. Exhibit 1-10 contains the **Standards of Ethical Conduct for Management Accountants** developed by the IMA. Professional accounting organizations have procedures for reviewing alleged behavior not consistent with the standards.

> **Standards of Ethical Conduct for Management Accountants** Codes of conduct developed by the Institute of Management Accountants, which include competence, confidentiality, integrity, and objectivity.

Preparing objective, accurate external and internal financial reports is primarily the responsibility of line managers. However, management accountants are also responsible for the reports. Ensuring that accounting systems, procedures, and compilations are reliable and free of manipulation is the responsibility of every accountant.

ETHICAL DILEMMAS

What makes an action by an accountant unethical? An unethical act is one that violates the ethical standards of the profession. The standards, however, leave much room for individual interpretation and judgment.

When one action is clearly unethical and another alternative is clearly ethical, managers and accountants should have no difficulty choosing between them. Unfortunately, most ethical dilemmas are not that clear-cut. The most difficult ethical situations arise when there is strong pressure to take an action that is borderline or when two ethical standards conflict.

Suppose you are an accountant who has been asked to supply the company's banker with a profit forecast for the coming year. A badly needed bank loan rides on the prediction. The company president is absolutely convinced that profits will be at least $500,000. Anything less than that and the loan is not likely to be approved.

Your analysis shows that if the planned introduction of a new product goes extraordinarily well, profits will exceed $500,000. The most likely outcome, however, is for a modestly successful introduction and a $100,000 profit. If the product fails, the company stands to lose $600,000. Without the loan, the new product cannot be taken to the market, and there is no way the company can avoid a loss for the year. Bankruptcy is even a possibility.

What forecast would you make? There is no easy answer. A forecast of less than $500,000 seems to guarantee financial problems, perhaps even bankruptcy. Stockholders, management, employees, suppliers, and customers may all be hurt. But a forecast of $500,000 may not be fair and objective. The bank may be misled by it. Still, the president apparently thinks a $500,000 forecast is reasonable, and you know that there is some

Exhibit 1-10

Standards of Ethical Conduct for Management Accountants

Management accountants have an obligation to the organizations they serve, their profession, the public, and themselves to maintain the highest standards of ethical conduct. In recognition of this obligation, the Institute of Management Accountants has adopted the following standards of ethical conduct for management accountants. Adherence to these standards is integral to achieving the objectives of management accounting. Management accountants shall not commit acts contrary to these standards nor shall they condone the commission of such acts by others within their organizations.

Competence

Management accountants have a responsibility to
- Maintain an appropriate level of professional competence by ongoing development of their knowledge and skills.
- Perform their professional duties in accordance with relevant laws, regulations, and technical standards.
- Prepare complete and clear reports and recommendations after appropriate analyses of relevant and reliable information.

Confidentiality

Management accountants have a responsibility to
- Refrain from disclosing confidential information acquired in the course of their work except when authorized, unless legally obligated to do so.
- Inform subordinates as appropriate regarding the confidentiality of information acquired in the course of their work and monitor their activities to assure the maintenance of that confidentiality.
- Refrain from using or appearing to use confidential information acquired in the course of their work for unethical or illegal advantage either personally or through third parties.

Objective 7

Explain a management accountant's ethical responsibilities.

Integrity

Management accountants have a responsibility to
- Avoid actual or apparent conflicts of interest and advise all appropriate parties of any potential conflict.
- Refrain from engaging in any activity that would prejudice their ability to carry out their duties ethically.
- Refuse any gift, favor, or hospitality that would influence or would appear to influence their actions.
- Refrain from either actively or passively subverting the attainment of the organization's legitimate and ethical objectives.
- Recognize and communicate professional limitations or other constraints that would preclude responsible judgment or successful performance of an activity.
- Communicate unfavorable as well as favorable information and professional judgments or opinions.
- Refrain from engaging in or supporting any activity that would discredit the profession.

Objectivity

Management accountants have a responsibility to
- Communicate information fairly and objectively.
- Disclose fully all relevant information that could reasonably be expected to influence an intended user's understanding of the reports, comments, and recommendations presented.

Ethics at General Motors

The importance of ethics to management accountants was emphasized when *Management Accounting*, the journal of the Institute of Management Accountants, put out a special issue on ethics in June 1990. Two thrusts run through the articles in the issue: (1) business schools must make students aware of the ethical dimension of the decisions they will face in the business world, and (2) business firms must recognize that establishing standards of ethical conduct for their employees is important to financial success. As a follow-up, *Management Accounting* instituted a regular column on ethics. A recent column presented a case on the ethics of planned obsolescence of products. Many readers submitted solutions to the case, some of which were published in *Management Accounting*, showing that ethical dilemmas generate a great deal of interest.

Roger B. Smith, former Chairman and Chief Executive Officer of General Motors, stated that "ethical practice is, quite simply, good business." Since 1977 GM has had a policy on personal integrity. But GM recognizes that making ethical decisions is not always easy. Because the world is complex, there are often competing obligations to shareholders, customers, suppliers, fellow managers, society, and self and family. As Smith says, "It is easy to do what is right; it is hard to know what is right." A basic rule used by GM is that employees "should never do anything [they] would be ashamed to explain to [their] families or be afraid to see on the front page of the local newspaper."

General Motors is not alone in promoting ethical conduct. Over half of the large companies in the United States have a "Corporate Code of Conduct." These codes provide support to employees who feel pressured to make decisions they believe to be unethical. They also provide training in the types of behavior expected of employees.

Sources: Adapted from Roger B. Smith, "Ethics in Business: An Essential Element of Success," *Management Accounting*, Special Issue on Ethics in Corporate America (June 1990), p. 50; Robert B. Sweeney and Howard L. Siers, "Ethics in America," *Management Accounting*, Special Issue on Ethics in Corporate America (June 1990); pp. 34–40; and James A. Healy and Roy L. Nersesian, "The Case of Planned Obsolescence," *Management Accounting* (February 1994), pp. 67–68.

chance it will be achieved. Perhaps the potential benefit to the company of an overly optimistic forecast is greater than the possible cost to the bank.

There is no right answer to this dilemma. The important point is to recognize the ethical dimensions and weigh them when forming your judgment.

The tone set by top management can have a great influence on managers' ethics. Complete integrity and outspoken support for ethical standards by senior managers is the single greatest motivator of ethical behavior throughout an organization. In the final analysis, however, ethical standards are personal and depend on the values of the individual.

SUMMARY PROBLEM FOR YOUR REVIEW

PROBLEM

Yang Electronics Company (YEC) developed a high-speed, low-cost copying machine. It marketed the machine primarily for home use. However, as YEC customers learned how easy and inexpensive it was to make copies with the YEC machine, its use by small businesses grew. Sales soared as some businesses ordered large numbers of the copiers. However, the heavier use by these companies caused breakdowns in a certain component of the equipment. The copiers were warrantied for two years, regardless of the amount of usage. Consequently, YEC experienced high costs for replacing the damaged components.

As the quarterly meeting of the Board of Directors of YEC approached, Mark Chua, assistant controller, was asked to prepare a report on the situation. Unfortunately, it was hard to predict the exact effects. However, it seemed that many business customers were starting to switch to more expensive copiers sold by competitors. And it was clear that the increased maintenance costs would significantly affect YEC's profitability. Mark summarized the situation as best he could for the Board.

Alice Martinez, the controller of YEC, was concerned about the impact of the report on the Board. She does not disagree with the analysis, but thinks it makes management look bad and might even lead the Board to discontinue the product. She is convinced from conversations with the head of engineering that the copier can be slightly redesigned to meet the needs of higher-volume users, so discontinuing it may pass up a potentially profitable opportunity.

Martinez called Chua into her office and asked him to delete the part of his report dealing with the component failures. She said it was all right to mention this orally to the Board, noting that engineering is nearing a solution to the problem. However, Chua feels strongly that such a revision in his report would mislead the Board about a potentially significant negative impact on the company's earnings.

Required Explain why Martinez's request to Chua is unethical. How should Chua resolve this situation?

SOLUTION

According to the Standards of Ethical Conduct for Management Accountants in Exhibit 1-10, Martinez's request violates requirements for competence, integrity, and objectivity. It violates competence because she is asking Chua to prepare a report that is not complete and clear, one that omits potentially relevant information. Therefore, the Board will not have all the information it should to make a decision about the component failure problem.

The request violates the integrity requirement because the revised report may subvert the attainment of the organization's objectives in order to achieve Martinez's objectives. Management accountants are specifically responsible for communicating unfavorable as well as favorable information.

Finally, the revised report would not be objective. It would not disclose all relevant information that could be expected to influence the Board's understanding of operations and therefore their decisions.

Chua's responsibility is to discuss this issue with increasingly higher levels of authority within YEC. First, he should let Martinez know about his misgivings. Possibly the issue can be resolved by her withdrawing the request. If not, he should inform her that he intends to take up the matter with her superior and then continue up to higher levels of authority, even to the Board, if necessary, until the issue is resolved. So that Chua does not violate the standard of confidentiality, he should not discuss the matter with persons outside of YEC.

Highlights to Remember

Describe the major users of accounting information. Accounting information is useful to internal managers for making short-term planning and control decisions, for making nonroutine decisions, and for formulating overall policies and long-range plans. Using accounting information, managers answer scorekeeping, attention-directing, and problem-solving questions.

Explain the cost-benefit and behavioral issues involved in designing an accounting system. Management accounting information systems are designed for the benefit of managers. These systems should be judged by a cost-benefit criterion—the benefits of better decisions should exceed the cost of the system. The benefit of a system will be affected by behavioral factors—how the system affects managers and their decisions.

Explain the role of budgets and performance reports in planning and control. Budgets and performance reports are essential tools for planning and control. Budgets result from the planning process and are a means of translating the organization's goals into action. A performance report compares actual results to the budget. Managers use these reports to monitor, evaluate, and reward performance and thus, exercise control.

Discuss the role accountants play in the company's value-chain functions. Accountants play a key role in planning and control. Throughout the company's value chain, accountants gather and report cost and revenue information for decision makers.

Contrast the functions of controllers and treasurers. Accountants are staff employees who provide information and advice for line managers. The head of accounting is often called the controller. Unlike the treasurer, who is concerned mainly with financial matters, the controller measures and reports on operating performance.

Identify current trends in management accounting. The future worth of an accounting system and accountants themselves will be affected by how easily and well they can adapt to change. Current trends affecting accounting systems include growth in the service sector of the economy, increased global competition, and advances in technology.

Explain a management accountant's ethical responsibilities. Both external and internal accountants are expected to adhere to standards of ethical conduct. Many ethical dilemmas, however, require value judgments, not the simple application of standards.

Understand how managerial accounting is used in companies. Management accounting plays a vital role in the achievement of company goals and objectives. Management accounting information is used across the entire value chain of activities as well as throughout the life cycle of products and services. In today's modern business environment, management accountants are playing an increasingly vital role because the need for accounting information to support decision making is greater than ever before.

Accounting Vocabulary

Vocabulary is an essential and often troublesome phase of the learning process. A fuzzy understanding of terms hampers the learning of concepts and the ability to solve accounting problems.

Before proceeding to the assignment material or to the next chapter, be sure you understand the words and terms listed below. Their meaning is explained in the chapter and in the glossary at the end of this book.

accounting system, p. 6
attention directing, p. 5
behavioral implications, p. 9
budget, p. 10
Certified Management
  Accountant (CMA), p. 20
Certified Public Accountant
  (CPA), p. 20
comptroller, p. 16
computer-integrated manufacturing (CIM) systems, p. 22
controller, p. 16
cost-benefit balance, p. 9

decision making, p. 9
financial accounting, p. 5
Foreign Corrupt Practices Act,
  p. 7
generally accepted accounting
  principles (GAAP), p. 6
Institute of Management
  Accountants (IMA), p. 20
just-in-time (JIT) philosophy,
  p. 22
line authority, p. 16
management accounting, p. 5
management audit, p. 7

management by exception,
  p. 11
performance reports, p. 10
problem solving, p. 5
product life cycle, p. 12
scorekeeping, p. 5
staff authority, p. 16
Standards of Ethical Conduct
  for Management Accoun-
  tants, p. 23
variances, p. 10
value chain, p. 13

Fundamental Assignment Material

The assignment material for each chapter is divided into two groups: *fundamental* and *additional*. The fundamental assignment material consists of two sets of parallel problems that convey the essential concepts and techniques of the chapter. The additional assignment material consists of questions, exercises, problems, cases, and collaborative learning exercises that cover the chapter in more detail.

1-A1 Scorekeeping, Attention Directing, and Problem Solving

For each of the activities listed below, identify the function that the accountant is performing—scorekeeping, attention directing, or problem solving—and explain why it fits that category.

1. Analyzing, for an Alcoa production superintendent, the impact on costs of some new drill presses.
2. Preparing a scrap report for the finishing department of a Mazda parts factory.
3. Preparing the budget for the maintenance department of Providence Hospital.
4. Interpreting why a Springfield foundry did not adhere to its production schedule.
5. Explaining the stamping department's performance report.
6. Preparing a monthly statement of European sales for the Ford marketing vice-president.
7. Preparing, for the manager of production control of an Inland Steel plant, a cost comparison of two computerized manufacturing control systems.
8. Interpreting variances on the Princeton University purchasing department's performance report.
9. Analyzing, for a Honda international manufacturing manager, the desirability of having some auto parts made in Korea.
10. Preparing a schedule of depreciation for forklift trucks in the receiving department of a General Electric factory in Scotland.

1-A2 Management by Exception

Beta Alpha Psi, the accounting honorary fraternity, held a homecoming party. The fraternity expected attendance of 80 persons and prepared the following budget:

Room rental	$ 150
Food	800
Entertainment	600
Decorations	220
Total	$1,770

After all bills for the party were paid, the total cost came to $1,948, or $178 over budget. Details are $150 for room rental; $1,013 for food; $600 for entertainment; and $185 for decorations. Ninety-five persons attended the party.

Required

1. Prepare a performance report for the party that shows how actual costs differed from the budget. That is, include in your report the budget amounts, actual amounts, and variances.
2. Suppose the fraternity uses a management-by-exception rule. Which costs deserve further examination? Why?

1-A3 Accounting's Position in the Organization: Line and Staff Functions

1. Of the following, who has line authority over a cost record clerk: budgetary accountant, head of accounting for current planning and control, head of gen-

eral accounting, controller, storekeeper, production superintendent, manufacturing vice-president, president, production control chief?

2. Of the following, who has line authority over an assembler: stamping manager, assembly manager, production superintendent, production control chief, storekeeper, manufacturing vice-president, engineering vice-president, president, controller, budgetary accountant, cost record clerk?

1-B1 Scorekeeping, Attention Directing, and Problem Solving

For each of the activities listed below identify the function the accountant is performing—scorekeeping, attention directing, or problem solving. Explain each of your answers.

1. Daily recording of material purchase vouchers.
2. Analyzing the costs of acquiring and using each of two alternate types of welding equipment.
3. Preparing a report of overtime labor costs by production departments.
4. Posting daily cash collections to customers' accounts.
5. Estimating the costs of moving corporate headquarters to another city.
6. Interpreting increases in nursing costs per patient-day in a hospital.
7. Analyzing deviations from the budget of the factory maintenance department.
8. Assisting in a study by the manufacturing vice-president to determine whether to buy certain parts needed in large quantities for manufacturing products or to acquire facilities for manufacturing these parts.
9. Allocating factory service department costs to production departments.
10. Recording overtime hours of the product finishing department.
11. Compiling data for a report showing the ratio of advertising expenses to sales for each branch store.
12. Investigating reasons for increased returns and allowances for drugs purchased by a hospital.
13. Preparing a schedule of fuel costs by months and government departments.
14. Estimating the operating costs and outputs that could be expected for each of two large metal-stamping machines offered for sale by different manufacturers. Only one of these machines is to be acquired by your company.
15. Computing and recording end-of-year adjustments for expired fire insurance on the factory warehouse for materials.

1-B2 Management by Exception

The Makah Indian Tribe sells fireworks for the 5 weeks preceding July 4th. The tribe's stand at the corner of Highway 104 and Eagle Drive was the largest, with budgeted sales for 19X8 of $80,000. Expected expenses were as follows:

Cost of fireworks	$40,000
Labor cost	15,000
Other costs	8,000
Total costs	$63,000

Actual sales were $79,860, almost equal to the budget. The tribe spent $44,000 for fireworks, $13,000 for labor, and $8,020 for other costs.

1. Compute budgeted profit and actual profit.

Required

2. Prepare a performance report to help identify those costs that were significantly different from the budget.

3. Suppose the tribe uses a management-by-exception rule. What costs deserve further explanation? Why?

1-B3 Accounting's Position in the Organization: Controller and Treasurer

For each of the following activities, indicate whether it is most likely to be performed by the controller or treasurer. Explain each answer.

1. Prepare credit checks on customers.
2. Help managers prepare budgets.
3. Advise which alternative action is least costly.
4. Prepare divisional financial statements.
5. Arrange short-term financing.
6. Prepare tax returns.
7. Arrange insurance coverage.
8. Meet with financial analysts from Wall Street.

Additional Assignment Material

QUESTIONS

1-1. Who uses information from an accounting system?

1-2. "The emphases of financial accounting and management accounting differ." Explain.

1-3. "The field is less sharply defined. There is heavier use of economics, decision sciences, and behavioral sciences." Identify the branch of accounting described in the quotation.

1-4. Distinguish among scorekeeping, attention directing, and problem solving.

1-5. "Additional government regulation assists the development of management accounting systems." Do you agree? Explain.

1-6. "The Foreign Corrupt Practices Act applies to bribes paid outside the United States." Do you agree? Explain.

1-7. Give three examples of service organizations. What distinguishes them from other types of organizations?

1-8. What two major considerations affect all accounting systems? Explain each.

1-9. "The accounting system is intertwined with operating management. Business operations would be a hopeless tangle without the paperwork that is so often regarded with disdain." Do you agree? Explain, giving examples.

1-10. Distinguish among a budget, a performance report, and a variance.

1-11. "Management by exception means abdicating management responsibility for planning and control." Do you agree? Explain.

1-12. "Good accounting provides automatic control of operations." Do you agree? Explain.

1-13. Why are accountants concerned about the product life cycle?

1-14. Name the six business functions that comprise the value chain.

1-15. "Accountants in every company should measure and report on every function in the company's value chain." Do you agree? Explain.

1-16. Distinguish between line and staff authority.

1-17. Distinguish between a controller and a treasurer. Does every company have both a controller and a treasurer? Explain.

1-18. "The controller does control in a special sense." Explain.

1-19. Describe the contents of the qualifying examination for becoming a CMA.

1-20. How are changes in technology affecting management accounting?

1-21. What is the essence of the JIT philosophy?

1-22. Standards of ethical conduct for management accountants have been divided into four major responsibilities. Describe each of the four in 20 words or less.

1-23. "Why are there ethical dilemmas? I thought accountants had standards that specified what is ethical behavior." Discuss.

EXERCISES

1-24 Management Accounting and Financial Accounting

Consider the following short descriptions. Indicate whether each description more closely relates to a major feature of financial accounting or management accounting.

1. Behavioral impact is secondary
2. Is constrained by generally accepted accounting principles
3. Has a future orientation
4. Is characterized by detailed reports
5. Field is more sharply defined
6. Has less flexibility
7. Provides internal consulting advice to managers

1-25 Line Versus Staff

For each of the following, indicate whether the employee has line (L) or staff (S) responsibility:

1. Production superintendent
2. Cost accountant
3. Market research analyst
4. District sales manager
5. Head of the legal department
6. President

1-26 Organization Chart

Draw an organization chart for a single-factory company with the personnel listed below. Which represent factory-service departments? Production departments?

Personnel vice-president
Maintenance manager
Sales vice-president
Production control chief
Production planning chief
Assembly manager
Purchasing agent
Secretary and treasurer
President
Punch press manager
Vice-president and controller
Scorekeeper
Drill press manager
Production superintendent
Chairman of the board
Engineering vice-president
Manufacturing vice-president

1-27 Objectives of Management Accounting

The Institute of Management Accountants (IMA) is composed of about 70,000 members. The IMA "Objectives of Management Accounting" states: "The management accountant participates, as part of management, in assuring that the organization operates as a unified whole in its long-run, intermediate, and short-run best interests."

Required

Based on your reading in this chapter, prepare a 100-word description of the principal ways that accountants participate in managing an entity.

PROBLEMS

1-28 Management and Financial Accounting

Judy Burkett, an able mechanical engineer, was informed that she would be promoted to assistant factory manager. Judy was pleased but uncomfortable. In particular, she knew little about accounting. She had taken one course in financial accounting.

Judy planned to enroll in a management accounting course as soon as possible. Meanwhile she asked Burt Greenspan, a cost accountant, to state three or four of the principal distinctions between financial and management accounting.

Prepare Burt's written response to Judy.

1-29   Use of Accounting Information in Hospitals

Most revenues of U.S. hospitals do not come directly from patients. Instead, revenues come through third parties such as insurance companies and government agencies. Until the 1980s, these payments generally reimbursed the hospital's costs of serving patients. Such payments, however, are now generally flat fees for specified services. For example, the hospital might receive $5,000 for an appendectomy or $25,000 for heart surgery—no more, no less.

Required

How might the method of payment change the demand for accounting information in hospitals? Relate your answer to the decisions of top management.

1-30   Costs and Benefits

Marks & Spencer, a huge retailer in the United Kingdom, was troubled by its paper bureaucracy. Looked at in isolation, each form seemed reasonable, but overall a researcher reported that there was substantial effort in each department to verify the information. Basically, the effort seemed out of proportion to any value received, and, eventually, many of the documents were simplified or eliminated.

Describe the rationale that should govern systems design.

1-31   Importance of Accounting

A news story reported:

> Rockwell's Anderson, a veteran of the company's automotive operations, recalls that when he sat in on meetings at Rockwell's North American Aircraft Operations 20 years ago, "there'd be 60 or 70 guys talking technical problems, with never a word on profits." Such inattention to financial management helped Rockwell lose the F-15 fighter to McDonnell Douglas, Pentagon sources say. Anderson brought in profit-oriented executives, and he has now transformed North American's staff meetings to the point that "you seldom hear talk of technical problems any more," he says. "It's all financial."

What is your reaction to Anderson's comments? Are his comments related to management accounting?

1-32   Changes in Accounting Systems

In the early 1990s, the Boeing Company undertook a large-scale study of its accounting system. The study led to several significant changes. None of these changes was required for reporting to external parties. Management thought, however, that the new system gave more accurate costs of the airplanes and other products produced.

Required

1. Boeing had been a very successful company using its old accounting system. What might have motivated it to change the system?
2. When Boeing changed its system, what criteria might its managers have used to decide whether to invest in the new system?
3. Is changing to a system that provides more accurate product costs always a good strategy? Why or why not?

1-33 Value Chain

Nike is an Oregon-based company that focuses on the design, development, and world-wide marketing of high quality footwear, apparel, equipment, and accessory products. Nike is the largest seller of athletic footwear and athletic apparel in the world. The Company sells its products to approximately 19,700 retail accounts in the United States and through a mix of independent distributors, licensees, and subsidiaries in approximately 110 countries around the world. Virtually all of the Company's products are manufactured by independent contractors. Most footwear products are produced outside the United States, while apparel products are produced both in the United States and abroad.

Required

1. Identify one decision that Nike managers make in each of the six value-chain functions.
2. For each decision in requirement 1, identify one piece of accounting information that would aid the manager's decision.

1-34 Role of Controller

Juanita Palencia, newly-hired controller of Braxton Industries, had been lured away from a competitor to revitalize the Controller's department. Her first day on the job proved to be an eye-opener. One of her first interviews was with Bill Belton, production supervisor in the Cleveland Factory. Belton commented: "I really don't want to talk to anyone from the Controller's office. The only time we see those accountants is when our costs go over their budget. They wave what they call a 'performance report,' but it's actually just a bunch of numbers they make up. It has nothing to do with what happens on the shop floor. Besides, my men can't afford the time to fill out all the paperwork those accountants want, so I just plug in some numbers and send it back. Now, if you'll let me get back to important matters. . . ." Palencia left quickly, but she was already planning for her next visit with Belton.

Required

1. Identify some of the problems in the relationship between the Controller's department and the production departments (assuming that the Cleveland Factory is representative of the production departments).
2. What should Juanita Palencia do next?

1-35 Ethical Issues

Suppose you are controller of a medium-sized oil exploration company in west Texas. You adhere to the standards of ethical conduct for management accountants. How would those standards affect your behavior in each of the following situations?

1. Late one Friday afternoon you receive a geologist's report on a newly purchased property. It indicates a much higher probability of oil than had previously been expected. You are the only one to read the report that day. At a party on Saturday night, a friend asks about the prospects for the property.
2. An oil industry stock analyst invites you and your spouse to spend a week in Hawaii free of charge. All she wants in return is to be the first to know about any financial information your company is about to announce to the public.
3. It is time to make a forecast of the company's annual earnings. You know that some additional losses will be recognized before the final statements are prepared. The company's president has asked you to ignore these losses in making your prediction because a lower-than-expected earnings forecast could adversely affect the chances of obtaining a loan that is being negotiated and will be completed before actual earnings are announced.

4. You do not know whether a particular expense is deductible for income tax purposes. You are debating whether to research the tax laws or simply to assume that the item is deductible. After all, if you are not audited, no one will ever know the difference. If you are audited, you can plead ignorance of the law.

 BUSINESS FIRST   www.prenhall.com/phlip

1-36   The Accountant's Role in an Organization

Marmon Company is a collection of 60 different operating companies with revenues of $6 billion. Its member companies manufacture such diverse products as copper tubing, water purification products, railroad tank cars, store fixtures, and provide services such as credit information for banks.

The introduction to this chapter described the role of accountants in Marmon. Others have described accountants as "internal consultants." Refer back to the discussion of Marmon on pages 3–4. Discuss how accountants at Marmon can act as internal consultants. What kind of background and knowledge would an accountant require to be an effective internal consultant?   ■

CASES

1-37   Line and Staff Authority (CMA adapted)

Electronic Equipment Leasing Company (EEL) leases office equipment to a variety of customers. The company's organization chart follows:

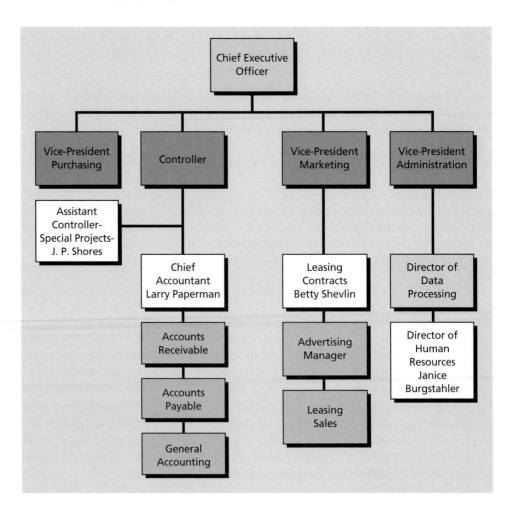

The four positions highlighted in the chart are described below:

- J. P. Shores, Assistant Controller–Special Projects. Shores works on projects assigned to him by the controller. The most recent project was to design a new accounts payable system.

- Betty Shevlin, Leasing Contracts Manager. Shevlin coordinates and implements leasing transactions. Her department handles all transactions after the sales department gets a signed contract. This includes requisitioning equipment from the purchasing department, maintaining appropriate insurance, delivering equipment, issuing billing statements, and seeking renewal of leases.

- Larry Paperman, Chief Accountant. Paperman supervises all the accounting functions. He produces reports for the four supervisors in the functional areas.

- Janice Burgstahler, Director of Human Resources. Burgstahler works with all departments of EEL in hiring of personnel. Her department advertises all positions and screens candidates, but the individual departments conduct interviews and make hiring decisions. Burgstahler also coordinates employee evaluations and administers the company's salary schedule and fringe benefit program.

Required

1. Distinguish between line and staff positions in an organization and discuss why conflicts might arise between line and staff managers.

2. For each of the four managers described, identify whether their position is a line or staff position and explain why you classified it that way. Also, indicate any potential conflicts that might arise with other managers in the organization.

1-38 Ethics and Accounting Personnel

Red Ball Beverage Company has an equal opportunity employment policy. This policy has the full support of the company's president, Beverly Chiapello, and is included in all advertisements for open positions.

Hiring in the accounting department is done by the controller, D. W. "Butch" Laughton. The assistant controller, Jack Myers, also interviews candidates, but Laughton makes all decisions. In the last year, the department hired five new persons. There had been a total of 175 applications for the open positions. From this set, thirteen had been interviewed, including four minority candidates. The five hired included three sons of close friends of Laughton and no minorities. Myers had felt that at least two of the minority candidates were very well qualified and that the three sons of Laughton's friends were definitely not among the most qualified.

When Myers questioned Laughton concerning his reservations about the hiring practices, he was told that these decisions were Laughton's and not his, so he should not question them.

Required

1. Explain why Laughton's hiring practices were probably unethical.

2. What should Myers do about this situation?

1-39 Professional Ethics and Toxic Waste

Yukon Mining Company extracts and processes a variety of ores and minerals. One of its operations is a coal cleaning plant that produces toxic wastes. For many years the wastes have been properly disposed of through National Disposal, a company experienced in disposing of such items. However, disposal of the toxic wastes was becoming an economic hardship because increasing government regulations had caused the cost of such disposal to quadruple in the last six years.

Rebecca Long, Director of Financial Reporting for Yukon Mining, was preparing the company's financial statements for the year ended June 30, 1998. In researching the material needed for preparing a footnote on environmental contingencies, Rebecca found the following note scribbled in pencil at the bottom of a memo to the General Manager of the coal cleaning plant. The body of the memo gave details on the increases in the cost of toxic waste disposals:

> *Ralph—We've got to keep these costs down or we won't meet budget. Can we mix more of these wastes with the shipments of refuse to the Oak Hill landfill? Nobody seems to notice the coal-cleaning fluids when we mix it in well.*

Rebecca was bothered by the note. She considered ignoring it, pretending that she had not seen it. But after a couple hours, her conscience would not let her do it. Therefore, she pondered the following three alternative courses of action:

   a. Seek the advice of her boss, the Vice-President, Finance of Yukon.

   b. Anonymously release the information to the local newspaper.

   c. Give the information to an outside member of the board of directors of Yukon who she knew because he lived in her neighborhood.

Required

   1. Discuss why Rebecca Long has an ethical responsibility to take some action about her suspicion of illegal dumping of toxic wastes.

   2. For each of the three alternative courses of action, explain whether the action is appropriate.

   3. Assume that Rebecca sought the advice of the Vice-President, Finance and discovered that he knew about and approved of the dumping of toxic wastes. What steps should she take to resolve the conflict in this situation?

COLLABORATIVE LEARNING EXERCISE

1-40 The Future Management Accountant

Form groups of four to six students each. Half of each group should read the first of the following articles and half should read the second article. (Alternatively, this exercise can be done as a total class, with half of the class reading each article.)

   1. Kulesza, C., and G. Siegel, "It's Not Your Father's Management Accounting," *Management Accounting* (May 1997), pp. 56–59.

   2. Siegel, G., and C. Kulesza, "The Practice Analysis of Management Accounting," *Management Accounting* (April 1996), pp. 20–28.

Required

   1. Individually write down the three most important lessons you learned from the article you read.

2. As a group, list all the lessons identified in requirement 1. Combine those that are essentially the same.

3. Prioritize the list you developed in requirement 2 in terms of their importance to one considering a career in management accounting.

4. Discuss whether this exercise has changed your impression of management accounting and, if so, how your impression has changed.

INTRODUCTION TO COST BEHAVIOR AND COST-VOLUME RELATIONSHIPS

Boeing's 767-300 ER has earned passenger ratings as one of the most preferred airplanes in every class of service. One reason is that 87% of the seats are next to a window or aisle.

Learning Objectives

When you have finished studying this chapter, you should be able to

1 Explain how cost drivers affect cost behavior.

2 Show how changes in cost-driver activity levels affect variable and fixed costs.

3 Calculate break-even sales volume in total dollars and total units.

4 Create a cost-volume-profit graph and understand the assumptions behind it.

5 Calculate sales volume in total dollars and total units to reach a target profit.

6 Distinguish between contribution margin and gross margin.

7 Explain the effects of sales mix on profits (Appendix 2A).

8 Compute cost-volume-profit relationships on an after-tax basis (Appendix 2B).

9 **Understand how cost behavior and cost-volume-profit analysis are used by managers.**

In 1915, William Boeing, a Seattle timberman, assembled his first airplane in a boathouse. Today, the Boeing Company produces more than 40 jetliners each month and has annual revenues of more than $22 billion. The company has two-thirds of the world's market share in airplane sales, but that could change as the competition steps up to meet growing demand. Over the next two decades, the airline industry will need 16,000 new airplanes worth over $1 trillion. How will Boeing maintain its competitive edge and profitability? With increased competition, Boeing knows that profits can be improved more by controlling (reducing) costs than by increasing prices to customers. So, should it build bigger airplanes or more of the existing size but with improvements in features and efficiencies that will lower customers' costs? Which alternative has lower costs for Boeing and its customers? To answer these questions, Boeing had to understand its own costs as well as the costs of its customers. The real question is what do its customers value in return for a price tag of $50+ million per airplane?

A case in point is the Boeing 747-X. In 1992, the company began its research and development program for this huge 500-passenger airplane. An important part of its research was the assessment of its customers' costs—both of operating their existing fleet of planes and of the reduced costs of the new 747-X planes. It formed a working group with 19 airline customers (for example, United and American Airlines, and British Airways) to look at their requirements in the 500+-seat market. By 1996, the company had completed the design of the new airplane and was faced with the final decision to launch. A decision to launch would involve a huge immediate investment in costly plant and equipment resources. In order to pay for these assets and make a profit, it had to be confident that its customers would demand the new plane.

The key question was whether customers wanted the latest, largest, and most costly airplane or one with the highest value? In 1997, Boeing made the final decision. According to Philip Condit, Chairman and Chief Executive Officer, "The prospective market for airplanes with over 500 seats was limited. We were at last in a position of balancing the significant cost of the program against the limited size of the market." Most of the company's customers needed more airplanes for the expected increase in the number of nonstop routes. In short, customers said, "We would rather have two new 250-seat airplanes that are more cost efficient than one 500-seat super airplane." So, the 747-X program was stopped. Instead, the company is concentrating on upgrading its existing aircraft. For example, Boeing's new model of the existing 747 will offer 16% more seats and up to 10% lower "seat-mile" costs.

How are the costs and revenues of an airline affected when one more passenger is added at the last moment, or when one more flight is added to the schedule? How should the budget request by the Arizona Department of Motor Vehicles be affected by the predicted increase in the state's population? These questions are really different forms of one common question: What will happen to financial results if a specified level of activity or volume changes?

Although financial results are based on revenues and costs, we will focus primarily on costs in this chapter. After all, as we saw in the case of Boeing, companies usually have more control over their costs than they do over their revenues. In fact, one of the main goals of management accounting is controlling (and reducing) costs. But managers cannot control costs unless they understand **cost behavior**—how costs are related to and affected by the activities of the organization.

cost behavior How costs are related to and affected by the activities of an organization.

ACTIVITIES, COSTS, AND COST DRIVERS

Different types of costs behave in different ways. Consider Boeing Company's costs of an existing plant that makes the 737 business jets. The cost of materials such as electrical wire, seats, and aluminum increase as the number of airplanes manufactured increases. But the cost of the plant and salaries of key managers stays the same regardless of the number of airplanes made. Associating cost behavior with units of product produced gives us an overall view of how costs behave, but it does little to help managers control costs on a day-to-day basis.

On a day-to-day basis, managers focus their efforts on managing the activities required to make products or deliver services—not on the products and services themselves. A production manager needs to know how routine activities such as machine maintenance and repairs affect costs. So, because understanding costs is so important for cost control, associating costs with activities is a key. For example, one of the activities performed at Boeing's plant is *receiving* parts to be installed on the airplane. Receiving managers need to know how their activities affect costs. Costs such as depreciation of the equipment used to move parts from one location in the plant to another do not change when receiving activity increases or decreases. However, costs such as fuel for the same moving equipment do change with activity changes. Actually, we should say that activities such as receiving require resources such as moving equipment and fuel and that these resources cost money.

Objective 1
Explain how cost drivers affect cost behavior.

But how exactly do accountants relate activities to resource costs in a way that makes cost control possible? Accountants determine output measures of both resources and

Exhibit 2-1

Examples of Value-Chain Functions, Costs, and Cost Drivers

Value-Chain Function and Example Costs	Example Cost Drivers
Research and development	
• Salaries of marketing research personnel, costs of market surveys	Number of new product proposals
• Salaries of product and process engineers	Complexity of proposed products
Design of products, services, and processes	
• Salaries of product and process engineers	Number of engineering hours
• Cost of computer-aided design equipment, cost to develop prototype of product for testing	Number of parts per product
Production	
• Labor wages	Labor hours
• Supervisory salaries	Number of people supervised
• Maintenance wages	Number of mechanic hours
• Depreciation of plant and machinery, supplies	Number of machine hours
• Energy	Kilowatt hours
Marketing	
• Cost of advertisements	Number of advertisements
• Salaries of marketing personnel, travel costs, entertainment costs	Sales dollars
Distribution	
• Wages of shipping personnel	Labor hours
• Transportation costs including depreciation of vehicles and fuel	Weight of items delivered
Customer service	
• Salaries of service personnel	Hours spent servicing products
• Costs of supplies, travel	Number of service calls

activities. These output measures (or factors) are called **cost drivers.** In our receiving example, the cost driver or output measure of receiving activity could be "number of parts received" or "weight of parts received." The receiving manager can easily understand how an increase in the number of parts received or the weight of parts received can increase or "drive" the use (and therefore cost) of fuel and moving equipment.

An organization has many cost drivers across its value chain. Exhibit 2-1 lists examples of costs and potential cost drivers for each of the value-chain functions. How well the accountant does at identifying the most appropriate cost drivers determines how well managers understand cost behavior and how well costs are controlled.

cost drivers Output measures of resources and activities.

COMPARISON OF VARIABLE AND FIXED COSTS

A key to understanding cost behavior is distinguishing *variable costs* from *fixed costs.* Costs are classified as variable or fixed depending on how much they change as the level of a particular cost driver changes. A **variable cost** is a cost that changes in direct proportion to changes in the cost driver. In contrast, a **fixed cost** is not immediately affected by changes in the cost driver. Suppose units of production is the cost driver of interest. A 10% increase in the units of production would produce a 10% increase in variable costs. However, the fixed costs would remain unchanged.

Consider some variable costs. Suppose Watkins Products pays its door-to-door sales personnel a 40% straight commission on sales. The total cost of sales commissions to Watkins is 40% of sales dollars—a variable cost with respect to sales revenues. Or suppose Dan's Bait Shop buys bags of fish bait for $2 each. The total cost of fish bait is $2 times the number of bags purchased—a variable cost with respect to units (number of

variable cost A cost that changes in direct proportion to changes in the cost driver.

fixed cost A cost that is not immediately affected by changes in the cost driver.

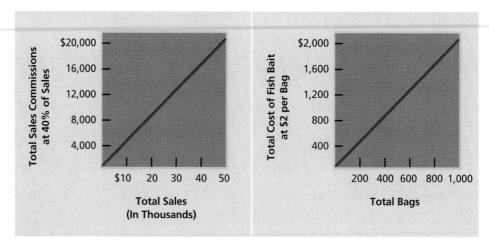

Exhibit 2-2

Variable-Cost Behavior

Objective 2

Show how changes in cost-driver activity levels affect variable and fixed costs.

bags) purchased. Notice that variable costs do not change *per unit,* but that the *total* costs change in direct proportion to the cost-driver activity. Exhibit 2-2 shows these relationships between cost and cost-driver activity graphically.

Now consider a fixed cost. Suppose Sony rents a factory to produce picture tubes for color television sets for $500,000 per year. The total cost of $500,000 is not affected by the number of picture tubes produced. The unit cost of rent applicable to each tube, however, does depend on the total number of tubes produced. If 100,000 tubes are produced, the unit cost will be $500,000 ÷ 100,000 = $5. If 50,000 tubes are produced, the unit cost will be $500,000 ÷ 50,000 = $10. Therefore, a fixed cost does not change in total, but it becomes progressively smaller on a per-unit basis as the volume increases.

Note carefully from these examples that the "variable" or "fixed" characteristic of a cost relates to its total dollar amount and not to its per-unit amount. The following table summarizes these relationships.

Type of Cost	If Cost-Driver Activity Level Increases (or Decreases)	
	Total Cost	*Cost Per Unit**
Fixed costs	No change	Decrease (or increase)
Variable costs	Increase (or decrease)	No change

*Per unit of activity volume, for example, product units, passenger-miles, sales dollars.

When analyzing costs, two rules of thumb are useful:

1. Think of fixed costs as a total. Total fixed costs remain unchanged regardless of changes in cost-driver activity.
2. Think of variable costs on a per-unit basis. The per-unit variable cost remains unchanged regardless of changes in cost-driver activity.

RELEVANT RANGE

Although we have just described fixed costs as unchanging regardless of changes in the given cost driver, this rule of thumb holds true only within reasonable limits. For example, rent costs, which are generally fixed, will rise if increased production requires a larger or additional building—or if the landlord just decides to raise the rent. Conversely, rent costs may go down if decreased production causes the company to move to a smaller plant. The **relevant range** is the limit of cost-driver activity within which a specific relationship between costs and the cost driver is valid. Even within the relevant range, though, a fixed cost remains fixed only over a given period of time—usually the budget period. Fixed costs may change from budget year to budget year solely because of changes in insurance and property tax rates, executive salary levels, or rent levels. But these items are unlikely to change within a given year.

relevant range The limit of cost-driver activity within which a specific relationship between costs and the cost driver is valid.

For example, suppose that a General Electric plant has a relevant range of between 40,000 and 85,000 cases of lightbulbs per month and that total monthly fixed costs within the relevant range are $100,000. Within the relevant range, fixed costs will remain the same. If production falls below 40,000 cases, changes in personnel and salaries would slash fixed costs to $60,000. If operations rise above 85,000 cases, increases in personnel and salaries would boost fixed costs to $115,000.

These assumptions—a given period and a given activity range—are shown graphically at the top of Exhibit 2-3. It is highly unusual, however, for monthly operations to be outside the relevant range. Therefore, the three-level refinement at the top of Exhibit 2-3 is usually not graphed. Instead, a single horizontal line is typically extended through the plotted activity levels, as at the bottom of the exhibit. Often a dashed line is used outside the relevant range.

The basic idea of a relevant range also applies to variable costs. That is, outside a relevant range, some variable costs, such as fuel consumed, may behave differently per unit of cost-driver activity. For example, the variable cost of a canning machine at Del Monte might be $5 for every hour it is used, assuming that it will be used between 30–50 hours each week. However, if it is used for more than 50 hours a week, the added wear and tear might increase variable costs to $6 for those hours beyond 50.

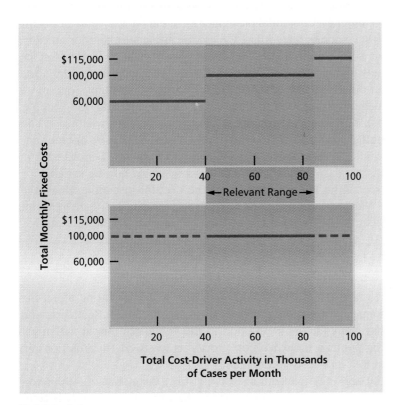

Exhibit 2-3

Fixed Costs and Relevant Range

DIFFERENCES IN CLASSIFYING COSTS

As you may suspect, it is often difficult to classify a cost as exactly variable or exactly fixed. Many complications arise including the possibility of costs behaving in some nonlinear way (not producing a straight line graph). For example, as tax preparers learn to process the new year's tax forms, their productivity rises. This means that total costs may actually behave as in Panel A that follows, not as in Panel B.

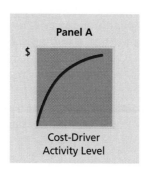

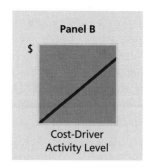

Moreover, costs may simultaneously be affected by more than one cost driver. For example, the costs of shipping labor may be affected by *both* the weight and the number of units handled. We shall investigate various facets of this problem in succeeding chapters; for now, we shall assume that any cost may be classified as either variable or fixed. We assume also that a given variable cost is associated with *only one* volume-related cost driver, and that relationship is linear.

Classifying costs as fixed or variable depends on the decision situation. More costs are fixed and fewer are variable when decisions involve very short time spans and very small changes in activity level. Suppose a United Airlines plane with several empty seats will depart from its gate in two minutes. A potential passenger is running down a corridor bearing a transferable ticket from a competing airline. Unless the airplane is held for an extra 30 seconds, the passenger will miss the departure and will not switch to United for the planned trip. What are the variable costs to United of delaying the departure and placing one more passenger in an otherwise empty seat? Variable costs (for example, one more meal) are negligible. Virtually all the costs in that decision situation are fixed (for example, maintenance crew salaries). Now in contrast, suppose United's decision is whether to add another flight, acquire another gate, add another city to its routes, or acquire another airplane. Many more costs would be regarded as variable and fewer as fixed. For example, in the case of adding a flight, the salaries of the maintenance crew would now be variable.

This example underscores the importance of how the decision situation affects the analysis of cost behavior. Whether costs are really "fixed" depends heavily on the relevant range, the length of the planning period in question, and the specific decision situation.

COST-VOLUME-PROFIT ANALYSIS

Managers often classify costs as fixed or variable when making decisions that affect the volume of output. The managers want to know how such decisions will affect costs and revenues. They realize that many factors in addition to the volume of output will affect costs. Yet, a useful starting point in their decision process is to specify the relationship between the volume of output and costs and revenues.

cost-volume-profit (CVP) analysis The study of the effects of output volume on revenue (sales), expenses (costs), and net income (net profit).

The managers of profit-seeking organizations usually study the effects of output volume on revenue (sales), expenses (costs), and net income (net profit). This study is commonly called **cost-volume-profit (CVP) analysis.** The managers of nonprofit organizations also benefit from the study of CVP relationships. Why? No organization has unlimited resources, and knowledge of how costs fluctuate as volume changes helps managers to understand how to control costs. For example, administrators of nonprofit hospitals are constantly concerned about the behavior of costs as the volume of patients fluctuates.

To apply CVP analysis, managers usually resort to some simplifying assumptions. The major simplification is to classify costs as either variable or fixed with respect to a single measure of the volume of output activity. This chapter focuses on such a simplified relationship.

CVP SCENARIO

Amy Winston, the manager of food services for Middletown Community College, is trying to decide whether to rent a line of snack vending machines. Although individual snack items have various acquisition costs and selling prices, Winston has decided that an average selling price of 50¢ per unit and an average acquisition cost of 40¢ per unit will suffice for purposes of this analysis. She predicts the following revenue and expense relationships.

	Per Unit	Percentage of Sales
Selling price	$ .50	100%
Variable cost of each item	.40	80
Selling price less variable cost	$ .10	20%
Monthly fixed expenses		
Rent	$1,000	
Wages for replenishing and servicing	4,500	
Other fixed expenses	500	
Total fixed expenses per month	$6,000	

We will now use these data in examining several applications of CVP analysis.

BREAK-EVEN POINT—CONTRIBUTION MARGIN AND EQUATION TECHNIQUES

The most basic CVP analysis computes the monthly break-even point in number of units and in dollar sales. The **break-even point** is the level of sales at which revenue equals expenses and net income is zero. The business press frequently refers to break-even points. For example, a news story on hotel occupancy rates in San Francisco in 1994 stated that "seventy percent [occupancy] is considered a break-even for hoteliers." Another news story stated that "the Big Three auto makers have slashed their sales break-even point in North America from 12.2 million cars and trucks to only 9.1 million this year." Finally, an article on Outboard Marine Corporation reported that, as a result of restructuring, the company's "break-even point will be $250 million lower than it was in 1993."

> **break-even point** The level of sales at which revenue equals expenses and net income is zero.

The study of cost-volume-profit relationships is often called break-even analysis. This term is misleading, because finding the break-even point is often just the first step in a planning decision. Managers usually concentrate on how the decision will affect sales, costs, and net income.

One direct use of the break-even point, however, is to assess possible risks. By comparing planned sales with the break-even point, managers can determine a **margin of safety:**

> **margin of safety** The planned unit sales less the break-even unit sales; it shows how far sales can fall below the planned level before losses occur.

margin of safety = planned unit sales − break-even unit sales

The margin of safety shows how far sales can fall below the planned level before losses occur.

There are two basic techniques for computing a break-even point: contribution margin and equation.

CONTRIBUTION-MARGIN TECHNIQUE Consider the following commonsense arithmetic approach. Every unit sold generates a **contribution margin** or **marginal income,** which

> **contribution margin (marginal income)** The sales price minus the variable cost per unit.

Break-Even in the Auto Industry

Increased worldwide competition in the automobile industry has made many companies acutely aware of their break-even points. In the early 1990s most auto companies were losing money. With dim prospects for large increases in volume of sales, the companies would be profitable only if they could decrease their break-even points. That is exactly what most companies did.

Break-even points vary greatly for different auto companies. The larger companies have high fixed costs and therefore must achieve higher sales to break even. For example, Chrysler must sell 1.6 million vehicles to break even. The break-even volume has dropped from 1.9 million vehicles in the late 1980s, and it is well below the 2.3 million sold in 1993. Still, the reduction of 16% in the break-even point is less than that achieved by some competitors.

Saab, a Swedish company, has focused on bringing down the number of production hours per car. A reduction from 120 hours to 45 hours has decreased the break-even volume from 125,000 vehicles to 83,000. This is still above 1993 sales of 73,605 cars, but well below the 135,000 vehicles projected for the mid-1990s.

The assembly operations for Jaguar, located 100 miles north of London, have had a dual focus: quality and production time. Quality improvements were expected to increase sales, and this appears to be working. Warranty costs in the United States alone are down 60%

and sales are up. Production improvements were intended to reduce the break-even volume. Since 1990, Jaguar has cut the time required to build a car by 54%. This has cut the break-even point from between 50,000 and 60,000 vehicles to 30,000 per year.

Another British company, Rolls-Royce, sells far fewer cars. In fact, sales dropped from 3,300 Rolls-Royces and Bentleys in 1990 to 1,360 in 1993. At a break-even volume of about 2,600 cars, the company was profitable in 1990. However, the company faced serious difficulty as sales plunged to 1,480 in 1991 and further to 1,360 by 1993. Yet, by trimming its worldwide staff from 5,000 to 2,300 people, Rolls-Royce reduced its break-even volume to 1,300 cars by 1993, providing a small profit after two years of losses.

It is clear that break-even volumes differ greatly among automobile companies. Rolls-Royce can generate a profit at a sales level of 1,300 vehicles, but Saab, Jaguar, and Chrysler would go out of business at that volume. Similarly, Chrysler could not survive selling at volumes that are highly profitable to Saab and Jaguar. Each company must compute its own break-even volume based on its own fixed and variable costs. If a company's sales fall below its break-even point, it must either find a way to get more sales or it must restructure its production operations to reduce its break-even point.

Sources: Adapted from Paul A. Eisenstein, "Jaguar Ledgers to Feature Black, Not Red, Ink Next Year," *The Washington Times*, September 16, 1994, p. D3; Mary Beth Vander Schaaf, "Saab Counts on V-6 to Boost 9000," *Automotive News*, September 26, 1994, p. 37; "GM's Saab Unit Climbs Back Into Black," *Investor's Business Daily*, September 27, 1994, p. A4; James Bennet, "Chrysler Chief's World View: Place to Sell, Not Build, Cars," *New York Times*, September 30, 1994, p. D1; Christopher Jensen, "Jaguar's Renaissance: Ford Helps Its British Acquisition Make Quality Job One," *The Plain Dealer*, October 9, 1994, p. 1H; Dan Jedlicka, "Rebounding Rolls Needs a Partner," *Chicago Sun-Times*, October 17, 1994, p. 47.

is the unit sales price minus the variable cost per unit. For the vending machine snack items, the contribution margin per unit is $.10:

Unit sales price	$.50
Unit variable cost	.40
Unit contribution margin to fixed costs and net income	$.10

Objective 3
Calculate break-even sales volume in total dollars and total units.

When is the break-even point reached? When enough units have been sold to generate a total contribution margin (total number of units sold × contribution margin per unit) equal to the total fixed costs. Divide the $6,000 in fixed costs by the $.10 unit contribution margin. The number of units that must be sold to break even is $6,000 ÷ $.10 = 60,000 units. The sales revenue at the break-even point is 60,000 units × $.50 per unit, or $30,000.

Think about the contribution margin of the snack items. Each unit purchased and sold generates extra revenue of $.50 and extra cost of $.40. Fixed costs are unaffected. If zero units were sold, a loss equal to the fixed cost of $6,000 would be incurred. Each unit reduces the loss by $.10 until sales reach the break-even point of 60,000 units. After that point, each unit adds (or *contributes*) $.10 to profit.

The condensed income statement at the break-even point is

	Total	Per Unit	Percentage
Units	60,000		
Sales	$30,000	$.50	100%
Variable costs	24,000	.40	80
Contribution margin*	$ 6,000	$.10	20%
Fixed costs	6,000		
Net income	$ 0		

*Sales less variable costs.

Sometimes the unit price and unit variable costs of a product are not known. This situation is common at companies that sell more than one product because no single price or variable cost applies to all products. For example, a grocery store sells hundreds of products at many different prices. A break-even point in overall units sold by the store would not be meaningful. In such cases, you can use total sales and total variable costs to calculate variable costs as a percentage of each sales dollar.

Consider our vending machine example:

Sales price	100%
Variable expenses as a percentage of dollar sales	80
Contribution-margin percentage	20%

Therefore, 20% of each sales dollar is available for the recovery of fixed expenses and the making of net income: $6,000 ÷ .20 = $30,000 sales are needed to break even. The contribution-margin percentage is based on dollar sales and is often expressed as a ratio (.20 instead of 20%). Using the contribution-margin percentage, you can compute the break-even volume in dollar sales without determining the break-even point in units.

EQUATION TECHNIQUE   The equation technique is the most general form of analysis, the one that may be adapted to any conceivable cost-volume-profit situation. You are familiar with a typical income statement. Any income statement can be expressed in equation form, or as a mathematical model, as follows:

$$\text{sales} - \text{variable expenses} - \text{fixed expenses} = \text{net income} \qquad (1)$$

That is,

$$\left(\begin{array}{c} \text{unit} \\ \text{sales} \\ \text{price} \end{array} \times \begin{array}{c} \text{number} \\ \text{of} \\ \text{units} \end{array} \right) - \left(\begin{array}{c} \text{unit} \\ \text{variable} \\ \text{cost} \end{array} \times \begin{array}{c} \text{number} \\ \text{of} \\ \text{units} \end{array} \right) - \begin{array}{c} \text{fixed} \\ \text{expenses} \end{array} = \begin{array}{c} \text{net} \\ \text{income} \end{array}$$

At the break-even point net income is zero:

$$\text{sales} - \text{variable expenses} - \text{fixed expenses} = 0$$

Let N = number of units to be sold to break even. Then, for the vending machine example,

$$\$.50N - \$.40N - \$6,000 = 0$$
$$\$.10N = \$6,000$$
$$N = \$6,000 \div \$.10$$
$$N = 60,000 \text{ units}$$

Total sales in the equation is a price-times-quantity relationship, which was expressed in our example as $.50N. To find the *dollar* sales, multiply 60,000 *units* by $.50, which would yield the break-even dollar sales of $30,000.

You can also solve the equation for sales dollars without computing the unit break-even point by using the relationship of variable costs and profits as a *percentage* of sales:

$$\text{variable-cost ratio or percentage} = \frac{\text{variable cost per unit}}{\text{sales price per unit}}$$

$$= \frac{\$.40}{\$.50}$$

$$= .80 \text{ or } 80\%$$

Let S = sales in dollars needed to break even. Then

$$S - .80S - \$6,000 = 0$$
$$.20S = \$6,000$$
$$S = \$6,000 \div .20$$
$$S = \$30,000$$

RELATIONSHIP BETWEEN THE TWO TECHNIQUES   You may have noticed that the contribution-margin technique is merely a shortcut version of the equation technique. Look at the last three lines in the two solutions given for equation 1. They read

Break-Even Volume	
Units	*Dollars*
$\$.10N = \$6,000$	$.20S = \$6,000$
$N = \dfrac{\$6,000}{\$.10}$	$S = \dfrac{\$6,000}{.20}$
$N = 60,000 \text{ units}$	$S = \$30,000$

From these equations, we can derive the following general shortcut formulas:

$$\text{break-even volume in units} = \frac{\text{fixed expenses}}{\text{contribution margin per unit}} \qquad (2)$$

$$\text{break-even volume in dollars} = \frac{\text{fixed expenses}}{\text{contribution-margin ratio}} \qquad (3)$$

Which should you use, the equation or the contribution-margin technique? Use either. Both yield the same results, so the choice is a matter of personal preference or convenience in a particular case.

BREAK-EVEN POINT—GRAPHICAL TECHNIQUES   Exhibit 2-4 is a graph of the cost-volume-profit relationship in our vending machine example. Study the graph as you read the procedure for constructing it.

Objective 4
Create a cost-volume-profit graph and understand the assumptions behind it.

1. Draw the axes. The horizontal axis is the sales volume, and the vertical axis is dollars of cost and revenue.
2. Plot sales volume. Select a convenient sales volume, say, 100,000 units, and plot point A for total sales dollars at that volume: 100,000 × $.50 = $50,000. Draw the revenue (that is, sales) line from point A to the origin, point 0.
3. Plot fixed expenses. Draw the line showing the $6,000 fixed portion of expenses. It should be a horizontal line intersecting the vertical axis at $6,000, point B.
4. Plot variable expenses. Determine the variable portion of expenses at a convenient level of activity: 100,000 units × $.40 = $40,000. Add this to the fixed expenses: $40,000 + $6,000 = $46,000. Plot point C for 100,000 units and $46,000. Then draw a line between this point and point B. This is the total expenses line.
5. Locate the break-even point. The break-even point is where the total expenses line crosses the sales line, 60,000 units or $30,000, namely, where total sales revenues exactly equal total costs, point D.

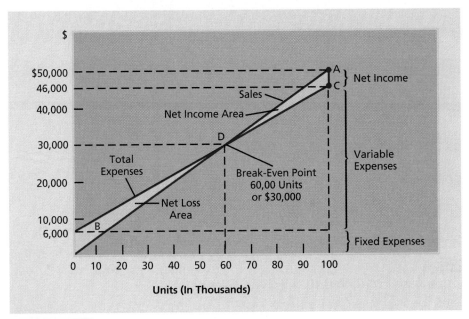

Exhibit 2-4

Cost-Volume-Profit Graph

The break-even point is only one part of this cost-volume-profit graph. The graph also shows the profit or loss at any rate of activity. At any given volume, the vertical distance between the sales line and the total expenses line measures the net income or net loss.

Managers often use break-even graphs because these graphs show potential profits over a wide range of volume more easily than numerical exhibits. Whether graphs or other presentations are used depends largely on management's preference.

Note that the concept of relevant range applies to the entire break-even graph. Almost all break-even graphs show revenue and cost lines extending back to the vertical axis as shown in Exhibit 2-5(A). This approach is misleading because the relationships depicted in such graphs are valid only within the relevant range that underlies the construction of the graph. Exhibit 2-5(B), a modification of the conventional break-even graph, partially demonstrates the multitude of assumptions that must be made in constructing the typical break-even graph. Some of these assumptions follow:

1. Expenses may be classified into variable and fixed categories. Total variable expenses vary directly with activity level. Total fixed expenses do not change with activity level.

2. The behavior of revenues and expenses is accurately portrayed and is linear over the relevant range. The principal differences between the accountant's break-even chart and the economist's are that (1) the accountant's sales line is drawn on the assumption that selling prices do not change with production or sales, and the economist assumes that reduced selling prices are normally associated with increased sales volume; and (2) the accountant usually assumes a constant variable expense per unit, and the economist assumes that variable expense per unit changes with production levels. Within the relevant range, the accountant's and the economist's sales and expense lines are usually close to one another, although the lines may diverge greatly outside the range.

3. Efficiency and productivity will be unchanged.

4. Sales mix will be constant. The **sales mix** is the relative proportions or combinations of quantities of products that constitute total sales. (See Appendix 2A for more on sales mixes.)

sales mix The relative proportions or combinations of quantities of products that constitute total sales.

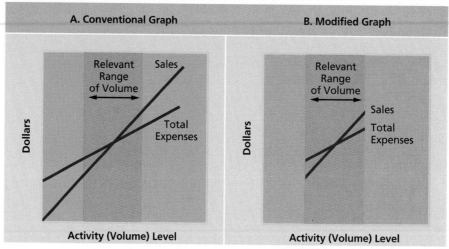

| A. Conventional Graph | B. Modified Graph |

Exhibit 2-5

Conventional and Modified Break-Even Graphs

5. The difference in inventory level at the beginning and at the end of a period is insignificant. (The impact of inventory changes on CVP analysis is discussed in Chapter 15.)

CHANGES IN FIXED EXPENSES   Changes in fixed expenses cause changes in the break-even point. For example, if the $1,000 monthly rent of the vending machines were doubled, what would be the monthly break-even point in number of units and dollar sales? The fixed expenses would increase from $6,000 to $7,000, so

$$\text{break-even volume in units} = \frac{\text{fixed expenses}}{\text{contribution margin per unit}} = \frac{\$7,000}{\$.10} = 70,000 \text{ units} \quad (2)$$

$$\text{break-even volume in dollars} = \frac{\text{fixed expenses}}{\text{contribution-margin ratio}} = \frac{\$7,000}{.20} = \$35,000 \quad (3)$$

Note that a one-sixth increase in fixed expenses altered the break-even point by one-sixth: from 60,000 to 70,000 units and from $30,000 to $35,000. This type of relationship always exists between fixed expenses and the break-even point if everything else remains constant.

Companies frequently lower their break-even points by reducing their total fixed costs. For example, closing or selling factories decreases property taxes, insurance, depreciation, and managers' salaries.

CHANGES IN CONTRIBUTION MARGIN PER UNIT   Changes in variable costs also cause the break-even point to shift. Companies can reduce their break-even points by increasing their contribution margins per unit of product through either increases in sales prices or decreases in unit variable costs, or both.

For example, assume that the fixed rent for the vending machines is still $1,000. (1) If the owner is paid 1¢ of rent per unit sold in addition to the fixed rent, find the monthly break-even point in number of units and in dollar sales. (2) If the selling price falls from 50¢ to 45¢ per unit, and the original variable expenses per unit are unchanged, find the monthly break-even point in number of units and in dollar sales.

Here's what happens to the break-even point:

1. The variable expenses would increase from 40¢ to 41¢, the unit contribution margin would decline from 10¢ to 9¢, and the contribution-margin ratio would become .18 ($.09 ÷ $.50).

The original fixed expenses of $6,000 would stay the same, but the denominators would change from those previously used. Thus,

$$\text{break-even point in units} = \frac{\$6,000}{\$.09} = 66,667 \text{ units} \qquad (2)$$

$$\text{break-even point in dollars} = \frac{\$6,000}{.18} = \$33,333 \qquad (3)$$

2. If the selling price fell from 50¢ to 45¢, and the original variable expenses were unchanged, the unit contribution would be reduced from 10¢ to 5¢ (that is, 45¢ − 40¢), and the break-even point would soar to 120,000 units ($6,000 ÷ $.05). The break-even point in dollars would also change because the selling price and contribution-margin ratio change. The contribution-margin ratio would be .1111 ($.05 ÷ $.45). The break-even point, in dollars, would be $54,000 (120,000 units × $.45) or, using the formula:

$$\text{break-even point in dollars} = \frac{\$6,000}{.1111} = \$54,000 \qquad (3)$$

TARGET NET PROFIT AND AN INCREMENTAL APPROACH

Managers can also use CVP analysis to determine the total sales, in units and dollars, needed to reach a target profit. For example, in our snack vending example, suppose Winston considers $480 per month the minimum acceptable net income. How many units will have to be sold to justify the adoption of the vending machine plan? How does this figure "translate" into dollar sales?

The method for computing desired or target sales volume in units and the desired or target net income is the same as was used in our earlier break-even computations. Now the targets, however, are expressed in the equations:

$$\text{target sales} - \text{variable expenses} - \text{fixed expenses} = \text{target net income} \qquad (4)$$

Objective 5
Calculate sales volume in total dollars and total units to reach a target profit.

or

$$\text{target sales volume in units} = \frac{\text{fixed expenses} + \text{target net income}}{\text{contribution margin per unit}} \qquad (5)$$

$$= \frac{\$6,000 + \$480}{\$.10} = 64,800 \text{ units}$$

Another way of getting the same answer is to use your knowledge of the break-even point and adopt an incremental approach. The phrase **incremental effect** is widely used in accounting. It refers to the change in total results (such as revenue, expenses, or income) under a new condition in comparison with some given or known condition.

In this case, the given condition is the 60,000-unit break-even point. All expenses would be recovered at that volume. Therefore the change or increment in net income for every unit beyond 60,000 would be equal to the contribution margin of $.50 − $.40 = $.10. If $480 were the target net profit, $480 ÷ $.10 would show that the target volume must exceed the break-even volume by 4,800 units; it would therefore be 60,000 + 4,800 = 64,800 units.

To find the answer in terms of dollar sales, multiply 64,800 units by $.50 or use the formula:

incremental effect The change in total results (such as revenue, expenses, or income) under a new condition in comparison with some given or known condition.

$$\text{target sales volume in dollars} = \frac{\text{fixed expenses} + \text{target net income}}{\text{contribution-margin ratio}} \qquad (6)$$

$$= \frac{\$6,000 + \$480}{.20} = \$32,400$$

To solve directly for sales dollars with the alternative incremental approach, we would start at the break-even point in dollar sales of $30,000. Every sales dollar beyond that point contributes $.20 to net profit. Divide $480 by .20. Dollar sales must exceed the break-even volume by $2,400 to produce a net profit of $480. Thus the total dollar sales would be $30,000 + $2,400 = $32,400.

The following table summarizes these computations:

	Break-Even Point	Increment	New Condition
Volume in units	60,000	4,800	64,800
Sales	$30,000	$2,400	$32,400
Variable expenses	24,000	1,920	25,920
Contribution margin	$ 6,000	$ 480	$ 6,480
Fixed expenses	6,000	—	6,000
Net income	$ 0	$ 480	$ 480

MULTIPLE CHANGES IN KEY FACTORS

So far, we have seen only changes in one CVP factor at a time. In the real world, managers often must make decisions about the probable effects of multiple factor changes. For instance, suppose that after the vending machines have been in place a while, Winston is considering locking them from 6:00 P.M. to 6:00 A.M., which she estimates will save $820 in wages monthly. However, the cutback from 24-hour service would hurt volume substantially because many nighttime employees use the machines. Should the machines remain available 24 hours per day? Assume that monthly sales would decline by 10,000 units from current sales. We will perform the analysis assuming two different levels of current sales volume: (1) 62,000 units and (2) 90,000 units. Consider two approaches. One approach is to construct and solve equations for conditions that prevail under each alternative and select the volume level that yields the highest net income.

Regardless of the current volume level, be it 62,000 or 90,000 units, if we accept the prediction that sales will decline by 10,000 units as accurate, the closing from 6:00 P.M. to 6:00 A.M. will decrease net income by $180.

	Decline from 62,000 to 52,000 Units		Decline from 90,000 to 80,000 Units	
Units	62,000	52,000	90,000	80,000
Sales	$31,000	$26,000	$45,000	$40,000
Variable expenses	24,800	20,800	36,000	32,000
Contribution margin	$ 6,200	$ 5,200	$ 9,000	$ 8,000
Fixed expenses	6,000	5,180	6,000	5,180
Net income	$ 200	$ 20	$ 3,000	$ 2,820
Change in net income		($180)		($180)

A second approach—an incremental approach—is quicker and simpler. Simplicity is important to managers because it keeps the analysis from being cluttered by irrelevant and potentially confusing data.

What does the insightful manager see in this situation? First, whether 62,000 or 90,000 units are being sold is irrelevant to the decision at hand. The issue is the decline in volume, which would be 10,000 units in either case. The essence of this decision is whether the prospective savings in fixed costs exceed the prospective loss in total contribution-margin dollars.

Lost total contribution margin, 10,000 units @ .10	$1,000
Savings in fixed expenses	$ 820
Prospective decline in net income	$ 180

Locking the vending machines from 6:00 P.M. to 6:00 A.M. would cause a $180 decrease in monthly net income. Whichever way you analyze it, locking the machines is not a sound financial decision.

CVP ANALYSIS IN THE COMPUTER AGE

As we have seen, cost-volume-profit analysis is based on a mathematical model, the equation.

sales − variable expenses − fixed expenses = net income

The CVP model is widely used as a planning model. Managers in a variety of organizations use a personal computer and a CVP modeling program to study combinations of changes in selling prices, unit variable costs, fixed costs, and desired profits. Many nonprofit organizations also use computerized CVP modeling. For example, some private universities have models that help measure how decisions such as raising tuition, adding programs, and closing dormitories during winter holidays will affect financial results. The computer quickly calculates the results of changes and can display them both numerically and graphically.

Exhibit 2-6 is a sample spreadsheet that shows what the sales level would have to be at three different fixed expense levels and three different variable expense levels to reach three different income levels. The computer calculates the 27 different sales levels rapidly and without error. Managers can insert any numbers they want for fixed expenses (column A), variable expense percentage (column B), target net income (row 3 of columns C, D, and E), or combinations thereof, and the computer will compute the required sales level.

In addition to speed and convenience, computers allow a more sophisticated approach to CVP analysis than the one illustrated in this chapter. The preceding assumptions listed on pages 49–50 are necessary to simplify the analysis enough for most managers to construct a CVP model by hand. Computer analysts, however, can construct a model that does not require all the simplifications. Computer models can include multiple cost drivers, nonlinear relationships between costs and cost drivers, varying sales mixes, and analyses that need not be restricted to a relevant range.

Use of computer models is a cost-benefit issue. Sometimes the costs of modeling are exceeded by the value of better decisions made using the models. However, the reliability

Exhibit 2-6
Spreadsheet Analysis of CVP Relationships

	A	B	C	D	E
1				Sales Required to Earn	
2	Fixed	Variable		Annual Net Income of	
3	Expenses	Expense %	$ 2,000	$ 4,000	$ 6,000
4					
5	$4,000	0.40	$10,000*	$13,333	$16,667
6	$4,000	0.44	$10,714*	$14,286	$17,857
7	$4,000	0.48	$11,538*	$15,385	$19,231
8	$6,000	0.40	$13,333	$16,667	$20,000
9	$6,000	0.44	$14,286	$17,857	$21,429
10	$6,000	0.48	$15,385	$19,231	$23,077
11	$8,000	0.40	$16,667	$20,000	$23,333
12	$8,000	0.44	$17,857	$21,429	$25,000
13	$8,000	0.48	$19,231	$23,077	$26,923
15					
16	*(A5 + C3)/(1 − B5) = ($4,000 + $2,000)/(1 − $.40) = $10,000				
17	(A6 + C3)/(1 − B6) = ($4,000 + $2,000)/(1 − $.44) = $10,714				
18	(A7 + C3)/(1 − B7) = ($4,000 + $2,000)/(1 − $.48) = $11,538				
19					

of these models depends on the accuracy of their underlying assumptions about how revenues and costs will actually be affected. Moreover, in small organizations, simplified CVP models often are accurate enough that more sophisticated modeling is unwarranted.

ADDITIONAL USES OF COST-VOLUME ANALYSIS

BEST COST STRUCTURE

Analyzing cost-volume-profit relationships is an important management responsibility. Managers usually try to find the most profitable cost structure—the combination of variable- and fixed-cost factors. For example, purchasing automated machinery may raise fixed costs but reduce labor cost per unit. Conversely, it may be wise to reduce fixed costs to obtain a more favorable combination. Thus, direct selling by a salaried sales force (a fixed cost) may be replaced by the use of salespeople who are compensated via sales commissions (variable costs).

Generally, companies that spend heavily for advertising are willing to do so because they have high contribution-margin percentages (airlines, cigarette and cosmetic companies). Conversely, companies with low contribution-margin percentages usually spend less for advertising and promotion (manufacturers of industrial equipment). As a result, two companies with the same unit sales volumes at the same unit prices could have different attitudes toward risking an advertising outlay. Assume the following:

	Perfume Company	Janitorial Service Company
Unit sales volume	100,000 bottles	100,000 square feet
Dollar sales at $20 per unit	$2,000,000	$2,000,000
Variable costs	200,000	1,700,000
Contribution margin	$1,800,000	$ 300,000
Contribution-margin percentage	90%	15%

Suppose each company wants to increase sales volume by 10%:

	Perfume Company	Janitorial Service Company
Increase in sales volume, 10,000 × $20	$200,000	$200,000
Increase in contribution margin, 90%, 15%	180,000	30,000

The perfume company would be inclined to increase advertising considerably to boost the contribution margin by $180,000. In contrast, the janitorial service company would be foolhardy to spend large amounts to increase the contribution margin by $30,000.

Note that when the contribution margin as a percentage of sales is low, great increases in volume are necessary before significant increases in net profits can occur. On the other hand as sales exceed the break-even point, a high contribution-margin percentage increases profits faster than does a small contribution-margin percentage.

OPERATING LEVERAGE

operating leverage A firm's ratio of fixed to variable costs.

In addition to weighing the varied effects of changes in fixed and variable costs, managers need to consider their firm's ratio of fixed to variable costs, called **operating leverage.** In highly leveraged companies—those with high fixed costs and low variable costs—small changes in sales volume result in large changes in net income. Companies with less lever-

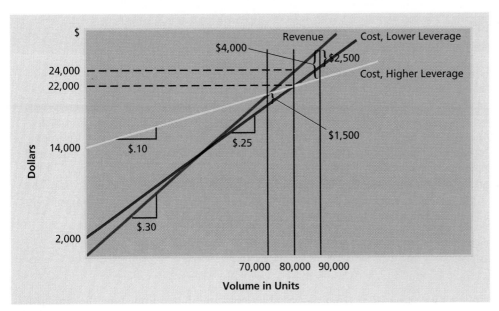

Exhibit 2-7

High Versus Low Leverage

age (that is, lower fixed costs and higher variable costs) are not affected as much by changes in sales volume.

Exhibit 2-7 shows cost behavior relationships at two firms, one highly leveraged and one with low leverage. The firm with higher leverage has fixed costs of $14,000 and variable cost per unit of $.10. The firm with lower leverage has fixed costs of only $2,000 but variable costs of $.25 per unit. Expected sales at both companies are 80,000 units at $.30 per unit. At this sales level, both firms would have net incomes of $2,000. If sales fall short of 80,000 units, profits drop most sharply for the highly leveraged business. If sales exceed 80,000 units, however, profits increase most sharply for the highly leveraged concern.

The highly leveraged alternative is more risky. Why? Because it provides the highest possible net income and the highest possible losses. In other words, net income is highly variable, depending on the actual level of sales. The low-leverage alternative is less risky because variations in sales lead to only small variability in net income. At sales of 90,000 units, net income is $4,000 for the higher-leveraged firm but only $2,500 for the lower-leveraged firm. At sales of 70,000 units, however, the higher-leveraged firm has zero profits, compared to $1,500 for the lower-leveraged firm.

CONTRIBUTION MARGIN AND GROSS MARGIN

Contribution margin may be expressed as a total absolute amount, a unit absolute amount, a ratio, and a percentage. The **variable-cost ratio** or **variable-cost percentage** is defined as all variable costs divided by sales. Thus a contribution-margin ratio of 20% means that the variable-cost ratio is 80%.

variable-cost ratio (variable-cost percentage) All variable costs divided by sales.

Too often people confuse the terms *contribution margin* and *gross margin*. **Gross margin** (which is also called **gross profit**) is the excess of sales over the **cost of goods sold** (that is, the cost of the merchandise that is acquired or manufactured and then sold). It is a widely used concept, particularly in the retailing industry.

gross margin (gross profit) The excess of sales over the total cost of goods sold.

Compare the gross margin with the contribution margin:

cost of goods sold The cost of the merchandise that is acquired or manufactured and resold.

gross margin = sales price − cost of goods sold
contribution margin = sales price − all variable expenses

One way that companies cope with hard economic times is to lower their break-even point. *Business Week* suggested that investors look for such firms "because efficiency gains at companies that have pared fixed costs as well as variable ones should be deep and lasting."

Why is lowering the break-even point important? Because a company that maintains its profitability in times of low sales is poised to take off when the economy improves. Baldwin, the piano maker, actually improved its profits in a time of decreasing sales by suc-cessfully cutting costs—especially fixed costs. If it maintains its new cost structure as sales rebound, profits will soar. Lowering fixed costs is especially important because these costs will not necessarily increase as production increases to meet renewed demand for sales.

Chrysler is another example of a company that pared its fixed costs in the slow sales period in the early 1990s. According to *Business Week*, it became "close to being the low-cost producer among the Big Three ... [and] will benefit most if an auto turnaround comes soon."

Source: Adapted from "Lots of Companies Are Lean, But Which Are Mean?" *Business Week*, February 3, 1992, p. 84.

Objective 6
Distinguish between contribution margin and gross margin

The following comparisons from our vending machine illustration show the similarities and differences between the contribution margin and the gross margin in a retail store:

Sales	$.50
Variable costs: acquisition cost of unit sold	.40
Contribution margin and gross margin are equal	$.10

Thus the original data resulted in no difference between the measure of contribution margin and gross margin. There would be a difference between the two, however, if the firm had to pay additional rent of 1¢ per unit sold:

	Contribution Margin	Gross Margin
Sales		$.50	$.50
Acquisition cost of unit sold	$.40		.40
Variable rent	.01		
Total variable expense		.41	
Contribution margin		$.09	
Gross margin			$.10

As the preceding tabulation indicates, contribution margin and gross margin are not the same concepts. Contribution margin focuses on sales in relation to all variable costs, whereas gross margin focuses on sales in relation to cost of goods sold. For example, consider MascoTech, a Detroit-based auto parts supplier. A newspaper article reported that MascoTech's "gross profit margin on sales is about 21% today, but for each additional sales dollar the contribution margin is more like 30%."

NONPROFIT APPLICATION

Consider how cost-volume-profit relationships apply to nonprofit organizations. Suppose a city has a $100,000 lump-sum budget appropriation to conduct a counseling program for drug addicts. The variable costs for drug prescriptions are $400 per patient per year. Fixed costs are $60,000 in the relevant range of 50 to 150 patients. If all of the budget appropriation is spent, how many patients can be served in a year?

We can use the break-even equation to solve the problem. Let N be the number of patients.

revenue − variable expenses − fixed expenses = 0 if budget is completely spent
$$\$100,000 \text{ lump sum} - \$400N - \$60,000 = 0$$
$$\$400N = \$100,000 - \$60,000$$
$$N = \$40,000 \div 400$$
$$N = 100 \text{ patients}$$

Suppose the total budget appropriation for the following year is cut by 10%. Fixed costs will be unaffected, but service will decline:

$$\text{revenue} - \text{variable expenses} - \text{fixed expenses} = 0$$
$$\$90,000 - \$400N - \$60,000 = 0$$
$$\$400N = \$90,000 - \$60,000$$
$$N = \$30,000 \div \$400$$
$$N = 75 \text{ patients}$$

The percentage reduction in service is more than the 10% reduction in the budget. Unless the city restructures its operations, the service volume must be reduced 25% (from 100 to 75 patients) to stay within budget. Note that lump-sum revenue is a horizontal line on the graph:

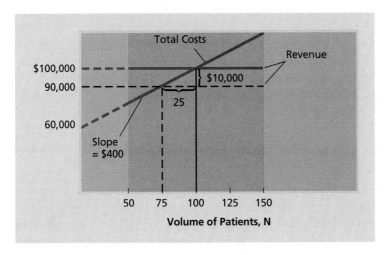

SUMMARY PROBLEM FOR YOUR REVIEW

PROBLEM

The budgeted income statement of Port Williams Gift Shop is summarized as follows:

Net revenue	$800,000
Less: expenses, including $400,000 of fixed expenses	880,000
Net loss	$(80,000)

The manager believes that an increase of $200,000 on advertising outlays will increase sales substantially.

Required

1. At what sales volume will the store break even after spending $200,000 on advertising?
2. What sales volume will result in a net profit of $40,000?

SOLUTION

1. Note that all data are expressed in dollars. No unit data are given. Most companies have many products, so the overall break-even analysis deals with dollar sales, not units. The variable expenses are $880,000 − $400,000, or $480,000. The variable-expense ratio is $480,000 ÷ $800,000, or .60. Therefore the contribution-margin ratio is .40. Let S = break-even sales in dollars. Then

$$S - \text{variable expenses} - \text{fixed expenses} = \text{net profit}$$
$$S - .60S - (\$400,000 + \$200,000) = 0$$
$$.40S = \$600,000$$
$$S = \frac{\$600,000}{.40} = \frac{\text{fixed expenses}}{\text{contribution-margin ratio}}$$
$$S = \$1,500,000$$

2.
$$\text{required sales} = \frac{\text{fixed expenses} + \text{target net profit}}{\text{contribution-margin ratio}}$$

$$\text{required sales} = \frac{\$600,000 + \$40,000}{.40} = \frac{\$640,000}{.40}$$
$$\text{required sales} = \$1,600,000$$

Alternatively, we can use an incremental approach and reason that all dollar sales beyond the $1.5 million break-even point will result in a 40% contribution to net profit. Divide $40,000 by .40. Sales must therefore be $100,000 beyond the $1.5 million break-even point to produce a net profit of $40,000.

Highlights to Remember

Explain how cost drivers affect cost behavior. A cost driver is an output measure of a resource or activity. When the use of a resource or the performance of an activity changes, the level of the cost driver or output measure will also change, causing changes in costs.

Show how changes in cost-driver activity levels affect variable and fixed costs. Different types of costs behave in different ways. If the costs of the resources used changes in proportion to changes in the cost driver level, the resource is a variable-cost resource (its costs are variable). If the cost of the resource used does not change because of cost driver level changes, the resource is a fixed-cost resource (its costs are fixed).

Calculate break-even sales volume in total dollars and total units. CVP analysis (sometimes called break-even analysis) can be approached graphically or with equations. To calculate the break-even point in total units, divide the fixed costs by the unit contribution margin. To calculate the break-even point in total dollars (sales dollars), divide the fixed costs by the contribution-margin ratio.

Create a cost-volume-profit graph and understand the assumptions behind it. A cost-volume-profit graph can be created by drawing revenue and total cost lines as functions of the cost-driver level. Be sure to recognize the limitations of CVP analysis and that it assumes constant efficiency, sales mix, and inventory levels.

Calculate sales volume in total dollars and total units to reach a target profit. Managers use CVP analysis to compute the sales needed to achieve a target profit or to examine the effects on profit of changes in factors such as fixed costs, variable costs, or cost driver volume.

Distinguish between contribution margin and gross margin. The contribution margin—the difference between sales price and variable costs—is an important concept. Do not confuse it with gross margin, the difference between sales price and cost of goods sold.

Understand how cost behavior and CVP analysis are used by managers. Understanding cost behavior patterns and cost-volume-profit (CVP) relationships can help guide a manager's decisions. Because one of the main goals of management accounting is controlling and reducing costs, understanding cost behavior is vital to the manager's decision-making role. CVP analysis is a technique that is used often by management accountants to both gain an understanding of the cost and profit structure in a company and to explain it to other managers.

Appendix 2A: Sales-Mix Analysis

To emphasize fundamental ideas, the cost-volume-profit analysis in this chapter has focused on a single product. Nearly all companies, however, sell more than one product. *Sales mix* is defined as the relative proportions or combinations of quantities of products that comprise total sales. If the proportions of the mix change, the cost-volume-profit relationships also change.

Objective 7
Explain the effects of sales mix on profits.

Suppose Ramos Company has two products, wallets (W) and key cases (K). The income budget follows:

	Wallets (W)	Key Cases (K)	Total
Sales in units	300,000	75,000	375,000
Sales @ $8 and $5	$2,400,000	$375,000	$2,775,000
Variable expenses @ $7 and $3	2,100,000	225,000	2,325,000
Contribution margins @ $1 and $2	$ 300,000	$150,000	$ 450,000
Fixed expenses			180,000
Net income			$ 270,000

For simplicity, ignore income taxes. What would be the break-even point? The typical answer assumes a constant mix of 4 units of W for every unit of K. Therefore, let K = number of units of product K to break even, and 4K = number of units of product W to break even:

$$\text{sales} - \text{variable expenses} - \text{fixed expenses} = \text{zero net income}$$
$$[\$8(4K) + \$5(K)] - [\$7(4K) + \$3(K)] - \$180,000 = 0$$
$$\$32K + \$5K - \$28K - \$3K - \$180,000 = 0$$
$$\$6K = \$180,000$$
$$K = 30,000$$
$$4K = 120,000 = W$$

The break-even point is 30,000K + 120,000W = 150,000 units.

This is the only break-even point for a sales mix of four wallets for every key case. Clearly, however, there are other break-even points for other sales mixes. For instance, suppose only key cases were sold, fixed expenses being unchanged:

$$\text{break-even point} = \frac{\text{fixed expenses}}{\text{contribution margin per unit}}$$
$$= \frac{\$180,000}{\$2}$$
$$= 90,000 \text{ key cases}$$

If only wallets were sold:

$$\text{break-even point} = \frac{180,000}{\$1}$$
$$= 180,000 \text{ wallets}$$

Managers are not interested in the break-even point for its own sake. Instead, they want to know how changes in a planned sales mix will affect net income. When the sales mix changes, the break-even point and the expected net income at various sales levels are altered. For example, suppose overall actual total sales were equal to the budget of 375,000 units. However, only 50,000 key cases were sold:

	Wallets (W)	Key Cases (K)	Total
Sales in units	325,000	50,000	375,000
Sales @ $8 and $5	$2,600,000	$250,000	$2,850,000
Variable expenses @ $7 and $3	2,275,000	150,000	2,425,000
Contribution margins @ $1 and $2	$ 325,000	$100,000	$ 425,000
Fixed expenses			180,000
Net income			$ 245,000

The change in sales mix has resulted in a $245,000 actual net income rather than the $270,000 budgeted net income, an unfavorable difference of $25,000. The budgeted and actual sales in number of units were identical, but the proportion of sales of the product bearing the higher unit contribution margin declined.

Managers usually want to maximize the sales of all their products. Faced with limited resources and time, however, executives prefer to generate the most profitable sales mix achievable. For example, consider a recent annual report of Deere & Co., a manufacturer of farm equipment: "The increase in the ratio of cost of goods sold to net sales resulted from higher production costs [and] a less favorable mix of products sold."

Profitability of a given product helps guide executives who must decide to emphasize or de-emphasize particular products. For example, given limited production facilities or limited time of sales personnel, should we emphasize wallets or key cases? These decisions may be affected by other factors beyond the contribution margin per unit of product. Chapter 5 explores some of these factors including the importance of the amount of profit per *unit of time* rather than per *unit of product*.

Appendix 2B: Impact of Income Taxes

Objective 8
Compute cost-volume-profit relationships on an after-tax basis.

Thus far we have (as so many people would like to) ignored income taxes. In most nations, however, private enterprises are subject to income taxes. Reconsider the vending machine example in this chapter. As part of our CVP analysis, we discussed the sales necessary to achieve a target income before income taxes of $480. If an income tax were levied at 40%, the new result would be

Income before income tax	$480	100%
Income tax	192	40
Net income	$288	60%

Note that

net income = income before income taxes − .40 (income before income taxes)
net income = .60 (income before income taxes)

$$\text{income before income taxes} = \frac{\text{net income}}{.60}$$

or

$$\text{target income before income taxes} = \frac{\text{target after-tax net income}}{1 - \text{tax rate}}$$

$$\text{target income before income taxes} = \frac{\$288}{1 - .40} = \frac{\$288}{.60} = \$480$$

Suppose the target net income after taxes was $288. The only change in the general equation approach would be on the right-hand side of the following equation:

$$\text{target sales} - \text{varible expenses} - \text{fixed expenses} = \frac{\text{target after-tax net income}}{1 - \text{tax rate}}$$

Thus, letting N be the number of units to be sold at $.50 each with a variable cost of $.40 each and total fixed costs of $6,000,

$$\$.50N - \$.40N - \$6,000 = \frac{\$288}{1 - .4}$$

$$\$.10N = \$6,000 + \frac{\$288}{.6}$$

$$\$.06N = \$3,600 + \$288 = 3,888$$

$$N = \$3,888 \div \$.06 = 64,800 \text{ units}$$

Sales of 64,800 units produce an after-tax profit of $288 as shown here and a before-tax profit of $480 as shown in the chapter.

Suppose the target net income after taxes was $480. The volume needed would rise to 68,000 units, as follows:

$$\$.50N - \$.40N - \$6,000 = \frac{\$480}{1 - .4}$$

$$\$.10N = \$6,000 + \frac{\$480}{.6}$$

$$\$.06N = \$3,600 + \$480 = \$4,080$$

$$N = \$4,080 \div \$.06 = 68,000 \text{ units}$$

As a shortcut to computing the effects of volume on the change in after-tax income, use the formula

$$\begin{array}{c}\text{change} \\ \text{in net} \\ \text{income}\end{array} = \left(\begin{array}{c}\text{change in volume} \\ \text{in units}\end{array}\right) \times \left(\begin{array}{c}\text{contribution margin} \\ \text{per unit}\end{array}\right) \times (1 - \text{tax rate})$$

In our example, suppose operations were at a level of 64,800 units and $288 after-tax net income. The manager is wondering how much after-tax net income would increase if sales become 68,000 units.

$$\begin{aligned}\text{change in net income} &= (68,000 - 64,800) \times \$.10 \times (1 - .4) \\ &= 3,200 \times \$.10 \times .60 = 3,200 \times \$.06 \\ &= \$192\end{aligned}$$

In brief, each unit beyond the break-even point adds to after-tax net profit at the unit contribution margin multiplied by (1 − income tax rate).

Throughout our illustration, the break-even point itself does not change. Why? Because *there is no income tax at a level of zero profits.*

Accounting Vocabulary

break-even point, p. 45

contribution margin, p. 45

cost behavior, p. 40

cost driver, p. 41

cost of goods sold, p. 55

cost-volume-profit (CVP)
  analysis, p. 44

fixed cost, p. 41

gross margin, p. 55

gross profit, p. 55

incremental effect, p. 51

marginal income, p. 45

margin of safety, p. 45

operating leverage, p. 54

relevant range, p. 43

sales mix, p. 49

variable cost, p. 41

variable-cost percentage, p. 55

variable-cost ratio, p. 55

Fundamental Assignment Material

2-A1 Cost-Volume-Profits and Vending Machines

Cola Food Services Company operates and services soft drink vending machines located in restaurants, gas stations, factories, etc., in four Southern states. The machines are rented from the manufacturer. In addition, Cola must rent the space occupied by its machines. The following expense and revenue relationships pertain to a contemplated expansion program of 20 machines.

Fixed monthly expenses follow:

Machine rental: 20 machines @ $43.50	$ 870
Space rental: 20 locations @ $28.80	576
Part-time wages to service the additional 20 machines	1,454
Other fixed costs	100
Total monthly fixed costs	$3,000

Other data follow:

	Per Unit	Per $100 of Sales
Selling price	$1.00	100%
Cost of snack	.80	80
Contribution margin	$ .20	20%

Required

These questions relate to the above data unless otherwise noted. Consider each question independently.

1. What is the monthly break-even point in number of units? In dollar sales?
2. If 18,000 units were sold, what would be the company's net income?
3. If the space rental cost were doubled, what would be the monthly break-even point in number of units? In dollar sales?
4. If, in addition to the fixed rent, Cola Food Services Company paid the vending machine manufacturer 2¢ per unit sold, what would be the monthly break-even point in number of units? In dollar sales? Refer to the original data.
5. If, in addition to the fixed rent, Cola paid the machine manufacturer 4¢ for each unit sold in excess of the break-even point, what would the new net income be if 18,000 units were sold? Refer to the original data.

2-A2 Exercises in Cost-Volume-Profit Relationships

The Global United Moving Company specializes in hauling heavy goods over long distances. The company's revenues and expenses depend on revenue miles, a measure that combines both weights and mileage. Summarized budget data for next year are based on predicted total revenue miles of 800,000.

	Per Revenue Mile
Average selling price (revenue)	$1.50
Average variable expenses	1.30
Fixed expenses, $120,000	

Required

1. Compute the budgeted net income. Ignore income taxes.
2. Management is trying to decide how various possible conditions or decisions might affect net income. Compute the new net income for each of the following changes. Consider each case independently.
   a. A 10% increase in revenue miles
   b. A 10% increase in sales price

c. A 10% increase in variable expenses

d. A 10% increase in fixed expenses

e. An average decrease in selling price of 3¢ per mile and a 5% increase in revenue miles. Refer to the original data

f. An average increase in selling price of 5% and a 10% decrease in revenue miles

g. A 10% increase in fixed expenses in the form of more advertising and a 5% increase in revenue miles

2-B1 Basic CVP Exercises

Each problem is unrelated to the others.

1. Given: Selling price per unit, $20; total fixed expenses, $6,000; variable expenses per unit, $15. Find break-even sales in units.

2. Given: Sales, $40,000; variable expenses, $30,000; fixed expenses, $7,500; net income, $2,500. Find break-even sales.

3. Given: Selling price per unit, $30; total fixed expenses, $37,000; variable expenses per unit, $14. Find total sales in units to achieve a profit of $7,000, assuming no change in selling price.

4. Given: Sales, $50,000; variable expenses, $20,000; fixed expenses, $20,000; net income, $10,000. Assume no change in selling price; find net income if activity volume increases 10%.

5. Given: Selling price per unit, $40; total fixed expenses, $80,000; variable expenses per unit, $30. Assume that variable expenses are reduced by 20% per unit, and the total fixed expenses are increased by 10%. Find the sales in units to achieve a profit of $24,000, assuming no change in selling price.

2-B2 Basic CVP Analysis

Carmen Guerrero opened Corner, a small day care facility, just over two years ago. After a rocky start, Carmen's has been thriving. Guerrero is now preparing a budget for November 19X9.

Monthly fixed costs for Carmen's are

Rent	$ 800
Salaries	1,500
Other fixed costs	100
Total fixed costs	$2,400

The salary is for Ann Penilla, the only employee, who works with Carmen in caring for the children. Guerrero does not pay herself a salary, but she receives the excess of revenues over costs each month.

The cost driver for variable costs is "child-days." One child-day is one day in day care for one child, and the variable cost is $10 per child-day. The facility is open 6:00 A.M. to 6:00 P.M. weekdays (that is, Monday through Friday), and there are 22 weekdays in November 19X9. An average day has 8 children attending Carmen's Corner. State law prohibits Carmen's from having more than 14 children, a limit it has never reached. Guerrero charges $30 per day per child, regardless of how long the child is at the facility.

Required

1. Suppose attendance for November 19X9 is equal to the average, resulting in 22 × 8 = 176 child-days. What amount will Guerrero have left after paying all her expenses?

2. Suppose both costs and attendance are difficult to predict. Compute the amount Guerrero will have left after paying all her expenses for each of the following situations. Consider each case independently.

   a. Average attendance is 9 children per day instead of 8, generating 198 child-days.

   b. Variable costs increase to $11 per child-day.

c. Rent is increased by $200 per month.

d. Guerrero spends $300 on advertising (a fixed cost) in November, which increases average daily attendance to 9.5 children.

e. Guerrero begins charging $33 per day on November 1, and average daily attendance slips to 7 children.

Additional Assignment Material

QUESTIONS

2-1. "Cost behavior is simply identification of cost drivers and their relationships to costs." Comment.

2-2. Give three examples of variable costs and of fixed costs.

2-3. "Fixed costs decline as volume increases." Do you agree? Explain.

2-4. "It is confusing to think of fixed costs on a per-unit basis." Do you agree? Why or why not?

2-5. "All costs are either fixed or variable. The only difficulty in cost analysis is determining which of the two categories each cost belongs to." Do you agree? Explain.

2-6. "The relevant range pertains to fixed costs, not variable costs." Do you agree? Explain.

2-7. Identify the major simplifying assumption that underlies CVP analysis.

2-8. "Classification of costs into variable and fixed categories depends on the decision situation." Explain.

2-9. "Contribution margin is the excess of sales over fixed costs." Do you agree? Explain.

2-10. Why is "break-even analysis" a misnomer?

2-11. "Companies in the same industry generally have about the same break-even point." Do you agree? Explain.

2-12. "It is essential to choose the right CVP technique— equation, contribution margin, or graphical. If you pick the wrong one, your analysis will be faulty." Do you agree? Explain.

2-13. Describe three ways of lowering a break-even point.

2-14. "Incremental analysis is quicker, but it has no other advantage over an analysis of all costs and revenues associated with each alternative." Do you agree? Why or why not?

2-15. "CVP analysis is a common management use of personal computers." Do you agree? Explain.

2-16. Explain operating leverage and why a highly leveraged company is risky.

2-17. "The contribution margin and gross margin are always equal." Do you agree? Explain.

2-18. "CVP relationships are unimportant in nonprofit organizations." Do you agree? Explain.

2-19. "Two products were sold. Total budgeted and actual total sales in number of units were identical to the units budgeted. Actual unit variable costs and sales prices were the same as budgeted. Actual contribution margin was lower than budgeted." What could be the reason for the lower contribution margin?

2-20. Given a target after-tax net income, present the CVP formula for computing the required income before income taxes.

2-21. Present the CVP formula for computing the effects of a change in volume on after-tax income.

2-22. "As I understand it, costs such as the salary of the vice president of transportation operations are variable because the more traffic you handle, the less your unit cost. In contrast, costs such as fuel are fixed because each ton-mile should entail consumption of the same amount of fuel and hence bear the same unit cost." Do you agree? Explain.

EXERCISES

2-23 Basic Review Exercises

Fill in the blanks for each of the following independent cases (ignore income taxes):

	Sales	Variable Expenses	Contribution Margin	Fixed Expenses	Net Income
1.	$900,000	$500,000	$ —	$275,000	$ —
2.	800,000	—	350,000	—	80,000
3.	—	600,000	340,000	260,000	—

2-24 Basic Review Exercises

Fill in the blanks for each of the following independent cases:

Case	(a) Selling Price per Unit	(b) Variable Cost per Unit	(c) Total Units Sold	(d) Total Contribution Margin	(e) Total Fixed Costs	(f) Net Income
1.	$30	$ —	120,000	$720,000	$640,000	$ —
2.	10	6	100,000	—	320,000	—
3.	20	15	—	100,000	—	15,000
4.	30	20	70,000	—	—	12,000
5.	—	9	80,000	160,000	120,000	—

2-25 Hospital Costs and Pricing

St. Theresa Hospital has overall variable costs of 20% of total revenue and fixed costs of $40 million per year.

Required

1. Compute the break-even point expressed in total revenue.
2. A patient-day is often used to measure the volume of a hospital. Suppose there are going to be 40,000 patient-days next year. Compute the average daily revenue per patient necessary to break even.

2-26 Motel Rentals

Suppose a Best Western Motel has annual fixed costs applicable to its rooms of $1.6 million for its 200-room motel, average daily room rents of $50, and average variable costs of $10 for each room rented. It operates 365 days per year.

Required

1. How much net income on rooms will be generated (1) if the motel is completely full throughout the entire year and (2) if the motel is half full?
2. Compute the break-even point in number of rooms rented. What percentage occupancy for the year is needed to break even?

2-27 Variable Cost to Break Even

General Mills makes Wheaties, Cheerios, Betty Crocker cake mixes, and many other food products. Suppose the product manager of a new General Mills cereal has determined that the appropriate wholesale price for a carton of the cereal is $48. Fixed costs of the production and marketing of the cereal is $15 million.

Required

1. The product manager estimates that she can sell 800,000 cartons at the $48 price. What is the largest variable cost per carton that can be paid and still achieve a profit of $1 million?
2. Suppose the variable cost is $30 per carton. What profit (or loss) would be expected?

2-28 Basic Relationships, Hotel

The Michigan Street Hotel in Chicago has 400 rooms, with a fixed cost of $350,000 per month during the busy season. Room rates average $65 per day with variable costs of $15 per rented room per day. Assume a 30-day month.

Required

1. How many rooms must be occupied per day to break even?
2. How many rooms must be occupied per month to make a monthly profit of $120,000?

3. Assume that the Michigan Street Hotel has these average contribution margins per month from use of space in its hotel:

Leased shops in hotel	$70,000
Meals served, conventions	40,000
Dining room and coffee shop	32,400
Bar and cocktail lounge	30,000

Fixed costs for the total hotel are $350,000 per month. Variable costs are $15 per day per rented room. The hotel has 400 rooms and averages 80% occupancy per day. What average rate per day must the hotel charge to make a profit of $120,000 per month?

2-29   Sales-Mix Analysis
Study Appendix 2A. Nakata Farms produces strawberries and raspberries. Annual fixed costs are $14,400. The cost driver for variable costs is pints of fruit produced. The variable cost is $.65 per pint of strawberries and $.85 per pint of raspberries. Strawberries sell for $1.00 per pint, raspberries for $1.35 per pint. Two pints of strawberries are produced for every pint of raspberries.

Required

1. Compute the number of pints of strawberries and the number of pints of raspberries produced and sold at the break-even point.
2. Suppose only strawberries are produced and sold. Compute the break-even point in pints.
3. Suppose only raspberries are produced and sold. Compute the break-even point in pints.

2-30   Income Taxes
Review the illustration in Appendix 2B. Suppose the income tax rate were 20% instead of 40%. How many units would have to be sold to achieve a target after-tax net income of (1) $288 and (2) $480? Show your computations.

2-31   Income Taxes and Cost-Volume-Profit Analysis
Study Appendix 2B. Suppose Manriquez Construction Company has a 40% income tax rate, a contribution-margin ratio of 30%, and fixed costs of $440,000. What sales volume is necessary to achieve an after-tax income of $42,000?

PROBLEMS

2-32   Fixed Costs and Relevant Range
Boulder Systems Group (BSG) has a substantial year-to-year fluctuation in billings to clients. Top management has the following policy regarding the employment of key professional personnel:

If Gross Annual Billings Are	Number of Persons to be Employed	Key Professional Annual Salaries and Related Expenses
$2,000,000 or less	10	$1,200,000
$2,000,001–2,400,000	11	1,320,000
$2,400,001–2,800,000	12	1,440,000

Top management believes that a minimum of 10 individuals should be retained for a year or more even if billings drop drastically below $2 million.

For the past five years, gross annual billings for BSG have fluctuated between $2,020,000 and $2,380,000. Expectations for next year are that gross billings will be between $2,100,000 and $2,300,000. What amounts should be budgeted for key professional personnel? Graph the relationships on an annual basis, using the two approaches illustrated in Exhibit 2-3. Indicate the relevant range on each graph. You need not use graph paper; simply approximate the graphical relationships.

2-33 Movie Manager

Malia Mertz is the manager of Stanford's traditional Sunday Flicks. Each Sunday a film has two showings. The admission price is deliberately set at a very low $3. A maximum of 500 tickets is sold for each showing. The rental of the auditorium is $330 and labor is $400, including $90 for Mertz. Mertz must pay the film distributor a guarantee, ranging from $300 to $900 or 50% of gross admission receipts, whichever is higher.

Before and during the show, refreshments are sold; these sales average 12% of gross admission receipts and yield a contribution margin of 40%.

1. On June 3, Mertz played *Air Force One*. The film grossed $2,250. The guarantee to the distributor was $750, or 50% of gross admission receipts, whichever is higher. What operating income was produced for the Students' Association, which sponsored the showings?

2. Recompute the results if the film grossed $1,350.

3. The "four-wall" concept is increasingly being adopted by movie producers. In this plan, the movie's producer pays a fixed rental to the theater owner for, say, a week's showing of a movie. As a theater owner, how would you evaluate a "four-wall" offer?

2-34 Promotion of a Rock Concert

NLR Productions, Ltd., is promoting a rock concert in London. The bands will receive a flat fee of £8 million in cash. The concert will be shown worldwide on closed-circuit television. NLR will collect 100% of the receipts and will return 30% to the individual local closed-circuit theater managers. NLR expects to sell 1.1 million seats at a net average price of £13 each. NLR will also receive £300,000 from the London arena (which has sold out its 19,500 seats, ranging from £150 for box seats down to £20 for general admission, for a gross revenue of £1.25 million); NLR will not share the £300,000 with the local promoters.

Required

1. The general manager of NLR Productions is trying to decide what amount to spend for advertising. What is the most NLR could spend and still break even on overall operations, assuming sales of 1.1 million tickets?

2. If NLR desired an operating income of £500,000, how many seats would have to be sold? Assume that the average price was £13 and the total fixed costs were £9 million.

2-35 Basic Relationships, Restaurant

Genevieve Giraud owns and operates a restaurant. Her fixed costs are $21,000 per month. She serves luncheons and dinners. The average total bill (excluding tax and tip) is $18 per customer. Giraud's present variable costs average $9.60 per meal.

Required

1. How many meals must be served to attain a profit before taxes of $8,400 per month?

2. What is the break-even point in number of meals served per month?

3. Giraud's rent and other fixed costs rise to a total of $29,400 per month. If variable costs also rise to $11.50 per meal. If Giraud increases her average price to $22, how many meals must be served to make $8,400 profit per month?

4. Ignore the changes in requirement 3. Giraud's accountant tells her she may lose 10% of her customers if she increases her prices. If this should happen, what would be Giraud's profit per month? Assume that the restaurant had been serving 3,500 customers per month.

5. To help offset the anticipated 10% loss of customers, Giraud hires a pianist to perform for four hours each night for $2,000 per month. Assume that this would increase the total monthly meals from 3,150 to 3,450. Would Giraud's total profit change? By how much?

2-36 Cost-Volume-Profit Analysis, Barbering

Andre's Hair Styling in Singapore has five barbers. (Andre is not one of them.) Each barber is paid $9.90 per hour and works a 40-hour week and a 50-week year, regardless of the number of haircuts. Rent and other fixed expenses are $1,750 per month. Assume that the only service performed is the giving of haircuts, the unit price of which is $12.

Required

1. Find the contribution margin per haircut. Assume that the barbers' compensation is a fixed cost.

2. Determine the annual break-even point, in number of haircuts.

3. What will be the operating income if 20,000 haircuts are sold?

4. Suppose Andre revises the compensation method. The barbers will receive $4 per hour plus $6 for each haircut. What is the new contribution margin per haircut? What is the annual break-even point (in number of haircuts)?

5. Ignore requirements 3 and 4 and assume that the barbers cease to be paid by the hour but receive $7 for each haircut. What is the new contribution margin per haircut? The annual break-even point (in number of haircuts)?

6. Refer to requirement 5. What would be the operating income if 20,000 haircuts are sold? Compare your answer with the answer in requirement 3.

7. Refer to requirement 5. If 20,000 haircuts are sold, at what rate of commission would Andre earn the same operating income as he earned in requirement 3?

2-37 CVP and Financial Statements

ConAgra, Inc., is an Omaha-based company that produces food products under brand names such as Healthy Choice, Armour, and Banquet. The company's 1997 income statement showed the following (in millions):

Net sales	$24,002
Costs of goods sold	20,442
Selling, administrative, and general expense	2,265
Interest expense	277
Income before income tax	$ 1,018

Suppose that the cost of goods sold is the only variable cost; selling, administrative, general, and interest expenses are fixed with respect to sales.

Required

Assume that ConAgra had a 10% increase in sales in 1998 and that there was no change in costs except for increases associated with the higher volume of sales. Compute the predicted 1998 operating profit for ConAgra and the percentage increase in operating profit.

Explain why the percentage increase in profit differs from the percentage increase in sales.

2-38 Bingo and Leverage

A California law permits bingo games when offered by specified nonprofit institutions, including churches. Reverend Wilbur Means, the pastor of a new parish in Orange County, is investigating the desirability of conducting weekly bingo nights. The parish has no hall, but a local hotel would be willing to commit its hall for a lump-sum rental of $800 per night. The rent would include cleaning, setting up and taking down the tables and chairs, and so on.

Required

1. A local printer would provide bingo cards in return for free advertising. Local merchants would donate door prizes. The services of clerks, callers, security force, and others would be donated by volunteers. Admission would be $4 per person, entitling the player to one card; extra cards would be $1.50 each. Many persons buy extra cards, so there would be an average of four cards played per person. What is the maximum in total cash prizes that the church may award and still break even if 200 persons attend each weekly session?

2. Suppose the total cash prizes are $900. What will be the church's operating income if 100 persons attend? If 200 persons attend? If 300 persons attend? Briefly explain the effects of the cost behavior on income.

3. After operating for 10 months, Reverend Means is thinking of negotiating a different rental arrangement but keeping the prize money unchanged at $900. Suppose the rent is $400 weekly plus $2 per person. Compute the operating income for attendance of 100, 200, and 300 persons, respectively. Explain why the results differ from those in requirement 2.

2-39 Adding a Product

Andy's Ale House, a pub located near State University, serves as a gathering place for the university's more social scholars. Andy sells beer on draft and all brands of bottled beer at a contribution margin of 60¢ a beer.

Andy is considering also selling hamburgers during selected hours. His reasons are twofold. First, sandwiches would attract daytime customers. A hamburger and a beer are a quick lunch. Second, he has to meet competition from other local bars, some of which provide more extensive menus.

Andy analyzed the costs as follows:

	Per Month			Per Hamburger
Monthly fixed expenses		Variable expenses		
Wages of part-time cook	$1,200	Rolls		$.12
Other	360	Meat @ $2.80 per pound		
Total	$1,560	(7 hamburgers per pound)		.40
		Other		.18
		Total		$.70

Andy planned a selling price of $1.10 per hamburger to lure many customers. For all questions, assume a 30-day month.

Required

1. What are the monthly and daily break-even points, in number of hamburgers?
2. What are the monthly and daily break-even points, in dollar sales?

3. At the end of two months, Andy finds he has sold 3,600 hamburgers. What is the operating profit per month on hamburgers?

4. Andy thinks that at least 60 extra beers are sold per day because he has these hamburgers available. This means that 60 extra people come to the bar or that 60 buy an extra beer because they are attracted by the hamburgers. How does this affect Andy's monthly operating income?

5. Refer to requirement 3. How many extra beers would have to be sold per day so that the overall effects of the hamburger sales on monthly operating income would be zero?

2-40 Cost-Volume-Profit Relationships and a Dog Track

The Miami Kennel Club is a dog-racing track. Its revenue is derived mainly from attendance and a fixed percentage of the parimutuel betting. Its expenses for a 90-day season are as follows:

Wages of cashiers and ticket takers	$160,000
Commissioner's salary	20,000
Maintenance (repairs, etc.)	20,000
Utilities	30,000
Other expenses (depreciation, insurance, advertising, etc.)	90,000
Purses: total prizes paid to winning racers	810,000

The track made a contract with PK Inc. to park the cars. PK charged the track $6.00 per car. A survey revealed that on the average three persons arrived in each car and that half the attendees arrived by private automobiles. The others arrived by taxi and public buses.

The track's sources of revenue are

Rights for concession and vending	$50,000
Admission charge (deliberately low)	$1 per person
Percentage of bets placed	10%

Required Assume that each person bets $27 a night.

1. **a.** How many persons have to be admitted for the track to break even for the season?
   b. If the desired operating profit for the year is $270,000, how many people would have to attend?

2. If a policy of free admission brought a 20% increase in attendance, what would be the new level of operating profit? Assume that the previous level of attendance was 600,000 people.

3. If the purses were doubled in an attempt to attract better dogs and thus increase attendance, what would be the new break-even point? Refer to the original data and assume that each person bets $27 a night.

2-41 Traveling Expenses

Yukio Nomo is a traveling inspector for the State Treasurer's Office. He uses his own car and the agency reimburses him at 23¢ per mile. Yukio Nomo claims he needs 27¢ per mile just to break even.

Marilyn McDyess, the district manager, looks into the matter and compiles the following information about Nomo's expenses:

Oil change every 3,000 miles	$ 30
Maintenance (other than oil) every 6,000 miles	240
Yearly insurance	700
Auto cost $13,500 with an average cash trade-in value of $6,000; has a useful life of three years.	
Gasoline is approximately $1.70 per gallon and Nomo averages 17 miles per gallon.	

When Nomo is on the road, he averages 120 miles a day. McDyess knows that Nomo does not work Saturdays or Sundays, has 10 working days vacation and 6 holidays, and spends approximately 15 working days in the office.

Required

1. How many miles per year would Nomo have to travel to break even at the current rate of reimbursement?
2. What would be an equitable mileage rate?

2-42 Government Organization

A social welfare agency has a government budget appropriation for 19X6 of $900,000. The agency's major mission is to help disabled persons who are unable to hold jobs. On the average, the agency supplements each person's other income by $5,000 annually. The agency's fixed costs are $290,000. There are no other costs.

Required

1. How many disabled persons were helped during 19X6?
2. For 19X7, the agency's budget appropriation has been reduced by 15%. If the agency continues the same level of monetary support per person, how many disabled persons will be helped in 19X7? Compute the percentage decline in the number of persons helped.
3. Assume a budget reduction of 15%, as in requirement 2. The manager of the agency has discretion as to how much to supplement each disabled person's income. She does not want to reduce the number of persons served. On the average, what is the amount of the supplement that can be given to each person? Compute the percentage decline in the annual supplement.

2-43 Airline CVP

Airline companies regularly provide operating statistics with their financial statements. In 1996 Continental Airlines reported that it had approximately 61,000 million seat-miles available, of which 68.1% were filled. (A seat-mile is one seat traveling one mile. For example, if an airplane with 100 seats traveled 400 miles, capacity would have been $100 \times 400 = 40,000$ seat miles.) The average revenue was $.1310 per revenue-passenger-mile, where a revenue-passenger-mile is one seat occupied by a passenger traveling one mile. In 1995, approximately the same number of seat-miles were available, but only 65.6% of them were filled at an average revenue of $.1251 per filled seat-mile. Continental calls the percentage of seat-miles available that are filled with passengers their load factor.

Required

1. Compute Continental's passenger revenue for 1996 and 1995.
2. Assume that Continental's variable costs were $.05 per revenue-passenger-mile in both 1995 and 1996 and that fixed costs are $3,000 million per year each year.

a. Compute Continental's break-even point at the 1995 level of revenue per passenger mile. Express it in both revenue-passenger-miles and as a load factor (that is, as a percentage of available capacity used).

b. Compute Continental's break-even point at the 1996 level of revenue per passenger mile. Express it in both revenue-passenger-miles and as a load factor (that is, as a percentage of available capacity used).

3. Suppose Continental maintained the same level of seat-miles available in 1997, had revenue of $.13 per revenue-passenger-mile, and maintained the same level of fixed and variable costs as in the previous two years. Compute the load factor necessary to achieve an operating income of $400 million.

2-44 Gross Margin and Contribution Margin

Eastman Kodak Company produces and sells cameras, film, and other imaging products. A condensed 1996 income statement follows (in millions):

Sales	$15,968
Costs of goods sold	8,326
Gross margin	7,642
Other operating expenses	6,086
Operating income	$ 1,556

Assume that $1,800 million of the cost of goods sold is a fixed cost representing depreciation and other production costs that do not change with the volume of production. In addition, $4,000 million of the other operating expenses is fixed.

Required

1. Compute the total contribution margin for 1996 and the contribution margin percentage. Explain why the contribution margin differs from the gross margin.

2. Suppose that sales for Eastman Kodak were predicted to increase by 10% in 1997 and that the cost behavior was expected to continue in 1997 as it did in 1996. Compute the predicted operating income for 1997. By what percentage did this predicted 1997 operating income exceed the 1996 operating income?

3. What assumptions were necessary to compute the predicted 1997 operating income in requirement 2?

2-45 Choosing Equipment for Different Volumes

(CMA, adapted.) Multiplex Cinema owns and operates a nationwide chain of movie theaters. The 500 properties in the Multiplex chain vary from low-volume, small-town, single-screen theaters to high-volume, big-city, multiscreen theaters.

The management is considering installing machines that will make popcorn on the premises. These machines would allow the theaters to sell popcorn that would be freshly popped daily rather than the prepopped corn that is currently purchased in large bags. This proposed feature would be properly advertised and is intended to increase patronage at the company's theaters.

The machines can be purchased in several different sizes. The annual rental costs and operating costs vary with the size of the machines. The machine capacities and costs are as follows:

	Popper Model		
	E5	R12	S30
Annual capacity	50,000 boxes	120,000 boxes	300,000 boxes
Costs			
Annual machine rental	$8,000	$11,200	$20,200
Popcorn cost per box	.14	.14	.14
Cost of each box	.09	.09	.09
Other variable costs per box	.22	.14	.05

Required

1. Calculate the volume level in boxes at which the E5 and R12 poppers would earn the same operating profit (loss).

2. The management can estimate the number of boxes to be sold at each of its theaters. Present a decision rule that would enable Multiplex management to select the most profitable machine without having to make a separate cost calculation for each theater. That is, at what anticipated range of unit sales should the E5 model be used? the R12 model? the S30 model?

3. Could the management use the average number of boxes sold per seat for the entire chain and the capacity of each theater to develop this decision rule? Explain your answer.

BUSINESS FIRST   www.prenhall.com/phlip

PHLIP

2-46   Boeing Break-Even

Boeing is the largest commercial airplane manufacturer in the world. In 1996 it began development of the 757-300, a 240-passenger plane with a range up to 4,010 miles. First deliveries will take place in 1999, and the price will be about $70 million per plane.

Assume that Boeing's annual fixed costs for the 757-300 are $950 million, and its variable cost per airplane is $45 million.

Required

1. Compute Boeing's break-even point in number of 757-300 airplanes and in dollars of sales.

2. Suppose Boeing plans to sell 42 757-300 airplanes in 1999. Compute Boeing's projected operating profit.

3. Suppose Boeing increased its fixed costs by $84 million and reduced variable costs per airplane by $2 million. Compute its operating profit if 42 757-300 airplanes are sold. Compute the break-even point. Comment on your results.

4. Ignore requirement 3. Suppose fixed costs do not change but variable costs increase by 10% before deliveries of 757-300 airplanes begin in 1999. Compute the new break-even point. What strategies might Boeing use to help assure profitable operations in light of increases in variable cost? ■

2-47   Sales-Mix Analysis

Study Appendix 2A. The New England Catering Company specializes in preparing tasty main courses that are frozen and shipped to the finer restaurants in the Boston area. When a diner orders the item, the restaurant heats and serves it. The budget data for 19X9 are

	Product	
	Chicken *Cordon Bleu*	*Veal* *Marsala*
Selling price to restaurants	$7	$9
Variable expenses	4	5
Contribution margin	$3	$4
Number of units	250,000	125,000

The items are prepared in the same kitchens, delivered in the same trucks, and so forth. Therefore, the fixed costs of $1,320,000 are unaffected by the specific products.

Required

1. Compute the planned net income for 19X9.
2. Compute the break-even point in units, assuming that the planned sales mix is maintained.
3. Compute the break-even point in units if only veal were sold and if only chicken were sold.
4. Suppose 99,000 units of veal and 297,000 units of chicken were sold. Compute the net income. Compute the new break-even point if these relationships persisted in 19X9. What is the major lesson of this problem?

2-48   Hospital Patient Mix
Study Appendix 2A. Hospitals measure their volume in terms of patient-days, which are defined as the number of patients multiplied by the number of days that the patients are hospitalized. Suppose a large hospital has fixed costs of $48 million per year and variable costs of $600 per patient-day. Daily revenues vary among classes of patients. For simplicity, assume that there are two classes: (1) self-pay patients (S) who pay an average of $1,000 per day and (2) non–self-pay patients (G) who are the responsibility of insurance companies and government agencies and who pay an average of $800 per day. Twenty percent of the patients are self-pay.

Required

1. Compute the break-even point in patient-days, assuming that the planned mix of patients is maintained.
2. Suppose that 200,000 patient-days were achieved but that 25% of the patient-days were self-pay (instead of 20%). Compute the net income. Compute the break-even point.

2-49   Income Taxes on Hotels
Study Appendix 2B. The All Seasons Hotel in downtown Denver has annual fixed costs applicable to rooms of $10 million for its 600-room hotel, average daily room rates of $105, and average variable costs of $25 for each room rented. It operates 365 days per year. The hotel is subject to an income tax rate of 40%.

Required

1. How many rooms must the hotel rent to earn a net income after taxes of $720,000? Of $360,000?
2. Compute the break-even point in number of rooms rented. What percentage occupancy for the year is needed to break even?
3. Assume that the volume level of rooms sold is 150,000. The manager is wondering how much income could be generated by adding sales of 15,000 rooms. Compute the additional net income after taxes.

2-50   Tax Effects, Multiple Choice
Study Appendix 2B. Raprock Company is a wholesaler of compact disks. The projected after-tax net income for the current year is $120,000 based on a sales volume of 200,000

CDs. Raprock has been selling the CDs at $16 each. The variable costs consist of the $10 unit purchase price and a handling cost of $2 per unit. Raprock's annual fixed costs are $600,000, and Raprock is subject to a 40% income tax rate.

Management is planning for the coming year when it expects that the unit purchase price will increase 30%.

1. Raprock Company's break-even point for the current year is (a) 150,000 units, (b) 100,000 units, (c) 50,000 units, (d) 60,000 units, and (e) some amount other than those given.

2. An increase of 10% in projected unit sales volume for the current year would result in an increased after-tax income for the current year of (a) $80,000, (b) $32,000, (c) $12,000, (d) $48,000, and (e) some amount other than those given.

3. The volume of sales in dollars that Raprock Company must achieve in the coming year to maintain the same after-tax net income as projected for the current year if unit selling price remains at $16 is (a) $12,800,000, (b) $14,400,000, (c) $11,520,000, (d) $32,000,000, or (e) some amount other than those given.

4. To cover a 30% increase in the unit purchase price for the coming year and still maintain the current contribution-margin ratio, Raprock Company must establish a selling price per unit for the coming year of (a) $19.60, (b) $20.00, (c) $20.80, (d) $19.00, or (e) some amount other than those given.

CASES

2-51 Hospital Costs

Metropolitan City Hospital is unionized. In 19X8 nurses received an average annual salary of $45,000. The hospital administrator is considering how the contract with nurses should be changed for 19X9. In turn, the charging of nursing costs to each department might also be changed.

Each department is accountable for its financial performance. Revenues and expenses are allocated to departments. Consider the expenses of the obstetrics department in 19X8:

Variable expenses (based on 19X8 patient-days) are

Meals	$ 510,000
Laundry	260,000
Laboratory	900,000
Pharmacy	800,000
Maintenance	150,000
Other	530,000
Total	$3,150,000

Fixed expenses (based on number of beds) are

Rent	$3,000,000
General administrative services	2,200,000
Janitorial	200,000
Maintenance	150,000
Other	350,000
Total	$5,900,000

Nurses are assigned to departments on the basis of annual patient-days as follows:

Volume Level in Patient-Days	Number of Nurses
10,000–12,000	30
12,000–16,000	35

Total patient-days are the number of patients multiplied by the number of days they are hospitalized. Each department is charged for the salaries of the nurses assigned to it.

During 19X8 the obstetrics department had a capacity of 60 beds, billed each patient an average of $800 per day, and had revenues of $12 million.

Required

1. Compute the 19X8 volume of activity in patient-days.
2. Compute the 19X8 patient-days that would have been necessary for the obstetrics department to recoup all fixed expenses except nursing expenses.
3. Compute the 19X8 patient-days that would have been necessary for the obstetrics department to break even including nurses' salaries as a fixed cost.
4. Suppose obstetrics must pay $200 per patient-day for nursing services. This plan would replace the two-level fixed-cost system employed in 19X8. Compute what the break-even point in patient-days would have been in 19X8 under this plan.

2-52 CVP and Prediction of Income

According to an article in *Business Week*, T.J. Izzo had a great idea after a bad back almost forced him to give up golf. His problem was carrying a golf bag, not swinging a club. So he designed a harness-like golf bag strap that distributed the weight equally on both shoulders. In April 1992 he formed Izzo Systems Inc. In 1993 Izzo made operating income of $12,000 on revenue of $1 million from selling 75,000 straps. In 1994 Izzo expected to sell 92,000 straps for $1.7 million.

Required

1. Suppose that variable costs per strap are $10. Compute total fixed and total variable costs for 1993.
2. Suppose the cost behavior in 1994 was the same as in 1993. Estimate Izzo's operating income for 1994 (a) with sales at the predicted 92,000 straps, (b) with unit sales 10% above the predicted level, and (c) with unit sales 10% below the predicted level.
3. Explain why the predicted 1994 operating income was so much greater than the 1993 operating income.

2-53 CVP in a Modern Manufacturing Environment

A division of Hewlett-Packard Company changed its production operations from one where a large labor force assembled electronic components to an automated production facility dominated by computer-controlled robots. The change was necessary because of fierce competitive pressures. Improvements in quality, reliability, and flexibility of production schedules were necessary just to match the competition. As a result of the change, variable costs fell and fixed costs increased, as shown in the following assumed budgets:

	Old Production Operation	New Production Operation
Unit variable cost		
Material	$ .88	$ .88
Labor	1.22	.22
Total per unit	$ 2.10	$ 1.10
Monthly fixed costs		
Rent and depreciation	$450,000	$ 875,000
Supervisory labor	85,000	175,000
Other	50,000	90,000
Total per month	$585,000	$1,140,000

Expected volume is 600,000 units per month, with each unit selling for $3.10. Capacity is 800,000 units.

Required

1. Compute the budgeted profit at the expected volume of 600,000 units under both the old and the new production environments.
2. Compute the budgeted break-even point under both the old and the new production environments.
3. Discuss the effect on profits if volume falls to 500,000 units under both the old and the new production environments.
4. Discuss the effect on profits if volume increases to 700,000 units under both the old and the new production environments.
5. Comment on the riskiness of the new operation versus the old operation.

2-54 Multiproduct Break-Even in a Restaurant

Study Appendix 2A. An article in *Washington Business* included an income statement for La Brasserie, a French restaurant in Washington, D.C. A simplified version of the statement follows:

Revenues	$2,098,400
Cost of sales, all variable	1,246,500
Gross profit	851,900
Operating expenses	
Variable	222,380
Fixed	170,700
Administrative expenses, all fixed	451,500
Net income	$ 7,320

The average dinner tab at La Brasserie is $40, and the average lunch tab is $20. Assume that the variable cost of preparing and serving dinner is also twice that of a lunch. The restaurant serves twice as many lunches as dinners. Assume that the restaurant is open 305 days a year.

Required

1. Compute the daily break-even volume in lunches and dinners for La Brasserie. Compare this to the actual volume reflected in the income statement.
2. Suppose that an extra annual advertising expenditure of $15,000 would increase the average daily volume by three dinners and six lunches, and that there is plenty of capacity to accommodate the extra business. Prepare an analysis for the management of La Brasserie explaining whether this would be desirable.

3. La Brasserie uses only premium food, and the cost of food makes up 25% of the restaurant's total variable costs. Use of average rather than premium ingredients could cut the food cost by 20%. Assume that La Brasserie uses average-quality ingredients and does not change its prices. How much of a drop-off in volume could it endure and still maintain the same net income? What factors in addition to revenue and costs would influence the decision about the quality of food to use?

2-55 Effects of Changes in Costs, Including Tax Effects

Study Appendix 2B. Pacific Fish Company is a wholesale distributor of salmon. The company services grocery stores in the Chicago area.

Small but steady growth in sales has been achieved by Pacific Fish over the past few years while salmon prices have been increasing. The company is formulating its plans for the coming fiscal year. Presented below are the data used to project the current year's after-tax net income of $138,000.

Average selling price per pound	$ 5.00
Average variable costs per pound	
Cost of salmon	$ 2.50
Shipping expenses	.50
Total	$ 3.00
Annual fixed costs	
Selling	$ 200,000
Administrative	350,000
Total	$ 550,000
Expected annual sales volume (390,000 pounds)	$1,950,000
Tax rate	40%

Fishing companies have announced that they will increase prices of their products an average of 15% in the coming year, owing mainly to increases in labor costs. Pacific Fish Company expects that all other costs will remain at the same rates or levels as in the current year.

1. What is Pacific Fish Company's break-even point in pounds of salmon for the current year?

2. What selling price per pound must Pacific Fish Company charge to cover the 15% increase in the cost of salmon and still maintain the current contribution-margin ratio?

3. What volume of sales in dollars must the Pacific Fish Company achieve in the coming year to maintain the same net income after taxes as projected for the current year if the selling price of salmon remains at $5 per pound and the cost of salmon increases 15%?

4. What strategies might Pacific Fish Company use to maintain the same net income after taxes as projected for the current year?

COLLABORATIVE LEARNING EXERCISE

2-56 CVP for a Small Business

Form a group of two to six students. Each group should select a very simple business, one with a single product or one with approximately the same contribution margin percentage for all products. Some possibilities are:

A child's lemonade stand

A retail video rental store

An expresso cart

A retail store selling compact disks

An athletic shoe store

A cookie stand in a mall

However, you are encouraged to use your imagination rather than just select one of these examples.

The following tasks might be split up among the group members.

Required

1. Make a list of all fixed costs associated with running the business you selected. Estimate the amount of each fixed cost per month (or per day or per year, if one of them is more appropriate for your business).

2. Make a list of all variable costs associated with making or obtaining the product or service your company is selling. Estimate the cost per unit for each variable cost.

3. Given the fixed and variable costs you have identified, compute the break-even point for your business in either units or dollar sales.

4. Assess the prospects of your business making a profit.

MEASUREMENT OF COST BEHAVIOR

An America West flight on final approach to San Diego's airport. America West serves the low cost/full service market at more than 90 destinations in the United States, Canada, and Mexico. Understanding the company's costs is an important factor in the company's competitive strategy.

Learning Objectives

When you have finished studying this chapter, you should be able to

1   Explain step- and mixed-cost behavior.

2   Explain management influences on cost behavior.

3   Measure and mathematically express cost functions and use them to predict costs.

4   Describe the importance of activity analysis for measuring cost functions.

5   Measure cost behavior using the account analysis, high-low, visual-fit, and least-squares regression methods.

6   **Understand the relationship between management decision making and cost behavior.**

With annual revenues of $1.9 billion, America West is the ninth largest U.S. commercial airline. The company focuses on the low-cost/full-service market with primary operations (hubs) in Phoenix, Las Vegas, and Columbus, Ohio. America West rode a booming economy to increased revenues in 1996 and 1997. As a result, management decided to expand by introducing service to new destinations including Acapulco, Miami, and Detroit, and by adding more daily flights to existing markets including Las Vegas, Mexico City, and Boston. To accomplish this, the company had to expand its labor force, add new aircraft, and spend over $40 million on new technology.

Management at America West did not take lightly the decision to invest large amounts of money in aircraft and equipment. They knew that their decision would have a significant influence on costs and thus profits for many years. They also knew that most of the costs would be fixed but the revenues would fluctuate with the economy. When the economy is bad, revenues may not cover these costs.

How does an airline protect itself against losses when the economy turns down? According to Richard Goodmanson, President and Chief Executive Officer of America West, "management has a goal to have from 5% to 10% of the fleet of aircraft leased and thus subject to annual renewal. This enhances the company's ability to decrease capacity (and related costs) in the event of an industry downturn." This example illustrates that understanding how costs behave, as well as how managers' decisions can influence costs, helped the airline improve its cost control.

Chapter 2 demonstrated the importance of understanding the cost structure of an organization and the relationships between an organization's activities and its costs,

measurement of cost behavior Understanding and quantifying how activities of an organization affect levels of costs.

revenues, and profits. This chapter focuses on **measurement of cost behavior,** which means understanding and quantifying how activities of an organization affect levels of costs. Recall that activities use resources and these resources have costs. We measure the relationship between activity and cost using output measures called cost drivers. Understanding relationships between costs and their cost drivers allows managers in all types of organizations—profit-seeking, nonprofit, and government—to

- Evaluate new manufacturing methods or service practices (Chapter 4)
- Make proper short-run marketing decisions (Chapter 5)
- Make short-run production decisions (Chapter 6)
- Plan or budget the effects of future activities (Chapters 7 and 8)
- Design effective management control systems (Chapters 9 and 10)
- Make proper long-run decisions (Chapter 11)
- Design accurate and useful product costing systems (Chapters 12 to 15)

As you can see, understanding cost behavior is fundamental to management accounting. There are numerous real-world cases in which managers have made very poor decisions to drop product lines, close manufacturing plants, or bid too high or too low on jobs because they had erroneous cost behavior information. This chapter, therefore, deserves careful study.

COST DRIVERS AND COST BEHAVIOR

linear-cost behavior Activity that can be graphed with a straight line because costs are assumed to be either fixed or variable.

Accountants and managers usually assume that cost behavior is linear over some relevant range of activities or change in cost drivers. **Linear-cost behavior** can be graphed with a straight line because costs are assumed to be either fixed or variable. Recall that the *relevant range* specifies the limits of cost driver activity within which a specific relationship between a cost and its cost driver will be valid. Managers usually define the relevant range based on their previous experience with different levels of activity and cost.

Many activities influence costs, but for some costs the volume of a product produced or service provided is the primary driver. These costs are easy to identify with, or trace to, products or services. Examples of volume-driven costs include the costs of printing labor, paper, ink, and binding to produce all the copies of this textbook. The number of copies printed obviously affects the total printing labor, paper, ink, and binding costs. Equally important, we could relatively easily trace the use of these resources to the copies of the text printed. Schedules, payroll records, and other documents show how much of each was used to produce the copies of this text.

Other costs are more affected by activities *not* directly related to volume and often have multiple cost drivers. Such costs are not easy to identify with or trace to outputs. Examples of costs that are difficult to trace include the wages and salaries of the editorial staff of the publisher of this textbook. These editorial personnel produce many different textbooks, and it would be very difficult to determine exactly what portion of their costs went into a specific book, such as *Introduction to Management Accounting*.

Understanding and measuring costs that are difficult to trace to outputs can be especially challenging. In practice, many organizations use a linear relationship with a single cost driver to describe each cost even though many have multiple causes. This approach is

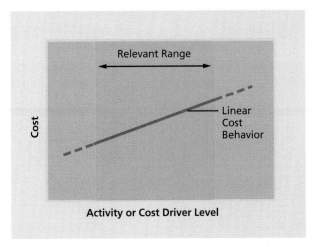

Exhibit 3-1
Linear-Cost Behavior

easier and less expensive than using nonlinear relationships or multiple cost drivers. Careful use of linear-cost behavior with a single cost driver often provides cost estimates that are accurate enough for most decisions. Linear-cost behavior with a single cost driver may seem at odds with reality and economic theory, but the added benefit of understanding "true" cost behavior may be less than the cost of determining "true" cost behavior.

For ease of communication and understanding, accountants usually describe cost behavior in visual or graphical terms. Exhibit 3-1 shows linear-cost behavior, the relevant range, and an activity or cost driver. Note the similarity to the CVP charts of Chapter 2.

STEP- AND MIXED-COST BEHAVIOR PATTERNS

Chapter 2 described two patterns of cost behavior: variable and fixed costs. Recall that a purely variable cost varies in proportion to the selected cost driver, while a purely fixed cost is not affected by the cost-driver level. In addition to these pure versions of cost, two additional types of costs combine characteristics of both fixed- and variable-cost behavior. These are step costs and mixed costs.

Objective 1
Explain step- and mixed-cost behavior.

STEP COSTS **Step costs** change abruptly at intervals of activity because the resources and their costs are only available in indivisible chunks. If the individual chunks of cost are relatively large and apply to a specific, broad range of activity, the cost is considered a fixed cost over that range of activity. An example is in panel (A) of Exhibit 3-2, which shows the cost of leasing oil and gas drilling equipment. When oil and gas exploration activity reaches a certain level in a given region, an entire additional rig must be leased. One level of oil and gas rig leasing, however, will support all volumes of exploration activity within a relevant range of drilling. Within each relevant range, this step cost behaves as a fixed cost. The total step cost at a level of activity is the amount of fixed cost appropriate for the range containing that activity level.

step costs Costs that change abruptly at intervals of activity because the resources and their costs come in indivisible chunks.

In contrast, accountants often describe step costs as variable when the individual chunks of costs are relatively small and apply to a narrow range of activity. Panel (B) of Exhibit 3-2 shows the wage cost of cashiers at a supermarket. Suppose one cashier can serve an average of 20 shoppers per hour and that within the relevant range of shopping activity, the number of shoppers can range from 40 per hour to 440 per hour. The corresponding number of cashiers would range between two and 22. Because the steps are relatively small, this step cost behaves much like a variable cost and could be used as such for planning with little loss of accuracy.

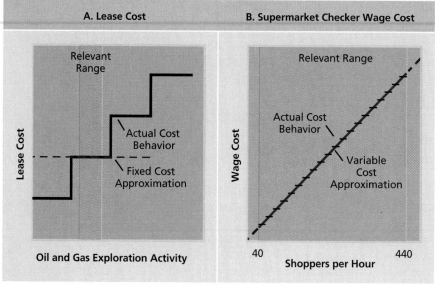

Exhibit 3-2

Step-Cost Behavior

mixed costs Costs that contain elements of both fixed- and variable-cost behavior.

MIXED COSTS **Mixed costs** contain elements of both fixed- and variable-cost behavior. As with step costs, the fixed element is determined by the planned range of activity level. Unlike step costs, though, usually in a mixed cost there is only one relevant range of activity and one level of fixed cost. The variable-cost element of the mixed cost is a purely variable cost that varies proportionately with activity within the single relevant range. In a mixed cost, the variable cost is incurred in addition to the fixed cost: the total mixed cost is the sum of the fixed cost plus the variable cost.

Many costs are mixed costs. For example, consider the monthly facilities maintenance department cost of the Parkview Medical Center, shown in Exhibit 3-3. Salaries of the maintenance personnel and costs of equipment are fixed at $10,000 per month. In addition, cleaning supplies and repair materials may vary at a rate of $5 per patient-day[1] delivered by the hospital.

An administrator at Parkview Medical Center could use knowledge of the facilities maintenance department cost behavior to:

1. Plan costs: Suppose the hospital expects to service 4,000 patient-days next month. The month's predicted facilities maintenance department costs are $10,000 fixed plus the variable cost of $20,000 (4,000 patient-days times $5 per patient-day), for a total of $30,000.

2. Provide feedback to managers: Suppose actual facilities maintenance costs were $34,000 in a month when 4,000 patient-days were serviced as planned. Managers would want to know why the hospital overspent by $4,000 ($34,000 less the planned $30,000) so that they could take corrective action.

3. Make decisions about the most efficient use of resources: For example, managers might weigh the long-run tradeoffs of increased fixed costs of highly automated floor cleaning equipment against the variable costs of extra hours needed to clean floors manually.

---

[1] A patient-day is one patient spending one day in the hospital. One patient spending five days in the hospital is five patient-days of service.

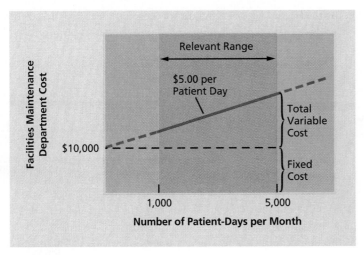

Exhibit 3-3
Mixed-Cost Behavior

MANAGEMENT INFLUENCE ON COST BEHAVIOR

In addition to measuring and evaluating current cost behavior, managers can influence cost behavior through decisions about such factors as product or service attributes, capacity, technology, and policies to create incentives to control costs.

PRODUCT AND SERVICE DECISIONS AND THE VALUE CHAIN

Throughout the value chain, managers influence cost behavior. This influence occurs through their choices of process and product design, quality levels, product features, distribution channels, and so on. Each of these decisions contributes to the organization's performance and should be made in a cost/benefit framework. For example, Hertz, the car rental company, would add a feature to its services only if the cost of the feature (for example, free mileage) could be justified (more than recovered in profit from increased business).

Objective 2
Explain management influences on cost behavior.

CAPACITY DECISIONS

Strategic decisions about the scale and scope of an organization's activities generally result in fixed levels of *capacity costs*. **Capacity costs** are the fixed costs of being able to achieve a desired level of production or to provide a desired level of service while maintaining product or service attributes, such as quality. Companies in industries with long-term variations in demand must be careful when making capacity decisions. Fixed-capacity costs cannot be recovered when demand falls during an economic downturn. Consider the dilemma facing Ford. In the mid-1980s, Ford was operating at full capacity. To meet demand, workers were on overtime and Ford even contracted with Mazda to produce some of its Probe cars. Ford had to choose between building new plants and assembly lines or continuing to pay premiums for overtime and outside production. Building new plants would enable Ford to produce cars at less cost but the fixed-capacity costs would not be controllable. Overtime and outsourcing production to Mazda was expensive, but Ford could control these variable costs much more easily during any business downturn. What did Ford do? According to executives at Ford, "We know in 1986 and 1987 we lost some sales. We could have probably had a higher market share. But we felt it was worth it to keep our costs under control. . . . Sooner or later there's going to be a downturn and we'll be running down days and short weeks even with the capacity we have." During the business downturn in the early 1990s, Ford was able to

capacity costs The fixed costs of being able to achieve a desired level of production or to provide a desired level of service while maintaining product or service attributes, such as quality.

exercise more control over its costs. Again, in the economic boom of the mid-1990s, Ford faced the same strategic decision concerning scale and scope of operations.

COMMITTED FIXED COSTS

committed fixed costs
Costs arising from the possession of facilities, equipment, and a basic organization: large, indivisible chunks of cost that the organization is obligated to incur or usually would not consider avoiding.

Even if, like Ford, a company has chosen to minimize fixed capacity costs, every organization has some costs to which it is committed, perhaps for quite a few years. **Committed fixed costs** usually arise from the possession of facilities, equipment, and a basic organization. These are large, indivisible chunks of cost that the organization is obligated to incur or usually would not consider avoiding. Committed fixed costs include mortgage or lease payments, interest payments on long-term debt, property taxes, insurance, and salaries of key personnel. Only major changes in the philosophy, scale, or scope of operations could change these committed fixed costs in future periods. Recall the example of the facilities maintenance department for the Parkview Medical Center. The capacity of the facilities maintenance department was a management decision, and in this case the decision determined the magnitude of the equipment cost. Suppose Parkview Medical Center were to increase permanently its patient-days per month beyond the relevant range of 5,000 patient-days. Because more capacity would be needed, the committed equipment cost would rise to a new level per month.

DISCRETIONARY FIXED COSTS

discretionary fixed costs
Costs determined by management as part of the periodic planning process in order to meet the organization's goals.

Some costs are fixed at certain levels only because management decided that these levels of cost should be incurred to meet the organization's goals. These **discretionary fixed costs** have no obvious relationship to levels of output activity but are determined as part of the periodic planning process. Each planning period, management will determine how much to spend on discretionary items such as advertising and promotion costs, public relations, research and development costs, charitable donations, employee training programs, and purchased management consulting services. These costs then become fixed until the next planning period.

Unlike committed fixed costs, managers can alter discretionary fixed costs easily—up or down—even within a budget period, if they decide that different levels of spending are desirable. Conceivably, managers could reduce such discretionary costs almost entirely for a given year in dire times, whereas they could not reduce committed costs. Discretionary fixed costs may be essential to the long-run achievement of the organization's goals, but managers can vary spending levels broadly in the short run.

Sometimes managers plan discretionary fixed costs, such as advertising or research and development, as a percentage of planned sales revenue. Of course, managers would not contract for advertising or conduct research and development only as current revenues are received. Rather, this planning is needed if the organization is to be able to pay for discretionary fixed costs.

Consider Marietta Corporation, which is experiencing financial difficulties. Sales for its major products are down, and Marietta's management is considering cutting back on costs temporarily. Marietta's management must determine which of the following fixed costs can be reduced or eliminated and how much money each would save:

Fixed Costs	Planned Amounts
Advertising and promotion	$ 30,000
Depreciation	400,000
Employee training	100,000
Management salaries	800,000
Mortgage payment	250,000
Property taxes	600,000
Research and development	1,500,000
Total	$3,680,000

Can Marietta reduce or eliminate any of these fixed costs? The answer depends on Marietta's long-run outlook. Marietta could reduce costs but also greatly reduce its ability to compete in the future if it cuts carelessly. Rearranging these costs by categories of committed and discretionary costs yields the following analysis:

Fixed Costs	Planned Amounts
Committed	
Depreciation	$ 400,000
Mortgage payment	250,000
Property taxes	600,000
Total committed	$1,250,000
Discretionary (potential savings)	
Advertising and promotion	$ 30,000
Employee training	100,000
Management salaries	800,000
Research and development	1,500,000
Total discretionary	$2,430,000
Total committed and discretionary	$3,680,000

Eliminating all discretionary fixed costs would save Marietta $2,430,000 per year. As is clear from Chapter 2, reducing fixed costs lowers the break-even point or increases the profit at a given level of sales, which might benefit Marietta at this time. Marietta would be unwise to cut all discretionary costs completely. Nevertheless, distinguishing committed and discretionary fixed costs would be the company's first step to identifying where costs could be reduced.

Technology Decisions

One of the most critical decisions that managers make is the type of technology that the organization will use to produce its products or deliver its services. Choice of technology (for example, labor-intensive versus robotic manufacturing or traditional banking services versus automated tellers) positions the organization to meet its current goals and to respond to changes in the environment (for example, changes in customer needs or actions by competitors). The use of high technology equipment rather than labor usually means a much greater fixed-cost component to the total cost. This type of cost behavior creates greater risks for companies with wide changes in demand. Not surprisingly, technology may have a great impact on the costs of products and services.

Cost-Control Incentives

Finally, future costs may be affected by the incentives that management creates for employees to control costs. Managers use their knowledge of cost behavior to set cost expectations, and employees may receive compensation or other rewards that are tied to meeting these expectations. For example, the administrator of Parkview Medical Center may give the supervisor of the facilities maintenance department a favorable evaluation if the supervisor maintained quality of service and kept department costs below the expected amount for the level of patient-days serviced. This strong form of feedback could cause the supervisor to watch department costs carefully and to find ways to reduce costs without reducing quality of service.

COST FUNCTIONS

The decision making, planning, and controlling activities of management accounting require accurate and useful estimates of future fixed and variable costs. The first step in estimating or predicting costs is **cost measurement** or *measuring cost behavior* as a

cost measurement
Estimating or predicting costs as a function of appropriate cost drivers.

Objective 3
Measure and mathematically express cost functions and use them to predict costs.

cost function An algebraic equation used by managers to describe the relationship between a cost and its cost driver(s).

function of appropriate cost drivers. The second step is to use these cost measures to estimate future costs at expected, future levels of cost-driver activity.

It is usually easy to measure costs that are obviously linked with a volume-related cost driver. Why? Because you can trace such costs to particular cost drivers, and measurement simply requires a system for identifying the costs. For example, systems for controlling inventories measure the amount of materials issued for a particular product or service. Similarly, payroll systems that use labor records or time cards may detail the amount of time each worker spends on a particular product or service.

In contrast, it is usually difficult to measure costs that have no obvious links to cost drivers, or those with multiple cost drivers. Assumed relationships between costs and cost drivers often are used because an observable link is not present.

FORM OF COST FUNCTIONS

To describe the relationship between a cost and its cost driver(s), managers often use an algebraic equation called a **cost function.** When there is only one cost driver, the cost function is similar to the algebraic CVP relationships discussed in Chapter 2. Consider the mixed cost graphed in Exhibit 3-3 on page 85, the facilities maintenance department cost:

$$\begin{matrix} \text{Total facilities maintenance} \\ \text{department costs} \end{matrix} = \begin{matrix} \text{Total fixed} \\ \text{maintenance cost} \end{matrix} + \begin{matrix} \text{Total variable} \\ \text{maintenance cost} \end{matrix}$$

$$= \begin{matrix} \text{Fixed maintenance} \\ \text{per month} \end{matrix} + \left(\begin{matrix} \text{Variable cost} \\ \text{per patient-day} \end{matrix} \times \begin{matrix} \text{Number of} \\ \text{patient-days} \end{matrix} \right)$$

Let

Y = total facilities maintenance department cost
F = fixed maintenance cost
V = variable cost per patient-day
X = cost-driver activity in number of patient-days

We can rewrite the mixed-cost function as

$$Y = F + VX, \text{ or}$$
$$Y = \$10,000 + \$5.00X$$

This mixed-cost function has the familiar form of a straight line—it is called a *linear-cost function.* When graphing a cost function, F is the intercept, the point on the vertical axis where the cost function begins. In Exhibit 3-3 the intercept is the $10,000 fixed cost per month. V, the variable cost per unit of activity, is the slope of the cost function. In Exhibit 3-3 the cost function slopes upward at the rate of $5 for each additional patient-day.

CRITERIA FOR CHOOSING FUNCTIONS

Managers should apply two principles to obtain accurate and useful cost functions: plausibility and reliability.

1. The cost function must be plausible or believable. Personal observation of costs and activities, when it is possible, provides the best evidence of a plausible relationship between a cost and its driver. Some cost relationships, by nature, are not directly observable, so the cost analyst must be confident that the proposed relationship is sound. Many costs may move together with a number of cost drivers, but no cause-and-effect relationships may exist. A cause-and-effect relationship (that is, X causes Y) is desirable for cost functions to be accurate and useful.

2. In addition to being plausible, a cost function's estimates of costs at actual levels of activity must reliably conform with actually observed costs. Reliability can be

assessed in terms of "goodness of fit"—how well the cost function explains past cost behavior. If the fit is good and conditions do not change, the cost function should be a reliable predictor of future costs.

Note especially that managers use these criteria together in choosing a cost function: each is a check on the other. Knowledge of operations and how costs are recorded is helpful in choosing a plausible and reliable cost function that links cause and effect. For example, maintenance is often performed when output is low, because that is when machines can be taken out of service. Lower output does not cause increased maintenance costs, however, nor does increased output cause lower maintenance costs. The timing of maintenance is somewhat discretionary. A more plausible explanation is that over a longer period increased output causes higher maintenance costs, but daily or weekly recording of maintenance costs may make it appear otherwise. Understanding the nature of maintenance costs should lead to a reliable, long-run cost function.

CHOICE OF COST DRIVERS: ACTIVITY ANALYSIS

How exactly do managers go about choosing reliable and plausible cost functions? Well, you cannot have a good cost function without knowing the right cost drivers, so choosing a cost function starts with choosing cost drivers. Managers use **activity analysis** to identify appropriate cost drivers and their effects on the costs of making a product or providing a service. The final product or service may have a number of cost drivers because a number of separate activities may be involved. The greatest benefit of activity analysis is that it directs management accountants to the appropriate cost drivers for each cost.

Activity analysis is especially important for measuring and predicting costs for which cost drivers are not obvious. **Cost prediction** applies cost measures to expected future activity levels to forecast future costs. Earlier in this chapter we said that a cost is fixed or variable with respect to a specific cost driver. A cost that appears fixed in relation to one cost driver could in fact be variable in relation to another cost driver. For example, suppose the Jupiter automobile plant uses automated painting equipment. The cost of adjusting this equipment may be fixed with respect to the total number of automobiles produced. That is, there is no clear cost relationship between these support costs and the number of automobiles produced. This same cost may vary greatly, however, with the number of different colors and types of finishes of automobiles produced. Activity analysis examines various potential cost drivers for plausibility and reliability. As always, the expected benefits of improved decision making from using more accurate cost behavior should exceed the expected costs of the cost-driver search.

Identifying the appropriate cost drivers is the most critical aspect of any method for measuring cost behavior. For many years, most organizations used only one cost driver: the amount of labor used. In essence, they assumed that the only activity affecting costs was the use of labor. In the past decade, however, we have learned that previously "hidden" activities greatly influence cost behavior. Often, analysts in both manufacturing and service companies find that activities related to the complexity of performing tasks affect costs more directly than do labor usage or other cost drivers that are related to the volume of output activity.

Consider Northwestern Computers, which makes two products for personal computers: a plug-in music board (Mozart-Plus) and a hard-disk drive (Powerdrive). When most of the work on Northwestern's products was done by hand, most costs, other than the cost of materials, were related to (driven by) labor cost. The use of computer-controlled assembly equipment, however, has increased the costs of support activities and has reduced labor cost. Labor cost is now only 5% of the total costs at Northwestern. Furthermore, activity analysis has shown that most of today's support costs are driven by the

activity analysis The process of identifying appropriate cost drivers and their effects on the costs of making a product or providing a service.

cost prediction The application of cost measures to expected future activity levels to forecast future costs.

Objective 4
Describe the importance of activity analysis for measuring cost functions.

number of components added to products (a measure of product complexity), not by labor cost. Mozart-Plus has five component parts, and Powerdrive has nine.

On average, support costs were twice as much as labor costs. Suppose Northwestern wants to predict how much support cost is incurred in producing one Mozart-Plus and how much for one Powerdrive. Using the old cost driver, labor cost, the prediction of support costs would be

	Mozart-Plus	Powerdrive
Labor cost	$ 8.50	$130.00
Support cost:		
2 × Direct labor cost	$17.00	$260.00

Using the more appropriate cost driver, the *number of components added to products,* the predicted support costs are

	Mozart-Plus	Powerdrive
Support cost		
at $20 per component		
$20 × 5 components	$100.00	
$20 × 9 components		$180.00
Difference in predicted support cost	$ 83.00	$ 80.00
	higher	lower

By using an appropriate cost driver, Northwestern can predict its support costs much more accurately. Managers will make better decisions with this more accurate information. For example, prices charged for products can be more closely related to the costs of production.

Activity Analysis at Hughes Aircraft Company

The regulatory and competitive environment of Hughes Aircraft Company has changed dramatically over the past several years. Government agencies demand better cost estimates, and shrinking defense spending means more competition among government contractors. Hughes Aircraft found that its 50-year-old financial reporting system provided irrelevant and inaccurate measures of cost behavior for management decision making. These cost measures were based on labor usage, which is no longer a relevant cost driver at Hughes.

Managers at Hughes spent considerable time and money analyzing the firm's service and manufacturing activities to find more appropriate cost drivers than labor usage. Among other things, they found that human resource service costs are driven in part by the number of new hires and the number of training hours rather than total direct labor usage. In fact, very few of Hughes' major activities were found to be driven by labor usage.

Managers also had to convince Hughes' employees, managers, auditors, and customers (primarily the U.S. government) that the new activity analysis produces plausible and reliable cost estimates. Toward that end, Hughes conducted pilot studies at a few sites before moving to company-wide implementation of activity analysis for cost measurement. These pilot studies demonstrated that activity analysis greatly improved cost predictions and also streamlined the cost-impact studies required by government agencies. Both managers at Hughes and government auditors are convinced that the activity-based cost information will be more relevant and will result in more effective management of government contracts.

Source: Adapted from Jack Haedicke and David Feil, "Hughes Aircraft Sets the Standard for ABC," *Management Accounting*, February 1991, pp. 29–33.

Once managers for a firm have determined the most plausible drivers behind different costs, they can choose from a broad selection of methods of approximating cost functions, including (1) engineering analysis, (2) account analysis, (3) high-low analysis, (4) visual-fit analysis, (5) simple least-squares regression, and (6) multiple least-squares regression. These methods are not mutually exclusive; managers frequently use two or more together to avoid major errors in measuring cost behavior. Some organizations use each of these methods in succession over the years as the need for more accurate measures becomes evident and more hard evidence becomes available. The first two methods may rely only on logical analysis, whereas the last four involve analysis of past costs. In this section, we will discuss each of these methods, with the exception of multiple least-squares regression, which is a bit more complex and not often used in practice.

ENGINEERING ANALYSIS

The first method, **engineering analysis,** measures cost behavior according to what costs should be, not by what costs have been. It entails a systematic review of materials, supplies, labor, support services, and facilities needed for products and services. Analysts can even use engineering analysis successfully for new products and services, as long as the organization has had experience with similar costs. Why? Because measures can be based on information from personnel who are directly involved with the product or service. In addition to actual experience, analysts learn about new costs from experiments with prototypes, accounting and industrial engineering literature, the experience of competitors, and the advice of management consultants. From this information, cost analysts determine what future costs should be. If the cost analysts are experienced and understand the activities of the organization, then their engineering cost predictions may be quite reliable and useful for decision making. The disadvantages of engineering cost analysis are that the efforts are costly and often not timely.

engineering analysis The systematic review of materials, supplies, labor, support services, and facilities needed for products and services; measuring cost behavior according to what costs should be, not by what costs have been.

Weyerhauser Company, producer of wood products, used engineering analysis to determine the cost functions for its 14 corporate service departments. These cost functions are used to measure the cost of corporate services used by three main business groups. For example, accounts payable costs for each division are a function of three cost drivers: the number of hours spent on each division, number of documents, and number of invoices. This approach to measuring cost behavior also could be used by nearly any service organization.

At Parkview Medical Center, introduced earlier, an assistant to the hospital administrator interviewed facilities maintenance personnel and observed their activities on several random days for a month. From these data, the assistant confirmed that the most plausible cost driver for facilities maintenance cost is the number of patient-days. The assistant also estimated from current department salaries and equipment charges that monthly fixed costs approximated $10,000 per month. From interviews and supplies usage during the month the assistant observed, the assistant estimated that variable costs are $5 per patient-day. The assistant gave this information to the hospital administrator but cautioned that the cost measures may be wrong because

1. The month observed may be abnormal.
2. The facilities maintenance personnel may have altered their normal work habits because the assistant was observing them.
3. The facilities maintenance personnel may not have told the complete truth about their activities because of their concerns about the use of the information they revealed.

However, if we assume the observed and estimated information is correct, facilities maintenance cost in any month could be predicted by first forecasting that month's expected patient-days and then entering that figure into the following algebraic, mixed-cost function:

$$Y = \$10,000 \text{ per month} + (\$5 \times \text{patient-days})$$

For example, if the administrator expects 4,000 patient-days next month, facilities maintenance costs are predicted to be:

$$Y = \$10,000 + (\$5 \times 4,000 \text{ patient-days}) = \underline{\$30,000}$$

ACCOUNT ANALYSIS

account analysis Selecting a volume-related cost driver and classifying each account as a variable cost or as a fixed cost.

In contrast to engineering analysis, users of account analysis look to the accounting system for information about cost behavior. The simplest method of **account analysis** selects a volume-related cost driver and classifies each account as a variable or fixed cost. The cost analyst then looks at each cost account balance and estimates either the variable cost per unit of cost-driver activity or the periodic fixed cost.

To illustrate this approach to account analysis, let's return to the facilities maintenance department at Parkview Medical Center and analyze costs for January 19X8. Recall that the most plausible driver for these costs is the number of patient-days serviced per month. The table below shows costs recorded in a month with 3,700 patient-days:

Monthly Cost	January 19X8 Amount
Supervisor's salary and benefits	$ 3,800
Hourly workers' wages and benefits	14,674
Equipment depreciation and rentals	5,873
Equipment repairs	5,604
Cleaning supplies	7,472
Total facilities maintenance cost	$37,423

Next, the analyst determines how much of each cost may be fixed and how much may be variable. Assume that the analyst has made the following judgments:

Monthly Cost	January 19X8 Amount	Fixed	Variable
Supervisor's salary and benefits	$ 3,800	$3,800	
Hourly workers' wages and benefits	14,674		$14,674
Equipment depreciation and rentals	5,873	5,873	
Equipment repairs	5,604		5,604
Cleaning supplies	7,472		7,472
Total facilities maintenance costs	$37,423	$9,673	$27,750

Objective 5
Measure cost behavior using the account analysis, high-low, visual-fit, and least-squares regression methods.

Measuring total facilities maintenance cost behavior, then, requires only simple arithmetic. Add all the fixed costs to get the total fixed cost per month. Divide the total variable costs by the units of cost-driver activity to get the variable cost per unit of cost driver.

$$\text{Fixed cost per month} = \underline{\$9,673}$$
$$\text{Variable cost per patient-day} = \$27,750 \div 3,700 \text{ patient-days}$$
$$= \underline{\$7.50 \text{ per patient-day}}$$

The algebraic, mixed-cost function, measured by account analysis, is

$$Y = \$9,673 \text{ per month} + (\$7.50 \times \text{patient-days})$$

Account-analysis methods are less expensive to conduct than engineering analysis, but they require recording of relevant cost accounts and cost drivers. In addition, account analysis, like engineering analysis, is subjective because the analyst decides whether each cost is variable or fixed based on judgment.

SUMMARY PROBLEM FOR YOUR REVIEW

ACTIVITY ANALYSIS

The Reliable Insurance Company processes a variety of insurance claims for losses, accidents, thefts, and so on. Account analysis has estimated the variable cost of processing each claim at 0.5% (.005) of the dollar value of the claim. This estimate seemed reasonable because higher claims often involve more analysis before settlement. To control processing costs better, however, Reliable Insurance conducted an activity analysis of claims processing. The analysis suggested that more appropriate cost drivers and behavior for automobile accident claims are

> 0.2% of Reliable Insurance policyholders' property claims
> \+ 0.6% of other parties' property claims
> \+ 0.8% of total personal injury claims

Data from two recent automobile accident claims follow:

	Automobile Claim No. 607788	Automobile Claim No. 607991
Policyholder claim	$ 4,500	$23,600
Other party claim	0	3,400
Personal injury claim	12,400	0
Total claim amount	$16,900	$27,000

Required

1. Estimate the cost of processing each claim using data from account analysis and then the activity analysis.
2. How would you recommend that Reliable Insurance estimate the cost of processing claims?

SOLUTION

1.

	Automobile Claim No. 607788		Automobile Claim No. 607991	
	Claim Amount	*Processing Cost*	*Claim Amount*	*Processing Cost*
Using account analysis				
Total claim amount	$16,900		$27,000	
Estimated processing cost at 0.5%		$ 84.50		$135.00
Using activity analysis				
Policyholder claim	$ 4,500		$23,600	
Estimated processing cost at 0.2%		$ 9.00		$ 47.20
Other party claim	0		3,400	
Estimated processing cost at 0.6%		0		20.40
Personal injury claim	12,400		0	
Estimated processing cost at 0.8%		99.20		0
Total estimated processing cost		$108.20		$ 67.60

2. The activity analysis estimates of processing costs are considerably different from those using cost account analysis. If the activity analyses are reliable, then automobile claims that include personal injury losses are more costly to process than property damage claims. If these estimates are relatively inexpensive to keep current and to use, then it seems reasonable to adopt the activity analysis approach. Reliable Insurance will have more accurate cost estimates and will be better able to plan its claims processing activities. Reliable Insurance processes many different types of claims, however. Extending activity analysis to all types of claims would result in a complicated system for predicting costs—much more complex (and costly) than simply using the total dollar value of claims. Whether to adopt the activity approach overall depends on cost-benefit considerations that may be estimated by first adopting activity analysis for one type of claim and assessing the usefulness and cost of the more accurate information.

HIGH-LOW, VISUAL-FIT, AND LEAST-SQUARES METHODS

When enough cost data are available, we can use historical data to measure the cost function mathematically. Three popular historical-cost methods are the high-low, visual-fit, and least-squares methods. All three of these methods are more objective than the engineering analysis method because each is based on hard evidence as well as on judgment. They also can be more objective than is account analysis because they use more than one period's cost and activity information. Account analysis and especially engineering analysis will probably remain primary methods of measuring cost behavior because the above three methods require more past cost data. Products, services, technologies, and organizations are changing rapidly in response to increased global competition. In some cases, by the time enough historical data are collected to support these analyses, the data are obsolete—the organization has changed, the production process has changed, or the product has changed. The cost analyst must be careful that the historical data are from a past environment that still closely resembles the future environment for which costs are being predicted. Another concern is that historical data may hide past inefficiencies that could be reduced if they are identified.

DATA FOR ILLUSTRATION   In discussing the high-low, visual-fit, and least-squares regression methods, we will continue to use one consistent example: Parkview Medical Center's facilities maintenance department costs. The following table shows monthly data collected on facilities maintenance department costs and on the number of patient-days serviced over the past year:

Facilities Maintenance Department Data, 19X8

Month	Facilities Maintenance Department Cost (Y)	Number of Patient-Days (X)
January	$37,000	3,700
February	23,000	1,600
March	37,000	4,100
April	47,000	4,900
May	33,000	3,300
June	39,000	4,400
July	32,000	3,500
August	33,000	4,000
September	17,000	1,200
October	18,000	1,300
November	22,000	1,800
December	20,000	1,600

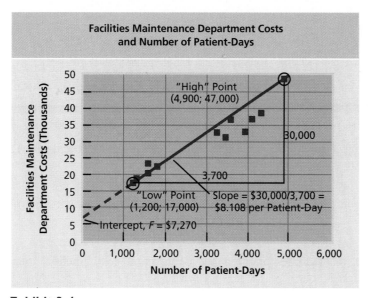

Exhibit 3-4

High-Low Method

HIGH-LOW METHOD   When sufficient cost data are available, the cost analyst may use historical data to measure the cost function mathematically. The simplest of the three methods to measure a linear-cost function from past cost data is the **high-low method** shown in Exhibit 3-4.

The first step in the high-low method is to plot the historical data points on a graph. This visual display helps the analyst see whether there are obvious errors in the data. Even though many points are plotted, the focus of the high-low method is on the highest- and lowest-activity points. Normally, the next step would be for us to draw a line through these two points. If one of these points is an "outlier" that seems in error or nonrepresentative of normal operations, however, we will need to use the next-highest or next-lowest activity point. For example, you should not use a point from a period with abnormally low activity caused by a labor strike or fire. Why? Because that point is not representative of a normal relationship between the cost and the cost driver.

After selecting the representative high and low points, we can draw a line between them, extending the line to the vertical (Y) axis of the graph. Note that this extension in Exhibit 3-4 is a dashed line as a reminder that costs may not be linear outside the relevant range. Also, managers usually are concerned with how costs behave within the relevant range, not with how they behave either at zero activity or at impossibly high activity (given current capacity). Measurements of costs within the relevant range probably are not reliable measures or predictors of costs outside the relevant range.

The point at which the line intersects the Y-axis is the intercept, F, or estimate of fixed cost. The slope of the line measures the variable cost, V, per patient-day. The clearest way to measure the intercept and slope with the high-low method is to use algebra:

high-low method   A simple method for measuring a linear-cost function from past cost data, focusing on the highest-activity and lowest-activity points and fitting a line through these two points.

Month	Facilities Maintenance Department Cost (Y)	Number of Patient-Days (X)
High: April	$47,000	4,900
Low: September	17,000	1,200
Difference	$30,000	3,700

Variable cost per patient-day,

$$V = \frac{\text{change in costs}}{\text{change in activity}} = \frac{\$47,000 - \$17,000}{4,900 - 1,200 \text{ patient-days}}$$

$$V = \frac{\$30,000}{3,700} = \underline{\$8.1081} \text{ per patient-day}$$

Fixed cost per month, F = Total mixed cost less total variable cost

at X (high): $F = \$47,000 - (\$8.1081 \times 4,900 \text{ patient-days})$
$= \$47,000 - \$39,730$
$= \underline{\$ \ 7,270}$ per month

at X (low): $F = \$17,000 - (\$8.1081 \times 1,200 \text{ patient-days})$
$= \$17,000 - \$9,730$
$= \underline{\$ \ 7,270}$ per month

Therefore, the facilities maintenance department cost function, measured by the high-low method, is

$$Y = \$7,270 \text{ per month} + (\$8.1081 \times \text{patient-days})$$

The high-low method is easy to use and illustrates mathematically how a change in a cost driver can change total cost. The cost function that resulted in this case is plausible. Before the widespread availability of computers, managers often used the high-low method to measure a cost function quickly. Today, however, the high-low method is not used often in practice because of its unreliability and because it makes inefficient use of information, using only two periods' cost experience, regardless of how many relevant data points have been collected.

SUMMARY PROBLEM FOR YOUR REVIEW

MEASUREMENT OF COST BEHAVIOR

The Reetz Company has its own photocopying department. Reetz's photocopying costs include costs of copy machines, operators, paper, toner, utilities, and so on. We have the following cost and activity data:

Month	Total Photocopying Cost	Number of Copies
1	$25,000	320,000
2	29,000	390,000
3	24,000	300,000
4	23,000	310,000
5	28,000	400,000

Required

1. Use the high-low method to measure the cost behavior of the photocopy department in formula form.

2. What are the benefits and disadvantages of using the high-low method for measuring cost behavior?

SOLUTION

1. The lowest and highest activity levels are in months 3 (300,000 copies) and 5 (400,000 copies).

$$\text{Variable cost per copy} = \frac{\text{change in cost}}{\text{change in activity}} = \frac{\$28,000 - \$24,000}{400,000 - 300,000}$$

$$= \frac{\$4,000}{100,000} = \underline{\$0.04} \text{ per copy}$$

Fixed cost per month = total cost less variable cost
at 400,000 copies: $28,000 − ($0.04 × 400,000) = $\underline{\underline{\$12,000}}$ per month
at 300,000 copies: $24,000 − ($0.04 × 300,000) = $\underline{\underline{\$12,000}}$ per month

Therefore, the photocopy cost function is:

Y (total cost) = $12,000 per month + $0.04 × number of copies

2. The benefits of using the high-low method are:

- The method is easy to use.
- Not many data are needed.

The disadvantages of using the high-low method are:

- The choice of the high and low points is subjective.
- The method does not use all available data.
- The method may not be reliable.

VISUAL-FIT METHOD   Because it can use all the available data instead of just two points, the **visual-fit method** is more reliable than is the high-low method. In the visual-fit method, we visually fit a straight line through a plot of all the available data, not just between the high point and the low point. If the cost function for the data is linear, it is possible to visualize a straight line through the scattered points that comes reasonably close to most of them and thus captures the general tendency of the data. We can extend that line back until it intersects the vertical axis of the graph.

Exhibit 3-5 shows this method applied to the facilities maintenance department cost data for the past 12 months. By measuring where the line intersects the cost axis, we can estimate the monthly fixed cost—in this case, about $10,000 per month. To find the variable cost per patient-day, select any activity level (say 1,000 patient-days) and find the total cost at that activity level ($17,000). Then divide the variable cost (which is total cost less fixed cost) by the units of activity.

$$\text{Variable cost per patient-day} = (\$17,000 - \$10,000) \div 1,000 \text{ patient-days}$$
$$= \$7 \text{ per patient-day}$$

The linear-cost function measured by the visual-fit method is:

$$Y = \$10,000 \text{ per month} + (\$7 \times \text{patient-days})$$

Although the visual-fit method can use all the data, the placement of the line and the measurement of the fixed and variable costs are subjective. This subjectivity is the main reason that the visual-fit method is now rarely used in practice, even though using computers to plot data and draw lines has made the method easier to implement. This method is a good introduction to what least-squares regression accomplishes with statistics.

LEAST-SQUARES REGRESSION METHOD   **Least-squares regression** measures a cost function more objectively (with statistics rather than human eyesight) using the same data. Least-squares regression analysis (or simply, regression analysis) uses statistics to fit a cost function to all the historical data. Regression analysis that uses one cost driver to measure a cost function is called *simple regression*. The use of multiple cost drivers for a single cost is called *multiple regression*. Only a basic discussion of simple regression analy-

visual-fit method   A method in which the cost analyst visually fits a straight line through a plot of all the available data, not just between the high point and the low point, making it more reliable than the high-low method.

least-squares regression (regression analysis) Measuring a cost function objectively by using statistics to fit a cost function to all the data.

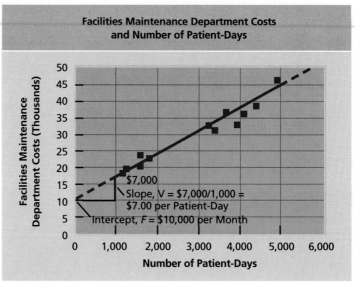

Exhibit 3-5

Visual-Fit Method

sis is presented in this section of the chapter. Some statistical properties of regression and using computer regression software are discussed in Appendix 3.

Regression analysis usually measures cost behavior more reliably than other cost measurement methods. In addition, regression analysis yields important statistical information about the reliability of cost estimates, so analysts can assess confidence in the cost measures and select the best cost driver. One such measure of reliability, or goodness of fit, is the **coefficient of determination,** R^2 (or R-squared), which measures how much of the fluctuation of a cost is explained by changes in the cost driver. Appendix 3 explains R^2 and discusses how to use it to select the best cost driver.

Exhibit 3-6 shows the linear, mixed-cost function for facilities maintenance costs as measured by simple regression analysis.

The fixed-cost measure is $9,329 per month. The variable-cost measure is $6.951 per patient-day. The linear-cost function is

Facilities maintenance department cost = $9,329 per month + $6.951 per patient-day

or

$$Y = \$9{,}329 + \$6.951 \times \text{patient-days}$$

Compare the cost measures produced by each of the five approaches:

Method	Fixed Cost per Month	Variable Cost per Patient-Day
Engineering analysis	$10,000	$5.000
Account analysis	9,673	7.500
High-low	7,270	8.108
Visual-fit	10,000	7.000
Regression	9,329	6.951

To see the differences in results between methods, we will use account-analysis and regression-analysis measures to predict total facilities maintenance department costs at 1,000 and 5,000 patient-days, the approximate limits of the relevant range:

coefficient of determination (R^2) A measurement of how much of the fluctuation of a cost is explained by changes in the cost driver.

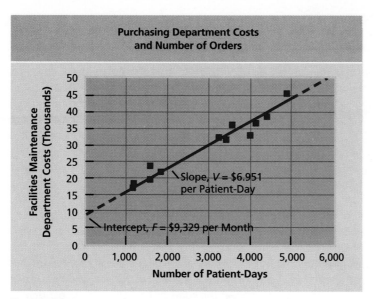

Exhibit 3-6

Least-Squares Regression Method

	Account Analysis	Regression Analysis	Difference
1,000 patient-days:			
Fixed cost	$ 9,673	$ 9,329	$ 344
Variable costs			
$7.500 × 1,000	7,500		
$6.951 × 1,000		6,951	549
Predicted total cost	$17,173	$16,280	$ 893
5,000 patient-days:			
Fixed cost	$ 9,673	$ 9,329	$ 344
Variable costs			
$7.500 × 5,000	37,500		
$6.951 × 5,000		34,755	2,745
Predicted total cost	$47,173	$44,084	$3,089

At lower levels of patient-day activity both methods yield similar cost predictions. At higher levels of patient-day activity, however, the account-analysis cost function predicts much higher facilities maintenance department costs. The difference between the predicted total costs is due primarily to the higher variable cost per patient-day (approximately $0.55 more) measured by account analysis, which increases the difference in predicted total variable costs proportionately as the number of planned patient-days increases. Because of their grounding in statistical analysis, the regression-cost measures are probably more reliable than are the other methods. Managers would thus have more confidence in cost predictions from the regression-cost function.

Consider how Hewlett-Packard (HP), the computer manufacturer, measured cost behavior as part of its companywide implementation of a new cost accounting system. HP used detailed engineering analysis to revise its accounting system at many of its manufacturing sites. The old cost system at HP used labor cost as the cost driver for all nonmaterial costs, regardless of the actual cost drivers. On average, labor costs were only 2% of total costs, so it was unlikely that they were the major cause of most other costs. The result of using labor cost was significant cost distortion—products with higher labor costs were overcosted whereas products with lower labor costs were undercosted. Managers did not have confidence in the product cost predictions using this labor-based system.

Cost analysts spent several years talking with managers and engineers and carefully observing facilities maintenance, manufacturing support, and other activities to identify more appropriate cost drivers and their relationships to cost behavior.

At HP's Surface Mount Center at Boise, the ABC system has been fully operational since early in 1993. This facility manufactures about 50 different electronic circuit boards for internal customers within HP. The selection of cost drivers at the Center resulted from an "intense analysis of the production process and cost behavior patterns by the accounting, production, and engineering staffs." This combination of account analysis and engineering analysis resulted in 10 different cost drivers.

One interesting aspect of the new cost accounting system is the continuous involvement of managers and engineers in improving the system. "An almost daily dialogue goes on among production, engineering, and the accountants about how the new cost system could be improved to reflect product costs more accurately."

A series of simple linear regressions between overhead dollars and cost driver volumes was conducted to test the statistical validity of the cost drivers. For example, one of the regressions was "all automatic placement overhead costs" versus the cost-driver "number of automatic placements," which had a coefficient of determination (R^2) of 92%. Another regression measured the relationship between "material procurement overhead costs" and the cost-driver "number of distinct parts" and had an R^2 of 91%. The regression analyses tended to confirm that the cost drivers selected indeed were correlated with overhead costs.

Source: Adapted from Mike Merz and Arlene Hardy, "ABC Puts Accountants on Design Team at HP," *Management Accounting*, September 1993, pp. 22–27.

Highlights to Remember

Explain step- and mixed-cost behavior.   Cost behavior refers to how costs change as levels of an organization's activities change. Costs can behave as fixed, variable, step, or mixed costs. Step and mixed costs both combine aspects of variable and fixed cost behavior. Step costs form graphs that look like steps. Costs will remain fixed within a given range of activity or cost-driver level, but then will rise or fall abruptly when activity or cost-driver level is outside this range. Mixed costs involve a fixed element and a variable element of cost behavior. Unlike step costs, mixed costs usually have only one range of activity or cost driver.

Explain management influences on cost behavior.   Managers can affect the costs and cost behavior patterns of their companies through the decisions they make. Decisions on product and service features, capacity, technology, and cost-control incentives, for example, can all affect cost behavior.

Measure and mathematically express cost functions and use them to predict costs.   The first step in estimating or predicting costs is measuring cost behavior. This is done by finding a cost function. This is an algebraic equation that describes the relationship between a cost and its cost driver(s). To be useful for decision-making purposes, cost functions should be plausible and reliable.

Describe the importance of activity analysis for measuring cost functions.   Activity analysis is the process of identifying the best cost drivers to use for cost estimation and prediction.

Measure cost behavior using the account analysis, high-low, visual-fit, and least-squares regression methods. Once cost drivers have been identified, one of several methods can be used to determine the cost function. Account analysis involves examining all accounts in terms of an appropriate cost driver and classifying each account as either fixed or variable (or mixed) with respect to the driver. The analyst then must estimate how much of each account cost is fixed and how much is variable. The variable cost is then unitized and added to the total fixed cost to provide a working cost function. The three methods, high-low, visual-fit, and least-squares methods, all use historical costs to determine cost functions. Of these three methods, high-low is the easiest, although least-squares is the most reliable.

Understand the relationship between management decision making and cost behavior. One of the key responsibilities of managers is making the best decisions possible for the company. Understanding cost behavior provides managers with valuable insights about how costs will respond to managers' decisions as well as to outside influences. In today's highly competitive business environment, successful cost management is a key to profitability. So, it follows that a solid understanding of how costs behave is a prerequisite to effective decision making.

Appendix 3: Use and Interpretation of Least-Squares Regression

Regression analysis of historical cost data can be accomplished with no more than a simple calculator. It would be unusual, however, to find cost analysts doing regression analysis by hand—computers are much faster and less prone to error. Therefore, we focus on using a computer to perform regression analysis and on interpretation of the results.

This appendix should not be considered a substitute for a good statistics class. More properly, this appendix should be seen as a motivator for studying statistics so that analysts can provide and managers can interpret top-quality cost estimates.

Assume that there are two potential cost drivers for the costs of the facilities maintenance department in Parkview Medical Center: (1) number of patient-days and (2) total value of hospital room charges. Regression analysis helps to determine which activity is the better cost driver. Exhibit 3-7 shows the past 12 months' cost and cost-driver data for the facilities maintenance department.

REGRESSION ANALYSIS PROCEDURES

Very good statistical software is available for both mainframes and personal computers (PCs). Most spreadsheet software available for PCs offers basic regression analysis in the "data" analysis or "tools" commands. We illustrate elements of these spreadsheet commands because many readers will be familiar with other aspects of spreadsheet software from work experience and from academic applications—not because spreadsheets are the best software to use for regression analysis. In general, sophisticated regression analysis, beyond what spreadsheets can offer, is easier with more specialized statistical software.

ENTERING DATA   First create a spreadsheet with the historical cost data in rows and columns. Each row should be data from one period. Each column should be a cost category or a cost driver. For ease of analysis, all the potential cost drivers should be in adjacent columns. Each row and column should be complete (no missing data) and without errors.

Exhibit 3-7

Facilities Maintenance Department Data

Month	Facilities Maintenance Cost (Y)	Number of Patient-Days (X_1)	Value of Room Charges (X_2)
January	$37,000	3,700	$2,983,000
February	23,000	1,600	3,535,000
March	37,000	4,100	3,766,000
April	47,000	4,900	3,646,000
May	33,000	3,300	3,767,000
June	39,000	4,400	3,780,000
July	32,000	3,500	3,823,000
August	33,000	4,000	3,152,000
September	17,000	1,200	2,625,000
October	18,000	1,300	2,315,000
November	22,000	1,800	2,347,000
December	20,000	1,600	2,917,000

PLOTTING DATA   There are two main reasons why the first step in regression analysis should be to plot the cost against each of the potential cost drivers: (1) Plots may show obvious nonlinear trends in the data; if so, linear regression analysis may not be appropriate for the entire range of the data. (2) Plots help identify "outliers"—costs that are in error or are otherwise obviously inappropriate. There is little agreement about what to do with any outliers that are not the result of data-entry errors or non-representative cost and activity levels (e.g., periods of labor strikes, natural catastrophes). After all, if the data are not in error and are representative, the process that is being studied generated them. Even so, some analysts might recommend removing outliers from the data set. Leaving these outliers in the data makes regression analysis statistically less appealing, because data far removed from the rest of the data set will not fit the line well. The most conservative action is to leave all data in the data set unless uncorrectable errors are detected or unless the data are known to be not representative of the process.

Plotting with spreadsheets uses "graph" commands on the columns of cost and cost-driver data. These graph commands typically offer many optional graph types (such as bar charts and pie charts), but the most useful plot for regression analysis usually is called the *XY* graph. This graph is the type shown earlier in this chapter—the *X*-axis is the cost driver, and the *Y*-axis is the cost. The *XY* graph should be displayed without lines drawn between the data points (called data symbols)—an optional command. (Consult your spreadsheet manual for details, because each spreadsheet program is different.)

REGRESSION OUTPUT   The regression output is generated by commands that are unique to each software package but they identify the cost to be explained ("dependent variable") and the cost driver(s) ("independent variable[s]").

Producing regression output with spreadsheets is simple: Just select the "regression" command, specify (or "highlight") the *X*-dimension[s] (the cost driver[s]), and specify the *Y*-dimension or "series" (the cost). Next specify a blank area on the spreadsheet where the output will be displayed, and select "go." Below is a regression analysis of facilities maintenance department costs using one of the two possible cost drivers, number of patient-days, X_1. Note that this output can be modified somewhat by the analyst, and the values in the output can be used elsewhere in the spreadsheet.

**Facilities Maintenance Department Cost
Explained by
Number of Patient-Days**

Regression Output

Constant	$9,329
Standard error of Y estimate	$2,145.875
R^2	0.9546625
No. of observations	12
Degrees of freedom	10
X coefficient(s)	6.9506726
Standard error of coefficient(s)	0.478994

INTERPRETATION OF REGRESSION OUTPUT   The fixed-cost measure is labeled "constant" or "intercept" and is $9,329 per month. The variable cost measure is labeled "X coefficient(s)" (or something similar in other spreadsheets) and is $6.9506726 per patient-day. The linear cost function (after rounding) is

$$Y = \$9{,}329 \text{ per month} + (\$6.951 \times \text{patient-days})$$

Typically, the computer output gives a number of statistical measures that indicate how well each cost driver explains the cost and how reliable the cost predictions are likely to be. A full explanation of the output is beyond the scope of this text. One of the most important statistics, the coefficient of determination or R^2, is very important to assessing the goodness of fit of the cost function to the actual cost data.

What the visual-fit method tried to do with eyesight, regression analysis has accomplished more reliably. In general, the better a cost driver is at explaining a cost, the closer the data points will lie to the line, and the higher will be the R^2, which varies between 0 and 1. An R^2 of 0 would mean that the cost driver does not explain the cost at all, whereas an R^2 of 1 would mean that the cost driver explains the cost perfectly. The R^2 of the relationship measured with number of patient-days as the cost driver is 0.955, which is quite high. This value indicates that number of patient-days explains facilities maintenance department cost extremely well and can be interpreted as meaning that number of patient-days explains 95.5% of the past fluctuation in facilities maintenance department cost.

In contrast, performing a regression analysis on the relationship between facilities maintenance department cost and value of hospital room charges produces the following results:

**Facilities Maintenance Department Cost
Explained by
Value of Hospital Room Charges**

Regression Output

Constant	−$8,627.01
Standard error of Y estimate	$7,045.371
R^2	0.511284
No. of observations	12
Degrees of freedom	10
X coefficient(s)	0.011939
Standard error of coefficient(s)	0.003691

The R^2 value, 0.511, indicates that the cost function using value of hospital room charges does not fit facilities maintenance department cost as well as the cost function using number of patient-days.

To use the information generated by regression analysis fully, an analyst must understand the meaning of the statistics and must be able to determine whether the statistical assumptions of regression are satisfied by the cost data. Indeed one of the major reasons why cost analysts study statistics is to understand the assumptions of regression analysis better. With this understanding, analysts can provide their organizations with top-quality estimates of cost behavior.

SUMMARY PROBLEM FOR YOUR REVIEW

PROBLEM

Comtell, Inc., makes computer peripherals (disk drives, tape drives, and printers). Until recently, production scheduling and control (PSC) costs were predicted to vary in proportion to labor costs according to the following cost function:

$$\text{PSC costs, } Y = 2 \times \text{labor cost (or 200\% of labor)}$$

Because PSC costs have been growing at the same time that labor cost has been shrinking, Comtell is concerned that its cost estimates are neither plausible nor reliable. Comtell's controller has just completed activity analysis to determine the most appropriate drivers of PSC costs. She obtained two cost functions using different cost drivers:

$$Y = 2 \times \text{labor cost}$$
$$R^2 = 0.233$$

and

$$Y = \$10,000/\text{month} + (11 \times \text{number of components used})$$
$$R^2 = 0.782$$

Required

1. What would be good tests of which cost function better predicts PSC costs?
2. During a subsequent month, labor costs were $12,000 and 2,000 product components were used. Actual PSC costs were $31,460. Using each of the preceding cost functions, prepare reports that show predicted and actual PSC costs, and the difference or variance between the two.
3. What is the meaning and importance of each cost variance?

SOLUTION

1. A statistical test of which function better explains past PSC costs compares the R^2 of each function. The second function, based on the number of components used, has a considerably higher R^2, so it better explains the past PSC costs. If the environment is essentially unchanged in the future, the second function probably will predict future PSC costs better than the first, too.

    A useful predictive test would be to compare the cost predictions of each cost function with actual costs for several months that were not used to measure the cost functions. The function that more closely predicted actual costs is probably the more reliable function.

2. Note that more actual cost data would be desirable for a better test, but the procedure would be the same.

    PSC cost predicted on a labor cost basis follows:

Predicted Cost	Actual Cost	Variance
2 × $12,000 = $24,000	$31,460	$7,460 underestimate

PSC cost predicted on a component basis follows:

Predicted Cost	Actual Cost	Variance
$10,000 + ($11 × 2,000) = $32,000	$31,460	$540 overestimate

3. The cost function that relies on labor cost underestimated PSC cost by $7,460. The cost function that uses the number of components closely predicted actual PSC costs (off by $540). Planning and control decisions would have been based on more accurate information using this prediction than using the labor cost-based prediction. An issue is whether the benefits of collecting data on the number of components used exceeded the added cost of so doing.

Accounting Vocabulary

account analysis, p. 92
activity analysis, p. 89
capacity costs, p. 85
coefficient of determination
  (R^2), p. 98
committed fixed costs, p. 86
cost function, p. 88

cost measurement, p. 87
cost prediction, p. 89
discretionary fixed costs, p. 86
engineering analysis, p. 91
high-low method, p. 95
least-squares regression, p. 97
linear-cost behavior, p. 82

measurement of cost behavior,
  p. 82
mixed cost, p. 84
regression analysis, p. 97
step costs, p. 83
visual-fit method, p. 97

Fundamental Assignment Material

3-A1 Types of Cost Behavior

Identify the following planned costs as (a) purely variable costs, (b) discretionary fixed costs, (c) committed fixed costs, (d) mixed costs, or (e) step costs. For purely variable costs and mixed costs, indicate the most likely cost driver.

1. Total repairs and maintenance of a school building.
2. Sales commissions based on revenue dollars. Payments to be made to advertising salespersons employed by radio station KVOD, Denver.
3. Jet fuel costs of United Airlines.
4. Total costs of renting trucks by the city of Detroit. Charge is a lump sum of $300 per month plus $.20 per mile.
5. Straight-line depreciation on desks in the office of an attorney.
6. Advertising costs, a lump sum planned by ABC, Inc.
7. Rental payment by the Federal Bureau of Investigation on a five-year lease for office space in a private office building.
8. Advertising allowance granted to wholesalers by Pepsi Bottling on a per-case basis.
9. Compensation of lawyers employed internally by Microsoft.
10. Crew supervisor in a Lands' End, Inc., mail-order house. A new supervisor is added for every 12 workers employed.
11. Public relations employee compensation to be paid by Chevron Oil Company.

3-A2 Activity Analysis

Evergreen Signs makes customized wooden signs for businesses and residences. These signs are made of wood, which the owner glues and carves by hand or with power tools.

After carving the signs, he paints them or applies a natural finish. He has a good sense of his labor and materials cost behavior, but he is concerned that he does not have good measures of other support costs. Currently, he predicts support costs to be 60% of the cost of materials. Close investigation of the business reveals that $40 times the number of power tool operations is a more plausible and reliable support cost relationship.

Consider estimated support costs of the following two signs that Evergreen Signs is making:

	SIGN A	SIGN B
Materials cost	$300	$150
Number of power tool operations	3	6
Support cost	?	?

Required

1. Prepare a report showing the support costs of both signs using each cost driver and showing the differences between the two.
2. What advice would you give Evergreen Signs about predicting support costs?

3-A3 Division of Mixed Costs into Variable and Fixed Components

Martina Fernandez, the president of Fernandez Tool Co., has asked for information about the cost behavior of manufacturing support costs. Specifically, she wants to know how much support cost is fixed and how much is variable. The following data are the only records available:

Month	Machine Hours	Support Costs
May	850	$ 9,000
June	1,400	12,500
July	1,000	7,900
August	1,250	11,000
September	1,750	13,500

Required

1. Find monthly fixed support cost and the variable support cost per machine hour by the high-low method.
2. A least-squares regression analysis gave the following output:

$$Y = \$2,728 + \$6.77X$$

What recommendations would you give the president based on these analyses?

3-B1 Identifying Cost Behavior Patterns

At a seminar, a cost accountant spoke on identification of different kinds of cost behavior. Carolyn Tom, a hospital administrator who heard the lecture, identified several hospital costs of concern to her. After her classification, Tom presented you with the following list of costs and asked you to (1) classify their behavior as one of the following: variable, step, mixed, discretionary fixed, committed fixed, and (2) to identify a likely cost driver for each variable or mixed cost.

1. Training costs of an administrative resident
2. Straight-line depreciation of operating room equipment
3. Costs of services of Lynn and Joss Hospital Consulting
4. Nursing supervisors' salaries (a supervisor is needed for each 45 nursing personnel)
5. Operating costs of x-ray equipment ($95,000 a year plus $3 per film)
6. Blue Cross insurance for all full-time employees
7. Costs incurred by Dr. Rath in cancer research
8. Repairs made on hospital furniture

3-B2 Activity Analysis

Boise Technology, an Idaho manufacturer of printed circuit boards, has always costed its circuits boards with a 100% "mark-up" over its material costs to cover its manufacturing support costs (which include labor). An activity analysis suggests that support costs are driven primarily by the number of manual operations performed on each board, estimated at $4 per manual operation. Compute the estimated support costs of two typical circuit boards below using the traditional mark-up and the activity analysis results:

	Board Z15	Board Q52
Material cost	$30.00	$55.00
Manual operations	16	7

Why are the cost estimates different?

3-B3 Division of Mixed Costs into Variable and Fixed Components

The president and the controller of Monterrey Transformer Company (Mexico) have agreed that refinement of the company's cost measurements will aid planning and control decisions. They have asked you to measure the function for mixed-cost behavior of repairs and maintenance from the following sparse data. Currency is the Mexican peso ($).

Monthly Activity in Machine Hours	Monthly Repair and Maintenance Cost
8,000	$190,000,000
12,000	$260,000,000

Additional Assignment Material

QUESTIONS

3-1. What is a cost driver? Give three examples of costs and their possible cost drivers.

3-2. Explain linear-cost behavior.

3-3. "Step costs can be fixed or variable depending on your perspective." Explain.

3-4. Explain how mixed costs are related to both fixed and variable costs.

3-5. How do management's product and service choices affect cost behavior?

3-6. Why are fixed costs also called capacity costs?

3-7. How do committed fixed costs differ from discretionary fixed costs?

3-8. Why are committed fixed costs the most difficult of the fixed costs to change?

3-9. What are the primary determinants of the level of committed costs? Discretionary costs?

3-10. "Planning is far more important than day-to-day control of discretionary costs." Do you agree? Explain.

3-11. How can a company's choice of technology affect its costs?

3-12. Explain the use of incentives to control cost.

3-13. What are the benefits of using "cost functions" to describe cost behavior?

3-14. Explain "plausibility" and "reliability" of cost functions. Which is preferred? Explain.

3-15. What is activity analysis?

3-16. What is engineering analysis? Account analysis?

3-17. Describe the methods for measuring cost functions using past cost data.

3-18. How could account analysis be combined with engineering analysis?

3-19. Explain the strengths and weaknesses of the high-low and visual-fit methods.

3-20. Why is regression analysis usually preferred to the high-low method?

3-21. "You never know how good your fixed- and variable-cost measures are if you use account analysis or if you visually fit a line on a data plot. That's why I like least-squares regression analysis." Explain.

3-22. (Appendix 3) Why should an analyst always plot cost data in addition to applying least-squares regression analysis?

3-23. (Appendix 3) What can we learn from R^2, the coefficient of determination?

3-24. At a conference, a consultant stated, "Before you can control, you must measure." An executive complained, "Why bother to measure when work rules and guaranteed employment provisions in labor contracts prevent discharging workers, using part-time employees, and using overtime?" Evaluate these comments. Summarize your personal attitudes toward the usefulness of engineering analysis.

EXERCISES

3-25 Various Cost-Behavior Patterns

In practice, there is often a tendency to simplify approximations of cost-behavior patterns, even though the "true" underlying behavior is not simple. Choose from the accompanying graphs A through H the one that matches the numbered items. Indicate by letter which graph best fits each of the situations described. Next to each number-letter pair, identify a likely cost driver for that cost.

The vertical axes of the graphs represent total dollars of costs incurred, and the horizontal axes represent levels of cost driver activity during a particular time period. The graphs may be used more than once.

1. Availability of quantity discounts, where the cost per unit falls as each price break is reached
2. Price of an increasingly scarce raw material as the quantity used increases
3. Guaranteed annual wage plan, whereby workers get paid for 40 hours of work per week even at zero or low levels of production that require working only a few hours weekly
4. Water bill, which entails a flat fee for the first 10,000 gallons used and then an increasing unit cost for every additional 10,000 gallons used
5. Cost of machining labor that tends to decrease as workers gain experience
6. Depreciation of office equipment
7. Cost of sheet steel for a manufacturer of farm implements
8. Salaries of supervisors, where one supervisor is added for every 12 phone solicitors
9. Natural gas bill consisting of a fixed component, plus a constant variable cost per thousand cubic feet after a specified number of cubic feet are used

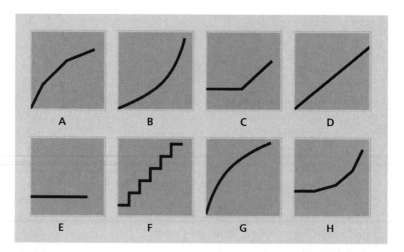

3-26 Predicting Costs

Given the following four cost behaviors and expected levels of cost-driver activity, predict total costs:

1. Fuel costs of driving vehicles, $.20 per mile, driven 15,000 miles per month

2. Equipment rental cost, $6,000 per piece of equipment per month for seven pieces for three months

3. Ambulance and EMT personnel cost for a soccer tournament, $1,100 for each 250 tournament participants; the tournament is expecting 2,400 participants

4. Purchasing department cost, $7,500 per month plus $4 per material order processed at 4,000 orders in one month

3-27 Identifying Discretionary and Committed Fixed Costs

Identify and compute total discretionary fixed and total committed fixed costs from the following list prepared by the accounting supervisor for Huang Building Supply, Inc.:

Advertising	$20,000
Depreciation	47,000
Company health insurance	15,000
Management salaries	85,000
Payment on long-term debt	50,000
Property tax	32,000
Grounds maintenance	9,000
Office remodeling	21,000
Research and development	36,000

3-28 Cost Effects of Technology

Recreational Sports, Inc., an outdoor sports retailer, is considering automating its order-taking process. The estimated costs of two alternative approaches are as follows:

	Alternative 1	Alternative 2
Annual fixed cost	$200,000	$400,000
Variable cost per order	$8	$4
Expected number of orders	70,000	70,000

At the expected level of orders, which automated approach has the lower cost? What is the indifference level of orders, or the "break-even" level of orders? What is the meaning of this level of orders?

3-29 Mixed Cost, Choosing Cost Drivers, High-Low and Visual-Fit Methods

Peoria Implements Company produces farm implements. Peoria is in the process of measuring its manufacturing costs and is particularly interested in the costs of the manufacturing maintenance activity since maintenance is a significant mixed cost. Activity analysis indicates that maintenance activity consists primarily of maintenance labor setting up machines using certain supplies. A setup consists of preparing the necessary machines for a particular production run of a product. During setup, machines must still be running, which consumes energy. Thus the costs associated with maintenance include labor, supplies, and energy. Unfortunately, Peoria's cost accounting system does not trace these costs to maintenance activity separately. Peoria employs two full-time maintenance mechanics to perform maintenance. The annual salary of a maintenance mechanic is $25,000 and is considered a fixed cost. Two plausible cost drivers have been suggested: units produced and number of setups.

Data had been collected for the past 12 months and a plot made for the cost driver—units of production. The maintenance cost figures collected include estimates for labor, supplies, and energy. Cory Fielder, controller at Peoria, recently attended an activity-based costing seminar where he learned that some types of activities are performed each time a batch of goods is processed rather than each time a unit is produced. Based on this concept, he has gathered data on the number of setups performed over the past 12 months. The plots of monthly maintenance costs versus the two potential cost drivers follow.

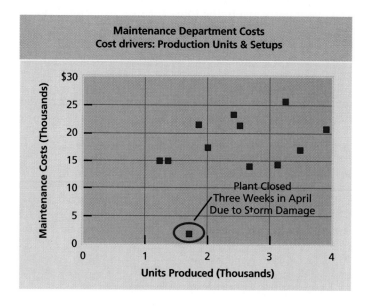

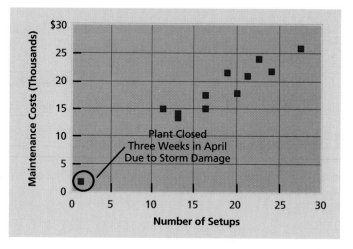

Required

1. Find monthly fixed maintenance cost and the variable maintenance cost per driver unit using the visual-fit method based on each potential cost driver. Explain how you treated the April data.

2. Find monthly fixed maintenance cost and the variable maintenance cost per driver unit using the high-low method based on each potential cost driver.

3. Which cost driver best meets the criteria for choosing cost functions? Explain.

3-30 Account Analysis

Genial Computers, Inc., is a company started by two university students to assemble and market personal computers to faculty and students. The company operates out of the garage of one of the student's homes. From the following costs of a recent month, compute the total cost function and total cost for the month.

- Telephone $ 50, fixed
- Utilities   260, 25% attributable to the garage, 75% to the house

- Advertising   75, fixed
- Insurance   80, fixed
- Materials   7,500, variable, for five computers
- Labor   1,800; $1,300 fixed plus $500 for hourly help for assembling five computers

3-31 Linear Cost Functions

Let Y = total costs, X_1 = production volume, and X_2 = number of setups. Which of the following are linear cost functions? Which are mixed cost functions?

  a. $Y = \$1,000$
  b. $Y = \$8X_1$
  c. $Y = \$5,000 + \$4X_1$
  d. $Y = \$3,000 + \$6X_1 + \$30X_2$
  e. $Y = \$9,000 + \$3X_1 \times \$2X_2$
  f. $Y = \$8,500 + \$1.50X_1^2$

3-32 High-Low Method

Southampton Foundry produced 45,000 tons in March at a cost of £1,100,000. In April, 35,000 tons were produced at a cost of £900,000. Using only these two data points, determine the cost function for Southampton.

3-33 Economic Plausibility of Regression Analysis Results

The head of the Warehousing Division of the Lachton Co. was concerned about some cost behavior information given to him by the new assistant controller, who was hired because of his recent training in cost analysis. His first assignment was to apply regression analysis to various costs in the department. One of the results was presented as follows:

"A regression on monthly data was run to explain building maintenance cost as a function of direct labor hours as the cost driver. The results are

$$Y = \$6,810 - \$.47X$$

I suggest that we use the building as intensively as possible to keep the maintenance costs down."

The department head was puzzled. How could increased use cause decreased maintenance cost? Explain this counterintuitive result to the department head. What step(s) did the assistant controller probably omit in applying and interpreting the regression analysis?

PROBLEMS

3-34 Controlling Risk, Capacity Decisions, Technology Decisions

Consider the previous discussion of Ford Motor on page 85 of the text. Ford had been outsourcing production to Mazda and using overtime for as much as 20% of production—Ford's plants and assembly lines were running at 100% of capacity and demand was sufficient for an additional 20%. Ford had considered building new highly automated assembly lines and plants to earn more profits since overtime premiums and outsourcing were costly. However, the investment in high technology and capacity expansion was rejected.

Assume that all material and labor costs are variable with respect to the level of production and that all other costs are fixed. Consider one of Ford's plants that makes Probes. The cost to convert the plant to use fully automated assembly lines is $20 million. The resulting labor costs would be significantly reduced. The costs, in millions of dollars, of the build option and the outsource/overtime option are given in the table below.

	Build Option		
Percent of capacity	60	100	120
Material costs	$18	$30	$36
Labor costs	6	10	12
Other costs	40	40	40
Total costs	$64	$80	$88

	Outsource/Overtime Option		
Percent of capacity	60	100	120
Material costs	$18	$30	$ 36
Labor costs	18	30	44
Other costs	20	20	20
Total costs	$56	$80	$100

Required

1. Prepare a line graph showing total costs for the two options: (1) build new assembly lines, and (2) continue to use overtime and outsource production of Probes. Give an explanation of the cost behavior of the two options.

2. Which option enables Ford management to control risk better? Explain. Assess the cost-benefit trade-offs associated with each option.

3. A solid understanding of cost behavior is an important prerequisite to effective managerial control of costs. Suppose you are an executive at Ford and currently the production (and sales) level is approaching the 100% level of capacity and the economy is expected to remain strong for at least 1 year. While sales and profits are good now, you are aware of the cyclical nature of the automobile business. Would you recommend committing Ford to building automated assembly lines in order to service potential near-term increases in demand or would you recommend against building, looking to the likely future downturn in business? Discuss your reasoning.

3-35 Step Costs

Atlantic County jail requires a staff of at least one guard for every four prisoners. The jail will hold 48 prisoners. Atlantic County has a beach that attracts numerous tourists and transients in the spring and summer. However, the county is rather sedate in the fall and winter. The fall–winter population of the jail is generally between 12 and 16 prisoners. The numbers in the spring and summer can fluctuate from 12 to 48, depending on the weather, among other factors (including phases of the moon, according to some longtime residents).

Atlantic County has four permanent guards hired on a year-round basis at an annual salary of $36,000 each. When additional guards are needed, they are hired on a weekly basis at a rate of $600 per week. (For simplicity, assume that each month has exactly four weeks.)

Required

1. Prepare a graph with the weekly planned cost of jail guards on the vertical axis and the number of prisoners on the horizontal axis.

2. What would be the budgeted amount for jail guards for the month of January? Would this be a fixed or variable cost?

3. Suppose the jail population of each of the four weeks in July was 25, 38, 26, and 43, respectively. The actual amount paid for jail guards in July was $19,800. Prepare a report comparing the actual amount paid for jail guards with the amount that would be expected with efficient scheduling and hiring.

4. Suppose Atlantic County treated jail-guard salaries for nonpermanent guards as a variable expense of $150 per week per prisoner. This variable cost was applied to the number of prisoners in excess of 16. Therefore, the weekly cost function was:

Weekly jail-guard cost = $3,000 + $150 × (total prisoners − 16)

Explain how this cost function was determined.

5. Prepare a report similar to that in requirement 3 except that the cost function in requirement 4 should be used to calculate the expected amount of jail-guard salaries. Which report, this one or the one in requirement 3, is more accurate? Is accuracy the only concern?

3-36 Government Service Cost Analysis

Auditors for the Internal Revenue Service scrutinize income tax returns after they have been prescreened with the help of computer tests for normal ranges of deductions claimed by taxpayers. The IRS uses an expected cost of $7 per tax return, based on measurement studies that allow 20 minutes per return. Each agent has a workweek of five days of eight hours per day. Twenty auditors are employed at a salary of $830 each per week.

The audit supervisor has the following data regarding performance for the most recent 4-week period, when 8,000 returns were processed:

Actual Cost of Auditors	Expected Cost for Processing Returns	Difference or Variance
$66,400	?	?

1. Compute the planned cost and the variance.
2. The supervisor believes that audit work should be conducted more productively and that superfluous personnel should be transferred to field audits. If the foregoing data are representative, how many auditors should be transferred? **Required**
3. List some possible reasons for the variance.
4. Describe some alternative cost drivers for processing income tax returns.

BUSINESS FIRST   www.prenhall.com/phlip

3-37 Cost Analysis at America West

America West is the nation's ninth largest commercial air carrier, with hubs in Phoenix, Las Vegas, and Columbus, Ohio. Listed below are some of the costs incurred by America West. For each cost, select an appropriate cost driver and indicate whether the cost is likely to be fixed, variable, or mixed in relation to your cost driver.

a. Pilots' salaries
b. Flight attendants' salaries

c. Baggage handlers' salaries

d. In-flight meals

e. Airplane fuel

f. Airplane depreciation

g. Advertising ∎

3-38 Separation of Drug Testing Laboratory Mixed Costs into Variable and Fixed Components

A staff meeting has been called at SportsLab, Inc., a drug-testing facility retained by several professional and college sport leagues and associations. The chief of testing, Dr. Mueller, has demanded an across-the-board increase in prices for a particular test because of the increased testing and precision that is now required.

The administrator of the laboratory has asked you to measure the mixed-cost behavior of this particular testing department and to prepare a short report she can present to Dr. Mueller. Consider the following limited data:

	Average Test Procedures per Month	Average Monthly Cost of Test Procedures
Monthly averages, 19X4	500	$ 60,000
Monthly averages, 19X5	600	70,000
Monthly averages, 19X6	700	144,000

3-39 University Cost Behavior

Metro Business College, a private institution, is preparing a planned income statement for the coming academic year ending August 31, 19X9. Tuition revenues for the past 2 years ending August 31 were 19X8: $720,000, and 19X7: $770,000. Total expenses for 19X8 were $710,000 and in 19X7 were $730,000. No tuition rate changes occurred in 19X7 or 19X8, nor are any expected to occur in 19X9. Tuition revenue is expected to be $710,000 for 19X9. What net income should be planned for 19X9, assuming that the implied cost behavior remains unchanged?

3-40 Activity Analysis

Des Moines Software develops and markets computer software for the agriculture industry. Because support costs comprise a large portion of the cost of software development, the director of cost operations of Des Moines, Shirley Danko, is especially concerned with understanding the effects of support cost behavior. Danko has completed a preliminary activity analysis of one of Des Moines's primary software products: FertiMix (software to manage fertilizer mixing). This product is a software "template" that is customized for specific customers, who are charged for the basic product plus customizing costs. The activity analysis is based on the number of customized lines of FertiMix code. Currently, support cost estimates are based on a fixed rate of 50% of the basic cost. Data are shown for two recent customers:

	Customer	
	West Acres Plants	Beautiful Blooms
Basic cost of FertiMix	$12,000	$12,000
Lines of customized code	490	180
Estimated cost per line of customized code	$23	$23

1. Compute the support cost of customizing FertiMix for each customer using each cost-estimating approach. Required
2. If the activity analysis is reliable, what are the pros and cons of adopting it for all of Des Moines's software products?

3-41 High-Low, Regression Analysis

On November 15, 1998, Sandra Cook, a newly-hired cost analyst at Demgren Company, was asked to predict overhead costs for the company's operations in 1999, when 500 units are expected to be produced. She collected the following quarterly data:

Quarter	Production in Units	Overhead Costs
1/95	76	$ 721
2/95	79	715
3/95	72	655
4/95	136	1,131
1/96	125	1,001
2/96	128	1,111
3/96	125	1,119
4/96	133	1,042
1/97	124	997
2/97	129	1,066
3/97	115	996
4/97	84	957
1/98	84	835
2/98	122	1,050
3/98	90	991

1. Using the high-low method to estimate costs, prepare a prediction of overhead costs for 1999. Required
2. Sandra ran a regression analysis using the data she collected. The result was:

$$Y = \$337 + \$5.75X$$

Using this cost function, predict costs for 1999.
3. Which prediction do you prefer? Why?

3-42 Interpretation of Regression Analysis

Study Appendix 3. The Sleeping Bag Division of General Outdoor Equipment Company has had difficulty controlling its use of supplies. The company has traditionally regarded supplies as a purely variable cost. Nearly every time production was above average, however, the division spent less than predicted for supplies; when production was below average, the division spent more than predicted. This pattern suggested to Yuki Li, the new controller, that part of the supplies cost was probably not related to production volume, or was fixed.

She decided to use regression analysis to explore this issue. After consulting with production personnel, she considered two cost drivers for supplies cost: (1) number of sleeping bags produced, and (2) square feet of material used. She obtained the following results based on monthly data:

	Cost Driver	
	Number of Sleeping Bags	*Square Feet of Material Used*
Constant	2,200	1,900
Variable coefficient	.033	.072
R^2	.220	.686

1. Which is the preferred cost function? Explain.
2. What percentage of the fluctuation of supplies cost depends on square feet of materials? Do fluctuations in supplies cost depend on anything other than square feet of materials? What proportion of the fluctuations are not explained by square feet of materials?

3-43 Regression Analysis

Study Appendix 3. Liao, Inc., a manufacturer of fine china and stoneware, is troubled by fluctuations in productivity and wants to compute how much manufacturing support costs are related to the various sizes of batches of output. The following data show the results of a random sample of 10 batches of one pattern of stoneware:

Sample	Batch Size, X	Support Costs, Y
1	15	$180
2	12	140
3	20	230
4	17	190
5	12	160
6	25	300
7	22	270
8	9	110
9	18	240
10	30	320

1. Plot support costs, Y, versus batch size, X.
2. Using regression analysis, measure the cost function of support costs and batch size.
3. Predict the support costs for a batch size of 30.
4. Using the high-low method, repeat requirements 2 and 3. Should the manager use the high-low or regression method? Explain.

3-44 Choice of Cost Driver

Study Appendix 3. Richard Ellis, the director of cost operations of Micro Devices, wishes to develop an accurate cost function to explain and predict support costs in the company's printed circuit board assembly operation. Mr. Ellis is concerned that the cost function that he currently uses—based on direct labor costs—is not accurate enough for proper planning and control of support costs. Mr. Ellis directed one of his financial analysts to obtain a random sample of 25 weeks of support costs and three possible cost drivers in the circuit-board assembly department: direct labor hours, number of boards assembled, and average cycle time of boards assembled. (Average cycle time is the average time between start and certified completion—after quality testing—of boards assembled during a week.) Much of the effort in this assembly operation is devoted to testing for quality and reworking defective boards, all of which increase the average cycle time in any period. Therefore, Mr. Ellis believes that average cycle time will be the best support cost driver. Mr. Ellis wants his analyst to use regression analysis to demonstrate which cost driver best explains support costs.

Week	Circuit Board Assembly Support Costs Y	Direct Labor Hours X_1	Number of Boards Completed X_2	Average Cycle Time (Hours) X_3
1	$66,402	7,619	2,983	186.44
2	56,943	7,678	2,830	139.14
3	60,337	7,816	2,413	151.13
4	50,096	7,659	2,221	138.30
5	64,241	7,646	2,701	158.63
6	60,846	7,765	2,656	148.71
7	43,119	7,685	2,495	105.85
8	63,412	7,962	2,128	174.02
9	59,283	7,793	2,127	155.30
10	60,070	7,732	2,127	162.20
11	53,345	7,771	2,338	142.97
12	65,027	7,842	2,685	176.08
13	58,220	7,940	2,602	150.19
14	65,406	7,750	2,029	194.06
15	35,268	7,954	2,136	100.51
16	46,394	7,768	2,046	137.47
17	71,877	7,764	2,786	197.44
18	61,903	7,635	2,822	164.69
19	50,009	7,849	2,178	141.95
20	49,327	7,869	2,244	123.37
21	44,703	7,576	2,195	128.25
22	45,582	7,557	2,370	106.16
23	43,818	7,569	2,016	131.41
24	62,122	7,672	2,515	154.88
25	52,403	7,653	2,942	140.07

Required

1. Plot support costs, Y, versus each of the possible cost drivers, X_1, X_2, and X_3.
2. Use regression analysis to measure cost functions using each of the cost drivers.
3. According to the criteria of plausibility and reliability, which is the best cost driver for support costs in the circuit board assembly department?
4. Interpret the economic meaning of the best cost function.

3-45 Use of Cost Functions for Pricing

Study Appendix 3. Read the previous problem. If you worked this problem, use your measured cost functions. If you did not work the previous problem, assume the following measured cost functions:

Y = $9,000/week + ($6 × direct labor hours); $R^2 = .10$
Y = $20,000/week + ($14 × number of boards completed); $R^2 = .40$
Y = $5,000/week + ($350 × average cycle time); $R^2 = .80$

Required

1. Which of the support cost functions would you expect to be the most reliable for explaining and predicting support costs? Why?

2. American Micro Devices prices its products by adding a percentage mark-up to its product costs. Product costs include assembly labor, components, and support costs. Using each of the cost functions, compute the circuit board portion of the support cost of an order that used the following resources:
   a. Effectively used the capacity of the assembly department for three weeks
   b. Assembly labor hours: 20,000
   c. Number of boards: 6,000
   d. Average cycle time: 180 hours
3. Which cost would you recommend that American Micro Devices use? Why?
4. Assume that the market for this product is extremely cost competitive. What do you think of American Micro Devices's pricing method?

CASES

3-46   Government Health Cost Behavior

Dr. Maxine Black, the chief administrator of St. Regis Clinic, a community mental health agency, is concerned about the dilemma of coping with reduced budgets next year and into the foreseeable future, but increasing demand for services. In order to plan for reduced budgets, she first must identify where costs can be cut or reduced and still keep the agency functioning. Below are some data from the past year.

Program Area	Costs
Administration	
Salaries	
Administrator	$60,000
Assistant	30,000
Two secretaries	42,000
Supplies	35,000
Advertising and promotion	9,000
Professional meetings, dues, and literature	14,000
Purchased services	
Accounting and billing	15,000
Custodial and maintenance	13,000
Security	12,000
Consulting	10,000
Community mental health services	
Salaries (two social workers)	46,000
Transportation	10,000
Outpatient mental health treatment	
Salaries	
Psychiatrist	85,000
Two social workers	70,000

Required

1. Identify which costs you think are likely to be discretionary or committed costs.
2. One possibility is to eliminate all discretionary costs. How much would be saved? What do you think of this recommendation?
3. How would you advise Dr. Black to prepare for reduced budgets?

3-47   Activity Analysis

The costs of the Systems Support (SS) department (and other service departments) of Southeast Pulp and Paper, Inc. have always been charged to the three business divisions

(Forest Management, Lumber Products, and Paper Products) based on the number of employees in each division. This measure is easy to obtain and update, and until recently none of the divisions had complained about the charges. The Paper Products division has recently automated many of its operations and has reduced the number of its employees. At the same time, however, to monitor its new process, Paper Products has increased its requests for various reports provided by the SS department. The other divisions have begun to complain that they are being charged more than their fair share of SS department costs. Based on activity analysis of possible cost drivers, cost analysts have suggested using the number of reports prepared as a means of charging for SS costs and have gathered the following information:

	Forest Management	Lumber Products	Paper Products
19X7 Number of employees	762	457	502
19X7 Number of reports	410	445	377
19X7 SS Costs: $300,000			
19X8 Number of employees	751	413	131
19X8 Number of reports	412	432	712
19X8 SS Costs: $385,000			

Required

1. Discuss the plausibility and probable reliability of each of the cost drivers—number of employees or number of reports.

2. What are the 19X7 and 19X8 SS costs per unit of cost driver for each division using each cost driver? Do the Forest Management and Lumber Products divisions have legitimate complaints? Explain.

3. What are the incentives that are implied by each cost driver?

4. Which cost driver should Southeast Pulp and Paper use to charge its divisions for SS services? For other services? Why?

3-48 Identifying Relevant Data

SuperByte Company manufactures palm-sized, portable computers. Because these very small computers compete with larger portable computers that have more functions and flexibility, understanding and using cost behavior is very critical to SuperByte's profitability. SuperByte's controller, Kelly Hudson, has kept meticulous files on various cost categories and possible cost drivers for most of the important functions and activities of SuperByte. Because most of the manufacturing at SuperByte is automated, labor cost is relatively fixed. Other support costs comprise most of SuperByte's costs. Partial data that Hudson has collected over the past 25 weeks on one of these support costs, logistics operations (materials purchasing, receiving, warehousing, and shipping), follow:

Week	Logistics Costs Y	Number of Orders X
1	$23,907	1,357
2	18,265	1,077
3	24,208	1,383
4	23,578	1,486
5	22,211	1,292
6	22,862	1,425
	(continued)	

Week	Logistics Costs Y	Number of Orders X
7	23,303	1,306
8	24,507	1,373
9	17,878	1,031
10	18,306	1,020
11	20,807	1,097
12	19,707	1,069
13	23,020	1,444
14	20,407	733
15	20,370	413
16	20,678	633
17	21,145	711
18	20,775	228
19	20,532	488
20	20,659	655
21	20,430	722
22	20,713	373
23	20,256	391
24	21,196	734
25	20,406	256

Required

1. Plot logistics cost, Y, versus number of orders, X. What cost behavior is evident? What do you think happened in week 14?

2. What is your recommendation to Kelly Hudson regarding the relevance of the past 25 weeks of logistics cost and number of orders for measuring logistics cost behavior?

3. Hudson remarks that one of the improvements that SuperByte has made in the past several months was to negotiate just-in-time deliveries from its suppliers. This was made possible by substituting an automated ordering system for the previous manual (labor-intensive) system. Although fixed costs increased, the variable cost of placing an order was expected to drop greatly. Do the data support this expectation? Do you believe that the change to the automated ordering system was justified? Why or why not?

COLLABORATIVE LEARNING EXERCISE

3-49 Cost-Behavior Examples

Select about 10 students to participate in a "cost-behavior bee." The game proceeds like a spelling bee—when a participant is unable to come up with a correct answer, he or she is eliminated from the game. The last one in the game is the winner.

The object of the game is to identify a type of cost that fits a particular cost-behavior pattern. The first player rolls a die.[1] If a 1 or 6 comes up, the die passes to the next player (and the roller makes it to the next round). If a 2, 3, 4, or 5 come up, the player has to identify one of the following types of costs:

---

[1]*Instead of rolling a die, players could draw one of the four cost categories out of a hat (or similar container) or from a deck of four 3 × 5 cards. This eliminates the chance element that can let some players proceed to a later round without having to give an example of a particular cost behavior. However, the chance element can add to the enjoyment of the game.*

If a 2 is rolled, identify a variable cost.

If a 3 is rolled, identify a fixed cost.

If a 4 is rolled, identify a mixed cost.

If a 5 is rolled, identify a step cost.

A scribe should label four columns on the board, one for each type of cost, and list the costs that are mentioned for each category. Once a particular cost has been used, it cannot be used again.

Each player has a time limit of 10 seconds to produce an example. (For a tougher game, make the time limit five seconds.) The instructor is the referee, judging if a particular example is acceptable. It is legitimate for the referee to ask a player to explain why he or she thinks the cost mentioned fits the category before making a judgment.

After each player has had a turn, a second round begins with the remaining players taking a turn in the same order as in the first round. The game continues through additional rounds until all but one player has failed to give an acceptable answer within the time limit. The remaining player is the winner.

COST MANAGEMENT SYSTEMS AND ACTIVITY-BASED COSTING

AT&T Wireless Services customers can use their phones in more than 5,500 locations across the United States and Canada and in Europe, Asia and Australia. People are able to call you nearly anywhere by dialing your local wireless number.

Learning Objectives

When you have finished studying this chapter, you should be able to

1 Explain the relationship between cost, cost objective, cost accumulation, and cost allocation.

2 Distinguish between direct and indirect costs.

3 Explain how the financial statements of merchandisers and manufacturers differ because of the types of goods they sell.

4 Construct income statements of a manufacturing company in both the absorption and contribution formats.

5 Identify the steps involved in the design and implementation of an activity-based-costing system.

6 Explain how JIT systems can reduce non-value-added activities.

7 **Understand how cost accounting fits into the value chain.**

A recent survey asked 1,000 adults for their two choices of a "really good company." The company named the most was AT&T. Chances are, AT&T has reached out and touched you. With 80 million customers, it has annual revenues of more than $52 billion and net income exceeding $6 billion.

There is a communications revolution taking place on a global scale. Today, we communicate using wireless cell phones and computer on-line services in addition to the traditional telephone. How does AT&T, a company that has been synonymous with communications for over 100 years, ensure that it remains competitive? Certainly, AT&T has the people, technology, brand, market presence, and financial resources to get the job done—but it takes more. Like any other company, AT&T's managers, from top executives to local service managers, must understand their customers and their costs. This understanding is a common theme for all successful businesses.

Consider AT&T's Business Communication Services unit (BCS). With annual revenue of more than $16 billion, BCS is responsible for domestic and international voice and data communications services. To keep the unit's competitive edge, management began using a new cost accounting system in 1992. Accountants and managers designed the new costing system "to help operating managers gain a better understanding of the costs of each kind of service (product)." The old cost system gathered financial data used primarily by top management and accountants. The new cost system measures the key business processes in the BCS and the activities the unit performs to support its various services.

One example of the results obtained using the new cost system is in the billing center. The BCS team computed the cost of investigating incorrect bills, a cost that was previously unknown. The cost was so high that BCS managers started a cost reduction effort. The result was an annual cost savings of about $500,000. The new cost system was an effective management tool for all operating managers, not just accountants.

Managers rely on accountants to design a cost accounting system that measures the cost of the goods and services the company produces. Consider the following commentaries on the modern role of management accountants:

> We (cost accountants) had to understand what the numbers mean, relate the numbers to business activity, and recommend alternative courses of action. Finally, we had to evaluate alternatives and make decisions to maximize business efficiency.
>
> —*South Central Bell*

> Because the ABC (Activity-Based Costing) system now mirrors the manufacturing process, the engineers and production staff believe the cost data produced by the accounting system. Engineering and production regularly ask accounting to help find the product design combination that will optimize costs. . . . The accountants now participate in product design decisions. They help engineering and production understand how costs behave. . . . The ABC system makes the professional lives of the accountants more rewarding.
>
> —*Hewlett-Packard Company*

The cost accounting system typically includes two processes:

cost accumulation
Collecting costs by some natural classification such as materials or labor.

1. **Cost accumulation:** Collecting costs by some "natural" classification such as materials or labor.
2. **Cost allocation:** Tracing and reassigning costs to one or more cost objectives such as activities, departments, customers, or products.

cost allocation Tracing and reassigning costs to one or more cost objectives such as activities, departments, customers, or products.

Exhibit 4-1 illustrates these processes. First, the costs of all raw materials are accumulated. Then they are allocated to the departments that use them and further to the specific items made by these departments. The total raw materials cost of a particular product is the sum of the raw materials costs allocated to it in the various departments.

To make intelligent decisions, managers want reliable measurements. Cost accounting systems that do not provide reliable information do not help managers make decisions. In fact, without reliable cost information, many decisions can be downright harmful. For example, an extremely large U.S. grocery chain, A&P, ran into profit difficulties and began retrenching by closing many stores. Management's lack of adequate cost information about individual store operations made the closing program a hit-or-miss affair. A news story reported the following:

> Because of the absence of detailed profit-and-loss statements, and a cost-allocation system that did not reflect true costs, A&P's strategists could not be sure whether an individual store was really unprofitable. For example, distribution costs were shared equally among all the stores in a marketing

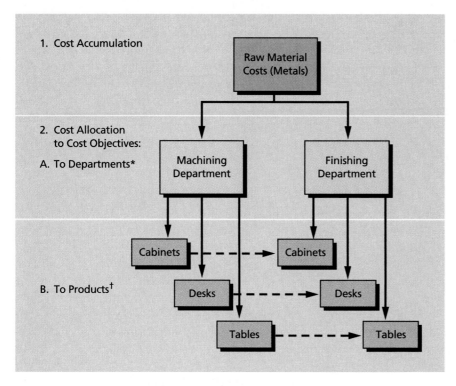

1. Cost Accumulation

2. Cost Allocation to Cost Objectives:

A. To Departments*

B. To Products†

*Purpose: to evaluate performance of manufacturing departments.
†Purpose: to obtain costs of various products for valuing inventory, determining income, and judging product profitability.

Exhibit 4-1

Cost Accumulation and Allocation

> *area without regard to such factors as a store's distance from the warehouse. Says one close observer of the company: "When they wanted to close a store, they had to wing it. They could not make rational decisions, because they did not have a fact basis."*

All kinds of organizations—manufacturing firms, service companies, and nonprofit organizations—need some form of **cost accounting,** that part of the accounting system that measures costs for the purposes of management decision making and financial reporting. Because it is the most general case, embracing production, marketing, and general administration functions, we will focus on cost accounting in a manufacturing setting. Remember, though, that you can apply this framework to any organization.

> **cost accounting** That part of the accounting system that measures costs for the purposes of management decision making and financial reporting.

CLASSIFICATIONS OF COSTS

Costs may be classified in many ways—far too many to be covered in a single chapter. We have already seen costs classified by their behavior—fixed, variable, step, and mixed. This section concentrates on the big picture of how manufacturing costs are accumulated and classified.

COST OBJECTIVES

A **cost** may be defined as a sacrifice or giving up of resources for a particular purpose. Costs are frequently measured by the monetary units (for example, dollars or francs) that must be paid for goods and services. Costs are initially recorded in elementary form (for

> **cost** A sacrifice or giving up of resources for a particular purpose, frequently measured by the monetary units that must be paid for goods and services.

example, repairs or advertising). Then these costs are grouped in different ways to help managers make decisions, such as evaluating subordinates and subunits of the organization, expanding or deleting products or territories, and replacing equipment.

To aid decisions, managers want to know the cost of something. This "something" is called a **cost objective** or **cost object,** defined as *anything for which a separate measurement of costs is desired.* Examples of cost objectives include departments, products, territories, miles driven, bricks laid, patients seen, tax bills sent, checks processed, student hours taught, and library books shelved.

cost objective (cost object)
Anything for which a separate measurement of costs is desired. Examples include departments, products, activities, and territories.

DIRECT AND INDIRECT COSTS

A major feature of costs in both manufacturing and nonmanufacturing activities is whether the costs have a direct or an indirect relationship to a particular cost objective. **Direct costs** can be identified specifically and exclusively with a given cost objective in an economically feasible way. In contrast, **indirect costs** cannot be identified specifically and exclusively with a given cost objective in an economically feasible way.

direct costs Costs that can be identified specifically and exclusively with a given cost objective in an economically feasible way.

Whenever it is "economically feasible," managers prefer to classify costs as direct rather than indirect. In this way, managers have greater confidence in the reported costs of products and services. "Economically feasible" means "cost effective," in the sense that managers do not want cost accounting to be too expensive in relation to expected benefits. For example, it may be economically feasible to trace the exact cost of steel and fabric (direct cost) to a specific lot of desk chairs, but it may be economically infeasible to trace the exact cost of rivets or thread (indirect costs) to the chairs.

indirect costs Costs that cannot be identified specifically and exclusively with a given cost objective in an economically feasible way.

Other factors also influence whether a cost is considered direct or indirect. The key is the particular cost objective. For example, consider a supervisor's salary in the maintenance department of a telephone company. If the cost objective is the department, the supervisor's salary is a direct cost. In contrast, if the cost objective is a service (the "product" of the company) such as a telephone call, the supervisor's salary is an indirect cost. In general, many more costs are direct when a department is the cost objective than when a service (a telephone call) or a physical product (a razor blade) is the cost objective.

Frequently managers want to know both the costs of running departments and the costs of products, services, activities, or resources. Costs are inevitably allocated to more than one cost objective. Thus a particular cost may simultaneously be direct and indirect. As you have just seen, a supervisor's salary can be both direct (with respect to his or her department) and indirect (with respect to the department's individual products or services).

CATEGORIES OF MANUFACTURING COSTS

Any raw material, labor, or other input used by any organization could, in theory, be identified as a direct or indirect cost, depending on the cost objective. In manufacturing operations, which transform materials into other goods through the use of labor and factory facilities, products are frequently the cost objective. Manufacturing operations, though, have their own way of classifying costs. All costs that are eventually allocated to products are classified as either (1) direct materials, (2) direct labor, and (3) indirect manufacturing.

direct-material costs The acquisition costs of all materials that are physically identified as a part of the manufactured goods and that may be traced to the manufactured goods in an economically feasible way.

1. **Direct-material costs** include the acquisition costs of all materials that are physically identified as a part of the manufactured goods and that may be traced to the manufactured goods in an economically feasible way. Examples are iron castings, lumber, aluminum sheets, and subassemblies. Direct materials often do not include minor items such as tacks or glue because the costs of tracing these items are greater than the possible benefits of having more precise product costs. Such items are usually called supplies or indirect materials, which are classified as a part of the factory overhead described in this list.

2. **Direct-labor costs** include the wages of all labor that can be traced specifically and exclusively to the manufactured goods in an economically feasible way. Examples are the wages of machine operators and assemblers. Much labor, such as that of janitors, forklift truck operators, plant guards, and storeroom clerks, is considered to be indirect labor because it is impossible or economically infeasible to trace such activity to specific products. Such indirect labor is classified as a part of factory overhead. In highly automated factories, there may be no direct labor costs. Why? Because it may be economically infeasible to physically trace any labor cost directly to specific products.

   direct-labor costs The wages of all labor that can be traced specifically and exclusively to the manufactured goods in an economically feasible way.

3. **Indirect manufacturing costs (or factory overhead)** include all costs associated with the manufacturing process that cannot be traced to the manufactured goods in an economically feasible way. Other terms used to describe this category are **factory burden** and **manufacturing overhead.** Because each of these terms are used often in practice, we will use them interchangeably throughout this textbook. Examples are power, supplies, indirect labor, supervisory salaries, property taxes, rent, insurance, and depreciation.

   indirect manufacturing costs (factory burden, factory overhead, manufacturing overhead) All costs other than direct material or direct labor that are associated with the manufacturing process.

In traditional accounting systems, all manufacturing overhead costs are considered to be indirect. However, computers have allowed modern systems to physically trace many overhead costs to products in an economically feasible manner. For example, meters wired to computers can monitor the electricity used to produce each product, and costs of setting up a batch production run can be traced to the items produced in the run. In general, the more overhead costs that can be traced directly to products, the more accurate the product cost.

PRIME COSTS, CONVERSION COSTS, AND DIRECT-LABOR COSTS

Exhibit 4-2 shows that direct labor is sometimes combined with one of the other types of manufacturing costs. The combined categories are **prime costs**—direct labor plus direct materials—or **conversion costs**—direct labor plus indirect manufacturing.

prime costs Direct labor costs plus direct materials costs.

The twofold categorization, direct materials and conversion costs, has replaced the threefold categorization, direct materials, direct labor, and indirect manufacturing, in many modern, automated manufacturing companies. Why? Because direct labor in such a company is a small part of costs and not worth tracing directly to the products. In fact, some companies call their two categories direct materials and indirect manufacturing, and simply include direct labor costs in the indirect manufacturing category.

conversion costs Direct labor costs plus factory overhead costs.

In addition to direct-material, direct-labor, and indirect manufacturing costs, all manufacturing companies also incur costs associated with the other value-chain functions

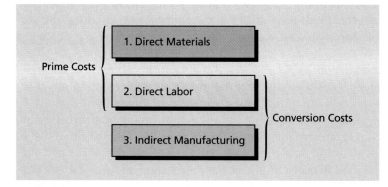

Exhibit 4-2

Relationships of Key Categories of Manufacturing Costs for Product-Costing Purposes

(research and development, design, marketing, distribution, and customer service). These costs are accumulated by departments such as R&D, advertising, and sales. These costs are often called selling and administrative costs. As you will see later in this chapter, most firms' financial statements do not allocate these costs to the physical units produced. In short, these costs do not become a part of the reported inventory cost of the manufactured products. To aid in decisions, however, managers often want to know all the costs associated with each product. Therefore, management reports often include such costs as product costs.

COST ACCOUNTING FOR FINANCIAL REPORTING

Regardless of the type of cost accounting system used, the resulting costs are used in a company's financial statements. This section discusses how financial reporting requirements influence the design of cost accounting systems.

Costs are reported on both the income statement, as cost of goods sold, and the balance sheet, as inventory amounts. If you are not familiar with income statements and balance sheets, or with terms such as cost of goods sold and inventory costs, you will find an overview of them in Chapter 16.

PRODUCT COSTS AND PERIOD COSTS

product costs Costs identified with goods produced or purchased for resale.

period costs Costs that are deducted as expenses during the current period without going through an inventory stage.

When preparing both income statements and balance sheets, accountants frequently distinguish between *product costs* and *period costs*. **Product costs** are costs identified with goods produced or purchased for resale. Product costs are initially identified as part of the inventory on hand. These product costs (inventoriable costs) become expenses (in the form of cost of goods sold) only when the inventory is sold. In contrast, **period costs** are costs that are deducted as expenses during the current period without going through an inventory stage.

For example, look at the top half of Exhibit 4-3. A merchandising company (retailer or wholesaler) acquires goods for resale without changing their basic form. The only product cost is the purchase cost of the merchandise. Unsold goods are held as merchandise inventory cost and are shown as an asset on a balance sheet. As the goods are sold, their costs become expenses in the form of "cost of goods sold."

A merchandising company also has a variety of selling and administrative expenses. These costs are period costs because they are deducted from revenue as expenses without ever being regarded as a part of inventory.

The bottom half of Exhibit 4-3 illustrates product and period costs in a manufacturing firm. Note that direct materials are transformed into salable form with the help of direct labor and indirect manufacturing. All these costs are product costs because they are allocated to inventory until the goods are sold. As in merchandising accounting, the selling and administrative expenses are not regarded as product costs but are treated as period costs.

Be sure you are clear on the differences between merchandising accounting and manufacturing accounting for such costs as insurance, depreciation, and wages. In merchandising accounting, all such items are period costs (expenses of the current period). In manufacturing accounting, many of these items are related to production activities and thus, as indirect manufacturing, are product costs (become expenses in the form of cost of goods sold as the inventory is sold).

In both merchandising and manufacturing accounting, selling and general administrative costs are period costs. Thus the inventory cost of a manufactured product excludes sales salaries, sales commissions, advertising, legal, public relations, and the president's salary. Manufacturing overhead is traditionally regarded as a part of finished-goods inventory cost, whereas selling expenses and general administrative expenses are not.

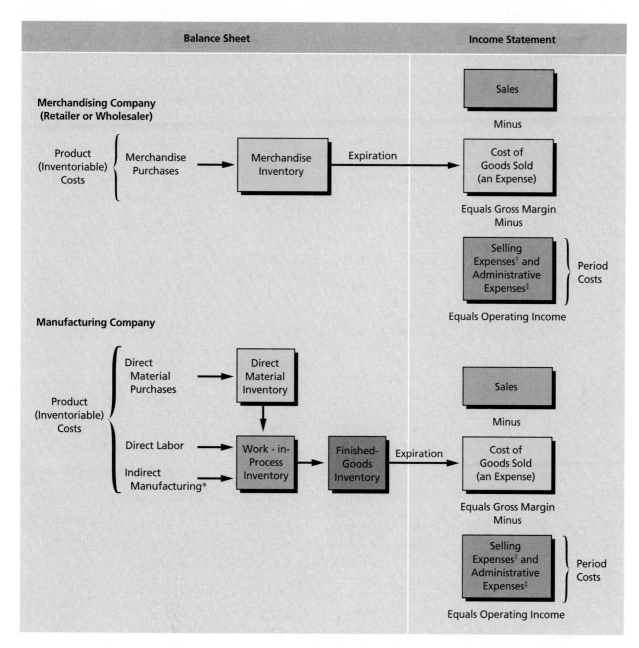

*Examples: indirect labor, factory supplies, insurance, and depreciation on plant.
†Examples: insurance on salespersons' cars, depreciation on salespersons' cars, salespersons' salaries.
‡Examples: insurance on corporate headquarters building, depreciation on office equipment, clerical salaries.

Note particularly that when insurance and depreciation relate to the manufacturing function, they are inventoriable, but when they relate to selling and administration, they are not inventoriable.

Exhibit 4-3
Relationships of Product Costs and Period Costs

BALANCE SHEET PRESENTATION

Examining both halves of Exhibit 4-3 together, you can see that the balance sheets of manufacturers and merchandisers differ with respect to inventories. The merchandiser's "inventory account" is supplanted in a manufacturing concern by three inventory classes that help managers trace all product costs through the production process to the time of sales.

Objective 3
Explain how the financial statements of merchandisers and manufacturers differ because of the types of goods they sell.

These classes are:

- *Direct-materials inventory:* Materials on hand and awaiting use in the production process.
- *Work-in-process inventory:* Goods undergoing the production process but not yet fully completed. Costs include appropriate amounts of the three major manufacturing costs (direct material, direct labor, and indirect manufacturing).
- *Finished-goods inventory:* Goods fully completed but not yet sold.

The only essential difference between the structure of the balance sheet of a manufacturer and that of a retailer or wholesaler would appear in their respective current asset sections:

Current Asset Sections of Balance Sheets

Manufacturer			Retailer or Wholesaler	
Cash		$ 4,000	Cash	$ 4,000
Receivables		25,000	Receivables	25,000
Finished goods	$32,000			
Work in process	22,000			
Direct material	23,000			
Total inventories		77,000	Merchandise inventories	77,000
Other current assets		1,000	Other current assets	1,000
Total current assets		$107,000	Total current assets	$107,000

UNIT COSTS FOR PRODUCT COSTING

Reporting cost of goods sold or inventory values requires costs to be assigned to units of product. Assume the following:

Total cost of goods manufactured	$40,000,000
Total units manufactured	10,000,000
Unit cost of product for inventory purposes ($40,000,000 ÷ 10,000,000)	$ 4

If some of the 10 million units manufactured are still unsold at the end of the period, $4 worth of costs for each unit not sold will be "held back" as a cost of the ending inventory of finished goods (and shown as an asset on a balance sheet). The remainder becomes "cost of goods sold" for the current period and is shown as an expense on the income statement.

COSTS AND INCOME STATEMENTS

In income statements, the detailed reporting of selling and administrative expenses is typically the same for manufacturing and merchandising organizations, but the cost of goods sold is different:

Manufacturer

Manufacturing cost of goods produced and then sold, usually composed of the three major categories of cost: direct materials, direct labor, and indirect manufacturing.

Retailer or Wholesaler

Merchandise cost of goods sold, usually composed of the purchase cost of items, including freight in, that are acquired and then resold.

Exhibit 4-4

Model Income Statement, Manufacturing Company

Sales (8,000,000 units @ $10)			$80,000,000
Cost of goods manufactured and sold			
Beginning finished-goods inventory		$ —0—	
Cost of goods manufactured			
Direct materials used	$20,000,000		
Direct labor	12,000,000		
Indirect manufacturing	8,000,000	40,000,000	
Cost of goods available for sale		$40,000,000	
Ending finished-goods inventory,			
2,000,000 units @ $4		8,000,000	
Cost of goods sold (an expense)			32,000,000
Gross margin or gross profit			$48,000,000
Less: other expenses			
Selling costs (an expense)		$30,000,000	
General and administrative costs			
(an expense)		8,000,000	38,000,000
Operating income*			$10,000,000

*Also net income in this example because other expenses such as interest and income taxes are ignored here for simplicity.

Consider the additional details as they are presented in the model income statement of a manufacturing company in Exhibit 4-4. The $40 million cost of goods manufactured is subdivided into the major components of direct materials, direct labor, and indirect manufacturing. In contrast, a wholesale or retail company would replace the entire "cost-of-goods-manufactured" section with a single line, "cost of goods purchased."

The terms "costs" and "expenses" are often used loosely by accountants and managers. Expenses denote all costs deducted from (matched against) revenue in a given period. On the other hand, costs is a much broader term and is used to describe both an asset (the cost of inventory) and an expense (the cost of goods sold). Thus manufacturing costs are funneled into an income statement as an expense (in the form of cost of goods sold) via the multistep inventory procedure shown earlier in Exhibit 4-3. In contrast, selling and general administrative costs are commonly deemed expenses immediately as they are incurred.

TRANSACTIONS AFFECTING INVENTORIES

The three manufacturing inventory accounts are affected by the following transactions:

- Direct-Materials Inventory
  Increased by purchases of direct materials
  Decreased by use of direct materials

- Work-in-Process Inventory
  Increased by use of direct materials, direct labor, or indirect manufacturing
  Decreased by transfer of completed goods to finished-goods inventory

- Finished-Goods Inventory
  Increased by transfers of completed goods from work-in-process inventory
  Decreased by the amount of cost of goods sold at time of sale

Direct labor and indirect manufacturing are used at the same time they are acquired. Therefore, they are entered directly into work-in-process inventory and have no separate inventory account. In contrast, direct materials are often purchased in advance of their use and held in inventory for some time.

Exhibit 4-5

Inventory Transactions (in millions)

Transaction	Direct-Materials Inventory	Work-in-Process Inventory	Finished-Goods Inventory
Beginning balance	$ 0	$ 0	$ 0
Purchase direct materials	+30	—	—
Use direct materials	−20	+20	—
Acquire and use direct labor	—	+12	—
Acquire and use factory overhead	—	+8	—
Complete production	—	−40	+40
Sell goods and record cost of goods sold	—	—	$−32
Ending balance	$ 10	$ 0	$ 8

Exhibit 4-5 traces the effects of each transaction. It uses the dollar amounts from Exhibit 4-4, with one exception. Purchases of direct materials totaled $30 million, with $20 million used in production (as shown in Exhibit 4-4) and $10 million left in inventory at the end of the period. As the bottom of Exhibit 4-5 indicates, the ending balance sheet amounts would be:

Direct-materials inventory	$10,000,000
Work-in-process inventory	0
Finished-goods inventory	8,000,000
Total inventories	$18,000,000

COST BEHAVIOR AND INCOME STATEMENTS

Manufacturers can differ not only from merchandisers in the form of the income statement, they can differ from one another as well. The difference does not appear in external financial statements, but in internal income statements. Some manufacturers like to track fixed and variable costs using the contribution approach, whereas others prefer the absorption approach used in external income statements. To highlight the different effects of these approaches, we will assume that in 19X8 the Samson Company has direct-material costs of $7 million and direct-labor costs of $4 million. Assume also that the company incurred the indirect manufacturing costs illustrated in Exhibit 4-6 and the selling and administrative expenses illustrated in Exhibit 4-7. Total sales were $20 million. Finally, assume that the units produced are equal to the units sold. That is, there is no change in inventory levels. (In this way, we avoid some complications that are unnecessary and unimportant at this stage.[1])

Note that Exhibits 4-6 and 4-7 subdivide costs as variable or fixed. Many companies do not make such subdivisions in their income statements. Furthermore, when such subdivisions are made, sometimes arbitrary decisions are necessary as to whether a given cost is variable, fixed, or partially fixed (for example, repairs). Nevertheless, to aid decision making, many companies are attempting to report the extent to which their costs are approximately variable or fixed.

[1] *These complexities are discussed in Chapters 14 and 15.*

Exhibit 4-6

Samson Company Schedules of Indirect Manufacturing Costs (Product Costs) for the Year Ended December 31, 19X8 (thousands of dollars)

Objective 4
Construct income statements of a manufacturing company in both the absorption and contribution formats.

Schedule 1: Variable Costs

Supplies (lubricants, expendable tools, coolants, sandpaper)	$ 150	
Material-handling labor (forklift operators)	700	
Repairs	100	
Power	50	$1,000

Schedule 2: Fixed Costs

Managers' salaries	$ 200	
Employee training	90	
Factory picnic and holiday party	10	
Supervisory salaries	700	
Depreciation, plant and equipment	1,800	
Property taxes	150	
Insurance	50	3,000
Total indirect manufacturing costs		$4,000

Exhibit 4-7

Samson Company Schedules of Selling and Administrative Expenses (Period Costs) for the Year Ended December 31, 19X8 (thousands of dollars)

Schedule 3: Selling Expenses

Variable		
Sales commissions	$ 700	
Shipping expenses for products sold	300	$1,000
Fixed		
Advertising	$ 700	
Sales salaries	1,000	
Other	300	2,000
Total selling expenses		$3,000

Schedule 4: Administrative Expenses

Variable		
Some clerical wages	$ 80	
Computer time rented	20	$ 100
Fixed		
Office salaries	$ 100	
Other salaries	200	
Depreciation on office facilities	100	
Public-accounting fees	40	
Legal fees	100	
Other	360	900
Total administrative expenses		$1,000

ABSORPTION APPROACH

Exhibit 4-8 presents Samson's income statement using the **absorption approach** (*absorption costing*), the approach used by most companies. Firms that take this approach consider all indirect manufacturing (both variable and fixed) to be product (inventoriable) costs that become an expense in the form of manufacturing cost of goods sold only as sales occur.

absorption approach
A costing approach that considers all factory overhead (both variable and fixed) to be product (inventoriable) costs that become an expense in the form of manufacturing cost of goods sold only as sales occur.

Exhibit 4-8

Samson Company Absorption Income Statement for the Year Ended December 31, 19X8 (thousands of dollars)

Sales		$20,000
Less: Manufacturing costs of goods sold		
Direct material	$7,000	
Direct labor	4,000	
Indirect manufacturing (Schedules 1 plus 2)*	4,000	15,000
Gross margin or gross profit		$ 5,000
Selling expenses (Schedule 3)	$3,000	
Administrative expenses (Schedule 4)	1,000	
Total selling and administrative expenses		4,000
Operating income		$ 1,000

*Note: Schedules 1 and 2 are in Exhibit 4-6. Schedules 3 and 4 are in Exhibit 4-7.

Note in Exhibit 4-8 that gross profit or gross margin is the difference between sales and the manufacturing cost of goods sold. Note too that the primary classifications of costs on the income statement are by three major management functions: manufacturing, selling, and administrative.

CONTRIBUTION APPROACH

contribution approach
A method of internal (management accounting) reporting that emphasizes the distinction between variable and fixed costs for the purpose of better decision making.

In contrast, Exhibit 4-9 presents Samson's income statement using the **contribution approach** (*variable costing* or *direct costing*). The contribution approach is not allowed for external financial reporting. However, many companies use this approach for internal (management accounting) purposes and an absorption format for external purposes, because they expect the benefits of making better decisions to exceed the extra costs of using different reporting systems simultaneously.

For decision purposes, the major difference between the contribution approach and the absorption approach is that the former emphasizes the distinction between variable and fixed costs. Its primary classifications of costs are by variable- and fixed-cost behavior patterns, not by business functions.

The contribution income statement provides a contribution margin, which is computed after deducting from revenue all variable costs including variable selling and administrative costs. This approach makes it easier to understand the impact of changes in sales demand on operating income. It also dovetails neatly with the CVP analysis illustrated in Chapter 2.

A major benefit of the contribution approach is that it stresses the role of fixed costs in net income. Before a company can earn income, it first must recoup the fixed costs it has incurred for manufacturing and other value-chain functions. This highlighting of total fixed costs focuses management attention on fixed-cost behavior and control in making both short-run and long-run plans. Remember that advocates of the contribution approach do not maintain that fixed costs are unimportant or irrelevant. They do stress, however, that the distinctions between behaviors of variable and fixed costs are crucial for certain decisions.

The difference between the gross margin (from the absorption approach) and the contribution margin (from the contribution approach) is striking in manufacturing companies. Why? Because fixed manufacturing costs are regarded as a part of cost of goods sold, and these fixed costs reduce the gross margin accordingly. However, fixed manufacturing costs do not reduce the contribution margin, which is affected solely by revenues and variable costs.

The implications of the absorption approach and the contribution approach for decision making in the marketing function of the value chain are discussed in the next chapter.

Exhibit 4-9

Samson Company Contribution Income Statement for the Year Ended December 31, 19X8 (thousands of dollars)

Sales		$20,000
Less: Variable expenses		
Direct material	$ 7,000	
Direct labor	4,000	
Variable indirect manufacturing costs (Schedule 1)*	1,000	
Total variable manufacturing cost of goods sold	$12,000	
Variable selling expenses (Schedule 3)	1,000	
Variable administrative expenses (Schedule 4)	100	
Total variable expenses		13,100
Contribution margin		$ 6,900
Less: fixed expenses		
Manufacturing (Schedule 2)	$ 3,000	
Selling (Schedule 3)	2,000	
Administrative (Schedule 4)	900	5,900
Operating income		$ 1,000

*Note: Schedules 1 and 2 are in Exhibit 4-6. Schedules 3 and 4 are in Exhibit 4-7.

SUMMARY PROBLEM FOR YOUR REVIEW

PROBLEM

1. Review the illustrations in Exhibits 4-6 through 4-9. Suppose that all variable costs fluctuate in direct proportion to units produced and sold, and that all fixed costs are unaffected over a wide range of production and sales. What would operating income have been if sales (at normal selling prices) had been $20.9 million instead of $20.0 million? Which statement, the absorption income statement or the contribution income statement, did you use as a framework for your answer? Why?

2. Suppose employee training (Exhibit 4-6) was regarded as a variable rather than a fixed cost at a rate of $90,000 ÷ 1,000,000 units, or $.09 per unit. How would your answer in part 1 change?

SOLUTION

1. Operating income would increase from $1,000,000 to $1,310,500, computed as follows:

Increase in revenue	$ 900,000
Increase in total contribution margin:	
Contribution-margin ratio in contribution income statement	
(Exhibit 4-9) is $6,900,000 ÷ $20,000,000 = .345	
Ratio times revenue increase is .345 × $900,000	$ 310,500
Increase in fixed expenses	0
Operating income before increase	1,000,000
New operating income	$1,310,500

Computations are easily made by using data from the contribution income statement. In contrast, the traditional absorption costing income statement must be analyzed and divided into variable and fixed categories before the effect on operating income can be estimated.

2. The original contribution-margin ratio would be lower because the variable costs would be higher by $.09 per unit: ($6,900,000 − $90,000) ÷ $20,000,000 = .3405.

	Given Level	Higher Level	Difference
Revenue	$20,000,000	$20,900,000	$900,000
Variable expense ($13,100,000 + $90,000)	13,190,000	13,783,550	593,550
Contribution margin at .3405	$ 6,810,000	$ 7,116,450	$306,450
Fixed expenses ($5,900,000 − $90,000)	5,810,000	5,810,000	—
Operating income	$ 1,000,000	$ 1,306,450	$306,450

ACTIVITY-BASED COSTING

In the past decade, many companies in the United States, struggling to keep up with competitors from Japan, Germany, and other countries, adopted new management philosophies and developed new production technologies. In many cases, these changes prompted corresponding changes in accounting systems.

For example, Borg-Warner's Automotive Chain Systems Operation transformed its manufacturing operation to a just-in-time manufacturing system with work cells. This change in the way manufacturing was done made the traditional accounting system obsolete. A new cost accounting system coupled with the new production systems "improved the overall reporting, controls, and efficiency dramatically."[2]

For the past two chapters, we have focused on traditional costing systems that work well with fairly simple production and operating systems. However, just as Borg-Warner did, many businesses have changed their operating systems in response to a more complex business environment and this has led to a need for new and improved costing systems. The most significant improvement in cost accounting system design has been activity-based costing (ABC). Let's take a look at how ABC differs from traditional costing.

ACTIVITY-BASED COSTING AND TRADITIONAL COSTING COMPARED

activity-based costing (ABC) A system that first accumulates overhead costs for each of the activities of an organization, and then assigns the costs of activities to the products, services, or other cost objects that caused that activity.

The primary focus of the changes in operations and accounting has been an increased attention to the cost of the activities undertaken to design, produce, sell, and deliver a company's products or services. **Activity-based-costing (ABC)** systems first accumulate overhead costs for each of the activities of an organization, and then assign the costs of activities to the products, services, or other cost objects that caused that activity.

Consider the Salem manufacturing plant of a producer of appliances for the home. Exhibit 4-10 contrasts the traditional costing system with an ABC system. In the traditional cost system, the portion of total overhead allocated to a product depends on the proportion of *total direct-labor-hours* consumed in making the product. In the ABC system, significant overhead activities (machine processing, assembly, quality inspections, and so on) are identified by operating managers. Then the costs of overhead resources used to perform these activities are traced to the activities using the most appropriate cost drivers (output measures). Finally, the pooled costs of each activity are allocated to products using cost drivers (sometimes called activity drivers). In effect, the ABC systems had taken one large cost (manufacturing overhead) and broken it down into several smaller costs, each associated with a key activity.

---

[2]*A. Phillips and Don Collins, "How Borg-Warner Made the Transition From Pile Accounting to JIT,"* Management Accounting, *October 1990, pp. 32–35.*

Since the 1950s a growing number of firms have used the contribution approach for internal income statements. However, with the emergence of activity-based costing (ABC) in the late 1980s, some ABC proponents suggested that absorption costing information from an ABC system was more appropriate than contribution-based information for decision making. Now in the 1990s, according to Robert Koehler, "the combination of activity-based costing . . . and the contribution-margin approach will give a true overview of the whole cost picture."

One company that has combined ABC with the contribution approach is the Elgin Sweeper Company, the leading manufacturer of motorized street sweepers in North America, with annual sales of $50 million. In the late 1980s Elgin set out to install a cost-management system so that the effects of management decisions on costs could be pinpointed. The first step was to perform a cost-behavior study to identify the costs of Elgin's various activities. The company compiled a list of cost drivers for its various activities. The cost drivers included actual labor dollars, actual labor hours, units shipped, units produced, purchase orders, service parts, sales dollars, service orders shipped, workdays, calendar days, completed engineering change notices, engineering

hours worked, and many others. Then costs that varied with each cost driver were identified and measured.

After measuring cost behavior, product-line contribution statements were prepared. These were designed to help managers see the results of their resource-allocation decisions and to assess the outcomes of strategic decisions. Each statement had three sections for each product line: (1) contribution margin, (2) direct margin, and (3) pretax income.

To measure contribution margin, costs driven by volume-related cost drivers were deducted from revenues to show the effects of volume on profits. The direct margin included a deduction of costs directly related to the product line but not necessarily related to volume. This provided a measure of the economic results of the full product line. Finally, pretax income included a deduction of all remaining fixed costs.

Elgin is still in the process of improving its cost-management system. Refinements of its product line contribution statements are planned, as are increased involvement of production supervisors with the cost-driver concept and the elimination of non-value-added activities. Elgin expects the result of its cost-management system to be "people making intelligent, informed, and cost-effective decisions."

Source: Adapted from R. W. Koehler, "Triple-Threat Strategy," *Management Accounting,* October 1991, pp. 30–34; and J. Callan, W. Tredup, and R. Wissinger, "Elgin Sweeper Company's Journey Toward Cost Management," *Management Accounting,* July 1991, pp. 24–27.

ILLUSTRATION OF ACTIVITY-BASED COSTING[3]

Consider the Billing Department at Portland Power Company (PPC), an electric utility. The Billing Department (BD) at PPC provides account inquiry and bill-printing services for two major classes of customers—residential and commercial. Currently, the BD services 120,000 residential and 20,000 commercial customer accounts.

Two factors are having a significant impact on PPC's profitability. First, deregulation of the power industry has led to increased competition and lower rates, so PPC must find ways of reducing its operating costs. Second, the demand for power in PPC's area will increase due to the addition of a large housing development and a shopping center. The marketing department estimates that residential demand will increase by almost 50% and commercial demand will increase by 10% during the next year. Since the BD is currently operating at full capacity, it needs to find ways to create capacity to service the expected increase in demand. A local service bureau has offered to take over the BD functions at an attractive lower cost (compared to the current cost) and proposes to provide all the functions of the BD at $3.50 per residential account and $8.50 per commercial account. To make an informed decision, the BD needs to know the cost per residential account and cost per commercial account from providing the service itself.

---

[3]*Much of the discussion in this section is based on an illustration used in "Implementing Activity-Based Costing—The Model Approach," a workshop sponsored by the Institute of Management Accountants and Sapling Corporation.*

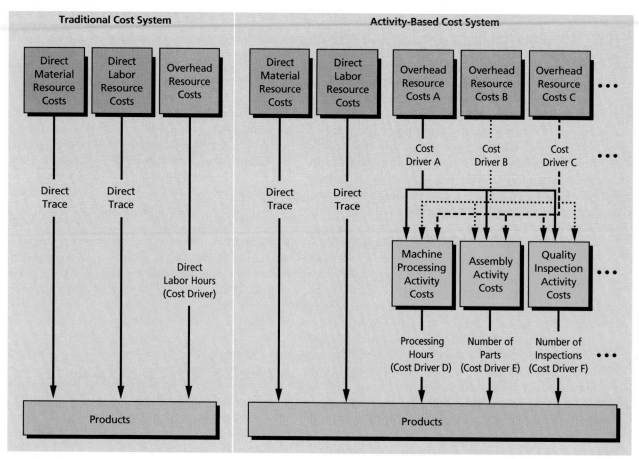

Exhibit 4-10

Traditional and Activity-Based Cost Systems

Exhibit 4-11 depicts the residential and commercial customer classes (cost objects) and the resources used to support the BD. The costs associated with the BD are all indirect—they cannot be identified specifically and exclusively with either customer class in an economically feasible way. The BD used a traditional costing system that allocated all support costs based on the number of account inquiries of the two customer classes. Exhibit 4-11 shows that the cost of the resources used in the BD last month was $565,340. BD received 23,000 account inquiries during the month, so the cost per inquiry was $565,340 ÷ 23,000 = $24.58. There were 18,000 residential account inquiries, 78.26% of the total. Thus residential accounts were charged with 78.26% of the support costs while commercial accounts were charged with 21.74%. The resulting cost per account is $3.69 and $6.15 for residential and commercial accounts, respectively.

Based on the costs provided by the traditional cost system, the BD management would be motivated to accept the service bureau's proposal to service all residential accounts because of the apparent savings of $.19 ($3.69 − $3.50) per account. The BD would continue to service its commercial accounts because its costs are $2.35 ($8.50 − $6.15) less than the service bureau's bid. However, management believed that the actual consumption of support resources was much greater than 22% for commercial accounts because of their complexity. For example, commercial accounts average 50 lines per bill compared with only 12 for residential accounts. Management was also concerned about activities such as correspondence (and supporting labor) resulting from customer inquiries because these activities are costly but do not add value to PPC's ser-

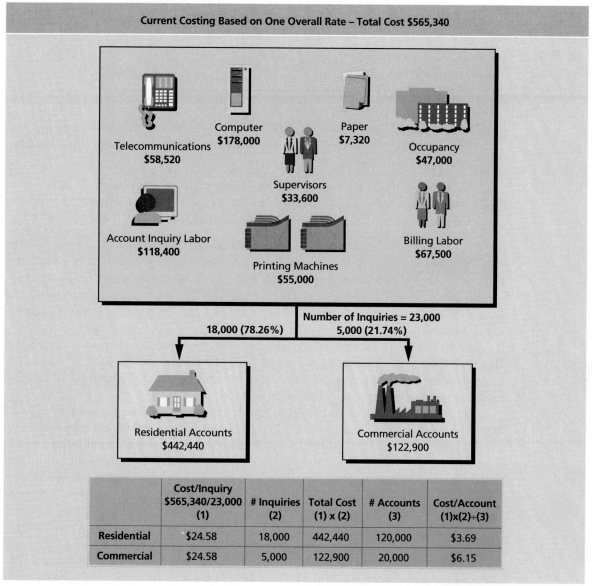

Current Costing Based on One Overall Rate – Total Cost $565,340

Telecommunications $58,520

Computer $178,000

Paper $7,320

Occupancy $47,000

Supervisors $33,600

Account Inquiry Labor $118,400

Printing Machines $55,000

Billing Labor $67,500

Number of Inquiries = 23,000

18,000 (78.26%)

5,000 (21.74%)

Residential Accounts $442,440

Commercial Accounts $122,900

	Cost/Inquiry $565,340/23,000 (1)	# Inquiries (2)	Total Cost (1) x (2)	# Accounts (3)	Cost/Account (1)x(2)÷(3)
Residential	$24.58	18,000	442,440	120,000	$3.69
Commercial	$24.58	5,000	122,900	20,000	$6.15

Exhibit 4-11

Current (Traditional) Costing System: Portland Power Company—Billing Department

vices from the customer's perspective. However, management wanted a more thorough understanding of key BD activities and their interrelationships before making important decisions that would impact PPC's profitability. The company decided to perform a study of the BD using activity-based costing. The following is a description of the study and its results.

The activity-based-costing study was performed by a team of managers from the BD and the chief financial officer from PPC. The team followed a four-step procedure to conduct the study.

Step 1: *Determine cost objectives, key activities, resources, and related cost drivers.* Management had set the objective for the study—determine the BD cost per account for each customer class. The team identified the following activities, and related cost drivers for the BD through interviews with appropriate personnel.

Objective 5
Identify the steps involved in the design and implementation of an activity-based-costing system.

Activity	Cost Driver
Account billing	Number of lines
Bill verification	Number of accounts
Account inquiry	Number of labor hours
Correspondence	Number of letters

The four key BD activities are *account billing, bill verification, account inquiry,* and *correspondence.* The resources shown in Exhibit 4-11 support these major activities. Cost drivers were selected based on two criteria:

1. There had to be a reasonable cause-effect relationship between the driver unit and the consumption of resources and/or the occurrence of supporting activities.
2. Data on the cost-driver units had to be available.

Step 2: *Develop a process-based map representing the flow of activities, resources, and their interrelationships.* An important phase of any activity-based analysis is identifying the interrelationships between key activities and the resources consumed. This is typically done by interviewing key personnel. Once the linkages between activities and resources are identified, a process map is drawn that provides a visual representation of the operations of the BD.

Exhibit 4-12 is a process map that depicts the flow of activities and resources at the BD. Note that there are no costs on Exhibit 4-12. The management team first focused on understanding business processes. Costs were not considered until Step 3, after the key interrelationships of the business were understood.

Consider residential accounts. Three key activities support these accounts: account inquiry, correspondence, and account billing. Account inquiry activity consumes account inquiry labor time. Account inquiry laborers, in turn, use telecommunication and computer resources, occupy space, and are supervised. Correspondence is sometimes necessary as a result of inquiries. This activity requires account inquiry laborers who are supervised. The account billing activity is performed by billing laborers using printing machines. The printing machines occupy space, and require paper and computer resources. Billing laborers also occupy space, use telecommunications, and are supervised. The costs of each of the resources consumed were determined during Step 3—data collection.

Step 3: *Collect relevant data concerning costs and the physical flow of the cost-driver units among resources and activities.* Using the process map as a guide, BD accountants collected the required cost and operational data by further interviews with relevant personnel. Sources of data include the accounting records, special studies, and sometimes "best estimates of managers."

Exhibit 4-13 is a graphical representation of the data collected for the four activities identified in Step 1. For each activity, data collected included traceable costs and the physical flow of cost-driver units. For example, Exhibit 4-13 shows traceable costs of $235,777 for the account billing activity. Traceable costs include the costs of the printing machines ($55,000 from Exhibit 4-11) plus portions of the costs of all other resources that support the billing activity (paper, occupancy, computer, and billing labor). Notice that the total traceable costs of $205,332 + $35,384 + $235,777 + $88,847 = $565,340 in Exhibit 4-13 equals the total indirect costs in Exhibit 4-11. Next, the physical flow of cost-driver units was determined for each activity or cost object. For each activity, the traceable costs were divided by the sum of the physical flows of cost-driver units to establish a cost per cost-driver unit.

Step 4: *Calculate and interpret the new activity-based information.* The activity-based cost per account for each customer class can be determined from the data in Step 3. Exhibit 4-14 shows the computations.

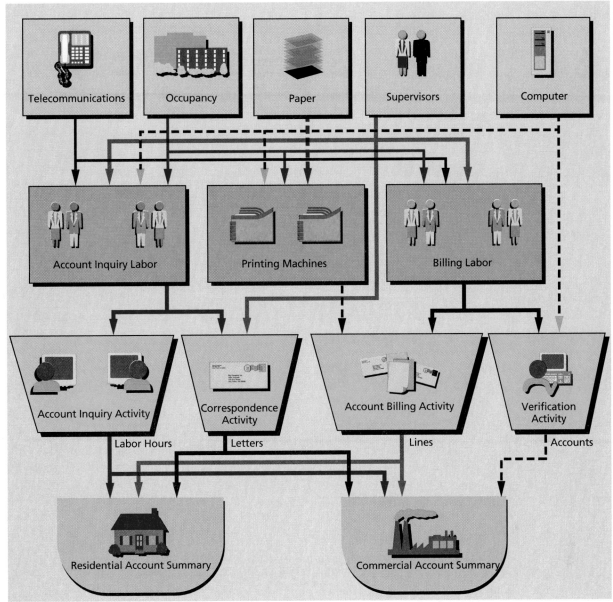

Exhibit 4-12

Process Map of Billing Department Activities

Examine the last two items in Exhibit 4-14. Notice that traditional costing overcosted the high-volume residential accounts and substantially undercosted the low-volume, complex commercial accounts. The cost per account for residential accounts using ABC is $2.28, which is $1.41 (or 38%) less than the $3.69 cost generated by the traditional costing system. The cost per account for commercial accounts is $14.57, which is $8.42 (or 137%) more than the $6.15 cost from the traditional cost system. Management's belief that traditional costing was undercosting commercial accounts was confirmed. PPC's management now has more accurate cost information for planning and decision-making purposes. We will return to the BD a bit later, but for now, think about what decision you would favor regarding the service bureau's proposal.

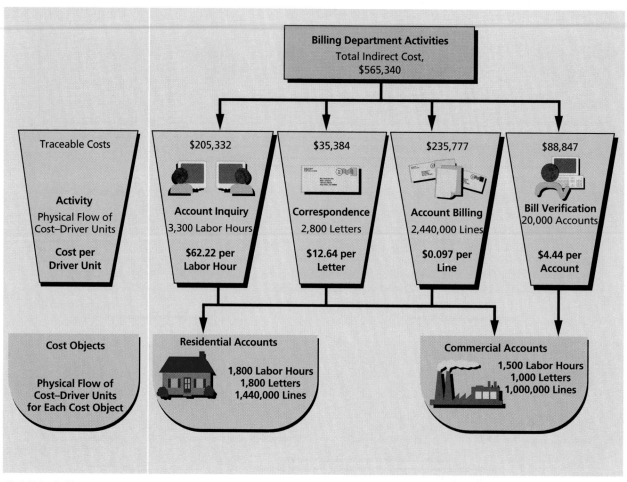

Exhibit 4-13

ABC System: Portland Power Company—Billing Department

These results are common when companies perform activity-based-costing studies—high volume cost objects with simple processes are overcosted when only one volume-based cost driver is used. In the BD, this volume-based cost driver was the number of inquiries. Which system makes more sense—the traditional allocation system that "spreads" all support costs to customer classes based solely on the number of inquiries, or the activity-based-costing system that identifies key activities and assigns costs based on the consumption of units of cost drivers chosen for each key activity? For PPC, the probable benefits of the new activity-based-costing system appear to outweigh the costs of implementing and maintaining the new cost system. However, the cost-benefit balance must be assessed on a case-by-case basis.

SUMMARY OF ACTIVITY-BASED COSTING

Activity-based accounting systems can turn many indirect manufacturing overhead costs into direct costs, costs identified specifically with given cost objectives. Appropriate selection of activities and cost drivers allows managers to trace many manufacturing overhead costs to cost objectives just as specifically as they have traced direct-material and direct-labor costs. Because activity-based accounting systems classify more costs as direct than do traditional systems, managers have greater confidence in the accuracy of the costs of products and services reported by activity-based systems.

Activity-based accounting systems are more complex and costly than traditional systems, so not all companies use them. But more and more organizations in both manufac-

Exhibit 4-14

Key Results of Activity-Based-Costing Study

Driver Costs

Activity/Resource (Driver Units)	Traceable Costs (From Exhibit 4-13)	Total Physical Flow of Driver Units (From Exhibit 4-13)	Cost per Driver Unit
	(1)	(2)	(1)÷(2)
Account inquiry (labor hours)	$205,332	3,300 Hours	$62.2218
Correspondence (letters)	35,384	2,800 Letters	12.6371
Account billing (lines)	235,777	2,440,000 Lines	0.09663
Bill verification (accounts)	88,847	20,000 Accounts	4.44235

Cost per Customer Class

		Residential		Commercial	
	Cost per Driver Unit	Physical Flow of Driver Units	Cost	Physical Flow of Driver Units	Cost
Account inquiry	$62.2218	1,800 Hrs.	$111,999	1,500 Hrs.	$ 93,333
Correspondence	$12.6371	1,800 Ltrs.	22,747	1,000 Ltrs.	12,637
Account billing	$0.09663	1,440,000 Lines	139,147	1,000,000 Lines	96,630
Bill verification	$4.44235			20,000 Accts.	88,847
Total cost			$273,893		$291,447
Number of accounts			120,000		20,000
Cost per account			$ 2.28		$ 14.57
Cost per account, traditional system from Exhibit 4-11			$ 3.69		$ 6.15

turing and nonmanufacturing industries are adopting activity-based systems for a variety of reasons:

- Fierce competitive pressure has resulted in shrinking profit margins. Companies may know their overall margin, but they often do not believe in the accuracy of the margins for individual products or services. Some are winners and some are losers—but which ones? Accurate costs are essential for answering this question.

- Business complexity has increased, which results in greater diversity in the types of products and services as well as customer classes. Therefore, the consumption of a company's shared resources also varies substantially across products and customers.

- New production techniques have increased the proportion of indirect costs—that is, indirect costs are far more important in today's world-class manufacturing environment. In many industries direct labor is being replaced by automated equipment. Indirect costs are sometimes more than 50% of total cost.

- The rapid pace of technological change has shortened product life cycles. Hence, companies do not have time to make price or cost adjustments once costing errors are discovered.

- The costs associated with bad decisions that result from inaccurate cost determinations are substantial (bids lost due to overcosted products, hidden losses from undercosted products, failure to detect activities that are not cost-effective, etc.). Companies with accurate costs have a huge advantage over those with inaccurate costs.

- Computer technology has reduced the costs of developing and operating cost systems that track many activities.

cost-management system
Identifies how management's decisions affect costs, by first measuring the resources used in performing the organization's activities and then assessing the effects on costs of changes in those activities.

activity-based management (ABM) Using an activity-based costing system to improve the operations of an organization.

value-added cost The necessary cost of an activity that cannot be eliminated without affecting a product's value to the customer.

non-value-added costs Costs that can be eliminated without affecting a product's value to the customer.

To support managers' decisions better, accountants go beyond simply determining the cost of products and services. They develop cost-management systems. A **cost-management system** identifies how management's decisions affect costs. To do so, it first measures the resources used in performing the organization's activities and then assesses the effects on costs of changes in those activities.

ACTIVITY-BASED MANAGEMENT

Recall that managers' day-to-day focus is on managing activities not costs. So, because ABC systems also focus on activities, they are very useful in cost management. Using an activity-based costing system to improve the operations of an organization is **activity-based management (ABM).** In the broadest terms, activity-based management aims to improve the value received by customers and to improve profits by providing this value.

The cornerstone of ABM is distinguishing between value-added costs and non-value-added costs. A **value-added cost** is the cost of an activity that cannot be eliminated without affecting a product's value to the customer. Value-added costs are necessary (as long as the activity that drives such costs is performed efficiently). In contrast, companies try to minimize **non-value-added costs,** costs that can be eliminated without affecting a product's value to the customer. Activities such as handling and storing inventories, transporting partly finished products from one part of the plant to another, and changing the setup of production-line operations to produce a different model of the product are all non-value-adding activities that can be reduced, if not eliminated, by careful redesign of the plant layout and the production process.

Let us return now to the Portland Power Company to see how the billing department could use the ABC system to improve its operation. Recall that the BD needed to find a way to increase its capacity to handle accounts due to an expected large increase in demand from a new housing development and a shopping center. BD managers also were interested (as always is the case) in reducing the operating costs of the department while not impairing the quality of the service it provided to its customers. To do so, they used the ABC information from Exhibit 4-14 to identify non-value-added activities that had significant costs. Account inquiry and bill verification activities are non-value-added and costly, so management asked for ideas for cost reductions. The new information provided by the ABC system generated the following ideas for improvement:

- Use the service bureau for commercial accounts because of the significant cost savings. From Exhibit 4-14, the service bureau's bid is for $8.50 per account compared to the BD's activity-based cost of $14.57, a difference of more than $6 per account! The freed-up capacity can be used to meet the expected increase in residential demand. Bill verification, a non-value-added activity, would also be eliminated because only commercial bills are verified.

- Exhibit 4-14 indicates that account inquiry activity is very costly, accounting for a significant portion of total BD costs. One idea is to make bills more descriptive in order to reduce the number of inquiries. Doing so would add lines to each bill, resulting in higher billing-activity costs, but the number of inquiries would be reduced, thus reducing a significant non-value-added cost. Whether this idea would result in a net cost reduction needs to be evaluated by the accountants with the help of the new ABC system.

Objective 6
Explain how JIT systems can reduce non-value-added activities.

JIT SYSTEMS

Attempts to minimize non-value-added costs have led many organizations to adopt JIT systems (see Chapter 1, page 22) to eliminate waste and improve quality. In a **just-in-time**

Identifying Activities, Resources, and Cost Drivers in the Health Care Industry

Arkansas Blue Cross Blue Shield (ABCBS) is the largest health insurer in the state of Arkansas with annual revenue of more than $450 million. Recently, ABCBS implemented activity-based management (ABM). ABM is using activity-based information in the decision-making process. The identification of key activities, resources, and cost drivers was one of the early steps performed.

- A pilot study was performed on one area of the firm—information management. The criteria for selection of a pilot area included significant costs, the possibility of improving the existing cost-allocation system, access to data, and a receptive staff.
- The cost objectives were defined—the internal customers of information management.
- Activities, resources, and cost drivers were identified based on meetings with managers. Examples of key activities are Production (job scheduling, production control), Electronic Media Claims Processing, Printing, and Mail Processing. Resources include Systems Programmers, Mail Labor, Print Labor, Tape Labor, Data Base Administrators, 3080 CPU, 3090 CPU, LSM (robotic cartridge system), DASD (hard disk storage), and Telecommunications. Cost drivers included CPU minutes, single-density volumes (DASD), number of tape/cartridge mounts (LSM), number of jobs, and number of CRTs (telecommunications).

- Once the key activities, resources, and drivers were identified, a process map of the operations of the information management function was developed by the project team. This map reflected the flow of activities and resources in support of the cost centers. The map also identified the data that needed to be collected to complete the study. The form of the process map is similar to Exhibit 4-12.
- Once the ABC model was built and validated, the results were interpreted and recommendations for improvement were made.

As a result of the ABC study, the following actions were taken by management:

- A separate utility meter was placed on the computer room.
- CRT purchases are now charged directly to the user. Maintenance costs for CRTs are now assigned based on CRT count.
- Three new cost centers were created: EMC Systems, Change Control, and Production Control.
- CPU was upgraded.

ABCBS is now in the process of expanding the new ABM system corporate-wide to include purchasing, actuarial, advertising, and claims processing. The company is also using the new ABM system for activity-based budgeting.

Source: Adapted from "Implementing Activity-Based Costing—The Model Approach," Institute of Management Accountants and Sapling Corporation, Orlando, November 1994.

(JIT) production system, an organization purchases materials and parts and produces components just when they are needed in the production process. Goods are not produced until it is time for them to be shipped to a customer. The goal is to have zero inventory, because holding inventory is a non-value-added activity.

JIT companies are customer-oriented because customer orders drive the production process. An order triggers the immediate delivery of materials, followed by production and delivery of the goods. Instead of producing inventory and hoping an order will come, a JIT system produces products directly for received orders. Several factors are crucial to the success of JIT systems:

1. *Focus on quality:* JIT companies try to involve all employees in controlling quality. Although any system can seek quality improvements, JIT systems emphasize total quality control (TQC) and continuous improvement in quality. Having all employees striving for zero defects minimizes non-value-added activities such as inspection and rework for defective items.

2. *Short* **production cycle times,** *the time from initiating production to delivering the goods to the customer:* Keeping production cycle times short allows timely

just-in-time (JIT) production system A system in which an organization purchases materials and parts and produces components just when they are needed in the production process, the goal being to have zero inventory, because holding inventory is a non-value-added activity.

production cycle time The time from initiating production to delivering the goods to the customer.

response to customer orders and reduces the level of inventories. Many JIT companies have achieved remarkable reductions in production cycle times. For example, applying JIT methods in one AT&T division cut production cycle time by a factor of 12.

3. *Smooth flow of production:* Fluctuations in production rates inevitably lead to delays in delivery to customers and excess inventories. To achieve smooth production flow, JIT companies simplify the production process to reduce the possibilities of delay, develop close relationships with suppliers to assure timely delivery and high quality of purchased materials, and perform routine maintenance on equipment to prevent costly breakdowns.

Many companies help achieve these objectives by improving the physical layout of their plants. In conventional manufacturing, similar machines (lathes, molding machines, drilling machines, and so on) are grouped together. Workers specialize in only one machine operation (operating either the molding or the drilling machine). There are at least two negative effects of such a layout. First, products must be moved from one area of the plant to another for required processing. This increases material handling costs and results in work-in-process inventories that can be substantial. These are non-value-added activities and costs. Second, the specialized labor resource is often idle—waiting for work-in-process. This wasted resource—labor time—is also non-value-added.

cellular manufacturing A production system in which machines are organized in cells according to the specific requirements of a product family.

In a JIT production system, machines are often organized in cells according to the specific requirements of a product family. This is called **cellular manufacturing.** Only the machines that are needed for the product family are in the cell, and these machines are located as close to each other as possible. Workers are trained to use all the cellular machines. Each cell (often shaped in the form of a "U") is a mini-factory or focused factory. Many problems associated with the conventional production layout are eliminated in cellular manufacturing. Work-in-process inventories are reduced or eliminated because there is no need for moving and storing inventory. Idle time is reduced or eliminated because workers are capable of moving from idle machine activity to needed activities. As a result, cycle times are reduced.

4. *Flexible production operations:* Two dimensions are important: facilities flexibility and employee flexibility. Facilities should be able to produce a variety of components and products to provide extra capacity when a particular product is in high demand and to avoid shut-down when a unique facility breaks down. Facilities should also require short setup times, the time it takes to switch from producing one product to another. Cross-training employees—training employees to do a variety of jobs—provides further flexibility. Multiskilled workers can fill in when a particular operation is overloaded and can reduce setup time. One company reported a reduction in setup time from 45 minutes to 1 minute by training production workers to perform the setup operations.

Accounting for a JIT system is often simpler than it is for other systems. Most cost accounting systems focus on determining product costs for inventory valuation. But JIT systems have minimal inventories, so there is less benefit from an elaborate inventory costing system. In true JIT systems, material, labor, and overhead costs can be charged directly to cost of goods sold because inventories are small enough to be ignored. All costs of production are assumed to apply to products that have already been sold. More details on accounting in JIT systems are found in Chapter 14.

Highlights to Remember

Explain the relationship between cost, cost objective, cost accumulation, and cost allocation. Cost accounting systems are designed to provide cost information about various types of objectives—products, customers, activities, and so on. To do this, resource costs are first accumulated by natural classifications such as materials, labor, and energy. Then costs are traced to cost objectives, either directly or indirectly through allocation.

Distinguish between direct and indirect costs. Direct costs can be identified specifically and exclusively with a cost object in an economically feasible way. When this is not possible, costs must be allocated to cost objectives using a cost driver. Such costs are called indirect costs. The greater the proportion of direct costs, the greater the accuracy of the cost system. When the proportion of indirect costs is significant, care must be taken to find the most appropriate cost drivers.

Explain how the financial statements of merchandisers and manufacturers differ because of the types of goods they sell. The primary difference between the financial statements of a merchandiser and a manufacturer is the reporting of inventories. A merchandiser has only one type of inventory whereas a manufacturer has three types of inventory—raw material, work-in-process, and finished goods.

Construct income statements of a manufacturing company in both the absorption and contribution formats. The major difference between the absorption and contribution formats for the income statement is that cost behavior (fixed and variable) is reported in the contribution format whereas the focus of the absorption format is in reporting costs by business functions. The contribution approach makes it easier for managers to evaluate the affects of changes in demand on income and thus it is better for planning and control purposes.

Identify the steps involved in the design and implementation of an activity-based-costing system. Designing and implementing an activity-based costing system involves four steps. First, managers determine the cost objectives, key activities, and resources used. Cost drivers (output measures) are also identified for each resource and activity. Second, a process-based map is drawn that represents the flow of activities and resources that support the cost objects. The third step is collecting cost and operating data. The last step is to calculate and interpret the new activity-based information. Often, this last step requires the use of a computer due to the complexity of many ABC systems. Using ABC information to improve operations is called activity-based management.

Explain how JIT systems can reduce non-value-added activities. Just-in-time (JIT) production systems are used to improve profitability of companies by eliminating waste and improving quality. JIT systems focus on quality, short production cycles, reducing inventory, and flexible use of operating assets and human resources. Each of these factors is associated with non-value-added activities and thus improvements result in reduced operating costs and improved profitability.

Understand how cost accounting fits into the value chain. A good cost accounting system is critical to all value-chain functions from research and development through customer service. Without accurate and timely cost information, decision making is poor at best. In today's complex business environment, the need for good cost information is critical to the success of the business. Improvements in the design of cost accounting systems through activity-based costing have expanded the role of the cost accountant to a position of strategic importance.

Accounting Vocabulary

absorption approach, p. 133

activity-based costing (ABC), p. 136

activity-based management (ABM), p. 144

cellular manufacturing, p. 146

contribution approach, p. 134

conversion costs, p. 127

cost, p. 125

cost accounting, p. 125

cost accumulation, p. 124

cost allocation, p. 124

cost-management system, p. 144

cost object, p. 126

cost objective, p. 126

direct costs, p. 126

direct-labor costs, p. 127

direct-material costs, p. 126

factory burden, p. 127

factory overhead, p. 127

indirect costs, p. 126

indirect manufacturing costs, p. 127

just-in-time (JIT) production system, p. 145

manufacturing overhead, p. 127

non-value-added costs, p. 144

period costs, p. 128

prime costs, p. 127

product costs, p. 128

production cycle time, p. 145

value-added cost, p. 144

Fundamental Assignment Material

4-A1 Straightforward Income Statements

The Columbia Company had the following manufacturing data for the year 19X9 (in thousands of dollars):

Beginning and ending inventories	None
Direct material used	$400
Direct labor	330
Supplies	20
Utilities—variable portion	40
Utilities—fixed portion	12
Indirect labor—variable portion	90
Indirect labor—fixed portion	40
Depreciation	110
Property taxes	20
Supervisory salaries	50

Selling expenses were $300,000 (including $60,000 that were variable) and general administrative expenses were $144,000 (including $24,000 that were variable). Sales were $1.8 million.

Direct labor and supplies are regarded as variable costs.

Required

1. Prepare two income statements, one using the contribution approach and one using the absorption approach.

2. Suppose that all variable costs fluctuate directly in proportion to sales, and that fixed costs are unaffected over a very wide range of sales. What would operating income have been if sales had been $2.0 million instead of $1.8 million? Which income statement did you use to help obtain your answer? Why?

4-A2 Meaning of Technical Terms

Refer to the absorption income statement of your solution to the preceding problem. Give the amounts of the following: (1) prime cost, (2) conversion cost, (3) factory burden, (4) factory overhead, (5) manufacturing overhead, and (6) indirect manufacturing cost.

4-A3 Cost Allocation, Activity-Based Costing, and Activity-Based Management

Reliable Machining Products (RMP) is a discrete automotive component supplier. RMP has been approached by Chrysler with a proposal to significantly increase production of

Part T151A to a total annual quantity of 100,000. Chrysler believes that by increasing the volume of production of Part T151A, RMP should realize the benefits of economies of scale and hence should accept a lower price than the current $6.00 per unit. Currently, RMP's gross margin on Part T151A is 3.3%, computed as follows:

	Total	Per Unit ($\div$100,000)
Direct materials	$150,000	$1.50
Direct labor	86,000	.86
Indirect manufacturing (400% $\times$ direct labor)	344,000	3.44
Total cost	$580,000	$5.80
Sales price		6.00
Gross margin		$ .20
Gross margin percentage		3.3%

Part T151A seems to be a marginal profit product. If additional volume of production of Part T151A is to be added, RMP management believes that the sales price must be increased, not reduced as requested by Chrysler. The management of RMP sees this quoting situation as an excellent opportunity to examine the effectiveness of their traditional costing system versus an activity-based-costing system. Data have been collected by a team consisting of accounting and engineering analysts.

Activity Center: Cost Drivers	Annual Cost-Driver Quantity
Quality: number of pieces scrapped	10,000
Production scheduling and setup: number of setups	500
Shipping: number of containers shipped	60,000
Shipping administration: number of shipments	1,000
Production: number of machine hours	10,000

Activity Center	Traceable Indirect Manufacturing Costs (Annual)
Quality	$ 800,000
Production scheduling	50,000
Setup	600,000
Shipping	300,000
Shipping administration	50,000
Production	1,500,000
Total costs	$3,300,000

The accounting and engineering team has provided the following cost-driver consumption estimates for the production of 100,000 units of Part T151A:

Cost Driver	Cost-Driver Consumption
Pieces scrapped	1,000
Setups	12
Containers shipped	500
Shipments	100
Machine hours	500

1. Prepare a schedule calculating the unit cost and gross margin of Part T151A using the activity-based-costing approach.

Required

2. Based on the ABC results, what course of action would you recommend regarding the proposal by Chrysler? List the benefits and costs associated with implementing an activity-based-costing system at RMP.

4-B1 Contribution and Absorption Income Statements

The following information is taken from the records of the Kingland Company for the year ending December 31, 19X9. There were no beginning or ending inventories.

Sales	$10,000,000	Long-term rent, factory	$ 100,000
Sales commissions	500,000	Factory superintendent's	
Advertising	200,000	salary	30,000
Shipping expenses	300,000	Supervisors' salaries	100,000
Administrative executive		Direct material used	4,000,000
salaries	100,000	Direct labor	2,000,000
Administrative clerical		Cutting bits used	60,000
salaries (variable)	400,000	Factory methods research	40,000
Fire insurance on		Abrasives for machining	100,000
factory equipment	2,000	Indirect labor	800,000
Property taxes on		Depreciation on	
factory equipment	10,000	equipment	300,000

Required

1. Prepare a contribution income statement and an absorption income statement. If you are in doubt about any cost behavior pattern, decide on the basis of whether the total cost in question will fluctuate substantially over a wide range of volume. Prepare a separate supporting schedule of indirect manufacturing costs subdivided between variable and fixed costs.

2. Suppose that all variable costs fluctuate directly in proportion to sales, and that fixed costs are unaffected over a wide range of sales. What would operating income have been if sales had been $10.5 million instead of $10 million? Which income statement did you use to help get your answer? Why?

4-B2 JIT and Non-Value-Added Activities

A motorcycle manufacturer was concerned with declining market share because of foreign competition. To become more efficient, the company was considering changing to a JIT production system. As a first step in analyzing the feasibility of the change, the company identified its major activities. Among the 120 activities were the following:

Materials receiving and inspection

Production scheduling

Production setup

Rear-wheel assembly

Movement of engine from fabrication to assembly building

Assembly of handlebars

Paint inspection

Reworking of defective brake assemblies

Installation of speedometer

Placement of completed motorcycle in finished goods storage

Required

1. From the preceding list of 10 activities, prepare two lists: one of value-added activities and one of non-value-added activities.

2. For each non-value-added activity, explain how a JIT production system might eliminate, or at least reduce, the cost of the activity.

4-B3 Activity-Based Costing

The cordless phone manufacturing division of a Denver-based consumer electronics company uses activity-based accounting. For simplicity, assume that its accountants have identified only the following three activities and related cost drivers for indirect manufacturing costs:

Activity	Cost Driver
Materials handling	Direct-materials cost
Engineering	Engineering change notices
Power	Kilowatt hours

Three types of cordless phones are produced: SA2, SA5, and SA9. Direct costs and cost-driver activity for each product for a recent month are as follows:

	SA2	SA5	SA9
Direct-materials cost	$25,000	$ 50,000	$125,000
Direct-labor cost	$ 4,000	$ 1,000	$ 3,000
Kilowatt hours	50,000	200,000	150,000
Engineering change notices	13	5	2

Indirect manufacturing cost for the month was:

Materials handling	$ 8,000
Engineering	20,000
Power	16,000
Total indirect manufacturing cost	$44,000

Required

1. Compute the indirect manufacturing cost allocated to each product with the activity-based accounting system.
2. Suppose all indirect manufacturing costs had been allocated to products in proportion to their direct-labor costs. Compute the indirect manufacturing allocated to each product.
3. In which product costs, those in requirement 1 or those in requirement 2, do you have the most confidence? Why?

Additional Assignment Material

QUESTIONS

4-1. Name four cost objectives or cost objects.

4-2. What is the major purpose of detailed cost-accounting systems?

4-3. "Departments are not cost objects or objects of costing." Do you agree? Explain.

4-4. "The same cost can be direct and indirect." Do you agree? Explain.

4-5. "Economic feasibility is an important guideline in designing cost-accounting systems." Do you agree? Explain.

4-6. How does the idea of economic feasibility relate to the distinction between direct and indirect costs?

4-7. Distinguish between prime costs and conversion costs.

4-8. "The typical accounting system does not allocate costs associated with value-chain functions other than production to units produced." Do you agree? Explain.

4-9. "For a furniture manufacturer, glue or tacks become an integral part of the finished product, so they would be direct material." Do you agree? Explain.

4-10. Many cost-accounting systems have a twofold instead of a threefold category of manufacturing costs. What are the items in the twofold category?

4-11. "Depreciation is an expense for financial statement purposes." Do you agree? Explain.

4-12. Distinguish between "costs" and "expenses."

4-13. "Unexpired costs are always inventory costs." Do you agree? Explain.

4-14. Why is there no direct-labor inventory account on a manufacturing company's balance sheet?

4-15. What is the advantage of the contribution approach as compared with the absorption approach?

4-16. Distinguish between manufacturing and merchandising companies.

4-17. "The primary classifications of costs are by variable- and fixed-cost behavior patterns, not by business functions." Name three commonly used terms that describe this type of income statement.

4-18. Refer to Exhibit 4-10. Cost drivers A, B, and C are sometimes called resource cost drivers whereas cost drivers D, E, and F are called activity cost drivers. Explain.

4-19. Refer to Exhibit 4-10. Suppose the appliance maker has two plants—the Salem plant and the Youngstown plant. The Youngstown plant produces only three appliances that are very similar in material and production requirements. Which type of costing system would you recommend for each plant (traditional or ABC)? Explain.

4-20. Name 4 steps in the design and implementation of an activity-based-costing system.

4-21. Refer to the Portland Power Company illustration on pages 137–144. Which BD resource costs depicted in Exhibit 4-11 would have variable cost behavior?

4-22. Why are more and more organizations adopting activity-based-costing systems?

4-23. Contrast activity-based costing (ABC) with activity-based management (ABM).

4-24. Why do managers want to distinguish between value-added activities and non-value-added activities?

4-25. Name four factors crucial to the success of JIT production systems.

4-26. "ABC and JIT are alternative techniques for achieving competitiveness." Do you agree?

EXERCISES

4-27 Meaning of Technical Terms
Refer to Exhibit 4-4, page 131. Give the amounts of the following with respect to the cost of goods available for sale: (1) prime costs, (2) conversion costs, (3) factory burden, and (4) indirect manufacturing costs.

4-28 Presence of Ending Work in Process
Refer to Exhibits 4-4 and 4-5 on pages 131–132. Suppose manufacturing costs were the same, but there was an ending work-in-process inventory of $3 million. The cost of the completed goods would therefore be $37 million instead of $40 million. Suppose also that the cost of goods sold is unchanged.

Required

1. Recast the income statement of Exhibit 4-4.
2. What lines and ending balances would change in Exhibit 4-5 and by how much?

4-29 Relating Costs to Cost Objectives
A company uses an absorption cost system. Prepare headings for two columns: (1) assembly department and (2) products assembled. Fill in the two columns with a *D* for direct and an *I* for indirect for each of the costs below. For example, if a specific cost is direct to the department but indirect to the product, place a *D* in column 1 and an *I* in column 2. The costs are: materials used, supplies used, assembly labor, material-handling labor (transporting materials between and within departments), depreciation—building, assembly supervisor's salary, and the building and grounds supervisor's salary.

4-30 Classification of Manufacturing Costs
Classify each of the following as direct or indirect (*D* or *I*) with respect to traceability to product and as variable or fixed (*V* or *F*) with respect to whether the cost fluctuates in total as activity or volume changes over wide ranges of activity. You will have two answers, *D* or *I* and *V* or *F*, for each of the 10 items.

1. Supervisor training program
2. Abrasives (sandpaper, etc.)
3. Cutting bits in a machinery department
4. Food for a factory cafeteria
5. Factory rent
6. Salary of a factory storeroom clerk
7. Workers' compensation insurance in a factory
8. Cement for a roadbuilder
9. Steel scrap for a blast furnace
10. Paper towels for a factory washroom

4-31 Variable Costs and Fixed Costs; Manufacturing and Other Costs

For each of the numbered items, choose the appropriate classifications for a manufacturing company. If in doubt about whether the cost behavior is basically variable or fixed, decide on the basis of whether the total cost will fluctuate substantially over a wide range of volume. Most items have two answers among the following possibilities with respect to the cost of a particular job:

a. Selling cost
b. Manufacturing costs, direct
c. Manufacturing costs, indirect
d. General and administrative cost
e. Fixed cost
f. Variable cost
g. Other (specify)

Sample answers:

Direct material	e, f
President's salary	d, e
Bond interest expense	e, g (financial expense)

Items for your consideration:

1. Factory power for machines
2. Salespersons' commissions
3. Salespersons' salaries
4. Welding supplies
5. Fire loss
6. Sandpaper
7. Supervisory salaries, production control
8. Supervisory salaries, assembly department
9. Supervisory salaries, factory storeroom
10. Company picnic costs
11. Overtime premium, punch press
12. Idle time, assembly
13. Freight out
14. Property taxes
15. Paint for finished products

16. Heat and air conditioning, factory

17. Material-handling labor, punch press

18. Straight-line depreciation, salespersons' automobiles

4-32 Inventory Transactions

Review Exhibit 4-9, page 135. Assume that the Slider Company had no beginning inventories. The following transactions occurred in 19X9 (in thousands):

1. Purchase of direct materials	$350
2. Direct materials used	300
3. Acquire direct labor	160
4. Acquire factory overhead	200
5. Complete all goods that were started	?
6. Cost of goods sold (half of the goods completed were sold)	?

Required

Prepare an analysis similar to Exhibit 4-9. What are the ending balances of direct materials, work-in-process, and finished-goods inventories?

4-33 Inventory Transactions

Refer to the preceding problem. Suppose goods were still in process that cost $100,000. Half the goods completed were sold. What are the balances of all the accounts in the ending balance sheet?

4-34 Straightforward Absorption Statement

The Pierce Company had the following data (in thousands) for a given period:

Sales	$700
Direct materials	210
Direct labor	150
Indirect manufacturing costs	170
Selling and administrative expenses	150

Required

There were no beginning or ending inventories. Compute the (1) manufacturing cost of goods sold, (2) gross profit, (3) operating income, (4) prime cost, and (5) conversion cost.

4-35 Straightforward Contribution Income Statement

Yoko Ltd. had the following data (in millions of yen) for a given period:

Sales	¥770
Direct materials	290
Direct labor	140
Variable factory overhead	60
Variable selling and administrative expenses	100
Fixed factory overhead	120
Fixed selling and administrative expenses	45

Required

There were no beginning or ending inventories. Compute the (1) variable manufacturing cost of goods sold, (2) contribution margin, and (3) operating income.

4-36 Straightforward Absorption and Contribution Statement

Anzola Company had the following data (in millions) for a recent period. Fill in the blanks. There were no beginning or ending inventories.

a. Sales	$920
b. Direct materials used	350
c. Direct labor	210
Indirect manufacturing costs:	
d. Variable	100
e. Fixed	50
f. Variable manufacturing cost of goods sold	—
g. Manufacturing cost of goods sold	—
Selling and administrative expenses:	
h. Variable	90
i. Fixed	80
j. Gross profit	—
k. Contribution margin	—
l. Prime costs	—
m. Conversion costs	—
n. Operating income	—

4-37 Absorption Statement

Raynard's Jewelry had the following data (in thousands) for a given period. Assume there are no inventories. Fill in the blanks.

Sales	$—
Direct materials	370
Direct labor	—
Indirect manufacturing	—
Manufacturing cost of goods sold	780
Gross margin	120
Selling and administrative expenses	—
Operating income	20
Conversion cost	—
Prime cost	600

4-38 Contribution Income Statement

Marlinski Company had the following data (in thousands) for a given period. Assume there are no inventories.

Direct labor	$170
Direct materials	210
Variable indirect manufacturing	110
Contribution margin	200
Fixed selling and administrative expenses	100
Operating income	10
Sales	970

Compute the (1) variable manufacturing cost of goods sold, (2) variable selling and administrative expenses, and (3) fixed indirect manufacturing costs.

Required

4-39 Value-Added Analysis in a Service Company

Refer to the Portland Power Company illustration and Exhibit 4-12 on page 141.

Some companies that perform value-added cost analysis subdivide non-value-added activities into two categories—essential and discretionary. An example of an essential but non-value-added activity is setting up the company's computer system for a billing run. An example of a discretionary non-value-added activity is monitoring telephone inquiries. Most non-value-added discretionary activities should be eliminated. Non-value-added essential activities are reduced through continuous improvement efforts. For each resource and activity listed below, indicate whether it is value-added (VA), non-value-added essential (NVA-E), or non-value-added discretionary (NVA-D). Also indicate appropriate managerial actions to control costs for each type of resource and activity based on its classification.

Resource/Activity
Telecommunications
Paper
Computer
Supervisors
Account inquiry activity
Billing labor

4-40 Cost Allocation and Activity-Based Costing

Refer to the Portland Power Company illustration and Exhibit 4-14 on page 143. The data used in the BD study are averages for each customer class. Based on the study results, the company conducted a thorough investigation of all commercial customers that received correspondence. On average, these accounts consumed 5 minutes of inquiry labor time and had 75 lines on the electric bill. What was the cost per account to service this customer class? (Assume only 1 letter per customer and that commercial accounts are verified only one time.)

PROBLEMS

4-41 Cost Accumulation and Allocation

Hwang Manufacturing Company has two departments, machining and finishing. For a given period, the following costs were incurred by the company as a whole: direct material, $120,000; direct labor, $60,000; and indirect manufacturing, $78,000. The grand total costs were $258,000.

The machining department incurred 80% of the direct-material costs, but only 30% of the direct-labor costs. As is commonplace, indirect manufacturing incurred by each department was allocated to products in proportion to the direct-labor costs of products within the departments.

Three products were produced.

Product	Direct Material	Direct Labor
X-1	50%	33⅓%
Y-1	25%	33⅓%
Z-1	25%	33⅓%
Total for the machining department	100%	100%
X-1	33⅓%	40%
Y-1	33⅓%	40%
Z-1	33⅓%	20%
Total added by finishing department	100%	100%

The indirect manufacturing incurred by the machining department and allocated to all products therein amounted to: machining, $36,000; finishing, $42,000.

Required

1. Compute the total costs incurred by the machining department and added by the finishing department.

2. Compute the total costs of each product that would be shown as finished-goods inventory if all the products were transferred to finished stock on completion. (There were no beginning inventories.)

4-42 Activity-Based Costing and Activity-Based Management

Reliable Machining Products (RMP) is an automotive component supplier. RMP has been approached by General Motors to consider expanding its production of part H707 to a total annual quantity of 2,000 units. This part is a low-volume, complex product with a high gross margin that is based on a proposed (quoted) unit sales price of $7.50. RMP uses a traditional costing system that allocates indirect manufacturing costs based on direct-labor costs. The rate currently used to allocate indirect manufacturing costs is 400% of direct-labor cost. This rate is based on the $3,300,000 annual factory overhead divided by $825,000 annual direct-labor cost. To produce 2,000 units of H707 requires $5,000 of direct materials and $1,000 of direct labor. The unit cost and gross margin percentage for Part H707 based on the traditional cost system are computed as follows:

	Total	Per Unit (÷2,000)
Direct material	$ 5,000	$ 2.50
Direct labor	1,000	.50
Indirect manufacturing: (400% × direct labor)	4,000	2.00
Total cost	$10,000	$ 5.00
Sales price quoted		7.50
Gross margin		$ 2.50
Gross margin percentage		33.3%

The management of RMP decided to examine the effectiveness of their traditional costing system versus an activity-based-costing system. The following data have been collected by a team consisting of accounting and engineering analysts:

Activity Center	Traceable Factory Overhead Costs (Annual)
Quality	$ 800,000
Production scheduling	50,000
Setup	600,000
Shipping	300,000
Shipping administration	50,000
Production	1,500,000
Total indirect manufacturing cost	$3,300,000

Activity Center: Cost Drivers	Annual Cost-Driver Quantity
Quality: number of pieces scrapped	10,000
Production scheduling and setup:	
number of setups	500
Shipping: number of containers shipped	60,000
Shipping administration: number of shipments	1,000
Production: number of machine hours	10,000

The accounting and engineering team has performed activity analysis and provides the following estimates for the total quantity of cost drivers to be used to produce 2,000 units of part H707:

Cost Driver	Cost-Driver Consumption
Pieces scrapped	120
Setups	4
Containers shipped	10
Shipments	5
Machine hours	15

Required

1. Prepare a schedule calculating the unit cost and gross margin of Part H707 using the activity-based-costing approach.

2. Based on the ABC results, which course of action would you recommend regarding the proposal by General Motors? List the benefits and costs associated with implementing an activity-based-costing system at RMP.

4-43   Financial Statements for Manufacturing and Merchandising Companies

Outdoor Equipment Company (OEC) and Mountain Supplies Inc. (MSI) both sell tents. OEC purchases its tents from a manufacturer for $90 each and sells them for $120. It purchased 10,000 tents in 19X9.

MSI produces its own tents. In 19X9 MSI produced 10,000 tents. Costs were as follows:

Direct materials purchased		$535,000
Direct materials used		$520,000
Direct labor		260,000
Indirect manufacturing:		
Depreciation	$40,000	
Indirect labor	50,000	
Other	30,000	120,000
Total cost of production		$900,000

Assume that MSI had no beginning inventory of direct materials. There was no beginning inventory of finished tents, but ending inventory consisted of 1,000 finished tents. Ending work-in-process inventory was negligible.

Each company sold 9,000 tents for $1,080,000 in 19X9 and incurred the following selling and administrative costs:

Sales salaries and commissions	$ 90,000
Depreciation on retail store	30,000
Advertising	20,000
Other	10,000
Total selling and administrative cost	$150,000

Required

1. Prepare the inventories section of the balance sheet for December 31, 19X9, for OEC.

2. Prepare the inventories section of the balance sheet for December 31, 19X9, for MSI.

3. Using Exhibit 4-4 on page 131 as a model, prepare an income statement for the year 19X9 for OEC.

4. Using Exhibit 4-4 on page 131 as a model, prepare an income statement for the year 19X9 for MSI.

5. Summarize the differences between the financial statements of OEC, a merchandiser, and MSI, a manufacturer.

4-44 Library Research in JIT, Activity-Based Costing, or Activity-Based Management

Select an article from *Management Accounting* or *Journal of Cost Management* (available in most libraries) that describes a particular company's application of either (1) a JIT production system, (2) an activity-based costing system, or (3) activity-based management. Prepare a summary of 300 words or less that includes the following:

Name of the company (if given)

Industry of the company

Description of the particular application

Assessment of the benefits the company received from the application

Any difficulties encountered in implementation

4-45 Review of Chapters 2 to 4

The Gomez Hosiery Company provides you with the following miscellaneous data regarding operations in 19X9:

Gross profit	$20,000
Net loss	(5,000)
Sales	100,000
Direct material used	35,000
Direct labor	25,000
Fixed manufacturing overhead	15,000
Fixed selling and administrative expenses	10,000

There are no beginning or ending inventories.

Required

Compute the (1) variable selling and administrative expenses, (2) contribution margin in dollars, (3) variable manufacturing overhead, (4) break-even point in sales dollars, and (5) manufacturing cost of goods sold.

4-46 Review of Chapters 2 to 4

Stephenson Corporation provides you with the following miscellaneous data regarding operations for 19X9:

Break-even point (in sales dollars)	$ 66,667
Direct material used	24,000
Gross profit	25,000
Contribution margin	30,000
Direct labor	28,000
Sales	100,000
Variable manufacturing overhead	5,000

There are no beginning or ending inventories.

Required

Compute the (1) fixed manufacturing overhead, (2) variable selling and administrative expenses, and (3) fixed selling and administrative expenses.

4-47 Review of Chapters 2 to 4

U. Grant Company manufactured and sold 1,000 sabres during November. Selected data for this month follow:

Sales	$100,000
Direct materials used	21,000
Direct labor	16,000
Variable manufacturing overhead	13,000
Fixed manufacturing overhead	14,000
Variable selling and administrative expenses	?
Fixed selling and administrative expenses	?
Contribution margin	40,000
Operating income	22,000

There were no beginning or ending inventories.

Required

1. What were the variable selling and administrative expenses for November?
2. What were the fixed selling and administrative expenses for November?
3. What was the cost of goods sold under absorption costing during November?
4. Without prejudice to your earlier answers, assume that the fixed selling and administrative expenses for November amounted to $14,000.
   a. What was the break-even point in units for November?
   b. How many units must be sold to earn a target operating income of $12,000?
   c. What would the selling price per unit have to be if the company wanted to earn an operating income of $17,000 on the sale of 900 units?

CASES

4-48 Identifying Activities, Resources, and Cost Drivers in Manufacturing

(*D. Sandison*) Extrusion Plastics is a multinational, diversified organization. One of its manufacturing divisions, Northeast Plastics Division, has become less profitable due to increased competition. The division produces three major lines of plastic products within its single plant. Product Line A is high-volume, simple pieces produced in large batches. Product Line B is medium-volume, more complex pieces. Product Line C is low-volume, small-order, highly complex pieces.

Currently, the division allocates indirect manufacturing costs based on direct labor. The V.P. Manufacturing is uncomfortable using the traditional cost figures. He thinks the company is under-pricing the more complex products. He decides to conduct an activity-based costing analysis of the business.

Interviews were conducted with the key managers in order to identify activities, resources, cost drivers, and their interrelationships.

Interviewee: Production Manager

Q1: What activities are carried out in your area?

A1: *All products are manufactured using three similar, complex, and expensive molding machines. Each molding machine can be used in the production of the three product lines. Each setup takes about the same time irrespective of the product.*

Q2: Who works in your area?

A2: *Last year, we employed thirty machine operators, two maintenance mechanics, and two supervisors.*

Q3: How are the operators used in the molding process?

A3: *It requires nine operators to support a machine during the actual production process.*

Q4: What do the maintenance mechanics do?

A4: *Their primary function is to perform machine setups. However, they were also required to provide machine maintenance during the molding process.*

Q5:   Where do the supervisors spend their time?

A5:   *They provide supervision for the machine operators and the maintenance mechanics. For the most part, the supervisors appear to spend the same amount of time with each of the employees that they supervise.*

Q6:   What other resources are used to support manufacturing?

A6:   *The molding machines use energy during the molding process and during the setups. We put meters on the molding machines to get a better understanding of their energy consumption. We discovered that for each hour that a machine ran, it used 6.3 kilowatts of energy. The machines also require consumable shop supplies (e.g., lubricants, hoses, etc.). We have found a direct correlation between the amount of supplies used and the actual processing time.*

Q7:   How is the building used, and what costs are associated with it?

A7:   *We have a 100,000-square-foot building. The total rent and insurance costs for the year were $675,000. These costs are allocated to production, sales, and administration based on square footage.*

Required

1.   Identify the activities, resources, and cost drivers for the division.
2.   For each resource identified in requirement 1, indicate its cost behavior with respect to the activities it supports (assume a planning period of 1 month).

4-49   Analysis with Contribution Income Statement
The following data have been condensed from LaGrande Corporation's report of 19X9 operations (in millions of French francs [FF]):

	Variable	Fixed	Total
Manufacturing cost of goods sold	FF400	FF180	FF580
Selling and administrative expenses	140	60	200
Sales			900

Required

1.   Prepare the 19X9 income statement in contribution form, ignoring income taxes.
2.   LaGrande's operations have been fairly stable from year to year. In planning for the future, top management is considering several options for changing the annual pattern of operations. You are asked to perform an analysis of their estimated effects. Use your contribution income statement as a framework to compute the estimated operating income (in millions) under each of the following separate and unrelated assumptions.
       a.   Assume that a 10% reduction in selling prices would cause a 30% increase in the physical volume of goods manufactured and sold.
       b.   Assume that an annual expenditure of FF30 million for a special sales promotion campaign would enable the company to increase its physical volume by 10% with no change in selling prices.
       c.   Assume that a basic redesign of manufacturing operations would increase annual fixed manufacturing costs by FF80 million and decrease variable manufacturing costs by 15% per product unit, but with no effect on physical volume or selling prices.
       d.   Assume that a basic redesign of selling and administrative operations would double the annual fixed expenses for selling and administration and increase

the variable expenses for selling and administration by 25% per product unit, but would also increase physical volume by 20%. Selling prices would be increased by 5%.

    e. Would you prefer to use the absorption form of income statement for the preceding analyses? Explain.

3. Discuss the desirability of alternatives a through d in requirement 2. If only one alternative could be selected, which would you choose? Explain.

BUSINESS FIRST   www.prenhall.com/phlip

4-50   Library Research and AT&T Corporation

AT&T Corporation was highlighted in the chapter-opening vignette on page 123. AT&T used the same approach as our chapter example Portland Power Company to implement activity-based management. A detailed description of AT&T's experience with ABM is given in the article, "Activity-Based Management at AT&T" by T. Hobdy, J. Thomson, and P. Sharman, *Management Accounting* (April 1994).

Required   Compare the approach to designing and implementing an ABC and ABM system described in the text (Portland Power Company) to that used by AT&T by answering the following questions.

1. At AT&T, how were "some billing costs" allocated to different customer classes (invoice types) prior to implementing the process modeling approach to ABC?

2. At AT&T, what business unit was selected for the pilot ABC project and what were the overall goals of the pilot study from the managers' perspective?

3. For AT&T, give examples of cost objects, activities, resources, and cost drivers.

4. For AT&T, "the cost of service support to these individual customers was determined by identifying *activity and driver consumption characteristics.*" For Portland Power's billing activity, describe what is meant by the cost consumption characteristics for the labor resource.

5. Exhibit 4-12 on page 141 shows the operations of the billing department at Portland Power Company. AT&T used a similar "flowchart." What function did it perform for AT&T?

6. At AT&T, "each cost object was costed by multiplying the quantity of driver units of each activity consumed by the cost per driver unit." Using the data from Exhibit 4-13, explain how this method applies to Portland Power Company for the residential customer class.

7. At AT&T, the ABC study revealed that "25% of total center costs were *assignable* to message investigation (account inquiry and correspondence)." For Portland Power Company, what is the percent of total billing department costs assigned to account inquiry investigation?

8. What process improvements were implemented at AT&T for the message investigation activity? ■

COLLABORATIVE LEARNING EXERCISE

4-51   Internet Research, ABC, and ABM

Form groups of from 3 to 5 persons each. Each member of the group should pick one of the following industries:

- Manufacturing
- Insurance
- Health care
- Government
- Service

Each person should explore the Internet for an example of a company that implemented activity-based costing and activity-based management. To do this, go to the following Internet cite—www.sapling.com/profiles.html, and choose one company from the industry chosen. Prepare and give a briefing for your group. Do this by completing the following:

1. Describe the company and its business.
2. What was the scope of the ABC/ABM project?
3. What were the goals for the ABC/ABM project?
4. Summarize the results of the project.

After each person has briefed the group on his/her company, discuss within your group the commonalities between the ABC/ABM applications.

5

Relevant Information & Decision Making: Marketing Decisions

The Grand Canyon Railway offers classic steam engine rides to the southern rim of the Grand Canyon. The train departs from the railway's Williams, Arizona depot for the 65-mile trip.

Learning Objectives

When you have finished studying this chapter, you should be able to

1   Discriminate between relevant and irrelevant information for making decisions.

2   Use the decision process to make business decisions.

3   Decide to accept or reject a special order using the contribution approach.

4   Decide to add or delete a product line using relevant information.

5   Compute a measure of product profitability when production is constrained by a scarce resource.

6   Discuss the factors that influence pricing decisions in practice.

7   Compute a target sales price by various approaches and compare the advantages and disadvantages of these approaches.

8   Use target costing to decide whether to add a new product.

9   **Understand how relevant information is used when making marketing decisions.**

While you are on vacation, the last thing you want to worry about is transportation. For visitors to Grand Canyon National Park, The Grand Canyon Railway provides a relaxing alternative to driving to the canyon. Why drive when you can sit back and enjoy the scenery across 65 miles of beautiful Arizona countryside from the comfort of a fully reconditioned steam engine? Strolling musicians serenade you, and western characters stage attacks and holdups that offer a glimpse into what train travel might have been like for old-west loggers, miners, and ranchers at the turn of the century. The Grand Canyon Railway thus offers a ride not only to the canyon itself but into the past as well.

Of course, rides into the past aren't exactly cheap. Tracks for the narrow-gauge train as well as the authentic steam engines and passenger cars cost an awful lot to buy new or to recondition. The company spent upwards of $20 million before opening in 1989. Recovering that initial investment while earning a profit is not easy. According to the company controller, Kevin Call, "Pricing is really the key in running a successful operation."

The railway offers five different classes of service, and choosing the pricing on each one determines the profit and return on investment the company's going to make. To set prices, management uses the contribution approach introduced in Chapter 4 and explained further in this chapter. Among the influences on pricing discussed in the chapter, costs and customer demands are the most important to the railway. The prices charged must not only ensure a reasonable profit but also must be attractive to the customer.

Costs are important in the marketing decisions of many types of companies. What price should a Safeway store charge for a pound of hamburger? What should Boeing charge for a 777 airplane? Should a clothing manufacturer accept a special discount order from Wal-Mart? Should an appliance manufacturer add a new product, say an automatic bread maker, to its product line? Or should an existing product be dropped? Marketing managers rely on accounting information to answer these questions and make important decisions on a daily basis. Without accounting information, it would be impossible for a firm to determine a marketing strategy. However, not all accounting information applies to each type of decision. In this chapter, we'll focus on identifying relevant information for marketing decisions. The ability to separate relevant from irrelevant information is often the difference between success and failure in modern business.[1]

THE CONCEPT OF RELEVANCE

Objective 1
Discriminate between relevant and irrelevant information for making decisions.

What information is relevant? That depends on the decision being made. Decision making essentially involves choosing among several courses of action. The available actions are determined by an often time-consuming formal or informal search and screening process, perhaps carried on by a company team that includes engineers, accountants, and operating executives. Accountants have an important role in the decision-making process, not as decision makers but as collectors and reporters of relevant information. (Although many managers want the accountant to recommend the proper decision, the final choice always rests with the operating executive.) The accountant's role in decision making is primarily that of a technical expert on financial analysis who helps managers focus on the relevant information that will lead to the best decision.

RELEVANCE DEFINED

relevant information The predicted future costs and revenues that will differ among alternative courses of action.

Making business decisions requires managers to compare two or more alternative courses of action. Accountants should use two criteria to determine if information is relevant: (1) it must be expected future revenue or cost, and (2) it must have an element of difference among the alternatives. **Relevant information** is the predicted future costs and revenues that will differ among the alternatives.

Note that relevant information is a prediction of the future, not a summary of the past. Historical (past) data have no *direct* bearing on a decision. Such data can have an *indirect* bearing on a decision because they may help in predicting the future. But past figures, in themselves, are irrelevant to the decision itself. Why? Because the decision cannot affect past data. Decisions affect the future. Nothing can alter what has already happened.

Of the expected future data, only those that will differ from alternative to alternative are relevant to the decision. Any item that will remain the same regardless of the alternative selected is irrelevant. For instance, if a department manager's salary will be the same regardless of the products stocked, the salary is irrelevant to the selection of products.

---

[1] *Throughout this and the next chapter, to concentrate on the fundamental ideas, we shall ignore the time value of money and income taxes (discussed in Chapter 11).*

EXAMPLES OF RELEVANCE

The following examples will help you clarify the sharp distinctions needed to discriminate between relevant and irrelevant information.

Suppose you always buy gasoline from either of two nearby gasoline stations. Yesterday you noticed that one station was selling gasoline at $1.50 per gallon. The other was selling at $1.40. Your automobile needs gasoline, and in making your choice of stations, you *assume* that these prices have not changed. The relevant costs are $1.50 and $1.40, the expected future costs that will differ between the alternatives. You use your past experience (that is, what you observed yesterday) for predicting today's price. Note that the relevant cost is not what you paid in the past, or what you observed yesterday, but what you expect to pay when you drive in to get gasoline. This cost meets our two criteria: (1) it is the expected future cost, and (2) it differs between the alternatives.

You may also plan to have your car lubricated. The recent price at each station was $12, and this is what you anticipate paying. This expected future cost is irrelevant because it will be the same under either alternative. It does not meet our second criterion.

On a business level, consider the following decision. A manufacturer is thinking of using aluminum instead of copper in making a line of ashtrays. The cost of direct material will decrease from 30¢ to 20¢ per ashtray.

The cost of copper used for this comparison probably came from historical cost records on the amount paid most recently for copper, but the *relevant* cost in the foregoing analysis is the expected future cost of copper compared with the expected future cost of aluminum.

The direct-labor cost will continue to be 70¢ per unit regardless of the material used. It is irrelevant because our second criterion—an element of difference between the alternatives—is not met.

	Aluminum	Copper	Difference
Direct material	$.20	$.30	$.10
Direct labor	.70	.70	—

Therefore we can safely exclude direct labor from the comparison of alternatives.

Exhibit 5-1 illustrates this simple decision, and it serves to show the appropriate framework for more complex decisions. Box 1(A) represents historical data from the accounting system. Box 1(B) represents other data, such as price indices or industry statistics, gathered from outside the accounting system. Regardless of their source, the data in step 1 help the formulation of *predictions* in step 2. (Remember that although historical data may act as a guide to predicting, they are irrelevant to the decision itself.)

Objective 2
Use the decision process to make business decisions.

In step 3 these predictions become inputs to the *decision model*. A **decision model** is any method used for making a choice. Such models sometimes require elaborate quantitative procedures, such as a petroleum refinery's mathematical method for choosing what products to manufacture for any given day or week. A decision model, however, may also be simple. It may be confined to a single comparison of costs for choosing between two materials. In this example our decision model is: Compare the predicted unit costs and select the alternative with the lesser cost.

decision model Any method for making a choice, sometimes requiring elaborate quantitative procedures.

We will be referring back to Exhibit 5-1 frequently because it illustrates the main concept in this chapter. In fact, this decision process applies to all business decisions, no matter how simple or complicated they may be. By using this process you will be able to focus squarely on the relevant information—the predicted future differences between alternatives—in any decision. In the rest of this chapter, we will use this decision process to apply the concept of relevance to several specific marketing decisions.

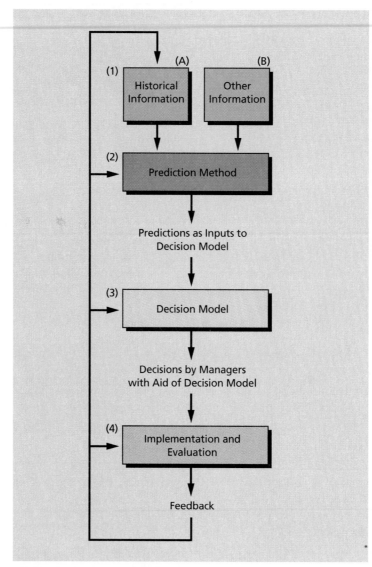

Exhibit 5-1

Decision Process and Role of Information

ACCURACY AND RELEVANCE

In the best of all possible worlds, information used for decision making would be perfectly relevant *and* accurate. However, in reality, such information is often too difficult or too costly to obtain. Accountants are thus forced to trade off relevance versus accuracy.

Precise but irrelevant information is worthless for decision making. For example, a university president's salary may be $140,000 per year, to the penny, but may have no bearing on the question of whether to buy or rent data processing equipment. However, imprecise but relevant information can be useful. For example, sales predictions for a new product may be subject to error, but they still are helpful to the decision of whether to manufacture the product. Of course, relevant information must be reasonably accurate but not precisely so.

The degree to which information is relevant or precise often depends on the degree to which it is *qualitative* or *quantitative*. Qualitative aspects are those for which measurement in dollars and cents is difficult and imprecise; quantitative aspects are those for which measurement is easy and precise. Accountants, statisticians, and mathematicians try to express as many decision factors as feasible in quantitative terms, because this approach reduces the number of qualitative factors to be judged. Just as we noted that relevance is more crucial than precision in decision making, so a qualitative aspect may easily carry more weight than a measurable (quantitative) financial impact in many decisions. For example, the extreme opposition of a militant union to new labor-saving machinery may cause a manager to not install such machinery even if it would save money. Alternatively, to avoid a long-run dependence on a particular supplier, a company may pass up the opportunity to purchase a component from the supplier at a price below the cost of producing it themselves.

Similarly, managers sometimes introduce new technology (for example, advanced computer systems or automated equipment) even though the expected quantitative results seem unattractive. Managers defend such decisions on the grounds that failure to keep abreast of new technology will surely bring unfavorable financial results sooner or later.

THE SPECIAL SALES ORDER

The first decision for which we examine relevant information is the special sales order.

ILLUSTRATIVE EXAMPLE

In our illustration we'll focus on our old friend, the Samson Company, from the previous chapter. Suppose 1 million units of product, such as some automobile replacement part, were made and sold. Under the absorption-costing approach, the unit manufacturing cost of the product would be $15,000,000 ÷ 1,000,000, or $15 per unit. Suppose a mail-order house near year-end offered Samson $13 per unit for a 100,000-unit special order that (1) would not affect Samson's regular business in any way, (2) would not raise any antitrust issues concerning price discrimination, (3) would not affect total fixed costs, (4) would not require any additional variable selling and administrative expenses, and (5) would use some otherwise idle manufacturing capacity. Should Samson accept the order? Perhaps the question should be stated more sharply: What is the difference in the short-run financial results between not accepting and accepting? As usual, the key question is: What are the differences between alternatives?

Exhibit 5-2 presents two income statements from Samson Company, one using the absorption approach (from Exhibit 4-8 in the previous chapter) and one using the contribution approach (from Exhibit 4-9 in the previous chapter). The difference in format between these two approaches may seem unimportant because the bottom line is the same in each. However, for decision-making purposes, we will need to choose the method that best tracks our relevant costs.

Objective 3
Decide to accept or reject a special order using the contribution approach.

Exhibit 5-2

Samson Company
Absorption and Contribution Forms of the Income Statement
Income Statement for the Year Ended December 31, 19X8 (thousands of dollars)

Absorption Form		Contribution Form		
Sales	$20,000	Sales		$20,000
Less: manufacturing cost		Less: variable expenses		
of goods sold	15,000	Manufacturing	$ 12,000	
Gross margin or gross profit	$ 5,000	Selling and		
Less: selling and admin-		administrative	1,100	13,100
istrative expenses	4,000	Contribution margin		$ 6,900
Operating income	$ 1,000	Less: fixed expenses		
		Manufacturing	$ 3,000	
		Selling and		
		administrative	2,900	5,900
		Operating income		$ 1,000

CORRECT ANALYSIS—FOCUS ON RELEVANT INFORMATION

The correct analysis focuses on determining relevant information and employs the contribution approach. As Exhibit 5-3 shows, only variable manufacturing costs are affected by the particular order, at a rate of $12 per unit. All other variable costs and all fixed costs are unaffected and thus irrelevant, so a manager may safely ignore them in making this special-order decision. Note how the contribution approach's distinction between variable- and fixed-cost behavior patterns aids the necessary cost analysis. Total short-run income will increase by $100,000 if the order is accepted—despite the fact that the unit selling price of $13 is less than the absorption manufacturing cost of $15. Why did we include fixed costs in Exhibit 5-3? After all, they are irrelevant. They were included because management wants to know the difference in short-run financial results between not accepting and accepting the special order. The analysis could have ended with the contribution margin line but we wanted to show how the difference will effect the "bottom line"—operating income. There will be occasions when irrelevant data will be included in the accountant's presentation of analysis. Why? To suit the preferences of managers who will use the information for decision making.

INCORRECT ANALYSIS—MISUSE OF UNIT COST

Faulty cost analysis sometimes occurs because of misinterpreting unit fixed costs. For instance, managers might erroneously use the $15 absorption manufacturing cost per unit to make the following prediction for the year:

Incorrect Analysis	Without Special Order 1,000,000 Units	Incorrect Effect of Special Order 100,000 Units	With Special Order 1,100,000 Units
Sales	$20,000,000	$1,300,000	$21,300,000
Less: manufacturing cost			
of goods sold @ $15	15,000,000	1,500,000	16,500,000
Gross margin	5,000,000	(200,000)	4,800,000
Selling and administrative			
expenses	4,000,000	—	4,000,000
Operating income	$ 1,000,000	$(200,000)	$ 800,000

The incorrect prediction of a $1.5 million increase in costs results from multiplying 100,000 units by $15. Of course, the fallacy in this approach is that it treats a fixed cost (fixed manufacturing cost) as if it were variable. Avoid the assumption that unit costs may be used indiscriminately as a basis for predicting how total costs will behave. Unit costs are useful for predicting variable costs but often misleading when used to predict fixed costs.

CONFUSION OF VARIABLE AND FIXED COSTS

Consider the relationship between total fixed manufacturing costs and a fixed manufacturing cost per unit of product:

$$\text{fixed cost per unit of product} = \frac{\text{total fixed manufacturing costs}}{\text{some selected volume level used as the denominator}}$$

$$= \frac{\$3,000,000}{1,000,000 \text{ units}} = \$3 \text{ per unit}$$

Exhibit 5-3

Samson Company
Comparative Predicted Income Statements, Contribution Approach
for Year Ended December 31, 19X2

	Without Special Order, 1,000,000 Units	Effect of Special Order 100,000 Units		With Special Order, 1,100,000 Units
		Total	*Per Unit*	
Sales	$20,000,000	$1,300,000	$13	$21,300,000
Less: variable expenses				
Manufacturing	$12,000,000	$1,200,000	$12	$13,200,000
Selling and administrative	1,100,000	—	—	1,100,000
Total variable expenses	$13,100,000	$1,200,000	$12	$14,300,000
Contribution margin	$ 6,900,000	$ 100,000	$ 1	$ 7,000,000
Less: fixed expenses				
Manufacturing	$ 3,000,000	—	—	$ 3,000,000
Selling and administrative	2,900,000	—	—	2,900,000
Total fixed expenses	$ 5,900,000	—	—	$ 5,900,000
Operating income	$ 1,000,000	$ 100,000	$ 1	$ 1,100,000

As noted in Chapter 2, the typical cost accounting system serves two purposes simultaneously: *planning and control* and *product costing.* The total fixed cost for *budgetary planning and control purposes* can be graphed as a lump sum:

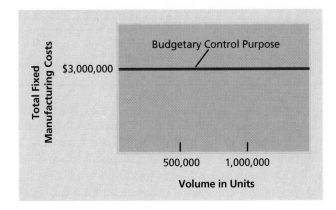

For *product-costing purposes,* however, the absorption-costing approach implies that these *fixed* costs have a *variable*-cost behavior pattern:

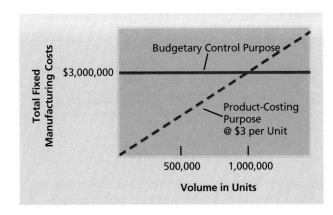

The addition of 100,000 units will not add any *total* fixed costs as long as total output is within the relevant range. The incorrect analysis, however, includes 100,000 × $3 = $300,000 of fixed cost in the predictions of increases in total costs.

In short, the increase in manufacturing costs should be computed by multiplying 1,000,000 units by $12, not by $15. The $15 includes a $3 component that will not affect the total manufacturing costs as volume changes.

ACTIVITY-BASED COSTING, SPECIAL ORDERS, AND RELEVANT COSTS

To identify relevant costs affected by a special order (or by other special decisions), more and more firms are going a step beyond simply identifying fixed and variable costs. As pointed out in Chapters 3 and 4, many different activities are associated with a company's operations. Businesses that have identified all their significant activities and related cost drivers can produce more detailed relevant information to predict the effects of special orders more accurately.

Suppose Samson Company examined its $12 million of variable costs very closely and identified two significant activities and related cost drivers: $9 million of processing activity that varies directly with *units produced* at a rate of $9 per unit and $3 million of setup activity that varies with the *number of production setups*. Normally, for processing 1,000,000 units, Samson has 500 setups at a cost of $6,000 per setup, with an average of 2,000 units processed for each setup. Additional sales generally require a proportional increase in the number of setups.

Now suppose the special order is for 100,000 units that vary only slightly in production specifications. Instead of the normal 50 setups, Samson will need only 5 setups, and processing 100,000 units will take only $930,000 of additional variable cost:

Additional unit-based variable cost, 100,000 × $9	$900,000
Additional setup-based variable cost, 5 × $6,000	30,000
Total additional variable cost	$930,000

Instead of the original estimate of 100,000 × $12 = $1,200,000 additional variable cost, the special order will cost only $930,000, or $270,000 less than the original estimate. Therefore, ABC allows managers to realize that the special order is $270,000 more profitable than predicted from the simple, unit-based assessment of variable cost.

A special order may also be more costly than predicted by a simple fixed- and variable-cost analysis. Suppose the 100,000-unit special order called for a variety of models and colors delivered at various times, so that 100 setups are required. The variable cost of the special order would be $1.5 million.

Additional unit-based variable cost, 100,000 × $9	$ 900,000
Additional setup-based variable cost, 100 × $6,000	600,000
Total additional variable cost	$1,500,000

SUMMARY PROBLEM FOR YOUR REVIEW

PROBLEM

1. Return to the basic illustration in Exhibit 5-3. Suppose Samson Co. received a special order for 250,000 units that had the following terms: selling price would

be $13.50 instead of $13.00, but a manufacturer's agent who had obtained the potential order would have to be paid a flat fee of $40,000 if the order were accepted. Should the special order be accepted?

2. What if the order was for 250,000 units at a selling price of $11.50 and there was no $40,000 agent's fee? Some managers have been known to argue for acceptance of such an order as follows: "Of course, we will lose $.50 each on the variable manufacturing costs, but we will gain $.60 per unit by spreading our fixed manufacturing costs over 1.25 million units instead of 1 million units. Consequently, we should take the offer because it represents an advantage of $.10 per unit."

Old fixed manufacturing cost per unit, $3,000,000 ÷ 1,000,000	$3.00
New fixed manufacturing cost per unit, $3,000,000 ÷ 1,250,000	2.40
"Saving" in fixed manufacturing cost per unit	$ .60
Loss on variable manufacturing cost per unit, $11.50 − $12.00	.50
Net saving per unit in manufacturing cost	$ .10

Explain why this is faulty thinking.

SOLUTION

1. Focus on relevant information—the *differences* in revenues and costs. In this problem, in addition to the difference in variable costs, there is a difference in fixed costs between the two alternatives.

Additional revenue, 100,000 units @ $13.50 per unit	$1,350,000
Less additional costs	
Variable costs, 100,000 units @ $12 per unit	1,200,000
Fixed costs, agent's fee	40,000
Increase in operating income from special order	$ 110,000

2. The faulty thinking comes from attributing a "savings" to the decrease in unit fixed costs. Regardless of how the fixed manufacturing costs are "unitized" or "spread" over the units produced, their *total* of $3 million will be *unchanged* by the special order. Remember, we have a negative contribution margin of $.50 per unit on this special order. Thus, there is no way we can cover any amount of fixed costs! Fixed costs are not relevant to this decision.

DELETION OR ADDITION OF PRODUCTS, SERVICES, OR DEPARTMENTS

Relevant information also plays an important role in decisions about adding or deleting products, services, or departments.

Objective 4
Decide to add or delete a product line using relevant information.

AVOIDABLE AND UNAVOIDABLE COSTS

Often existing businesses will want to expand or contract their operations to improve profitability. How can a manufacturer decide whether to add or drop products? The same way a retailer decides whether to add or drop departments: by examining all the relevant cost and revenue information. For example, consider a discount department store that has three major departments: groceries, general merchandise, and drugs. Management is considering dropping the grocery department, which has consistently shown an operating loss. The following table reports the store's present annual operating income (in thousands of dollars).

		Departments		
	Total	Groceries	General Merchandise	Drugs
Sales	$1,900	$1,000	$800	$100
Variable cost of goods sold and expenses*	1,420	800	560	60
Contribution margin	$ 480 (25%)	$ 200 (20%)	$240 (30%)	$ 40 (40%)
Fixed expenses (salaries, depreciation, insurance, property taxes, and so on):				
Avoidable	$ 265	$ 150	$100	$ 15
Unavoidable	180	60	100	20
Total fixed expenses	$ 445	$ 210	$200	$ 35
Operating income	$ 35	$ (10)	$ 40	$ 5

*Examples of variable expenses include paper shipping bags and sales commissions.

avoidable costs Costs that will not continue if an ongoing operation is changed or deleted.

unavoidable costs Costs that continue even if an operation is halted.

common costs Those costs of facilities and services that are shared by users.

Notice that the fixed expenses are divided into two categories, *avoidable* and *unavoidable*. **Avoidable costs**—costs that will *not* continue if an ongoing operation is changed or deleted—are relevant. In our example, avoidable costs include department salaries and other costs that could be eliminated by not operating the specific department. **Unavoidable costs**—costs that continue even if an operation is halted—are not relevant in our example because they are not affected by a decision to delete the department. Unavoidable costs include many **common costs,** which are those costs of facilities and services that are shared by users.[2] For example, store depreciation, heating, air conditioning, and general management expenses are costs of resources used by all departments. For our example, assume first that the only alternatives to be considered are dropping or continuing the grocery department, which shows a loss of $10,000. Assume further that the total assets invested would be unaffected by the decision. The vacated space would be idle, and the unavoidable costs would continue. Which alternative would you recommend? An analysis (in thousands of dollars) follows:

	Store as a Whole		
Income Statements	Total Before Change (a)	Effect of Dropping Groceries (b)	Total After Change (a) – (b)
Sales	$1,900	$1,000	$900
Variable expenses	1,420	800	620
Contribution margin	$ 480	$ 200	$280
Avoidable fixed expenses	265	150	115
Profit contribution to common space and other unavoidable costs	$ 215	$ 50	$165
Common space and other unavoidable costs	180	—	180
Operating income	$ 35	$ 50	$(15)

[2]*The concept of avoidable cost is used by government regulators as well as business executives. For example, Amtrak divides its costs into avoidable—costs that "would cease if the route were eliminated"—and fixed—costs that would "remain relatively constant if a single route were discontinued." The U.S. Interstate Commerce Commission then considers the avoidable costs when considering approval of a railroad's request to abandon a route. Similarly, the Canadian government looks at the avoidable cost when determining the amount of subsidy to give to the country's passenger-rail system. The Montreal Gazette reported that in 1993 revenues covered only 35% of the "$7 million in avoidable costs (costs that wouldn't exist if the train disappeared tomorrow—things like staff salaries, food, fuel, and upkeep of train stations)."*

The preceding analysis shows that matters would be worse, rather than better, if groceries were dropped and the vacated facilities left idle. In short, as the income statement shows, groceries bring in a contribution margin of $200,000, which is $50,000 more than the $150,000 fixed expenses that would be saved by closing the grocery department. The grocery department showed a loss in the first income statement because of the unavoidable fixed costs charged to it.

Of course, most companies do not like having space left idle, so perhaps the preceding example was a bit too basic. Assume now that the space made available by the dropping of groceries could be used to expand the general merchandise department. The space would be occupied by merchandise that would increase sales by $500,000, generate a 30% contribution-margin percentage, and have avoidable fixed costs of $70,000. The $80,000 increase in operating income of general merchandise more than offsets the $50,000 decline from eliminating groceries, providing an overall increase in operating income of $65,000 − $35,000 = $30,000.

| | **Effects of Changes** | | | |
| | Total Before Change (a) | Drop Groceries (b) | Expand General Merchandise (c) | Total After Changes (a) − (b) + (c) |
(In thousands of dollars)				
Sales	$1,900	$1,000	$500	$1,400
Variable expenses	1,420	800	350	970
Contribution margin	$ 480	$ 200	$150	$ 430
Avoidable fixed expenses	265	150	70	185
Contribution to common space and other unavoidable costs	$ 215	$ 50	$ 80	$ 245
Common space and other unavoidable costs*	180	—	—	180
Operating income	$ 35	$ 50	$ 80	$ 65

*Includes the $60,000 of former grocery fixed costs, which were allocations of unavoidable common costs that will continue regardless of how the space is occupied.

The purpose in deciding whether to add or drop new products, services, or departments is to obtain the greatest contribution possible to pay unavoidable costs. The unavoidable costs will remain the same regardless of any decision, so the key is picking the alternative that will contribute the most toward paying off these costs. The following analysis illustrates this concept for our example:

| | **Profit Contribution of Given Space (in thousands of dollars)** | | |
	Groceries	Expansion of General Merchandise	Difference
Sales	$1,000	$500	$500 U
Variable expenses	800	350	450 F
Contribution margin	$ 200	$150	$ 50 U
Avoidable fixed expenses	150	70	80 F
Contribution to common space and other unavoidable costs	$ 50	$ 80	$ 30 F

F = Favorable difference resulting from replacing groceries with general merchandise.
U = Unfavorable difference.

In our example, the general merchandise will not achieve the dollar sales volume that groceries will, but the higher contribution margin percentage and the lower wage costs (mostly because of the diminished need for stocking and checkout clerks) combine to produce a more favorable bottom line.

This example should show you that relevant costs are not always variable. In the special order decision, the relevant costs were the variable costs, which might have led you to believe that you should always ignore fixed costs and focus only on variable costs. However, the key to decision making is not relying on a hard and fast rule about what to ignore and what not to ignore. Rather, you need to analyze all pertinent cost and revenue data to determine what is and is not relevant. In this case, the relevant costs included the fixed avoidable costs.

OPTIMAL USE OF LIMITED RESOURCES

limiting factor (scarce resource) The item that restricts or constrains the production or sale of a product or service.

When a plant that makes more than one product is being operated at capacity, managers often must decide which orders to accept. The contribution approach also applies here, because the product to be emphasized or the order to be accepted is the one that makes the biggest *total* profit contribution per unit of the limiting factor. A **limiting factor** or **scarce resource** restricts or constrains the production or sale of a product or service. Limiting factors include labor-hours and machine-hours that limit production and hence sales in manufacturing firms, and square feet of floor space or cubic meters of display space that limit sales in department stores.

The contribution approach must be used wisely, however. Managers sometimes mistakenly favor those products with the biggest contribution margin or gross margin per sales dollar, without regard to scarce resources.

Assume that a company has two products: a plain cellular phone and a fancier cellular phone with many special features. Unit data follow:

	Plain Phone	Fancy Phone
Selling price	$80	$120
Variable costs	64	84
Contribution margin	$16	$ 36
Contribution-margin ratio	20%	30%

Objective 5
Compute a measure of product profitability when production is constrained by a scarce resource.

Which product is more profitable? On which should the firm spend its resources? The correct answer is: It depends. If sales are restricted by demand for only a limited *number* of phones, fancy phones are more profitable. Why? Because sale of a plain phone adds $16 to profit; sale of a fancy phone adds $36. Thus, if the limiting factor is *units* of sales, the more profitable product is the one with the higher contribution *per unit*.

Now suppose annual demand for phones of both types is more than the company can produce in the next year. Productive capacity is the limiting factor because only 10,000 hours of capacity are available. If in one hour plant workers can make either three plain phones or one fancy phone, the plain phone is more profitable. Why? Because it contributes more profit *per hour* of capacity:

	Plain Phone	Fancy Phone
1. Units per hour	3	1
2. Contribution margin per unit	$ 16	$ 36
Contribution margin per hour (1) × (2)	$ 48	$ 36
Total contribution for 10,000 hours	$480,000	$360,000

Exhibit 5-4

Effect of Turnover on Profit

	Regular Department Store	Discount Department Store
Retail price	$4.00	$3.50
Cost of merchandise and other variable costs	3.00	3.00
Contribution to profit per unit	$1.00 (25%)	$ .50 (14%)
Units sold per year	10,000	22,000
Total contribution to profit, assuming the same space allotment in both stores	$10,000	$11,000

As we said earlier, the criterion for maximizing profits when one factor limits sales is to obtain the greatest possible contribution to profit for each unit of the limiting or scarce factor. However, the product that is most profitable when one particular factor limits sales may be the least profitable if a different factor restricts sales.

In retail sales, the limiting resource is often floor space. Thus, retail stores must either focus on products taking up less space or using the space for shorter periods of time— greater **inventory turnover** (number of times the average inventory is sold per year). Consider an example of two department stores. The conventional gross profit percentage (gross profit ÷ selling price) is an insufficient clue to profitability because, as we said, profits depend on the space occupied and the inventory turnover. Discount department stores such as Wal-Mart, Target, and Kmart have succeeded while using lower markups than traditional department stores because they have been able to increase turnover and thus increase the contribution to profit per unit of space. Exhibit 5-4 illustrates the same product, taking up the same amount of space, in each of two stores. The contribution margins per unit and per sales dollar are less in the discount store, but faster turnover makes the same product a more profitable use of space in the discount store. In general, retail companies seek faster inventory turnover. A survey of retail shoe stores showed that those with above-average financial performance had an inventory turnover of 2.6 times per year compared to an industry average of 2.0.

> **inventory turnover** The number of times the average inventory is sold per year.

PRICING DECISIONS

One of the major decisions managers face is pricing. Actually, pricing can take many forms. Among the many pricing decisions to be made are:

1. Setting the price of a new or refined product
2. Setting the price of products sold under private labels
3. Responding to a new price of a competitor
4. Pricing bids in both sealed and open bidding situations

Pricing decisions are so important, in fact, that we will spend the rest of the chapter discussing the many aspects of pricing. Let us now take a look at some of the basic concepts behind pricing.

THE CONCEPT OF PRICING

Pricing decisions depend on the characteristics of the market a firm faces. In **perfect competition,** all competing firms sell the same type of product at the same price. Thus, a firm can sell as much of a product as it can produce, all at a single market price. If it charges more, no

> **perfect competition** A market in which a firm can sell as much of a product as it can produce, all at a single market price.

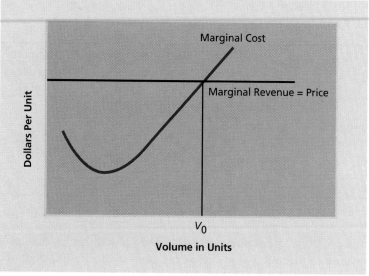

Exhibit 5-5

Marginal Revenue and Cost in Perfect Competition

customer will buy. If it charges less, it sacrifices profits. Therefore, every firm in such a market will charge the market price, and the only decision for managers is how much to produce.

Although costs do not directly influence prices in perfect competition, they do affect the production decision. Consider the *marginal cost curve* in Exhibit 5-5. The **marginal cost** is the additional cost resulting from producing and selling one additional unit. The marginal cost often decreases as production increases up to a point because of efficiencies created by larger amounts. At some point, however, marginal costs begin to rise with increases in production because facilities begin to be overcrowded or overused, resulting in inefficiencies.

Exhibit 5-5 also includes a *marginal revenue curve*. The **marginal revenue** is the additional revenue resulting from the sale of an additional unit. In perfect competition, the marginal revenue curve is a horizontal line equal to the price per unit at all volumes of sales.

As long as the marginal cost is less than the marginal revenue (price), additional production and sales are profitable. When marginal cost exceeds price, however, the firm loses money on each additional unit. Therefore, the profit-maximizing volume is the quantity at which marginal cost equals price. In Exhibit 5-5, the firm should produce V_0 units. Producing fewer units passes up profitable opportunities and producing more units reduces profit because each additional unit costs more to produce than it generates in revenue.

In **imperfect competition,** the price a firm charges for a unit will influence the quantity of units it sells. At some point, the firm must reduce prices to generate additional sales. Exhibit 5-6 contains a demand curve (also called the average revenue curve) for imperfect competition that shows the volume of sales at each possible price. To sell additional units, the price of *all units sold* must be reduced. Therefore, the marginal revenue curve, also shown in Exhibit 5-6, is below the demand curve. That is, the marginal revenue for selling one additional unit is less than the price at which it is sold because the price of all other units falls as well. For example, suppose 10 units can be sold for $50 per unit. The price must be dropped to $49 per unit to sell 11 units, to $48 to sell 12 units, and to $47 to sell 13 units. The fourth column of Exhibit 5-7 shows the marginal revenue for units 11 through 13. Notice that the marginal revenue decreases as volume increases.

To estimate marginal revenue, managers must predict the effect of price changes on sales volume, which is called **price elasticity.** If small price increases cause large volume declines, demand is highly *elastic.* If prices have little or no effect on volume, demand is highly *inelastic.*

marginal cost The additional cost resulting from producing and selling one additional unit.

marginal revenue The additional revenue resulting from the sale of an additional unit.

imperfect competition A market in which the price a firm charges for a unit will influence the quantity of units it sells.

price elasticity The effect of price changes on sales volume.

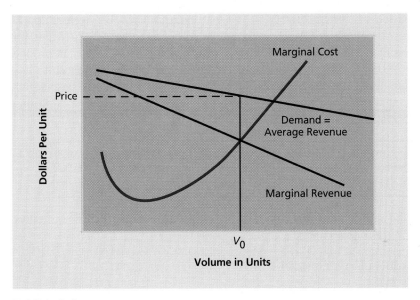

Exhibit 5-6

Marginal Revenue and Cost in Imperfect Competition

Exhibit 5-7

Profit Maximization in Imperfect Competition

Units Sold	Price per Unit	Total Revenue	Marginal Revenue	Marginal Cost	Profit from Production and Sale of Additional Unit
10	$50	10 × $50 = $500			
11	49	11 × 49 = 539	$539 − $500 = $39	$35	$39 − $35 = $4
12	48	12 × 48 = 576	576 − 539 = 37	36	37 − 36 = 1
13	47	13 × 47 = 611	611 − 576 = 35	37	35 − 37 = (2)

For the marginal costs shown in the fifth column of Exhibit 5-7, the optimal production and sales level would be 12 units. The last column of that exhibit illustrates that the 11th unit adds $4 to profit, and the 12th adds $1, but production and sale of the 13th unit would *decrease* profit by $2. In general, firms should produce and sell units until the marginal revenue equals the marginal cost, represented by volume V_0 in Exhibit 5-6. The optimal price charged will be the amount that creates a demand for V_0 units.

Notice that the *marginal cost* is relevant for pricing decisions. In managerial accounting, marginal cost is essentially the *variable cost*. What is the major difference between marginal cost and variable cost? Variable cost is assumed to be constant within a relevant range of volume, whereas marginal cost may change with each unit produced. Within large ranges of production volume, however, changes in marginal cost are often small. Therefore, using variable cost can be a reasonable approximation to marginal cost in many situations.

PRICING AND ACCOUNTING

Accountants seldom compute marginal revenue curves and marginal cost curves. Instead, they use estimates based on judgment to predict the effects of additional production and sales on profits. In addition, they examine selected volumes, not the whole range of possible volumes. Such simplifications are justified because the cost of a more sophisticated analysis would exceed the benefits.

Consider a division of General Electric (GE) that makes microwave ovens. Suppose market researchers estimate that 700,000 ovens can be sold if priced at $200 per unit, but 1,000,000 could be sold at $180. The variable cost of production is $130 per unit at production levels of both 700,000 and 1,000,000. Both volumes are also within the relevant range so that fixed costs are unaffected by the changes in volume. Which price should be charged?

GE's accountant would determine the relevant revenues and costs. The additional revenue and additional costs of the 300,000 additional units of sales at the $180 price:

Additional revenue: (1,000,000 × $180) − (700,000 × $200) =	$40,000,000
− Additional costs: 300,000 × $130 =	39,000,000
Additional profit:	$ 1,000,000

Alternatively, the accountant could compare the total contribution for each alternative:

Contribution at $180: ($180 − $130) × 1,000,000 =	$50,000,000
Contribution at $200: ($200 − $130) × 700,000 =	49,000,000
Difference:	$ 1,000,000

Notice that comparing the total contributions is essentially the same as computing the additional revenues and costs—both use the same relevant information. Further, both approaches correctly ignore fixed costs, which are unaffected by this pricing decision.

GENERAL INFLUENCES ON PRICING IN PRACTICE

Objective 6
Discuss the factors that influence pricing decisions in practice.

Several factors interact to shape the market in which managers make pricing decisions. Legal requirements, competitors' actions, and customer demands all influence pricing.

LEGAL REQUIREMENTS

Pricing decisions must be made within constraints imposed by U.S. and international laws. These laws are generally aimed at protecting consumers, but they also help protect other companies from *predatory* and *discriminatory* pricing.

predatory pricing
Establishing prices so low that competitors are driven out of the market. The predatory pricer then has no significant competition and can raise prices dramatically.

Predatory pricing involves establishing prices so low that competitors are driven out of the market. The predatory pricer then has no significant competition and can raise prices dramatically. For example, Wal-Mart has been accused of predatory pricing—selling at low cost to drive out local competitors (in a 4-to-3 vote, the court ruled in favor of Wal-Mart). U.S. courts have generally ruled that pricing is predatory only if companies set prices below their average variable cost and actually lose money in order to drive their competitors out of business.

discriminatory pricing
Charging different prices to different customers for the same product or service.

Discriminatory pricing is charging different prices to different customers for the same product or service. For example, a large group of retail druggists and big drugstore chains sued several large drug companies, alleging that their practice of allowing discounts to mail-order drug companies, health maintenance organizations, and other managed-care entities constitutes discriminatory pricing. The discounts were as large as 40%. However, pricing is not discriminatory if it reflects a cost differential incurred in providing the good or service. A tentative settlement to the $600 million class action suit was reached but it did not require the drug companies to alter their pricing practices.

COMPETITORS' ACTIONS

Competitors usually react to the price changes of their rivals. Many companies will gather information regarding a rival's capacity, technology, and operating policies. In this way, managers make more informed predictions of competitors' reactions to a company's prices. The study of game theory, for which two economists won the 1994 Nobel Prize, focuses on predicting and reacting to competitors' actions.

Tinkering with prices is often most heavily affected by the price setter's expectations of competitors' reactions and of the overall effects on the total industry demand for the good or service in question. For example, an airline might cut prices even if it expects price cuts from its rivals, hoping that total customer demand for the tickets of all airlines will increase sufficiently to offset the reduction in the price per ticket.

Competition is becoming increasingly international. Overcapacity in some countries often causes aggressive pricing policies, particularly for a company's exported goods.

CUSTOMER DEMANDS

More than ever before, managers are recognizing the needs of customers. Pricing is no exception. If customers believe a price is too high, they may turn to other sources for the product or service, substitute a different product, or decide to produce the item themselves.

ROLE OF COSTS IN PRICING DECISIONS

The influence of accounting on pricing is through costs. The exact role costs play in pricing decisions depends on both the market conditions and the company's approach to pricing. Two pricing approaches used by companies are cost-plus pricing and target costing.

COST-PLUS PRICING

Many managers say that their prices are set by *cost-plus pricing*. For example, Grand Canyon Railway sets its prices by computing an average cost and then adding a desired **markup** (that is, the amount by which price exceeds cost) that will generate a target return on investment. The key, however, is the "plus" in cost plus. Instead of being a fixed markup, the "plus" will usually depend on both costs and the demands of customers. For example, the railway has a standard (rack rate) price that does not change during the year, but the company does offer discounts during the slow winter season.

markup The amount by which price exceeds cost.

Prices are most directly related to costs in industries where revenue is based on cost reimbursement. Cost-reimbursement contracts generally specify how costs should be measured and what costs are allowable. For example, only coach-class (not first-class) fares are reimbursable for business air travel on government projects, such as defense contracts.

Ultimately, though, the market sets prices. Why? Because the price as set by a cost-plus formula is inevitably adjusted "in light of market conditions." The maximum price that may be charged is the one that does not drive the customer away. The minimum price might be considered to be zero (for example, companies may give out free samples to gain entry into a market). A more practical guide is that, in the short run, the minimum price to be quoted, subject to consideration of long-run effects, should be equal to the costs that may be avoided by not landing the order—often all variable costs of producing, selling, and distributing the good or service. In the long run, the price must be high enough to cover all costs, including fixed costs.

COST BASES FOR COST-PLUS PRICING

Cost plus is often the basis for target prices. The size of the "plus" depends on target (desired) operating incomes. Target prices can be based on a host of different markups, that are in turn based on a host of different definitions of cost. Thus, there are many ways to arrive at the *same target price*.

Exhibit 5-8 displays the relationships of costs to target selling prices, assuming a target operating income of $1 million. The percentages there represent four popular markup

Objective 7
Compute a target sales price by various approaches and compare the advantages and disadvantages of these approaches.

Exhibit 5-8

Relationships of Costs to Same Target Selling Prices

		Alternative Markup Percentages to Achieve Same Target Sales Prices
Target sales price	$20.00	
Variable costs		
(1) Manufacturing	$12.00*	($20.00 − $12.00) ÷ $12.00 = 66.67%
Selling and administrative[†]	1.10	
(2) Unit variable costs	$13.10	($20.00 − $13.10) ÷ $13.10 = 52.67%
Fixed costs:		
Manufacturing	$ 3.00*	
Selling and administrative	2.90	
Unit fixed costs	$ 5.90	
(3) Full costs	$19.00	($20.00 − $19.00) ÷ $19.00 = 5.26%
Target operating income	$ 1.00	

*(4) A frequently used formula is based on absorption costs:
[$20.00 − ($12.00 + $3.00)] ÷ $15.00 = 33.33%.
[†]Selling and administrative costs includes costs of value-chain functions other than production.

formulas for pricing: (1) as a percentage of variable manufacturing costs, (2) as a percentage of total variable costs, (3) as a percentage of full costs, and (4) as a percentage of absorption costs.

full cost (fully allocated cost) The total of all manufacturing costs plus the total of all selling and administrative costs.

Note particularly that **full cost** or **fully allocated cost** means the total of all manufacturing costs plus the total of all selling and administrative costs. As noted in earlier chapters, we use "selling and administrative" to include value-chain functions other than production. Of course, the percentages differ. For instance, the markup on variable manufacturing costs is 66.67%, and on absorption costs it is 33.33%. Regardless of the formula used, the pricing decision maker will be led toward the same target price. For a volume of 1 million units, assume that the target selling price is $20 per unit. If the decision maker is unable to obtain such a price consistently, the company will not achieve its $1 million operating income objective.

We have seen that prices can be based on various types of cost information, from variable costs to absorption costs to full costs. Each of these costs can be relevant to the pricing decision. Each approach has advantages and disadvantages.

ADVANTAGES OF CONTRIBUTION APPROACH IN COST-PLUS PRICING

Prices based on variable costs represent a contribution approach to pricing. When used intelligently, the contribution approach has some advantages over the absorption-costing and full-cost approaches, because the latter two often fail to highlight different cost behavior patterns.

Obviously, the contribution approach offers more detailed information because it displays variable- and fixed-cost behavior patterns separately. Because the contribution approach is sensitive to cost-volume-profit relationships, it is a helpful basis for developing pricing formulas. As a result, this approach allows managers to prepare price schedules at different volume levels.

The correct analysis in Exhibit 5-9 shows how changes in volume affect operating income. The contribution approach helps managers with pricing decisions by readily displaying the interrelationships among variable costs, fixed costs, and potential changes in selling prices.

In contrast, target pricing with absorption costing or full costing presumes a given volume level. When volume changes, the unit cost used at the original planned volume may mislead managers. As our preceding "incorrect analysis" example showed, managers

Exhibit 5-9

Analyses of Effects of Changes in Volume on Operating Income

	Correct Analysis			Incorrect Analysis		
Volume in units	900,000	1,000,000	1,100,000	900,000	1,000,000	1,100,000
Sales @ $20.00	$18,000,000	$20,000,000	$22,000,000	$18,000,000	$20,000,000	$22,000,000
Unit variable costs @ $13.10*	11,790,000	13,100,000	14,410,000			
Contribution margin	6,210,000	6,900,000	7,590,000			
Fixed costs[†]	5,900,000	5,900,000	5,900,000			
Full costs @ $19.00*				17,100,000	19,000,000	20,900,000
Operating income	$ 310,000	$ 1,000,000	$ 1,690,000	$ 900,000	$ 1,000,000	$ 1,100,000

*From Exhibit 5-8.

[†]Fixed manufacturing costs	$3,000,000
Fixed selling and administrative costs	2,900,000
Total fixed costs	$5,900,000

sometimes erroneously assume that the change in total costs may be computed by multiplying any change in volume by the full unit cost.

The incorrect analysis in Exhibit 5-9 shows how managers may be misled if the $19 full cost per unit is used to predict effects of volume changes on operating income. Suppose a manager uses the $19 figure to predict an operating income of $900,000 if the company sells 900,000 instead of 1,000,000 units. If actual operating income is $310,000 instead, as the correct analysis predicts, that manager may be stunned—and possibly looking for a new job.

The contribution approach also offers insight into the short-run versus long-run effects of cutting prices on special orders. For example, assume the same cost behavior patterns as in the Samson Co. example in Exhibit 5-3 (page 171). The 100,000-unit order added $100,000 to operating income at a selling price of $13, which was $7 below the target selling price of $20 and $2 below the absorption manufacturing cost of $15. Given all the stated assumptions, accepting the order appeared to be the better choice. As you saw earlier, the relevant information was more easily generated by the contribution approach. Consider the contribution and absorption-costing approaches:

	Contribution Approach	Absorption-Costing Approach
Sales, 100,000 units @ $13	$1,300,000	$1,300,000
Variable manufacturing costs @ $12	1,200,000	
Absorption manufacturing costs @ $15		1,500,000
Apparent change in operating income	$ 100,000	($ 200,000)

Under the absorption approach, the offer is definitely unattractive because the price of $13 is $2 below absorption costs.

Under the contribution approach, the decision maker sees a short-run advantage of $100,000 from accepting the offer. Fixed costs will be unaffected by whatever decision is made and operating income will increase by $100,000. Still, there often are long-run effects to consider. Will acceptance of the offer undermine the long-run price structure? In other words, is the short-run advantage of $100,000 more than offset by highly probable long-run financial disadvantages? The decision maker may think so and may reject the offer. But— and this is important—by doing so the decision maker is, in effect, forgoing $100,000 now to protect certain long-run market advantages. Generally, the decision maker can assess problems of this sort by asking whether the probability of long-run benefits is worth an "investment" equal to the forgone contribution margin ($100,000 in this case). Under absorption approaches, the decision maker must ordinarily conduct a special study to find the immediate effects. Under the contribution approach, the manager has a system that will routinely and more surely provide such information.

ADVANTAGES OF ABSORPTION-COST OR FULL-COST APPROACHES IN COST-PLUS PRICING

Frequently, managers do not employ a contribution approach because they fear that variable costs will be substituted indiscriminately for full costs and will therefore lead to suicidal price cutting. This problem should *not* arise if the data are used wisely. However, if top managers perceive a pronounced danger of underpricing when variable-cost data are revealed, they may justifiably prefer an absorption-cost approach or a full-cost approach for guiding pricing decisions.

Actually, absorption costs or full costs are far more widely used in practice than is the contribution approach. Why? In addition to the reasons already mentioned, managers have cited the following reasons:

1. In the long run, all costs must be recovered to stay in business. Sooner or later fixed costs do indeed fluctuate as volume changes. Therefore it is prudent to assume that all costs are variable (even if some are fixed in the short run).

2. Computing target prices based on cost plus may indicate what competitors might charge, especially if they have approximately the same level of efficiency as you and also aim at recovering all costs in the long run.

3. Absorption-cost or full-cost formula pricing meets the cost-benefit test. It is too expensive to conduct individual cost-volume tests for the many products (sometimes thousands) that a company offers.

4. There is much uncertainty about the shape of the demand curves and the correct price-output decisions. Absorption-cost or full-cost pricing copes with this uncertainty by not encouraging managers to take too much marginal business.

5. Absorption-cost or full-cost pricing tends to promote price stability. Managers prefer price stability because it eases their professional lives, primarily because planning is more dependable.

6. Absorption-cost pricing or full-cost pricing provides the most defensible basis for justifying prices to all interested parties including government antitrust investigators.

7. Absorption-cost or full-cost pricing provides convenient reference (target) points to simplify hundreds or thousands of pricing decisions.

USING MULTIPLE APPROACHES

To say that either a contribution approach or an absorption-cost approach or a full-cost approach provides the "best" guide to pricing decisions is a dangerous oversimplification of one of the most perplexing problems in business. Lack of understanding and judgment can lead to unprofitable pricing regardless of the kind of cost data available or cost accounting system used.

Basically, no single method of pricing is always best. An interview study of executives reported that companies often use *both* full-cost and variable-cost information in pricing decisions: "The full-vs.-variable-cost pricing controversy is not one of either black or white. The companies we studied used both approaches."[3]

---

[3]*T. Bruegelmann, G. Haessly, C. Wolfangel, and M. Schiff, "How Variable Costing is Used in Pricing Decisions,"* Management Accounting, *Vol. 65, no. 10, p. 65.*

The history of accounting reveals that most companies' systems have gathered costs via some form of full-manufacturing-cost system because this is what is required for financial reporting. In recent years, when systems have changed, variable costs and fixed costs were often identified. But managers have regarded this change as an addition to the existing full-manufacturing-cost system. That is, many managers insist on having information regarding both variable costs per unit and the allocated fixed costs per unit before setting selling prices. If the accounting system routinely gathers data regarding both variable and fixed costs, such data can readily be provided. However, most absorption-costing systems in practice do not organize their data collection so as to distinguish between variable and fixed costs. As a result, special studies or educated guessing must be used to designate costs as variable or fixed.

Managers are especially reluctant to focus on variable costs and ignore allocated fixed costs when their performance evaluations, and possibly their bonuses, are based on income shown in published financial statements. Why? Because such statements are based on absorption costing and thus are affected by allocations of fixed costs.

FORMATS FOR PRICING

Exhibit 5-8 showed how to compute alternative general markup percentages that would produce the same selling prices if used day after day. In practice, the format and arithmetic of quote sheets, job proposals, or similar records vary considerably.

Exhibit 5-10 is from an actual quote sheet used by the manager of a small job shop that bids on welding machinery orders in a highly competitive industry. The Exhibit 5-10 approach is a tool for informed pricing decisions. Notice that the *maximum* price is not a matter of cost at all. It is what you think you can obtain. The *minimum* price is the total variable cost.

Of course, the manager will rarely bid the minimum price. Businesses do need to make a profit. Still, the manager wants to know the effect of a job on the company's total variable costs. Occasionally, a company will bid near that minimum price to establish a presence in new markets or with a new customer.

Note that Exhibit 5-10 classifies costs especially for the pricing task. Pricing decisions may be made by more than one person. The accountant's responsibility is to prepare an understandable format that involves a minimum of computations. Exhibit 5-10 combines direct labor and variable manufacturing overhead. All fixed costs, whether manufacturing, selling, or administrative, are lumped together and applied to the job using a single fixed-overhead rate per direct-labor-hour. Obviously, if more accuracy is desired, many more detailed cost items and overhead rates could be formulated. To obtain the desired accuracy, many companies are turning to activity-based costing.

Exhibit 5-10
Quote Sheet for Pricing

Direct materials, at cost	$25,000
Direct labor and variable manufacturing overhead, 600 direct-labor-hours × $30	18,000
Sales commission (varies with job)	2,000
Total variable costs—minimum price*	45,000
Add fixed costs allocated to job, 600 direct-labor-hours × $20	12,000
Total costs	57,000
Add desired markup	30,000
Selling price—maximum price that you think you can obtain*	$87,000

*This sheet shows two prices, maximum and minimum. Any amount you can get above the minimum price is a contribution margin.

Some managers, particularly in construction and service industries such as auto repair, compile separate categories of costs of (1) direct materials, parts, and supplies and (2) direct labor. These managers then use different markup rates for each category. These rates are developed to provide revenue for both related overhead costs and operating profit. For example, an automobile repair shop might have the following format for each job:

	Billed to Customers
Auto parts ($200 cost plus 40% markup)	$280
Direct labor (Cost is $20 per hour. Bill at 300% to recover overhead and provide for operating profit. Billing rate is $20 × 300% = $60 per hour. Total billed for 10 hours is $60 × 10 = $600)	600
Total billed to customer	$880

Another example is an Italian printing company in Milan that wants to price its jobs so that each one generates a margin of 28% of revenues—14% to cover selling and administrative expenses and 14% for profit. To achieve this margin, the manager uses a pricing formula of 140% times predicted materials cost plus 25,000 Italian Lira (abbreviated Lit.) per hour of production time. The latter covers labor and overhead costs of Lit. 18,000 per hour. For a product with Lit.400,000 of materials cost and 30 hours of production time, the price would be Lit.1,310,000:

	Cost	Price	Profit
Materials	Lit. 400,000	Lit. 560,000	Lit. 160,000
Labor and overhead	540,000	750,000	210,000
Total	Lit. 940,000	Lit. 1,310,000	Lit. 370,000

The profit of Lit.370,000 is approximately 40% of the cost of Lit.940,000 and 28% of the price of Lit.1,310,000.

Thus there are numerous ways to compute selling prices. However, some general words of caution are appropriate here. Managers are better able to understand their options and the effects of their decisions on profits if they know their costs. That is, it is more informative to pinpoint costs first, before adding markups, than to have a variety of markups already embedded in the "costs" used as guides for setting selling prices. For example, if materials cost $1,000, they should be shown on a price quotation guide at $1,000, not at, say, a marked-up $1,400 because that is what the seller hopes to get.

TARGET COSTING

Consider the situation when a company is deciding whether to develop and market a *new product*. In evaluating the feasibility of the new product, management must determine both the price it can charge and the expected cost. As we have seen, both the price and cost of the new product are affected by market conditions and actions of management. The degree that price and cost can be affected by management actions determines the most effective approach to use for pricing and cost management purposes. Cost-plus pricing is used for products where management actions (for example, advertising) can influence the market price. Although cost management is important in this case, there is a strong focus on marketing and the revenue side of the profit equation.

But what if the market conditions are such that management cannot influence prices? If management's desired profit is to be achieved, the company must then focus on the product's cost. What management needs is an effective tool to reduce costs without reducing value to the customer. Many companies faced with this situation are adopting target costing. **Target costing** is a cost management tool for making cost reduction a key focus throughout the life of a product. A desired, or target, cost is set before the product is created or even designed. Managers must then try to reduce and control costs so that the product's cost does not exceed its target cost. Target costing is most effective at reducing costs during the product design phase when the vast majority of costs are committed. For example, the costs of resources such as new machinery, materials, parts, and even future refinements are largely determined by the design of the product and the associated production processes. These costs are not easily reduced once production begins. So, the emphasis of target costing is on proactive, up-front planning throughout every activity of the new product *development* process.

target costing A cost management tool for making cost a key focus throughout the life of a product.

TARGET COSTING AND NEW PRODUCT DEVELOPMENT

Exhibit 5-11 shows the target costing process for a new product. Based on the existing technology and related cost structure, the product has three parts, requires direct labor, and has four types of indirect costs. The first step in the target costing process is the determination of market price. This price is set by the market. Management sets the gross margin for the new product. The difference between the gross margin and the market price is the target cost for the new product. The existing cost structure for the product is determined by building up costs on an individual component level. This product has two components. Component 1 consists of parts A and B. Component 2 consists of part C. Direct labor is needed for both components and final assembly. The indirect costs are associated with activities necessary to plan and process the product.

Marketing might appear to have a limited role in target costing because the price is set by competitive market conditions. Actually, market research from the marketing department at the beginning of the target costing activity guides the whole product development

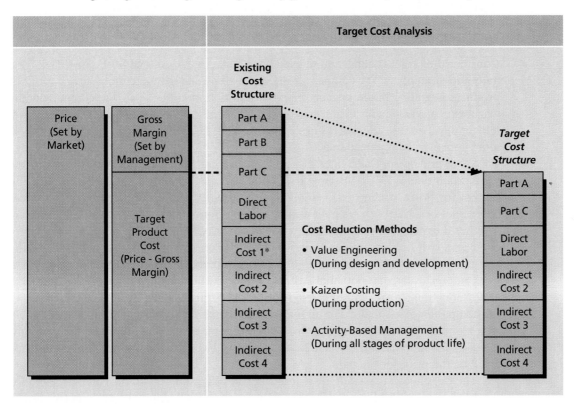

*Each indirect cost is associated with an indirect activity. Indirect Cost 1 was eliminated in the cost reduction process.

Exhibit 5-11

The Target Costing Process

process by supplying information on customer demands and requirements. In fact, one of the key characteristics of successful target costing is a strong emphasis on understanding customer demands

In the example in Exhibit 5-11, the existing cost is too large to generate the desired profit. Does this mean that the new product is not feasible? Not necessarily. A cross-functional team consisting of engineers, sales personnel, and accountants now must determine if cost reductions can be implemented that will reduce the costs enough to meet the target cost.

In the example in Exhibit 5-11, in the target cost structure, the cost of parts was reduced by changing the design of the product so that part C could be used in place of part B. Suppliers of parts A and C were also asked to reduce their costs. Design and process engineers were also able to eliminate the activity, generating the first type of indirect cost. These cost reductions resulted from **value engineering**—a cost-reduction technique, used primarily during the design stage, that uses information about all value-chain functions to satisfy customer needs while reducing costs. In total, the planned cost reductions were adequate to reduce costs to the target. However, not all the reductions in cost take place before production begins. **Kaizen costing** is the Japanese word for continuous improvement during manufacturing. How is kaizen costing applied? Kaizen goals are established each year as part of the planning process. Examples include the continual reduction in setup times and processing times due to employee experience. In total, target costing during design and kaizen costing during manufacturing enables the achievement of the target cost over the product's life.

Underlying these cost-reduction methods is the need for accurate cost information. Activity-based costing provides this information. Activity-based management (ABM) is then used to identify and eliminate non-value-added activities, waste, and their related costs. ABM is applied throughout both the design and manufacturing stages of the product's life.

ILLUSTRATION OF TARGET COSTING

Consider the target-costing system used by ITT Automotive—one of the world's largest automotive suppliers. The company designs, develops, and manufactures a broad range of products, including brake systems, electric motors, and lamps. Also, the company is the worldwide market leader in anti-lock braking systems (ABS), producing 20,000 such systems a day. Because these ABS are computerized, ITT Automotive actually ships 30% more computers daily than does Compaq!

What pricing approach does ITT Automotive use for the ABS? The pricing process starts when one of ITT's customers, say Mercedes-Benz, sends an invitation to bid. The market for brake systems is so competitive that very little variance exists in the prices companies can ask (bid). A target costing group is formed and charged with determining whether the price and costs allow for enough of a profit margin. This group is made up of engineers, cost accountants, and sales personnel. Factors considered in determining the feasibility of earning the desired target profit margin include competitor pricing, inflation rates, interest rates, and potential cost reductions during both the design (target costing) and production stages (kaizen costing) of the ABS product life. ITT purchases many of the component parts that make up the ABS. Thus, the target costing group works closely with suppliers. After product and process design improvements are made and commitments from suppliers are received, the company has the cost information needed for deciding the price for the bid.

The target-costing system has worked well at ITT Automotive. The company's bid for the ABS resulted in Mercedes-Benz U.S. International selecting ITT Automotive as the developer and supplier of ABS for the automaker's M-Class All-Activity Vehicle.[4]

---

[4] Sources: G. Schmeize, R. Greier, and E. Buttross, "Target Costing at ITT Automotive," Management Accounting, December 1996, pp. 26–30; News release, ITT Automotive, August 6, 1996, Auburn Hills, Mich.

value engineering A cost-reduction technique, used primarily during design, that uses information about all value-chain functions to satisfy customer needs while reducing costs.

kaizen costing The Japanese word for continuous improvement during manufacturing.

SOLUTION

The purpose of this problem is to emphasize that many different approaches to pricing might be used that, properly employed, would achieve the same target selling prices. To achieve $250,000 of profit, the desired revenue for 19X9 is $1,250,000 + $250,000 = $1,500,000. The target markup percentages are

1. Percent of prime cost $= \dfrac{(\$1,500,000 - \$600,000)}{(\$600,000)} = 150\%$

2. Percent of variable production cost of jobs $= \dfrac{(\$1,500,000 - \$900,000)}{(\$900,000)} = 66.7\%$

3. Percent of total production cost of jobs $= \dfrac{(\$1,500,000 - \$1,050,000)}{(\$1,050,000)} = 42.9\%$

4. Percent of all variable costs $= \dfrac{(\$1,500,000 - \$975,000)}{(\$975,000)} = 53.8\%$

5. Percent of all costs $= \dfrac{(\$1,500,000 - \$1,250,000)}{(\$1,250,000)} = 20\%$

Highlights to Remember

Discriminate between relevant and irrelevant information for making decisions. To be relevant to a particular decision, a cost (or revenue) must meet two criteria: (1) it must be an expected future cost (or revenue), and (2) it must have an element of difference among the alternative courses of action.

Use the decision process to make business decisions. All managers make business decisions based on some decision process. The best processes help decision making by focusing the manager's attention on relevant information.

Decide to accept or reject a special order using the contribution approach. Decisions to accept or reject a special sales order should use the contribution approach and focus on the additional revenues and additional costs of the order.

Decide to add or delete a product line using relevant information. Relevant information also plays an important role in decisions about adding or deleting products, services, or departments. Decisions on whether to delete a department or product line require analysis of the revenues forgone and the costs saved from the deletion.

Compute a measure of product profitability when production is constrained by a scarce resource. When production is constrained by a limiting resource, the key to obtaining the maximum profit from a given capacity is to obtain the greatest possible contribution to profit per unit of the limiting or scarce resource.

Discuss the factors that influence pricing decisions in practice. Pricing decisions are influenced by market conditions, the law, customers, competitors, and costs. The degree that price and cost can be affected by management actions determines the most effective approach to use for pricing and cost management purposes.

Compute a target sales price by various approaches and compare the advantages and disadvantages of these approaches. Cost-plus pricing is used for products when management actions can influence the market price. Profit markups can be added to a variety of cost bases including variable manufacturing costs, all variable costs, absorption (full manufacturing) costs, or all costs. The contribution approach to pricing has the advantage of providing detailed cost behavior information that is consistent with cost-volume-profit analysis.

Use target costing to decide whether to add a new product. When market conditions are such that management cannot influence prices, the focus must be on cost control and reduction. Target costing is used primarily for new products during the design phase of the value chain. A desired target margin is deducted from the market-established price to determine the target cost. The focus of cost management is then on controlling and reducing costs over the product's life cycle.

Understand how relevant information is used when making marketing decisions. Accountants and managers must have a thorough understanding of relevant information, especially costs, when making marketing decisions. Each of the marketing-related decision situations discussed in this chapter (special sales order, adding or deleting a product, service, or department, product emphasis when resources constrain capacity, and pricing) involve determining revenue and cost information that is relevant. The accountant's role in decision making is primarily that of a technical expert on both financial and managerial analyses. The accountant's responsibility is to help the manager use relevant data as guidance for decisions.

Accounting Vocabulary

avoidable costs, p. 174	inventory turnover, p. 177	predatory pricing, p. 180
common costs, p. 174	kaizen costing, p. 188	price elasticity, p. 178
decision model, p. 167	limiting factor, p. 176	relevant information, p. 166
discriminatory pricing, p. 180	marginal cost, p. 178	scarce resource, p. 176
full cost, p. 182	marginal revenue, p. 178	target costing, p. 187
fully allocated cost, p. 182	markup, p. 181	unavoidable costs, p. 174
imperfect competition, p. 178	perfect competition, p. 177	value engineering, p. 188

Fundamental Assignment Material

5-A1   Special Order

Consider the following details of the income statement of the Pocket Calculator Division (PCD) of the Kim Electronics Company for the year ended December 31, 19X6:

Sales	$10,000,000
Less manufacturing cost of goods sold	6,000,000
Gross margin or gross profit	$ 4,000,000
Less selling and administrative expenses	3,300,000
Operating income	$ 700,000

PCD's fixed manufacturing costs were $2.4 million and its fixed selling and administrative costs were $2.5 million. Sales commissions of 3% of sales are included in selling and administrative expenses.

The division had sold 2 million calculators. Near the end of the year, Burger King offered to buy 150,000 calculators on a special order. To fill the order, a special Burger King logo would have to be added to each calculator. Burger King intended to use the calculators in special promotions in an eastern city during early 19X7.

Even though PCD had some idle plant capacity, the president rejected the Burger King offer of $660,000 for the 150,000 calculators. He said:

> The Burger King offer is too low. We'd avoid paying sales commissions, but we'd have to incur an extra cost of $.20 per calculator to add the logo. If PCD sells below its regular selling prices, it will begin a chain reaction

of competitors' price cutting and of customers wanting special deals. I believe in pricing at no lower than 8% above our full costs of $9,300,000 ÷ 2,000,000 units = $4.65 per unit plus the extra $.20 per calculator less the savings in commissions.

Required

1. Using the contribution approach, prepare an analysis similar to that in Exhibit 5-3, page 171. Use four columns: without the special order, the effect of the special order (total and per unit), and totals with the special order.

2. By what percentage would operating income increase or decrease if the order had been accepted? Do you agree with the president's decision? Why?

5-A2 Choice of Products

The Ibunez Tool Company has two products: a plain circular saw and a fancy circular saw. The plain saw sells for $66 and has a variable cost of $50. The fancy saw sells for $100 and has a variable cost of $70.

Required

1. Compute contribution margins and contribution-margin ratios for plain and fancy circular saws.

2. The demand is for more units than the company can produce. There are only 20,000 machine-hours of manufacturing capacity available. Two plain saws can be produced in the same average time (1 hour) needed to produce one fancy saw. Compute the total contribution margin for 20,000 hours for plain saws only and for fancy saws only.

3. Use two or three sentences to state the major lesson of this problem.

5-A3 Formulas for Pricing

Randy Azarski, a building contractor, constructs houses in tracts, often building as many as 20 homes simultaneously. Azarski has budgeted costs for an expected number of houses in 19X9 as follows.

Direct materials	$3,500,000
Direct labor	1,000,000
Job construction overhead	1,500,000
Cost of jobs	$6,000,000
Selling and administrative costs	1,500,000
Total costs	$7,500,000

The job construction overhead includes approximately $600,000 of fixed costs, such as the salaries of supervisors and depreciation on equipment. The selling and administrative costs include $300,000 of variable costs, such as sales commissions and bonuses that depend fundamentally on overall profitability.

Azarski wants an operating income of $1.5 million for 19X9.

Compute the average target markup percentage for setting prices as a percentage of

Required

1. Prime costs (direct materials plus direct labor)
2. The full "cost of jobs"
3. The variable "cost of jobs"
4. The full "cost of jobs" plus selling and administrative costs
5. The variable "cost of jobs" plus variable selling and administrative costs

5-B1 Special Order, Terminology, and Unit Costs

Following is the income statement of a manufacturer of men's shirts:

Hunter Company
Income Statement for the Year Ended December 31, 19X7

	Total	Per Unit
Sales	$40,000,000	$20.00
Less manufacturing cost of goods sold	24,000,000	12.00
Gross margin	$16,000,000	$ 8.00
Less selling and administrative expenses	14,000,000	7.00
Operating income	$ 2,000,000	$ 1.00

Hunter had manufactured 2 million shirts, which had been sold to various clothing whole-salers and department stores. At the start of 19X8, the president, Rosie Valenzuela, died from a stroke. Her son, Ricardo, became the new president. Ricardo had worked for 15 years in the marketing phases of the business. He knew very little about accounting and manufacturing, which were his mother's strengths. Ricardo has several questions for you including inquiries regarding the pricing of special orders.

Required

1. To prepare better answers, you decide to recast the income statement in contribution form. Variable manufacturing cost was $19 million. Variable selling and administrative expenses, which were mostly sales commissions, shipping expenses, and advertising allowances paid to customers based on units sold, were $9 million.

2. Ricardo asks, "I can't understand financial statements until I know the meaning of various terms. In scanning my mother's assorted notes, I found the following pertaining to both total and unit costs: *absorption cost, full manufacturing cost, variable cost, full cost, fully allocated cost, gross margin,* and *contribution margin.* Using our data for 19X7, please give me a list of these costs, their total amounts, and their per-unit amounts."

3. "Near the end of 19X7, I brought in a special order from Costco for 100,000 shirts at $17 each. I said I'd accept a flat $20,000 sales commission instead of the usual 6% of selling price, but my mother refused the order. She usually upheld a relatively rigid pricing policy, saying that it was bad business to accept orders that did not at least generate full manufacturing cost plus 80% of full manufacturing cost.

   "That policy bothered me. We had idle capacity. The way I figured, our manufacturing costs would go up by 100,000 × $12 = $1,200,000, but our selling and administrative expenses would go up by only $20,000. That would mean additional operating income of 100,000 × ($17 − $12) minus $20,000, or $500,000 minus $20,000, or $480,000. That's too much money to give up just to maintain a general pricing policy. Was my analysis of the impact on operating income correct? If not, please show me the correct additional operating income."

4. After receiving the explanations offered in requirements 2 and 3, Ricardo said: "Forget that I had the Costco order. I had an even bigger order from Lands' End. It was for 500,000 units and would have filled the plant completely. I told my mother I'd settle for no commission. There would have been no selling and administrative costs whatsoever because Lands' End would pay for the shipping and would not get any advertising allowances.

   "Lands' End offered $9.20 per unit. Our fixed manufacturing costs would have been spread over 2.5 million instead of 2 million units. Wouldn't it have been advantageous to accept the offer? Our old fixed manufacturing costs were $2.50 per unit. The added volume would reduce that cost more than our loss on our variable costs per unit.

   "Am I correct? What would have been the impact on total operating income if we had accepted the order?"

5-B2 Unit Costs and Capacity

Fargo Manufacturing Company produces two industrial solvents for which the following data have been tabulated. Fixed manufacturing cost is applied to products at a rate of $1.00 per machine-hour.

Per Unit	XY-7	XZ-8
Selling price	$6.00	$4.00
Variable manufacturing costs	3.00	1.40
Fixed manufacturing cost	.80	.20
Variable selling cost	2.00	2.00

The sales manager has had a $160,000 increase in her budget allotment for advertising and wants to apply the money on the most profitable product. The solvents are not substitutes for one another in the eyes of the company's customers.

Required

1. How many machine-hours does it take to produce one XY-7? To produce one XZ-8? (Hint: Focus on applied fixed manufacturing cost.)

2. Suppose Fargo has only 100,000 machine-hours that can be made available to produce XY-7 and XZ-8. If the potential increase in sales units for either product resulting from advertising is far in excess of these production capabilities, which product should be produced and advertised and what is the estimated increase in contribution margin earned?

5-B3 Dropping a Product Line

Hambley's Toy Store is on Regent Street in London. It has a magic department near the main door. Suppose that management is considering dropping the magic department, which has consistently shown an operating loss. The predicted income statements, in thousands of pounds (£), follow (for ease of analysis, only three product lines are shown):

	Total	General Merchandise	Electronic Products	Magic Department
Sales	£6,000	£5,000	£400	£ 600
Variable expenses	4,090	3,500	200	390
Contribution margin	£1,910 (32%)	£1,500 (30%)	£200 (50%)	£ 210 (35%)
Fixed expenses (compensation, depreciation, property taxes, insurance, etc.)	1,110	750	50	310
Operating income	£ 800	£ 750	£150	£(100)

The £310,000 of magic department fixed expenses include the compensation of employees of £100,000. These employees will be released if the magic department is abandoned. All equipment is fully depreciated, so none of the £310,000 pertains to such items. Furthermore, disposal values of equipment will be exactly offset by the costs of removal and remodeling.

If the magic department is dropped, the manager will use the vacated space for either more general merchandise or more electronic products. The expansion of general merchandise would not entail hiring any additional salaried help, but more electronic products would require an additional person at an annual cost of £25,000. The manager thinks that sales of general merchandise would increase by £300,000; electronic products, by £200,000. The manager's modest predictions are partially based on the fact that she thinks the magic department has helped lure customers to the store and thus improved overall sales. If the magic department is closed, that lure would be gone.

Should the magic department be closed? Explain, showing computations.

Required

Additional Assignment Material

QUESTIONS

5-1. "The distinction between precision and relevance should be kept in mind." Explain.

5-2. Distinguish between the quantitative and qualitative aspects of decisions.

5-3. Describe the accountant's role in decision making.

5-4. "Any future cost is relevant." Do you agree? Explain.

5-5. Why are historical or past data irrelevant to special decisions?

5-6. Describe the role of past or historical costs in the decision process. That is, how do these costs relate to the prediction method and the decision model?

5-7. "There is a commonality of approach to various special decisions." Explain.

5-8. "In relevant-cost analysis, beware of unit costs." Explain.

5-9. "Increasing sales will decrease fixed costs because it spreads them over more units." Do you agree? Explain.

5-10. "The key to decisions to delete a product or department is identifying avoidable costs." Do you agree? Explain.

5-11. "Avoidable costs are variable costs." Do you agree? Explain.

5-12. Give four examples of limiting or scarce factors.

5-13. Compare and contrast *marginal cost* and *variable cost*.

5-14. Describe the major factors that influence pricing decisions.

5-15. Why are customers one of the factors influencing price decisions?

5-16. "In target costing, prices determine costs rather than vice versa." Explain.

5-17. "Basing pricing on only the variable costs of a job results in suicidal underpricing." Do you agree? Why?

5-18. Provide three examples of pricing decisions other than the special order.

5-19. List four popular markup formulas for pricing.

5-20. Describe two long-run effects that may lead to managers rejecting opportunities to cut prices and obtain increases in short-run profits.

5-21. Give two reasons why full costs are far more widely used than variable costs for guiding pricing.

5-22. Why do most executives use both full-cost and variable-cost information for pricing decisions?

EXERCISES

5-23 Pinpointing of Relevant Costs

Today you are planning to see a motion picture and you can attend either of two theaters. You have only a small budget for entertainment, so prices are important. You have attended both theaters recently. One charged $6 for admission; the other charged $7. You habitually buy popcorn in the theater—each theater charges $2. The motion pictures now being shown are equally attractive to you, but you are virtually certain that you will never see the picture that you reject today.

Required   Identify the relevant costs. Explain your answer.

5-24 Information and Decisions

Suppose the historical costs for the manufacture of a calculator by Texas Instruments were as follows: direct materials, $5.00 per unit; direct labor, $3.00 per unit. Management is trying to decide whether to replace some materials with different materials. The replacement should cut material costs by 5% per unit. However, direct-labor time will increase by 5% per unit. Moreover, direct-labor rates will be affected by a recent 10% wage increase.

Prepare an exhibit like Exhibit 5-1 (p. 168), showing where and how the data about direct material and direct labor fit in the decision process.

5-25 Identification of Relevant Costs

Sankar and Raji Ramaswamy were trying to decide whether to go to the symphony or to the baseball game. They already have two nonrefundable tickets to "Pops Night at the

Symphony" that cost $40 each. This is the only concert of the season they considered attending because it is the only one with the type of music they enjoy. The baseball game is the last one of the season, and it will decide the league championship. They can purchase tickets for $20 each.

The Ramaswamys will drive 50 miles round trip to either event. Variable costs for operating their auto are $.14 per mile, and fixed costs average $.15 per mile for the 20,000 miles they drive annually. Parking at the symphony is free, but it costs $6 at the baseball game.

To attend either event, Sankar and Raji will hire a baby-sitter at $4 per hour. They expect to be gone 5 hours to attend the baseball game but only 4 hours to attend the symphony.

Required Compare the cost of attending the baseball game to the cost of attending the symphony. Focus on relevant costs. Compute the difference in cost, and indicate which alternative is more costly to the Ramaswamys.

5-26 Special-Order Decision

Belltown Athletic Supply (BAS) makes game jerseys for athletic teams. The F. C. Kitsap soccer club has offered to buy 100 jerseys for the teams in its league for $15 per jersey. The team price for such jerseys normally is $18, an 80% markup over BAS's purchase price of $10 per jersey. BAS adds a name and number to each jersey at a variable cost of $2 per jersey. The annual fixed cost of equipment used in the printing process is $6,000 and other fixed costs allocated to jerseys is $2,000. BAS makes about 2,000 jerseys per year, so the fixed cost is $4 per jersey. The equipment is used only for printing jerseys and stands idle 75% of the usable time.

The manager of BAS turned down the offer, saying, "If we sell at $15 and our cost is $16, we lose money on each jersey we sell. We would like to help your league, but we can't afford to lose money on the sale."

Required

1. Compute the amount by which the operating income of BAS would change if the F. C. Kitsap's offer were accepted.

2. Suppose you were the manager of BAS. Would you accept the offer? In addition to considering the quantitative impact computed in requirement 1, list two qualitative considerations that would influence your decision—one qualitative factor supporting acceptance of the offer and one supporting rejection.

5-27 Unit Costs and Total Costs

You are a CPA who belongs to a downtown luncheon club. Annual dues are $150. You use the club solely for lunches, which cost $6 each. You have not used the club much in recent years and you are wondering whether to continue your membership.

Required

1. You are confronted with a variable-cost plus a fixed-cost behavior pattern. Plot each on a graph, where the vertical axis is total cost and the horizontal axis is annual volume in number of lunches. Also plot a third graph that combines the previous two graphs.

2. What is the cost per lunch if you pay for your own lunch once a year? Twelve times a year? Two hundred times a year?

3. Suppose the average price of lunches elsewhere is $11. (a) How many lunches must you have at the luncheon club so that the total costs of the lunches would be the same regardless of where you ate for that number of lunches? (b) Suppose you ate 250 lunches a year at the club. How much would you save in relation to the total costs of eating elsewhere?

5-28 Advertising Expenditures and Nonprofit Organizations

Many colleges and universities have been extensively advertising their services. For example, a university in Philadelphia used a biplane to pull a sign promoting its evening program, and one in Mississippi designed bumper stickers and slogans as well as innovative programs.

Suppose Wilton College charges a comprehensive annual fee of $15,000 for tuition, room, and board, and it has capacity for 2,500 students. Costs per student for the 19X1 academic year are:

	Variable	Fixed	Total
Educational programs	$5,000	$4,200	$ 9,200
Room	1,300	2,200	3,500
Board	2,600	600	3,200
	$8,900	$7,000*	$15,900

*Based on 2,000 to 2,500 students for the year.

The admissions department predicts enrollment of 2,000 students for 19X1. The assistant director of admissions has proposed a two-month advertising campaign, however, using radio and television advertisements together with an extensive direct mailing of brochures.

Required

1. Suppose the advertising campaign will cost $1.83 million. What is the minimum number of additional students the campaign must attract to make the campaign break even?

2. Suppose the admissions department predicts that the campaign will attract 360 additional students. What is the most Wilton should pay for the campaign and still break even?

3. Suppose a three-month (instead of two-month) campaign will attract 450 instead of 360 additional students. What is the most Wilton should pay for the one-month extension of the campaign and still break even?

5-29 Variety of Cost Terms

Consider the following data:

Variable selling and administrative costs per unit	$ 3.00
Total fixed selling and administrative costs	$2,900,000
Total fixed manufacturing costs	$3,000,000
Variable manufacturing costs per unit	$ 10.00
Units produced and sold	500,000

Required

1. Compute the following per unit of product: (a) total variable costs, (b) absorption cost, (c) full cost.

2. Give a synonym for full cost.

5-30 Profit per Unit of Space

1. Several successful chains of warehouse stores such as Costco and Sam's Club have merchandising policies that differ considerably from those of traditional department stores. Name some characteristics of these warehouse stores that have contributed to their success.

2. Food chains such as Safeway have typically regarded approximately 20% of selling price as an average target gross profit on canned goods and similar grocery items. What are the limitations of such an approach? Be specific.

5-31 Deletion of Product Line

Zurich American School is an international private elementary school. In addition to regular classes, after-school care is provided between 3:00 and 6:00 P.M. at SF12 per child per hour. Financial results for the after-school care for a representative month are:

Revenue, 600 hours @ SF12 per hour		SF7,200
Less		
Teacher salaries	SF5,200	
Supplies	800	
Depreciation	1,300	
Sanitary engineering	100	
Other fixed costs	200	7,600
Operating income (loss)		SF (400)

The director of Zurich American School is considering discontinuing the after-school care services because it is not fair to the other students to subsidize the after-school care program. He thinks that eliminating the program will free up SF400 a month to be used in the regular classes.

1. Compute the financial impact on Zurich American School from discontinuing the after-school care program. **Required**

2. List three qualitative factors that would influence your decision.

5-32 Acceptance of Low Bid
The Velasquez Company, a maker of a variety of metal and plastic products, is in the midst of a business downturn and is saddled with many idle facilities. Columbia Health Care has approached Velasquez to produce 300,000 nonslide serving trays. Columbia will pay $1.30 each.

Velasquez predicts that its variable costs will be $1.40 each. Its fixed costs, which had been averaging $1 per unit on a variety of other products, will now be spread over twice as much volume, however. The president commented, "Sure we'll lose $.10 each on the variable costs, but we'll gain $.50 per unit by spreading our fixed costs. Therefore, we should take the offer, because it represents an advantage of $.40 per unit."

Suppose the regular business had a current volume of 300,000 units, sales of $600,000, variable costs of $420,000, and fixed costs of $300,000. Do you agree with the president? Why? **Required**

5-33 Pricing by Auto Dealer
Many automobile dealers have an operating pattern similar to that of Austin Motors, a dealer in Texas. Each month, Austin initially aims at a unit volume quota that approximates a break-even point. Until the break-even point is reached, Austin has a policy of relatively lofty pricing, whereby the "minimum deal" must contain a sufficiently high markup to ensure a contribution to profit of no less than $400. After the break-even point is attained, Austin tends to quote lower prices for the remainder of the month.

What is your opinion of this policy? As a prospective customer, how would you react to this policy? **Required**

5-34 Pricing to Maximize Contribution
Reynolds Company produces and sells picture frames. One particular frame for 8 × 10 photos was an instant success in the market, but recently competitors have come out with comparable frames. Reynolds has been charging $12 wholesale for the frames, and sales have fallen from 10,000 units last year to 7,000 units this year. The product manager in charge of this frame is considering lowering the price to $10 per frame. He believes sales will rebound to 10,000 units at the lower price, but they will fall to 6,000 units at the $12 price. The unit variable cost of producing and selling the frames is $6, and $40,000 of fixed cost is assigned to the frames.

1. Assuming that the only prices under consideration are $10 and $12 per frame, which price will lead to the largest profit for Reynolds? Explain why? **Required**

2. What subjective considerations might affect your pricing decision?

5-35 Target Selling Prices

Consider the following data from Klastorin Company's budgeted income statement (in thousands of dollars):

Target sales	$60,000
Variable costs	
Manufacturing	30,000
Selling and administrative	6,000
Total variable costs	36,000
Fixed costs	
Manufacturing	8,000
Selling and administrative	6,000
Total fixed costs	14,000
Total of all costs	50,000
Operating income	$10,000

Required   Compute the following markup formulas that would be used for obtaining the same target sales as a percentage of (1) total variable costs, (2) full costs, (3) variable manufacturing costs, and (4) absorption costs.

5-36 Competitive Bids

Griffey, Rodriguez, and Martinez, a CPA firm, is preparing to bid for a consulting job. Although Alicia Martinez will use her judgment about the market in finalizing the bid, she has asked you to prepare a cost analysis to help in the bidding. You have estimated the costs for the consulting job to be:

Materials and supplies, at cost	$ 28,000
Hourly pay for consultants, 2,000 hours @ $36 per hour	72,000
Fringe benefits for consultants, 2,000 hours @ $12 per hour	24,000
Total variable costs	124,000
Fixed costs allocated to the job	
Based on labor, 2,000 hours @ $10.80 per hour	21,600
Based on materials and supplies, 80% of 28,000	22,400
Total cost	$168,000

Of the $44,000 allocated fixed costs, $35,000 will be incurred even if the job is not undertaken.

Alicia normally bids jobs at the sum of (1) 150% of the estimated materials and supplies cost and (2) $75 per estimated labor-hour.

Required

1. Prepare a bid using the normal formula.

2. Prepare a minimum bid equal to the additional costs expected to be incurred to complete the job.

3. Prepare a bid that will cover full costs plus a markup for profit equal to 20% of full cost.

PROBLEMS

5-37 Pricing, Ethics, and the Law

Great Lakes Pharmaceuticals, Inc. (GLPI), produces both prescription and over-the-counter medications. In January GLPI introduced a new prescription drug, Capestan, to relieve the pain of arthritis. The company spent more than $50 million over the last five years developing the drug, and advertising alone during the first year of introduction will exceed $10 million. Production cost for a bottle of 100 tablets is approximately $12. Sales in the first three years are predicted to be 500,000, 750,000, and 1,000,000 bottles, respectively. To achieve these sales, GLPI plans to distribute the medicine through three sources: directly from physicians, through hospital pharmacies, and through retail pharmacies. Initially, the bottles will be given free to physicians to give to patients, hospital pharmacies will pay $25 per bottle, and retail pharmacies will pay $40 per bottle. In the second and third year, the company plans to phase out the free distributions to physicians and move all other customers toward a $50 per bottle sales price.

Required

Comment on the pricing and promotion policies of GLPI. Pay particular attention to the legal and ethical issues involved.

5-38 Pricing and Contribution Approach

The Transnational Trucking Company has the following operating results to date for 19X3:

Operating revenues	$50,000,000
Operating costs	40,000,000
Operating income	$10,000,000

A large Boston manufacturer has inquired about whether Transnational would be interested in trucking a large order of its parts to Chicago. Steve Goldmark, operations manager, investigated the situation and estimated that the "fully allocated" costs of servicing the order would be $45,000. Using his general pricing formula, he quoted a price of $50,000. The manufacturer replied: "We'll give you $39,000, take it or leave it. If you do not want our business, we'll truck it ourselves or go elsewhere."

A cost analyst had recently been conducting studies of how Transnational's operating costs tended to behave. She found that $32 million of the $40 million could be characterized as variable costs. Goldmark discussed the matter with her and decided that this order would probably generate cost behavior little different from Transnational's general operations.

Required

1. Using a contribution format, prepare an analysis for Transnational.
2. Should Transnational accept the order? Explain.

5-39 Cost Analysis and Pricing

The budget for the Oxford University Printing Company for 19X5 follows:

Sales		£1,100,000
Direct material	£280,000	
Direct labor	320,000	
Overhead	400,000	1,000,000
Net income		£ 100,000

The company typically uses a so-called cost-plus pricing system. Direct-material and direct-labor costs are computed, overhead is added at a rate of 125% of direct labor, and 10% of the total cost is added to obtain the selling price.

Edith Smythe, the sales manager, has placed a £22,000 bid on a particularly large order with a cost of £5,600 direct material and £6,400 direct labor. The customer informs her that she can have the business for £19,800, take it or leave it. If Smythe accepts the order, total sales for 19X5 will be £1,119,800.

Smythe refuses the order, saying: "I sell on a cost-plus basis. It is bad policy to accept orders at below cost. I would lose £2,000 on the job."

The company's annual fixed overhead is £160,000.

Required

1. What would net income have been with the order? Without the order? Show your computations.

2. Give a short description of a contribution approach to pricing that Smythe might follow. Include a stipulation of the pricing formula that Smythe should routinely use if she hopes to obtain a target net income of £100,000.

5-40 Pricing of Education

You are the director of continuing education programs for a state university. Courses for executives are especially popular, and you have developed an extensive menu of one-day and two-day courses that are presented in various locations throughout the state. The performance of these courses for the current fiscal year, excluding the final course, which is scheduled for the next Saturday, is:

Tuition revenue	$2,000,000
Costs of courses	800,000
Contribution margin	1,200,000
General administrative expenses	400,000
Operating income	$ 800,000

The costs of the courses include fees for instructors, rentals of classrooms, advertising, and any other items, such as travel, that can be easily and exclusively identified as being caused by a particular course.

The general administrative expenses include your salary, your secretary's compensation, and related expenses, such as a lump-sum payment to the university's central offices as a share of university overhead.

The enrollment for your final course of the year is 30 students, who have paid $200 each. Two days before the course is to begin, a city manager telephones your office. "Do you offer discounts to nonprofit institutions?" he asks. "If so, we'll send 10 managers. But our budget will not justify our spending more than $100 per person." The extra cost of including these ten managers would entail lunches at $20 each and course materials at $40 each.

Required

1. Prepare a tabulation of the performance for the full year including the final course. Assume that the costs of the final course for the 30 enrollees' instruction, travel, advertising, rental of hotel classroom, lunches, and course materials would be $4,000. Show a tabulation in four columns: before final course, final course with 30 registrants, effect of 10 more registrants, and grand totals.

2. What major considerations would probably influence the pricing policies for these courses? For setting regular university tuition in private universities?

5-41 Videotape Sales and Rental Markets

Is it more profitable to sell your product for $50 or $15? This is a difficult question for many movie studio executives. Consider a movie that cost $60 million to produce and required another $40 million to promote. After its theater release, the studio must determine whether to sell videotapes directly to the public at a wholesale price of about $15 per tape or to sell to video rental store distributors for about $50 per tape. The distributors will then sell to about 14,000 video rental stores in the United States.

Assume that the variable cost to produce and ship one video tape is $2.00.

Required

1. Suppose each video rental store would purchase 10 tapes of this movie. How many tapes would need to be sold directly to customers to make direct sales a more profitable option than sales to video store distributors?

2. How does the cost of producing and promoting the movie affect this decision?

3. Disney elected to sell *The Lion King* directly to consumers, and it sold 30 million copies at an average price of $15.50 per tape. How many tapes would each video rental store have to purchase to provide Disney as much profit as the company

received from direct sales? Assume that Disney would receive $50 per tape from the distributors.

5-42 Use of Passenger Jets

In a recent year Continental Air Lines, Inc. filled about 50% of the available seats on its flights, a record about 15 percentage points below the national average.

Continental could have eliminated about 4% of its runs and raised its average load considerably. The improved load factor would have reduced profits, however. Give reasons for or against this elimination. What factors should influence an airline's scheduling policies?

When you answer this question, suppose that Continental had a basic package of 3,000 flights per month that had an average of 100 seats available per flight. Also suppose that 52% of the seats were filled at an average ticket price of $200 per flight. Variable costs are about 70% of revenue.

Continental also had a marginal package of 120 flights per month that had an average of 100 seats available per flight. Suppose that only 20% of the seats were filled at an average ticket price of $100 per flight. Variable costs are about 50% of this revenue. Prepare a tabulation of the basic package, marginal package, and total package, showing percentage of seats filled, revenue, variable expenses, and contribution margin.

5-43 Effects of Volume on Operating Income

The Wittred Division of Melbourne Sports Company manufactures boomerangs, which are sold to wholesalers and retailers. The division manager has set a target of 250,000 boomerangs for next month's production and sales. The manager, however, has prepared an analysis of the effects on operating income of deviations from the target:

Volume in units	200,000	250,000	300,000
Sales @ $3.00	$600,000	$750,000	$900,000
Full costs @ $2.50	500,000	625,000	750,000
Operating income	$100,000	$125,000	$150,000

The costs have the following characteristics. Variable manufacturing costs are $.90 per boomerang; variable selling costs are $.20 per boomerang. Fixed manufacturing costs per month are $300,000; fixed selling and administrative costs, $50,000.

Required 1. Prepare a correct analysis of the changes in volume on operating income. Prepare a tabulated set of income statements at levels of 200,000, 250,000, and 300,000 boomerangs. Also show percentages of operating income in relation to sales.

2. Compare your tabulation with the manager's tabulation. Why is the manager's tabulation incorrect?

BUSINESS FIRST   www.prenhall.com/phlip

5-44 Pricing at The Grand Canyon Railway

Suppose a tour guide approached the general manager of The Grand Canyon Railway with a proposal to offer a special guided tour to the agent's clients. The tour would occur 20 times each summer and be part of a larger itinerary that the agent is putting together. The agent presented two options: (1) a special 65-mile tour with the agent's 30 clients as the only passengers on the train, or (2) adding a car to an existing train to accommodate the 30 clients on the 65-mile tour.

Under either option Grand Canyon would hire a tour guide for $150 for the trip. Grand Canyon has extra cars in its switching yard, and it would cost $40 to move a car to the main track and hook it up. The extra fuel cost to pull one extra car is $.20 per mile. To run an engine and a passenger car on the trip would cost $2.20 per mile, and an engineer would be paid $400 for the trip.

Depreciation on passenger cars is $5,000 per year, and depreciation on engines is $20,000 per year. Each passenger car and each engine travels about 50,000 miles a year. They are replaced every 8 years.

The agent offered to pay $30 per passenger for the special tour and $15 per passenger for simply adding an extra car.

Required

1. Which of the two options is more profitable to Grand Canyon? Comment on which costs are irrelevant to this decision.

2. Should Grand Canyon accept the proposal for the option you found best in requirement 1? Comment on what costs are relevant for this decision but not for the decision in requirement 1. ∎

5-45 Pricing of Special Order

The Drosselmeier Corporation, located in Munich, makes Christmas Nutcrackers and has an annual plant capacity of 2,400 product units. Its predicted operating results (in German marks) for the year are:

Production and sales of 2,000 units, total sales	DM180,000
Manufacturing costs	
Fixed (total)	60,000
Variable (per unit)	26
Selling and administrative expenses	
Fixed (total)	30,000
Variable (per unit)	10

Required

Compute the following, ignoring income taxes:

1. If the company accepts a special order for 300 units at a selling price of DM40 each, how would the *total* predicted net income for the year be affected, assuming no effect on regular sales at regular prices?

2. Without decreasing its total net income, what is the lowest unit price for which the Drosselmeier Corporation could sell an additional 100 units not subject to any variable selling and administrative expenses, assuming no effect on regular sales at regular prices?

3. List the numbers given in the problem that are irrelevant (not relevant) in solving requirement 2.

4. Compute the expected annual net income (with no special orders) if plant capacity can be doubled by adding additional facilities at a cost of DM500,000. Assume that these facilities have an estimated life of five years with no residual scrap value, and that the current unit selling price can be maintained for all sales. Total sales are expected to equal the new plant capacity each year. No changes are expected in variable costs per unit or in total fixed costs except for depreciation.

5-46 Pricing and Confusing Variable and Fixed Costs

Diaz Telecom had a fixed factory overhead budget for 19X8 of $1 million. The company planned to make and sell 200,000 units of a particular communications device. All variable manufacturing costs per unit were $10. The budgeted income statement contained the following (in thousands):

Sales	$4,000
Manufacturing cost of goods sold	3,000
Gross margin	1,000
Deduct selling and administrative expenses	400
Operating income	$ 600

For simplicity, assume that the actual variable costs per unit and the total fixed costs were exactly as budgeted.

Required

1. Compute Diaz's budgeted fixed factory overhead per unit.

2. Near the end of 19X8, a large computer manufacturer offered to buy 10,000 units for $120,000 on a one-time special order. The president of Diaz stated: "The offer is a bad deal. It's foolish to sell below full manufacturing costs per unit. I realize that this order will have only a modest effect on selling and administrative costs. They will increase by a $1,000 fee paid to our sales agent." Compute the effect on operating income if the offer is accepted.

3. What factors should the president of Diaz consider before finally deciding whether to accept the offer?

4. Suppose the original budget for fixed manufacturing costs was $1 million, but budgeted units of product were 100,000. How would your answers to requirements 1 and 2 change? Be specific.

5-47 Demand Analysis

Zimmerman Manufacturing Limited produces and sells one product, a three-foot Canadian flag. During 19X8, the company manufactured and sold 50,000 flags at $25 each. Existing production capacity is 60,000 flags per year.

In formulating the 19X9 budget, management is faced with a number of decisions concerning product pricing and output. The following information is available:

1. A market survey shows that the sales volume depends on the selling price. For each $1 drop in selling price, sales volume would increase by 10,000 flags.

2. The company's expected cost structure for 19X9 is as follows:

   a. Fixed cost (regardless of production or sales activities), $360,000

   b. Variable costs per flag (including production, selling, and administrative expenses), $16

3. To increase annual capacity from the present 60,000 to 90,000 flags, additional investment for plant, building, equipment, and the like, of $200,000 would be necessary. The estimated average life of the additional investment would be 10 years, so the fixed costs would increase by an average of $20,000 per year. (Expansion of less than 30,000 additional units of capacity would cost only slightly less than $200,000.)

Required

Indicate, with reasons, what the level of production and the selling price should be for the coming year. Also indicate whether the company should approve the plant expansion. Show your calculations. Ignore income tax considerations and the time value of money.

5-48 Choice of Products

Gulf Coast Fashions sells both designer and moderately priced women's wear in Tampa. Profits have been volatile. Top management is trying to decide which product line to drop. Accountants have reported the following data:

	Per Item	
	Designer	*Moderately Priced*
Average selling price	$240	$150
Average variable expenses	120	85
Average contribution margin	$120	$ 65
Average contribution-margin percentage	50%	43%

The store has 8,000 square feet of floor space. If moderately priced goods are sold exclusively, 400 items can be displayed. If designer goods are sold exclusively, only 300 items can be displayed. Moreover, the rate of sale (turnover) of the designer items will be two-thirds the rate of moderately priced goods.

Required
1. Prepare an analysis to show which product to drop.
2. What other considerations might affect your decision in requirement 1?

5-49 Analysis of Unit Costs

Home Appliance Company manufactures small appliances, such as electric can openers, toasters, food mixers, and irons. The peak season is at hand, and the president is trying to decide whether to produce more of the company's standard line of can openers or its premium line that includes a built-in knife sharpener, a better finish, and a higher-quality motor. The unit data follow:

	Product	
	Standard	*Premium*
Selling price	$28	$38
Direct material	$ 8	$13
Direct labor	2	1
Variable factory overhead	4	6
Fixed factory overhead	6	9
Total cost of goods sold	$20	$29
Gross profit per unit	$ 8	$ 9

The sales outlook is very encouraging. The plant could operate at full capacity by producing either product or both products. Both the standard and the premium products are processed through the same departments. Selling and administrative costs will not be affected by this decision, so they may be ignored.

Many of the parts are produced on automatic machinery. The factory overhead is allocated to products by developing separate rates per machine-hour for variable and fixed overhead. For example, the total fixed overhead is divided by the total machine-hours to get a rate per hour. Thus the amount of overhead allocated to products is dependent on the number of machine-hours used by the product. It takes one hour of machine time to produce one unit of the standard product.

Direct labor may not be proportionate with overhead because many workers operate two or more machines simultaneously.

Required
Which product should be produced? If more than one should be produced, indicate the proportions of each. Show computations. Explain your answers briefly.

5-50 Use of Available Facilities

The Oahu Audio Company manufactures electronic subcomponents that can be sold directly or can be processed further into "plug-in" assemblies for a variety of intricate electronic equipment. The entire output of subcomponents can be sold at a market price of $2.20 per unit. The plug-in assemblies have been generating a sales price of $5.70 for three years, but the price has recently fallen to $5.30 on assorted orders.

Janet Oh, the vice president of marketing, has analyzed the markets and the costs. She thinks that production of plug-in assemblies should be dropped whenever the price falls below $4.70 per unit. However, at the current price of $5.30, the total available capacity should currently be devoted to producing plug-in assemblies. She has cited the data in Exhibit 5-12.

Direct-materials and direct-labor costs are variable. The total overhead is fixed; it is allocated to units produced by predicting the total overhead for the coming year and dividing this total by the total hours of capacity available.

Exhibit 5-12

Oahu Audio Company

Product Profitability Data

		Sub-components
Selling price, after deducting relevant selling costs		$2.20
Direct materials	$ 1.10	
Direct labor	.30	
Manufacturing overhead	.60	
Cost per unit		2.00
Operating profit		$ .20

		Plug-In Assemblies
Selling price, after deducting relevant selling costs		$5.30
Transferred-in variable cost for subcomponents	$1.40	
Additional direct materials	1.45	
Direct labor	.45	
Manufacturing overhead	1.20*	
Cost per unit		4.50
Operating profit		$ .80

*For additional processing to make and test plug-in assemblies.

The total hours of capacity available are 600,000. It takes 1 hour to make 60 subcomponents and 2 hours of additional processing and testing to make 60 plug-in assemblies.

1. If the price of plug-in assemblies for the coming year is going to be $5.30, should sales of subcomponents be dropped and all facilities devoted to the production of plug-in assemblies? Show computations.

2. Prepare a report for the vice president of marketing to show the lowest possible price for plug-in assemblies that would be acceptable.

3. Suppose 40% of the manufacturing overhead is variable with respect to processing and testing time. Repeat requirements 1 and 2. Do your answers change? If so, how?

Required

5-51 Target Costing

Memphis Electrical, Inc., makes small electric motors for a variety of home appliances. Memphis sells the motors to appliance makers, who assemble and sell the appliances to retail outlets. Although Memphis makes dozens of different motors, it does not currently make one to be used in garage-door openers. The company's market research department has discovered a market for such a motor.

The market research department has indicated that a motor for garage-door openers would likely sell for $25. A similar motor currently being produced has the following manufacturing costs:

Direct materials	$13.00
Direct labor	6.00
Overhead	8.00
Total	$27.00

Memphis desires a gross margin of 15% of the manufacturing cost.

1. Suppose Memphis used cost-plus pricing, setting the price 15% above the manufacturing cost. What price would be charged for the motor? Would you produce such a motor if you were a manager at Memphis? Explain.

2. Suppose Memphis uses target costing. What price would the company charge for a garage-door-opener motor? What is the highest acceptable manufacturing cost for which Memphis would be willing to produce the motor?

3. As a user of target costing, what steps would Memphis managers take to try to make production of this product feasible?

5-52 Target Costing Over Product Life Cycle

Southeast Equipment, Inc. makes a variety of motor-driven products for the home and small businesses. The market research department recently identified power lawn mowers as a potentially lucrative market. As a first entry into this market, Southeast is considering a riding lawn mower that is smaller and less expensive than those of most of the competition. Market research indicates that such a lawn mower would sell for about $995 at retail and $800 wholesale. At that price, Southeast expects life cycle sales as follows:

19X1	1,000
19X2	5,000
19X3	10,000
19X4	10,000
19X5	8,000
19X6	6,000
19X7	4,000

The production department has estimated that the variable cost of production will be $475 per lawn mower, and annual fixed costs will be $900,000 per year for each of the 7 years. Variable selling costs will be $25 per lawn mower and fixed selling costs will be $50,000 per year. In addition, the product development department estimates that $5 million of development costs will be necessary to design the lawn mower and the production process for it.

1. Compute the expected profit over the entire product life cycle of the proposed riding lawn mower.

2. Suppose Southeast expects pretax profits equal to 10% of sales on new products. Would the company undertake production and selling of the riding lawn mower?

3. Southeast Equipment uses a target costing approach to new products. What steps would management take to try to make a profitable product of the riding lawn mower?

CASES

5-53 Use of Capacity

St. Tropez S. A. manufactures several different styles of jewelry cases in southern France. Management estimates that during the second quarter of 1999 the company will be operating at 80% of normal capacity. Because the company desires a higher utilization of plant capacity, it will consider a special order.

St. Tropez has received special-order inquiries from two companies. The first is from Lyon, Inc., which would like to market a jewelry case similar to one of St. Tropez's cases. The Lyon jewelry case would be marketed under Lyon's own label. Lyon, Inc., has offered St. Tropez FF67.5 per jewelry case for 20,000 cases to be shipped by July 1, 1999. The cost data for the St. Tropez jewelry case, which would be similar to the specifications of the Lyon special order, are as follows:

Regular selling price per unit	FF100
Costs per unit:	
Raw materials	FF35
Direct labor, .5 hr @ FF60	30
Overhead, .25 machine-hr @ FF40	10
Total costs	FF75

According to the specifications provided by Lyon, Inc., the special-order case requires less expensive raw materials, which will cost only FF32.5 per case. Management has estimated that the remaining costs, labor time, and machine time will be the same as those for the St. Tropez jewelry case.

The second special order was submitted by the Avignon Co. for 7,500 jewelry cases at FF85 per case. These cases would be marketed under the Avignon label and would have to be shipped by July 1, 1999. The Avignon jewelry case is different from any jewelry case in the St. Tropez line. Its estimated per-unit costs are as follows:

Raw materials	FF42.5
Direct labor, .5 hr @ FF60	30
Overhead, .5 machine-hr @ FF40	20
Total costs	FF92.5

In addition, St. Tropez will incur FF15,000 in additional setup costs and will have to purchase a FF25,000 special device to manufacture these cases; this device will be discarded once the special order is completed.

The St. Tropez manufacturing capabilities are limited by the total machine-hours available. The plant capacity under normal operations is 90,000 machine-hours per year, or 7,500 machine-hours per month. The budgeted fixed overhead for 1999 amounts to FF2.16 million, or FF24 per hour. All manufacturing overhead costs are applied to production on the basis of machine-hours at FF40 per hour.

St. Tropez will have the entire second quarter to work on the special orders. Management does not expect any repeat sales to be generated from either special order. Company practice precludes St. Tropez from subcontracting any portion of an order when special orders are not expected to generate repeat sales.

Required

Should St. Tropez accept either special order? Justify your answer and show your calculations. (Hint: Distinguish between variable and fixed overhead.)

5-54 Review of Chapters 2-5

The San Juan Bottling Company is a processor of mineral water. Sales are made principally in liter bottles to grocery stores throughout the region.

The company's income statements for the past year and the coming year are being analyzed by top management and are shown in Exhibit 5-13.

Required

Consider each requirement independently. Unless otherwise stated, assume that all unit costs of inputs such as material and labor are unchanged. Also, assume that efficiency is unchanged—that is, the labor and quantity of material consumed per unit of output are unchanged. Unless otherwise stated, assume that there are no changes in fixed costs.

1. The president has just returned from a management conference at a local university, where he heard an accounting professor criticize conventional income statements. The professor had asserted that knowledge of cost behavior patterns was of key importance in determining managerial strategies. The president now feels that the income statement should be recast to harmonize with cost-volume-profit analysis—that is, the statement should have three major sections: sales,

Exhibit 5-13

San Juan Company
Income Statements

	For the Year 1998 Just Ended		For the Year 1999 Tentative Budget	
Sales 1,500,000 units in 1998		$900,000		$1,000,000
Cost of goods sold				
Direct material	$450,000		$495,000	
Direct labor	90,000		99,000	
Factory overhead				
Variable	18,000		19,800	
Fixed	50,000	608,000	50,000	663,800
Gross margin		$292,000		$ 336,200
Selling expenses				
Variable				
Sales commissions (based on dollar sales)	$ 45,000		$ 50,000	
Shipping and other	90,000		99,000	
Fixed				
Salaries, advertising, etc.	110,000		138,000	
Administrative expenses				
Variable	12,000		13,200	
Fixed	40,000	297,000	40,000	340,200
Operating income		$ (5,000)		$ (4,000)

variable costs, and fixed costs. Using the 1998 data, prepare such a statement, showing the contribution margin as well as operating income.

2. Comment on the changes in each item in the 1999 income statement compared to the 1998 statement. What are the most likely causes for each increase? For example, have selling prices been changed for 1999? How do sales commissions fluctuate in relation to units sold or in relation to dollar sales?

3. The president is unimpressed with the 1999 budget: "We need to take a fresh look in order to begin moving toward profitable operations. Let's tear up the 1999 budget, concentrate on 1998 results, and prepare a new comparative 1999 budget under each of the following assumptions:

    a. A 5% average price cut will increase unit sales by 20%.

    b. A 5% average price increase will decrease unit sales by 10%.

    c. A sales commission rate of 10% and a 3⅓% price increase will boost unit sales by 10%.

    Prepare the budgets for 1999, using a contribution-margin format and three columns. Assume that there are no changes in fixed costs.

4. The advertising manager maintains that the advertising budget should be increased by $130,000 and that prices should be increased by 10%. Resulting unit sales will soar by 25%. What would be the expected operating income under such circumstances?

5. A nearby distillery has offered to buy 300,000 units in 1999 if the unit price is low enough. The San Juan Company would not have to incur sales commissions or shipping costs on this special order, and regular business would be undisturbed. Assuming that 1999's regular operations will be exactly like 1998's, what unit price should be quoted in order for the San Juan Company to earn an operating income of $10,000 in 1999?

6. The company chemist wants to add a special ingredient, an exotic flavoring that will add $.03 per bottle to the mineral water costs. Assuming no other changes in cost behavior, how many units must be sold to earn an operating income of $10,000 in 1999? How should the San Juan managers decide whether to add the flavoring to all the company's mineral water?

COLLABORATIVE LEARNING EXERCISE

5-55 Understanding Pricing Decisions

Form a group of three to six students. Each team should contact and meet with a manager responsible for pricing in a company in your area. This could be a product manager or brand manager for a large company or a Vice President of Marketing or Sales for a smaller company.

Explore with the manager how his or her company sets prices. Among the questions you might ask are:

- How do costs influence your prices? Do you set prices by adding a markup to costs? If so, what measure of costs do you use? How do you determine the appropriate markup?
- How do you adjust prices to meet market competition? How do you measure the effects of price on sales level?
- Do you use target costing? That is, do you find out what a product will sell for and then try to design the product and production process to make a desired profit on the product?
- What is your goal in setting prices? Do you try to maximize revenue, market penetration, contribution margin, gross margin, or some combination of these, or do you have other goals when setting prices?

After each team has its interview, it would be desirable, if time permits, to get together as a class and share your findings. How many different pricing policies did the groups find? Can you explain why policies differ across companies? Are there characteristics of different industries or different management philosophies that explain the different pricing policies?

6

RELEVANT INFORMATION AND DECISION MAKING: PRODUCTION DECISIONS

"Starbucks Coffee—a place to meet a friend, somewhere between home and work."

Learning Objectives

When you have finished studying this chapter, you should be able to

1 Use opportunity cost to analyze the income effects of a given alternative.

2 Decide whether to make or buy certain parts or products.

3 Decide whether a joint product should be processed beyond the split-off point.

4 Identify irrelevant information in disposal of obsolete inventory and equipment replacement decisions.

5 Explain how unit costs can be misleading.

6 Discuss how performance measures can affect decision making.

7 **Understand the relationship between accounting information and decisions in the production stage of the value chain.**

From a single coffee shop in Seattle in 1971 to more than 1,660 stores in 1998 with annual revenue of more than 1 billion, Starbucks Coffee Company is an amazing success story. In 1997 alone, the company's sales increased by almost 40%. The company has a goal of operating more than 2,000 stores in North America by the year 2000.

Starbucks purchases and roasts high-quality whole bean coffees and sells them, along with fresh, rich-brewed coffees and Italian-style espresso beverages, through its company-operated stores. At the end of 1996, stores were located in 21 states, Canada, and Tokyo. The company also has alliances with other businesses to provide its coffee, including United Airlines, University of Florida, Boeing, and Citicorp. Though the company derives the majority of its revenues from the sale of coffee and espresso beverages, it has a growing specialty line that includes bottled Frappuccino™ and coffee-flavored ice creams such as Caffé Almond Fudge and Dark Roast Expresso Swirl.

Any business that is growing as fast as Starbucks is faced with important production-related decisions on a regular basis. In 1996, the company had to decide whether to launch a new bottled Frappuccino™ coffee drink. Their analysis included quantifiable factors such as the cost of production facilities and subjective factors such as product quality. The company decided to proceed with the launch and to build new production facilities partly because they believed this would be the best way to assure the highest quality production standards. But more importantly, says Orin Smith, president and chief operating officer, "we knew that we had developed a platform for bigger product innovations."

As with Starbucks, managers in other companies must make similar decisions. Should Chrysler make the tires it mounts on its cars, or should it buy them from suppliers? Should General Mills sell the flour it mills, or should it use the flour to make more breakfast cereal? Should American Airlines add routes to use idle airplanes, or should it sell the planes? These decisions all require a good deal of accounting information. But what information will be relevant to each decision? In Chapter 5, we needed to identify relevant information for decisions in the marketing stage of the value chain. We now need to determine relevance in the production stage. The basic framework for identifying relevant information remains the same for production as it was for marketing. We are still looking only for future costs that differ among alternatives. However, we now expand our analysis by introducing the concepts of opportunity and differential costs.

OPPORTUNITY, OUTLAY, AND DIFFERENTIAL COSTS

opportunity cost The maximum available contribution to profit foregone (or passed up) by using limited resources for a particular purpose.

outlay cost A cost that requires a cash disbursement.

The concept of opportunity cost is often used by decision makers. An **opportunity cost** is the maximum available contribution to profit foregone (or passed up) by using limited resources for a particular purpose. This definition indicates that opportunity cost is not the usual outlay cost recorded in financial accounting ledgers. An **outlay cost,** which requires a cash disbursement sooner or later, is the typical cost recorded by accountants.

An example of an opportunity cost is the salary foregone by a person who quits a job to start a business. Consider Maria Morales, a certified public accountant employed by a large accounting firm at $60,000 per year. She is yearning to have her own independent practice.

Maria's alternatives may be framed in more than one way. A straightforward comparison follows:

Objective 1
Use opportunity cost to analyze the income effects of a given alternative.

	Alternatives Under Consideration		
	Remain as Employee	Open an Independent Practice	Difference
Revenues	$60,000	$200,000	$140,000
Outlay costs (operating expenses)	—	120,000	120,000
Income effects per year	$60,000	$ 80,000	$ 20,000

The annual difference of $20,000 favors Maria's choosing independent practice.

This tabulation is sometimes called a *differential analysis*. The *differential revenue* is $140,000, the *differential cost* is $120,000, and the *differential income* is $20,000. Each amount is the difference between the corresponding items under each alternative being considered. **Differential cost** and **incremental cost** are widely used synonyms. They are defined as the difference in total cost between two alternatives. For instance, the differential costs or incremental costs of increasing production from 1,000 automobiles to 1,200 automobiles per week would be the additional costs of producing the additional 200 automobiles each week. In the reverse situation, the decline in costs caused by reducing production from 1,200 to 1,000 automobiles per week would often be called *differential* or *incremental savings*.

differential cost (incremental cost) The difference in total cost between two alternatives.

Let's assume that Maria goes ahead and starts her own business. In her first year she makes a full $200,000—quite a bit more than she would have made as an employee of the large firm. However, getting started cost her $120,000 up front for equipment, advertising, renting office space, and so on. Still, she seems to have made quite a tidy profit. But there is another cost to consider. Had Maria remained an employee, she would have made $60,000. By starting her own company, Maria has foregone this profit, thus it counts as an opportunity cost of starting her own business. Considering all the costs, did Maria make the right decision? Yes, as we can see in the following table.

		Alternative Chosen: Independent Practice
Revenue		$200,000
Expenses		
Outlay costs (operating expenses)	$120,000	
Opportunity cost of employee salary	60,000	180,000
Income effects per year		$ 20,000

Ponder the two preceding tabulations. Each produces the correct key difference between alternatives, $20,000. The first tabulation does not mention opportunity cost because the economic impacts (in the form of revenues and outlay costs) are individually measured for each of the alternatives (two in this case). Neither alternative has been excluded from consideration. The second tabulation mentions opportunity cost because the $60,000 annual economic impact of the *best excluded* alternative is included as a cost of the chosen alternative. The failure to recognize opportunity cost in the second tabulation will misstate the difference between alternatives.

Suppose Morales prefers less risk and chooses to stay as an employee:

		Alternative Chosen: Remain as Employee
Revenue		$ 60,000
Expenses		
Outlay costs	$ 0	
Opportunity cost of independent practice	80,000	80,000
Decrease in income per year		$(20,000)

If the employee alternative is selected, the key difference in favor of independent practice is again $20,000. The opportunity cost is $80,000, the annual operating income foregone by rejecting the best excluded alternative. Morales is sacrificing $20,000 annually to avoid the risks of an independent practice. In sum, the opportunity cost is the contribution of the best alternative that is excluded from consideration.

The major message here is straightforward: Do not overlook opportunity costs. Consider a homeowner who has made the final payment on the mortgage. While celebrating, the owner says, "It's a wonderful feeling to know that future occupancy is free of any interest cost!" Many owners have similar thoughts. Why? Because no future outlay costs for interest are required. Nevertheless, there is an opportunity cost of continuing to live in the home. After all, an alternative would be to sell the home, place the proceeds in some other investment, and rent an apartment. The owner forgoes the interest in the other investment, so this foregone interest income becomes an opportunity cost of home ownership.

Managers often must decide whether to produce a product or service within the firm or purchase it from an outside supplier. They apply relevant cost analysis to a variety of such make-or-buy decisions, including:

- Boeing must decide whether to buy or make many of the tools used in assembling 777 airplanes.

- IBM must decide whether to develop its own operating system for a new computer or to buy it from a software vendor.

BASIC MAKE-OR-BUY AND IDLE FACILITIES

Objective 2
Decide whether to make or buy certain parts or products.

The basic make-or-buy question is whether a company should make its own parts to be used in its products or buy them from vendors. Sometimes the answer to this question is based on qualitative factors. For example, some manufacturers always make parts because they want to control quality. Alternatively, some companies always purchase parts to protect long-run relationships with their suppliers. These companies may deliberately buy from vendors even during slack times to avoid difficulties in obtaining needed parts during boom times, when there may well be shortages of materials and workers, but no shortage of sales orders.

What quantitative factors are relevant to the decision of whether to make or buy? The answer, again, depends on the situation. A key factor is whether there are idle facilities. Many companies make parts only when their facilities cannot be used to better advantage.

Assume that the following costs are reported:

General Electric Company
Cost of Making Part No. 900

	Total Cost for 20,000 Units	Cost per Unit
Direct material	$ 20,000	$ 1
Direct labor	80,000	4
Variable factory overhead	40,000	2
Fixed factory overhead	80,000	4
Total costs	$220,000	$11

Another manufacturer offers to sell General Electric (GE) the same part for $10. Should GE make or buy the part?

Although the $11 unit cost shown seemingly indicates that the company should buy, the answer is rarely so obvious. The essential question is the difference in expected future costs between the alternatives. If the $4 fixed overhead per unit consists of costs that will continue regardless of the decision, the entire $4 becomes irrelevant. Examples of such costs include depreciation, property taxes, insurance, and allocated executive salaries.

Again, are only the variable costs relevant? No. Perhaps $20,000 of the fixed costs will be eliminated if the parts are bought instead of made. For example, a supervisor with a $20,000 salary might be released. In other words, fixed costs that may be avoided in the future are relevant.

For the moment, suppose the capacity now used to make parts will become idle if the parts are purchased and the $20,000 supervisor's salary is the only fixed cost that would be eliminated. The relevant computations follow:

	Make		Buy	
	Total	*Per Unit*	*Total*	*Per Unit*
Purchase cost			$200,000	$10
Direct material	$ 20,000	$ 1		
Direct labor	80,000	4		
Variable factory overhead	40,000	2		
Fixed factory overhead that can be avoided by not making (supervisor's salary)	20,000*	1*		
Total relevant costs	$160,000	$ 8	$200,000	$10
Difference in favor of making	$ 40,000	$ 2		

*Note that unavoidable fixed costs of $80,000 − $20,000 = $60,000 are irrelevant. Thus the irrelevant costs per unit are $4 − $1 = $3.

The key to make-or-buy decisions is identifying the *additional costs* for making (or the *costs avoided* by buying) a part or subcomponent. Activity analysis, described in Chapter 3, helps identify these costs. Production of a product requires a set of activities. A company with accurate measurements of the costs of its various activities can better estimate the additional costs incurred to produce an item. GE's activities for production of part number 900 were measured by two cost drivers, units of production of $8 per unit and supervision at a $20,000 fixed cost. Sometimes identification and measurement of additional cost drivers, especially non-volume-related cost drivers, can improve the predictions of the additional cost to produce a part or subcomponent.

MAKE OR BUY AND THE USE OF FACILITIES

Make-or-buy decisions are rarely as simple as is the one in our GE example. As we said earlier, the use of facilities is a key to the make-or-buy decision. For simplicity, we assumed that the GE facilities would remain idle if the company chose to buy the product. Of course, in most cases companies will not leave their facilities idle. Instead, they will often put idle facilities to some other use, and we must consider the financial outcomes of these uses when choosing to make or buy.

Suppose the released facilities in our example can be used advantageously in some other manufacturing activity (to produce a contribution to profits of, say, $55,000) or can be rented out (say, for $35,000). We now have four alternatives to consider (figures are in thousands):

	Make	Buy and Leave Facilities Idle	Buy and Rent out Facilities	Buy and Use Facilities for Other Products
Rent revenue	$—	$ —	$ 35	$ —
Contribution from other products	—	—	—	55
Obtaining of parts	(160)	(200)	(200)	(200)
Net relevant costs	$(160)	$(200)	$(165)	$(145)

The final column indicates that buying the parts and using the vacated facilities for the production of other products would yield the lowest net costs in this case.

In sum, the make-or-buy decision should focus on relevant costs in a particular decision situation. In all cases, companies should relate make-or-buy decisions to the long-run policies for the use of capacity.

An Example of Make or Buy: Outsourcing

Make-or-buy decisions apply to services as well as to products. One type of make-or-buy decision faced by many companies in the mid-1990s was whether to buy data processing and computer network services or to provide them internally. Many companies eliminated their internal departments and "outsourced" (or bought) data processing services and network services from companies such as Electronic Data Systems.

One of the first major companies to outsource its data processing was Eastman Kodak. By hiring IBM and Digital Equipment, Kodak was able to eliminate 1,000 jobs and avoid huge capital investments. Another example is J. P. Morgan & Co., which hired BT North America to link 26 Morgan offices in 14 countries. The five-year, $20-million contract is expected to save Morgan $12.5 million. Other outsourcing agreements include Sprint running Unilever's network, MCI handling Sun Micro-system's Pacific Rim network, AT&T working on Chevron's network, and GE Information Services operating the Vatican's global data network. Some companies, such as Sun Microsystems, outsource everything except their core technologies. Sun focuses on hardware and software design and outsources nearly everything else. Its employees do not actually produce any of the products that bear the company's name.

The driving forces behind most outsourcing decisions are access to technology and cost savings. As the complexity of data processing and especially net-working has grown, companies have found it harder and harder to keep current with the technology. Instead of investing huge sums in personnel and equipment and diverting attention from the value-added activities of their own businesses, many firms have found outsourcing financially attractive. The big stumbling block to outsourcing has been subjective factors, such as control. To make outsourcing attractive, the services must be reliable, be available when needed, and be flexible enough to adapt to changing conditions. Companies that have successful outsourcing arrangements have been careful to include the subjective factors in their decisions.

Outsourcing has become so profitable that 77% of the Fortune 500 companies outsource some aspect of their business support services. The total value of outsourcing contracts in the United States is more than $10 billion. An association, the Outsourcing Institute, was formed to provide "objective, independent information on the strategic use of outside resources." The institute regularly sponsors a special advertising section in *Fortune* magazine.

Sources: Adapted from "Telecommunications: More Firms 'Outsource' Data Networks," The *Wall Street Journal*, March 11, 1992, p. B1; R. Suh, "Guaranteeing that Outsourcing Serves Your Business Strategy," *Information Strategy: The Executive's Journal*, Spring 1992, pp. 39–42; R. Zahler, "Identifying the Key Issues for Assessing Outsourcing," *Network World*, March 30, 1992, pp. 21, 23; J. Radigan, "All Wired Up at Morgan," *Bank Systems & Technology*, March 1992, pp. 25, 27; R.E. Drtina, "The Outsourcing Decision," *Management Accounting*, March, 1994, pp. 56–62; and M.F. Corbett, "Outsourcing: Redefining the Corporation of the Future," *Fortune*, December 12, 1994, pp. 51–92.

To illustrate, suppose a company uses its facilities, *on average,* 80% of the time. However, because of seasonal changes in the demand for its product, the actual demand for the facilities varies from 60% in the off season to over 100% in the peak season. During the off season, the company may decide to perform special projects for other manufacturers (on a subcontract). There is profit on these projects but not enough to justify expanding the capacity of the facilities. During the peak season, the company meets the high volume by purchasing some parts. Again, the cost of purchased parts is higher than the cost to make them in the company's own facilities if there were idle capacity, but purchasing the parts is less costly than buying the facilities to produce them.

JOINT PRODUCT COSTS

NATURE OF JOINT PRODUCTS

joint products Two or more manufactured products that (1) have relatively significant sales values and (2) are not separately identifiable as individual products until their split-off point.

When two or more manufactured products (1) have relatively significant sales values and (2) are not separately identifiable as individual products until their split-off point, they are called **joint products.** The **split-off point** is that juncture of manufacturing where the joint products become individually identifiable. Any costs beyond that stage are called **separable costs** because they are not part of the joint process and can be exclusively identified with individual products. The costs of manufacturing joint products before the split-off point are called **joint costs.** Examples of joint products include chemicals, lumber, flour, and the products of petroleum refining and meat packing. A meat-packing company cannot kill a sirloin steak; it has to slaughter a steer, which supplies various cuts of dressed meat, hides, and trimmings.

To illustrate joint costs, suppose Dow Chemical Company produces two chemical products, X and Y, as a result of a particular joint process. The joint processing cost is $100,000. This includes raw material costs and the cost of processing to the point where X and Y go their separate ways. Both products are sold to the petroleum industry to be used as ingredients of gasoline. The relationships follow:

split-off point The juncture of manufacturing where the joint products become individually identifiable.

separable costs Any cost beyond the split-off point.

joint costs The costs of manufacturing joint products prior to the split-off point.

SELL OR PROCESS FURTHER

Managers frequently face decisions of whether to sell joint products at split-off or to process some or all products further. Suppose the 500,000 liters of Y can be processed further and sold to the plastics industry as product YA, an ingredient for plastic sheeting. The additional processing cost would be $.08 per liter for manufacturing and distribution, a total of $40,000 for 500,000 liters. The net sales price of YA would be $.16 per liter, a total of $80,000.

Product X cannot be processed further and will be sold at the split-off point, but management is undecided about Product Y. Should Y be sold or should it be processed into YA? To answer this question we need to find the relevant costs involved. Because the joint costs must be incurred to reach the split-off point, they might seem relevant. However, they cannot affect anything *beyond* the split-off point. Therefore, they do not differ between alternatives and are completely irrelevant to the question of whether to sell or process further. The only approach that will yield valid results is to concentrate on the separable costs and revenue beyond split-off, as shown in Exhibit 6-1.

This analysis shows that it would be $10,000 more profitable to process Y beyond split-off than to sell Y at split-off. Briefly, it is profitable to extend processing or to incur additional distribution costs on a joint product *if* the additional revenue exceeds the additional expenses.

Exhibit 6-2 illustrates another way to compare the alternatives of (1) selling Y at the split-off point and (2) processing Y beyond split-off. It includes the joint costs, which are the same for each alternative and therefore do not affect the difference.

The allocation of joint costs would not affect the decision, as Exhibit 6-2 demonstrates. The joint costs are not allocated in the exhibit, but no matter how they might be allocated, the total income effects would be unchanged. Additional coverage of joint costs and inventory valuation can be found in Chapter 12.

Objective 3
Decide whether a joint product should be processed beyond the split-off point.

Exhibit 6-1

Illustration of Sell or Process Further

	Sell at Split-Off as Y	Process Further and Sell as YA	Difference
Revenues	$30,000	$80,000	$50,000
Separable costs beyond split-off @ $.08	—	40,000	40,000
Income effects	$30,000	$40,000	$10,000

Exhibit 6-2

Sell or Process Further Analysis—Firm as Whole

	(1) Alternative One			(2) Alternative Two			(3)
	X	Y	Total	X	YA	Total	Differential Effects
Revenues	$90,000	$30,000	$120,000	$90,000	$80,000	$170,000	$50,000
Joint costs			$100,000			$100,000	—
Separable costs			—		40,000	40,000	40,000
Total costs			$100,000			$140,000	$40,000
Income effects			$ 20,000			$ 30,000	$10,000

IRRELEVANCE OF PAST COSTS

The ability to recognize and thereby ignore irrelevant costs is sometimes just as important to decision makers as identifying relevant costs. How do we know that past costs, although sometimes predictors, are irrelevant in decision making? Consider such past costs as obsolete inventory and the book value of old equipment to see why they are irrelevant to decisions.

OBSOLETE INVENTORY

Objective 4
Identify irrelevant information in disposal of obsolete inventory and equipment replacement decisions.

Suppose General Dynamics has 100 obsolete aircraft parts in its inventory. The original manufacturing cost of these parts was $100,000. General Dynamics can (1) remachine the parts for $30,000 and then sell them for $50,000 or (2) scrap them for $5,000. Which should it do?

This is an unfortunate situation, yet the $100,000 past cost is irrelevant to the decision to remachine or scrap. The only relevant factors are the expected future revenues and costs:

	Remachine	Scrap	Difference
Expected future revenue	$ 50,000	$ 5,000	$45,000
Expected future costs	30,000	—	30,000
Relevant excess of revenue over costs	$ 20,000	$ 5,000	$15,000
Accumulated historical inventory cost*	100,000	100,000	—
Net overall loss on project	$ (80,000)	$(95,000)	$15,000

* Irrelevant because it is unaffected by the decision.

As you can see from the fourth line of the preceding table, we can completely ignore the $100,000 historical cost and still arrive at the $15,000 difference, the key figure in the analysis.

BOOK VALUE OF OLD EQUIPMENT

Like obsolete parts, the book value of equipment is not a relevant consideration in deciding whether to replace the equipment. Why? Because it is a past cost, not a future cost. When equipment is purchased, its cost is spread over (or charged to) the future periods in which the equipment is expected to be used. This periodic cost is called **depreciation.** The equipment's **book value** (or **net book value**) is the original cost less accumulated depreciation, which is the sum of all depreciation charged to past periods. For example, suppose a $10,000 machine with a 10-year life has depreciation of $1,000 per year. At the end of six years, accumulated depreciation is $6 \times \$1,000 = \$6,000$, and the book value is $\$10,000 - \$6,000 = \$4,000$.

Consider the following data for a decision whether to replace an old machine:

depreciation The periodic cost of equipment which is spread over (or charged to) the future periods in which the equipment is expected to be used.

book value (net book value) The original cost of equipment less accumulated depreciation, which is the summation of depreciation charged to past periods.

	Old Machine	Replacement Machine
Original cost	$10,000	$8,000
Useful life in years	10	4
Current age in years	6	0
Useful life remaining in years	4	4
Accumulated depreciation	$ 6,000	0
Book value	$ 4,000	Not acquired yet
Disposal value (in cash) now	$ 2,500	Not acquired yet
Disposal value in 4 years	0	0
Annual cash operating costs (maintenance, power, repairs, coolants, and so on)	$ 5,000	$3,000

We have been asked to prepare a comparative analysis of the two alternatives. Before proceeding, consider some important concepts. The most widely misunderstood facet of replacement decision making is the role of the book value of the old equipment in the decision. The book value, in this context, is sometimes called a **sunk cost,** which is really just another term for *historical* or *past cost,* a cost that has already been incurred and, therefore, is irrelevant to the decision-making process. At one time or another, we all try to soothe the wounded pride arising from having made a bad purchase decision by using an item instead of replacing it. It is a serious mistake to think, however, that a current or future action can influence the long-run impact of a past outlay. All past costs are down the drain. Nothing can change what has already happened.

sunk cost A cost that has already been incurred and, therefore, is irrelevant to the decision making process.

The irrelevance of past costs for decisions does not mean that knowledge of past costs is useless. Often managers use past costs to help predict future costs. In addition, past costs affect future payments for income taxes (as explained in Chapter 11). However, the past cost itself is not relevant. The only relevant cost is the predicted future cost.

In deciding whether to replace or keep existing equipment, we must consider the relevance of four commonly encountered items:[1]

- *Book value of old equipment:* Irrelevant, because it is a past (historical) cost. Therefore, depreciation on old equipment is irrelevant.

- *Disposal value of old equipment:* Relevant (ordinarily), because it is an expected future inflow that usually differs among alternatives.

---

[1] *For simplicity, we ignore income tax considerations and the effects of the interest value of money in this chapter. Book value is irrelevant even if income taxes are considered, however, because the relevant item is then the tax cash flow, not the book value. The book value is essential information for predicting the amount and timing of future tax cash flows, but, by itself, the book value is irrelevant. For elaboration, see Chapter 11.*

Exhibit 6-3

Cost Comparison—Replacement of Equipment Including Relevant and Irrelevant Items

	Four Years Together		
	Keep	*Replace*	*Difference*
Cash operating costs	$20,000	$12,000	$ 8,000
Old equipment (book value)			
Periodic write-off as depreciation	4,000	—	
or			—
Lump-sum write-off		4,000*	
Disposal value	—	−2,500*	2,500
New machine			
Acquisition cost	—	8,000†	−8,000
Total costs	$24,000	$21,500	$ 2,500
The advantage of replacement is $2,500 for the four years together.			

* In a formal income statement, these two items would be combined as "loss on disposal" of $4,000 − $2,500 = $1,500.

† In a formal income statement, written off as straight-line depreciation of $8,000 ÷ 4 = $2,000 for each of four years.

- *Gain or loss on disposal:* This is the difference between book value and disposal value. It is therefore a meaningless combination of irrelevant and relevant items. The combination form, loss (or gain) on disposal, blurs the distinction between the irrelevant book value and the relevant disposal value. Consequently, it is best to think of each separately.
- *Cost of new equipment:* Relevant, because it is an expected future outflow that will differ among alternatives. Therefore depreciation on new equipment is relevant.

Exhibit 6-3 shows the relevance of these items in our example. Book value of old equipment is irrelevant regardless of the decision-making technique used. The "difference" column in Exhibit 6-3 shows that the $4,000 book value of the *old* equipment does not differ between alternatives. It should be completely ignored for decision-making purposes. The difference is merely one of timing. The amount written off is still $4,000, regardless of any available alternative. The $4,000 appears on the income statement either as a $4,000 deduction from the $2,500 cash proceeds received to obtain a $1,500 loss on disposal in the first year or as $1,000 of depreciation in each of 4 years. But how it appears is irrelevant to the replacement decision. In contrast, the $2,000 annual depreciation on the new equipment is relevant because the total $8,000 depreciation is a future cost that may be avoided by not replacing. The three relevant items, operating costs, disposal value, and acquisition cost, give replacement a net advantage of $2,500.

EXAMINATION OF ALTERNATIVES OVER THE LONG RUN

Exhibit 6-3 is the first example that looks beyond one year. Examining the alternatives over the entire lives ensures that peculiar nonrecurring items (such as loss on disposal) will not obstruct the long-run view vital to many managerial decisions.[2]

Exhibit 6-4 concentrates on relevant items only: the cash operating costs, the disposal value of the old equipment, and the depreciation on the new equipment. To demonstrate that the amount of the old equipment's book value will not affect the answer, suppose the book value of the old equipment is $500,000 rather than $4,000. Your final answer will not

---

[2] *A more complete analysis that includes the timing of revenues and costs appears in Chapter 11.*

Exhibit 6-4

Cost Comparison—Replacement of Equipment, Relevant Items Only

	Four Years Together		
	Keep	Replace	Difference
Cash operating costs	$20,000	$12,000	$8,000
Disposal value of old machine	—	−2,500	2,500
New machine, acquisition cost	—	8,000	−8,000
Total relevant costs	$20,000	$17,500	$2,500

change. The cumulative advantage of replacement is still $2,500. (If you are in doubt, rework this example, using $500,000 as the book value.)

IRRELEVANCE OF FUTURE COSTS THAT WILL NOT DIFFER

In addition to past costs, some *future* costs may be irrelevant because they will be the same under all feasible alternatives. These, too, may be safely ignored for a particular decision. The salaries of many members of top management are examples of expected future costs that will be unaffected by the decision at hand.

Other irrelevant future costs include fixed costs that will be unchanged by such considerations as whether machine X or machine Y is selected. However, it is not merely a case of saying that fixed costs are irrelevant and variable costs are relevant. Variable costs can be irrelevant, and fixed costs can be relevant. For instance, sales commissions might

Sunk Costs and Government Contracts

It is easy to agree that—in theory—sunk costs should be ignored when making decisions. But in practice sunk costs often influence important decisions, especially when a decision maker doesn't want to admit that a previous decision to invest funds was a bad decision.

Consider two examples from the *St. Louis Post Dispatch*: (1) Larry O. Welch, the air force chief of staff, was quoted as saying that "the B-2 already is into production; cancel it and the $17 billion front end investment is lost." (2) Les Aspin, chairman of the House Armed Services Committee, was quoted as stating that "with $17 billion already invested in it, the B-2 is too costly to cancel."

The $17 billion already invested in the B-2 is a sunk cost. It is "lost" regardless of whether production of the B-2 is canceled or not. And whether B-2 production is too costly to continue depends only on the future costs necessary to complete production compared to the value of the completed B-2s. The $17 billion was relevant when the original decision to begin development of the B-2 was made, but now that the money has been spent, it is no longer relevant. No decision can affect it.

Why would intelligent leaders consider the $17 billion relevant to the decision on continuing production of the B-2? Probably because it is difficult to admit that no benefit would be derived from the $17 billion investment. Those who favor canceling production of the B-2 would consider the outcome of the original investment decision to be unfavorable. With perfect hindsight, they believe the investment should not have been made. It is human nature to find unpleasant the task of admitting that $17 billion was wasted. Yet, it is more important to avoid throwing good money after bad—that is, if the value of the B-2 is not at least equal to the future investment in it, production should be terminated, regardless of the amount spent to date.

Failure to ignore sunk costs is not unique to the U.S. government. In reference to Russia's store of bomb-grade plutonium, the country's Minister of Atomic Energy stated, "We have spent too much money making this material to just mix it with radioactive wastes and bury it." Burying the plutonium may or may not be the best decision, but the amount already spent is not relevant to the decision.

Sources: Adapted from J. Berg, J. Dickhaut, and C. Kanodia, "The Role of Private Information in the Sunk Cost Phenomenon," unpublished paper, November 12, 1991; M. Wald and M. Gordon, "Russia Treasures Plutonium, But U.S. Wants to Destroy It," *New York Times*, August 19, 1994, p. A1.

be paid on an order regardless of whether the order was filled from plant G or plant H. Variable costs are irrelevant whenever they do not differ among the alternatives at hand, and fixed costs are relevant whenever they differ between the alternatives at hand.

BEWARE OF UNIT COSTS

Objective 5
Explain how unit costs can be misleading.

The pricing illustration in Chapter 5 showed that unit costs should be analyzed with care in decision making. There are two major ways to go wrong: (1) the inclusion of irrelevant costs, such as the $3 allocation of unavoidable fixed costs in the General Electric make-or-buy example (p. 216) that would result in a unit cost of $11 instead of the relevant unit cost of $8, and (2) comparisons of unit costs not computed on the same volume basis, as the following example demonstrates. Machinery sales personnel, for example, often brag about the low unit costs of using the new machines. Sometimes they neglect to point out that the unit costs are based on outputs far in excess of the volume of activity of their prospective customer. Assume that a new $100,000 machine with a five-year life can produce 100,000 units a year at a variable cost of $1 per unit, as opposed to a variable cost per unit of $1.50 with an old machine. A sales representative claims that the new machine will reduce cost by $.30 per unit. Is the new machine a worthwhile acquisition?

The new machine is attractive at first glance. If the customer's expected volume is 100,000 units, unit-cost comparisons are valid, provided that new depreciation is also considered. Assume that the disposal value of the old equipment is zero. Because depreciation is an allocation of historical cost, the depreciation on the old machine is irrelevant. In contrast, the depreciation on the new machine is relevant because the new machine entails a future cost that can be avoided by not acquiring it:

	Old Machine	New Machine
Units	100,000	100,000
Variable costs	$150,000	$100,000
Straight-line depreciation	—	20,000
Total relevant costs	$150,000	$120,000
Unit relevant costs	$ 1.50	$ 1.20

Apparently, the sales representative is correct. However, if the customer's expected volume is only 30,000 units per year, the unit costs change in favor of the old machine:

	Old Machine	New Machine
Units	30,000	30,000
Variable costs	$45,000	$30,000
Straight-line depreciation	—	20,000
Total relevant costs	$45,000	$50,000
Unit relevant costs	$ 1.50	$1.6667

Generally, be wary of unit fixed costs. Use total costs rather than unit costs. Then, if desired, the totals may be unitized.

CONFLICTS BETWEEN DECISION MAKING AND PERFORMANCE EVALUATION

You should now know how to make good decisions based on relevant data. However, knowing how to make these decisions and actually making them are two different things. Managers might be tempted to make decisions they know are poor if the performance measures in place will reward them for those decisions. To motivate managers to make optimal decisions, methods of evaluating the performance of managers should be consistent with the decision analysis.

Consider the replacement decision shown in Exhibit 6-4 on page 223, where replacing the machine had a $2,500 advantage over keeping it. To motivate managers to make the right choice, the method used to evaluate performance should be consistent with the decision model—that is, it should show better performance when managers replace the machine than when they keep it. Because performance is often measured by accounting income, consider the accounting income in the first year after replacement compared with that in years 2, 3, and 4.

Objective 6
Discuss how performance measures can affect decision making.

	Year 1		Years 2, 3, and 4	
	Keep	*Replace*	*Keep*	*Replace*
Cash operating costs	$5,000	$3,000	$5,000	$3,000
Depreciation	1,000	2,000	1,000	2,000
Loss on disposal ($4,000 − $2,500)	—	$1,500	—	—
Total charges against revenue	$6,000	$6,500	$6,000	$5,000

If the machine is kept rather than replaced, first-year costs will be $6,500 − $6,000 = $500 lower, and first-year income will be $500 higher. Because managers naturally want to make decisions that maximize the measure of their performance, they may be inclined to keep the machine. This is an example of a conflict between the analysis for decision making and the method used to evaluate performance.

The conflict is especially severe if managers are transferred often from one position to another. Why? Because the $500 first-year advantage for keeping will be offset by a $1,000 annual advantage of replacing in years 2 to 4. (Note that the net difference of $2,500 in favor of replacement over the four years together is the same as in Exhibit 6-4.) A manager who moves to a new position after the first year, however, bears the entire loss on disposal without reaping the benefits of lower operating costs in years 2 to 4.

The decision to replace a machine earlier than planned also reveals that the original decision to purchase the machine may have been flawed. The old machine was bought six years ago for $10,000. Its expected life was 10 years. However, if a better machine is now available, then the useful life of the old machine was really six years, not 10. This feedback on the actual life of the old machine has two possible effects, the first good and the second bad. First, managers might learn from the earlier mistake. If the useful life of the old machine was overestimated, how believable is the prediction that the new machine will have a four-year life? Feedback can help avoid repeating past mistakes. Second, another mistake might be made to cover up the earlier one. A "loss on disposal" could alert superiors to the incorrect economic-life prediction used in the earlier decision. By avoiding replacement, the $4,000 remaining book value is spread over the future as "depreciation," a more appealing term than "loss on disposal." The superiors may never find out about the incorrect prediction of economic life. The accounting income approach to performance evaluation mixes the financial effects of various decisions, hiding both the earlier misestimation of useful life and the current failure to replace.

The conflict between decision making and performance evaluation is a widespread problem in practice. Unfortunately, there are no easy solutions. In theory, accountants could evaluate performance in a manner consistent with decision making. In our equipment example, this would mean predicting year-by-year income effects over the planning horizon of four years, noting that the first year would be poor, and evaluating actual performance against the predictions.

The trouble is that evaluating performance, decision by decision, is a costly procedure. Therefore aggregate measures are used. For example, an income statement shows the results of many decisions, not just the single decision of buying a machine. Consequently, in many cases like our equipment example, managers may be most heavily influenced by the first-year effects on the income statement. Thus managers refrain from taking the longer view that would benefit the company.

SUMMARY PROBLEM FOR YOUR REVIEW

PROBLEM

Exhibit 6-5 contains data for the Block Company for the year just ended. The company makes industrial power drills. Exhibit 6-5 shows the costs of the plastic housing separately from the costs of the electrical and mechanical components.

Required

1. During the year, a prospective customer in an unrelated market offered $82,000 for 1,000 drills. The latter would be in addition to the 100,000 units sold. The regular sales commission rate would have been paid. The president rejected the order because "it was below our costs of $97 per unit." What would operating income have been if the order had been accepted?

2. A supplier offered to manufacture the year's supply of 100,000 plastic housings for $13.50 each. What would be the effect on operating income if the Block Company purchased rather than made the housings? Assume that $350,000 of the separable fixed costs assigned to housings would have been avoided if the housings were purchased.

3. The company could have purchased the housings for $13.50 each and used the vacated space for the manufacture of a deluxe version of its drill. Assume that 20,000 deluxe units could have been made (and sold in addition to the 100,000 regular units) at a unit variable cost of $90, exclusive of housings and exclusive of the 10% sales commission. The 20,000 extra plastic housings could also be purchased for $13.50 each. The sales price would have been $130. All the fixed costs pertaining to the plastic housings would have continued, because these costs related primarily to the manufacturing facilities used. What would operating income have been if Block had bought the housings and made and sold the deluxe units?

Exhibit 6-5
Block Company Cost of Industrial Drills

	A	B	A + B
	Electrical and Mechanical Components*	**Plastic Housing**	**Industrial Drills**
Sales: 100,000 units, @ $100			$10,000,000
Variable costs			
Direct material	$4,400,000	$ 500,000	$ 4,900,000
Direct labor	400,000	300,000	700,000
Variable factory overhead	100,000	200,000	300,000
Other variable costs	100,000	—	100,000
Sales commissions, @ 10% of sales	1,000,000	—	1,000,000
Total variable costs	$6,000,000	$1,000,000	$ 7,000,000
Contribution margin			$ 3,000,000
Separable fixed costs	$1,900,000	$ 400,000	$ 2,300,000
Common fixed costs	320,000	80,000	400,000
Total fixed costs	$2,220,000	$ 480,000	$ 2,700,000
Operating income			$ 300,000

*Not including the costs of plastic housing (column B).

SOLUTION

1. The costs of filling the special order follow:

Direct material	$49,000
Direct labor	7,000
Variable factory overhead	3,000
Other variable costs	1,000
Sales commission @ 10% of $82,000	8,200
Total variable costs	$68,200
Selling price	82,000
Contribution margin	$13,800

Operating income would have been $300,000 + $13,800, or $313,800, if the order had been accepted. In a sense, the decision to reject the offer implies that the Block Company is willing to invest $13,800 in immediate gains foregone (an opportunity cost) in order to preserve the long-run selling-price structure.

2. Assuming that $350,000 of the fixed costs could have been avoided by not making the housings and that the other fixed costs would have continued, the alternatives can be summarized as follows:

	Make	Buy
Purchase cost		$1,350,000
Variable costs	$1,000,000	
Avoidable fixed costs	350,000	
Total relevant costs	$1,350,000	$1,350,000

If the facilities used for plastic housings became idle, the Block Company would be indifferent as to whether to make or buy. Operating income would be unaffected.

3. The effect of purchasing the plastic housings and using the vacated facilities for the manufacture of a deluxe version of its drill is:

Sales would increase by 20,000 units, @ $130			$2,600,000
Variable costs exclusive of parts would increase by			
20,000 units, @ $90		$1,800,000	
Plus: sales commission, 10% of $2,600,000		260,000	2,060,000
Contribution margin on 20,000 units			$ 540,000
Housings: 120,000 rather than 100,000 would			
be needed			
Buy 120,000 @ $13.50		$1,620,000	
Make 100,000 @ $10 (only the variable costs			
are relevant)		1,000,000	
Excess cost of outside purchase			620,000
Fixed costs, unchanged			—
Disadvantage of making deluxe units			$ 80,000

Operating income would decline to $220,000 ($300,000 − $80,000). The deluxe units bring in a contribution margin of $540,000, but the additional costs of buying rather than making housings is $620,000, leading to a net disadvantage of $80,000.

Highlights to Remember

Use opportunity cost to analyze the income effects of a given alternative. Opportunity costs should always be considered when deciding on the use of limited resources. The opportunity cost of a course of action is the maximum profit foregone from other alternative actions. Decision makers may fail to consider opportunity costs because they are not reported in the financial accounting system.

Decide whether to make or buy certain parts or products. One of the most important production decisions is the make-buy decision. Should a company make its own parts or products or should it buy them from outside sources? Both qualitative and quantitative factors affect this decision. In applying relevant cost analysis to a make-buy situation, a key factor to consider is the use of facilities.

Decide whether a joint product should be processed beyond the split-off point. Another typical production situation is deciding whether to process further a joint product or sell it at the split-off point. The relevant information for this decision includes the costs that differ beyond the split-off point. Joint costs that occur before split-off are irrelevant.

Identify irrelevant information in disposal of obsolete inventory and equipment replacement decisions. In certain production decisions, it is important to recognize and identify irrelevant costs. In the decision to dispose of obsolete inventory, the original cost of the inventory is irrelevant because the resources used to get the inventory cannot be restored. The book value of old equipment is also irrelevant to the equipment replacement decision. This sunk cost is a past or historical cost that has already been incurred.

Explain how unit costs can be misleading. Unit fixed costs can be misleading because of the differences in the assumed level of volume on which they are based. The more units a company makes, the lower the unit fixed cost will be. If a salesperson assumes 100,000 units will be produced and only 30,000 are actually made, the unit costs will be understated. You can avoid being misled by unit costs by always using total fixed costs.

Discuss how performance measures can affect decision making. If companies evaluate managers using performance measures that are not in line with relevant decision criteria, there could be a conflict of interest. Managers often make decisions based on how the decision affects their performance measures. Thus, performance measures work best when they are consistent with the long-term good of the company.

Understand the relationship between accounting information and decisions in the production stage of the value chain. In the production stage of the value chain, managers make decisions about product mix, production equipment, labor, and all other factors that affect the creation of goods and services. Managers need timely and relevant accounting information to make these decisions on an objective, quantifiable basis. The accounting information used must be relevant to the decision at hand, so accountants must take extra care in determining which factors affect future costs that differ between alternatives.

Accounting Vocabulary

book value, p. 221	joint costs, p. 219	outlay cost, p. 214
depreciation, p. 221	joint products, p. 218	separable costs, p. 219
differential cost, p. 214	net book value, p. 221	split-off point, p. 219
incremental cost, p. 214	opportunity cost, p. 214	sunk cost, p. 221

Fundamental Assignment Material

6-A1 Role of Old Equipment Replacement

On January 2, 19X9, the S. H. Park Company installed a brand new $87,000 special molding machine for producing a new product. The product and the machine have an expected life of three years. The machine's expected disposal value at the end of three years is zero.

On January 3, 19X9, Kimiyo Lee, a star salesperson for a machine tool manufacturer, tells Mr. Park: "I wish I had known earlier of your purchase plans. I can supply you with a technically superior machine for $99,000. The machine you just purchased can be sold for $16,000. I guarantee that our machine will save $35,000 per year in cash operating costs, although it too will have no disposal value at the end of three years."

Park examines some technical data. Although he has confidence in Lee's claims, Park contends: "I'm locked in now. My alternatives are clear: (a) disposal will result in a loss, (b) keeping and using the 'old' equipment avoids such a loss. I have brains enough to avoid a loss when my other alternative is recognizing a loss. We've got to use that equipment until we get our money out of it."

The annual operating costs of the old machine are expected to be $60,000, exclusive of depreciation. Sales, all in cash, will be $910,000 per year. Other annual cash expenses will be $810,000 regardless of this decision. Assume that the equipment in question is the company's only fixed asset.

Ignore income taxes and the time value of money.

Required

1. Prepare statements of cash receipts and disbursements as they would appear in each of the next three years under both alternatives. What is the total cumulative increase or decrease in cash for the three years?

2. Prepare income statements as they would appear in each of the next three years under both alternatives. Assume straight-line depreciation. What is the cumulative increase or decrease in net income for the three years?

3. Assume that the cost of the "old" equipment was $1 million rather than $87,000. Would the net difference computed in requirements 1 and 2 change? Explain.

4. As Kimiyo Lee, reply to Mr. Park's contentions.

5. What are the irrelevant items in each of your presentations for requirements 1 and 2? Why are they irrelevant?

6-A2 Make or Buy

Sunshine State Fruit Company sells premium quality oranges and other citrus fruits by mail-order. Protecting the fruit during shipping is important, so the company has designed and produces shipping boxes. The annual cost of 80,000 boxes is:

Materials	$120,000
Labor	20,000
Overhead	
Variable	16,000
Fixed	60,000
Total	$216,000

Therefore, the cost per box averages $2.70.

Suppose Georgia-Pacific submits a bid to supply Sunshine State with boxes for $2.40 per box. Sunshine State must give Georgia-Pacific the box design specifications, and the boxes will be made according to those specs.

1. How much, if any, would Sunshine State save by buying the boxes from Georgia-Pacific?

2. What subjective factors should affect Sunshine State's decision whether to make or buy the boxes?

3. Suppose all the fixed costs represent depreciation on equipment that was purchased for $600,000 and is just about at the end of its 10-year life. New replacement equipment will cost $1 million and is also expected to last 10 years. In this case, how much, if any, would Sunshine State save by buying the boxes from Georgia-Pacific?

6-A3   Hospital Opportunity Cost

An administrator at Sacred Heart Hospital is considering how to use some space made available when the outpatient clinic moved to a new building. She has narrowed her choices as follows:

a. Use the space to expand laboratory testing. Expected future annual revenue would be $320,000; future costs, $290,000.

b. Use the space to expand the eye clinic. Expected future annual revenue would be $500,000; future costs, $480,000.

c. The gift shop is rented by an independent retailer who wants to expand into the vacated space. The retailer has offered an $11,000 yearly rental for the space. All operating expenses will be borne by the retailer.

The administrator's planning horizon is unsettled. However, she has decided that the yearly data given will suffice for guiding her decision.

Tabulate the total relevant data regarding the decision alternatives. Omit the concept of opportunity cost in one tabulation, but use the concept in a second tabulation. As the administrator, which tabulation would you prefer if you could receive only one?

6-A4   Joint Products: Sell or Process Further

The Mussina Chemical Company produced three joint products at a joint cost of $117,000. These products were processed further and sold as follows:

Chemical Product	Sales	Additional Processing Costs
A	$230,000	$190,000
B	330,000	300,000
C	175,000	100,000

The company has had an opportunity to sell at split-off directly to other processors. If that alternative had been selected, sales would have been: A, $54,000; B, $28,000; and C, $54,000.

The company expects to operate at the same level of production and sales in the forthcoming year.

Consider all the available information, and assume that all costs incurred after split-off are variable.

1. Could the company increase operating income by altering its processing decisions? If so, what would be the expected overall operating income?

2. Which products should be processed further and which should be sold at split-off?

6-B1 Replacing Old Equipment

Consider these data regarding Douglas County's photocopying requirements:

	Old Equipment	Proposed Replacement Equipment
Useful life, in years	5	3
Current age, in years	2	0
Useful life remaining, in years	3	3
Original cost	$30,000	$15,000
Accumulated depreciation	12,000	0
Book value	18,000	Not acquired yet
Disposal value (in cash) now	3,000	Not acquired yet
Disposal value in 2 years	0	0
Annual cash operating costs for power, maintenance, toner, and supplies	14,000	7,500

The county administrator is trying to decide whether to replace the old equipment. Because of rapid changes in technology, she expects the replacement equipment to have only a three-year useful life. Ignore the effects of taxes.

Required

1. Tabulate a cost comparison that includes both relevant and irrelevant items for the next three years together. (*Hint:* See Exhibit 6-3, page 222.)
2. Tabulate a cost comparison of all relevant items for the next three years together. Which tabulation is clearer, this one or the one in requirement 1? (*Hint:* See Exhibit 6-4, page 223.)
3. Prepare a simple "shortcut" or direct analysis to support your choice of alternatives.

6-B2 Decision and Performance Models

Refer to the preceding problem.

1. Suppose the "decision model" favored by top management consisted of a comparison of a three-year accumulation of cash under each alternative. As the manager of office operations, which alternative would you choose? Why?
2. Suppose the "performance evaluation model" emphasized the minimization of overall costs of photocopying operations for the first year. Which alternative would you choose?

6-B3 Make or Buy

Suppose a BMW executive in Germany is trying to decide whether the company should continue to manufacture an engine component or purchase it from Mainz Corporation for 50 deutsche marks (DM) each. Demand for the coming year is expected to be the same as for the current year, 200,000 units. Data for the current year follow:

Direct material	DM 5,000,000
Direct labor	1,900,000
Factory overhead, variable	1,100,000
Factory overhead, fixed	2,500,000
Total costs	DM10,500,000

If BMW makes the components, the unit costs of direct material will increase 10%.

If BMW buys the components, 40% of the fixed costs will be avoided. The other 60% will continue regardless of whether the components are manufactured or purchased. Assume that variable overhead varies with output volume.

Required

1. Tabulate a comparison of the make-or-buy alternatives. Show totals and amounts per unit. Compute the numerical difference between making and buying. Assume that the capacity now used to make the components will become idle if the components are purchased.

2. Assume also that the BMW capacity in question can be rented to a local electronics firm for DM1,250,000 for the coming year. Tabulate a comparison of the net relevant costs of the three alternatives: make, buy and leave capacity idle, buy and rent. Which is the most favorable alternative? By how much in total?

6-B4 Sell or Process Further

ConAgra, Inc. produces meat products with brand names such as Swift, Armour, and Butterball. Suppose one of the company's plants processes beef cattle into various products. For simplicity, assume that there are only three products: steak, hamburger, and hides, and that the average steer costs $700. The three products emerge from a process that costs $100 per steer to run, and output from one steer can be sold for the following net amounts:

Steak (100 pounds)	$ 400
Hamburger (500 pounds)	600
Hide (120 pounds)	100
Total	$1,100

Assume that each of these three products can be sold immediately or processed further in another ConAgra plant. The steak can be the main course in frozen dinners sold under the Healthy Choice label. The vegetables and desserts in the 400 dinners produced from the 100 pounds of steak would cost $120, and production, sales, and other costs for the 400 meals would total $350. Each meal would be sold wholesale for $2.15.

The hamburger could be made into frozen Salisbury Steak patties sold under the Armour label. The only additional cost would be a $200 processing cost for the 500 pounds of hamburger. Frozen Salisbury Steaks sell wholesale for $1.70 per pound.

The hide can be sold before or after tanning. The cost of tanning one hide is $80, and a tanned hide can be sold for $175.

Required

1. Compute the total profit if all three products are sold at the split-off point.

2. Compute the total profit if all three products are processed further before being sold.

3. Which products should be sold at the split-off point? Which should be processed further?

4. Compute the total profit if your plan in requirement 3 is followed.

Additional Assignment Material

QUESTIONS

6-1. Distinguish between an opportunity cost and an outlay cost.

6-2. "I had a chance to rent my summer home for two weeks for $800. But I chose to have it idle. I didn't want strangers living in my summer house." What term in this chapter describes the $800? Why?

6-3. "Accountants do not ordinarily record opportunity costs in the formal accounting records." Why?

232 PART ONE FOCUS ON DECISION MAKING

6-4. Distinguish between an incremental cost and a differential cost.

6-5. "Incremental cost is the addition to costs from the manufacture of one unit." Do you agree? Explain.

6-6. "The differential costs or incremental costs of increasing production from 1,000 automobiles to 1,200 automobiles per week would be the additional costs of producing the additional 200 automobiles." If production were reduced from 1,200 to 1,000 automobiles per week, what would the decline in costs be called?

6-7. "Qualitative factors generally favor making over buying a component." Do you agree? Explain.

6-8. "Choices are often mislabeled as simply *make* or *buy*." Do you agree? Explain.

6-9. What is the split-off point and why is it important in analyzing joint costs?

6-10. "No technique used to assign the joint cost to individual products should be used for management decisions regarding whether a product should be sold at the split-off point or processed further." Do you agree? Explain.

6-11. "Inventory that was purchased for $5,000 should not be sold for less than $5,000 because such a sale would result in a loss." Do you agree? Explain.

6-12. "Recovering sunk costs is a major objective when replacing equipment." Do you agree? Explain.

6-13. "Past costs are indeed relevant in most instances because they provide the point of departure for the entire decision process." Do you agree? Why?

6-14. Which of the following items are relevant to replacement decisions? Explain.
  a. Book value of old equipment
  b. Disposal value of old equipment
  c. Cost of new equipment

6-15. "Some expected future costs may be irrelevant." Do you agree? Explain.

6-16. "Variable costs are irrelevant whenever they do not differ among the alternatives at hand." Do you agree? Explain.

6-17. There are two major reasons why unit costs should be analyzed with care in decision making. What are they?

6-18. "Machinery sales personnel sometimes erroneously brag about the low unit costs of using their machines." Identify one source of an error concerning the estimation of unit costs.

6-19. Give an example of a situation in which the performance evaluation model is not consistent with the decision model.

6-20. "Evaluating performance, decision by decision, is costly. Aggregate measures, like the income statement, are frequently used." How might the wide use of income statements affect managers' decisions about buying equipment?

EXERCISES

6-21 Opportunity Costs

Martina Bridgeman is an attorney employed by a large law firm at $90,000 per year. She is considering whether to become a sole practitioner, which would probably generate annually $320,000 in operating revenues and $220,000 in operating expenses.

  1. Present two tabulations of the annual income effects of these alternatives. The second tabulation should include the opportunity cost of Bridgeman's compensation as an employee.

  2. Suppose Bridgeman prefers less risk and chooses to stay as an employee. Show a tabulation of the income effects of rejecting the opportunity of independent practice.

Required

6-22 Opportunity Cost of Home Ownership

Oliver Kemp has just made the final payment on his mortgage. He could continue to live in the home; cash expenses for repairs and maintenance (after any tax effects) would be $500 monthly. Alternatively, he could sell the home for $200,000 (net of taxes), invest the proceeds in 8% municipal tax-free bonds, and rent an apartment for $14,000 annually. The landlord would then pay for repairs and maintenance.

Prepare two analyses of Kemp's alternatives, one showing no explicit opportunity cost and the second showing the explicit opportunity cost of the decision to hold the present home.

Required

6-23 Make Or Buy

Assume that a division of NEC makes an electronic component for its speakers. Its manufacturing process for the component is a highly automated part of a just-in-time production system. All labor is considered to be an overhead cost, and all overhead is regarded as fixed with respect to output volume. Production costs for 100,000 units of the component are as follows:

Direct materials		$300,000
Factory overhead		
Indirect labor	$80,000	
Supplies	30,000	
Allocated occupancy cost	40,000	150,000
Total cost		$450,000

A small, local company has offered to supply the components at a price of $3.40 each. If the division discontinued its production of the component, it would save two-thirds of the supplies cost and $30,000 of indirect labor cost. All other overhead costs would continue.

The division manager recently attended a seminar on cost behavior and learned about fixed and variable costs. He wants to continue to make the component because the variable cost of $3.00 is below the $3.40 bid.

Required

1. Compute the relevant cost of (a) making and (b) purchasing the component. Which alternative is less costly and by how much?

2. What qualitative factors might influence the decision about whether to make or buy the component?

6-24 Sell or Process Further

An Exxon petrochemical factory produces two products, L and M, as a result of a particular joint process. Both products are sold to manufacturers as ingredients for assorted chemical products.

Product L sells at split-off for $.25 per gallon; M, for $.30 per gallon. Data for April follow:

Joint processing cost	$1,600,000
Gallons produced and sold	
L	4,000,000
M	2,500,000

Suppose that in April the 2,500,000 gallons of M could have been processed further into Super M at an additional cost of $225,000. The Super M output would be sold for $.38 per gallon. Product L would be sold at split-off in any event.

Required   Should M have been processed further in April and sold as Super M? Show computations.

6-25 Joint Products, Multiple Choice

From a particular joint process, Edgerton Company produces three products, A, B, and C. Each product may be sold at the point of split-off or processed further. Additional processing requires no special facilities, and production costs of further processing are entirely variable and traceable to the products involved. In 19X8 all three products were processed beyond split-off. Joint production costs for the year were $72,000. Sales values and costs needed to evaluate Edgerton's 19X8 production policy follow:

Product	Units Produced	Net Realizable Values (Sales Values) at Split-Off	Additional Costs and Sales Values if Processed Further	
			Sales Values	Added Costs
A	6,000	$25,000	$42,000	$9,000
B	4,000	41,000	45,000	7,000
C	2,000	24,000	32,000	8,000

Answer the following multiple-choice questions:

Required

1. For units of C, the unit production cost most relevant to a sell-or-process-further decision is (a) $5, (b) $12, (c) $4, (d) $9.
2. To maximize profits, Edgerton should subject the following products to additional processing (a) A only, (b) A, B, and C, (c) B and C only, (d) C only.

6-26   Obsolete Inventory

The local bookstore bought more Garfield calendars than it could sell. It was nearly June and 200 calendars remained in stock. The store paid $4.50 each for the calendars and normally sold them for $8.95. Since February, they had been on sale for $6.00, and two weeks ago the price was dropped to $5.00. Still, few calendars were being sold. The bookstore manager thought it was no longer worthwhile using shelf space for the calendars.

The proprietor of Mac's Collectibles offered to buy all 200 calendars for $250. He intended to store them a few years and then sell them as novelty items.

The bookstore manager was not sure she wanted to sell for $1.25 calendars that cost $4.50. The only alternative, however, was to scrap them because the publisher would not take them back.

Required

1. Compute the difference in profit between accepting the $250 offer and scrapping the calendars.
2. Describe how the $4.50 × 200 = $900 paid for the calendars affects your decision.

6-27   Replacement of Old Equipment

Three years ago the Oak Street TCBY bought a frozen yogurt machine for $8,000. A salesman has just suggested to the TCBY manager that she replace the machine with a new, $12,500 machine. The manager has gathered the following data:

	Old Machine	New Machine
Original cost	$8,000	$12,500
Useful life in years	8	5
Current age in years	3	0
Useful life remaining in years	5	5
Accumulated depreciation	$3,000	Not acquired yet
Book value	$5,000	Not acquired yet
Disposal value (in cash) now	$2,000	Not acquired yet
Disposal value in 5 years	0	0
Annual cash operating cost	$4,500	$2,000

1. Compute the difference in total costs over the next five years under both alternatives, that is, keeping the original machine or replacing it with the new machine. Ignore taxes.

2. Suppose the Oak Street TCBY manager replaces the original machine. Compute the "loss on disposal" of the original machine. How does this amount affect your computation in requirement 1? Explain.

6-28 Unit Costs

Brandon Company produces and sells a product that has variable costs of $9 per unit and fixed costs of $110,000 per year.

1. Compute the unit cost at a production and sales level of 10,000 units per year.

2. Compute the unit cost at a production and sales level of 20,000 units per year.

3. Which of these unit costs is most accurate? Explain.

6-29 Relevant Investment

Roberta Thomas had obtained a new truck with a list price, including options, of $21,000. The dealer had given her a "generous trade-in allowance" of $4,500 on her old truck that had a wholesale price of $3,000. Sales tax was $1,260.

The annual cash operating costs of the old truck were $4,200. The new truck was expected to reduce these costs by one-third.

Compute the amount of the original investment in the new truck. Explain your reasoning.

6-30 Weak Division

Lake Forest Electronics Company paid $7 million in cash four years ago to acquire a company that manufactures CD-ROM drives. This company has been operated as a division of Lake Forest and has lost $500,000 each year since its acquisition.

The minimum desired return for this division is that, when a new product is fully developed, it should return a net profit of $500,000 per year for the foreseeable future.

Recently the IBM Corporation offered to purchase the division from Lake Forest for $5 million. The president of Lake Forest commented, "I've got an investment of $9 million to recoup ($7 million plus losses of $500,000 for each of four years). I have finally got this situation turned around, so I oppose selling the division now."

Prepare a response to the president's remarks. Indicate how to make this decision. Be as specific as possible.

6-31 Opportunity Cost

Renee Behr, M.D., is a psychiatrist who is in heavy demand. Even though she has raised her fees considerably during the past five years, Dr. Behr still cannot accommodate all the patients who wish to see her.

Behr has conducted six hours of appointments a day, six days a week, for 48 weeks a year. Her fee averages $140 per hour.

Her variable costs are negligible and may be ignored for decision purposes. Ignore income taxes.

1. Behr is weary of working a six-day week. She is considering taking every other Saturday off. What would be her annual income (a) if she worked every Saturday and (b) if she worked every other Saturday?

2. What would be her opportunity cost for the year of not working every other Saturday?

3. Assume that Dr. Behr has definitely decided to take every other Saturday off. She loves to repair her sports car by doing the work herself. If she works on her car during half a Saturday when she otherwise would not see patients, what is her opportunity cost?

PROBLEMS

6-32 Hotel Rooms and Opportunity Costs

The Marriott Corporation operates many hotels throughout the world. Suppose one of its Chicago hotels is facing difficult times because of the opening of several new competing hotels.

To accommodate its flight personnel, Northwest Airlines has offered Marriott a contract for the coming year that provides a rate of $50 per night per room for a minimum of 50 rooms for 365 nights. This contract would assure Marriott of selling 50 rooms of space nightly, even if some of the rooms are vacant on some nights.

The Marriott manager has mixed feelings about the contract. On several peak nights during the year, the hotel could sell the same space for $100 per room.

1. Suppose the contract is signed. What is the opportunity cost of the 50 rooms on October 20, the night of a big convention of retailers when every nearby hotel room is occupied? What is the opportunity cost on December 28, when only 10 of these rooms would be expected to be rented at an average rate of $80?   **Required**

2. If the year-round rate per room averaged $90, what percentage of occupancy of the 50 rooms in question would have to be rented to make Marriott indifferent about accepting the offer?

6-33 Extension of Preceding Problem

Assume the same facts as in the preceding problem. However, also assume that the variable costs per room per day are $10.

1. Suppose the best estimate is a 53% general occupancy rate for the 50 rooms at an average $90 room rate for the next year. Should Marriott accept the contract?   **Required**

2. What percentage of occupancy of the 50 rooms in question would make Marriott indifferent about accepting the offer?

6-34 Make or Buy

Dana Corporation manufactures automobile parts. It frequently subcontracts work to other manufacturers, depending on whether Dana's facilities are fully occupied. Dana is about to make some final decisions regarding the use of its manufacturing facilities for the coming year.

The following are the costs of making part EC113, a key component of an emission control system:

	Total Cost for 50,000 Units	Cost per Unit
Direct material	$ 400,000	$ 8
Direct labor	300,000	6
Variable factory overhead	150,000	3
Fixed factory overhead	300,000	6
Total manufacturing costs	$1,150,000	$23

Another manufacturer has offered to sell the same part to Dana for $21 each. The fixed overhead consists of depreciation, property taxes, insurance, and supervisory salaries. All the fixed overhead would continue if Dana bought the component except that the cost of $100,000 pertaining to some supervisory and custodial personnel could be avoided.

Required

1. Assume that the capacity now used to make parts will become idle if the parts are purchased. Should the parts be made or bought? Show computations.

2. Assume that the capacity now used to make parts will either (a) be rented to a nearby manufacturer for $65,000 for the year or (b) be used to make oil filters that will yield a profit contribution of $200,000. Should part EC113 be made or bought? Show computations.

6-35 Relevant-Cost Analysis

Following are the unit costs of making and selling a single product at a normal level of 5,000 units per month and a current unit selling price of $90:

Manufacturing costs	
Direct material	$35
Direct labor	12
Variable overhead	8
Fixed overhead (total for the year, $300,000)	5
Selling and administrative expenses	
Variable	15
Fixed (total for the year, $480,000)	8

Required

Consider each requirement separately. Label all computations, and present your solutions in a form that will be comprehensible to the company president.

1. This product is usually sold at a rate of 60,000 units per year. It is predicted that a rise in price to $98 will decrease volume by 10%. How much may advertising be increased under this plan without having annual operating income fall below the current level?

2. The company has received a proposal from an outside supplier to make and ship this item directly to the company's customers as sales orders are forwarded. Variable selling and administrative costs would fall 40%. If the supplier's proposal is accepted, the company will use its own plant to produce a new product. The new product would be sold through manufacturer's agents at a 10% commission based on a selling price of $40 each. The cost characteristics of this product, based on predicted yearly normal volume, are as follows:

	Per Unit
Direct material	$ 6
Direct labor	12
Variable overhead	8
Fixed overhead	6
Manufacturing costs	$32
Selling and administrative expenses	
Variable (commission)	10% of selling price
Fixed	$ 2

What is the maximum price per unit that the company can afford to pay to the supplier for subcontracting production of the entire old product? Assume the following:

- Total fixed factory overhead and total fixed selling expenses will not change if the new product line is added.
- The supplier's proposal will not be considered unless the present annual net income can be maintained.
- Selling price of the old product will remain unchanged.
- All $300,000 of fixed manufacturing overhead will be assigned to the new product.

6-36 Hotel Pricing and Use of Capacity

A growing corporation in a large city has offered a 200-room Embassy Suites Hotel a 1-year contract to rent 40 rooms at reduced rates of $50 per room instead of the regular rate of $85 per room. The corporation will sign the contract for 365-day occupancy because its visiting manufacturing and marketing personnel are virtually certain to use all the space each night.

Each room occupied has a variable cost of $10 per night (for cleaning, laundry, lost linens, and extra electricity).

The motel manager expects an 85% occupancy rate for the year, so she is reluctant to sign the contract. If the contract is signed, the occupancy rate on the remaining 160 rooms will be 95%.

Required

1. Compute the total contribution margin for the year with and without the contract.
2. Compute the lowest room rate that the motel should accept on the contract so that the total contribution margin would be the same with or without the contract.

6-37 Special Air Fares

The manager of operations of Frontier Airlines is trying to decide whether to adopt a new discount fare. Focus on one 134-seat 737 airplane now operating at a 56% load factor. That is, on the average the airplane has $.56 \times 134 = 75$ passengers. The regular fares produce an average revenue of 12¢ per passenger mile.

Suppose an average 40% fare discount (which is subject to restrictions regarding time of departure and length of stay) will produce three new additional passengers. Also suppose that three of the previously committed passengers accept the restrictions and switch to the discount fare from the regular fare.

Required

1. Compute the total revenue per airplane mile with and without the discount fares.
2. Suppose the maximum allowed allocation to new discount fares is 50 seats. These will be filled. As before, some previously committed passengers will accept the restrictions and switch to the discount fare from the regular fare. How many will have to switch so that the total revenue per mile will be the same either with or without the discount plan?

6-38 Joint Costs and Incremental Analysis

Jacque de Paris, a high-fashion women's dress manufacturer, is planning to market a new cocktail dress for the coming season. Jacque de Paris supplies retailers in Europe and the United States.

Four yards of material are required to lay out the dress pattern. Some material remains after cutting, which can be sold as remnants. The leftover material could also be used to manufacture a matching cape and handbag. However, if the leftover material is to be used for the cape and handbag, more care will be required in the cutting, which will increase the cutting costs.

The company expects to sell 1,250 dresses if no matching cape or handbag is available. Market research reveals that dress sales will be 20% higher if a matching cape and handbag are available. The market research indicates that the cape and handbag will not be sold individually, but only as accessories with the dress. The various combinations of dresses, capes, and handbags that are expected to be sold by retailers are as follows:

	Percent of Total
Complete sets of dress, cape, and handbag	70%
Dress and cape	6%
Dress and handbag	15%
Dress only	9%
Total	100%

The material used in the dress costs FF75 a yard, or FF300 for each dress. The cost of cutting the dress if the cape and handbag are not manufactured is estimated at FF100 a dress, and the resulting remnants can be sold for FF25 for each dress cut out. If the cape and handbag are to be manufactured, the cutting costs will be increased by FF36 per dress. There will be no salable remnants if the capes and handbags are manufactured in the quantities estimated. The selling prices and the costs to complete the three items once they are cut are as follows:

	Selling Price per Unit	Unit Cost to Complete (Excludes Cost of Material and Cutting Operation)
Dress	FF1,050	FF400
Cape	140	100
Handbag	50	30

Required

1. Calculate the incremental profit or loss to Jacque de Paris from manufacturing the capes and handbags in conjunction with the dresses.
2. Identify any nonquantitative factors that could influence the company's management in its decision to manufacture the capes and handbags that match the dress.

6-39   Relevant Cost

Antonio Company's unit costs of manufacturing and selling a given item at the planned activity level of 10,000 units per month are

Manufacturing costs	
Direct materials	$4.10
Direct labor	.60
Variable overhead	.70
Fixed overhead	.80
Selling expenses	
Variable	3.00
Fixed	1.10

Ignore income taxes in all requirements. These four parts have no connection with each other.

1. Compute the planned annual operating income at a selling price of $12 per unit.

2. Compute the expected annual operating income if the volume can be increased by 20% when the selling price is reduced to $11. Assume the implied cost behavior patterns are correct.

3. The company desires to seek an order for 5,000 units from a foreign customer. The variable selling expenses for the order will be 40% less than usual, but the fixed costs for obtaining the order will be $6,000. Domestic sales will not be affected. Compute the minimum break-even price per unit to be considered.

4. The company has an inventory of 2,000 units of this item left over from last year's model. These must be sold through regular channels at reduced prices. The inventory will be valueless unless sold this way. What unit cost is relevant for establishing the minimum selling price of these 2,000 units?

6-40 New Machine

A new $300,000 machine is expected to have a five-year life and a terminal value of zero. It can produce 40,000 units a year at a variable cost of $4 per unit. The variable cost is $6 per unit with an old machine, which has a book value of $100,000. It is being depreciated on a straight-line basis at $20,000 per year. It too is expected to have a terminal value of zero. Its current disposal value is also zero because it is highly specialized equipment.

The salesman of the new machine prepared the following comparison:

	New Machine	Old Machine
Units	40,000	40,000
Variable costs	$160,000	$240,000
Straight-line depreciation	60,000	20,000
Total cost	$220,000	$260,000
Unit cost	$ 5.50	$ 6.50

He said, "The new machine is obviously a worthwhile acquisition. You will save $1.00 for every unit you produce."

1. Do you agree with the salesman's analysis? If not, how would you change it? Be specific. Ignore taxes.

2. Prepare an analysis of total and unit costs if the annual volume is 20,000 units.

3. At what annual volume would both the old and new machines have the same total relevant costs?

6-41 Conceptual Approach

A large automobile-parts plant was constructed four years ago in an Ohio city served by two railroads. The PC Railroad purchased 40 specialized 60-foot freight cars as a direct result of the additional traffic generated by the new plant. The investment was based on an estimated useful life of 20 years.

Now the competing railroad has offered to service the plant with new 86-foot freight cars, which would enable more efficient shipping operations at the plant. The automobile company has threatened to switch carriers unless PC Railroad buys 10 new 86-foot freight cars.

CHAPTER 6   RELEVANT INFORMATION AND DESIGN MAKING: PRODUCTION DECISIONS   241

The PC marketing management wants to buy the new cars, but PC operating management says, "The new investment is undesirable. It really consists of the new outlay plus the loss on the old freight cars. The old cars must be written down to a low salvage value if they cannot be used as originally intended."

Required Evaluate the comments. What is the correct conceptual approach to the quantitative analysis in this decision?

6-42 Book Value of Old Equipment
Consider the following data:

	Old Equipment	Proposed New Equipment
Original cost	$24,000	$12,000
Useful life in years	8	3
Current age in years	5	0
Useful life remaining in years	3	3
Accumulated depreciation	$15,000	0
Book value	9,000	*
Disposal value (in cash) now	3,000	*
Annual cash operating costs (maintenance, power, repairs, lubricants, etc.)	$10,000	$ 6,000

*Not acquired yet.

Required

1. Prepare a cost comparison of all relevant items for the next three years together. Ignore taxes.

2. Prepare a cost comparison that includes both relevant and irrelevant items. (See Exhibit 6-3, p. 222.)

3. Prepare a comparative statement of the total charges against revenue for the first year. Would the manager be inclined to buy the new equipment? Explain.

6-43 Decision and Performance Models
Refer back to problem 6-A1.

1. Suppose the "decision model" favored by top management consisted of a comparison of a three-year accumulation of wealth under each alternative. Which alternative would you choose? Why? (Accumulation of wealth means cumulative increase in cash.)

2. Suppose the "performance evaluation model" emphasized the net income of a subunit (such as a division) each year rather than considering each project, one by one. Which alternative would you expect a manager to choose? Why?

3. Suppose the same quantitative data existed, but the "enterprise" was a city and the "machine" was a computer in the treasurer's department. Would your answers to the first two parts change? Why?

6-44 Review of Relevant Costs
The *New York Times* reported that Neil Simon planned to open his play, *London Suite*, off Broadway. Why? For financial reasons. Producer Emanuel Azenberg predicted the following costs before the play even opened:

	On Broadway	Off Broadway
Sets, costumes, lights	$ 357,000	$ 87,000
Loading in (building set, etc.)	175,000	8,000
Rehearsal salaries	102,000	63,000
Director and designer fees	126,000	61,000
Advertising	300,000	121,000
Administration	235,000	100,000
Total	$1,295,000	$440,000

Broadway ticket prices average $55, and theaters can seat about 1,000 persons per show. Off-Broadway prices average only $40, and the theaters seat only 500. Normally plays run eight times a week, both on and off Broadway. Weekly operating expenses off Broadway average $82,000; they average an extra $124,000 on Broadway for a weekly total of $206,000.

Required

1. Suppose 400 persons attended each show, whether on or off Broadway. Compare the weekly financial results from a Broadway production to one produced off Broadway.

2. Suppose attendance averaged 75% of capacity, whether on or off Broadway. Compare the weekly financial results from a Broadway production to one produced off Broadway.

3. Compute the attendance per show required just to cover weekly expenses (a) on Broadway and (b) off Broadway.

4. Suppose average attendance on Broadway was 600 per show and off Broadway was 400. Compute the total net profit for a 26-week run (a) on Broadway and (b) off Broadway. Be sure to include the pre-opening costs.

5. Repeat requirement 4 for a 100-week run.

6. Using attendance figures from requirements 4 and 5, compute (a) the number of weeks a Broadway production must run before it breaks even, and (b) the number of weeks an off-Broadway production must run before it breaks even.

7. Using attendance figures from requirements 4 and 5, determine how long a play must run before the profit from a Broadway production exceeds that from an off-Broadway production.

8. If you were Neil Simon, would you prefer *London Suite* to play on Broadway or off Broadway? Explain.

6-45 Make or Buy, Opportunity Costs, and Ethics

Agribiz Food Products, Inc., produces a wide variety of food and related products. The company's tomato canning operation relies partly on tomatoes grown on Agribiz's own farms and partly on tomatoes bought from other growers.

Agribiz's tomato farm is on the edge of Sharpestown, a fast-growing medium-sized city. It produces 8 million pounds of tomatoes a year and employs 55 persons. The annual costs of tomatoes grown on this farm are:

Variable production costs	$ 550,000
Fixed production costs	1,200,000
Shipping costs (all variable)	200,000
Total costs	$1,950,000

Fixed production costs include depreciation on machinery and equipment, but not on land because land should not be depreciated. Agribiz owns the land, which was purchased for $600,000 many years ago. A recent appraisal placed the value of the land at $15 million because it was prime land for development of an industrial park and shopping center.

Agribiz could purchase all the tomatoes it needs on the market for $.25 per pound delivered to its factory. If it did this, it would sell the farmland and shut down the operations in Sharpestown. If the farm were sold, $300,000 of the annual fixed costs would be saved. Agribiz can invest excess cash and earn an annual rate of 10%.

Required

1. How much does it cost Agribiz annually for the land used by the tomato farm?
2. How much would Agribiz save annually if it closed the tomato farm? Is this more or less than would be paid to purchase the tomatoes on the market?
3. What ethical issues are involved with the decision of whether to shut down the tomato farm?

BUSINESS FIRST   www.prenhall.com/phlip

6-46 Irrelevance of Past Costs at Starbucks

Starbucks purchases and roasts high-quality whole bean coffees and sells them, along with other coffee-related products, primarily through its company-operated retail stores. The company is known for its high-quality coffees.

Suppose that the quality-control manager at Starbucks discovered a 1,000-pound batch of roasted beans that did not meet the company's quality standards. Company policy would not allow such beans to be sold with the Starbucks name on it. However, it could be reprocessed, at which time it could be sold by Starbucks' retail stores, or it could be sold as-is on the wholesale coffee-bean market.

Assume that the beans were initially purchased for $2,000, and the total cost of roasting the batch was $1,500, including $500 of variable cost and $1,000 of fixed costs (primarily depreciation on the equipment).

The wholesale price at which Starbucks could sell the beans was $2.75 per pound. Purchasers would pay the shipping costs from the Starbucks plant to their warehouse.

If the beans were reprocessed, the processing cost would be $600 because the beans would not require as much processing as new beans. All $600 would be additional costs, that is, costs that would not be incurred without the reprocessing. The beans would be sold to the retail stores for $3.70 per pound, and Starbucks would have to pay an average of $.20 per pound to ship the beans to the stores.

Required

1. Should Starbucks sell the beans on the market as-is for $2.75 per pound, or should the company reprocess the beans and sell them through its own retail stores? Why?
2. Compute the amount of extra profit Starbucks earns from the alternative you selected in requirement 1 compared to what it would earn from the other alternative.
3. What cost numbers in the problem were irrelevant to your analysis? Explain why they were irrelevant. ■

CASES

6-47 Make or Buy

The Minnetonka Corporation, which produces and sells to wholesalers a highly successful line of water skis, has decided to diversify to stabilize sales throughout the year. The company is considering the production of cross-country skis.

After considerable research, a cross-country ski line has been developed. Because of the conservative nature of the company management, however, Minnetonka's president has decided to introduce only one type of the new skis for this coming winter. If the product is a success, further expansion in future years will be initiated.

The ski selected is a mass-market ski that comes with a special binding. It will be sold to wholesalers for $80 per pair. Because of available capacity, no additional fixed charges will be incurred to produce the skis. A $100,000 fixed charge will be absorbed by the skis, however, to allocate a fair share of the company's present fixed costs to the new product.

Using the estimated sales and production of 10,000 pair of skis as the expected volume, the accounting department has developed the following costs per pair of skis and bindings:

Direct labor	$35
Direct material	30
Total overhead	15
Total	$80

Minnetonka has approached a subcontractor to discuss the possibility of purchasing the bindings. The purchase price of the bindings from the subcontractor would be $5.25 per binding, or $10.50 per pair. If the Minnetonka Corporation accepts the purchase proposal, it is predicted that direct-labor and variable-overhead costs would be reduced by 10% and direct-material costs would be reduced by 20%.

Required

1. Should the Minnetonka Corporation make or buy the bindings? Show calculations to support your answer.

2. What would be the maximum purchase price acceptable to the Minnetonka Corporation for the bindings? Support your answer with an appropriate explanation.

3. Instead of sales of 10,000 pair of skis, revised estimates show sales volume at 12,500 pair. At this new volume, additional equipment, at an annual rental of $10,000, must be acquired to manufacture the bindings. This incremental cost would be the only additional fixed cost required even if sales increased to 30,000 pair. (The 30,000 level is the goal for the third year of production.) Under these circumstances, should the Minnetonka Corporation make or buy the bindings? Show calculations to support your answer.

4. The company has the option of making and buying at the same time. What would be your answer to requirement 3 if this alternative were considered? Show calculations to support your answer.

5. What nonquantifiable factors should the Minnetonka Corporation consider in determining whether they should make or buy the bindings?

6-48 Make or Buy

The Rohr Company's old equipment for making subassemblies is worn out. The company is considering two courses of action: (a) completely replacing the old equipment with new equipment or (b) buying subassemblies from a reliable outside supplier, who has quoted a unit price of $1 on a seven-year contract for a minimum of 50,000 units per year.

Production was 60,000 units in each of the past two years. Future needs for the next seven years are not expected to fluctuate beyond 50,000 to 70,000 units per year. Cost records for the past two years reveal the following unit costs of manufacturing the subassembly:

Direct material	$ .30
Direct labor	.35
Variable overhead	.10
Fixed overhead (including $.10 depreciation and $.10 for direct departmental fixed overhead)	.25
	$1.00

The new equipment will cost $188,000 cash, will last seven years, and will have a disposal value of $20,000. The current disposal value of the old equipment is $10,000.

The sales representative for the new equipment has summarized her position as follows: The increase in machine speeds will reduce direct labor and variable overhead by 35¢ per unit. Consider last year's experience of one of your major competitors with identical equipment. They produced 100,000 units under operating conditions very comparable to yours and showed the following unit costs:

Direct material	$.30
Direct labor	.05
Variable overhead	.05
Fixed overhead, including depreciation of $.24	.40
	$.80

Required

For purposes of this case, assume that any idle facilities cannot be put to alternative use. Also assume that 5¢ of the old Rohr unit cost is allocated fixed overhead that will be unaffected by the decision.

1. The president asks you to compare the alternatives on a total-annual-cost basis and on a per-unit basis for annual needs of 60,000 units. Which alternative seems more attractive?

2. Would your answer to requirement 1 change if the needs were 50,000 units? 70,000 units? At what volume level would Rohr be indifferent between making and buying subassemblies? Show your computations.

3. What factors, other than the preceding ones, should the accountant bring to the attention of management to assist them in making their decision? Include the considerations that might be applied to the outside supplier.

COLLABORATIVE LEARNING EXERCISE

6-49 Outsourcing

A popular term for make or buy decisions is "outsourcing" decisions. There are many examples of outsourcing, from Nike's outsourcing of nearly all its production activities to small firms' outsourcing of their payroll activities. Especially popular outsourcing activities are warehousing and computer systems.

The purpose of this exercise is to share information on different types of outsourcing decisions. It can be done in small groups or as an entire class. Each student should pick an article from the literature that tells about a particular company's outsourcing decision. There are many such articles: a recent electronic search of the business literature turned up more than 4,000 articles. An easy way to find such an article is to search an electronic database of business literature. Magazines that have had outsourcing articles include *For-*

tune, Forbes, Business Week, and *Management Accounting.* Many business sections of newspapers also have published such articles. The *Wall Street Journal* usually has a couple articles on outsourcing each month.

Required

1. List as many details about the outsourcing decision as you can. Include the type of activity that is being outsourced, the size of the outsourcing, and the type of company providing the outsourcing service.

2. Explain why the company decided to outsource the activity. If reasons are not given in the article, prepare a list of reasons that you think influenced the decision.

3. What disadvantages are there to outsourcing the activity?

4. Be prepared to make a 3- to 5-minute presentation to the rest of the group or to the class covering your answers to requirements 1, 2, and 3.

7

THE MASTER BUDGET

An outdoor pool and jacuzzi
add to the elegance of this
Ritz-Carlton hotel.

Learning Objectives

When you have finished studying this chapter, you should be able to

1   Explain the major features and advantages of a master budget.

2   Follow the principal steps in preparing a master budget.

3   Use sales and other cost drivers in preparing budgets.

4   Prepare the operating budget and the supporting schedules.

5   Prepare the financial budget.

6   Understand the difficulties of sales forecasting.

7   Anticipate possible human relations problems caused by budgets.

8   Use a spreadsheet to develop a budget (Appendix 7).

9   **Understand the importance of budgeting to managers.**

If you have ever traveled, you will know that there is a big difference between staying in a cheap motel and staying in a five-star world-class hotel. You can think of the difference as that of riding in an old Ford Pinto versus riding in a Rolls Royce. The first takes care of your basic needs, but the second surrounds you in comfort and luxury, taking care of your every whim. The experience of staying in a luxurious hotel can simply take your breath away, and no one knows that better than the managers of the Ritz-Carlton chain of hotels. After all, the word "ritzy," which means glamorous and luxurious, is actually derived from the name of the Ritz Hotel. Thanks to fierce competition in the industry, though, Ritz-Carlton managers have their share of challenges in running successful hotels.

What does it take to run a world-class hotel successfully? Good location, exquisite food, luxury, personalized service, and quality are essential ingredients. But you might be surprised to learn that at the Ritz-Carlton hotels, the budgeting process is also a key success factor. According to Ralph Vick, general manager of the Phoenix Ritz-Carlton, "Budgets are crucial to the ultimate financial success of our hotels." Why are budgets so important? Mainly because they serve as a roadmap toward achieving goals. Budgets are a manager's tool to understand, plan, and control operations, and Ritz-Carlton wants to give its managers the best tools possible. As a result, the company takes the budgeting process very seriously.

At the Ritz-Carlton hotels, all employees, from the hotel manager, to the controller, to the newest housekeeper, are involved in the budgeting process. Working in teams, they set budget targets for the expenses they can control. These target figures help not only in planning, but also in controlling and evaluating employee performance. Actual results are compared with previously budgeted target figures, and workers are evaluated based on the differences. Even nonfinancial measures of performance are important. Ritz-Carlton managers use nonfinancial measures of quality and customer satisfaction in addition to financial reports to evaluate and reward employees.

Planning is the key to good management. This statement is certainly true for Ritz-Carlton, and it is also true for other types of business organizations—small family-owned companies, large corporations, government agencies, and nonprofit organizations—as well as for individuals. For example, most successful students who earn good grades, finance their education, and finish their degrees in a reasonable amount of time do so because they plan their time, their work, and their recreation. These students are *budgeting* their scarce resources to make the best use of their time, money, and energy. Similarly, business owners and managers need to budget their resources—which includes everything from raw materials to human resources to facilities and even time—to make the best and most profitable use of what they have to work with. Budgeting can cover such diverse issues as how much time to spend sanding a piece of wood to how much money the company will allot to research and development in the coming year. However, company budgets always aim to get the most out of available resources.

In this chapter we will look at the uses and benefits of budgets and consider the construction of the master budget.

BUDGETS AND THE ORGANIZATION

Most people associate the word "budget" with the approving, rejecting, or arguing over various budgets. Taxpayers demand that governments plan the effective use of their hard-earned tax dollars, and budgets not only allow governments to plan spending, but also allow taxpayers to see exactly where and how their money is being spent. Governments and government agencies, however, tend to use budgets only as a means of limiting spending. In contrast, most business organizations use budgets to focus attention on company operations and finances, not just to limit spending. Budgets highlight potential problems and advantages early, allowing management to take steps to avoid these problems or use the advantages wisely. Thus, a budget is a tool that helps managers in both their planning and control functions.

Interestingly, budgets help managers with their control function not only by looking forward but also by looking backward. Budgets, of course, deal with what managers plan for the future. However, they also can be used to evaluate what happened in the past. Budgets can be used as a benchmark that allows managers to compare actual performance with estimated or desired performance. Keeping score is an American tradition, whether on the football field or in the boardroom, and budgets provide the standards for evaluating and "scoring" the company "players."

Recent surveys show just how valuable budgets can be. Study after study have shown budgets to be the most widely used and highest rated tool for cost reduction and control. Advocates of budgeting go so far as to claim that the process of budgeting forces a manager to become a better administrator and puts planning in the forefront of the manager's mind. Actually, many seemingly healthy businesses have died because managers failed to draw up, monitor, and adjust budgets to changing conditions.

ADVANTAGES OF BUDGETS

Objective 1
Explain the major features and advantages of a master budget.

Budgets are a formal business plan. All managers do some kind of planning. Sometimes plans are unwritten, especially in small organizations. Unwritten plans might work in a small organization, but as an organization grows, informal, seat-of-the-pants planning is not enough. A more formal plan—a budgetary system—becomes a necessity.

Skeptical managers have claimed, "I face too many uncertainties and complications to make budgeting worthwhile for me." Be wary of such claims. Planning and budgeting are especially important in uncertain environments. A budget allows *systematic rather than chaotic reaction to change*. For example, the Natural Resources Group of W. R. Grace & Co. greatly reduced its planned expansion in reaction to a worldwide abundance of oil and gas. A top executive, quoted in the company's annual report, stated that "management used the business planning process to adjust to changes in operating conditions."

Three major benefits of budgeting are as follows:

1. Budgeting compels managers to think ahead by formalizing their responsibilities for planning.
2. Budgeting provides definite expectations that are the best framework for judging subsequent performance.
3. Budgeting aids managers in coordinating their efforts, so that the objectives of the organization as a whole match the objectives of its parts.

Let's look more closely at each of these benefits.

FORMALIZATION OF PLANNING

Budgeting forces managers to think ahead—to anticipate and prepare for changing conditions. The budgeting process makes planning an *explicit* management responsibility. Too often, managers operate from day-to-day, extinguishing one business brush fire after another. They simply have "no time" for any tough-minded thinking beyond the next day's problems. Planning takes a back seat to or is actually obliterated by daily pressures.

The trouble with the day-to-day approach to managing an organization is that objectives are never crystallized. Managers react to current events rather than plan for the future. To prepare a budget, a manager should set goals and objectives, and establish policies to aid their achievement. The objectives are the destination points, and budgets are the road maps guiding us to those destinations. Without goals and objectives, company operations lack direction; problems are not foreseen; and results are difficult to interpret afterward.

FRAMEWORK FOR JUDGING PERFORMANCE

Budgeted goals and performance are generally a better basis for judging actual results than is past performance. The news that a company had sales of $100 million this year, as compared with $80 million the previous year, may or may not indicate that the company has been effective and has met company objectives. Perhaps sales should have been $110 million this year. The major drawback of using historical results for judging current performance is that inefficiencies may be concealed in the past performance. Changes in economic conditions, technology, personnel, competition, and so forth also limit the usefulness of comparisons with the past.

COMMUNICATION AND COORDINATION

Budgets tell employees what is expected of them. Nobody likes to drift along, not knowing what "the boss" expects or hopes to achieve. A good budget process communicates both from the top down and from the bottom up. Top management makes clear the goals and objectives of the organization in its budgetary directives. Employees and lower-level managers then inform higher-level managers how they plan to achieve the goals and objectives.

Budgets also help managers coordinate objectives. For example, a budget forces purchasing personnel to integrate their plans with production requirements, while production managers use the sales budget and delivery schedule to help them anticipate and plan for the employees and physical facilities they will need. Similarly, financial officers use the sales budget, purchasing requirements, and so forth to anticipate the company's need for cash. Thus the budgetary process forces managers to visualize the relationship of their department's activities to other departments and to the company as a whole.

TYPES OF BUDGETS

strategic plan A plan that sets the overall goals and objectives of the organization.

long-range planning Producing forecasted financial statements for five- to ten-year periods.

capital budget A budget that details the planned expenditures for facilities, equipment, new products, and other long-term investments.

master budget (pro forma statement) A budget that summarizes the planned activities of all subunits of an organization.

There are several different types of budgets used by businesses. The most forward-looking budget is the **strategic plan,** which sets the overall goals and objectives of the organization. Some business analysts won't classify the strategic plan as an actual budget, though, because it does not deal with a specific time frame, and it does not produce forecasted financial statements. In any case, the strategic plan leads to **long-range planning,** which produces forecasted financial statements for five- to ten-year periods. The financial statements are estimates of what management would like to see in the company's future financial statements. Decisions made during long-range planning include addition or deletion of product lines, design and location of new plants, acquisitions of buildings and equipment, and other long-term commitments. Long-range plans are coordinated with **capital budgets,** which detail the planned expenditures for facilities, equipment, new products, and other long-term investments.

Long-range plans and budgets give the company direction and goals for the future, while short-term plans and budgets guide day-to-day operations. Managers who pay attention to only short-term budgets will quickly lose sight of long-term goals. Similarly, managers who pay attention to only the long-term budget could wind up mismanaging day-to-day operations. There has to be a happy medium that allows managers to pay attention to their short-term budgets while still keeping an eye on long-term plans. Enter the master budget. The master budget is an extensive analysis of the first year of the long-range plan. A **master budget** summarizes the planned activities of all subunits of an organization—sales, production, distribution, and finance. The master budget quantifies targets for sales, cost-driver activity, purchases, production, net income, cash position, and any other objective that management specifies. It expresses these amounts in the form of forecasted financial statements and supporting operating schedules. These supporting schedules provide the information that is too highly detailed to appear in the actual financial statements. *Thus, the master budget is a periodic business plan that includes a coordinated set of detailed operating schedules and financial statements.* It includes forecasts of sales, expenses, cash receipts and disbursements, and balance sheets. Master budgets (also called **pro forma statements,** another term for forecasted financial statements) might consist of 12 monthly budgets for the year or perhaps monthly budgets for only the first quarter and quarterly budgets for the three remaining quarters.

continuous budget (rolling budget) A common form of master budget that adds a month in the future as the month just ended is dropped.

Continuous budgets or **rolling budgets** are a very common form of master budgets that simply add a month in the future as the month just ended is dropped. Budgeting thus becomes an ongoing instead of periodic process. Continuous budgets force managers to always think about the next 12 months, not just the remaining months in a fixed budgeting cycle. As they add a new twelfth month to a continuous budget, managers may update the other 11 months as well. Then they can compare actual monthly results with both the original plan and the most recently revised plan.

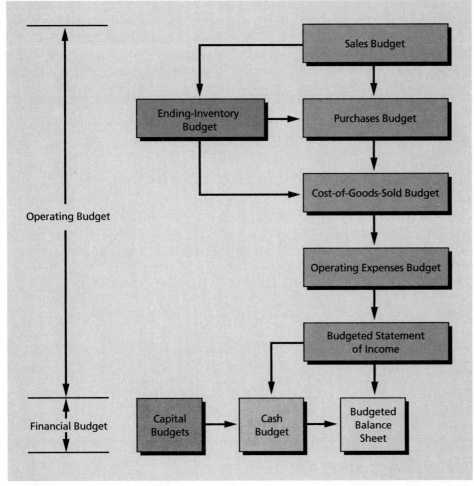

Exhibit 7-1

Preparation of Master Budget for Nonmanufacturing Company

COMPONENTS OF MASTER BUDGET

The terms used to describe specific budget schedules vary from organization to organization. However, most master budgets have common elements. The usual master budget for a nonmanufacturing company has the following components:

A. Operating budget
   1. Sales budget (and other cost-driver budgets as necessary)
   2. Purchases budget
   3. Cost-of-goods-sold budget
   4. Operating expenses budget
   5. Budgeted income statement

B. Financial budget
   1. Capital budget
   2. Cash budget
   3. Budgeted balance sheet

Exhibit 7-1 presents a condensed diagram of the relationships among the various parts of a master budget for a nonmanufacturing company. In addition to these categories, manufacturing companies that maintain physical product inventories prepare ending inventory budgets and additional budgets for each type of resource activity (such as labor, materials, and factory overhead).

operating budget (profit plan) A major part of a master budget that focuses on the income statement and its supporting schedules.

The two major parts of a master budget are the operating budget and the financial budget. The **operating budget** focuses on the income statement and its supporting schedules. Though sometimes called the **profit plan,** an operating budget may show a budgeted *loss,* or even be used to budget expenses in an organization or agency with no sales revenues. In contrast, the **financial budget** focuses on the effects that the operating budget and other plans (such as capital budgets and repayments of debt) will have on cash.

In addition to the master budget, there are countless forms of special budgets and related reports. For example, a report might detail goals and objectives for improvements in quality or customer satisfaction during the budget period.

PREPARING THE MASTER BUDGET

financial budget The part of a master budget that focuses on the effects that the operating budget and other plans (such as capital budgets and repayments of debt) will have on cash.

Let's return to Exhibit 7-1 and trace the preparation of the master budget components. *Follow each step carefully and completely.* Although the process may seem largely mechanical, remember that the master-budgeting process generates key decisions regarding all aspects of the company's value chain. Therefore, the first draft of the budget leads to decisions that prompt subsequent drafts before a final budget is chosen.

THE COOKING HUT

To illustrate the budgeting process we will use as an example the Cooking Hut Company (CHC), a local retailer of a wide variety of kitchen and dining room items such as coffeemakers, silverware, and table linens. The company rents a retail store in a midsized community near Denver. CHC's management prepares a continuous budget to aid financial and operating decisions. For simplicity in this illustration, the planning horizon is only four months, April through July. In the past, sales have increased during this season. However, the company's collections have always lagged well behind its sales. As a result, the company has often found itself pressed to come up with the cash for purchases, employee wages, and other operating outlays. To help meet this cash squeeze, CHC has used short-term loans from local banks, paying them back when cash comes in. CHC plans to keep on using this system.

Exhibit 7-2 is the closing balance sheet for the fiscal year ending March 31, 19X9. Sales in March were $40,000. Monthly sales are forecasted as follows:

April	$50,000
May	$80,000
June	$60,000
July	$50,000
August	$40,000

Management expects future sales collections to follow past experience: 60% of the sales should be in cash and 40% on credit. All credit accounts are collected in the month following the sales. The $16,000 of accounts receivable on March 31 represents credit sales made in March (40% of $40,000). Uncollectible accounts are negligible and thus ignored. For simplicity's sake, we will ignore all local, state, and federal taxes for this illustration.

Because deliveries from suppliers and customer demands are uncertain, at the end of each month, CHC wants to have on hand a basic inventory of items valued at $20,000 plus 80% of the expected cost of goods sold for the following month. The cost of merchandise sold averages 70% of sales. Therefore, the inventory on March 31 is $20,000 + .7(.8 × April sales of $50,000) = $20,000 + $28,000 = $48,000. The purchase terms available to CHC are net, 30 days. CHC pays for each month's purchases as follows: 50% during that month and 50% during the next month. Therefore, the accounts payable balance on March 31 is 50% of March's purchases, or $33,600 × .5 = $16,800.

Photon Sees the Light

Photon Technology International, Inc., manufactures electro-optical instruments used for medical research and diagnostic procedures. Its products are state-of-the-art, but until recently, Photon did not have a formal budgeting procedure and found itself on the verge of financial failure. Collection of sales from customers was slow, research and development outlays were high, and Photon was fast running out of cash.

Photon hired a professional financial manager who has instituted a budget process that links cash flow, intensive high-technology research and development, customer training and education, and on-site customizing of the products. Coordination of all of these factors is absolutely critical in this new, high-technology firm. This budget process develops three "what-if" scenarios: (1) a best-case budget where everything goes as hoped, (2) a worst-case budget that predicts just the opposite, and (3) a most-likely-case budget where each budget forecast (sales, sales collections, cost-driver activity, cost behavior, and so on) is examined and set at a realistic level. This budget process allows Photon to anticipate cash flow problems before they threaten the company's survival and to communicate critical resource needs within the company. Photon believes that implementing a formal budget process is a critical step in its transition from a start-up to a maturing company.

Source: Adapted from Charles L. Grant, "High-Tech Budgeting," *Management Accounting*, May 1991, pp. 30–31.

Exhibit 7-2

The Cooking Hut Company
Balance Sheet March 31, 19X9

Assets

Current assets		
Cash	$10,000	
Accounts receivable, net (.4 × March sales of $40,000)	16,000	
Merchandise inventory, $20,000 +.7 (.8 × April sales of $50,000)	48,000	
Unexpired insurance	1,800	$ 75,800
Plant assets		
Equipment, fixtures, and other	$37,000	
Accumulated depreciation	12,800	24,200
Total assets		$100,000

Liabilities and Owners' Equity

Current liabilities		
Accounts payable (.5 × March purchases of $33,600)	$16,800	
Accrued wages and commissions payable ($1,250 + $3,000)	4,250	$ 21,050
Owners' equity		78,950
Total liabilities and owners' equity		$100,000

CHC pays wages and commissions semimonthly, half a month after they are earned. They are divided into two portions: monthly fixed wages of $2,500 and commissions, equal to 15% of sales, which we will assume are uniform throughout each month. Therefore, the March 31 balance of accrued wages and commissions payable is (.5 × $2,500) + .5(.15 × $40,000) = $1,250 + $3,000 = $4,250. CHC will pay this $4,250 on April 15.

In addition to buying new fixtures for $3,000 cash in April, CHC's other monthly expenses are as follows:

Miscellaneous expenses	5% of sales, paid as incurred
Rent	$2,000, paid as incurred
Insurance	$200 expiration per month
Depreciation, including new fixtures	$500 per month

The company wants a minimum of $10,000 as a cash balance at the end of each month. To keep this simple, we will assume that CHC can borrow or repay loans in multiples of $1,000. Management plans to borrow no more cash than necessary and to repay as promptly as possible. Assume that borrowing occurs at the beginning and repayment at the end of the months in question. Interest is paid, under the terms of this credit arrangement, when the related loan is repaid. The interest rate is 18% per year.

STEPS IN PREPARING THE MASTER BUDGET

The principal steps in preparing the master budget are:

Objective 2
Follow the principal steps in preparing a master budget.

Operating Budget

1. Using the data given, prepare the following detailed schedules for each of the months of the planning horizon:
   a. Sales budget
   b. Cash collections from customers
   c. Purchases budget
   d. Disbursements for purchases
   e. Operating expense budget
   f. Disbursements for operating expenses
2. Using these schedules, prepare a budgeted income statement for the 4 months ending July 31, 19X9 (Exhibit 7-3).

Financial Budget

3. Using the data given and the supporting schedules, prepare the following forecasted financial statements:
   a. Capital budget
   b. Cash budget including details of borrowings, repayments, and interest for each month of the planning horizon (Exhibit 7-4)
   c. Budgeted balance sheet as of July 31, 19X9 (Exhibit 7-5)

Organizations with effective budget systems have specific guidelines for the steps and timing of budget preparation. Although the details differ, the guidelines invariably include the preceding steps. As we follow these steps to prepare CHC's master budget, *be sure that you understand the source of each figure in each schedule and budget.*

STEP 1: PREPARING THE OPERATING BUDGET

Step 1a: Sales Budget

Objective 3
Use sales and other cost drivers in preparing budgets.

The sales budget (Schedule a in the following table) is the starting point for budgeting because inventory levels, purchases, and operating expenses are geared to the rate of sales activities (and other cost drivers that are not present in this example). Accurate sales and cost-driver activity forecasting is essential to effective budgeting; sales forecasting is considered in a later section of this chapter. March sales are included in Schedule a because they affect cash collections in April. Trace the final column in Schedule a to the first row of Exhibit 7-3 on page 259. In nonprofit organizations, forecasts of revenue or some level of services are also the focal points for budgeting. Examples are patient revenues and government reimbursement expected by hospitals and donations expected by churches. If no revenues are generated, as in the case of municipal fire protection, a desired level of service is predetermined.

Step 1b: Cash Collections from Customers

It is easiest to prepare Schedule b, cash collections, at the same time as we prepare the sales budget. Cash collections from customers include the current month's cash sales plus the previous month's credit sales. We will use total collections in preparing the cash budget—see Exhibit 7-4 on page 260.

	March	April	May	June	July	April–July Total
Schedule a: Sales Budget						
Credit sales, 40%	$16,000	$20,000	$32,000	$24,000	$20,000	
Plus cash sales, 60%	24,000	30,000	48,000	36,000	30,000	
Total sales	$40,000	$50,000	$80,000	$60,000	$50,000	$240,000
Schedule b: Cash Collections						
Cash sales this month		$30,000	$48,000	$36,000	$30,000	
Plus 100% of last month's credit sales		16,000	20,000	32,000	24,000	
Total collections		$46,000	$68,000	$68,000	$54,000	

Step 1c: Purchases Budget

After sales are budgeted, we prepare the purchases budget (Schedule c). The total merchandise needed will be the sum of the desired ending inventory plus the amount needed to fulfill budgeted sales demand. The total need will be partially met by the beginning inventory; the remainder must come from planned purchases. These purchases are computed as follows:

budgeted purchases = desired ending inventory + cost of goods sold − beginning inventory

Objective 4
Prepare the operating budget and the supporting schedules.

Trace the total purchases figure in the final column of Schedule c to the second row of Exhibit 7-3 on page 259.

	March	April	May	June	July	April–July Total
Schedule c: Purchases Budget						
Desired ending inventory	$48,000*	$64,800	$ 53,600	$48,000	$42,400	
Plus cost of goods sold[†]	28,000	35,000	56,000	42,000	35,000	$168,000
Total needed	$76,000	$99,800	$109,600	$90,000	$77,400	
Less beginning inventory	42,400[‡]	48,000	64,800	53,600	48,000	
Purchases	$33,600	$51,800	$ 44,800	$36,400	$29,400	
Schedule d: Disbursements for Purchases						
50% of last month's purchases		$16,800	$ 25,900	$22,400	$18,200	
Plus 50% of this month's purchases		25,900	22,400	18,200	14,700	
Disbursements for purchases		$42,700	$ 48,300	$40,600	$32,900	

*$20,000 + (.8 × April cost of goods sold) = $20,000 + .8($35,000) = $48,000.
[†].7 × March sales of $40,000 = $28,000; .7 × April sales of $50,000 = $35,000, and so on.
[‡]$20,000 + (.8 × March cost of goods sold of $28,000) = $20,000 + $22,400 = $42,400.

Step 1d: Disbursements for Purchases

Schedule d, disbursements for purchases, is based on the purchases budget. In our example disbursements include 50% of the current month's purchases and 50% of the previous month's purchases. We will use total disbursements in preparing the cash budget, Exhibit 7-4, for the financial budget.

Step 1e: Operating Expense Budget

The budgeting of operating expenses depends on several factors. Month-to-month changes in sales volume and other cost-driver activities directly influence many operating expenses. Examples of expenses driven by sales volume include sales commissions and many delivery expenses. Other expenses are not influenced by sales or other cost-driver activity (such as rent, insurance, depreciation, and salaries) within appropriate relevant ranges and are regarded as fixed. Trace the total operating expenses in the final column of Schedule e, which summarizes these expenses, to the budgeted income statement, Exhibit 7-3.

	March	April	May	June	July	April–July Total
Schedule e: Operating Expense Budget						
Wages (fixed)	$2,500	$2,500	$ 2,500	$2,500	$ 2,500	
Commissions (15% of current month's sales)	6,000	7,500	12,000	9,000	7,500	
Total wages and commissions	$8,500	$10,000	$14,500	$11,500	$10,000	$46,000
Miscellaneous expenses (5% of current sales)		2,500	4,000	3,000	2,500	12,000
Rent (fixed)		2,000	2,000	2,000	2,000	8,000
Insurance (fixed)		200	200	200	200	800
Depreciation (fixed)		500	500	500	500	2,000
Total operating expenses		$15,200	$21,200	$17,200	$15,200	$68,800

Step 1f: Disbursements for Operating Expenses

Disbursements for operating expenses are based on the operating expense budget. Disbursements include 50% of last month's and this month's wages and commissions, and miscellaneous and rent expenses. We will use the total of these disbursements in preparing the cash budget, Exhibit 7-4.

	March	April	May	June	July	April–July Total
Schedule f: Disbursements for Operating Expenses						
Wages and commission						
50% of last month's expenses		$ 4,250	$ 5,000	$ 7,250	$ 5,750	
50% of this month's expenses		5,000	7,250	5,750	5,000	
Total wages and commissions		$ 9,250	$12,250	$13,000	$10,750	
Miscellaneous expenses		2,500	4,000	3,000	2,500	
Rent		2,000	2,000	2,000	2,000	
Total disbursements		$13,750	$18,250	$18,000	$15,250	

STEP 2: PREPARING THE BUDGETED INCOME STATEMENT

Steps 1a through 1f provide enough information to construct a budgeted income statement *from operations* (Exhibit 7-3). The income statement will be complete after addition of the interest expense, which is computed after the cash budget has been prepared. Budgeted income from operations is often a benchmark for judging management performance.

Exhibit 7-3

The Cooking Hut Company
Budgeted Income Statement for 4 Months Ending July 31, 19X9

	Data		Source of Data
Sales		$240,000	Schedule a
Cost of goods sold		168,000	Schedule c
Gross margin		$ 72,000	
Operation expenses:			
Wages and commissions	$46,000		Schedule e
Rent	8,000		Schedule e
Miscellaneous	12,000		Schedule e
Insurance	800		Schedule e
Depreciation	2,000	68,800	Schedule e
Income from operations		$ 3,200	
Interest expense		675	Exhibit 7-4
Net income		$ 2,525	

STEP 3: PREPARATION OF FINANCIAL BUDGET

The second major part of the master budget is the financial budget, which consists of the capital budget, cash budget, and ending balance sheet. This chapter focuses on the cash budget and the ending balance sheet. Chapter 11 discusses the capital budget. In our illustration, the $3,000 purchase of new fixtures would be included in the capital budget.

Objective 5
Prepare the financial budget.

Step 3b: Cash Budget

The **cash budget** is a statement of planned cash receipts and disbursements. The cash budget is heavily affected by the level of operations summarized in the budgeted income statement. The cash budget has the following major sections, where the letters *w, x, y,* and *z* refer to the lines in Exhibit 7-4 that summarize the effects of that section:

cash budget A statement of planned cash receipts and disbursements.

- The *total cash available before financing (w)* equals the beginning cash balance plus cash receipts. Cash receipts depend on collections from customers' accounts receivable and cash sales and on other operating income sources. Trace total collections from Schedule b to Exhibit 7-4.

- *Cash disbursements (x)* for
  1. Purchases depend on the credit terms extended by suppliers and the bill-paying habits of the buyer (disbursements for merchandise from Schedule d should be traced to Exhibit 7-4).
  2. Payroll depends on wage, salary, and commission terms and on payroll dates (wages and commissions from Schedule f should be traced to Exhibit 7-4).
  3. Some costs and expenses depend on contractual terms for installment payments, mortgage payments, rents, leases, and miscellaneous items (miscellaneous and rent from Schedule f should be traced to Exhibit 7-4).
  4. Other disbursements include outlays for fixed assets, long-term investments, dividends, and the like (the $3,000 expenditure for new fixtures).

- Management determines the *minimum cash balance desired (y)* depending on the nature of the business and credit arrangements.

- *Financing requirements (z)* depend on how the *total cash available, w* in Exhibit 7-4, compares with the *total cash needed.* Needs include the disbursements, *x,* plus the desired ending cash balance, *y.* If the total cash available is less than the cash needed, borrowing is necessary—Exhibit 7-4 shows that CHC will borrow

Exhibit 7-4

The Cooking Hut Company
Cash Budget for 4 Months Ending July 31, 19X9

	April	May	June	July
Beginning cash balance	$ 10,000	$ 10,550	$10,970	$10,965
Cash receipts				
Collections from customers (Schedule b)	46,000	68,000	68,000	54,000
Total cash available, before financing (w)*	$ 56,000	$ 78,550	$78,970	$64,965
Cash disbursements				
Merchandise (Schedule d)	42,700	48,300	40,600	32,900
Operating expenses (Schedule f)	13,750	18,250	18,000	15,250
Purchase of new fixtures (given)	3,000	—	—	—
Total disbursements (x)	$ 59,450	$ 66,550	$58,600	$48,150
Minimum cash balance desired (y)	10,000	10,000	10,000	10,000
Total cash needed	69,450	$ 76,550	$68,600	$58,150
Excess (deficiency) of total cash available over total cash needed before financing (w − x − y)	$ (13,450)	$ 2,000	$10,370	$ 6,815
Financing				
Borrowing (at beginning of month)	$ 14,000†			
Repayments (at end of month)	—	$ (1,000)	$(9,000)	$ (4,000)
Interest (at 18% per year‡)	—	(30)	(405)	(240)
Total cash increase (decrease) from financing (z)	$ 14,000	$ (1,030)	$(9,405)	$(4,240)
Ending cash balance (w − x + z)	$ 10,550	$ 10,970	$10,965	$12,575

*Letters are keyed to the explanation in the text.

†Borrowing and repayment of principal are made in multiples of $1,000, at an interest rate of 18% per year.

‡Interest computations: $.18 \times \$1,000 \times 2/12; .18 \times \$9,000 \times 3/12; .18 \times \$4,000 \times 4/12$.

$14,000 in April to cover the planned deficiency. If there is an excess, loans may be repaid—$1,000, $9,000, and $4,000 are repaid in May, June, and July, respectively. The pertinent outlays for interest expenses are usually contained in this section of the cash budget. Trace the calculated interest expense to Exhibit 7-3, which then will be complete.

- The *ending cash balance* is $w - x + z$. Financing, z, has either a positive (borrowing) or a negative (repayment) effect on the cash balance. The illustrative cash budget shows the pattern of short-term, "self-liquidating" financing. Seasonal peaks often result in heavy drains on cash—for merchandise purchases and operating expenses—before the sales are made and cash is collected from customers. The resulting loan is "self-liquidating"—that is, the borrowed money is used to acquire merchandise for sale, and the proceeds from sales are used to repay the loan. This "working capital cycle" moves from cash to inventory to receivables and back to cash.

Cash budgets help management to avoid having unnecessary idle cash, on the one hand, and unnecessary cash deficiencies, on the other. A well-managed financing program keeps cash balances from becoming too large or too small.

Step 3c: Budgeted Balance Sheet

The final step in preparing the master budget is to construct the budgeted balance sheet (Exhibit 7-5) that projects each balance sheet item in accordance with the business plan as expressed in the previous schedules. Specifically, the beginning balances at March 31 would be increased or decreased in light of the expected cash receipts and cash disbursements in Exhibit 7-4 and in light of the effects of noncash items appearing on the income

Exhibit 7-5

The Cooking Hut Company
Budgeted Balance Sheet July 31, 19X9

Assets

Current Assets

Cash (Exhibit 7-4)	$ 12,575	
Accounts receivable, net (.4 × July sales of $50,000, Schedule a)	20,000	
Merchandise inventory (Schedule c)	42,400	
Unexpired insurance ($1,800 − $800)	1,000	$ 75,975

Plant assets

Equipment, fixtures, and other ($37,000 + $3,000 fixtures)	$ 40,000	
Accumulated depreciation ($12,800 + $2,000 depreciation expense)	(14,800)	25,200
Total assets		$101,175

Liabilities and Owners' Equity

Current liabilities

Accounts payable (.5 × July purchases of $29,400, Schedule c)	$ 14,700	
Accrued wages and commissions payable (.5 × $10,000, Schedule e)	5,000	$ 19,700
Owners' equity ($78,950 + $2,525 net income)		81,475
Total liabilities and owners' equity		$101,175

Note: Beginning balances are used as a start for the computations of unexpired insurance, plant, and owners' equity.

The Budgeting Process at Daihatsu

Daihatsu Motor Company is a Japanese-based mini-car manufacturer owned in part by Toyota. Daihatsu ranks seventh of the nine Japanese automakers in terms of their domestic sales volume. The annual budgeting process (short-term profit-planning process) at Daihatsu is the first-year segment of the five-year long-range plan.

Each year departments prepare six plans that are combined to form an operating profit budget. A brief description of these six plans follows:

1. Production, Distribution, and Sales
2. Projected Parts and Materials Costs
3. Plant Rationalization (projected reductions in variable costs)
4. Personnel (direct labor and service department)

5. Facility Investment (capital budget)
6. Fixed Expense (design costs, maintenance costs, advertising, general and administrative costs)

The starting point for each plan is the actual cost performance of the previous year—*actual cost performance of the previous year is used as the standard for the coming year.* The six plans are combined as follows:

Sales forecast	Plan 1
Less expected variable costs (standards)	Plan 1
Contribution margin	
Less expected changes in variable costs	Plans 2 and 3
Adjusted contribution margin	
Less expected fixed costs	Plans 4, 5, and 6
Budgeted operating profit	

Source: Adapted from Y. Monden and J. Lee, "How a Japanese Auto Maker Reduces Costs," *Management Accounting*, August 1993, pp. 22–26.

---

statement in Exhibit 7-3. For example, unexpired insurance would decrease from its balance of $1,800 on March 31 to $1,000 on July 31, even though it is a noncash item.

When the complete master budget is formulated, management can consider all the major financial statements as a basis for changing the course of events. For example, the initial formulation of the financial statements may prompt management to try new sales strategies to generate more demand. Alternatively, management may explore the effects of various adjustments in the timing of receipts and disbursements. The large cash deficiency in April, for example, may lead to an emphasis on cash sales or an attempt to speed up collection of accounts receivable. In any event, the first draft of the master budget is rarely the final draft. As it is reworked, the budgeting process becomes an integral part of the management process itself—budgeting is planning and communicating.

DIFFICULTIES OF SALES FORECASTING

As you saw in the CHC example, the sales budget is the foundation of the entire master budget. The accuracy of estimated purchases budgets, production schedules, and costs depends on the detail and accuracy (in dollars, units, and mix) of the budgeted sales. At the Ritz-Carlton hotels, the process of developing the sales budget involves forecasting levels of room occupancy, group events, banquets, and other activities. Upper management initially sets the costs of these activities. Then, employee teams in each department provide ideas for improvements (cost reductions). Managers prepare monthly departmental budgets based on the annual master budget.

Objective 6
Understand the difficulties of sales forecasting.

sales forecast A prediction of sales under a given set of conditions.

sales budget The result of decisions to create conditions that will generate a desired level of sales.

As we stated earlier, and as you might have noticed from the Ritz-Carlton's budgeting practices, the sales budget depends entirely on sales forecasts. Although "sales budget" and "sales forecast" sound as if they might be the same thing, be aware that a forecast and a budget are not necessarily identical. A **sales forecast** is a *prediction* of sales under a given set of conditions. A **sales budget** is the result of *decisions* to create the conditions that will generate a *desired* level of sales. For example, you may have forecasts of sales at various levels of advertising. The forecast for the one level you decide to implement becomes the budget.

Sales forecasts are usually prepared under the direction of the top sales executive. Important factors considered by sales forecasters include the following:

1. *Past patterns of sales:* Past experience combined with detailed past sales by product line, geographical region, and type of customer can help predict future sales.
2. *Estimates made by the sales force:* A company's sales force is often the best source of information about the desires and plans of customers.
3. *General economic conditions:* Predictions for many economic indicators, such as gross domestic product and industrial production indexes (local and foreign), are published regularly. Knowledge of how sales relate to these indicators can aid sales forecasting.
4. *Competitors' actions:* Sales depend on the strength and actions of competitors. To forecast sales, a company should consider the likely strategies and reactions of competitors, such as changes in their prices, product quality, or services.
5. *Changes in the firm's prices:* Sales can be increased by decreasing prices and vice versa. A company should consider the effects of price changes on customer demand (see Chapter 5).
6. *Changes in product mix:* Changing the mix of products often can affect not only sales levels but also overall contribution margin. Identifying the most profitable products and devising methods to increase their sales is a key part of successful management.
7. *Market research studies:* Some companies hire market experts to gather information about market conditions and customer preferences. Such information is useful to managers making sales forecasts and product mix decisions.
8. *Advertising and sales promotion plans:* Advertising and other promotional costs affect sales levels. A sales forecast should be based on anticipated effects of promotional activities.

Sales forecasting usually combines various techniques. In addition to the opinions of the sales staff, statistical analysis of correlations between sales and economic indicators (prepared by economists and members of the market research staff) provide valuable help. The opinions of line management also heavily influence the final sales forecasts. Ultimately, no matter how many technical experts are used in forecasting, the sales budget is the responsibility of line management.

Sales forecasting is still somewhat mystical, but its procedures are becoming more formalized and are being reviewed more seriously because of the intensity of global competitive pressures. Although this book does not include a detailed discussion of the preparation of the sales budget, the importance of an accurate sales forecast cannot be overstressed.

Interestingly, governments and other nonprofit organizations also face a problem similar to sales forecasting. For example, the budget for city revenues may depend on a variety of factors, such as predicted property taxes, traffic fines, parking fees, license fees, and city income taxes. In turn, property taxes depend on the extent of new construction and, in most localities, general increases in real estate values. Thus, a municipal budget may require forecasting that is just as sophisticated as that required by a private firm.

GETTING EMPLOYEES TO ACCEPT THE BUDGET

No matter how accurate sales forecasts are, if budgets are to benefit an organization, they need the support of all the firm's employees. Lower-level workers and managers' attitudes toward budgets will be heavily influenced by the attitude of top management. Even with the support of top management, however, budgets—and the managers who implement them—can run into opposition.

Objective 7
Anticipate possible human relations problems caused by budgets.

Managers often compare actual results with budgets in evaluating subordinates. Few individuals are immediately ecstatic about techniques used to check their performance. Lower-level managers sometimes regard budgets as embodiments of restrictive, negative top-management attitudes. Accountants reinforce this view if they use a budget only to point out managers' failings. Such negative attitudes are even greater when the budget's primary purpose is to limit spending. For example, budgets are generally unpopular in government agencies where their only use is to request and authorize funding. To avoid negative attitudes toward budgets, accountants and top management must demonstrate how budgets can help each manager and employee achieve better results. Only then will the budgets become a positive aid in motivating employees at all levels to work toward goals, set objectives, measure results accurately, and direct attention to the areas that need investigation.

Another serious human relations problem that can negate the benefits of budgeting arises if budgets stress one set of performance goals but employees and managers are rewarded for different performance measures. For example, a budget may concentrate on current costs of production, but managers and employees may be rewarded on quality of production (defect rate) and on timely delivery of products to customers (percent on time). These measures of performance could be in direct conflict.

The overriding importance of the human aspects of budgeting cannot be overemphasized. Too often, top management and accountants are overly concerned with the mechanics of budgets, ignoring the fact that the effectiveness of any budgeting system depends directly on whether the affected managers and employees understand and accept the budget. Budgets created with the active participation of all affected employees are generally more effective than budgets imposed on subordinates. This involvement is usually called **participative budgeting.**

participative budgeting
Budgets formulated with the active participation of all affected employees.

For example, Ritz-Carlton's budgeting system includes all hotel employees and is thus a participative system. In fact, employee "buy-in" to the budget is so important at Ritz-Carlton that self-directed employee teams at all levels of the company have the authority to change operations based on budgets as they see fit.

FINANCIAL PLANNING MODELS

financial planning models
Mathematical models of the master budget that can react to any set of assumptions about sales, costs, or product mix.

Because a well-made budget considers all aspects of the company (the entire value chain), it serves as an effective model for decision making. For example, managers can use the master budget to predict how various decisions might affect the company in both the long and short run. Using the master budget in this way is a step-by-step process in which tentative plans are revised as managers exchange views on various aspects of expected activities.

Today, most large companies have developed **financial planning models,** mathematical models of the master budget that can react to any set of assumptions about sales, costs, product mix, and so on. For instance, Dow Chemical's model uses 140 separate, constantly revised cost inputs that are based on several different cost drivers.

Activity-Based Budgeting

Financial planning models can use activity-based costs for budgeting, and such information can provide managers with a more useful view of costs than can traditional information. Let's compare methods using a company's purchasing department as an example. The purchasing department's previous-year results might appear as follows, based on a traditional view of costs:

Purchasing Department	
Salaries	$200,000
Benefits	75,000
Supplies	30,000
Travel	10,000
Total	$315,000

If management wants to reduce costs by 10% overall ($31,500) using the traditional view of costs, purchasing may simply reduce each cost category by 10%. This method of cost reduction is sometimes referred to as "slash and burn." However, it is the managers who often wind up getting burnt by this technique. For example, at Borg-Warner Automotive, virtually all managers expressed dissatisfaction with the budgeting process. Each year managers made cost estimates as part of the annual budgeting procedure. But because the company used a slash and burn cost-cutting technique, these budgets were "almost surely" returned with a directive to cut costs across the board. Managers got so frustrated that they started overestimating costs to compensate for the cuts they knew were coming.

Using activity-based cost information, the purchasing department's budget would appear as follows:

Purchasing Department	
Activity	
Certify 10 new vendors	$ 65,450
Issue 450 purchase orders	184,640
Issue 275 releases	64,910
	$315,000

Activity-based budgeting links financial data with the activity that consumed the related resource. Instead of using the "slash and burn" method, the department now targets specific activities that can be reduced without hurting its overall effectiveness. For example, the department may be able to reduce the number of vendor certifications to five. Assuming that vendor certification costs are variable with respect to the number of vendors, this would reduce certification costs by $5 \times (\$65,450 \div 10)$ or $32,725, enabling the department to meet or exceed its budget target.

Many companies that implement activity-based costing primarily for product costing purposes realize many more benefits after implementation. For example, a snack-food processor used one financial planning model for activity-based product costing purposes but, after implementing the model, the company now uses it for budgeting, manpower projections, new pricing strategies, and product rationalization.

Sources: Adapted from "Implementing Activity-Based Costing: The Model Approach," Institute of Management Accounting and Sapling Corporation, November 1994; G. Hanks, M. Fried, and J. Huber, "Shifting Gears at Borg-Warner Automotive," *Management Accounting*, February 1994, pp. 25–29..

By mathematically describing the relationships among all the operating and financial activities covered in the master budget and among the other major internal and external factors that can affect the results of management decisions, financial planning models allow managers to assess the predicted impacts of various alternatives before final decisions are selected. For example, a manager might want to predict the consequences of changing the mix of products offered for sale to emphasize several products with the highest prospects for growth. A financial planning model would provide operational and financial budgets well into the future under alternative assumptions about the product mix, sales levels, production constraints, quality levels, scheduling, and so on. Most importantly, managers can get answers to "what if" questions, such as "What if sales are 10% below forecasts? What if material prices increase 8% instead of 4% as expected? What if the new union contract grants a 6% raise in consideration for productivity improvements?"

Financial planning models have shortened managers' reaction times dramatically. A revised plan for a large company that took many accountants many days to prepare by hand can be prepared in minutes. Public Service Electric & Gas, a New Jersey utility company, can run its total master budget several times a day, if necessary.

Warning: The use of spreadsheet software on personal computers has put financial planning models within reach of even the smallest organizations. The ready access to powerful modeling, however, does not guarantee plausible or reliable results. Financial planning models are only as good as the assumptions and the inputs used to build and manipulate them—what computer specialists call GIGO (garbage in, garbage out). Nearly every chief financial officer has a horror story to tell about following bad advice from a faulty financial planning model.

SUMMARY PROBLEM FOR YOUR REVIEW

Do not attempt to solve this problem until you understand every step in this chapter's CHC example.

PROBLEM

The Country Store is a retail outlet for a variety of hardware and homewares. The owner of the Country Store is anxious to prepare a budget for the next quarter, which is typically quite busy. She is most concerned with her cash position because she expects that she will have to borrow to finance purchases in anticipation of sales. She has gathered all the data necessary to prepare a simplified budget as listed in Exhibit 7-6. In addition, equipment will be purchased in April for $19,750 cash, and dividends of $4,000 will be paid in June. Review the structure of the example in the chapter and then prepare the Country Store's master budget for the months of April, May, and June. The solution follows after the budget data. Note that there are a few minor differences between this example and the one in the chapter. These are identified in Exhibit 7-6 and in the solution. The primary difference is in the payment of interest on borrowing. Borrowing occurs at the end of a month when cash is needed. Repayments (if appropriate) occur at the end of a month when cash is available. Interest also is paid in cash at the end of the month at an annual rate of 12% on the amount of note payable outstanding during that month.

Exhibit 7-6

The Country Store
Budget Data

Balance Sheet as of March 31, 19X9

Assets		
Cash	$ 9,000	
Accounts receivable	48,000	
Inventory	12,600	
Plant and equipment (net)	200,000	
Total assets	$269,600	
Liabilities and equities		
Interest payable	0	
Note payable	0	
Accounts payable	18,300	
Capital stock	180,000	
Retained earnings	71,300	
Total liabilities and equities	$269,600	

Budgeted expenses (per month)		
Wages and salaries	$ 7,500	
Freight out as a % of sales	6%	
Advertising	$ 6,000	
Depreciation	$ 2,000	
Other expense as a % of sales	4%	

Minimum inventory policy as a % of next month's cost of goods sold	30%

Budgeted Sales	
March (actual)	$60,000
April	70,000
May	85,000
June	90,000
July	50,000
Required minimum cash balance	$ 8,000
Sales mix, cash/credit:	
Cash sales	20%
Credit sales (collected the following month)	80%
Gross profit rate	40%
Loan interest rate (interest paid in cash monthly)	12%
Inventory paid for in:	
Month purchased	50%
Month after purchase	50%

SOLUTION

Schedule a: Sales budget

	April	May	June	Total
Credit sales, 80%	$56,000	$68,000	$72,000	$196,000
Cash sales, 20%	14,000	17,000	18,000	49,000
Total sales	$70,000	$85,000	$90,000	$245,000

Schedule b: Cash collections

	April	May	June	Total
Cash sales	$14,000	$17,000	$18,000	$ 49,000
Collections from prior month	48,000	56,000	68,000	172,000
Total collections	$62,000	$73,000	$86,000	$221,000

Schedule c: Purchases budget

	April	May	June	Total
Desired ending inventory	$15,300	$16,200	$ 9,000	$ 40,500
Plus cost of goods sold	42,000	51,000	54,000	147,000
Total needed	$57,300	$67,200	$63,000	$187,500
Less beginning inventory	12,600	15,300	16,200	44,100
Total purchases	$44,700	$51,900	$46,800	$143,400

get. Advantages of budgets include formalization of planning, providing a framework for judging performance, and aiding managers in coordinating their efforts.

Follow the principal steps in preparing a master budget. Master budgets typically cover relatively short periods—usually 1 month to 1 year. The steps involved in preparing the master budget vary across organizations but follow the general outline given on page 256. Invariably, the first step is to forecast sales or service levels. The next step should be to forecast cost-driver activity levels, given expected sales and service. From these forecasts and knowledge of cost behavior, collection patterns, and so on, the operating and financing budgets can be prepared.

Use sales and other cost drivers in preparing budgets. Accurate sales and cost-driver activity forecasts are essential to effective budgeting.

Prepare the operating budget and the supporting schedules. The operating budget is the income statement for the budget period. It is prepared from the following supporting schedules: sales budget, cash collections, purchases budget, disbursements for purchases, operating expenses, and disbursements for operating expenses.

Prepare the financial budget. The second major part of the master budget is the financial budget. The financial budget consists of a capital budget and a budgeted balance sheet.

Understand the difficulties of sales forecasting. Sales forecasting combines various techniques as well as opinions of sales staff and management. Many factors (such as past patterns of sales, economic conditions, and competitors' actions) must be considered by sales forecasters. Sales forecasting is difficult because of its complexity and the rapid changes in the business environment in which most companies operate.

Anticipate possible human relations problems caused by budgets. The success of a budget depends heavily on employee reaction to it. Negative attitudes toward budgets usually prevent realization of many of the benefits of budgeting. Such attitudes are usually caused by managers who use budgets to force behavior or to punish employees. Budgets generally are more useful when they are formulated with the willing participation of all affected parties.

Understand the importance of budgeting to managers. The budgetary process compels managers to think and to prepare for changing conditions. Budgets are aids in planning, communicating, setting standards of performance, motivating personnel toward goals, measuring results, and directing attention to problem areas that need investigation.

Appendix 7: Use of Spreadsheets for Budgeting

Spreadsheet software for personal computers is an extremely powerful and flexible tool for budgeting. An obvious advantage of the spreadsheet is that arithmetic errors are virtually nonexistent. The real value of spreadsheets, however, is that they can be used to make a mathematical model (a financial planning model) of the organization. This model can be used repeatedly at a very low cost and can be altered to reflect possible changes in expected sales, cost drivers, cost functions, and so on. The objective of this appendix is to illustrate *sensitivity analysis,* one aspect of the power and flexibility of spreadsheet software that has made this software an indispensable budgeting tool.

Recall the chapter's CHC example. Suppose CHC has prepared its master budget using spreadsheet software. To simplify making changes to the budget, the relevant forecasts and other budgeting details have been placed in Exhibit 7-7. Note that for simplification, only the data necessary for the purchases budget have been shown here. The full master budget would require a larger table with all the data given in the chapter. Each part of the table can be identified by its column and row intersection or "cell address." For example, the beginning inventory for the budget period can be located with the cell address "D4," which is shown as $48,000.

By referencing the budget data's cell addresses, you can generate the purchases budget (Exhibit 7-8) within the same spreadsheet by entering formulas instead of

Exhibit 7-7

The Cooking Hut Company

Budget Data (Column and row labels are given by the spreadsheet)

	A	B	C	D	E	F	G
1	Budget data						
2	Sales forecasts		Other information				
3							
4	March (actual)	$40,000	Beginning inventory	$48,000			
5	April	50,000	Desired ending inventory: Base amount	$20,000			
6	May	80,000	Plus percent of next				
7	June	60,000	month's cost of				
8	July	50,000	goods sold	80%			
9	August	40,000	Cost of goods sold				
10			as percent of sales	70%			

numbers into the schedule. Consider Exhibit 7-8. Instead of typing $48,000 as April's beginning inventory in the purchases budget at cell D17, type a "formula" with the cell address for the beginning inventory from the preceding table, + D4 (the cell address preceded by a "+" sign—a spreadsheet rule to identify a formula; some spreadsheets use "=" to indicate a formula). Likewise, all the cells of the purchases budget will be composed of formulas containing cell addresses instead of numbers. The total needed in April (D16) is + D13 + D14, and purchases in April (D19) are budgeted to be + D16 − D17. The figures for May, June, and July are computed similarly within the respective columns. This approach gives the spreadsheet the most flexibility, because you could change any number in the budget data in Exhibit 7-7 (for example, a sales forecast), and the software automatically recalculates the numbers in the entire purchases budget. Exhibit 7-8 shows the formulas used for the purchases budget. Exhibit 7-9 is the purchases budget displaying the numbers generated by the formulas in Exhibit 7-8.

Now, what if sales could be 10% higher than initially forecasted during April through August? What effect will this alternative forecast have on budgeted purchases? Even to revise this simple purchases budget would require a considerable number of manual recalculations. Merely changing the sales forecasts in spreadsheet Exhibit 7-7, however, results in a nearly instantaneous revision of the purchases budget. Exhibit 7-10 shows the alternative sales forecasts (in colored type) and other unchanged data along with the revised purchases budget. We could alter every piece of budget data in the table, and easily view or print out the effects on purchases. This sort of analysis, assessing the effects of varying one of the budget inputs, up or down, is called sensitivity analysis. **Sensitivity analysis** for budgeting is the systematic varying of budget data input to determine the effects of each change on the budget. This type of "what if" analysis is one of the most powerful uses of spreadsheets for financial planning models. Note, though, that it is not generally a good idea to vary more than one of the types of budget inputs at a time, unless they are obviously related, because doing so makes it difficult to isolate the effect of each change.

sensitivity analysis The systematic varying of budget data input to determine the effects of each change on the budget.

Exhibit 7-8

The Cooking Hut Company

Purchases Budget Formulas

	A	B	C	D	E	F	G
11	Schedule c						
12	Purchases budget			April	May	June	July
13	Desired ending inventory			+ D5 + D8 D10*B6	+ D5 + D8 D10*B7	+ D5 + D8 D10*B8	+ D5 + D8 D10*B9
14	Plus cost of goods sold			+ D10*B5	+ D10*B6	+ D10*B7	+ D10*B8
15							
16	Total needed			+ D13 + D14	+ E13 + E14	+ F13 + F14	+ G13 + G14
17	Less beginning inventory			+D4	+D13	+E13	+F13
18							
19	Purchases			+ D16 − D17	+ E16 − E17	+ F16 − F17	+ G16 − G17
20							

Exhibit 7-9

The Cooking Hut Company

Purchases Budget

	A	B	C	D	E	F	G
11	Schedule c						
12	Purchases budget			April	May	June	July
13	Desired ending inventory			$64,800	$ 53,600	$48,000	$42,400
14	Plus cost of goods sold			35,000	56,000	42,000	35,000
15							
16	Total needed			99,800	109,600	90,000	77,400
17	Less beginning inventory			48,000	64,800	53,600	48,000
18							
19	Purchases			$51,800	$ 44,800	$36,400	$29,400
20							

Every schedule, operating budget, and financial budget of the master budget can be prepared on the spreadsheet. Each schedule would be linked by the appropriate cell addresses just as the budget input data (Exhibit 7-7) are linked to the purchases budget (Exhibits 7-8 and 7-9). As in the purchases budget, ideally all cells in the master budget are formulas, not numbers. That way, every budget input can be the subject of sensitivity analysis, if desired, by simply changing the budget data in Exhibit 7-7.

Preparing the master budget on a spreadsheet is time-consuming—the first time. After that, the time savings and planning capabilities through sensitivity analysis are enormous compared with a manual approach. A problem can occur, however, if the master budget model is not well documented when a person other than the author attempts to modify the spreadsheet model. Any assumptions that are made should be described either within the spreadsheet or in a separate budget preparation document.

Exhibit 7-10

The Cooking Hut Company
Purchases Budget

	A	B	C	D	E	F	G
1	Budgeted data						
2	Sales forecasts		Other information				
3							
4	March (actual)	$40,000	Beginning inventory	$ 48,000			
5	April	55,000	Desired ending inventory: Base amount	$ 20,000			
6	May	88,000	Plus percent of next				
7	June	66,000	month's cost of				
8	July	55,000	goods sold	80%			
9	August	44,000	Cost of goods sold				
10			as percent of sales	70%			
11	Schedule c						
12	Purchases budget			April	May	June	July
13	Desired ending inventory			$ 69,280	$ 56,960	$50,800	$44,640
14	Plus cost of goods sold			38,500	61,600	46,200	38,500
15							
16	Total needed			107,780	118,560	97,000	83,140
17	Beginning inventory			48,000	69,280	56,960	50,800
18							
19	Purchases			59,780	49,280	$40,040	$32,340
20							

Accounting Vocabulary

capital budget, p. 252
cash budget, p. 259
continuous budget, p. 252
financial budget, p. 254
financial planning model, p. 264

long-range planning, p. 252
master budget, p. 252
operating budget, p. 254
participative budgeting, p. 263
profit plan, p. 254
pro forma statements, p. 252

rolling budget, p. 252
sales budget, p. 262
sales forecast, p. 262
sensitivity analysis, p. 270
strategic plan, p. 252

Fundamental Assignment Material

Special note: Problems 7-A1 and 7-B1 provide single-problem reviews of most of the chapter topics. Those readers who prefer to concentrate on the fundamentals in smaller chunks should consider any of the other problems.

7-A1   Prepare Master Budget

Computer Superstores, Inc. has a strong belief in using highly decentralized management. You are the new manager of one of its small "computer boutiques" in Las Vegas. You know much about how to buy, how to display, how to sell, and how to reduce shoplifting. You know little about accounting and finance, however.

Top management is convinced that training for higher management should include the active participation of store managers in the budgeting process. You have been asked to prepare a complete master budget for your store for June, July, and August. You are responsible for its actual full preparation. All accounting is done centrally, so you have no expert help on the premises. In addition, tomorrow the branch manager and the assistant controller will be here to examine your work; at that time they will assist you in formulating the final budget document. The idea is to have you prepare the budget a few times so that you gain more confidence about accounting matters. You want to make a favorable impression on your superiors, so you gather the following data as of May 31, 19X6:

		Recent and Projected Sales	
Cash	$ 29,000		
Inventory	420,000	April	$300,000
Accounts receivable	369,000	May	350,000
Net furniture and fixtures	168,000	June	700,000
Total assets	$986,000	July	400,000
Accounts payable	$475,000	August	400,000
Owners' equity	511,000	September	300,000
Total liabilities and owners' equities	$986,000		

Credit sales are 90% of total sales. Credit accounts are collected 80% in the month following the sale and 20% in the following month. Assume that bad debts are negligible and can be ignored. The accounts receivable on May 31 are the result of the credit sales for April and May: (.20 ×.90 × $300,000 = $54,000) + (1.0 ×.90 × $350,000 = $315,000) = $369,000. The average gross profit on sales is 40%.

The policy is to acquire enough inventory each month to equal the following month's projected sales. All purchases are paid for in the month following purchase.

Salaries, wages, and commissions average 20% of sales; all other variable expenses are 4% of sales. Fixed expenses for rent, property taxes, and miscellaneous payroll and other items are $55,000 monthly. Assume that these variable and fixed expenses require cash disbursements each month. Depreciation is $2,500 monthly.

In June, $55,000 is going to be disbursed for fixtures acquired in May. The May 31 balance of accounts payable includes this amount.

Assume that a minimum cash balance of $25,000 is to be maintained. Also assume that all borrowings are effective at the beginning of the month and all repayments are made at the end of the month of repayment. Interest is paid only at the time of repaying principal. The interest rate is 10% per annum; round interest computations to the nearest ten dollars. All loans and repayments of principal must be made in multiples of a thousand dollars.

1. Prepare a budgeted income statement for the coming quarter, a budgeted statement of monthly cash receipts and disbursements (for the next three months), and a budgeted balance sheet for August 31, 19X6. All operations are evaluated on a before-income-tax basis, so income taxes may be ignored here.

Required

2. Explain why there is a need for a bank loan and what operating sources supply cash for repaying the bank loan.

7-B1 Prepare Master Budget

Victoria Kite Company, a small Melbourne firm, wants a master budget for the next three months, beginning January 1, 19X9. It desires an ending minimum cash balance of $5,000 each month. Sales are forecasted at an average selling price of $8 per kite. In January, Victoria Kite is beginning JIT deliveries from suppliers, which means that purchases equal expected sales. On January 1, purchases will cease until inventory reaches $6,000, after which time purchases will equal sales. Merchandise costs are $4 per kite. Purchases during any given month are paid in full during the following month. All sales are on credit, payable within 30 days, but experience has shown that 60% of current sales is collected in the current month, 30% in the next month, and 10% in the month thereafter. Bad debts are negligible.

Monthly operating expenses are as follows:

Wages and salaries	$15,000
Insurance expired	125
Depreciation	250
Miscellaneous	2,500
Rent	250/month + 10% of quarterly sales over $10,000

Cash dividends of $1,500 are to be paid quarterly, beginning January 15, and are declared on the 15th of the previous month. All operating expenses are paid as incurred, except insurance, depreciation, and rent. Rent of $250 is paid at the beginning of each month, and the additional 10% of sales is paid quarterly on the 10th of the month following the end of the quarter. The next settlement is due January 10.

The company plans to buy some new fixtures for $3,000 cash in March.

Money can be borrowed and repaid in multiples of $500 at an interest rate of 10% per annum. Management wants to minimize borrowing and repay rapidly. Interest is computed and paid when the principal is repaid. Assume that borrowing occurs at the beginning, and repayments at the end, of the months in question. Money is never borrowed at the beginning and repaid at the end of the *same* month. Compute interest to the nearest dollar.

Assets as of December 31, 19X8		Liabilities as of December 31, 19X8	
Cash	$ 5,000	Accounts payable	
Accounts receivable	12,500	(merchandise)	$35,550
Inventory*	39,050	Dividends payable	1,500
Unexpired insurance	1,500	Rent payable	7,800
Fixed assets, net	12,500		$44,850
	$70,550		

*November 30 inventory balance = $16,000.

Recent and forecasted sales:

October	$38,000	December	$25,000	February	$75,000	April	$45,000
November	25,000	January	62,000	March	38,000		

Required

1. Prepare a master budget including a budgeted income statement, balance sheet, statement of cash receipts and disbursements, and supporting schedules for the months January through March 19X9.

2. Explain why there is a need for a bank loan and what operating sources provide the cash for the repayment of the bank loan.

Additional Assignment Material

QUESTIONS

7-1. Is budgeting used primarily for scorekeeping, attention directing, or problem solving?

7-2. "Budgets are primarily a tool used to limit expenditures." Do you agree? Explain.

7-3. How do strategic planning, long-range planning, and budgeting differ?

7-4. "Capital budgets are plans for managing long-term debt and common stock." Do you agree? Explain.

7-5. "I oppose continuous budgets because they provide a moving target. Managers never know what to aim at." Discuss.

7-6. "Pro forma statements are those statements prepared in conjunction with continuous budgets." Do you agree? Explain.

7-7. Why is budgeted performance better than past performance as a basis for judging actual results?

7-8. "Budgets are okay in relatively certain environments. But everything changes so quickly in the electronics industry that budgeting is a waste of time." Comment on this statement.

7-9. What are the major benefits of budgeting?

7-10. "Budgeting is an unnecessary burden on many managers. It takes time away from important day-to-day problems." Do you agree? Explain.

7-11. Differentiate between an operating budget and a financial budget.

7-12. Why is the sales forecast the starting point for budgeting?

7-13. Explain the relationship between the sales (or service) forecast and cost-driver activity.

7-14. Distinguish between operating expenses and disbursements for operating expenses.

7-15. What is the principal objective of a cash budget?

7-16. Differentiate between a sales forecast and a sales budget.

7-17. What factors influence the sales forecast?

7-18. "Education and salesmanship are key features of budgeting." Explain.

7-19. What are financial planning models?

7-20. "Financial planning models guide managers through the budget process so that managers do not need to really understand budgeting." Do you agree? Explain.

7-21. "I cannot be bothered with setting up my monthly budget on a spreadsheet. It just takes too long to be worth the effort." Comment.

7-22. How do spreadsheets aid the application of sensitivity analysis?

EXERCISES

7-23 Fill In The Blanks

Enter the word or phrase that best completes the following:

1. The financial budget process includes the following budgets:

   a. _____

   b. _____

   c. _____

   d. _____

2. The master budget process usually begins with the _____ budget.

3. The production budget process usually begins with the _____ budget.

4. A _____ budget is a plan that is revised monthly or quarterly, dropping one period and adding another.

5. Strategic planning sets the _____.

7-24 Purchases and Cost of Goods Sold

The Northfield Co., a wholesaler of food products, budgeted the following sales for the indicated months:

	June 19X6	July 19X6	August 19X6
Sales on account	$1,800,000	$1,920,000	$2,040,000
Cash sales	240,000	250,000	260,000
Total sales	$2,040,000	$2,170,000	$2,300,000

All merchandise is marked up to sell at its invoice cost plus 25%. Merchandise inventories at the beginning of each month are at 30% of that month's projected cost of goods sold.

Required

1. Compute the budgeted cost of goods sold for the month of June 19X6.
2. Compute the budgeted merchandise purchases for July 19X6.

7-25 Purchases and Sales Budgets

All sales of Dunn's Building Supplies (DBS) are made on credit. Sales are billed twice monthly, on the 10th of the month for the last half of the prior month's sales and on the 20th of the month for the first half of the current month's sales. The terms of all sales are 2/10, net 30. Based on past experience, the collection experience of accounts receivable is as follows:

Within the discount period	80%
On the 30th day	18%
Uncollectible	2%

The sales value of shipments for May 19X8 was $750,000. The forecast sales for the next 4 months are:

June	800,000
July	900,000
August	900,000
September	600,000

DBS's average markup on its products is 20% of the sales price.

DBS purchases merchandise for resale to meet the current month's sales demand and to maintain a desired monthly ending inventory of 25% of the next month's sales. All purchases are on credit with terms of net 30. DBS pays for one-half of a month's purchases in the month of purchase and the other half in the month following the purchase.

All sales and purchases occur uniformly throughout the month.

Required

1. How much cash can DBS plan to collect from accounts receivable collections during July 19X8?
2. How much can DBS plan to collect in September from sales made in August 19X8?
3. Compute the budgeted dollar value of DBS inventory on August 31, 19X8.
4. How much merchandise should DBS plan to purchase during June 19X8?
5. How much should DBS budget in August 19X8 for the payment for merchandise purchased?

7-26 Sales Budget

Suppose a division of Nike has the following data:

- Accounts receivable, May 31: (.3 × May sales of $400,000) = $120,000
- Monthly forecasted sales: June, $400,000; July, $440,000; August, $500,000; September, $530,000

Sales consist of 70% cash and 30% credit. All credit accounts are collected in the month following the sales. Uncollectible accounts are negligible and may be ignored.

Required Prepare a sales budget schedule and a cash collections budget schedule for June, July, and August.

7-27 Sales Budget

A Tokyo wholesaler was preparing its sales budget for the first quarter of 19X8. Forecast sales are (in thousands of yen)

January	¥180,000
February	¥210,000
March	¥240,000

Sales are 20% cash and 80% on credit. Fifty percent of the credit accounts are collected in the month of sale, 40% in the month following the sale, and 10% in the following month. No uncollectible accounts are anticipated. Accounts receivable at the beginning of 19X8 are ¥96 million (10% × November credit sales of ¥180 million and 50% of December credit sales of ¥156 million).

Required

Prepare a schedule showing sales and cash collections for January, February, and March, 19X8.

7-28 Cash Collection Budget

Pioneer Square Carpets has found that cash collections from customers tend to occur in the following pattern:

Collected within cash discount period in month of sale	50%
Collected within cash discount period in first month after month of sale	10
Collected after cash discount period in first month after month of sale	25
Collected after cash discount period in second month after month of sale	12
Never collected	3
Total sales in any month (before cash discounts)	100%
Cash discount allowable as a percentage of invoice price	1%

Compute the total cash budgeted to be collected in March if sales are predicted as $300,000 for January, $400,000 for February, and $450,000 for March.

7-29 Purchase Budget

Fernandez Furniture Mart plans inventory levels (at cost) at the end of each month as follows: May, $250,000; June, $220,000; July, $270,000; August, $250,000.

Sales are expected to be: June, $440,000; July, $350,000; August, $400,000. Cost of goods sold is 60% of sales.

Purchases in April were $250,000; in May, $180,000. A given month's purchases are paid as follows: 10% during that month; 80% the next month; and the final 10% the next month.

Required

Prepare budget schedules for June, July, and August for purchases and for disbursements for purchases.

7-30 Purchase Budget

The inventory of the Belfast Appliance Company was £200,000 on May 31. The manager was upset because the inventory was too high. She has adopted the following policies regarding merchandise purchases and inventory. At the end of any month, the inventory should be £15,000 plus 90% of the cost of goods to be sold during the following month. The cost of merchandise sold averages 60% of sales. Purchase terms are generally net, 30 days. A given month's purchases are paid as follows: 20% during that month and 80% during the following month.

Purchases in May had been £150,000. Sales are expected to be: June, £300,000; July, £280,000; August, £340,000; and September, £400,000.

Required

1. Compute the amount by which the inventory on May 31 exceeded the manager's policies.
2. Prepare budget schedules for June, July, and August for purchases and for disbursements for purchases.

7-31 Cash Budget

Consider the income statement in Exhibit 7-11.

The cash balance, May 31, 19X6, is $15,000. Sales proceeds are collected as follows: 80% month of sale, 10% second month, 10% third month.

Exhibit 7-11

Raleigh Company

Budgeted Income Statement for the Month Ended June 30,
19X6 (in thousands)

Sales		$290
Inventory, May 31	$ 50	
Purchases	192	
Available for sale	242	
Inventory, June 30	40	
Cost of goods sold		202
Gross margin		$ 88
Operating expenses		
Wages	$ 36	
Utilities	5	
Advertising	10	
Depreciation	1	
Office expenses	4	
Insurance and property taxes	3	59
Operating income		$ 29

Accounts receivable are $40,000 on May 31, 19X6, consisting of $16,000 from April sales and $24,000 from May sales.

Accounts payable on May 31, 19X6, are $145,000. Raleigh Company pays 25% of purchases during the month of purchase and the remainder during the following month. All operating expenses requiring cash are paid during the month of recognition. Insurance and property taxes are paid annually in December, however.

Required Prepare a cash budget for June. Confine your analysis to the given data. Ignore income taxes and other possible items that might affect cash.

PROBLEMS

7-32 Cash Budget

Catherine O'Shea is the manager of an extremely successful gift shop, Kate's Gifts, which is operated for the benefit of local charities. From the following data, she wants a cash budget showing expected cash receipts and disbursements for the month of April, and the cash balance expected as of April 30, 19X7:

- Bank note due April 10: $90,000 plus $4,500 interest
- Depreciation for April: $2,100
- Two-year insurance policy due April 14 for renewal: $1,500, to be paid in cash
- Planned cash balance, March 31, 19X7: $80,000
- Merchandise purchases for April: $500,000, 40% paid in month of purchase, 60% paid in next month
- Customer receivables as of March 31: $60,000 from February sales, $450,000 from March sales
- Payrolls due in April: $90,000
- Other expenses for April, payable in April: $45,000
- Accrued taxes for April, payable in June: $7,500
- Sales for April: $1,000,000, half collected in month of sale, 40% in next month, 10% in third month
- Accounts payable, March 31, 19X7: $460,000

Required Prepare the cash budget.

7-33 Cash Budget

Prepare a statement of estimated cash receipts and disbursements for October 19X7 for the Aquarius Company, which sells one product, herbal soap, by the case. On October 1, 19X7, part of the trial balance showed:

Cash	$ 4,800	
Accounts receivable	15,600	
Allowance for bad debts		$1,900
Merchandise inventory	11,500	
Accounts payable, merchandise		7,200

The company pays for its purchases within 10 days. Assume that one-third of the purchases of any month are due and paid for in the following month.

The cost of the merchandise purchased is $12 per case. At the end of each month it is desired to have an inventory equal in units to 50% of the following month's sales in units.

Sales terms include a 1% discount if payment is made by the end of the calendar month. Past experience indicates that 60% of the billings will be collected during the month of the sale, 30% in the following calendar month, 6% in the next following calendar month. Four percent will be uncollectible. The company's fiscal year begins August 1.

Unit selling price	$	20
August actual sales		12,000
September actual sales		36,000
October estimated sales		30,000
November estimated sales		22,000
Total sales expected in the fiscal year		$360,000

Exclusive of bad debts, total budgeted selling and general administrative expenses for the fiscal year are estimated at $55,500, of which $18,000 is fixed expense (which includes a $7,200 annual depreciation charge). Aquarius incurs these fixed expenses uniformly throughout the year. The balance of the selling and general administrative expenses varies with sales. Expenses are paid as incurred.

BUSINESS FIRST   www.prenhall.com/phlip

7-34 Budgeting at Ritz-Carlton

Suppose Ritz-Carlton has a 300-room hotel in a tropical climate. Management expects occupancy rates to be 95% in December, January, and February, 85% in November, March, and April, and 70% the rest of the year. The average room rental is $250 per night. Of this, on average 10% is received as a deposit the month before the stay, 60% is received in the month of the stay, and 28% is collected the month after. The remaining 2% is never collected.

Most of the costs of running the hotel are fixed. The variable costs are only $30 per occupied room per night. Fixed salaries (including benefits) run $400,000 per month, depreciation is $350,000 a month, other fixed operating costs are $120,000 per month, and interest expense is $500,000 per month. Variable costs and salaries are paid in the month they are incurred, depreciation is recorded at the end of each quarter, other fixed operating costs are paid as incurred, and interest is paid each June and December.

Required

1. Prepare a monthly cash budget for this Ritz-Carlton hotel. For simplicity, assume that there are 30 days in each month.

2. How much would the hotel's annual profit increase if occupancy rates increased by five percentage points each month in the off-season (that is, from 70% to 75% in May through October)? ■

7-35 Activity-Based Budgeting

A recent directive from Helen Prescott, CEO of Comtel, had instructed each department to cut its costs by 10%. The traditional budget for the Warehousing Department was as follows:

Salaries, 4 employees @ $42,000	$168,000
Benefits @ 20%	33,600
Depreciation, straight-line basis	76,000
Parts and supplies	42,400
Overhead @ 35% of direct costs	112,000
Total	$432,000

Therefore, the Warehousing Division needed to find $43,200 to cut.

Tom Procter, a recent MBA graduate, was asked to pare $43,200 from the Warehousing Department's budget. As a first step, he recast the traditional budget into an activity-based budget:

Receiving, 620,000 pounds	$ 93,000
Shipping, 402,000 boxes	201,000
Handling, 11,200 moves	112,000
Record-keeping, 65,000 transactions	26,000
Total	$432,000

Required

1. What actions might Procter suggest to attain a $43,200 budget cut? Why would these be the best actions to pursue?

2. Which budget helped you most in answering requirement 1? Explain.

7-36 Budgeting, Behavior, and Ethics

Since Stan Legree had become President of Alberta Mining, Ltd., budgets had become a major focus for managers. In fact, making budget was such an important goal that the only two managers who had missed their budgets in 19X8 (by 2% and 4%, respectively) had been summarily fired. This caused all managers to be wary when setting their 19X9 budgets.

The GSL Copper Division of Alberta Mining had the following results for 19X8:

Sales, 1.6 million pounds @ $.95/pound	$1,520,000
Variable costs	880,000
Fixed costs, primarily depreciation	450,000
Pretax profit	$ 190,000

Sheila Masur, General Manager of GSL, received a memo from Legree that contained the following:

> "We expect your profit for 19X9 to be at least $209,000. Prepare a budget showing how you plan to accomplish this."

Masur was concerned because the market for copper had recently softened. Her market research staff forecast that sales would be at or below the 19X8 level and prices would likely be between $.92 and $.94 per pound. Her manufacturing manager reported that most of the fixed costs were committed and there were few efficiencies to be gained in the variable costs. He indicated that perhaps a 2% savings might be achievable, but certainly no more.

Required

1. Prepare a budget for Masur to submit to headquarters. What dilemmas does Masur face in preparing this budget?

2. What problems do you see in the budgeting process at Alberta Mining?

3. Suppose Masur submitted a budget showing a $209,000 profit. It is now late in 19X9, and she has had a good year. Despite an industrywide decline in sales, GSL's sales matched last year's 1.6 million pounds, and the average price per pound was $.945, nearly at last year's level and well above that forecast. Variable costs were cut by 2% through extensive efforts. Still, profit projections were more than $9,000 below budget. Masur was concerned for her job, so she approached the controller and requested that depreciation schedules be changed. By extending the lives of some equipment for 2 years, $15,000 of depreciation could be saved in 19X9. Estimating the economic lives of equipment is difficult, and it would be hard to prove that the old lives were better than the new proposed lives. What should the controller do? What ethical issues does this raise?

7-37 Spreadsheets and Sensitivity Analysis of Income Statement
Study Appendix 7. The Speedy-Mart Store has the following budgeted sales, which are uniform throughout the month:

May	$450,000
June	375,000
July	330,000
August	420,000

Cost of goods sold averages 70% of sales and is purchased essentially as needed. Employees earn fixed salaries of $22,000 (total) monthly and commissions of 10% of the current month's sales, paid as earned. Other expenses are rent, $6,000, paid on the first of each month for that month's occupancy; miscellaneous expenses, 6% of sales, paid as incurred; insurance, $450 per month, from a one-year policy that was paid for on January 2; and depreciation, $2,850 per month.

1. Using spreadsheet software, prepare a table of budget data for the Speedy-Mart **Required** Store.

2. Continue the spreadsheet in part 1 to prepare budget schedules for (a) disbursements for operating expenses and (b) operating income for June, July, and August.

3. Adjust the budget data appropriately for each of the following scenarios independently and recompute operating income using the spreadsheet:

   a. A sales promotion that will cost $30,000 in May could increase sales in each of the following three months by 5%.

   b. Eliminating the sales commissions and increasing employees' salaries to $52,500 per month could decrease sales thereafter by a net of 2%.

7-38 Spreadsheets and Sensitivity Analysis of Operating Expenses
Study Appendix 7. The CD-ROM Division (CDRD) of Micro Storage, Inc., produces highest quality CD-ROM drives for personal computers. The drives are assembled from purchased components. The costs (value) added by CDRD are indirect costs (which include assembly labor), packaging, and shipping. CDRD produces two speeds of drives: 5X and 10X. Cost behavior of CDRD is as follows:

	Fixed	Variable
Purchased components		
10X Drives		$100 per component
5X Drives		40 per component
Indirect costs	$40,000	16 per component
Packaging	8,000	4 per drive
Shipping	8,000	2 per drive

Both CD-ROM drives require five components. Therefore, the total cost of components for 10X drives is $500 and for 5X drives is $200. CDRD uses a six-month continuous budget that is revised monthly. Sales forecasts for the next eight months are as follows:

	10X Drives	5X Drives
October	3,200 units	4,000 units
November	2,400	3,000
December	5,600	7,000
January	3,200	4,000
February	3,200	4,000
March	2,400	3,000
April	2,400	3,000
May	2,800	3,500

Required   Treat each event in succession.

1. Use spreadsheet software to prepare a table of budgeting information and an operating expense budget for the CD-ROM Division for October through March. Incorporate the expectation that sales of 5X drives will be 125% of 10X drives. Prepare a spreadsheet that can be revised easily for succeeding months.

2. October's actual sales were 2,800 10X drives and 3,600 5X drives. This outcome has caused CDRD to revise its sales forecasts downward by 10%. Revise the operating expense budget for November through April.

3. At the end of November, CDRD decides that the proportion of 10X to 5X is changing. Sales of 5X drives are expected to be 150% of 10X drive sales. Expected sales of 10X drives are unchanged from part 2. Revise the operating expense budget for December through May.

CASES

7-39 Cash Budgeting for Hospital

Mercy Hospital provides a wide range of health services in its community. Mercy's board of directors has authorized the following capital expenditures:

Intraaortic balloon pump	$1,300,000
Computed tomographic scanner	850,000
X-ray equipment	550,000
Laboratory equipment	1,200,000
	$3,900,000

The expenditures are planned for October 1, 19X7, and the board wishes to know the amount of borrowing, if any, necessary on that date. Jill Todd, hospital controller, has gathered the following information to be used in preparing an analysis of future cash flows.

1. Billings, made in the month of service, for the first 6 months of 19X7 are:

Month	Actual Amount
January	$5,300,000
February	5,300,000
March	5,400,000
April	5,400,000
May	6,000,000
June	6,000,000

Ninety percent of Mercy's billings are made to third parties such as Blue Cross, federal or state governments, and private insurance companies. The remaining 10% of the billings are made directly to patients. Historical patterns of billing collections are:

	Third-Party Billings	Direct Patient Billings
Month of service	20%	10%
Month following service	50	40
Second month following service	20	40
Uncollectible	10	10

Estimated billings for the last six months of 19X7 are listed next. Todd expects the same billing and collection patterns that have been experienced during the first six months of 19X7 to continue during the last six months of the year.

Month	Estimated Amount
July	$5,400,000
August	6,000,000
September	6,600,000
October	6,800,000
November	7,000,000
December	6,600,000

2. The following schedule presents the purchases that have been made during the past three months and the planned purchases for the last six months of 19X7.

Month	Amount
April	$1,300,000
May	1,450,000
June	1,450,000
July	1,500,000
August	1,800,000
September	2,200,000
October	2,350,000
November	2,700,000
December	2,100,000

All purchases are made on account, and accounts payable are remitted in the month following the purchase.

3. Salaries for each month during the remainder of 19X7 are expected to be $1,800,000 per month plus 20% of that month's billings. Salaries are paid in the month of service.

4. Mercy's monthly depreciation charges are $150,000.

5. Mercy incurs interest expenses of $180,000 per month and makes interest payments of $540,000 on the last day of each calendar quarter.

6. Endowment fund income is expected to continue to total $210,000 per month.

7. Mercy has a cash balance of $350,000 on July 1, 19X7, and has a policy of maintaining a minimum end-of-month cash balance of 10% of the current month's purchases.

8. Mercy Hospital employs a calendar-year reporting period.

1. Prepare a schedule of budgeted cash receipts by month for the third quarter of 19X7.

2. Prepare a schedule of budgeted cash disbursements by month for the third quarter of 19X7.

3. Determine the amount of borrowing, if any, necessary on October 1, 19X7, to acquire the capital items totaling $3,900,000.

7-40 Comprehensive Budgeting for University

Suppose you are the controller of Western Wyoming State University. The university president, Willa Redcloud, is preparing for her annual fund-raising campaign for 19X8–X9. To set an appropriate target, she has asked you to prepare a budget for the academic year. You have collected the following data for the current year (19X7–X8):

1.	Undergraduate Division	Graduate Division
Average salary of faculty member	$46,000	$46,000
Average faculty teaching load in semester credit hours per year (eight undergraduate or six graduate courses)	24	18
Average number of students per class	30	20
Total enrollment (full-time and part-time students)	3,600	1,800
Average number of semester credit hours carried each year per student	25	20
Full-time load, semester hours per year	30	24

For 19X8–X9, all faculty and staff will receive a 6% salary increase. Undergraduate enrollment is expected to decline by 2%, but graduate enrollment is expected to increase by 5%.

2. The 19X7–X8 budget for operation and maintenance of facilities is $500,000, which includes $240,000 for salaries and wages. Experience so far this year indicates that the budget is accurate. Salaries and wages will increase by 6% and other operating costs will increase by $12,000 in 19X8–X9.

3. The 19X7–X8 and 19X8–X9 budgets for the remaining expenditures are:

	19X7–X8	19X8–X9
General administrative	$500,000	$525,000
Library		
Acquisitions	150,000	155,000
Operations	190,000	200,000
Health services	48,000	50,000
Intramural athletics	56,000	60,000
Intercollegiate athletics	240,000	245,000
Insurance and retirement	520,000	560,000
Interest	75,000	75,000

4. Tuition is $70 per credit hour. In addition, the state legislature provides $780 per full-time-equivalent student. (A full-time equivalent is 30 undergraduate hours or 24 graduate hours.) Tuition scholarships are given to 30 *full-time* undergraduates and 50 *full-time* graduate students.

5. Revenues other than tuition and the legislative apportionment are:

	19X7–X8	19X8–X9
Endowment income	$200,000	$210,000
Net income from auxiliary services	325,000	335,000
Intercollegiate athletic receipts	290,000	300,000

6. The chemistry/physics classroom building needs remodeling during the 19X8–X9 period. Projected cost is $550,000.

Required

1. Prepare a schedule for 19X8–X9 that shows, by division, (a) expected enrollment, (b) total credit hours, (c) full-time-equivalent enrollment, and (d) number of faculty members needed. Assume that part-time faculty can be hired at one-half the salary per credit hour as full-time faculty.

2. Calculate the budget for faculty salaries for 19X8–X9 by division.

3. Calculate the budget for tuition revenue and legislative apportionment for 19X8–X9 by division.

4. Prepare a schedule for President Redcloud showing the amount that must be raised by the annual fund-raising campaign.

COLLABORATIVE LEARNING EXERCISE

7-41 Personal Budgeting

Budgeting is useful to many different types of entities. One is the individual. Consider the entity that you know best, the college or university student. Form a group of two to six students, and pool the information that you have about what it costs to spend a year as a full-time student.

Prepare a revenue and expense budget for an average prospective full-time student at your college or university. Identify possible sources of revenue and the amount to be received from each. Identify the costs a student is likely to incur during the year. You can assume that cash disbursements are made immediately for all expenses, so the budgeted income statement and cash budget are identical.

When all groups have completed their budgets, compare those budgets. What are the differences? What assumptions led to the differences?

FLEXIBLE BUDGETS AND VARIANCE ANALYSIS

Eating under the arches in Tokyo. McDonald's restaurants are located in more than 100 countries.

Learning Objectives

When you have finished studying this chapter, you should be able to

1   Distinguish between flexible budgets and master (static) budgets.

2   Use flexible-budget formulas to construct a flexible budget based on the volume of sales.

3   Prepare an activity-based flexible budget.

4   Understand the performance evaluation relationship between master (static) budgets and flexible budgets.

5   Compute flexible-budget variances and sales-activity variances.

6   Compute and interpret price and usage variances for inputs based on cost-driver activity.

7   Compute variable overhead spending and efficiency variances.

8   **Understand how management uses flexible budgets to evaluate the company's financial performance.**

I n 1996, McDonald's was ranked the world's greatest brand. More than 2,400 new restaurants were opened in 1997 and about 70% of these were outside the United States. You can eat a Big Mac under the Golden Arches in more than 100 countries.

With revenues exceeding $30 billion and more than 21,000 restaurants, the challenge is to ensure that the taste of each Big Mac is the same. How does McDonald's maintain cost and quality control? How does it ensure that each of the 35 million customers it serves daily receives the same value? It uses standards, budgets, and variance analysis. For example, the standards for material are the same for hamburgers wherever they are sold—1 bun, 1 hamburger patty, 1 pickle slice, 1/8 tablespoon of dehydrated onion, 1/4 tablespoon mustard, and 1/2 oz. of ketchup. Material variances are computed for each of these ingredients by computing the amount actually used compared to what should have been used, given the number and type of sandwiches sold.

McDonald's managers budget sales for each hour during the day. Based on the sales budgeted, labor is scheduled. If sales are lower than budgeted, managers can control labor cost by sending some employees home early.

McDonald's also uses nonfinancial standards to help achieve its quality and service goals. For example, the standard time for a drive-through customer is 310 seconds from pulling up to the menu board to driving away. Cooked meat that is not used in a sandwich within 30 minutes is destroyed. Once a sandwich is made and placed in the transfer bin, it must be sold within 10 minutes or it will be thrown away.

As is the case at McDonald's, managers and employees of any organization want to know how they are doing in meeting their goals. Upper-level managers also want to know how the organization is meeting its financial objectives. Knowing what went wrong and what went right should help managers plan and manage more effectively in future periods.

This chapter introduces flexible budgets, which are budgets designed to direct management to areas of actual financial performance that deserve attention. Managers can apply this same basic process to control other important areas of performance such as quality and service.

FLEXIBLE BUDGETS: BRIDGE BETWEEN STATIC BUDGETS AND ACTUAL RESULTS

STATIC BUDGETS

Static budget is really just another name for *master budget.* All the *master budgets* discussed in Chapter 7 are *static* or inflexible, because even though they may be easily revised, these budgets assume fixed levels of activity. In other words, a master budget is prepared for only one level of a given type of activity. For example, consider a company using a traditional costing system with only one cost driver. The Dominion Company is a one-department firm in Toronto that manufactures and sells a wheeled, collapsible suitcase carrier that is popular with airline flight crews. Manufacture of this suitcase carrier requires several manual and machine operations. The product has some variations, but may be viewed for our purposes essentially as a single product bearing one selling price. Assume that the cost driver is sales volume (that is, units sold), and the projected level of activity (sales volume) is 9,000 units. All of the budget figures are then based on projected sales of 9,000 units.

All *actual* results could be compared with the original budgeted amounts, even though, for example, sales volume turned out to be only 7,000 units instead of the originally planned 9,000 units. The master (static) budget for June 19X8 included the condensed income statement shown in Exhibit 8-1, column 2. The actual results for June 19X8 are in column 1. Differences or variances between actual results and the master budget are in column 3. The master budget called for production and sales of 9,000 units, but only 7,000 units were actually produced and sold. There were no beginning or ending inventories, so the units made in June were sold in June.

master budget variance (static budget variance) The variance of actual results from the master budget.

The performance report in Exhibit 8-1 compares the actual results with the master budget. *Performance report* is a generic term that usually means a comparison of actual results with some budget. A helpful performance report will include variances that direct upper management's attention to significant deviations from expected results, allowing *management by exception.* Recall that a *variance* is a deviation of an actual amount from the expected or budgeted amount. Exhibit 8-1 shows variances of actual results from the master budget; these are called **master (static) budget variances.** Actual revenues that exceed expected revenues result in favorable revenue variances. When actual revenues are below expected revenues, variances are unfavorable. Similarly, actual expenses that exceed budgeted expenses result in **unfavorable expense variances,** and actual expenses

unfavorable expense variance A variance that occurs when actual expenses are more than budgeted expenses.

Exhibit 8-1
Dominion Company
Performance Report Using Master Budget For the Month Ended June 30, 19X8

	Actual (1)	Master Budget (2)	Master Budget Variances (3)
Units	7,000	9,000	2,000
Sales	$ 217,000	$279,000	$62,000 U
Variable expenses			
Variable manufacturing expenses	$ 151,270	$189,000	$37,730 F
Shipping expenses (selling)	5,000	5,400	400 F
Administrative expenses	2,000	1,800	200 U
Total variable expenses	$ 158,270	$196,200	$37,930 F
Contribution margin	$ 58,730	$ 82,800	$24,070 U
Fixed expenses			
Fixed manufacturing expenses	$ 37,300	$ 37,000	$ 300 U
Fixed selling and administrative expenses	33,000	33,000	—
Total fixed expenses	$ 70,300	$ 70,000	$ 300 U
Operating income (loss)	$ (11,570)	$ 12,800	$24,370 U

U = Unfavorable expense variances occur when actual expenses are more than budgeted expenses.

F = Favorable expense variances occur when actual expenses are less than budgeted expenses.

that are less than budgeted expenses, result in **favorable expense variances.** Each significant variance should cause a manager to ask "Why?" By explaining why a variance occurs, managers are forced to recognize changes that have affected costs and that might affect future decisions.

Suppose the president of Dominion Company asks you to explain why there was an operating loss of $11,570 when a profit of $12,800 was budgeted. Clearly, sales were below expectations, but the favorable variances for the variable costs are misleading. Considering the lower-than-projected level of sales activity, was cost control really satisfactory? The comparison of actual results with a master budget does not give much help in answering that question. Master budget variances are not very useful for management by exception.

favorable expense variance A variance that occurs when actual expenses are less than budgeted expenses.

FLEXIBLE BUDGETS

A more helpful benchmark for analysis is the *flexible budget.* A **flexible budget** (sometimes called **variable budget**) is a budget that adjusts for changes in sales volume and other cost-driver activities. The flexible budget is identical to the master budget in format, but managers may prepare it for any level of activity. So, when sales turn out to be 7,000 units instead of 9,000, managers can use the flexible budget to prepare a new budget *based on this new cost-driver level.* We can then see what the total variable expenses should be based on a sales level of 7,000 and compare this amount to the actual result. For performance evaluation, the flexible budget would be prepared at the actual levels of activity achieved. In contrast, the master budget is kept fixed or static to serve as the primary benchmark for evaluating performance. It shows revenues and costs at only the *originally planned* levels of activity.

The flexible-budget approach says, "Give me any activity level you choose, and I'll provide a budget tailored to that particular level." Many companies routinely "flex" their budgets to help evaluate recent financial performance. For example, Ritz-Carlton managers evaluate monthly financial performance of all the company's hotels by comparing actual results to new, flexible budgets that are prepared for actual levels of activity.

flexible budget (variable budget) A budget that adjusts for changes in sales volume and other cost-driver activities.

Objective 1
Distinguish between flexible budgets and master (static) budgets.

Exhibit 8-2

Dominion Company
Flexible Budgets

	Flexible Budget Formula	Flexible Budgets for Various Levels of Sales/Production Activity		
BUDGET FORMULA PER UNIT				
Units		7,000	8,000	9,000
Sales	$ 31.00	$217,000	$248,000	$279,000
Variable costs/expense				
Variable manufacturing costs	$ 21.00	$147,000	$168,000	$189,000
Shipping expenses (selling)	.60	4,200	4,800	5,400
Administrative	.20	1,400	1,600	1,800
Total variable costs/expenses	$ 21.80	$152,600	$174,400	$196,200
Contribution margin	$ 9.20	$ 64,400	$ 73,600	$ 82,800
BUDGET FORMULA PER MONTH				
Fixed costs				
Fixed manufacturing costs	$37,000	$ 37,000	$ 37,000	$ 37,000
Fixed selling and administrative costs	33,000	33,000	33,000	33,000
Total fixed costs	$70,000	$ 70,000	$ 70,000	$ 70,000
Operating income (loss)		$ (5,600)	$ 3,600	$ 12,800

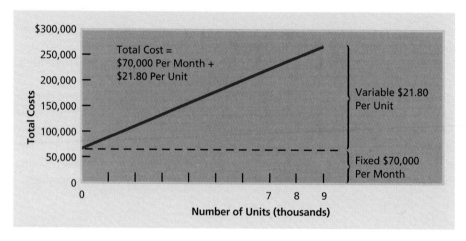

Exhibit 8-3

Dominion Company
Graph of Flexible Budget of Costs

FLEXIBLE-BUDGET FORMULAS

Objective 2
Use flexible-budget formulas to construct a flexible budget based on the volume of sales.

The flexible budget is based on the same assumptions of revenue and cost behavior (within the relevant range) as is the master budget. It is based on knowledge of cost behavior regarding appropriate cost drivers—cost functions or flexible-budget formulas. The cost functions that you used in Chapter 2 and estimated in Chapter 3 can be used as flexible-budget formulas. The flexible budget incorporates effects on each cost and revenue caused by changes in activity. Exhibits 8-2 and 8-3 show Dominion Company's simple flexible budget, which has a single cost driver, units of output. Dominion Company's cost functions or flexible budget formulas are believed to be valid within the relevant range of 7,000 to 9,000 units. Be sure that you understand that each column of Exhibit 8-2 (7,000, 8,000, and 9,000 units, respectively) is prepared using the same flexible-budget formulas—and any activity level within this range could be used, as shown in the graph in Exhibit 8-3. Note that fixed costs are expected to be constant across this range of activity.

ACTIVITY-BASED FLEXIBLE BUDGETS

The flexible budget for Dominion Company shown in Exhibit 8-2 is based on a single cost driver—units of product. For companies that use a traditional, volume-based costing system, this is an appropriate approach to flexible budgeting.

Companies that use an activity-based costing system use a more detailed approach. An **activity-based flexible budget** is based on budgeted costs for each activity and related cost driver. Exhibit 8-4 shows an activity-based flexible budget for the Dominion Company. There are four activities: processing, setup, marketing, and administration. Within each activity, costs depend on an appropriate cost driver. Compare the traditional flexible budget (Exhibit 8-2) and the activity-based flexible budget (Exhibit 8-4). The key difference is that some manufacturing costs that are fixed with respect to *units* are variable with respect to more appropriate cost-driver *setups*. The fixed manufacturing costs ($37,000) in Exhibit 8-2 includes setup costs that are largely fixed with respect to "units produced" but that vary with respect to the "number of setups." An example is the cost of supplies used to set up the production run. Each time a setup is done, supplies are used. Therefore, the cost of supplies varies directly with the number of setups. However, no setup supplies are used during production, so there is little change in the cost of supplies over wide ranges of units produced. This basic difference is why the total costs differ using the two approaches—activity-based flexible budgets provide more accurate measures of cost behavior.

When should a company use activity-based flexible budgets? When a significant portion of its costs vary with cost drivers other than units of production. In our Dominion example, the $500 per setup is the only such cost. For the rest of this chapter we will ignore the fact that this cost varies with number of setups, and go back to assuming that Dominion's operations are simple enough that a traditional flexible budget with a single cost driver is appropriate.

Objective 3
Prepare an activity-based flexible budget.

activity-based flexible budget A budget based on budgeted costs for each activity and related cost driver.

EVALUATION OF FINANCIAL PERFORMANCE USING FLEXIBLE BUDGETS

Comparing the flexible budget to actual results accomplishes an important performance evaluation purpose. There are basically two reasons why actual results might differ from the master budget. One is that sales and other cost-driver activities were not the same as originally forecasted. The second is that revenues or variable costs per unit of activity and fixed costs per period were not as expected. Though these reasons may not be completely independent (for example, higher sales prices may have caused lower sales levels), it is useful to separate these effects because different people may be responsible for each and because different management actions may be indicated. The intent of using the flexible budget for performance evaluation is to isolate unexpected effects on actual results that can be corrected if adverse or enhanced if beneficial. Because the flexible budget is prepared at the actual levels of activity (in our example, sales volume), any variances between the flexible budget and actual results cannot be due to activity levels (again, assuming cost and revenue functions are valid). These *variances between the flexible budget and actual results* are called **flexible-budget variances** and must be due to *departures of actual costs or revenues from flexible-budget formula amounts*—because of pricing or cost control. In contrast, any differences or *variances between the master budget and the flexible budget are due to activity levels,* not cost control. These latter differences between the master budget amounts and the amounts in the flexible budget are called **activity-level variances.** In other words, the origi-

Objective 4
Understand the performance evaluation relationship between master (static) budgets and flexible budgets.

flexible-budget variances
The variances between the flexible budget and the actual results.

activity-level variances
The differences between the master budget amounts and the amounts in the flexible budget.

Exhibit 8-4

Dominion Company
Activity-Based Flexible Budget for the Month Ended June 30, 19X8

	BUDGET FORMULA	Units		
		7,000	8,000	9,000
Sales	$31.00	$217,000	$248,000	$279,000

ACTIVITY

Processing

		Cost Driver: Number of Machine Hours		
Cost-Driver Level		14,000	16,000	18,000
Variable Costs	$10.50	$147,000	$168,000	$189,000
Fixed Costs	$13,000	13,000	13,000	13,000
Total Costs of Processing Activity		$160,000	$181,000	$202,000

Setup

		Cost Driver: Number of Setups		
Cost-Driver Level		21	24	27
Variable Costs	$500	$ 10,500	$ 12,000	$ 13,500
Fixed Costs	$12,000	12,000	12,000	12,000
Total Costs of Setup Activity		$ 22,500	$ 24,000	$ 25,500

Marketing

		Cost Driver: Number of Orders		
Cost-Driver Level		350	400	450
Variable Costs	$12.00	$ 4,200	$ 4,800	$ 5,400
Fixed Costs	$15,000	15,000	15,000	15,000
Total Costs of Marketing Activity		$ 19,200	$ 19,800	$ 20,400

Administration

		Cost Driver: Number of Units		
Cost Driver Level		7,000	8,000	9,000
Variable Costs	$.20	$ 1,400	$ 1,600	$ 1,800
Fixed Costs	$18,000	18,000	18,000	18,000
Total Costs of Administration Activity		$ 19,400	$ 19,600	$ 19,800

Total Costs		$221,100	$244,400	$267,700
Operating Income (loss)		$ (4,100)	$ 3,600	$ 11,300

nal difference we saw between actual results and the original master budget, which we earlier could not fully explain, actually has two components: the sales-activity variance and the flexible-budget variance.

Consider Exhibit 8-5. The flexible budget (column 3) taken from Exhibit 8-2 (and simplified) provides an explanatory bridge between the master budget (column 5) and the

Exhibit 8-5

Dominion Company
Summary of Performance for the Month Ended June 30, 19X8

	Actual Results at Actual Activity Level* (1)	Flexible-Budget Variances† (2) = (1) − (3)	Flexible Budget for Actual Sales Activity‡ (3)	Sales-Activity Variances (4) = (3) − (5)	Master Budget (5)
Units	7,000	—	7,000	2,000 U	9,000
Sales	$ 217,000	—	$217,000	$62,000 U	$279,000
Variable costs	158,270	5,670 U	152,600	43,600 F	196,200
Contribution margin	$ 58,730	$5,670 U	$ 64,400	$18,400 U	$ 82,800
Fixed costs	70,300	300 U	70,000	—	70,000
Operating income	$ (11,570)	$5,970 U	$ (5,600)	$18,400 U	$ 12,800

Total flexible-budget variances, $5,970 U

Total sales-activity variances, $18,400 U

Total master budget variances, $24,370 U

U = Unfavorable. F = Favorable.

* Figures are from Exhibit 8-1.

† Figures are shown in more detail in Exhibit 8-6.

‡ Figures are from the 7,000-unit column in Exhibit 8-2.

actual results (column 1). The variances for operating income are summarized at the bottom of Exhibit 8-5. Note that the sum of the activity-level variances (here sales-activity variances because sales is the only activity used as a cost driver) and the flexible-budget variances equals the total of the master budget variances.

ISOLATING THE CAUSES OF VARIANCES

Managers use comparisons between actual results, master budgets, and flexible budgets to evaluate organizational performance. When evaluating performance, it is useful to distinguish between **effectiveness**—the degree to which a goal, objective, or target is met— and **efficiency**—the degree to which inputs are used in relation to a given level of outputs.

effectiveness The degree to which a goal, objective, or target is met.

Performance may be effective, efficient, both, or neither. For example, Dominion Company set a master budget objective of manufacturing and selling 9,000 units. Only 7,000 units were actually made and sold, however. Performance, as measured by sales-activity variances, was ineffective because the sales objective was not met.

efficiency The degree to which inputs are used in relation to a given level of outputs.

Was Dominion's performance efficient? Managers judge the degree of efficiency by comparing actual outputs achieved (7,000 units) with actual inputs (such as the costs of direct materials and direct labor). *The less input used to produce a given output, the more efficient the operation.* As indicated by the flexible-budget variances, Dominion was inefficient in its use of a number of inputs. Later in this chapter we consider in detail direct material, direct labor, and variable overhead flexible-budget variances. For now, though, we will look at the causes of both flexible-budget and activity-level variances.

FLEXIBLE-BUDGET VARIANCES

Objective 5
Compute flexible-budget variances and sales-activity variances.

Flexible-budget variances measure the efficiency of operations at the actual level of activity. The first three columns of Exhibit 8-5 compare the actual results with the flexible-budget amounts. The flexible-budget variances are the differences between columns 1 and 3, which total $5,970 unfavorable:

$$\text{total flexible-budget variance} = \text{total actual results} - \text{total flexible budget, planned results}$$
$$= (-\$11,570) - (-\$5,600)$$
$$= \$-5,970, \text{ or } \$5,970 \text{ unfavorable}$$

The total flexible-budget variance arises from sales prices received and the variable and fixed costs incurred. Dominion Company had no difference between actual sales price and the flexible-budgeted sales price, so we must focus on the differences between actual costs and flexible-budgeted costs at the actual 7,000-unit level of activity. Without the flexible budget in column 3, we cannot separate the effects of differences in cost behavior from the effects of changes in sales activity. The flexible-budget variances indicate whether operations were efficient or not, and may form the basis for periodic performance evaluation. Operations managers are in the best position to explain flexible-budget variances.

Companies that use variances primarily to fix blame often find that managers resort to cheating and subversion to beat the system. Managers of operations usually have more information about those operations than higher-level managers. If that information is used against them, lower-level managers can be expected to withhold or misstate valuable information for their own self-protection. For example, one manufacturing firm actually reduced the next period's departmental budget by the amount of the department's unfavorable variances in the current period. If a division had a $50,000 expense budget and experienced a $2,000 unfavorable variance, the following period's budget would be set at $48,000. This system led managers to cheat and to falsify reports to avoid unfavorable variances. We can criticize departmental managers' ethics, but the system was as much at fault as the managers.

Exhibit 8-6 gives an expanded, line-by-line computation of variances for all master budget items at Dominion. Note how most of the costs that had seemingly favorable variances when a master budget was used as a basis for comparison (see Exhibit 8-1) have, in reality, unfavorable variances. Do not conclude automatically that favorable flexible-budget variances are good and unfavorable flexible-budget variances are bad. Instead, interpret all variances as signals that actual operations have not occurred exactly as anticipated when the flexible-budget formulas were set. Any cost that differs significantly from the flexible budget deserves an explanation. The last column of Exhibit 8-6 gives possible explanations for Dominion Company's variances.

SALES-ACTIVITY VARIANCES

sales-activity variances
Variances that measure how effective managers have been in meeting the planned sales objective, calculated as actual unit sales less master budget unit sales times the budgeted unit contribution margin.

Sales-activity variances measure how effective managers have been in meeting the planned sales objective. In Dominion Company, sales activity fell 2,000 units short of the planned level. The final three columns of Exhibit 8-5 clearly show how the sales-activity variances (totaling $18,400 U) are unaffected by any changes in unit prices or variable costs. Why? Because the same budgeted unit prices and variable costs are used in constructing both the flexible and master budgets. Therefore, all unit prices and variable costs are held constant in columns 3 through 5.

The total of the sales-activity variances informs the manager that falling short of the sales target by 2,000 units caused operating income to be $18,400 lower than initially budgeted (a $5,600 loss instead of a $12,800 profit). In summary, the shortfall of sales by 2,000 units caused Dominion Company to incur a total sales activity variance of 2,000 units at a contribution margin of $9.20 per unit (from the first column of Exhibit 8-2):

Exhibit 8-6

Dominion Company

Cost-Control Performance Report for the Month Ended June 30, 19X8

	Actual Costs Incurred	Flexible Budget*	Flexible-Budget Variances[†]	Explanation
Units	7,000	7,000	—	
Variable costs				
Direct material	$69,920	$70,000	$ 80 F	Lower prices but higher usage
Direct labor	61,500	56,000	5,500 U	Higher wage rates and higher usage
Indirect labor	9,100	11,900	2,800 F	Decreased setup time
Idle time	3,550	2,800	750 U	Excessive machine breakdowns
Cleanup time	2,500	2,100	400 U	Cleanup of spilled solvent
Supplies	4,700	4,200	500 U	Higher prices and higher usage
Variable manufacturing costs	$151,270	$147,000	$4,270 U	
Shipping	5,000	4,200	800 U	Use of air freight to meet delivery
Administration	2,000	1,400	600 U	Excessive copying and long distance calls
Total variable costs	$158,270	$152,600	$5,670 U	
Fixed costs				
Factory supervision	$ 14,700	$ 14,400	$ 300 U	Salary increase
Factory rent	5,000	5,000	—	
Equipment depreciation	15,000	15,000	—	
Other fixed factory costs	2,600	2,600	—	
Fixed manufacturing costs	$ 37,300	$ 37,000	$ 300 U	
Fixed selling and administrative costs	33,000	33,000	—	
Total fixed costs	$ 70,300	$ 70,000	$ 300 U	
Total variable and fixed costs	$228,570	$222,600	$5,970 U	

* From 7,000-unit column of Exhibit 8-2.

[†] This is a line-by-line breakout of the variances in column 2 of Exhibit 8-5.

$$\text{total sales-activity variance} = \left(\begin{array}{c} \text{actual sales units} - \\ \text{master budgeted sales units} \end{array} \right) \times \left(\begin{array}{c} \text{budgeted contribution} \\ \text{margin per unit} \end{array} \right)$$

$$= (9,000 - 7,000) \times \$9.20$$
$$= \$18,400 \text{ Unfavorable}$$

Who has responsibility for the sales-activity variance? Marketing managers usually have the primary responsibility for reaching the sales level specified in the static budget. Of course variations in sales may be attributable to many factors.[1] Nevertheless, marketing managers are typically in the best position to explain why sales activities attained differed from plans.

EXPECTATIONS, STANDARD COSTS, AND STANDARD COST SYSTEMS

Expectations or standard costs are the building blocks of a planning and control system. An **expected cost** is the cost that is most likely to be attained. A **standard cost** is a carefully developed cost per unit that *should be* attained. It is often synonymous with the

expected cost The cost most likely to be attained.

standard cost A carefully determined cost per unit that should be attained.

---

[1] For example, sales-activity variances can be subdivided into sales quantity, sales mix, market size, and market share variances. This more advanced treatment of sales-activity variances is covered in Charles T. Horngren, George Foster, and Srikant M. Datar, Cost Accounting: A Managerial Emphasis (Upper Saddle River, NJ: Prentice Hall, 1997), pp. 583–587. These sales-activity variances might result from changes in the product, changes in customer demand, effective advertising, and so on.

standard cost systems
Accounting systems that value products according to standard costs only.

expected cost, but some companies intentionally set standards above or below expected costs to create desired incentives. Do not confuse having expectations or standards with having *a standard cost system*. **Standard cost systems** value products according to standard costs only. These inventory valuation systems simplify financial reporting, but in most companies they are expensive to install and to maintain. Therefore, standard costs may not be revised often enough to be useful for management decision making regarding specific products or services. (Ideally, only one cost system should be necessary in any organization, but in practice many organizations have developed multiple cost systems.) The expected costs used in flexible budgets also may be called standards because they are benchmarks or objectives to be attained. The fact that they are called standards does not imply that the organization also must have a standard cost system for inventory valuation or that it must use the standard cost system for planning and control.

CURRENT ATTAINABILITY: MOST WIDELY USED STANDARD

What standard of expected performance should be used in flexible budgets? Should it be so strict that it is rarely, if ever, attained? Should it be attainable 50% of the time? 90%? 20%? Individuals who have worked a lifetime setting and evaluating standards for performance disagree, so there are no universal answers to this question.

perfection standards (ideal standards) Expressions of the most efficient performance possible under the best conceivable conditions, using existing specifications and equipment.

Perfection standards (also called **ideal standards**) are expressions of the most efficient performance possible under the best conceivable conditions, using existing specifications and equipment. No provision is made for waste, spoilage, machine breakdowns, and the like. Those who favor using perfection standards maintain that the resulting unfavorable variances will constantly remind personnel of the continuous need for improvement in all phases of operations. Though concern for continuous improvement is wide-

*C*aterpillar Tracks Multiple Cost Systems Through Master Budget

Caterpillar, Inc., the worldwide manufacturer of heavy construction equipment, found that its standard cost system, while efficient for financial reporting, was too cumbersome to support its many decision-making needs. For example, a product designer, who recognizes that most of a product's costs are determined at the design stage, could not determine what expected costs of alternative designs would be for a new product. Current or expected costs would be more useful for decision making, but Caterpillar determined that developing a standard cost system that reflected current or expected costs would be infeasible. Caterpillar decided instead to use three cost systems, linked through the master budget, to meet all its accounting and decision-making needs.

Caterpillar retained the standard cost system for financial reporting, but developed two additional cost systems. To support planning and decision making,

Caterpillar has a separate product costing system based on activity-based costing (discussed in Chapter 4). This system is kept current to reflect changes in activities and cost drivers. Caterpillar also developed an operational control system for evaluating performance. This system compares actual performance to budgets and targets, computing new flexible budgets for changes in product mix, quantities, and other operations.

The new cost systems provide immediate cost feedback to product development, component design, sourcing decisions, quality and cost improvements, investment analysis, pricing, competitive cost analyses, and manufacturing design and process improvements. As a result, cost estimates are more reliable, and the time to make critical decisions has been shortened considerably—both critical components of effective decision making in a competitive environment.

Source: Adapted from Lou F. Jones, "Product Costing at Caterpillar," *Management Accounting*, February 1991, pp. 34–42.

spread, these standards are not widely used because they have an adverse effect on employee motivation. Employees tend to ignore unreasonable goals, especially if they would not share the gains from meeting imposed perfection standards. Organizations that apply the JIT philosophy (discussed in Chapter 4) attempt to achieve continuous improvement from "the bottom up," not by prescribing what should be achieved via perfection standards.

Currently attainable standards are levels of performance that can be achieved by realistic levels of effort. Allowances are made for normal defectives, spoilage, waste, and nonproductive time. There are at least two popular interpretations of the meaning of currently attainable standards. The first interpretation has standards set just tightly enough that employees regard their attainment as highly probable if normal effort and diligence are exercised. That is, variances should be random and negligible. Hence, the standards are predictions of what will likely occur, anticipating some inefficiencies. Managers accept the standards as being reasonable goals. The major reasons for "reasonable" standards, then, are:

currently attainable standards Levels of performance that can be achieved by realistic levels of effort.

1. The resulting standards serve multiple purposes. For example, the same cost can be used for financial budgeting, inventory valuation, and budgeting departmental performance. In contrast, perfection standards cannot be used for inventory valuation or financial budgeting, because the costs are known to be inaccurate.

2. Reasonable standards have a desirable motivational impact on employees, especially when combined with incentives for continuous improvement. The standard represents reasonable future performance, not fanciful goals. Therefore, unfavorable variances direct attention to performance that is not meeting reasonable expectations.

A second interpretation of currently attainable standards is that standards are set tightly. That is, employees regard their fulfillment as possible, though unlikely. Standards can be achieved only by very efficient operations. Variances tend to be unfavorable; nevertheless, employees accept the standards as being tough but not unreasonable goals. Is it possible to achieve continuous improvement using currently attainable standards? Yes, but expectations must reflect improved productivity and must be tied to incentive systems that reward continuous improvement.

TRADE-OFFS AMONG VARIANCES

Because the operations of organizations are linked, the level of performance in one area of operations will affect performance in other areas. Nearly any combination of effects is possible: Improvements in one area could lead to improvements in others and vice versa. Likewise, substandard performance in one area may be balanced by superior performance in others. For example, a service organization may generate favorable labor variances by hiring less-skilled and thus lower-paid customer representatives, but this favorable variance may lead to unfavorable customer satisfaction and future unfavorable sales-activity variances. In another situation, a manufacturer may experience unfavorable materials variances by purchasing higher-quality materials at a higher than planned price, but this variance may be more than offset by the favorable variances caused by lower inventory handling costs (for example, inspections) and higher-quality products (such as favorable scrap and rework variances).

Because of the many interdependencies among activities, an "unfavorable" or "favorable" label should not lead the manager to jump to conclusions. By themselves, such labels merely raise questions and provide clues to the causes of performance. They are attention directors, not problem solvers. Furthermore, the cause of variances might be faulty expectations rather than the execution of plans by managers. One of the first questions a manager should consider when explaining a large variance is whether expectations were valid.

WHEN TO INVESTIGATE VARIANCES

When should variances be investigated? Managers recognize that, even if everything operates as planned, variances are unlikely to be exactly zero. They predict a range of "normal" variances; this range may be based on economic criteria (that is, how big a variance must be before investigation could be worth the effort) or on statistical criteria. For some critical items, any deviation may prompt a follow-up. For most items, a minimum dollar or percentage deviation from budget may be necessary before investigations are expected to be worthwhile. For example, a 4% variance in a $1 million material cost may deserve more attention than a 20% variance in a $10,000 repair cost. Because knowing exactly when to investigate is difficult, many organizations have developed such rules of thumb as, "Investigate all variances exceeding $5,000 or 25% of expected cost, whichever is lower."

COMPARISONS WITH PRIOR PERIOD'S RESULTS

Some organizations compare the most recent budget period's actual results with last year's results for the same period rather than use flexible budget benchmarks. For example, an organization might compare June 19X8's actual results to June 19X7's actual results. In general these comparisons are not as useful for evaluating performance of an organization as comparisons of actual outcomes with planned results for the same period. Why? Because many changes probably have occurred in the environment and in the organization that make a comparison across years invalid. Very few organizations and environments are so stable that the only difference between now and a year ago is merely the passage of time. Even comparisons with last month's actual results may not be as useful as comparisons with flexible budgets. Comparisons over time may be useful for analyzing trends in such key variables as sales volume, market share, and product mix, but they do not help answer questions such as "Why did we have a loss of $11,570 in June, when we expected a profit of $12,800?"

SUMMARY PROBLEM FOR YOUR REVIEW

PROBLEM

Refer to the data contained in Exhibits 8-1 and 8-2. Suppose actual production and sales were 8,500 units instead of 7,000 units; actual variable costs were $188,800; and actual fixed costs were $71,200. The selling price remained at $31 per unit.

Required

1. Compute the master budget variance. What does this tell you about the efficiency of operations? The effectiveness of operations?
2. Compute the sales-activity variance. Is the performance of the marketing function the sole explanation for this variance? Why?
3. Using a flexible budget at the actual activity level, compute the budgeted contribution margin, budgeted operating income, and flexible-budget variance. What do you learn from this variance?

SOLUTION

1.
$$\text{actual operating income} = (8{,}500 \times \$31) - \$188{,}800 - \$71{,}200 = \$3{,}500$$
$$\text{master budget operating income} = \$12{,}800 \text{ (from Exhibit 8-1)}$$
$$\text{master budget variance} = \$12{,}800 - \$3{,}500 = \$9{,}300 \text{ U}$$

Three factors affect the master budget variance: sales activity, efficiency, and price changes. There is no way to tell from the master budget variance alone how much of the $9,300 U was caused by each of these factors.

2. sales-activity variance = budgeted unit contribution margin × difference between
the master budget unit sales and the actual unit sales
= $9.20 per unit CM × (9,000 − 8,500)
= $4,600 U

This variance is labeled as a sales-activity variance because it quantifies the impact on operating income of the deviation from an original sales target while holding price and efficiency factors constant. This is a measure of the effectiveness of the operations—Dominion was ineffective in meeting its sales objective. Of course, the failure to reach target sales may be traceable to several causes beyond the control of marketing personnel, including material shortages, factory breakdowns, and so on.

3. The budget formulas in Exhibit 8-2 are the basis for the following answers:

flexible-budget contribution margin = $9.20 × 8,500 = $78,200
flexible-budget operating income = $78,200 − $70,000 fixed costs = $8,200
actual operating income = $3,500 (from requirement 1)
flexible-budget variance = $8,200 − $3,500 = $4,700 U

The flexible-budget variance shows that the company spent $4,700 more to produce and sell the 8,500 units than it should have if operations had been efficient and unit costs had not changed. Note that this variance plus the $4,600 U sales-activity variance total to the $9,300 U master budget variance.

FLEXIBLE-BUDGET VARIANCES IN DETAIL

The rest of this chapter probes the flexible budget variance in detail. The emphasis is on subdividing labor, material, and overhead cost variances into usage and price or spending components. Note that in companies where direct-labor costs are small in relation to total costs (that is, in highly automated companies) direct-labor costs may be treated as an overhead-cost item, so separate labor standards, budgets, or variances need not be analyzed.

Objective 6
Compute and interpret price and usage variances for inputs based on cost-driver activity.

VARIANCES FROM MATERIAL AND LABOR STANDARDS

Consider Dominion Company's $10 standard cost of direct materials and $8 standard cost of direct labor. These standards per unit are derived from two components: a standard quantity of an input and a standard price for the input.

	Standards		
	Standard Inputs Expected per Unit of Output	*Standard Price Expected per Unit of Input*	*Standard Cost Expected per Unit of Output*
Direct material	5 pounds	$ 2/pound	$10
Direct labor	1/2 hour	16/hour	8

Once standards are set and actual results are observed, we can measure variances from the flexible budget. To show how the analysis of variances can be pursued more fully, we will reconsider Dominion's direct-material and direct-labor costs, as shown in Exhibit 8-6, and assume that the following actually occurred for the production of 7,000 units of output:

- *Direct material:* 36,800 pounds of material were purchased and used at an actual unit price of $1.90 for a total actual cost of $69,920.

- *Direct labor:* 3,750 hours of labor were used at an actual hourly price (rate) of $16.40, for a total cost of $61,500.

Note that the flexible-budget variances for direct labor and direct material can be attributed to (1) using more or less of the resource than planned for the actual level of output achieved and (2) paying more or less for the resource than planned. These additional data enable us to subdivide the flexible-budget variances (column 3) from Exhibit 8-6 into the separate usage and price components, which are shown as follows in columns 4 and 5.

	(1) Actual Costs	(2) Flexible Budget	(3) Flexible-Budget Variance	(4) Price Variance*	(5) Usage Variance*
Direct material	$69,920	$70,000	$ 80 F	$3,680 F	$3,600 U
Direct labor	61,500	56,000	5,500 U	1,500 U	4,000 U

* Computations to be explained shortly.

The flexible-budget totals for direct materials and direct labor are the amounts that would have been spent with expected efficiency. They are often labeled total *standard costs allowed,* computed as follows:

$$\begin{matrix} \text{flexible} \\ \text{budget or} \\ \text{total standard} \\ \text{cost allowed} \end{matrix} = \begin{matrix} \text{units of good} \\ \text{output} \\ \text{achieved} \end{matrix} \times \begin{matrix} \text{input allowed} \\ \text{per unit of} \\ \text{output} \end{matrix} \times \begin{matrix} \text{standard unit} \\ \text{price of input} \end{matrix}$$

$$\begin{matrix} \text{standard direct-materials} \\ \text{cost allowed} \end{matrix} = 7,000 \text{ units} \times 5 \text{ pounds} \times \$2.00 \text{ per pound} = \$70,000$$

$$\begin{matrix} \text{standard direct-labor cost} \\ \text{allowed} \end{matrix} = 7,000 \text{ units} \times \tfrac{1}{2} \text{ hour} \times \$16.00 \text{ per hour} = \$56,000$$

Before reading on, note particularly that the flexible-budget amounts (that is, the standard costs allowed) are tied to an initial question: What was the output achieved? Always ask yourself: What was the good output? Then proceed with your computations of the total standard cost allowed for the good output achieved.

PRICE AND USAGE VARIANCES

As noted earlier, we computed the flexible-budget amounts using the flexible-budget formulas, or currently attainable standards. Flexible-budget variances measure the relative efficiency of achieving the actual output. Price and usage variances subdivide each flexible-budget variance into the following:

price variance The difference between actual input prices and expected input prices multiplied by the actual quantity of inputs used.

1. **Price variance**—difference between actual input prices and standard input prices multiplied by the actual quantity of inputs used.
2. **Usage variance**—difference between the quantity of inputs actually used and the quantity of inputs that should have been used to achieve the actual quantity of output multiplied by the expected price of the input (also called a **quantity variance** or **efficiency variance**).

usage variance (quantity variance, efficiency variance) The difference between the quantity of inputs actually used and the quantity of inputs that should have been used to achieve the actual quantity of output multiplied by the expected price of the input.

When feasible, you should separate the variances that are subject to a manager's direct influence from those that are not. The usual approach is to separate price factors from usage factors. Price factors are less subject to immediate control than are usage factors, principally because of external forces, such as general economic conditions, that can influence prices. Even when price factors are regarded as being outside management control, isolating them helps to focus on the efficient usage of inputs. For example, the commodity prices of wheat, oats, corn, and rice are outside the control of General Mills. By separating price variances from usage variances, the breakfast cereal maker can focus on whether grain was used efficiently.

Price and usage variances are helpful because they provide feedback to those responsible for inputs. These variances should not be the only information used for decision making, control, or evaluation, however. Exclusive focus on material price variances by purchasing agents or buyers, for example, can work against an organization's JIT and total quality management goals. A buyer may be motivated to earn favorable material price variances by buying in large quantities and by buying low-quality material. The result could then be excessive inventory-handling and opportunity costs and increased manufacturing defects owing to faulty material. Similarly, exclusive focus on labor price and usage variances could motivate supervisors to use lower-skilled workers or to rush workers through critical tasks, both of which could impair quality of products and services.

PRICE AND USAGE VARIANCE COMPUTATIONS

We now consider the detailed calculation of price and usage variances. The objective of these variance calculations is to hold either price or usage constant so that the effect of the other can be isolated. When calculating the price variance, you hold use of inputs constant at the actual level of usage. When calculating the usage variance, you hold price constant at the standard price. For Dominion Company the price variances are:

$$\text{Direct-material price variance} = (\text{actual price} - \text{standard price}) \times \text{actual quantity}$$
$$= (\$1.90 - \$2.00) \text{ per pound} \times 36,800 \text{ pounds}$$
$$= \$3,680 \text{ favorable}$$

$$\text{Direct-labor price variance} = (\text{actual price} - \text{standard price}) \times \text{actual quantity}$$
$$= (\$16.40 - \$16.00) \text{ per hour} \times 3,750 \text{ hours}$$
$$= \$1,500 \text{ unfavorable}$$

The usage variances are:

$$\text{Direct-material usage variance} = (\text{actual quantity used} - \text{standard quantity allowed})$$
$$\times \text{standard price}$$
$$= [36,800 - (7,000 \times 5)] \text{ pounds} \times \$2.00 \text{ per pound}$$
$$= (36,800 - 35,000) \times \$2$$
$$= \$3,600 \text{ unfavorable}$$

$$\text{Direct-labor usage variance} = (\text{actual quantity used} - \text{standard quantity allowed})$$
$$\times \text{standard price}$$
$$= [3,750 - (7,000 \times 1/2)] \text{ hours} \times \$16 \text{ per hour}$$
$$= (3,750 - 3,500) \times \$16$$
$$= \$4,000 \text{ unfavorable}$$

To determine whether a variance is favorable or unfavorable, use logic rather than memorizing a formula. A price variance is favorable if the actual price is less than the standard. A usage variance is favorable if the actual quantity used is less than the standard quantity allowed. The opposite relationships imply unfavorable variances.

Note that the sum of the direct-labor price and usage variances equals the direct-labor flexible-budget variance. Furthermore, the sum of the direct-material price and usage variances equals the total direct-material flexible-budget variance.

$$\text{Direct-materials flexible-budget variance} = \$3,680 \text{ favorable} + \$3,600 \text{ unfavorable}$$
$$= \$80 \text{ favorable}$$

$$\text{Direct-labor flexible-budget variance} = \$1,500 \text{ unfavorable} + \$4,000 \text{ unfavorable}$$
$$= \$5,500 \text{ unfavorable}$$

Variances themselves do not show why the budgeted operating income was not achieved. They raise questions, provide clues, and direct attention, however. For instance, one possible explanation for this set of variances is that a manager might have made a trade-off—the manager might have purchased at a favorable price some materials that

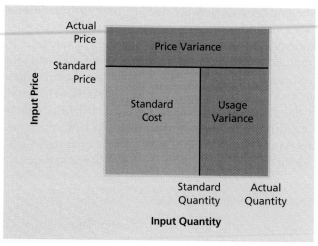

Exhibit 8-7

Graphical Representation of Price and Usage Variances for Labor

were substandard quality, saving $3,680 (the materials price variance). Excessive waste might have nearly offset this savings, as indicated by the $3,600 unfavorable material usage variance and net flexible-budget variance of $80 favorable. The material waste also might have caused at least part of the excess use of direct labor. Suppose more than $80 of the $4,000 unfavorable direct-labor usage variance was caused by reworking units with defective materials. Then the manager's trade-off was not successful. The cost inefficiencies caused by using substandard materials exceeded the savings from the favorable price.

Exhibit 8-7 shows the price and usage variance computations for labor graphically. The standard cost (or flexible budget) is the standard quantity multiplied by the standard price—the rectangle shaded light blue. The price variance is the difference between the unit prices, actual and standard, multiplied by actual quantity used—the rectangle shaded dark blue. The usage variance is the standard price multiplied by the difference between the actual quantity used and the standard quantity allowed for the good output achieved—the rectangle shaded light brown. (Note that for clarity the graph portrays only unfavorable variances.)

EFFECTS OF INVENTORIES

Analysis of Dominion Company was simplified because (1) there were no finished goods inventories—any units produced were sold in the same period—and (2) there was no direct-material inventory—the materials were purchased and used in the same period.

What if production does not equal sales? The sales-activity variance then is the difference between the static budget and the flexible budget for the number of units sold. In contrast, the flexible-budget cost variances compare actual costs with flexible-budgeted costs for the number of units *produced*.

Generally managers want quick feedback and want variances to be identified as early as is practical. In the case of the price of direct materials, that time is when the materials are purchased rather than when they are used, which may be much later. Therefore, the material price variance is usually based on the quantity purchased, measured at the time of purchase. The material usage variance remains based on the quantity used. Suppose Dominion Company purchased 40,000 pounds of material (rather than the 36,800 pounds used) at $1.90 per pound. The material price variance would be (actual price − standard price) × material *purchased* = ($1.90 − $2.00) per pound × 40,000 pounds = $4,000 favorable. The material usage variance would remain at $3,600 unfavorable because it is based on the material *used*.

We have just seen that direct-material and direct-labor variances are often subdivided into price and usage components. In contrast, many organizations believe that it is not worthwhile to monitor individual overhead items to the same extent. Therefore, overhead variances often are not subdivided beyond the flexible-budget variances—the complexity of the analysis may not be worth the effort.

Objective 7
Compute variable overhead spending and efficiency variables.

But in some cases, it may be worthwhile to subdivide the flexible-budget overhead variances, especially those for variable overhead. Part of the variable-overhead flexible-budget variance is related to control of the cost driver and part to the control of overhead spending itself. When actual cost-driver activity differs from the standard amount allowed for the actual output achieved, a **variable-overhead efficiency variance** will occur. Suppose that Dominion Company's cost of supplies, a variable-overhead cost, is driven by direct-labor hours. A variable-overhead cost rate of $.60 per unit at Dominion would be equivalent to $1.20 per direct-labor hour (because 1/2 hour is allowed per unit of output). Of the $500 unfavorable variance, $300 unfavorable is due to using 3,750 direct-labor hours rather than the 3,500 allowed by the flexible budget, as calculated below:

variable-overhead efficiency variance An overhead variance caused by actual cost-driver activity differing from the standard amount allowed for the actual output achieved.

$$\begin{matrix} \text{Variable-overhead} \\ \text{efficiency variance} \\ \text{for supplies} \end{matrix} = \left(\begin{matrix} \text{actual direct-} \\ \text{labor hours} \end{matrix} - \begin{matrix} \text{standard direct-labor} \\ \text{hours allowed} \end{matrix} \right) \times \begin{matrix} \text{standard} \\ \text{variable-overhead} \\ \text{rate per hour} \end{matrix}$$

$$= \left(\begin{matrix} \text{3,750 actual} \\ \text{hours} \end{matrix} - \begin{matrix} \text{3,500 standard} \\ \text{hours allowed} \end{matrix} \right) \times \ \$1.20 \text{ per hour}$$

$$= \ \$300 \text{ unfavorable}$$

This $300 excess usage of supplies is attributable to inefficient use of cost-driver activity, direct-labor hours. Whenever actual cost-driver activity exceeds that allowed for the actual output achieved, overhead efficiency variances will be unfavorable and vice versa. In essence this efficiency variance tells management the cost of *not* controlling the use of cost-driver activity. The remainder of the flexible-budget variance measures control of overhead spending itself, given actual cost-driver activity.

$$\begin{matrix} \text{variable-overhead spending} \\ \text{variance for supplies} \end{matrix} = \begin{matrix} \text{actual variable} \\ \text{overhead} \end{matrix} - \left(\begin{matrix} \text{standard variable-} \\ \text{overhead rate} \end{matrix} \times \begin{matrix} \text{actual direct-} \\ \text{labor hours used} \end{matrix} \right)$$

$$= \$4,700 - (\$1.20 \times 3,750 \text{ hours})$$

$$= \$4,700 - \$4,500$$

$$= \$200 \text{ unfavorable}$$

That is, the **variable-overhead spending variance** is the difference between the actual variable overhead and the amount of variable overhead budgeted for the actual level of cost-driver activity.

variable-overhead spending variance The difference between the actual variable overhead and the amount of variable overhead budgeted for the actual level of cost-driver activity.

As with other variances, the overhead variances by themselves cannot identify causes for results that differ from the static and flexible budgets. The only way for management to discover why overhead performance did not agree with the budget is to investigate possible causes. The distinction between spending and usage variances provides a springboard for more investigation, however.

GENERAL APPROACH

Exhibit 8-8 presents the analysis of direct material and direct labor in a format that deserves close study. The general approach is at the top of the exhibit. The specific applications then follow. Even though the exhibit may seem unnecessarily complex at first, its repeated use will solidify your understanding of variance analysis. Of course, the other

Exhibit 8-8

General Approach to Analysis of Direct-Labor and Direct-Material Variances

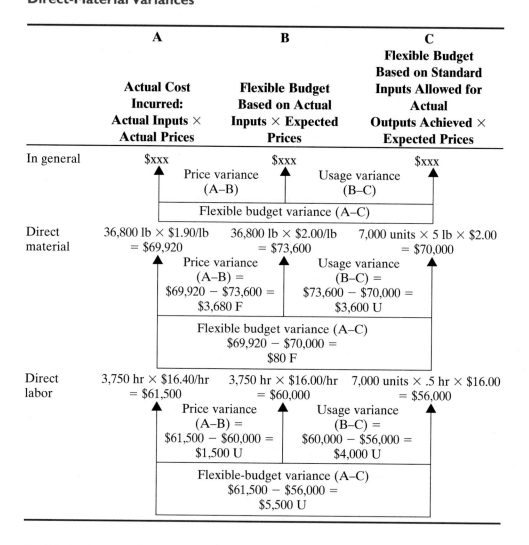

	A	**B**	**C**
	Actual Cost Incurred: Actual Inputs × Actual Prices	**Flexible Budget Based on Actual Inputs × Expected Prices**	**Flexible Budget Based on Standard Inputs Allowed for Actual Outputs Achieved × Expected Prices**
In general	$xxx	$xxx	$xxx
	Price variance (A–B)	Usage variance (B–C)	
	Flexible budget variance (A–C)		
Direct material	36,800 lb × $1.90/lb = $69,920	36,800 lb × $2.00/lb = $73,600	7,000 units × 5 lb × $2.00 = $70,000
	Price variance (A–B) = $69,920 − $73,600 = $3,680 F	Usage variance (B–C) = $73,600 − $70,000 = $3,600 U	
	Flexible budget variance (A–C) $69,920 − $70,000 = $80 F		
Direct labor	3,750 hr × $16.40/hr = $61,500	3,750 hr × $16.00/hr = $60,000	7,000 units × .5 hr × $16.00 = $56,000
	Price variance (A–B) = $61,500 − $60,000 = $1,500 U	Usage variance (B–C) = $60,000 − $56,000 = $4,000 U	
	Flexible-budget variance (A–C) $61,500 − $56,000 = $5,500 U		

flexible-budget variances in Exhibit 8-6 could be further analyzed in the same manner in which direct labor and direct material are analyzed in Exhibit 8-8. Such a detailed investigation depends on the manager's perception of whether the extra benefits will exceed the extra costs of the analysis.

Column A of Exhibit 8-8 contains the actual costs incurred for the inputs during the budget period being evaluated. Column B is the flexible-budgeted costs for the inputs *given the actual inputs used,* using expected prices but actual usage. Column C is the flexible-budget amount using both expected prices and expected usage for the outputs actually achieved. (This is the flexible-budget amount from Exhibit 8-6 for 7,000 units.) Column B is inserted between A and C by using *expected* prices and *actual* usage. The difference between columns A and B is attributed to changing prices because usage is held constant between A and B at actual levels. The difference between columns B and C is attributed to changing usage because price is held constant between B and C at expected levels.

Actual output achieved in column C is measured in units of product. However, most organizations manufacture a variety of products. When the variety of units are added together, the sum is frequently a nonsensical number (it is like adding apples and oranges). Therefore, all units of output are often expressed in terms of the standard inputs allowed for their production, such as pounds of fruit. Labor hours may also become the

Exhibit 8-9

General Approach to Analysis of Overhead Variances

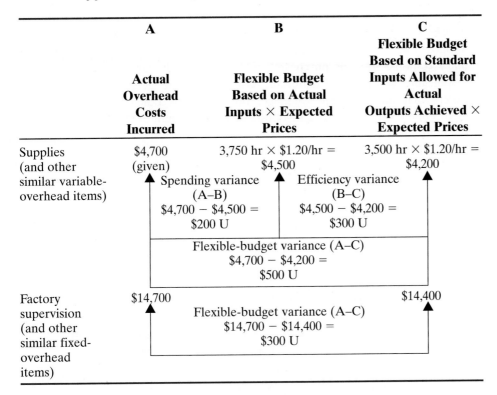

	A	B	C
	Actual Overhead Costs Incurred	**Flexible Budget Based on Actual Inputs × Expected Prices**	**Flexible Budget Based on Standard Inputs Allowed for Actual Outputs Achieved × Expected Prices**
Supplies (and other similar variable-overhead items)	$4,700 (given)	3,750 hr × $1.20/hr = $4,500	3,500 hr × $1.20/hr = $4,200

Spending variance (A–B)
$4,700 − $4,500 = $200 U

Efficiency variance (B–C)
$4,500 − $4,200 = $300 U

Flexible-budget variance (A–C)
$4,700 − $4,200 = $500 U

Factory supervision (and other similar fixed-overhead items) — $14,700 ... $14,400

Flexible-budget variance (A–C)
$14,700 − $14,400 = $300 U

common denominator for measuring total output volume. Thus production, instead of being expressed as 12,000 chairs and 3,000 sofas, could be expressed as 20,000 standard hours allowed (or more accurately as standard hours of input allowed for outputs achieved). Remember that standard hours allowed is a measure of actual output achieved. A key idea illustrated in Exhibit 8-8 is the versatility of the flexible budget. A flexible budget is geared to activity volume, and Exhibit 8-8 shows that activity volume can be measured in terms of either actual inputs used (columns A and B) or standard inputs allowed for actual outputs achieved (column C).

Exhibit 8-9 summarizes the general approach to overhead variances. The flexible-budget variances for fixed-overhead items are not subdivided here. Fixed-overhead flexible-budget variances are discussed in more detail in Chapter 15. Note that the sales activity variance for fixed overhead is zero, because as long as activities remain within relevant ranges, the fixed-overhead budget is the same at both planned and actual levels of activity.

SUMMARY PROBLEM FOR YOUR REVIEW

PROBLEM

The following questions are based on the data contained in the Dominion Company illustration used in this chapter.

- Direct materials: standard, 5 pounds per unit @ $2 per pound
- Direct labor: standard, 1/2 hour @ $16 per hour

Suppose the following were the actual results for production of 8,500 units:

- Direct material: 46,000 pounds purchased and used at an actual unit price of $1.85 per pound, for an actual total cost of $85,100

- Direct labor: 4,125 hours of labor used at an actual hourly rate of $16.80, for a total actual cost of $69,300

Required

1. Compute the flexible-budget variance and the price and usage variances for direct labor and direct material.

2. Suppose the company is organized so that the purchasing manager bears the primary responsibility for purchasing materials, and the production manager is responsible for the use of materials. Assume the same facts as in requirement 1 except that the purchasing manager bought 60,000 pounds of material. This means that there is an ending inventory of 14,000 pounds of material. Recompute the materials variances.

SOLUTION

1. The variances are:

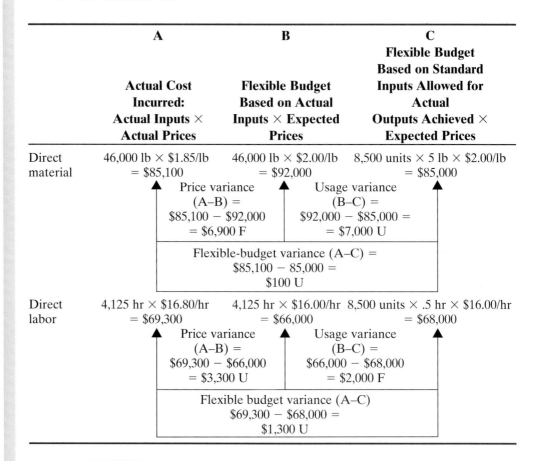

2. Price variances are isolated at the most logical control point—time of purchase rather than time of use. In turn, the operating departments that later use the materials are generally charged at some predetermined budget, expected or standard price rather than at actual prices. This represents a slight modification of the approach in requirement 1 as shown at the top of the next page.

Note that this favorable price variance on balance may not be a good outcome—Dominion Company may not desire the extra inventory in excess of its immediate needs, and the favorable price variance may reflect that quality of the material is lower than planned. Note also that the usage variance is the same in requirements 1 and 2.

Typically, the price and usage variances for materials now would be reported separately and not added together because they are based on different measures of volume. The price variance is based on inputs *purchased,* but the usage variance is based on inputs *used.*

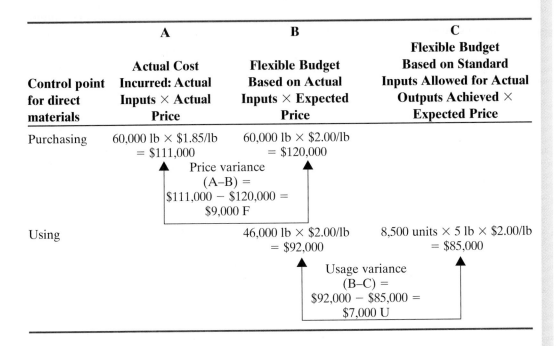

Control point for direct materials	A Actual Cost Incurred: Actual Inputs × Actual Price	B Flexible Budget Based on Actual Inputs × Expected Price	C Flexible Budget Based on Standard Inputs Allowed for Actual Outputs Achieved × Expected Price
Purchasing	60,000 lb × $1.85/lb = $111,000	60,000 lb × $2.00/lb = $120,000	
		Price variance (A–B) = $111,000 − $120,000 = $9,000 F	
Using		46,000 lb × $2.00/lb = $92,000	8,500 units × 5 lb × $2.00/lb = $85,000
		Usage variance (B–C) = $92,000 − $85,000 = $7,000 U	

Highlights to Remember

Distinguish between flexible budgets and master (static) budgets. Flexible budgets are geared to changing levels of cost-driver activity rather than to the single static level of the master (static) budget. Flexible budgets may be tailored to particular levels of sales or cost-driver activity—before or after the fact. They tell how much revenue and cost to expect for any level of activity.

Use flexible-budget formulas to construct a flexible budget based on the volume of sales. Cost functions, or flexible-budget formulas, reflect fixed- and variable-cost behavior and allow managers to compute budgets for any desired output or cost-driver activity level. The flexible-budget amounts are computed by multiplying the variable cost per cost-driver unit times the level of activity, as measured in cost-driver units.

Prepare an activity-based flexible budget. When a significant portion of operating costs vary with cost drivers other than units of production, a company benefits from using activity-based flexible budgets. These budgets are based on budgeted costs for each activity and related cost driver.

Understand the performance evaluation relationship between master (static) budgets and flexible budgets. The differences or variances between the master budget and the flexible budget are due to activity levels, not cost control. These variances are called activity-level variances.

Compute flexible-budget variances and sales-activity variances. The flexible-budget variance is the difference between the total actual results and the total flexible budget amounts. Sales-activity variances are calculated as actual unit sales less master budget unit sales times the budgeted unit contribution margin.

Compute and interpret price and usage variances for inputs based on cost-driver activity. Flexible-budget variances for variable inputs can be further broken down into price (or spending) and usage (or efficiency) variances. Price variances reflect the effects of changing input prices, holding usage of inputs (measured in cost-driver units) constant at actual input use. Usage variances reflect the effects of different levels of input usage (measured in cost-driver units), holding prices constant at expected prices.

Compute variable overhead spending and efficiency variances. The variable-overhead spending variance is the difference between the actual variable overhead and the amount of variable overhead budgeted for the actual level of cost-driver activity. The variable-overhead efficiency variance is the difference between the actual cost-driver activity and the amount allowed for the actual output achieved, costed at the standard variable-overhead rate.

Understand how management uses flexible budgets to evaluate the company's financial performance. The evaluation of performance is aided by feedback that compares actual results with budgeted expectations. The flexible-budget helps managers explain why the master budget was not achieved. Master budget variances are divided into (sales) activity and flexible-budget variances. Activity variances reflect the organization's effectiveness in meeting financial plans. Flexible-budget variances reflect the organization's efficiency at actual levels of activity.

Accounting Vocabulary

activity-based flexible budget, p. 291
activity-level variances, p. 291
currently attainable standards, p. 297
effectiveness, p. 293
efficiency, p. 293
efficiency variance, p. 300
expected cost, p. 295
favorable expense variance, p. 289

flexible budget, p. 289
flexible-budget variances, p. 291
ideal standards, p. 296
master (static) budget variances, p. 288
perfection standards, p. 296
price variance, p. 300
quantity variance, p. 300
sales-activity variances, p. 294
standard cost, p. 295

standard cost systems, p. 296
static budget variance, p. 288
unfavorable expense variance, p. 288
usage variance, p. 300
variable budget, p. 289
variable-overhead spending variance, p. 303
variable-overhead efficiency variance, p. 303

Fundamental Assignment Material

8-A1 Flexible and Static Budgets

Coast-to-Coast Shipping Company's general manager reports quarterly to the company president on the firm's operating performance. The company uses a budget based on detailed expectations for the forthcoming quarter. The general manager has just received the condensed quarterly performance report shown in exhibit 8-10.

Although the general manager was upset about not obtaining enough revenue, she was happy that her cost performance was favorable; otherwise her net operating income would be even worse.

The president was totally unhappy and remarked: "I can see some merit in comparing actual performance with budgeted performance because we can see whether actual revenue coincided with our best guess for budget purposes. But I can't see how this performance report helps me evaluate cost control performance."

Required

1. Prepare a columnar flexible budget for Coast-to-Coast Shipping at revenue levels of $7,000,000, $8,000,000 and $9,000,000. Use the format of the last three

Exhibit 8-10

Coast-to-Coast Shipping Operating Performance Report
Second Quarter, 19X8

	Budget	Actual	Variance
Net revenue	$8,000,000	$7,600,000	$400,000 U
Fuel	$ 160,000	$ 157,000	$ 3,000 F
Repairs and maintenance	80,000	78,000	2,000 F
Supplies and miscellaneous	800,000	788,000	12,000 F
Variable payroll	5,360,000	5,200,000	160,000 F
Total variable costs*	$6,400,000	$6,223,000	$177,000 F
Supervision	$ 160,000	$ 164,000	4,000 U
Rent	160,000	160,000	—
Depreciation	480,000	480,000	—
Other fixed costs	160,000	158,000	2,000 F
Total fixed costs	$ 960,000	$ 962,000	$ 2,000 U
Total costs charged against revenue	$7,360,000	$7,185,000	$175,000 F
Operating income	$ 640,000	$ 415,000	$225,000 U

U = Unfavorable. F = Favorable.

* For purposes of this analysis, assume that all these costs are totally variable with respect to sales revenue. In practice, many are mixed and have to be subdivided into variable and fixed components before a meaningful analysis can be made. Also assume that the prices and mix of services sold remain unchanged.

columns of Exhibit 8-2, page 290. Assume that the prices and mix of products sold are equal to the budgeted prices and mix.

2. Express the flexible budget for costs in formula form.

3. Prepare a condensed table showing the master (static) budget variance, the sales activity variance, and the flexible-budget variance. Use the format of Exhibit 8-5, page 293.

8-A2 Activity Level Variances

The systems consulting department of Vermont Textiles designs data collecting, encoding, and reporting systems to fit the needs of other departments within the company. An overall cost driver is the number of requests made to the systems consulting department. The expected variable cost of handling a request was $600, and the number of requests expected for June 19X8 was 75. Monthly fixed costs for the department (salaries, equipment depreciation, space costs) were budgeted at $70,000.

The actual number of requests serviced by systems consulting in June 19X8 was 90, and the total costs incurred by the department was $123,000. Of that amount, $78,000 was for fixed costs.

Required

Compute the master (static) budget variances and the flexible-budget variances for variable and fixed costs for the systems consulting department for June 19X8.

8-A3 Direct-Material and Direct-Labor Variances

Artistic Metalworks, Inc. manufactures sculpted metal railings, lamp posts, and other ornaments. The following standards were developed for a line of lamp posts:

	Standard Inputs Expected for Each Unit of Output Achieved	Standard Price per Unit of Input
Direct materials	10 pounds	$ 5 per pound
Direct labor	5 hours	$25 per hour

During April, 550 lamp posts were scheduled for production. However, only 525 were actually produced.

Direct materials purchased and used amounted to 5,500 pounds at a unit price of $4.25 per pound. Direct labor actually paid was $26.00 per hour, and 2,850 hours were used.

Required

1. Compute the standard cost per lamp post for direct materials and direct labor.

2. Compute the price variances and usage variances for direct materials and direct labor.

3. Based on these sketchy data, what clues for investigation are provided by the variances?

8-B1 Summary Performance Reports

Consider the following data for Express Tax Preparation Services, Inc.:

1. Master budget data: sales, 2,500 clients at $350 each; variable costs, $250 per client; fixed costs, $150,000.

2. Actual results at actual prices: sales, 3,000 clients at $360 per client; variable costs, $800,000; fixed costs, $157,500.

Required

1. Prepare a summary performance report similar to Exhibit 8-4, page 292.

2. Fill in the blanks:

Master budget operating income	$ —
Variances	
Sales-activity variances	$ —
Flexible-budget variances	—
Actual operating income	$ —

8-B2 Material and Labor Variances

Consider the following data:

	Direct Material	Direct Labor
Actual price per unit of input (lb and hr)	$16	$12
Standard price per unit of input	$14	$13
Standard inputs allowed per unit of output	5	2
Actual units of input	56,000	30,000
Actual units of output (product)	14,400	14,400

Required

1. Compute the price, usage, and flexible-budget variances for direct material and direct labor. Use U or F to indicate whether the variances are unfavorable or favorable.

2. Prepare a plausible explanation for the performance.

8-B3 Variable-Overhead Variances

You have been asked to prepare an analysis of the overhead costs in the order processing department of a mail-order clothing company. As an initial step, you prepare a summary of some events that bear on overhead for the most recent period. The variable-overhead flexible-budget variance was $6,000 unfavorable. The standard variable-overhead price per order was $.06. Ten orders per hour is regarded as standard productivity per clerk. The total overhead incurred was $202,200, of which $133,500 was fixed. There were no variances for fixed overhead. The variable-overhead spending variance was $1,500 favorable.

Find the following:

Required

1. Variable-overhead efficiency variance
2. Actual hours of input
3. Standard hours allowed for output achieved

Additional Assignment Material

QUESTIONS

8-1. Distinguish between favorable and unfavorable variances.

8-2. "The flex in the flexible budget relates solely to variable costs." Do you agree? Explain.

8-3. "We want a flexible budget because costs are difficult to predict. We need the flexibility to change budgeted costs as input prices change." Does a flexible budget serve this purpose? Explain.

8-4. Explain the role of understanding cost behavior and cost-driver activities for flexible budgeting.

8-5. "An activity-based flexible budget has a "flex" for every activity." Do you agree? Explain.

8-6. "Effectiveness and efficiency go hand in hand. You can't have one without the other." Do you agree? Explain.

8-7. Differentiate between a master-budget variance and a flexible-budget variance.

8-8. "Managers should be rewarded for favorable variances and punished for unfavorable variances." Do you agree? Explain.

8-9. "A good control system places the blame for every unfavorable variance on someone in the organization. Without affixing blame, no one will take responsibility for cost control." Do you agree? Explain.

8-10. Who is usually responsible for sales-activity variances? Why?

8-11. Differentiate between perfection standards and currently attainable standards.

8-12. What are two possible interpretations of "currently attainable standards"?

8-13. "A standard is one point in a band or range of acceptable outcomes." Evaluate this statement.

8-14. "Price variances should be computed even if prices are regarded as being outside of company control." Do you agree? Explain.

8-15. What are some common causes of usage variances?

8-16. "Failure to meet price standards is the responsibility of the purchasing officer." Do you agree? Explain.

8-17. Are direct-material price variances generally recognized when the materials are purchased or when they are used? Why?

8-18. Why do the techniques for controlling overhead differ from those for controlling direct materials?

8-19. How does the variable-overhead spending variance differ from the direct-labor price variance?

EXERCISES

8-20 Flexible Budget

Ralston Sports Equipment Company made 20,000 basketballs in a given year. Its manufacturing costs were $170,000 variable and $70,000 fixed. Assume that no price changes will occur in the following year and that no changes in production methods are applicable. Compute the budgeted cost for producing 25,000 basketballs in the following year.

8-21 Basic Flexible Budget

The superintendent of police of the city of Nashville is attempting to predict the costs of operating a fleet of police cars. Among the items of concern are fuel, $.15 per mile, and depreciation, $6,000 per car per year.

The manager is preparing a flexible budget for the coming year. Prepare the flexible-budget amounts for fuel and depreciation for each car at a level of 30,000, 40,000, and 50,000 miles.

Required

8-22 Flexible Budget

Wisconsin Woolens has a department that makes wool scarves. Consider the following data for a recent month:

	Budget Formula per Unit	Various Levels of Output		
Units	—	6,000	7,000	8,000
Sales	$18	$?	$?	$?
Variable costs				
Direct material	?	48,000	?	?
Fuel	2	?	?	?
Fixed costs				
Depreciation		?	15,000	?
Salaries		?	?	40,000

Required Fill in the unknowns.

8-23 Basic Flexible Budget

The budgeted prices for materials and direct labor per unit of finished product are $12 and $5, respectively. The production manager is delighted about the following data:

	Master (Static) Budget	Actual Costs	Variance
Direct materials	$96,000	$90,000	$6,000 F
Direct labor	40,000	37,600	2,400 F

Required Is the manager's happiness justified? Prepare a report that might provide a more detailed explanation of why the static (master) budget was not achieved. Good output was 6,800 units.

8-24 Activity-Level Variances

Materials support costs for the Industrial Equipment Manufacturing Company (IEMC) are variable costs that depend on the weight of material (plate steel, castings, etc.) moved. For the current budget period and based on scheduled production, IEMC expected to move 750,000 pounds of material at a cost of $.25 per pound. Several orders were canceled by customers, and IEMC moved only 650,000 pounds of material. Total materials support costs for the period were $175,000.

Required Compare actual support costs to the master-budget support costs by computing master budget, activity-level, and flexible-budget variances for materials support costs.

8-25 Direct-Material Variances

Tailored Shirt Company uses a special fabric in the production of dress shirts. During August, Tailored Shirt purchased 10,000 square yards of the fabric @ $6.90 per yard and used 7,900 square yards in the production of 3,800 jackets. The standard allows 2 yards @ $7.10 per yard for each jacket.

Required Calculate the material price variance and the material usage variance.

8-26 Labor Variances

The city of Tampa has a sign shop where street signs of all kinds are manufactured and repaired. The manager of the shop uses standards to judge performance. Because a clerk mistakenly discarded some labor records, however, the manager has only partial data for April. She knows that the total direct-labor variance was $1,855 favorable, and that the standard labor price was $14 per hour. Moreover, a recent pay raise produced an unfavorable labor price variance for April of $945. The actual hours of input were 1,750.

Required

1. Find the actual labor price per hour.
2. Determine the standard hours allowed for the output achieved.

8-27 Usage Variances

Pacific Toy Company produced 9,000 stuffed bears. The standard direct-material allowance is two pounds per bear, at a cost per pound of $3. Actually, 17,000 pounds of materials (input) were used to produce the 9,000 bears (output).

Similarly, it is supposed to take 5 direct-labor hours to produce one bear, and the standard hourly labor cost is $3. But 46,500 hours (input) were used to produce the 9,000 bears in this Hong Kong factory.

Compute the usage variances for direct material and direct labor.

Required

8-28 Labor and Material Variances

Standard direct-labor rate	$ 13.50	Standard unit price of materials	$ 4.50
Actual direct-labor rate	$ 12.20	Actual quantity purchased	1,800
Standard direct-labor-hours	12,000	Standard quantity allowed	
Direct-labor usage		for actual production	1,650
variance—unfavorable	$13,500	Materials purchase price	
		variance—favorable	$ 288

Required

1. Compute the actual hours worked, rounded to the nearest hour.
2. Compute the actual purchase price per unit of materials, rounded to the nearest penny.

8-29 Material and Labor Variances

Consider the following data:

	Direct Material	Direct Labor
Costs incurred: actual inputs × actual prices incurred	$153,000	$79,000
Actual inputs × expected prices	165,000	74,000
Standard inputs allowed for actual outputs achieved × expected prices	172,500	71,300

Compute the price, usage, and flexible-budget variances for direct material and direct labor. Use *U* or *F* to indicate whether the variances are unfavorable or favorable.

Required

PROBLEMS

8-30 National Park Service

The National Park Service prepared the following budget for one of its national parks for 19X8:

Revenue from fees	$5,000,000
Variable costs (miscellaneous)	500,000
Contribution margin	$4,500,000
Fixed costs (miscellaneous)	4,500,000
Operating income	$ 0

The fees were based on an average of 25,000 vehicle-admission days (vehicles multiplied by number of days in parks) per week for the 20-week season, multiplied by average entry and other fees of $10 per vehicle-admission day.

The season was booming for the first four weeks. There were major forest fires during the fifth week, however. A large percentage of the park was scarred by the fires. As a result, the number of visitors to the park dropped sharply during the remainder of the season.

Total revenue fell $1 million short of the original budget. Variable costs fell as expected, and fixed costs were unaffected except for hiring extra firefighters at a cost of $360,000.

Required

Prepare a columnar summary of performance, showing the original (static) budget, sales-activity variances, flexible budget, flexible-budget variances, and actual results.

8-31 Flexible and Static Budgets

Beta Alpha Psi, the accounting fraternity, recently held a dinner dance. The original (static) budget and actual results were as follows:

	Budget	Actual	Variance
Attendees	75	90	
Revenue	$2,625	$3,255	$630 F
Chicken dinners @ $17.60	1,320	1,668	348 U
Beverages, $6 per person	450	466	16 U
Club rental, $75 plus 8% tax	81	81	0
Music, 3 hours @ $240 per hour	720	840	120 U
Profit	$54	$ 200	$ 146 F

Required

1. Subdivide each variance into a sales activity variance portion and a flexible-budget variance portion. Use the format of Exhibit 8-5, page 293.
2. Provide possible explanations for the variances.

8-32 Summary Explanation

Wilcox Company produced 80,000 units, 8,000 more than budgeted. Production data are as follows. Except for physical units, all quantities are in dollars:

	Actual Results at Actual Prices	Flexible-Budget Variances	Flexible Budget	Sales-Activity Variances	Static (Master) Budget
Physical units	80,000	—	?	?	72,000
Sales	?	6,400 F	?	?	720,000
Variable costs	492,000	?	480,000	?	?
Contribution margin	?	?	?	?	?
Fixed costs	?	8,000 U	?	?	195,000
Operating income	?	?	?	?	?

1. Fill in the unknowns.

2. Give a brief summary explanation of why the original target operating income was not attained.

8-33 Explanation of Variance in Income

Diaz Credit Services produces reports for consumers about their credit ratings. The company's standard contribution margins average 70% of dollar sales, and average selling prices are $50 per report. Average productivity is four reports per hour. Some preparers work for sales commissions and others for an hourly rate. The master budget for 19X8 had predicted processing 800,000 reports, but only 700,000 reports were processed.

Fixed costs of rent, supervision, advertising, and other items were budgeted at $21.5 million, but the budget was exceeded by $700,000 because of extra advertising in an attempt to boost revenue.

There were no variances from the average selling prices, but the actual commissions paid to preparers and the actual productivity per hour resulted in flexible-budget variances (i.e., total price and efficiency variances) for variable costs of $900,000 unfavorable.

The president of Diaz was unhappy because the budgeted operating income of $6.5 million was not achieved. He said, "Sure, we had unfavorable variable-cost variances, but our operating income was down far more than that. Please explain why."

Explain why the budgeted operating income was not attained. Use a presentation similar to Exhibit 8-5, page 293. Enough data have been given to permit you to construct the complete exhibit by filling in the known items and then computing the unknown. Complete your explanation by summarizing what happened, using no more than three sentences.

BUSINESS FIRST   www.prenhall.com/phlip

PHLIP

8-34 Activity and Flexible-Budget Variances at McDonald's

Suppose a McDonald's franchise in Bangkok had budgeted sales for 1996 of B7.3 million (where B stands for baht, the Thai unit of currency). Cost of goods sold and other variable costs were expected to be 70% of sales. Budgeted annual fixed costs were B1.8 million. A booming Thai economy caused actual 1996 sales to soar to B9.3 million and actual profits to increase to B600,000. Fixed costs in 1996 were as budgeted. The franchise was pleased with the increase in profit.

1. Compute the sales activity variance and the flexible budget variance for 1996. What can the franchisee learn from these variances?

2. In 1997 the Thai economy plummeted, and the franchise's sales fell back to the B7.3 million level. Given what happened in 1996, what do you expect to happen to profits in 1997? ■

8-35 Summary of Airline Performance

Consider the performance (in thousands of dollars) of Economy Airlines for a given year in the following table.

	Actual Results at Actual Prices	Master Budget	Variance
Revenue	$?	$300,000	$?
Variable expenses	200,000	195,000*	5,000U
Contribution margin	?	105,000	?
Fixed expenses	77,000	75,000	2,000U
Operating income	$?	30,000	$?

* Includes jet fuel of $90,000.

The master budget had been based on a budget of $.20 per revenue passenger mile. A revenue passenger mile is one paying passenger flown one mile. An average airfare decrease of 8% had helped generate an increase in passenger miles flown that was 10% in excess of the static budget for the year.

The price per gallon of jet fuel rose above the price used to formulate the static budget. The average jet fuel price increase for the year was 12%.

Required

1. As an explanation for the president, prepare a summary performance report that is similar to Exhibit 8-5, page 293.

2. Assume that jet fuel costs are purely variable and the use of fuel was at the same level of efficiency as predicted in the static budget. What part of the flexible-budget variance for variable expenses is attributable to jet fuel expenses? Explain.

8-36 University Flexible Budgeting

The University of Liverpool offers an extensive continuing education program in many cities throughout Britain. For the convenience of its faculty and administrative staff and also to save costs, the university operates a motor pool. The motor pool operated with 25 vehicles until February of this year, when an additional automobile was acquired. The motor pool furnishes gasoline, oil, and other supplies for the cars and hires one mechanic who does routine maintenance and minor repairs. Major repairs are done at a nearby commercial garage. A supervisor manages the operations.

Each year the supervisor prepares an operating budget, informing university management of the funds needed to operate the pool. Depreciation on the automobiles is recorded in the budget in order to determine the cost per kilometre.

The schedule below presents the annual budget approved by the university. The actual costs for March are compared with one-twelfth of the annual budget.

University Motor Pool
Budget Report for March 19X6

	Annual Budget	One-Month Budget	March Actual	Over (Under)
Gasoline	£ 75,000	£ 6,250	£ 7,500	£1,250
Oil, minor repairs, parts, and supplies	15,000	1,250	1,300	50
Outside repairs	2,700	225	50	(175)
Insurance	4,800	400	416	16
Salaries and benefits	21,600	1,800	1,800	—
Depreciation	22,800	1,900	1,976	76
	£ 141,900	£ 11,825	£ 13,042	£1,217
Total kilometres	1,500,000	125,000	140,000	
Cost per kilometre	£ .0946	£ .0946	£ .0932	
Number of automobiles	25	25	26	

The annual budget was constructed based on the following assumptions:

1. 25 automobiles in the pool
2. 60,000 kilometres per year per automobile
3. 8 kilometres per liter for each automobile

4. £0.4 per liter of gas

5. £.01 per kilometre for oil, minor repairs, parts, and supplies

6. £108 per automobile in outside repairs

The supervisor is unhappy with the monthly report comparing budget and actual costs for March; he claims it presents his performance unfairly. His previous employer used flexible budgeting to compare actual costs with budgeted amounts.

Required

1. Employing flexible-budgeting techniques, prepare a report that shows budgeted amounts, actual costs, and monthly variation for March.

2. Explain briefly the basis of your budget figure for outside repairs.

8-37 Activity-Based Flexible Budget

Cost behavior analysis for the four activity centers in the Billing Department of Portland Power Company is given below.

Activity Center	Traceable Costs Variable	Traceable Costs Fixed	Cost-Driver Activity
Account inquiry	$ 79,910	$155,270	3,300 labor hours
Correspondence	$ 9,800	$ 25,584	2,800 letters
Account billing	$154,377	$ 81,400	2,440,000 lines
Bill verification	$ 10,797	$ 78,050	20,000 accounts

The Billing Department constructs a flexible budget for each activity center based on the following ranges of cost-driver activity:

Activity Center	Cost Driver	Relevant Range	
Account inquiry	Labor hours	3,000	5,000
Correspondence	Letters	2,500	3,500
Account billing	Lines	2,000,000	3,000,000
Bill verification	Accounts	15,000	25,000

Required

1. Develop flexible-budget formulas for each of the four activity centers.

2. Compute the budgeted total cost in each activity center for each of these levels of cost driver activity: (a) the smallest activity in the relevant range, (b) the midpoint of the relevant range, and (c) the highest activity in the relevant range.

3. Determine the total cost function for the Billing Department.

4. The following table gives the actual results for the Billing Department. Prepare a cost-control performance report comparing the flexible budget to actual results for each activity center. Compute flexible budget variances.

Activity Center	Cost-Driver Level (Actual)	Actual Cost
Account inquiry	4,400 labor hours	$229,890
Correspondence	3,250 letters	$ 38,020
Account billing	2,900,000 lines	$285,000
Bill verification	22,500 accounts	$105,320

8-38 Straightforward Variance Analysis

Beringer Metals, Inc. uses a standard cost system. The month's data regarding its iron castings follow:

- Material purchased and used, 3,400 pounds
- Direct-labor costs incurred, 5,500 hours, $20,900
- Variable-overhead costs incurred, $4,780
- Finished units produced, 1,000
- Actual material cost, $.95 per pound
- Variable-overhead rate, $.80 per hour
- Standard direct-labor cost, $4 per hour
- Standard material cost, $1 per pound
- Standard pounds of material in a finished unit, 3
- Standard direct-labor hours per finished unit, 5

Required Prepare schedules of all variances, using the formats of Exhibits 8-8 and 8-9 on pages 304 and 305.

8-39 Variance Analysis

The Geneva Chocolate Company uses standard costs and a flexible budget to control its manufacture of fine chocolates. The purchasing agent is responsible for material price variances, and the production manager is responsible for all other variances. Operating data for the past week are summarized as follows:

1. Finished units produced: 4,000 boxes of chocolates.
2. Direct material: Purchases, 6,400 pounds of chocolate @ 15.5 Swiss francs (SF) per pound; standard price is 16 SF per pound. Used, 4,300 pounds. Standard allowed per box produced, 1 pound.
3. Direct labor: Actual costs, 6,400 hours @ 30.5 SF, or 195,200 SF. Standard allowed per box produced, 1½ hours. Standard price per direct-labor-hour, 30 SF.
4. Variable manufacturing overhead: Actual costs, 69,500 SF. Budget formula is 10 SF per standard direct-labor-hour.

Required Compute the following:

1. a. Material purchase-price variance
   b. Material usage variance
   c. Direct-labor price variance
   d. Direct-labor usage variance
   e. Variable manufacturing-overhead spending variance
   f. Variable manufacturing-overhead efficiency variance

(*Hint:* For format, see the solution to the Summary Problem for Your Review, pages 306–308.)

2. a. What is the budget allowance for direct labor?
   b. Would it be any different if production were 5,000 boxes?

8-40 Similarity of Direct-Labor and Variable-Overhead Variances

The L. Ming Company has had great difficulty controlling costs in Singapore during the past 3 years. Last month a standard cost and flexible-budget system was installed. A condensation of results for a department follows:

	Expected Cost per Standard Direct-Labor-Hour	Flexible-Budget Variance
Lubricants	$ .60	$300 F
Other supplies	.30	225 U
Rework	.60	450 U
Other indirect labor	1.50	450 U
Total variable overhead	$3.00	$825 U

F = Favorable. U = Unfavorable.

The department had initially planned to manufacture 9,000 audio speaker assemblies in 6,000 standard direct-labor-hours allowed. Material shortages and a heat wave resulted in the production of 8,100 units in 5,700 actual direct-labor-hours. The standard wage rate is $5.25 per hour, which was $.20 higher than the actual average hourly rate.

1. Prepare a detailed performance report with two major sections: direct labor and variable overhead.

2. Prepare a summary analysis of price and usage variances for direct labor and spending and efficiency variances for variable overhead.

3. Explain the similarities and differences between the direct-labor and variable-overhead variances. What are some of the likely causes of the overhead variances?

Required

8-41 Material, Labor, and Overhead Variances

Belfair Kayak Company makes molded plastic kayaks. Standard cost for an entry-level whitewater kayak are:

Direct materials, 60 lbs. @ $5.50 per pound	$330
Direct labor, 1.5 hours @ $16 per hour	24
Overhead, @ $12 per kayak	12
Total	$366

The overhead rate assumes production of 450 kayaks per month. The overhead cost function is $2,808 + $5.76 × number of kayaks.

During March, Belfair produced 430 kayaks and had the following actual results:

Direct materials purchased:	28,000 pounds @ $5.30/lb.
Direct materials used	27,000 pounds
Direct labor	660 hours @ $15.90/hr.
Actual overhead	$ 5,320

1. Compute material, labor, and overhead variances.

2. Interpret the variances.

3. Suppose variable overhead was $3.84 per labor hour instead of $5.76 per kayak. Compute the variable-overhead efficiency variance and the total overhead spending variance. Would these variances lead you to a different interpretation of the overhead variances from the interpretation in requirement 2? Explain.

Required

8-42 Automation and Direct Labor as Overhead

Ohio Precision Machining has a highly automated manufacturing process for producing a variety of auto parts. Through the use of computer-aided manufacturing and robotics, the company has reduced its labor costs to only 5% of total manufacturing costs. Consequently, labor is not accounted for as a separate item but is considered part of overhead.

Consider a part used in antilock braking systems. The static budget for producing 750 units in March 19X8 is:

Direct materials	$18,000*
Overhead	
Supplies	1,875
Power	1,310
Rent and other building services	2,815
Factory labor	1,500
Depreciation	4,500
Total manufacturing costs	$30,000

* 3 pounds per unit × $8 per pound × 750 units

Supplies and power are considered to be variable overhead. The other overhead items are fixed costs.

Actual costs in March 19X8 for producing 900 units of the brake part were:

Direct materials	$21,645*
Overhead	
Supplies	2,125
Power	1,612
Rent and other building services	2,775
Factory labor	1,625
Depreciation	4,500
Total manufacturing costs	$34,282

* 2,775 pounds purchased and used @ $7.80 per pound

1. Compute (a) the direct-materials price and usage variances and (b) the flexible-budget variance for each overhead item.

2. Comment on the way Ohio Precision Machining accounts for and controls factory labor.

8-43 Standard Material Allowances

Geiger Company is a chemical manufacturer that supplies industrial users. You have been asked to develop a standard product cost for a new solution the company plans to introduce.

The new chemical solution is made by combining altium and bollium, boiling the mixture, adding credix, and bottling the resulting solution in 20-liter containers. The initial mix, which is 20 liters in volume, consists of 24 kilograms of altium and 19.2 liters of bollium. A 20% reduction in volume occurs during the boiling process. The solution is then cooled slightly before 10 kilograms of credix are added; the addition of credix does not affect the total liquid volume.

The purchase prices of the raw materials used in the manufacture of this new chemical solution are as follows:

Altium	$2.05 per kilogram
Bollium	1.90 per liter
Credix	2.80 per kilogram

Determine the standard quantity for each of the raw materials needed to produce 20 liters of Geiger Company's new chemical solution and the standard materials cost of 20 liters of the new product.

Required

8-44 Role of Defective Units and Nonproductive Time in Setting Standards

Sung Park owns and operates Transpac Machining, a subcontractor to several aerospace industry contractors. When Mr. Park wins a bid to produce a piece of equipment, he sets standard costs for the production of the item. He then compares actual manufacturing costs with the standards to judge the efficiency of production.

In April 19X8, Transpac won a bid to produce 15,000 units of a shielded component used in a navigation device. Specifications for the components were very tight, and Mr. Park expected that 20% of the components would fail his final inspection, even if every care was exercised in production. There was no way to identify defective items before production was complete. Therefore 18,750 units had to be produced to get 15,000 good components. Standards were set to include an allowance for the expected number of defective items.

Each final component contained 2.8 pounds of direct materials, and normal scrap from production was expected to average an additional .4 pounds per unit. The direct material was expected to cost $11.25 per pound plus $.75 per pound for shipping and handling.

Machining of the components required close attention by skilled machinists. Each component required four hours of machining time. The machinists were paid $22 per hour and worked 40-hour weeks. Of the 40 hours, an average of 32 hours was spent directly on production. The other eight hours consisted of time for breaks and waiting time when machines were broken down or there was no work to be done. Nevertheless, all payments to machinists were considered direct labor, whether or not they were for time spent directly on production. In addition to the basic wage rate, Transpac paid fringe benefits averaging $5 per hour and payroll taxes of 10% of the basic wages.

Determine the standard cost of direct materials and direct labor for each good unit of output.

Required

8-45 Review of Major Points in Chapter

The following questions are based on the Dominion Company data contained in Exhibit 8-1 (p. 289) and in the table on p. 299.

1. Suppose actual production and sales were 8,000 units instead of 7,000 units. (a) Compute the sales-activity variance. Is the performance of the marketing function the sole explanation for this variance? Why? (b) Using a flexible budget, compute the budgeted contribution margin, the budgeted operating income, budgeted direct material, and budgeted direct labor.

Required

2. Suppose the following were the actual results for the production of 8,000 units:

   Direct material: 42,000 pounds were used at an actual unit price of $1.85, for a total actual cost of $77,700.

   Direct labor: 4,125 hours were used at an actual hourly rate of $16.40, for a total actual cost of $67,650.

   Compute the flexible-budget variance and the price and usage variances for direct materials and direct labor. Present your answers in the form shown in Exhibit 8-8, p. 304.

3. Suppose the company is organized so that the purchasing manager bears the primary responsibility for the acquisition prices of materials, and the production manager bears the primary responsibility for usage but not responsibility for unit prices. Assume the same facts as in requirement 2 except that the purchasing manager acquired 60,000 pounds of materials at $1.85 per pound. This means that

there is an ending inventory of 18,000 pounds. Would your variance analysis of materials in requirement 2 change? Why? Show computations.

8-46 Review Problem on Standards and Flexible Budgets; Answers Are Provided
The Cowboy Leather Company makes a variety of leather goods. It uses standard costs and a flexible budget to aid planning and control. Budgeted variable overhead at a 45,000-direct-labor-hour level is $27,000.

During April the company had an unfavorable variable-overhead efficiency variance of $1,150. Material purchases were $241,900. Actual direct-labor costs incurred were $140,700. The direct-labor usage variance was $5,100 unfavorable. The actual average wage rate was $.20 lower than the average standard wage rate.

The company uses a variable-overhead rate of 20% of standard direct-labor cost for flexible-budgeting purposes. Actual variable overhead for the month was $30,750.

Required Compute the following amounts; use U or F to indicate whether variances are unfavorable or favorable.

1. Standard direct-labor cost per hour
2. Actual direct-labor hours worked
3. Total direct-labor price variance
4. Total flexible budget for direct-labor costs
5. Total direct-labor variance
6. Variable-overhead spending variance in total

Answers to Problem 8-46

1. $3. The variable-overhead rate is $.60, obtained by dividing $27,000 by 45,000 hours. Therefore the direct-labor rate must be $.60 ÷ .20 = $3.
2. 50,250 hours. Actual costs, $140,700 ÷ ($3 − $.20) = 50,250 hours.
3. $10,050 F.   50,250 actual hours × $.20 = $10,050.
4. $145,650. Usage variance was $5,100 U. Therefore, excess hours must have been $5,100 ÷ $3 = 1,700. Consequently, standard hours allowed must be 50,250 − 1,700 = 48,550. Flexible budget = 48,550 × $3 = $145,650.
5. $4,950 F. $145,650 − $140,700 = $4,950 F; or $10,050 F − $5,100 U = $4,950 F.
6. $470 U. Flexible budget = 48,550 × $.60 = $29,130. Total variance = $30,750 − $29,130 = $1,620 U. Price variance = $1,620 − $1,150. Efficiency variance = $470 U.

8-47 Hospital Costs and Explanation of Variances
The emergency room at Providence Hospital uses a flexible budget based on patients seen as a measure of activity. An adequate staff of attending and on-call physicians must be maintained at all times, so physician scheduling is unaffected by patient activity. Nurse scheduling varies as volume changes, however. A standard of .5 nurse-hours per patient visit was set. Average hourly pay for nurses is $14, ranging from $8 to $17 per hour. All materials are considered to be supplies, a part of overhead; there are no direct materials. A statistical study showed that the cost of supplies and other variable overhead is more closely associated with nurse-hours than with patient visits. The standard for supplies and other variable overhead is $10 per nursing hour.

The head physician of the emergency room unit, Beverly McCaffrey, is responsible for control of costs. During October the emergency room unit treated 4,000 patients. The budget and actual costs were as follows:

	Budget	Actual	Variance
Patient visits	3,800	4,000	200
Nursing hours	1,900	2,075	175
Nursing cost	$ 26,600	$ 31,050	$4,450
Supplies and other			
variable overhead	19,000	20,320	1,320
Fixed costs	92,600	92,600	0
Total cost	$138,200	$143,970	$5,770

Required

1. Calculate price and usage variances for nursing costs.
2. Calculate spending and efficiency variances for supplies and other variable overhead.
3. Dr. McCaffrey has been asked to explain the variances to the chief of staff. Provide possible explanations.

8-48 Activity-Based Costing and Flexible Budgeting

The new printing department provides printing services to the other departments of Madison Avenue Advertising, Inc. Before the establishment of the in-house printing department, the departments contracted with external printers for their printing work. The Madison Avenue printing policy is to charge using departments for the variable printing costs on the basis of number of pages printed. Fixed costs are recovered in pricing of external jobs.

The first year's budget for the printing department was based on the department's expected total costs divided by the planned number of pages to be printed.

The projected annual number of pages to be printed was 420,000, and total variable costs were budgeted to be $420,000. Most government accounts and all internal jobs were expected to use only single color printing. Commercial accounts were primarily color printing. Variable costs were estimated based on the average variable cost of printing a four-color page that is one-fourth graphics and three-fourths text. The expected annual costs for each division were as follows:

Department	Planned Pages Printed	Variable Cost per Page	Budgeted Charges
Government accounts	120,000	$1	$ 90,000
Commercial accounts	250,000	1	300,000
Central administration	50,000	1	30,000
Total	420,000		$420,000

After the first month of using the internal printing department, the printing department announced that its variable cost estimate of $1 per page was too low. The first month's actual costs were $50,000 to print 40,000 pages.

Government accounts	9,000 pages
Commercial accounts	27,500
Central administration	3,500

Three reasons were cited for higher than expected costs: All departments were using more printing services than planned, and government and internal jobs were using more four-color printing and more graphics than expected. The printing department also argued that additional four-color printing equipment would have to be purchased if demand for four-color printing continued to grow.

Required

1. Compare the printing department actual results, static budget, and flexible budget for the month just completed.

2. Discuss possible reasons why the printing department static budget was inaccurate.

3. An activity-based costing (ABC) study completed by a consultant indicated that printing costs are driven by number of pages (@ $.30 per page), and use of colors @ $1 extra per page for color.

   a. Discuss the likely effects of using the ABC results for budgeting and control of printing department use.

   b. Discuss the assumptions regarding cost behavior implied in the ABC study results.

   c. Commercial accounts during the first month (27,500 pages) used four colors per page. Compare the cost of central administration accounts under the old and the proposed ABC system.

COLLABORATIVE LEARNING EXERCISE

8-49   Setting Standards
Form groups of two to six persons each. The groups should each select a simple product or service. Be creative, but do not pick a product or service that is too complex. For those having difficulty choosing a product or service, some possibilities are:

- One dozen chocolate-chip cookies
- A 10-mile taxi ride
- One copy of a 100-page course syllabus
- A machine-knit wool sweater
- A hand-knit wool sweater
- One hour of lawn mowing and fertilizing
- A hammer

Required

1. Each student should individually estimate the direct materials and direct labor inputs needed to produce the product or service. For each type of direct material and direct labor, determine the standard quantity and standard price. Also, identify the overhead support needed, and determine the standard overhead cost of the product or service. The result should be a total standard cost for the product or service.

2. Each group should compare the estimates of its members. Where estimates differ, determine why there were differences. Did assumptions differ? Did some members have more knowledge about the product or service than others? Form a group estimate of the standard cost of the product or service.

3. After the group has agreed on a standard cost, discuss the process used to arrive at the cost. What assumptions did the group make? Is the standard cost an "ideal" standard or a "currently attainable" standard? Note how widely standard costs can vary depending on assumptions and knowledge of the production process.

MANAGEMENT CONTROL SYSTEMS AND RESPONSIBILITY ACCOUNTING

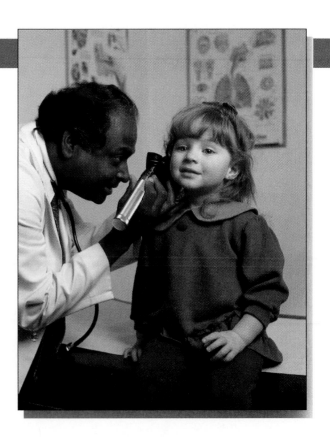

Doctors and patients at Foundation Health Systems benefit from the latest, state-of-the-art medical management system, offering the highest quality health care at an affordable price.

Learning Objectives

When you have finished studying this chapter, you should be able to

1   Describe the relationship of management control systems to organizational goals.

2   Use responsibility accounting to define an organizational subunit as a cost center, a profit center, or an investment center.

3   Compare financial and nonfinancial performance, and explain why planning and control systems should consider both.

4   Explain the importance of evaluating performance and how it impacts motivation, goal congruence, and employee effort.

5   Prepare segment income statements for evaluating profit and investment centers using the contribution margin and controllable-cost concepts.

6   Measure performance against quality, cycle time, and productivity objectives.

7   Describe the difficulties of management control in service and nonprofit organizations.

8   Understand how a management control system uses accounting information.

It's 2:30 a.m. You don't feel well. Should you call your doctor? Go to the emergency room? Is what you're feeling really something to worry about? What you need is good quality health care and you need it now, not tomorrow morning, and you do not want to worry about its cost. Sound familiar? This is a dilemma that we have all faced at some time. One health care organization that has a solution to this common problem is Foundation Health Systems, Inc. (FHS).

Foundation Health Systems, Inc. is one of the largest managed health care organizations in the United States. With more than 15,000 employees and 1997 revenues of more than $9 billion, FHS provides coverage to more than five million members.

Health care organizations must compete just as any other business, offering high quality health care at an affordable cost, and when it is needed. In order to maintain its competitive advantage, FHS started a major information systems development program called "fourth generation medical management." According to Dr. Malik Hasan, chairman and chief executive officer of FHS, this new management control system was created "because the greatest opportunity for increasing overall quality and decreasing the cost of health care lies in managing patient care by seamlessly linking the entire health care delivery system electronically." The system "gives physicians and health care providers instant, user-friendly electronic access to comprehensive information about a patient's medical history and the best clinical treatments recommended."

The result? A fast and pre-approved referral to the best clinical resource, whether it be a specialist, the emergency room or urgent care center, your regular physician, or safe self-care. In other words, a satisfied customer! And as a bonus, costs are reduced. As Medical Director John Danaher, M.D. explains, "paper charting and duplicative lab and radiology test are eliminated."

The previous chapters have presented many important tools of management accounting. Tools such as activity-based costing, relevant costing, budgeting, and variance analysis are each useful by themselves. They are most useful, however, when they are parts of an integrated system—an orderly, logical plan to coordinate and evaluate all the activities of the organization's value chain. Just as in the case of FHS, managers of most organizations today realize that long-run success depends on focusing on cost, quality, and service—three components of the competitive edge. This chapter considers how management accounting tools help the management control system focus resources and talents of the individuals in an organization on such goals as cost, quality, and service. As you will see, no single management control system is inherently superior to another. The "best" system is the one that consistently leads to decisions that meet the organization's goals and objectives.

This chapter builds on previous ones to present how the individual tools of management accounting are blended systematically to help achieve organizational goals.

MANAGEMENT CONTROL SYSTEMS

management control system A logical integration of techniques to gather and use information to make planning and control decisions, to motivate employee behavior, and to evaluate performance.

A **management control system** is a logical integration of techniques to gather and use information to make planning and control decisions, to motivate employee behavior, and to evaluate performance. The purposes of a management control system are:

- to clearly communicate the organization's goals;
- to ensure that managers and employees understand the specific actions required of them to achieve organizational goals;
- to communicate results of actions across the organization; and
- to ensure that the management control system adjusts to changes in the environment.

Exhibit 9-1 shows the components of a management control system. We will refer to Exhibit 9-1 often in this chapter as we consider the design and operation of management control systems.

MANAGEMENT CONTROL SYSTEMS AND ORGANIZATIONAL GOALS

Objective 1
Describe the relationship of management control systems to organizational goals.

A well-designed management control system aids and coordinates the process of making decisions and motivates individuals throughout the organization to act in concert. It also facilitates forecasting revenue- and cost-driver levels, budgeting, and measuring and evaluating performance.

The first and most basic component in a management control system is the organization's goals. Why? Because the focus of the management control system is on internal

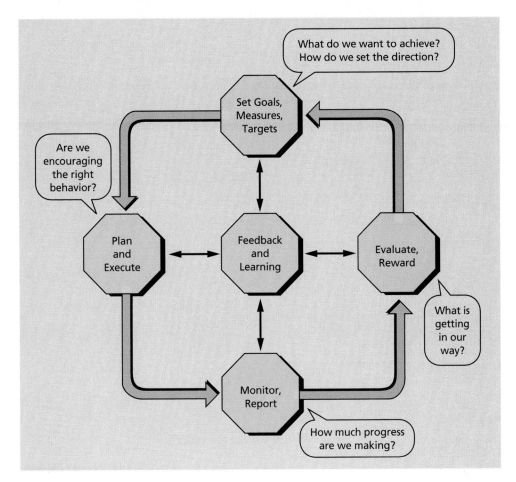

Exhibit 9-1

The Management Control System

management decision making and motivating (and then evaluating) performance consistent with the organization's goals. As shown in Exhibit 9-2, setting goals, objectives, and performance measures involves managers at all levels.

Exhibit 9-2 shows that top management sets organization-wide (overall company) goals, performance measures, and targets. Management reviews these goals on a periodic basis, usually once a year, but normally they do not change them. These goals provide a long-term framework around which an organization will form its comprehensive plan for positioning itself in the market. As Exhibit 9-1 shows, goals answer the question, "What do we want to achieve?" However, goals without performance measures do not motivate managers.

The purpose of performance measures is to set direction and to motivate managers. For example, a major luxury hotel chain, Luxury Suites, has the following goals and related performance measures:

Organizational Goals	**Performance Measures**
Exceed guest expectations	• Satisfaction index
	• Number of repeat stays
Maximize revenue yield	• Occupancy rate
	• Room rate
	• Income before fixed costs
Focus on innovation	• New products/services implemented per year
	• Number of employee suggestions

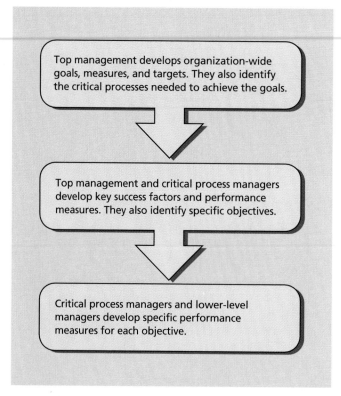

Exhibit 9-2

Setting Goals, Objectives, and Performance Measures

Targets for goals are specific quantified levels of the measures. For example, a target for the performance measure *occupancy rate* might be "at least 70 percent."

As you can see, goals and their related performance measures are very broad. In fact, they are often too vague to guide managers and employees. As a result, top managers also identify critical processes and key success factors. A **critical process** is a series of related activities that directly affects the achievement of organizational goals. For example, the Luxury Suites goal "exceed guest expectations" would have "produce and deliver services" as a critical process. The next step in goal setting is for both top managers and the managers of the critical processes to develop subgoals or key success factors and related performance measures. **Key success factors** are actions that must be done well in order to drive the organization towards its goals. Again consider Luxury Suites. An example of a critical success factor for the *produce and deliver services* process is *timeliness.* Performance measures for timeliness would include *check-in time, check-out time,* and *response time to guest requests* (for example, number of rings before pickup).

Although key success factors and related performance measures give managers more focus than do overall, organization-wide goals, they still do not give lower-level managers and employees the direction they need to guide their daily actions. As shown in Exhibit 9-2, to set this direction, critical process managers work with lower-level managers within the appropriate business unit to establish objectives—specific tangible actions (or activities) that can be observed on a short-term basis. Examples of specific actions related to timeliness are *implementing an express check-in system* and *training staff* to use the new check-in system.

Balancing the various objectives is an important part of management control. Sometimes the management control system ignores critical success factors or inadvertently emphasizes the wrong factors. Managers often face trade-off decisions. For example, a

critical process A series of related activities that directly affects the achievement of organizational goals.

key success factor Actions that must be done well in order to drive the organization towards its goals.

sales manager can increase the "employee satisfaction" measure (a survey of employees) by setting lower standards for responding to customer inquiries. This action may improve the employee satisfaction measure of the manager but result in unsatisfied customers.

DESIGNING MANAGEMENT CONTROL SYSTEMS

To create a management control system that meets the organization's needs, designers need to recognize existing constraints, identify responsibility centers, weigh costs and benefits, and provide motivation to achieve goal congruence and managerial effort.

WORKING WITHIN THE ORGANIZATIONAL STRUCTURE

Every management control system needs to fit the organization's goals. As shown in Exhibit 9-1, developing plans and then executing them is the second major function of a management control system. One of the primary purposes of planning (budgeting) is to encourage managers throughout the organization to take actions that aim to achieve overall organizational goals. To achieve this, the management control system must fit into the organization's structure. Some firms are organized primarily by functions such as manufacturing, sales, and service. Others are organized by divisions that bear profit responsibility along product or geographical lines. Still others may be organized by some hybrid arrangement.

IDENTIFICATION OF RESPONSIBILITY CENTERS

In addition to organizational structures, designers of management control systems must consider the desired responsibility centers in an organization. A **responsibility center** is a set of activities assigned to a manager, a group of managers, or other employees. A set of machines and machining tasks, for example, may be a responsibility center for a production supervisor. The full production department may be a responsibility center for the department head. Finally, the entire organization may be a responsibility center for the president. In some organizations, management responsibility is shared by groups of employees to create wide "ownership" of management decisions, allow creative decision making, and prevent one person's concern (or lack of concern) for risks of failure to dominate decisions.

An effective management control system gives each lower-level manager responsibility for a group of activities and objectives and then, as shown in Exhibit 9-1, monitors, and reports on (1) the results of the activities, and (2) the manager's influence on those results. Such a system has innate appeal for most top managers because it helps them delegate decision making and frees them to plan and control. Lower-level managers appreciate the autonomy of decision making they inherit. Thus system designers apply **responsibility accounting** to identify what parts of the organization have primary responsibility for each objective, develop performance measures and targets to achieve, and design reports of these measures by organization subunit or responsibility center. Responsibility centers usually have multiple objectives that the management control system monitors. Responsibility centers usually are classified according to their financial responsibility as cost centers, profit centers, or investment centers.

COST, PROFIT, AND INVESTMENT CENTERS

A **cost center** is a responsibility center in which a manager is accountable for costs only. Its financial responsibilities are to control and report costs only. An entire department may be considered a single cost center, or a department may contain several cost centers. For example, although an assembly department may be supervised by one manager, it may contain several assembly lines and regard each assembly line as a separate cost center.

responsibility center A set of activities assigned to a manager, a group of managers, or other employees.

responsibility accounting Identifying what parts of the organization have primary responsibility for each objective, developing measures and targets to achieve, and creating reports of these measures by organization subunit or responsibility center.

Objective 2
Use responsibility accounting to define an organizational subunit as a cost center, a profit center, or an investment center.

cost center A responsibility center in which a manager is accountable for costs only.

profit center A responsibility center for controlling revenues as well as costs (or expenses)—that is, profitability.

investment center A responsibility center whose success is measured not only by its income but also by relating that income to its invested capital, as in a ratio of income to the value of the capital employed.

Objective 3
Compare financial and nonfinancial performance, and explain why planning and control systems should consider both.

Likewise, within each line, separate machines or test equipment may be regarded as separate cost centers. The determination of the number of cost centers depends on cost-benefit considerations—do the benefits of smaller cost centers (for planning, control, and evaluation) exceed the higher costs of reporting?

Unlike cost centers, **profit centers** have responsibility for controlling revenues as well as costs (or expenses)—that is, profitability. Despite the name, a profit center can exist in nonprofit organizations (though it might not be referred to as such) when a responsibility center receives revenues for its services. For example, the Western Area Power Authority (WAPA) is charged with recovering its costs of operations through sales of power to electric utilities in the western United States. WAPA essentially is a profit center with the objective of breaking even. All profit center managers are responsible for both revenues and costs, but they may not be expected to maximize profits.

An **investment center** goes a step further than a profit center does. Its success is measured not only by its income but also by relating that income to its invested capital, as in a ratio of income to the value of the capital employed. In practice, the term *investment center* is not widely used. Instead, the term *profit center* is used indiscriminately to describe centers that are always assigned responsibility for revenues and expenses, but may or may not be assigned responsibility for the capital investment.

DEVELOPMENT OF MEASURES OF PERFORMANCE

Because most responsibility centers have multiple objectives, only some of these objectives are expressed in financial terms, such as operations budgets, profit targets, or required return on investment, depending on the financial classification of the center. Other objectives, which are to be achieved concurrently, are nonfinancial in nature. For example, many companies list environmental stewardship and social responsibility as key objectives. The well-designed management control system functions alike for both financial and nonfinancial objectives to develop and report measures of performance. Good performance measures will:

1. Relate to the goals of the organization
2. Balance long-term and short-term concerns
3. Reflect the management of key actions and activities
4. Be affected by actions of managers and employees
5. Be readily understood by employees
6. Be used in evaluating and rewarding managers and employees
7. Be reasonably objective and easily measured
8. Be used consistently and regularly

Both financial and nonfinancial performance measures are important. Sometimes accountants and managers focus too much on financial measures such as profit or cost variances because they are readily available from the accounting system. Managers, however, can improve operational control by also considering nonfinancial measures of performance. Such measures may be more timely and more closely affected by employees at lower levels of the organization, where the product is made or the service is rendered. Nonfinancial measures are often easier to quantify and understand. Hence, employees can be easily motivated toward achieving performance goals. For example, AT&T Universal Card Services, which was awarded the prestigious Baldrige National Quality Award (presented by the U.S. Department of Commerce), uses 18 performance measures for its customer inquiries process. These measures include average speed of answer, abandon rate, and application processing time (three days compared to the industry average of 34 days).

Often the effects of poor nonfinancial performance (quality, productivity, and customer satisfaction) do not show up in the financial measures until considerable ground has been lost. Financial measures often are lagging indicators that arrive too late to help

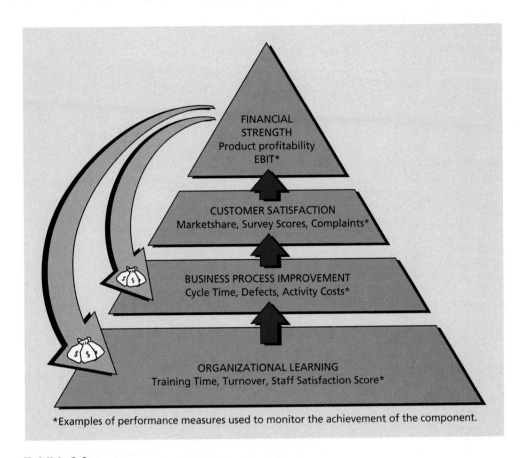

*Examples of performance measures used to monitor the achievement of the component.

Exhibit 9-3

The Components of a Successful Organization and Measures of Achievement

prevent problems and ensure the organization's health. What is needed are leading indicators. As a result, many companies now stress management of the activities that drive revenues and costs rather than waiting to explain the revenues or costs themselves after the activities have occurred. Superior financial performance usually follows from superior nonfinancial performance.

MONITORING AND REPORTING RESULTS AND THE BALANCED SCORECARD

Notice that Exhibit 9-1 has feedback and learning at the center of the management control system. At all points in the planning and control process, it is vital that effective communication exist between all levels of management and employees. In fact, organization-wide learning is a foundation for gaining and maintaining financial strength. Exhibit 9-3 shows how organizational learning leads to financial strength. Organizational learning is monitored by measures such as training time, employee turnover, and staff satisfaction scores on employee surveys. The result of learning is continuous process improvement that is monitored by measures such as cycle time, number of defects (quality), and activity cost. Customers will value improved response (lower cycle time), higher quality, and lower prices, and thus increase their demand for products and services. Increased demand, combined with lower costs to make and deliver products and services, results in financial strength as monitored by such measures as product profitability and earnings before interest and taxes (EBIT). It is important to note that the successful organization does not stop with one cycle of learning → process improvement → increased customer satisfaction → improved financial strength. The benefits of improved financial strength, financial resources, must be rein-

Exhibit 9-4

Balanced Scorecard for Luxury Suites Hotels

Component and Measures	Target	Result
Financial Strength		
Revenue (millions of dollars) per new service	$50	$58
Revenue per arrival	$75	$81
Customer Satisfaction		
Customer satisfaction index	95	88
Brand loyalty index	60	40
Business Process Improvement		
Number of improvements	8	8
Average cycle time (minutes) for checkin and checkout	15	12
Organizational Learning		
Percent of staff re-trained	80	85
Training hours per employee	30	25

vested within the organization by supporting both continuous learning and continuous process improvement.

As shown in Exhibit 9-1, monitoring and reporting the results of business activities is a key component of a management control system. Exhibit 9-2 indicates that managers identify actions and related performance measures that are linked to the achievement of goals and objectives. Once these performance measures and actions are identified, an organization must obtain information on the achievement of desired outcomes. This is done through the performance-reporting system. Effective performance reports align results with managers' goals and objectives, provide guidance to managers, communicate goals and their level of attainment throughout the organization, and enable organizations to anticipate and respond to change in a timely manner.

THE BALANCED SCORECARD There are several approaches to performance reporting. Each approach attempts to link organizational strategy to actions of managers and employees. One popular approach to performance reporting is the balanced scorecard. A **balanced scorecard** is a performance measurement and reporting system that strikes a balance between financial and operating measures, links performance to rewards, and gives explicit recognition to the diversity of organizational goals. Companies such as Champion International, AT&T, Allstate, and Apple Computer use the balanced scorecard to focus management's attention on items subject to action on a month-by-month and day-to-day basis.

One advantage of the balanced scorecard approach is that line managers can see the relationship between nonfinancial measures, which they often can relate more easily to their own actions, and the financial measures that relate to organizational goals. Another advantage of the balanced scorecard is its focus on performance measures from each of the four components of the successful organization shown in Exhibit 9-3. This enhances the learning process because managers learn the results of their actions and how these actions are linked to the organizational goals.

What does a balanced scorecard look like? Exhibit 9-4 shows a balanced scorecard for Luxury Suites hotels. This scorecard is for the organization as a whole. It has performance measures for all four components of organizational success. There are many scorecards for an organization. In fact, each area of responsibility will have its own scorecard. Scorecards for some lower-level responsibility centers that are focused strictly on day-to-day operations may be totally focused on only one of the four components. We should also note that not all performance measures appear on scorecards. Managers of responsibility centers include only those measures that are **key performance indicators**—measures that drive the organization to achieve its goals. For example, top management at

balanced scorecard A performance measurement and reporting system that strikes a balance between financial and operating measures, links performance to rewards, and gives explicit recognition to the diversity of organizational goals.

key performance indicators Measures that drive the organization to achieve its goals.

Luxury Suites set "exceed guest expectations" as one organizational goal. The balanced scorecard should have at least one key performance indicator that is linked to this goal. The customer satisfaction index, brand loyalty index, number of improvements, and average cycle time for checkin and checkout measures all are linked to this goal.

SUMMARY PROBLEM FOR YOUR REVIEW

PROBLEM

Consider our example, the Luxury Suites hotel chain. As we have noted, top management established "*exceed guest expectations*" as one organization-wide goal. The critical process for this goal is *produce and deliver services*. Among the key success factors for this critical process are *timelines of customer service* and *quality of personalized service*. Susan Pierce, the Vice President of Sales, is the manager responsible for the *produce and deliver services* critical process. She has already identified one action (objective) for the coming year—upgrade customer service department capabilities.

Required

1. Identify several possible performance measures for the quality of *personalized service* key success factor.
2. Recommend several specific actions or activities associated with upgrading customer service department capabilities that would drive Luxury Suites towards its goal of exceeding customer expectations.

SOLUTION

1. Performance measures for the *quality of personalized service* key success factor include number of changes to registration, rating on the "friendly, knowledgeable staff" question on the guest survey, number of complaints, percent return guests, and percent of customers with completed customer profile (profiles special needs of customers).
2. Specific actions or activities include training employees, implementing a call checklist (list of services and options available to guest) and monitoring compliance with the list, developing a customer satisfaction survey, and reengineering the guest registration and reservation processes.

WEIGHING OF COSTS AND BENEFITS

The designer of the management control system must also weigh the costs and benefits of various alternatives, given the organization's needs. No system is perfect, but one system may be better than another if it can improve operating decisions at a reasonable cost.

Both benefits and costs of management control systems are often difficult to measure, and both may become apparent only after experimentation or use. For example, the director of accounting policy of Citicorp has stated that, after several years of experience with a very detailed management control system, the system has proved to be too costly to administer relative to the perceived benefits. Accordingly, Citicorp planned to return to a simpler, less costly—though less precise—management control system.

MOTIVATION OF EMPLOYEES TO ACHIEVE GOAL CONGRUENCE AND EXERT MANAGERIAL EFFORT THROUGH REWARDS

goal congruence A condition where employees, working in their own personal interests, make decisions that help meet the overall goals of the organization.

To achieve maximum benefits at minimum cost, a management control system must foster goal congruence and managerial effort. **Goal congruence** exists when individuals and groups aim at the same organizational goals. Goal congruence is achieved when employees, working in their own perceived best interests, make decisions that help meet the over-

managerial effort
Exertion toward a goal or objective including all conscious actions (such as supervising, planning, and thinking) that result in more efficiency and effectiveness.

Objective 4
Explain the importance of evaluating performance and how it impacts motivation, goal congruence, and employee effort.

all goals of the organization. **Managerial effort** is defined as exertion toward a goal or objective. Effort here means not merely working faster but also working better. As a result, effort includes all conscious actions (such as supervising, planning, and thinking) that result in more efficiency and effectiveness. Effort is a matter of degree—it is optimized when individuals and groups strive for their objectives.

Goal congruence can exist with little accompanying effort, and vice versa, but rewards are necessary for both to be achieved. As shown in Exhibit 9-1, the challenge of management control system design is to specify objectives and a performance evaluation and reward system that induce (or at least do not discourage) employee decisions that would achieve organizational goals. For example, an organization may specify one of its subgoals to be continuous improvement in employee efficiency and effectiveness. Employees, however, might perceive that continuous improvements will result in tighter standards, faster pace of work, and loss of jobs. Even though they may agree with management that continuous improvements are competitively necessary, they should not be expected to exert effort for continuous improvements unless rewards are in place to make this effort in their own best interests.

As another example, students may enroll in a college course because their goal is to learn about management accounting. The faculty and the students share the same goal, but goal congruence is not enough. Faculty also introduce rewards in the form of a grading system to spur student effort. Grading is a form of *performance evaluation,* as is use of management control reports for raises, promotions, and other forms of rewards in other settings. Performance evaluation is a widely used means of improving congruence and effort, because most individuals tend to perform better when they receive feedback that is tied to their own self-interest. Thus Allen-Bradley Co., Corning, and other manufacturers who set quality improvements as critical subgoals put quality objectives into the bonus plans of top managers. Corning has quality incentives for factory workers as well.

motivation The drive for some selected goal that creates effort and action toward that goal.

To achieve goal congruence and managerial effort, designers of management control systems focus on motivating employees. **Motivation** has been defined as a drive toward some selected goal that creates effort and action toward that goal. Yet employees differ widely in their motivations. The system designer's task is more complex, ill structured, and more affected by human behavior than many people believe at first. The system designer must align individuals' self-interest with the goals of the organization. Thus the designer must focus on the different motivational impact—how each system will cause people to respond—of one management control system versus another.

Responsibility accounting, budgets, variances, and the entire inventory of management control tools should constructively influence behavior. They may, however, be misused as negative weapons to punish, place blame, or find fault. Viewed positively, they assist employees to improve decisions. Used negatively, they pose a threat to employees, who will resist and undermine the use of such techniques.

To see how failure to anticipate motivational impact can cause problems, consider that some years ago in Russia, managers of the Moscow Cable Company decided to reduce copper wastage and actually slashed it by 60% that year. As a result they had only $40,000 worth of scrap instead of the $100,000 originally budgeted. Top management in the central government then fined the plant $45,000 for not meeting its scrap budget. What do you think this did to the cable company managers' motivation to control waste?

CONTROLLABILITY AND MEASUREMENT OF FINANCIAL PERFORMANCE

Management control systems often distinguish between controllable and uncontrollable events and between controllable and uncontrollable costs. Usually, responsibility center managers are in the best position to explain their center's results even if the managers had little influence over them. For example, an importer of grapes from Chile to the United

States suffered a sudden loss of sales several years ago after a few of the grapes were found to contain poisonous cyanide. The tampering was beyond the importer's control, so the importer's management control system compared actual profits to flexible-budgeted profits (see Chapter 8), given that actual sales were unusually low. This comparison separated effects of activity volume—sales levels—from effects of efficiency, and reported the importer's profitability given the uncontrollable drop in sales.

An **uncontrollable cost** is any cost that cannot be affected by the management of a responsibility center within a given time span. For example, a mail-order supervisor may be responsible only for costs of labor, shipping costs, ordering errors and adjustments, and customer satisfaction. The supervisor would not be responsible for costs of the supporting information system because the supervisor cannot control that cost.

Controllable costs should include all costs that are influenced by a manager's decision and actions. For example, the costs of the mail-order information system, though uncontrollable by the mail-order supervisor, are controllable by the manager in charge of information systems.

In a sense, the term "controllable" is a misnomer because no cost is completely under the control of a manager. The term is widely used, however, to refer to any cost that is affected by a manager's decisions, even if not totally "controlled." Thus the cost of operating the mail-order information system may be affected by equipment or software failures that are not completely—but are partially—under the control of the manager of information systems, who would be held responsible for all of the costs of the information system, even the costs of downtime.

The distinction between controllable and uncontrollable costs serves an information purpose. Costs that are completely uncontrollable tell nothing about a manager's decisions and actions because, by definition, nothing the manager does will affect the costs. Such costs should be ignored in evaluating the responsibility center manager's performance. In contrast, reporting controllable costs provides evidence about a manager's performance.

Because responsibility for costs may be widespread, systems designers must depend on understanding cost behavior to help identify controllable costs. This understanding is increasingly gained through activity-based costing (see Chapters 3 and 4). Both Procter & Gamble and Upjohn, Inc., for example, are experimenting with activity-based costing systems in some divisions. Procter & Gamble credits its experimental activity-based management control system for identifying controllable costs in one of its detergent divisions, which led to major strategic changes.

> **uncontrollable cost** Any cost that cannot be affected by the management of a responsibility center within a given time span.

> **controllable cost** Any cost that is influenced by a manager's decisions and actions.

CONTRIBUTION MARGIN

Many organizations combine the contribution approach to measuring income with responsibility accounting—that is, they report by cost behavior as well as by degrees of controllability.

Exhibit 9-5 displays the contribution approach to measuring the financial performance of the various organizational units (or segments) of Barleycorn, Inc., a retail grocery company. **Segments** are responsibility centers for which a separate measure of revenues and costs is obtained. Study this exhibit carefully. It provides perspective on how a management control system can be designed to stress cost behavior, controllability, manager performance, and responsibility center performance simultaneously.

Line a in Exhibit 9-5 shows the contribution margin, sales revenues less all variable expenses. The contribution margin is especially helpful for predicting the impact on income of short-run changes in activity volume. Managers may quickly calculate any expected changes in income by multiplying increases in dollar sales by the contribution margin ratio. The contribution margin ratio for meats in the West Division is $180 ÷ $900 = .20. Thus a $1,000 increase in sales of meats in the West Division should produce a $200 increase in income (.20 × $1,000 = $200) if there are no changes in selling prices, per unit operating expenses, or mix of sales between stores 1 and 2.

> **Objective 5**
> Prepare segment income statements for evaluating profit and investment centers using the contribution-margin and controllable-cost concepts.

> **segments** Responsibility centers for which a separate measure of revenues and costs is obtained.

CONTRIBUTION CONTROLLABLE BY SEGMENT MANAGERS

Lines b and c in Exhibit 9-5 separate the contribution that is controllable by segment managers (b) from the overall segment contribution (c). Designers of management control systems distinguish between the segment as an economic investment and the manager as a professional decision maker. For instance, an extended period of drought coupled with an aging population may adversely affect the desirability of continued economic investment in a ski resort, but the resort manager may be doing an excellent job under the circumstances.

The manager of store 1 may have influence over some local advertising but not other advertising, some fixed salaries but not other salaries, and so forth. Moreover, the meat manager at both the division and store levels may have zero influence over store depreciation or the president's salary. Therefore, Exhibit 9-5 separates costs by controllability. Managers on all levels are asked to explain the total segment contribution but are held responsible only for the controllable contribution.

Note that fixed costs controllable by the segment managers are deducted from the contribution margin to obtain the contribution controllable by segment managers. These controllable costs are usually discretionary fixed costs such as local advertising and some salaries, but not the manager's own salary. Other, noncontrollable, fixed costs (shown between lines a and b) are not allocated in the breakdown because they are not considered controllable this far down in the organization. That is, of the $160,000 fixed cost that is controllable by the manager of the West Division, $140,000 is also controllable by subordinates (grocery, produce, and meat managers), but $20,000 is not. The latter is controllable by the West Division manager but not by lower managers. Similarly, the $30,000 in that same line are costs that are attributable to the meat department of the West Division but not to individual stores.

In many organizations, managers have latitude to trade off some variable costs for fixed costs. To save variable material and labor costs, managers might make heavier outlays for automation, quality management and employee training programs, and so on. Moreover, decisions on advertising, research, and sales promotion have effects on sales activity and hence on contribution margins. The controllable contribution includes these expenses and attempts to capture the results of these trade-offs.

The distinctions in Exhibit 9-5 among which items belong in what cost classification are inevitably not clear-cut. For example, determining controllability is always a problem when service department costs are allocated to other departments. Should the store manager bear a part of the division headquarters costs? If so, how much and on what basis? How much, if any, store depreciation or lease rentals should be deducted in computing the controllable contribution? There are no easy answers to these questions. Each organization picks ways that benefit it most with the lowest relative cost (unlike the situation in external financial accounting systems, which must follow strict regulations).

CONTRIBUTION BY SEGMENTS

The contribution by segments, line c in Exhibit 9-5, is an attempt to approximate the financial performance of the segment, as distinguished from the financial performance of its manager, which is measured in line b. The "fixed costs controllable by others" typically include committed costs (such as depreciation and property taxes) and discretionary costs (such as the segment manager's salary). These costs are attributable to the segment but primarily are controllable only at higher levels of management.

UNALLOCATED COSTS

Exhibit 9-5 shows "unallocated costs" immediately before line d. They might include central corporate costs such as the costs of top management and some corporate-level services (for example, legal and taxation). When a persuasive cause and effect or activity-

Exhibit 9-5

Barleycorn, Inc.

Contribution Approach: Model Income Statement, by Segments* (thousands of dollars)

	Company as a Whole	Company Breakdown into Two Divisions		Breakdown of West Division Only				Breakdown of West Division, Meats Only		
		East Division	West Division	Not Allocated†	Groceries	Produce	Meats	Not Allocated†	Store 1	Store 2
Net sales	$4,000	$1,500	$2,500	—	$1,300	$300	$900	—	$600	$300
Variable costs										
Cost of merchandise sold	$3,000	$1,100	$1,900	—	$1,000	$230	$670	—	$450	$220
Variable operating expenses‡	260	100	160	—	100	10	50	—	35	15
Total variable costs	$3,260	$1,200	$2,060	—	$1,100	$240	$720	—	$485	$235
(a) Contribution margin	$ 740	$ 300	$ 440	—	$ 200	$ 60	$ 180	—	$115	$ 65
Less: fixed costs controllable by segment managers§	260	100	160	$ 20	40	10	90	$ 30	35	25
(b) Contribution controllable by segment managers	$ 480	$ 200	$ 280	$(20)	$ 160	$ 50	$ 90	$(30)	$ 80	$ 40
Less: fixed costs controllable by others¶	200	90	110	20	40	10	40	10	22	8
(c) Contribution by segments	$ 280	$ 110	$ 170	$(40)	$ 120	$ 40	$ 50	$(40)	$ 58	$ 32
Less: unallocated costs‖	100									
(d) Income before income taxes	$ 180									

*Three different types of segments are illustrated here: divisions, product lines, and stores. As you read across, note that the focus becomes narrower; from East and West divisions to West Division only, to meats in West Division only.

†Only those costs clearly identifiable to a product line should be allocated.

‡Principally wages and payroll-related costs.

§Examples are certain advertising, sales promotion, salespersons' salaries, management consulting, training and supervision costs.

¶Examples are depreciation, property taxes, insurance, and perhaps the segment manager's salary.

‖These costs are not clearly or practically allocable to any segment except by some highly questionable allocation base.

based justification for allocating such costs cannot be found, many organizations favor not allocating them to segments.

The contribution approach highlights the relative objectivity of various means of measuring financial performance. The contribution margin itself tends to be the most objective. As you read downward in the report, the allocations become more subjective, and the resulting measures of contributions or income become more subject to dispute. Though such disputes may be unproductive uses of management time, the allocations do direct managers' attention to the costs of the entire organization and lead to organizational cost control.

NONFINANCIAL MEASURES OF PERFORMANCE

Objective 6
Measure performance against quality, cycle time, and productivity objectives.

For many years organizations have monitored their nonfinancial performance. For example, sales organizations have followed up on customers to ensure their satisfaction and manufacturers have tracked manufacturing defects and product performance. In recent years, most organizations have developed a new awareness of the importance of controlling such nonfinancial performance as quality, cycle time, and productivity.

CONTROL OF QUALITY

quality control The effort to ensure that products and services perform to customer requirements.

Quality control is the effort to ensure that products and services perform to customer requirements. In essence, customers or clients define quality by comparing their needs to the attributes of the product or service. For example, buyers judge the quality of an automobile based on reliability, performance, styling, safety, and image relative to their needs, budget, and the alternatives. Defining quality in terms of customer requirements is only half the battle. There remains the problem of reaching and maintaining the desired level of quality. There are many approaches to controlling quality. The traditional approach in the United States was to inspect products after they were completed, and reject or rework those that failed the inspections. Because testing is expensive, often only a sample of products were inspected. The process was judged to be in control as long as the number of defective products did not exceed an *acceptable quality level*. This meant that some defective products could still make their way to customers.

In recent years, however, U.S. companies, confronted with the success of Japanese products, have learned that this is a very costly way to control quality. All the resources consumed to make a defective product and to detect it are wasted, or considerable rework may be necessary to correct the defects. In addition, it is very costly to repair products in use by a customer or to win back a dissatisfied customer. IBM's former Chief Executive Officer John Akers was quoted in the *Wall Street Journal* as saying, "I am sick and tired of visiting plants to hear nothing but great things about quality and cycle time—and then to visit customers who tell me of problems."[1] The high costs of achieving quality by "inspecting it in" are evident in a **cost of quality report,** which displays the financial impact of quality. The quality cost report shown in Exhibit 9-6 measures four categories of quality costs:

cost of quality report A report that displays the financial impact of quality.

1. Prevention—costs incurred to prevent the production of defective products or delivery of substandard services including engineering analyses to improve product design for better manufacturing, improvements in production processes, increased quality of material inputs, and programs to train personnel

2. Appraisal—costs incurred to identify defective products or services including inspection and testing

---

[1] *Quoted in Graham Sharman, "When Quality Control Gets in the Way of Quality,"* Wall Street Journal, *February 24, 1992, p. A14.*

Exhibit 9-6
Eastside Manufacturing Company
Quality Cost Report* (thousands of dollars)

Month			Quality Cost Area	Year to Date		
Actual	*Plan*	*Variance*		*Actual*	*Plan*	*Variance*
			1. Prevention Cost			
3	2	1	A. Quality—administration	5	4	1
16	18	(2)	B. Quality—engineering	37	38	(1)
7	6	1	C. Quality—planning by others	14	12	2
5	7	(2)	D. Supplier assurance	13	14	(1)
31	33	(2)	Total prevention cost	69	68	1
5.5%	6.1%		% of Total quality cost	6.2%	6.3%	
			2. Appraisal cost			
31	26	5	A. Inspection	55	52	3
12	14	(2)	B. Test	24	28	(4)
7	6	1	C. Insp. & test of purchased mat.	15	12	3
11	11	0	D. Product quality audits	23	22	1
3	2	1	E. Maint. of insp. & test equip.	4	4	0
2	2	0	F. Mat. consumed in insp. & test	5	4	1
66	61	5	Total appraisal cost	126	122	4
11.8%	11.3%		% of Total quality cost	11.4%	11.3%	
			3. Internal failure cost			
144	140	4	A. Scrap & rework—manuf.	295	280	15
55	53	2	B. Scrap & rework—engineering	103	106	(3)
28	30	(2)	C. Scrap & rework—supplier	55	60	(5)
21	22	(1)	D. Failure investigation	44	44	0
248	245	3	Total internal failure cost	497	490	7
44.3%	45.4%		% of Total quality cost	44.9%	45.3%	
345	339	6	Total internal quality cost (1 + 2 + 3)	692	680	12
61.6%	62.8%		% of Total quality cost	62.6%	62.8%	
			4. External failure quality cost			
75	66	9	A. Warranty exp.—manuf.	141	132	9
41	40	1	B. Warranty exp.—engineering	84	80	4
35	35	0	C. Warranty exp.—sales	69	70	(1)
46	40	6	D. Field warranty cost	83	80	3
18	20	(2)	E. Failure investigation	37	40	(3)
215	201	14	Total external failure cost	414	402	12
38.4%	37.2%		% of Total quality cost	37.4%	37.2%	
560	540	20	Total quality cost	1,106	1,082	24
9,872	9,800		Total product cost	20,170	19,600	
5.7%	5.5%		%Tot. qual. cost to tot. prod. cost	5.5%	5.5%	

*Adapted from Allen H. Seed III, *Adapting Management Accounting Practice to an Advanced Manufacturing Environment* (National Association of Accountants, 1988). Table 5-2, p. 76.

3. Internal failure—costs of defective components and final products or services that are scrapped or reworked; also costs of delays caused by defective products or services

4. External failure—costs caused by delivery of defective products or services to customers, such as field repairs, returns, and warranty expenses

This report shows that most of the costs incurred by Eastside Manufacturing Company are due to internal or external failures. These costs almost certainly are understated, however. Poor quality can result in large opportunity costs because of internal delays and

Poor Quality Nearly Short-Circuits Electronics Company

Penril DataComm, a Maryland designer and maker of data communications equipment, was on the brink of financial disaster resulting from the cost of poor quality. Penril was performing 100% inspection in many of its manufacturing processes and reworking or scrapping one-third of everything it produced. Penril turned its financial fortunes around based on a total quality effort. The results of a customized quality program included:

1. 1,266% increase in profits per employee
2. 95% increase in revenues
3. 81% decrease in defects per unit
4. 83% decrease in out-of-box failures (failures during the first three months in the field)
5. 73% decrease in first-year warranty service repairs
6. reduced response time to customer's orders from 10 weeks to 3 days

Penril's new mission is "to build an environment where internal and external customer expectations are met in every transaction." Penril supports this mission by following six principles:

1. Quality is the number-one priority. This requires a shift from short-term to long-term thinking. Resources are allocated for quality efforts, and quality teams are rewarded for improvements.
2. Customer focus. Customers and suppliers serve on concurrent engineering teams to "build the voice of the customer into all aspects of the business."
3. Emphasize prevention and continuous improvement. "Inspection only maintains the status quo." Total quality means reforming designs, modifying policies and procedures, and training people in correct practices.
4. Management using data. Statistical analysis is used for control of processes.
5. Total employee involvement. According to Penril, the most important measure in the race for quality leadership is the rate of improvement, and this rate is maximized by involving everyone on a team. The team concept at Penril unleashes employee energy that improves morale, communication, respect, and trust. Training includes job skills, total quality management concepts, statistics, statistical process control, problem-solving skills, presentation skills, and communication skills.
6. Cross-functional management. Processes cross departments so each cross-functional team includes members from all areas involved in the process. Communication is enhanced by frequent meetings and newsletters. Employees present quality reports that document improvement efforts.

Perhaps the best measure of the success of Penril's new quality focus is in customer reaction—business has doubled in the three years since the program began. "We know of no greater testimony to a company's quality than to have another company ask it to design a product for them, build it for them, and put the customer's name on it."

Source: Adapted from "Poor Quality Nearly Short-Circuits Electronics Company," in Chet Marchwinski ed., *Productivity*, February 1993, pp. 1–3.

---

lost sales. For example, quality problems in American-built automobiles in the 1970s and 1980s probably caused forgone sales that were significantly more costly than the tangible costs measured in any quality cost report.

In recent years, more and more U.S. companies have been rethinking this approach to quality control. Instead, they have adopted an approach first espoused by an American, W. Edwards Deming, and embraced by Japanese companies decades ago: *total quality management* (TQM). Following the old adage, "an ounce of prevention is worth a pound of cure," it focuses on prevention of defects and on customer satisfaction. The TQM approach is based on the assumption that the cost of quality is minimized when a firm achieves high quality levels. **Total quality management** is the application of quality principles to all of the organization's endeavors to satisfy customers. The U.S. Department of Commerce presents the Baldrige Award to companies that excel in quality, based on their customer-oriented quality achievements. TQM has significant implications for organization goals, structure, and management control systems. For TQM to work, though,

total quality management (TQM) The application of quality principles to all of the organization's endeavors to satisfy customers.

Measuring the Cost of Quality

Often, companies do not invest in equipment that promotes quality because it is difficult to quantify all the benefits and costs of using such equipment. One company has developed a software program that enables a better measurement of these benefits and costs. Perceptron, Inc., based in Farmington Hills, Michigan, produces industrial measurement systems such as laser-based, optical, noncontact systems for automotive, appliance, aerospace, and furniture companies. These systems are used to measure product assembly accuracy. Assembly-line technicians can use the data provided by Perceptron's equipment to take preventive action to correct problems immediately, virtually eliminating the need for highly paid quality control inspectors.

Perceptron developed a computer software program that helps plant personnel to identify and quantify the hidden benefits and costs of acquiring and using quality equipment. Some of the major benefits and costs of the investment in in-line measurement systems and associated preventive activities are

QUANTIFIABLE BENEFITS	COSTS
quicker response to variation problems, leading to reduced average cost of manufacturing process problems	acquisition cost of equipment including transportation and installation
reduced production costs of scrap and repair from early detection of defects	training
reduced work-in-process and parts inventories lower the carrying costs of inventory and the costs of obsolescence because of engineering changes	initial programming labor
higher uptime and throughput from more stable processes reduces the costs of overtime and outsourcing	maintenance
reduced downstream production and warranty costs	measurement labor
higher quality of supplier parts due to early in-process detection of defects	process inspection

Source: Adapted from Alahassane Diallon Zafar, U. Khan, and Curtis F. Vail, "Measuring the Cost of Investment in Quality Equipment," *Management Accounting*, August 1994, pp. 32–35.

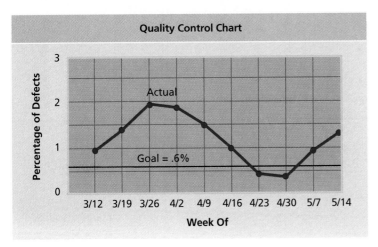

Exhibit 9-7

Eastside Manufacturing Company
Quality-Control Chart

employees must be very well trained in the process, the product or service, and the use of quality-control information.

To implement TQM, employees are trained to prepare, interpret, and act on *quality-control charts*, such as that shown in Exhibit 9-7. The **quality-control chart** is a statistical plot of measures of various product dimensions or attributes. This plot helps detect process deviations before the process generates defects. These plots also identify excessive variation in

quality-control chart The statistical plot of measures of various product dimensions or attributes.

product dimensions or attributes that should be addressed by process or design engineers. The chart in Exhibit 9-7 shows that the Eastside Manufacturing Company generally is not meeting its defects objective of .6% defects (which is a relatively high defect rate). A manager looking at this chart would know that corrective action must be taken.

CONTROL OF CYCLE TIME

cycle time The time taken to complete a product or service, or any of the components of a product or service.

One key to improving quality is to reduce cycle time. **Cycle time,** or throughput time, is the time taken to complete a product or service, or any of the components of a product or service. It is a summary measure of manufacturing or service efficiency and effectiveness, and an important cost driver. The longer a product or service is in process, the more costs are consumed. Low cycle time means quick completion of a product or service (without defects). Lowering cycle time requires smooth-running processes and high quality, and also creates increased flexibility and quicker reactions to customer needs. As cycle time is decreased, quality problems become apparent throughout the process and must be solved if quality is to be improved. Decreasing cycle time also results in bringing products or services more quickly to customers, a product or service characteristic customers value.

Firms measure cycle time for the important stages of a process and for the process as a whole. An effective means of measuring cycle time is to use barcoding, where a barcode (similar to symbols on most grocery products) is attached to each component or product, and read at the end of each stage of completion. Cycle time is measured for each stage as the time between readings of barcodes. Barcoding also permits effective tracking of materials and products for inventories, scheduling, and delivery.

Exhibit 9-8 shows a sample cycle-time report. (Cycle time can also be displayed on a control chart.) This report shows that Eastside Manufacturing Company is meeting its cycle-time objectives at two of its five production process stages. This report is similar to the flexible budget reports of Chapter 8. Explanations of the variances indicate that poor quality materials and poor design led to extensive rework and retesting.

Exhibit 9-8

Eastside Manufacturing Company
Cycle Time Report for the Second Week of May, 19X8

Process Stage	Actual Cycle Time*	Standard Cycle Time	Variance	Explanation
Materials processing	2.1	2.5	0.4 F	
Circuit board assembly	44.7	28.8	15.9 U	Poor quality materials caused rework
Power unit assembly	59.6	36.2	23.4 U	Engineering change required rebuilding all power units
Product assembly	14.6	14.7	0.1 F	
Functional and environmental test	53.3	32.0	21.3 U	Software failure in test procedures required retesting

F = Favorable.

U = Unfavorable.

*Average time per stage over the week.

CONTROL OF PRODUCTIVITY

More than half the companies in the United States manage productivity as part of the effort to improve their competitiveness. **Productivity** is a measure of outputs divided by inputs. The fewer inputs needed to produce a given output, the more productive the organization. This simple definition, however, raises difficult measurement questions. How should outputs and inputs be measured? Specific management control problems usually determine the most appropriate measures of inputs and outputs. Labor-intensive (especially service) organizations are concerned with increasing the productivity of labor, so labor-based measures are appropriate. Highly automated companies are concerned with machine use and productivity of capital investments, so capacity-based measures, such as the percentage of time machines are available, may be most important to them. Manufacturing companies in general are concerned with the efficient use of materials, and so for them measures of material *yield* (a ratio of material outputs over material inputs) may be useful indicators of productivity. In all cases of productivity ratios, a measure of the resource that management wishes to control is in the denominator (the input) and some measure of the objective of using the resource is in the numerator (the output).

Exhibit 9-9 shows 12 possible productivity measures. As you can see, they vary widely according to the type of resource with which management is concerned.

productivity A measure of outputs divided by inputs.

CHOICE OF PRODUCTIVITY MEASURES

Which productivity measures should a company choose to manage? The choice depends on the behaviors desired. Managers generally concentrate on achieving the performance levels desired by their superiors. Thus, if top management evaluates subordinates' performance based on direct-labor productivity, lower-level managers will focus on improving that specific measure.

The challenge in choosing productivity measures is that a manager may be able to improve a single measure but hurt performance elsewhere in the organization. For example, long production runs may improve machine productivity but result in excessive inventories. Alternatively, improved labor productivity in the short run may be accompanied by a high rate of product defects.

Exhibit 9-9

Measures of Productivity

Resource	Possible Outputs (Numerator)		Possible Inputs (Denominator)
Labor	Standard direct labor hours allowed for good output	÷	Actual direct labor hours used
	Sales revenue	÷	Number of employees
	Sales revenue	÷	Direct labor costs
	Bank deposit/loan activity (by a bank)		Number of employees
	Service calls	÷	Number of employees
	Customer orders	÷	Number of employees
Materials	Weight of output	÷	Weight of input
	Number of good units	÷	Total number of units
Equipment, capital, physical capacity	Time (e.g., hours) used	÷	Time available for use
	Time available for use	÷	Time (e.g., 24 hours per day)
	Expected machine hours for good output	÷	Actual machine hours
	Sales revenue	÷	Direct labor cost

For the fourth year in a row, Nissan's plant in Smyrna, Tennessee has been rated as the most productive assembly plant in North America.[1] The measure used was the number of workers per vehicle. Nissan used 2.23 workers compared to Ford's 3.09, Chrysler's 3.29, and GM's 3.47 workers per vehicle.

How did they do it? The key is a "highly motivated workforce" according to Barry Watson, Nissan's Smyrna plant department manager. A number of "simple but effective" efforts are at the heart of the plant's success. These efforts include:

- Social events such as family day and picnics.
- Continuous training.
- Manager and employee involvement through group meetings at the start of every shift. These open, two-way discussions focus on ideas for improving productivity and reducing costs.
- Impact teams of managers and employees evaluate and implement ideas.

For example, an idea was submitted to build a special table that would significantly reduce the time it takes to change equipment between production runs. The idea was implemented and resulted in a 15% increase in the number of units assembled on each production run.

[1]Source: Harbour and Associates, Inc., *Auto Manufacturing Productivity Report*, June, 1997.

Use of a single measure of productivity is unlikely to result in overall improvements in performance. The choice of management controls requires balancing trade-offs that employees can be expected to make to improve their performance evaluations. Many organizations focus management control on more fundamental activities, such as control of quality and service, and use productivity measures to monitor the actual benefits of improvements in these activities.

PRODUCTIVITY MEASURES OVER TIME

Be careful with comparing productivity measures over time. Changes in the process or in the rate of inflation can prove misleading. For example, consider labor productivity at Ameritech Corporation (the Midwest U.S. telecommunications company). One measure of productivity tracked by Ameritech is *sales revenue per employee.*

	1997	1995	Percent Change
Total revenue (millions)	$ 15,998	$ 13,428	+19.1%
Employees	74,359	65,345	+13.8%
Revenue per employee (unadjusted for inflation)	$215,145	$205,494	+ 4.7%

By this measure, Ameritech appears to have achieved a 4.7% increase in the productivity of labor. Total revenue has not been adjusted for the effects of inflation, however. Because of inflation, each 1995 dollar was equivalent to 1.053 1997 dollars. Therefore, Ameritech's 1995 sales revenue, expressed in 1997 dollars (to be equivalent with 1997 sales revenue) is $13,428 × 1.053 = $14,140. The adjusted 1995 sales revenue per employee is as follows:

	1997	1995 (Adjusted)	Percent Change
Total revenue (millions)	$ 15,998	$ 14,140	+13.1%
Employees	74,359	65,345	+13.8%
Revenue per employee (adjusted for inflation)	$215,145	$216,390	− 0.6%

Adjusting for the effects of inflation reveals that Ameritech's labor productivity has dropped rather than improved. This is a signal to management that corrective action should be taken to reverse this slide—such as raising prices or reducing the number of employees.

MANAGEMENT CONTROL SYSTEMS IN SERVICE, GOVERNMENT, AND NONPROFIT ORGANIZATIONS

Objective 7
Describe the difficulties of management control in service and nonprofit organizations.

Most service, government, and nonprofit organizations have more difficulty implementing management control systems than do manufacturing firms. Why? The main problem is that the outputs of service and nonprofit organizations are more difficult to measure than are the cars or computers that are produced by manufacturers. As a result, it may be more difficult to know whether the service provided is, for example, of top quality until (long) after the service has already been delivered.

The key to successful management control in any organization is proper training and motivation of employees to achieve goal congruence and effort, followed by consistent monitoring of objectives set in accordance with critical processes and success factors, but it is even more important in service-oriented organizations. For example, MBNA America, a large issuer of bank credit cards, identifies customer retention as its primary key success factor. MBNA trains its customer representatives carefully, each day measures and reports performance on 14 objectives consistent with customer retention (such as answering every call by the second ring, keeping the computer up 100% of the time, processing credit-line requests within 1 hour), and rewards every employee based on those 14 objectives. Employees have earned bonuses as high as 20% of their annual salaries by meeting those objectives.

Nonprofit and government organizations also have additional problems designing and implementing an objective that is similar to the financial "bottom line" that often serves as a powerful incentive in private industry. Furthermore, many people seek positions in nonprofit organizations primarily for other than monetary rewards. For example, volunteers in the Peace Corps receive very little pay but derive much satisfaction from helping to improve conditions in underdeveloped countries. Thus monetary incentives are generally less effective in nonprofit organizations. Control systems in nonprofit organizations probably will never be as highly developed as are those in profit-seeking firms because:

1. Organizational goals and objectives are less clear. Moreover, they are often multiple, requiring difficult trade-offs.

2. Professionals (for example, teachers, attorneys, physicians, scientists, economists) tend to dominate nonprofit organizations. Because of their perceived professional status, they have been less receptive to the installation or improvement of formal control systems.

3. Measurements are more difficult because
   a. There is no profit measure.
   b. There are heavy amounts of discretionary fixed costs, which make the relationships of inputs to outputs difficult to specify and measure.

4. There is less competitive pressure from other organizations or "owners" to improve management control systems. As a result, for example, many cities in the United States are "privatizing" some essential services such as sanitation by contracting with private firms.

5. The role of budgeting is often more a matter of playing bargaining games with sources of funding to get the largest possible authorization than it is rigorous planning.

6. Motivations and incentives of individuals may differ from those in for-profit organizations.

As organizations mature and as environments change, managers must expand and refine their management control tools. The management control techniques that were quite satisfactory 10 or 20 years ago may not be adequate for many organizations today.

A changing environment often means that organizations must set different subgoals or key success factors. Different subgoals create different objectives to be used as targets and create different benchmarks for evaluating performance. Obviously, the management control system must evolve, too, or the organization may not manage its resources effectively or efficiently. Thus the management control tools presented in this text may not be adequate even a short time from now.

Does this mean that the time spent studying this material has been wasted? No. Certain management control principles that will always be important and that can guide the redesign of systems to meet new management needs follow:

1. Always expect that individuals will be pulled in the direction of their own self-interest. You may be pleasantly surprised that some individuals will act selflessly, but management control systems should be designed to take advantage of more typical human behavior. Be aware that self-interest may be perceived differently in different cultures.

2. Design incentives so that individuals who pursue their own self-interest are also achieving the organization's objectives. If there are multiple objectives (as is usually the case), then multiple incentives are appropriate. Do not underestimate the difficulty of balancing these incentives—some experimentation may be necessary to achieve multiple objectives.

3. Evaluate actual performance based on expected or planned performance, revised, if possible, for actual output achieved. The concept of flexible budgeting can be applied to most subgoals and objectives, both financial and nonfinancial.

4. Consider nonfinancial performance to be just as important as financial performance. In the short run, a manager may be able to generate good financial performance while neglecting nonfinancial performance, but it is not likely over a longer haul.

5. Array performance measures across the entire value chain of the company. This ensures that all activities that are critical to the long-run success of the company are integrated into the management control system.

6. Periodically review the success of the management control system. Are objectives being met? Does meeting the objectives mean that subgoals and goals are being met, too? Do individuals have, understand, and use the management control information effectively?

7. Learn from the management control successes (and failures) of competitors around the world. Despite cultural differences, human behavior is remarkably similar. Successful applications of new technology and management controls may be observed in the performance of others.

SUMMARY PROBLEM FOR YOUR REVIEW

PROBLEM

The Book & Game Company has two bookstores: Auntie's and Merlin's. Each store has managers who have a great deal of decision authority over their store. Advertising, market research, acquisition of books, legal services, and other staff functions, however, are handled by a central office. The Book & Game Company's current accounting system allocates all costs to the stores. Results for 19X9 were

Item	Total Company	Auntie's	Merlin's
Sales revenue	$700,000	$350,000	$350,000
Cost of merchandise sold	450,000	225,000	225,000
Gross margin	250,000	125,000	125,000
Operating expenses			
Salaries and wages	63,000	30,000	33,000
Supplies	45,000	22,500	22,500
Rent and utilities	60,000	40,000	20,000
Depreciation	15,000	7,000	8,000
Allocated staff costs	60,000	30,000	30,000
Total operating expenses	243,000	129,500	113,500
Operating income (loss)	$ 7,000	$ (4,500)	$ 11,500

Each bookstore manager makes decisions that affect salaries and wages, supplies, and depreciation. In contrast, rent and utilities are beyond the managers' control because the managers did not choose the location or the size of the store.

Supplies are variable costs. Variable salaries and wages are equal to 8% of the cost of merchandise sold; the remainder of salaries and wages is a fixed cost. Rent, utilities, and depreciation also are fixed costs. Allocated staff costs are unaffected by any events at the bookstores, but they are allocated as a proportion of sales revenue.

1. Using the contribution approach, prepare a performance report that distinguishes the performance of each bookstore from that of the bookstore manager. **Required**
2. Evaluate the financial performance of each bookstore.
3. Evaluate the financial performance of each manager.

SOLUTION

1. See Exhibit 9-10.
2. The financial performances of the bookstores (that is, segments of the company) are best evaluated by the line "contribution by bookstore." Merlin's has a substantially

Exhibit 9-10

The Book & Game Company
Performance Report

Item	Total Company	Auntie's	Merlin's
Sales revenue	$700,000	$350,000	$350,000
Variable costs			
Cost of merchandise sold	450,000	225,000	225,000
Salaries and wages	36,000	18,000	18,000
Supplies	45,000	22,500	22,500
Total variable costs	531,000	265,500	265,500
Contribution margin by bookstore	169,000	84,500	84,500
Less: fixed costs controllable by			
bookstore managers			
Salaries and wages	27,000	12,000	15,000
Depreciation	15,000	7,000	8,000
Total controllable fixed costs	42,000	19,000	23,000
Contribution controllable by managers	127,000	65,500	61,500
Less: fixed costs controllable by others			
Rent and utilities	60,000	40,000	20,000
Contribution by bookstore	67,000	$ 25,500	$ 41,500
Unallocated costs	60,000		
Operating income	$ 7,000		

higher contribution, despite equal levels of sales revenues in the two stores. The major reason for this advantage is the lower rent and utilities paid by Merlin's.

3. The financial performance by managers is best judged by the line "contribution controllable by managers." By this measure, the performance of Auntie's manager is better than that of Merlin's. The contribution margin is the same for each store, but Merlin's manager paid $4,000 more in controllable fixed costs than did Auntie's manager. Of course, this decision could be beneficial in the long run. What is missing from each of these segment reports is the year's master budget and a flexible budget, which would be the best benchmark for evaluating both bookstore and bookstore manager.

Highlights to Remember

Describe the relationship of management control systems to organizational goals. The starting point for designing and evaluating a management control system is the identification of organizational goals as specified by top management.

Use responsibility accounting to define an organizational subunit as a cost center, a profit center, or an investment center. Responsibility accounting assigns particular revenue or cost objectives to the management of the subunit that has the greatest influence over them. Cost centers focus on costs only, profit centers on both revenues and costs, and investments center on profits relative to the amount invested.

Compare financial and nonfinancial performance, and explain why planning and control systems should consider both. Nonfinancial performance is as important as financial performance. In fact, nonfinancial performance usually leads to financial performance in time.

Explain the importance of evaluating performance and how it impacts motivation, goal congruence, and employee effort. The way performance is measured and evaluated affects individuals' behavior. The more rewards are tied to performance measures, the more incentive there is to improve the measures. Poorly designed or balanced measures may actually work against the organization's goals.

Prepare segment income statements for evaluating profit and investment centers using the contribution margin and controllable-cost concepts. The contribution approach to measuring a segment's income aids performance evaluation by separating a segment's costs into those controllable by the segment management and those beyond management's control.

Measure performance against quality, cycle time, and productivity objectives. Measuring performance in areas such as quality, cycle time, and productivity causes employees to direct attention to those areas.

Describe the difficulties of management control in service and nonprofit organizations. Management control in service and nonprofit organizations is difficult because of a number of factors, chief of which is a relative lack of clearly observable outcomes.

Understand how a management control system uses accounting information. A management control system uses management accounting tools such as budgets and performance reports to focus resources and talents of the individuals in an organization on such goals as quality, cost and service.

Accounting Vocabulary

balanced scorecard, p. 334
controllable cost, p. 337
cost center, p. 332
cost of quality report, p. 340
critical process, p. 330

cycle time, p. 344
goal congruence, p. 335
investment center, p. 332
key success factor, p. 330
key performance indicators, p. 334

management control system, p. 328
managerial effort, p. 336
motivation, p. 336
productivity, p. 345
profit center, p. 332

quality control, p. 340
quality-control chart, p. 343
responsibility accounting,
  p. 331

responsibility center,
  p. 331
segments, p. 337

total quality management
  (TQM), p. 342
uncontrollable cost, p. 337

Fundamental Assignment Material

9-A1 Responsibility of Purchasing Agent

GL Interiors, Inc., a privately held enterprise has a subcontract to produce overhead storage bins for a Boeing airplane. Although GL was a low bidder, Boeing was reluctant to award the business to GL, a newcomer to this kind of activity. Consequently, GL assured Boeing of its financial strength by submitting its audited financial statements. Moreover, GL agreed to a penalty clause of $5,000 per day to be paid by GL for each day of late delivery for whatever cause.

Leesa Martinson, the GL purchasing agent, is responsible for acquiring materials and parts in time to meet production schedules. She placed an order with a GL supplier for a critical manufactured component. The supplier, who had a reliable record for meeting schedules, gave Martinson an acceptable delivery date. Martinson checked up several times and was assured that the component would arrive at GL on schedule.

On the date specified by the supplier for shipment to GL, Martinson was informed that the component had been damaged during final inspection. It was delivered 10 days late. Martinson had allowed four extra days for possible delays, but GL was six days late in delivering to Boeing and so had to pay a penalty of $30,000.

Required   What department should bear the penalty? Why?

9-A2 Contribution Approach to Responsibility Accounting

Mile High Enterprises operates a small chain of convenience stores in Denver and Colorado Springs. The company's organization chart follows:

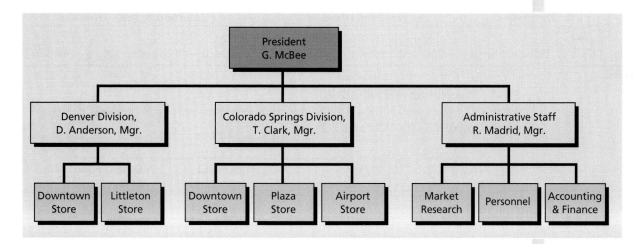

Mile High had the following financial results for 19X8 (in thousands):

Sales revenue	$6,000
Cost of merchandise sold	3,750
Gross margin	2,250
Operating expenses	1,650
Income before income taxes	$ 600

The following data about 19X8 operations were also available:

1. All five stores used the same pricing formula; therefore all had the same gross margin percentage.
2. Sales were largest in the two Downtown stores, with 30% of the total sales volume in each. The Plaza and Airport stores each provided 15% of total sales volume, and the Littleton store provided 10%.
3. Variable operating costs at the stores were 10% of revenue for the Downtown stores. The other stores had lower variable and higher fixed costs. Their variable operating costs were only 5% of sales revenue.
4. The fixed costs over which the store managers had control were $94,000 in each of the Downtown stores, $120,000 at Plaza and Airport, and $60,000 at Littleton.
5. The remaining $682,000 of operating costs consisted of
   a. $135,000 controllable by the Colorado Springs division manager, but not by individual stores
   b. $97,000 controllable by the Denver division manager, but not by individual stores
   c. $450,000 controllable by the administrative staff
6. Of the $450,000 spent by the administrative staff, $260,000 directly supported the Colorado Springs division, with 20% for the Downtown store, 30% for each of the Plaza and Airport stores, and 20% for Colorado Springs operations in general. Another $112,000 supported the Denver division, 50% for the Downtown store, 25% for the Littleton store, and 25% supporting Denver operations in general. The other $78,000 was for general corporate expenses.

Required Prepare an income statement by segments using the contribution approach to responsibility accounting. Use the format of Exhibit 9-5, page 339. Column headings should be

	Breakdown into Two Divisions		Breakdown of Denver Division			Breakdown of Colorado Springs Division			
Company as a Whole	Denver	Colorado Springs	Not allocated	Downtown	Littleton	Not allocated	Downtown	Plaza	Airport

9-A3 Comparison of Productivity

Lakeland Foods and National Food and Beverage are consumer products companies. Comparative data for 1992 and 1998 are

		Lakeland Foods	National Food and Beverage
Sales revenue	1992	$5,924,000,000	$7,658,000,000
	1998	$6,764,000,000	$9,667,000,000
Number of employees	1992	56,600	75,900
	1998	54,800	76,200

Assume that each 1992 dollar is equivalent to 1.2 1998 dollars, owing to inflation.

Required

1. Compute 1992 and 1998 productivity measures in terms of revenues per employee for Lakeland Foods and National Food and Beverage.
2. Compare the change in productivity between 1992 and 1998 for Lakeland Foods with that for National Food and Beverage.

9-B1 Responsibility Accounting

The LaCrosse Manufacturing Company produces precision machine parts. LaCrosse uses a standard cost system, calculates standard cost variances for each department, and reports them to department managers. Managers use the information to improve their operations. Superiors use the same information to evaluate managers' performance.

Roberta Dahl was recently appointed manager of the assembly department of the company. She has complained that the system as designed is disadvantageous to her department. Included among the variances charged to the departments is one for rejected units. The inspection occurs at the end of the assembly department. The inspectors attempt to identify the cause of the rejection so that the department where the error occurred can be charged with it. Not all errors can easily be identified with a department, however. The nonidentified units are totaled and apportioned to the departments according to the number of identified errors. The variance for rejected units in each department is a combination of the errors caused by the department plus a portion of the unidentified causes of rejects.

Required

1. Is Dahl's complaint valid? Explain the reason(s) for your answer.
2. What would you recommend that the company do to solve its problem with Dahl and her complaint?

9-B2 Divisional Contribution, Performance, and Segment Margins

The board of directors of Atlantic Coast Railroad wants to obtain an overview of the company's operations, particularly with respect to comparing freight and passenger business. The board chairman has heard about "contribution" approaches to cost allocations that emphasize cost behavior patterns and contribution margins, contributions controllable by segment managers, and contributions by segments. The board has hired you as a consultant to help them. They gave you the following information.

Total revenue in 19X8 was $80 million, of which $72 million was freight traffic and $8 million was passenger traffic. Fifty percent of the latter was generated by Division 1; 40% by Division 2; and 10% by Division 3.

Total variable costs were $45 million, of which $36 million was caused by freight traffic. Of the $9 million allocable to passenger traffic, $3.3, $2.8, and $2.9 million could be allocated to Divisions 1, 2, and 3, respectively.

Total separable discretionary fixed costs were $8 million, of which $7.6 million applied to freight traffic. Of the remainder, $80,000 could not be allocated to specific divisions, although it was clearly traceable to passenger traffic in general. Divisions 1, 2, and 3 should be allocated $240,000, $60,000, and $20,000, respectively.

Total separable committed costs, which were not regarded as being controllable by segment managers, were $25 million, of which 90% was allocable to freight traffic. Of the 10% traceable to passenger traffic, Divisions 1, 2, and 3 should be allocated $1.5 million, $350,000, and $150,000, respectively; the balance was unallocable to a specific division.

The common fixed costs not clearly allocable to any part of the company amounted to $750,000.

Required

1. The board asks you to prepare statements, dividing the data for the company as a whole between the freight and passenger traffic and then subdividing the passenger traffic into three divisions.
2. Some competing railroads actively promote a series of one-day sightseeing tours on summer weekends. Most often, these tours are timed so that the cars with the tourists are hitched on with regularly scheduled passenger trains. What costs are relevant for making decisions to run such tours? Other railroads, facing the same general cost picture, refuse to conduct such sightseeing tours. Why?
3. For purposes of this analysis, even though the numbers may be unrealistic, suppose that Division 2's figures represented a specific run for a train instead of a

division. Suppose further that the railroad has petitioned government authorities for permission to drop Division 2. What would be the effect on overall company net income for 19X9, assuming that the figures are accurate and that 19X9 operations are in all other respects a duplication of 19X8 operations?

9-B3   Quality Cost Report

Dayton Manufacturing Company makes a variety of auto parts. The company prepares monthly reports on quality costs. In early 19X8, Dayton's president asked you, the controller, to compare quality costs in 19X7 to those in 19X5. He wanted to see only total annual numbers for 19X7 compared with 19X5. You have prepared the report shown in Exhibit 9-11.

Required

1. For each of the four quality cost areas, explain what types of costs are included and how those costs have changed between 19X5 and 19X7.

2. Assess overall quality performance in 19X7 compared with 19X5. What do you suppose has caused the changes observed in quality costs?

Exhibit 9-11

Dayton Manufacturing Company
Quality Cost Report (thousands of dollars)

Quality Cost Area	19X5 Cost	19X7 Cost
1. Prevention cost	45	107
% of Total quality cost	3.3%	12.4%
2. Appraisal cost	124	132
% of Total quality cost	9.1%	15.2%
3. Internal failure cost	503	368
% of Total quality cost	36.9%	42.5%
Total internal quality cost (1 + 2 + 3)	672	607
% of Total quality cost	49.3%	70.1%
4. External failure cost	691	259
% of Total quality cost	50.7%	29.9%
Total quality cost	1,363	866
Total product cost	22,168	23,462

Additional Assignment Material

QUESTIONS

9-1. What are the purposes of a management control system?

9-2. "Goals are useless without performance measures." Do you agree? Explain.

9-3. "There are corporate objectives other than profit." Name three.

9-4. How does management determine its key success factors?

9-5. Give three examples of how managers may improve short-run performance to the detriment of long-run results.

9-6. Name three kinds of responsibility centers.

9-7. How do profit centers and investment centers differ?

9-8. "Performance evaluation seeks to achieve *goal congruence* and *managerial effort*." Describe what is meant by this statement.

9-9. Why do accountants need to consider behavioral factors when designing a management control system?

9-10. List five characteristics of a good performance measure.

9-11. "Managers of profit centers should be held responsible for the center's entire profit. They are responsible for profit even if they cannot control all factors affecting it." Discuss.

9-12. What is a balanced scorecard and why are more and more companies using one?

9-13. What are four nonfinancial measures of performance that managers find useful?

9-14. "Variable costs are controllable and fixed costs are uncontrollable." Do you agree? Explain.

9-15. "The contribution margin is the best measure of short-run performance." Do you agree? Explain.

9-16. Give four examples of segments.

9-17. "Always try to distinguish between the performance of a segment and its manager." Why?

9-18. "The contribution margin approach to performance evaluation is flawed because focusing on only the contribution margin ignores important aspects of performance." Do you agree? Explain.

9-19. There are four categories of cost in the quality cost report; explain them.

9-20. Why are companies increasing their quality control emphasis on the *prevention* of defects?

9-21. Discuss how quality, cycle time, and productivity are related.

9-22. "Nonfinancial measures of performance can be controlled just like financial measures." Do you agree? Explain.

9-23. Identify three measures of labor productivity, one using all physical measures, one using all financial measures, and one that mixes physical and financial measures.

9-24. Discuss the difficulties of comparing productivity measures over time.

9-25. "Control systems in nonprofit organizations will never be as highly developed as in profit-seeking organizations." Do you agree? Explain.

EXERCISES

9-26 Management Control Systems and Innovation

The president of a fast-growing high-technology firm remarked, "Developing budgets and comparing performance with the budgets may be fine for some firms. But we want to encourage innovations and entrepreneurship. Budgets go with bureaucracy, not innovation." Do you agree? How can a management control system encourage innovation and entrepreneurship?

9-27 Municipal Responsibility Accounting

In 1975 New York City barely avoided bankruptcy. By the 1990s it had one of the most sophisticated budgeting and reporting systems of any municipality, and its budgetary problems had nearly disappeared. The Integrated Financial Management System (IFMS), "clearly identifies managers in line agencies, and correlates allocations and expenditures with organizational structure. . . . In addition, managers have more time to take corrective measures when variances between budgeted and actual expenditures start to develop." (*FE—The Magazine for Financial Executives*, vol. 1, no. 8, p. 26.)

Discuss how a responsibility accounting system such as IFMS can help manage a municipality such as New York City.

9-28 Responsibility for Stable Employment Policy

The Sargent Metal Fabricating Company has been manufacturing machine tools for a number of years and has had an industrywide reputation for doing high-quality work. The company has been faced with irregularity of output over the years. It has been company policy to lay off welders as soon as there was insufficient work to keep them busy and to rehire them when demand warranted. The company, however, now has poor labor relations and finds it very difficult to hire good welders because of its layoff policy. Consequently, the quality of the work has been declining steadily.

The plant manager has proposed that the welders, who earn $20 per hour, be retained during slow periods to do menial plant maintenance work that is normally performed by workers earning $13 per hour in the plant maintenance department.

You, as controller, must decide the most appropriate accounting procedure to handle the wages of the welders doing plant maintenance work. What department(s) should be charged with this work, and at what rate? Discuss the implications of your plan.

9-29   Salesclerk's Compensation Plan

You are manager of a department store in Kyoto. Sales are subject to month-to-month variations, depending on the individual salesclerk's efforts. A new salary-plus-bonus plan has been in effect for four months, and you are reviewing a sales performance report. The plan provides for a base salary of ¥45,000 per month, a ¥58,000 bonus each month if the monthly sales quota is met, and an additional commission of 5% of all sales over the monthly quota. The quota is set approximately 3% above the previous month's sales to motivate clerks toward increasing sales (in thousands):

		Salesclerk A	Salesclerk B	Salesclerk C
January	Quota	¥4,500	¥1,500	¥7,500
	Actual	1,500	1,500	9,000
February	Quota	¥1,545	¥1,545	¥9,270
	Actual	3,000	1,545	3,000
March	Quota	¥3,090	¥1,590	¥3,090
	Actual	5,250	750	9,000
April	Quota	¥5,400	¥ 775	¥9,270
	Actual	1,500	780	4,050

Required

1. Compute the compensation for each salesclerk for each month.
2. Evaluate the compensation plan. Be specific. What changes would you recommend?

BUSINESS FIRST   www.prenhall.com/phlip

9-30   Goals and Objectives at Foundation Health Systems

Foundation Health Systems, Inc. (FHS) provides health care to more than five million members. As a managed health care organization, the company strives to provide high-quality health care at a reasonable cost. Many stakeholders have an interest in FHS's operations, including doctors and other medical personnel, patients, insurance companies, government regulators, and the general public.

Required

Prepare a goal and one measure for assessing achievement of that goal for each of the following key areas:

Customer satisfaction

Efficient use of lab tests

Usage of physician time

Maintain state-of-the-art facilities

Overall financial performance ■

9-31   Performance Evaluation

Lynch, Barney, and Schwab is a stock brokerage firm that evaluates its employees on sales activity generated. Recently the firm also began evaluating its stockbrokers on the number of new accounts generated.

Required

Discuss how these two performance measures are consistent and how they may conflict. Do you believe that these measures are appropriate for the long-term goal of profitability?

9-32   Quality Theories Compared

Sketch the two graphs as they appear below. Compare the total quality management approach to the traditional theory of quality. Which theory do you believe represents the current realities of today's global competitive environment? Explain.

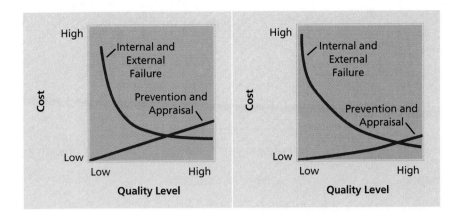

9-33 Quality Control Chart

Baffin Manufacturing Company was concerned about a growing number of defective units being produced. At one time the company had the percentage of defective units down to less than 50 per thousand, but recently rates of defects have been near, or even above, 1%. The company decided to graph its defects for the last eight weeks (40 working days), beginning Monday, September 1 through Friday, October 31. The graph is shown in Exhibit 9-12.

1. Identify two important trends evident in the quality control chart.
2. What might management of Baffin do to deal with each trend.

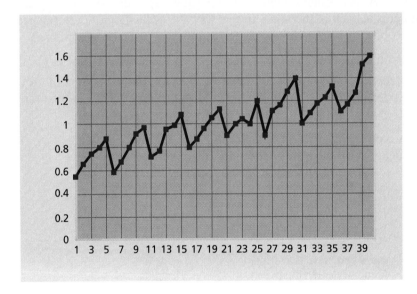

Exhibit 9-12

Baffin Manufacturing Company
Quality Control Chart for September 1 through October 31

9-34 Cycle-Time Reporting

Digital Processors, Inc., monitors its cycle time closely to prevent schedule delays and excessive costs. The standard cycle time for the manufacture of printed circuit boards for one of its computers is 26.4 hours. Consider the following cycle time data from the past six weeks of circuit board production:

Week	Units Completed	Total Cycle Time
1	564	14,108 hours
2	544	14,592
3	553	15,152
4	571	16,598
5	547	17,104
6	552	16,673

Required

Analyze circuit board cycle time performance in light of the 26.4-hour objective.

PROBLEMS

9-35 Multiple Goals and Profitability

The following multiple goals were identified by the General Electric company:

Profitability   Employee attitudes

Market position   Public responsibility

Productivity   Balance between short-range and

Product leadership   long-range goals

Personnel development

General Electric is a huge, highly decentralized corporation. At the time it developed these goals, GE had approximately 170 responsibility centers called "departments," but that is a deceiving term. In most other companies, these departments would be called divisions. For example, some GE departments had sales of more than $500 million.

Each department manager's performance is evaluated annually in relation to the specified multiple goals. A special measurements group was set up to devise ways of quantifying accomplishments in each of the areas. In this way, the evaluation of performance would become more objective as the various measures were developed and improved.

Required

1. How would you measure performance in each of these areas? Be specific.
2. Can the other goals be encompassed as ingredients of a formal measure of profitability? In other words, can profitability per se be defined to include the other goals?

9-36 Responsibility Accounting, Profit Centers, and Contribution Approach

Consider the following data for the year's operations of an automobile dealer:

Sales of vehicles	$2,600,000
Sales of parts and service	600,000
Cost of vehicle sales	2,120,000
Parts and service materials	180,000
Parts and service labor	240,000
Parts and service overhead	60,000
General dealership overhead	120,000
Advertising of vehicles	120,000
Sales commissions, vehicles	48,000
Sales salaries, vehicles	60,000

The president of the dealership has long regarded the markup on material and labor for the parts and service activity as the amount that is supposed to cover all parts and service overhead plus all general overhead of the dealership. In other words, the parts and service department is viewed as a cost-recovery operation, and the sales of vehicles as the income-producing activity.

Required

1. Prepare a departmentalized operating statement that harmonizes with the views of the president.

2. Prepare an alternative operating statement that would reflect a different view of the dealership operations. Assume that $15,000 and $60,000 of the $120,000 general overhead can be allocated with confidence to the parts and service department and to sales of vehicles, respectively. The remaining $45,000 cannot be allocated except in some highly arbitrary manner.

3. Comment on the relative merits of requirements 1 and 2.

9-37 Incentives in Former Soviet Union

Before the country's breakup, officials in what had been the Soviet Union had been rewarding managers for exceeding a five-year-plan target for production quantities. A problem arose, however, because managers naturally tended to predict low volumes so that the targets would be set low. This hindered planning; good information about production possibilities was lacking.

The Soviets then devised a new performance evaluation measure. Suppose F is the forecast of production, A is actual production, and X, Y, and Z are positive constants set by top officials, with $X, Y, Z > 0$. The following performance measure was designed to motivate both high production and accurate forecasts.

$$\text{performance} = \begin{cases} (Y \times F) + [X \times (A - F)] \text{ if } F \leq A \\ (Y \times F) - [Z \times (F - A)] \text{ if } F > A \end{cases}$$

Consider the Moscow Automotive Factory. During 19X6 the factory manager, Nicolai Konstantin, had to predict the number of automobiles that could be produced during the next year. He was confident that at least 700,000 autos could be produced in 19X7, and most likely they could produce 800,000 autos. With good luck, they might even produce 900,000. Government officials told him that the new performance evaluation measure would be used, and that $X = .50$, $Y = .80$, and $Z = 1.00$ for 1997 and 1998.

Required

1. Suppose Konstantin predicted production of 800,000 autos and 800,000 were produced. Calculate the performance measure.

2. Suppose again that 800,000 autos were produced. Calculate the performance measure if Konstantin had been conservative and predicted only 700,000 autos. Also calculate the performance measure if he had predicted 900,000 autos.

3. Now suppose it is November 19X7 and it is clear that the 800,000 target cannot be achieved. Does the performance measure motivate continued efforts to increase production? Suppose it is clear that the 800,000 target will be met easily. Will the system motivate continued effort to increase production?

9-38 Balanced Scorecard

Zenon Medical Instruments Company (ZMIC) recently revised its performance evaluation system. The company identified four major goals and several objectives required to meet each goal. Ruth Sanchez, controller of ZMIC, suggested that a balanced scorecard be used to report on progress toward meeting the objectives. At a recent meeting, she told the managers of ZMIC that listing the objectives was only the first step in installing a new performance measurement system. Each objective has to be accompanied by one or more measures to monitor progress toward achieving the objectives. She asked the help of the managers in identifying appropriate measures.

The goals and objectives determined by the top management of ZMIC are:

1. Maintain strong financial health
   a. Keep sufficient cash balances to assure financial survival
   b. Achieve consistent growth in sales and income
   c. Provide excellent returns to shareholders

2. Provide excellent service to customers
    a. Provide products that meet the needs of customers
    b. Meet customer needs on a timely basis
    c. Meet customer quality requirements
    d. Be the preferred supplier to customers
3. Be among the industry leaders in product and process innovations
    a. Bring new products to market before competition
    b. Lead competition in production process innovation
4. Develop and maintain efficient, state-of-the-art productions processes
    a. Excel in manufacturing efficiency
    b. Design products efficiently and quickly
    c. Meet or beat product introduction schedules

Required Propose at least one measure of performance for each of the objectives of ZMIC.

9-39 Productivity

Global Telecom, a U.S.-based international telephone communications company, purchased the controlling interest in Eurotel Corporation in an eastern European country. A key productivity measure monitored by Global Telecom is the number of customer telephone lines per employee. Consider the following data:

	19X6 without Eurotel	19X6 with Eurotel	19X5
Customer lines	15,054,000	19,994,000	14,315,000
Employees	74,520	114,590	70,866
Lines per employee	202	174	202

Required
1. What are Global Telecom's 19X5 productivity and its 19X6 productivity without Eurotel?
2. What are Global Telecom's 19X6 productivity with Eurotel and Eurotel's 19X6 productivity?
3. What difficulties do you foresee if Global Telecom brings Eurotel's productivity in line?

9-40 Productivity Measurement

Crystal Cleaners had the following results in 19X4 and 19X7:

	19X4	19X7
Pounds of laundry processed	680,000 pounds	762,000 pounds
Sales revenue	$360,000	$697,000
Direct-labor-hours worked	22,550 hours	23,325 hours
Direct-labor cost	$158,000	$249,000

Crystal used the same facilities in 19X7 as in 19X4. During the past 3 years, however, the company put more effort into training its employees. The manager of Crystal was curious about whether the training had increased labor productivity.

Required
1. Compute a measure of labor productivity for 19X7 based entirely on physical measures. Do the same for 19X4. That is, from the data given, choose measures of physical output and physical input, and use them to compare the physical productivity of labor in 19X7 with that in 19X4.
2. Compute a measure of labor productivity for 19X7 based entirely on financial measures. Do the same for 19X4. That is, from the data given, choose measures

of financial output and financial input, and use them to compare the financial productivity of labor in 19X7 with that in 19X4.

3. Suppose the following productivity measure were used:

$$\text{productivity} = \frac{\text{sales revenue}}{\text{direct labor hours worked}}$$

Because of inflation, each 19X4 dollar is equivalent to 1.4 19X7 dollars. Compute appropriate productivity numbers for comparing 19X7 productivity with 19X4 productivity.

CASES

9-41 Trade-Offs among Objectives

Computer Data Services (CDS) performs routine and custom information systems services for many companies in a large midwestern metropolitan area. CDS has built a reputation for high-quality customer service and job security for its employees. Quality service and customer satisfaction have been CDS's primary subgoals—retaining a skilled and motivated work force has been an important factor in achieving those goals. In the past, temporary downturns in business did not mean layoffs of employees, though some employees were required to perform other than their usual tasks. In anticipation of growth in business, CDS leased new equipment that, beginning in August, added $10,000 per month in operating costs. Three months ago, however, a new competitor began offering the same services to CDS customers at prices averaging 20% lower than those of CDS. Rico Estrada, the company founder and president, believes that a significant price reduction is necessary to maintain the company's market share and avoid financial ruin, but he is puzzled about how to achieve it without compromising quality, service, and the goodwill of his work force.

CDS has a productivity objective of 20 accounts per employee. Estrada does not think that he can increase this productivity and still maintain both quality and flexibility to customer needs. CDS also monitors average cost per account and the number of customer satisfaction adjustments (resolutions of complaints). The average billing markup rate is 25%. Consider the following data from the past six months:

	June	July	August	September	October	November
Number of accounts	797	803	869	784	723	680
Number of employees	40	41	44	43	43	41
Average cost per account	$153	$153	$158	$173	$187	$191
Average salary per employee	$3,000	$3,000	$3,000	$3,000	$3,000	$3,000

1. Discuss the trade-offs facing Rico Estrada.
2. Can you suggest solutions to his trade-off dilemma?

9-42 Review of Chapters 1–9

Ben Gleneagle, general manager of the Boulder Division of Colorado Enterprises, Inc., was preparing for a management meeting. His divisional controller gave him the following information:

1. The master budget for the fiscal year just ended on June 30, 19X8:

Sales (50,000 units of A and 70,000 units of B)	$850,000
Manufacturing cost of goods sold	670,000
Manufacturing margin	$180,000
Selling and administrative expenses	120,000
Operating income	$ 60,000

2. The standard variable manufacturing cost per unit:

	Product A		Product B	
Direct material	10 pieces @ $0.25	$2.50	5 pounds @ $0.10	$0.50
Direct labor	1 hour @ $3.00	3.00	.3 hours @ $2.50	0.75
Variable overhead	1 hour @ $2.00	2.00	.3 hours @ $2.50	0.75
		$7.50		$2.00

3. All budgeted selling and administrative expenses are common, fixed expenses; 60% are discretionary expenses.

4. The actual income statement for the fiscal year ended June 30, 19X8:

Sales (53,000 units of A and 64,000 units of B)	$850,000
Manufacturing cost of goods sold	685,200
Manufacturing margin	$164,800
Selling and administrative expenses	116,000
Operating income	$ 48,800

5. The budgeted sales prices for products A and B were $10 and $5, respectively. Actual sales prices equaled budgeted sales prices.

6. The schedule of the actual variable manufacturing cost of goods sold by product (actual quantities in parentheses):

Product A:	Material	$134,500	(538,000 pieces)
	Labor	156,350	(53,000 hours)
	Overhead	108,650	(53,000 hours)
Product B:	Material	38,400	(320,000 pounds)
	Labor	50,000	(20,000 hours)
	Overhead	50,000	(20,000 hours)
		$537,900	

7. Products A and B are manufactured in separate facilities. Of the budgeted fixed manufacturing cost, $130,000 is separable as follows: $45,000 to product A and $85,000 to product B. Ten percent of these separate costs are discretionary. All other budgeted fixed manufacturing expenses, separable and common, are committed.

8. There are no beginning or ending inventories.

During the upcoming management meeting it is quite likely that some of the information from your controller will be discussed. In anticipation you set out to prepare answers to possible questions.

Required

1. Determine the firm's budgeted break-even point in dollars, overall contribution-margin ratio, and contribution margins per unit by product.

2. Considering products A and B as segments of the firm, find the budgeted "contribution by segments" for each.

3. It is decided to allocate the budgeted selling and administrative expenses to the segments (in requirement 2) as follows: committed costs on the basis of budgeted unit sales mix and discretionary costs on the basis of actual unit sales mix. What are the final expense allocations? Briefly appraise the allocation method.

4. How would you respond to a proposal to base commissions to salespersons on the sales (revenue) value of orders received? Assume all salespersons have the opportunity to sell both products.

5. Determine the firm's actual "contribution margin" and "contribution controllable by segment managers" for the fiscal year ended June 30, 19X8. Assume no variances in committed fixed costs.

6. Determine the "sales-activity variance" for each product for the fiscal year ended June 30, 19X8.

7. Determine and identify all variances in variable manufacturing costs by product for the fiscal year ended June 30, 19X8.

COLLABORATIVE LEARNING EXERCISE

9-43 Goals, Objectives, and Performance Measures

There is increasing pressure on colleges and universities to develop measures of accountability. The objective is to specify goals and objectives and to develop measures to assess the achievement of those goals and objectives.

Form a group of four to six students to be a consulting team to the accounting department at your college or university. (If you are not using this book as part of a course in an accounting department, select any department at a local college or university.) Based on your collective knowledge of the department, its mission, and its activities, formulate a statement of goals for the department. From that statement, develop several specific objectives, each of which can be measured. Then develop one or more measures of performance for each objective.

An optional second step in this exercise is to meet with a faculty member from the department, and ask him or her to critique your objectives and measures. As a member of the department, do the objectives make sense? Are the proposed measures feasible, and will they correctly measure attainment of the objectives? Will they provide proper incentives to the faculty? If the department has created objectives and performance measures, compare them to those your group developed.

MANAGEMENT CONTROL IN DECENTRALIZED ORGANIZATIONS

The Niketown store in New York City is a well-known landmark. Just say "Niketown" to a cab driver—it is just like saying "airport."

Learning Objectives

When you have finished studying this chapter, you should be able to

1 *Define decentralization and identify its expected benefits and costs.*

2 *Distinguish between profit centers and decentralization.*

3 *Define transfer prices and identify their purpose.*

4 *Identify the relative advantages and disadvantages of basing transfer prices on total costs, variable costs, and market prices.*

5 *Identify the factors affecting multinational transfer prices.*

6 *Explain how the linking of rewards to responsibility center results affects incentives and risk.*

7 *Compute ROI, residual income, and economic value added (EVA) and contrast them as criteria for judging the performance of organization segments.*

8 *Compare the advantages and disadvantages of various bases for measuring the invested capital used by organization segments.*

9 **Understand the role of management control systems in decentralized organizations.**

Philip Knight, chief executive officer of Nike, tells a story. Recently, one of Nike's officers was in New York City and managed to get a cab with a driver who did not speak English (not that difficult in New York). He made several attempts at making his directions understood, all without success. Then he asked, "Where's NIKETOWN?" Clearly, as if he had just graduated from speech class, the driver said: "NIKETOWN! 57th and Fifth!"

From 1986 to 1997, Nike's revenues increased from $1 billion to more than $9 billion. During this same period, the percentage of revenues from outside the United States increased from 25% to 40%. Global apparel sales account for more than one-third of Nike's revenue. A sampling of endorsements (promotional contracts with famous sports teams, individuals, and organizations) gives another perspective of the company's global presence: Michael Jordan, the Italian National Soccer team, German tennis star Michael Stich, golf star Tiger Woods—in fact, watch almost any sports event on television and you are likely to see the Nike Swoosh logo.

Nike made a conscious decision to go global—a ten-year process that is now generating substantial financial rewards. What are some of the keys to success when a company such as Nike decides to significantly expand its operations abroad? One critical element is understanding the relevance of the brand to local markets. Nike has gained this understanding by delegating management decision making to the local market level.

For example, the decision to sign an endorsement contract with world champion race car driver Michael Schumacher was made at the local level in Germany. According to Philip Knight, "Five years ago it would have taken a move from within the company headquarters to strike such a deal.... But this time it was a decision made in country." The local German manager knew that Schumacher was extremely relevant to the German market and that this would be a "profit driven, culturally significant, and brand enhancing move." Knight credits this move toward decentralization for Nike's 36% increase in international sales. "It is a great example of what we are trying to do: Make decisions on the ground in faraway places."

As organizations like Nike grow and undertake more diverse and complex activities, many elect to delegate decision-making authority to managers throughout the organization. This delegation of the freedom to make decisions is called **decentralization.** The lower in the organization that this freedom exists, the greater the decentralization. Decentralization is a matter of degree along a continuum:

decentralization The delegation of freedom to make decisions. The lower in the organization that this freedom exists, the greater the decentralization.

This chapter focuses on the role of management control systems in decentralized organizations. After providing an overview of decentralization, the chapter addresses the special problems created when one segment of an organization charges another for providing goods or services. Then it discusses how performance measures can be used to motivate managers. Finally, measures used to assess the profitability of decentralized units are introduced and compared.

Increasing sophistication of telecommunications—especially e-mail and fax machines—aids decentralization. Geographical separation no longer must mean lack of access to information. Both sales and production units are being relocated far from headquarters without top management losing knowledge of what is happening in the units.

CENTRALIZATION VERSUS DECENTRALIZATION

Decentralization is not right for every firm. Consider the international airline industry in the mid-1990s. Most airlines, such as South China Airlines, Iberia Airlines, and Air France, were decentralizing. In contrast, at the same time, Sabena, Belgium's state-owned airline, was reorganizing to reverse its trend toward decentralization. In the insurance industry, Aetna was decentralizing at the same time Equitable was centralizing. Let's take a look at some of the reasons why companies choose to (or not to) decentralize.

COSTS AND BENEFITS

There are many benefits of at least some decentralization for most organizations. First, lower-level managers have the best information concerning local conditions and therefore may be able to make better decisions than their superiors. Second, decentralization gives managers decision-making ability and other management skills that help them move upward in the organization, ensuring continuity of leadership. In addition, managers enjoy higher status from being independent and thus are better motivated.

Objective 1
Define decentralization and identify its expected benefits and costs.

Of course, decentralization has its costs. Managers may make decisions that are not in the organization's best interests, either because they act to improve their own segment's performance at the expense of the organization or because they are not aware of relevant facts from other segments. Managers in decentralized organizations also tend to duplicate services that might be less expensive if centralized (e.g., accounting, advertising, and personnel). Furthermore, under decentralization, costs of accumulating and processing information frequently rise because responsibility accounting reports are needed for top management to learn about and evaluate decentralized units and their managers. Finally, managers in decentralized units may waste time negotiating with other units about goods or services one unit provides to the other.

Decentralization is more popular in profit-seeking organizations—where outputs and inputs can be measured—than it is in nonprofit organizations. Managers can be given more freedom when the results of their decisions are measurable so that they can be held accountable for them. Poor decisions in a profit-seeking firm become apparent from the inadequate profit generated. Most nonprofit organizations lack such a reliable performance measure, so granting their managers freedom is more risky.

MIDDLE GROUND

Philosophies of decentralization differ considerably. Cost-benefit considerations usually require that some management decisions be highly decentralized and others centralized. To illustrate, much of the controller's problem-solving and attention-directing functions may be decentralized and handled at lower levels, whereas income tax planning and mass scorekeeping such as payroll may be highly centralized.

Decentralization in the 1990s

Many companies moved to decentralize their operations in one way or another during the 1990s, among them PepsiCo, DuPont, and Procter & Gamble. But one company that stood out in its efforts to decentralize was Johnson & Johnson.

Johnson & Johnson (1997 sales of $20 billion, 87,000 employees, and operations in 50 countries), maker of Tylenol, Band Aids, Johnson's Baby Powder, PEPCID AC, and many other products, has a long history of decentralization, beginning in the 1930s. Its 166 companies are empowered to act independently. Although ultimately accountable to executives at J & J headquarters in New Brunswick, New Jersey, some segment presidents see their bosses as few as four times a year. An article in *Business Week* called J & J "a model of how to make decentralization work." CEO Ralph Larson says that decentralization "provides a sense of ownership and responsibility for a business that you simply cannot get any other way." Larson sees his role as providing direction but giving managers creative freedom. J & J spent the early 1990s fine-tuning its decentralized system to erase costly mistakes that could have been avoided with more guidance from top management. Also, J & J had incurred high overhead costs as independent units duplicated many functions. Larson introduced methods of coordinating the independent units while still preserving the basics of decentralization. Although perhaps toning down the degree of decentralization, Larson vows that J & J "will never give up the principle of decentralization, which is to give our operating executives ownership of a business. They are ultimately responsible."

Source: Adapted from "A Big Company That Works," *Business Week*, May 4, 1992, pp. 124–130.

Decentralization is most successful when an organization's segments are relatively independent of one another—that is, the decisions of a manager in one segment will not affect the fortunes of another segment. If segments do much internal buying or selling, much buying from the same outside suppliers, or much selling to the same outside markets, they are candidates for heavier centralization.

In Chapter 9, we stressed that cost-benefit tests, goal congruence, and managerial effort must all be considered when designing a control system. If management has decided in favor of heavy decentralization, **segment autonomy,** the delegation of decision-making power to managers of segments of an organization, is also crucial. For decentralization to work, however, this autonomy must be real, not just lip service. In most circumstances, top managers must be willing to abide by decisions made by segment managers.

segment autonomy The delegation of decision-making power to managers of segments of an organization.

PROFIT CENTERS AND DECENTRALIZATION

Objective 2
Distinguish between profit centers and decentralization.

Do not confuse profit centers (accountability for revenue and expenses) with decentralization (freedom to make decisions). They are entirely separate concepts. Although profit centers can aid decentralization, one can exist without the other. Some profit center managers possess vast freedom to make decisions concerning labor contracts, supplier choices, equipment purchases, personnel decisions, and so on. In contrast, other profit center managers may need top-management approval for almost all the decisions just mentioned. Indeed, cost centers may be more heavily decentralized than profit centers if cost center managers have more freedom to make decisions.

The literature contains many criticisms of profit centers on the grounds that managers are given profit responsibility without commensurate authority. Therefore, the criticism continues, the profit center is "artificial" because the manager is not free to make a sufficient number of the decisions that affect profit.

Such criticisms confuse profit centers and decentralization. The fundamental question in deciding between using a cost center or a profit center for a given segment is not whether heavy decentralization exists. Instead, the fundamental question is: Will a profit center better solve the problems of goal congruence and management effort than a cost center? In other words, do I predict that a profit center will induce the managers to make a better collective set of decisions from the viewpoint of the organization as a whole?

All control systems are imperfect. Judgments about their merits should concentrate on which alternative system will bring more of the actions top management seeks. For example, a plant may seem to be a "natural" cost center because the plant manager has no influence over decisions concerning the marketing of its products. Still, some companies evaluate a plant manager by the plant's profitability. Why? Because this broader evaluation base will affect the plant manager's behavior. Instead of being concerned solely with running an efficient cost center, the plant manager now "naturally" considers quality control more carefully and reacts to customers' special requests more sympathetically. A profit center may thus obtain the desired plant-manager behavior that a cost center cannot. In designing accounting control systems, top managers must consider the system's impact on behavior desired by the organization.

TRANSFER PRICING

Objective 3
Define transfer prices and identify their purpose.

Very few problems arise in decentralized organizations when all the segments are independent of one another. Segment managers can then focus only on their own segments without hurting the organization as a whole. In contrast, when segments interact greatly, there is an increased possibility that what is best for one segment hurts another segment badly enough to have a negative effect on the entire organization. Such a situation may occur when one segment provides products or services to another segment and charges that segment a transfer price. **Transfer prices** are the amounts charged by one segment of an organization for a product or service that it supplies to another segment of the same organization. Most often, the term is associated with materials, parts, or finished goods. The transfer price is revenue to the segment producing the product or service, and it is a cost to the acquiring segment.

transfer price The amount charged by one segment of an organization for a product or service that it supplies to another segment of the same organization.

PURPOSES OF TRANSFER PRICING

Why do transfer-pricing systems exist? The principal reason is to communicate data that will lead to goal-congruent decisions. For example, transfer prices should guide managers to make the best possible decisions regarding whether to buy or sell products and services inside or outside the total organization. Another important reason is to evaluate segment performance and thus motivate both the selling manager and the buying manager toward goal-congruent decisions. Finally, multinational companies use transfer pricing to minimize their worldwide taxes, duties, and tariffs. These are easy goals to describe, but they are difficult goals to achieve.

Organizations solve their problems by using cost-based prices for some transfers, market-based prices for other transfers, and negotiated prices for others. Therefore, do not expect to obtain a single, universally applicable answer in the area of transfer pricing. It is a subject of continuous concern to top management. Whenever there is a lull in a conversation with a manager, try asking, "Do you have any transfer-pricing problems?" The response is usually, "Let me tell you about the peculiar transfer-pricing difficulties in my organization." A manager in a large wood products firm called transfer pricing his firm's most troublesome management control issue.

TRANSFERS AT COST

About half of the major companies in the world transfer items at cost. However, there are many possible definitions of cost. Some companies use only variable cost, others use full cost, and still others use full cost plus a profit markup. Some use standard costs and some use actual costs.

When the transfer price is some version of cost, transfer pricing is nearly identical to cost allocation (see Chapters 4 and 12). Costs are accumulated in one segment and then assigned to (or transferred to) another segment. Details of this process are covered in Chapter 12, but two important points deserve mention here.

First, transferring or allocating costs can disguise a cost's behavior pattern. Consider a computer manufacturer, such as Apple, that makes keyboards in one division and transfers them to another division for assembly into personal computers. The manager of the Keyboard Division may have good knowledge of the cost drivers affecting the costs of keyboards. But if a single transfer price per unit is charged when transferring the keyboards to the Assembly Division, the only cost driver affecting the cost to the Assembly Division is "units of keyboards." Cost drivers other than units produced are ignored, and distinctions between fixed and variable costs are blurred. The Assembly Division manager sees the entire cost of keyboards as a variable cost, regardless of what the true cost behavior is.

Other problems arise if actual cost is used as a transfer price. Because actual cost cannot be known in advance, the buying segment will not be able to plan its costs. More important, because a transfer price based on actual costs merely passes cost inefficiencies along to the buying division, the supplying division lacks incentive to control its costs. Thus, using budgeted or standard costs instead of actual costs is recommended for both cost allocation and transfer pricing.

Objective 4
Identify the relative advantages and disadvantages of basing transfer prices on total costs, variable costs, and market prices.

Teva Pharmaceutical Industries Ltd. is a worldwide manufacturer of proprietary drugs. It is headquartered in Israel and had 1996 sales of $954 million. Teva entered the lucrative generic drug market in the mid-1980s. As part of its strategy, the company decentralized its pharmaceutical business into cost and profit centers as shown below.

Each of the marketing divisions purchases generic drugs from the manufacturing division. Prior to decentralization, each marketing division was a revenue center. With the new organizational structure, management had to decide how to measure marketing division costs because profits were now the key financial performance measure.

A key cost to the marketing divisions is the transfer price paid for drugs purchased from the manufacturing division. Management considered several alternative bases for the company's transfer prices. Market price was rejected because there was not a ready market. Negotiated price was rejected because management believed that the resulting debates over the proper price would be lengthy and disruptive. Variable cost (raw material and packaging costs) was adopted for a short time. Eventually, however, it was rejected because it did not lead to congruent decisions—products using many scarce resources were not differentiated from those using few. Further, when a local source for the drug did exist, the market price was always above the variable-cost transfer price. Thus, managers in Teva's manufacturing division had little incentive to keep costs low.

Full cost was rejected because the traditional costing system did not capture the actual cost structure of the manufacturing division. Specifically, the system undercosted the low volume products and overcosted the large volume products. The system traced only raw materials directly to products. The remaining manufacturing costs were divided into two cost pools and allocated based on labor hours and machine hours. One problem with the traditional system was its inability to capture and correctly allocate the non-value-added cost of setup activity. The size of the errors in product cost was not known, but the lack of confidence in the traditional cost system led to full cost being rejected as the transfer-price base.

Teva's management adopted an activity-based costing system to improve the accuracy of its product costs.

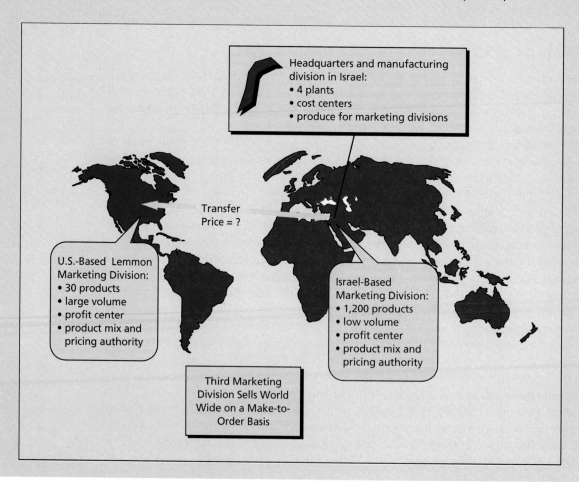

The ABC system has five activity centers and related cost pools: receiving, manufacturing, packaging, quality assurance, and shipping. Because of the dramatic increase in costing accuracy, management was able to adopt full activity-based cost as the transfer price.

Teva's managers are pleased with their transfer pricing system. The benefits include increased confidence that the costs being transferred are closely aligned with the actual short- and long-run costs being incurred, increased communication between divisions, and an increased awareness of the costs of low-volume products and the costs of capacity required to support these products.

Source: Adapted from Robert Kaplan, Dan Weiss, and Eyal Desheh, "Transfer Pricing with ABC," *Management Accounting*, May, 1997, pp. 20–28.

MARKET-BASED TRANSFER PRICES

If there is a competitive market for the product or service being transferred internally, using the market price as a transfer price will generally lead to the desired goal congruence and managerial effort. The market price may come from published price lists for similar products or services, or it may be the price charged by the producing division to its external customers. If the latter, the internal transfer price may be the external market price less the selling and delivery expenses that are not incurred on internal business. The major drawback to market-based prices is that market prices are not always available for items transferred internally.

Consider Outdoor Equipment Company, Inc. (OEC), a major outdoor equipment manufacturer that makes clothing and gear for all kinds of outdoor activities. One division of OEC makes fabrics that are used in many final products as well as being sold directly to external customers, and another division makes tents. A particular tent requires five square yards of a special waterproof fabric. Should the Tent Division obtain the fabric from the Fabric Division of the company or purchase it from an external supplier?

Suppose the market price of the fabric is $10 per square yard, or $50 per tent, and assume for the moment that the Fabric Division can sell its entire production to external customers without incurring any marketing or shipping costs. The Tent Division manager will refuse to pay a transfer price greater than $50 for the fabric for each tent. Why? Because if the transfer price is greater than $50, she will purchase the fabric from the external supplier in order to maximize her division's profit.

Furthermore, the manager of the Fabric Division will not sell five square yards of fabric for less than $50. Why? Because he can sell it on the market for $50, so any lower price will reduce his division's profit. The only transfer price that allows both managers to maximize their division's profit is $50, the market price. If the managers had autonomy to make decisions, one of them would decline the internal production of fabric at any transfer price other than $50.

Now suppose the Fabric Division incurs a $1 per square yard marketing and shipping cost that can be avoided by transferring the fabric to the Tent Division instead of marketing it to outside customers. Most companies would then use a transfer price of $9 per square yard, or $45 per tent, often called a "market-price-minus" transfer price. The Fabric Division would get the same net amount from the transfer ($45 with no marketing or shipping costs) as from an external sale ($50 less $5 marketing and shipping costs), whereas the Tent Division saves $5 per tent. Thus OEC overall benefits.

VARIABLE-COST PRICING

Market prices have innate appeal in a profit-center context, but they are not cure-all answers to transfer-pricing problems. Sometimes market prices do not exist, are inapplicable, or are impossible to determine. For example, no intermediate markets may exist for specialized

Exhibit 10-1

Data for Analysis of Transfer Prices

Sell Fabric Outside		Use Fabric to Make Tent			
Market price per yard of fabric to outsiders	$10	Sales price of finished tent			$100
Variable costs per yard of fabric	8	Variable costs: Fabric Division			
Contribution margin per yard	$ 2	(5 yds @ $8) Tent Division		$40	
Total contribution for 50,000 yards	$100,000	Processing	$41		
		Selling	12	53	93
		Contribution margin			$ 7
		Total contribution for 10,000 tents			$70,000

parts, or markets may be too thin or scattered to permit the determination of a credible price. When market prices cannot be used, versions of "cost-plus-a-profit" are often used as a fair substitute. To illustrate, consider Outdoor Equipment Company again. Exhibit 10-1 shows its selling prices and variable costs per unit. In this example, the Fabric Division's variable costs of $8 per yard are the only costs affected by producing the additional fabric for transfer to the Tent Division. On receiving five yards of fabric, the Tent Division spends an additional $53 to process and sell each tent. Whether the fabric should be manufactured and transferred to the Tent Division depends on the existence of idle capacity in the Fabric Division (insufficient demand from outside customers).

As Exhibit 10-1 shows, if there were no idle capacity in the Fabric Division, the optimum action for the company as a whole would be for the Fabric Division to sell outside at $50, because the Tent Division would incur $53 of additional variable costs but add only $50 of additional revenue ($100 − $50). Using market price would provide the correct motivation for such a decision because, if the fabric were transferred, the Tent Division's cost would be $50 + $53 or $103, which would be $3 higher than its prospective revenue of $100 per unit. So the Tent Division would choose not to buy from the Fabric Division at the $50 market price. Of course, the Tent Division also would not buy from outside suppliers at a price of $50. If fabric is not available at less than $50 per tent, this particular tent will not be produced.

What if the Fabric Division has idle capacity sufficient to meet all the Tent Division's requirements? The optimum action would be to produce the fabric and transfer it to the Tent Division. Idle capacity implies that the Fabric Division could not sell the fabric to external customers and therefore would have zero contribution. If there were no production and transfer, the Tent Division and the company as a whole would forgo a total contribution of $70,000. In this situation, variable cost would be the better basis for transfer pricing and would lead to the optimum decision for the firm as a whole. To be more precise, the transfer price would be all additional costs that will be incurred by the production of the fabric to be transferred. For example, if a lump-sum setup cost is required to produce the 50,000 square yards of fabric required, the setup cost should be added to the variable cost in calculating the appropriate transfer price. (In the example there is no such cost.)

NEGOTIATED TRANSFER PRICES

Companies heavily committed to segment autonomy often allow managers to negotiate transfer prices. The managers may consider both costs and market prices in their negotiations, but no policy requires them to do so. Supporters of negotiated transfer prices maintain that the managers involved have the best knowledge of what the company will gain or lose by producing and transferring the product or service, so open negotiation allows the managers to make optimal decisions. Critics of negotiated prices focus on the time and effort spent negotiating, an activity that adds nothing directly to the profits of the company.

DYSFUNCTIONAL BEHAVIOR

Virtually any type of transfer pricing policy can lead to **dysfunctional behavior**—actions taken in conflict with organizational goals. Gulf Oil provides a clear example. Segments tried to make their results look good at each other's expense. One widespread result: inflated transfer payments among the Gulf segments as each one vied to boost its own bottom line. A top manager, recognizing the problem, was quoted in *Business Week,* "Gulf doesn't ring the cash register until we've made an outside sale."

dysfunctional behavior
Any action taken in conflict with organizational goals.

What prompts such behavior? Reconsider the situation shown in Exhibit 10-1. Suppose the Fabric Division has idle capacity. As we saw earlier, when there is idle capacity, the optimal transfer price is the variable cost of $40 (that is, $8 per yard). As long as the fabric is worth at least $40 to the Tent Division, the company as a whole is better off with the transfer. Nevertheless, in a decentralized company the Fabric Division manager, working in the division's best interests, may argue that the transfer price should be based on the market price instead of variable cost. If the division is a profit center, its objective is to obtain as high a price as possible because such a price maximizes the contribution to the division's profit. (This strategy assumes that the number of units transferred will be unaffected by the transfer price—an assumption that is often shaky.)

If the company uses a market-based transfer-pricing policy when the Fabric Division has idle capacity, dysfunctional behavior can occur. At a $50 transfer price, the Tent Division manager will not purchase the fabric and make the tent. Why? Because at a transfer price of $50 and with additional processing costs of $53, the division's cost of $103 will exceed the tent's $100 selling price. Because the true additional cost of the fabric to the company is $40, the company forgoes a contribution of $100 − ($40 + $53) = $7 per tent.

Now suppose the Fabric Division has no idle capacity. A variable-cost transfer-pricing policy can lead to dysfunctional decisions. The Tent Division manager might argue for a variable-cost-based transfer price. After all, the lowest possible transfer price will maximize the Tent Division's profit. But such a policy will not motivate the Fabric Division to produce fabric for the Tent Division. As long as output can be sold on the outside market for any price above the variable cost, the Fabric Division will use its capacity to produce for the market, regardless of how valuable the fabric might be to the Tent Division.

How are such dilemmas resolved? One possibility is for top management to impose a "fair" transfer price and insist that a transfer be made. But managers in a decentralized company often regard such orders as undermining their autonomy.

Alternatively, managers might be given the freedom to negotiate transfer prices on their own. The Tent Division manager might look at the selling price of the tent, $100, less the additional cost the division incurs in making it, $53, and decide to purchase fabric at any transfer price less than $100 − $53 = $47. The Tent Division will add to its profit by making the tent if the transfer price is below $47.

Similarly, the Fabric Division manager will look at what it costs to produce and transfer the fabric. If there is idle capacity, any transfer price above $40 will increase the Fabric Division's profit. However, if there is no idle capacity, so that transferring a unit causes the division to give up an external sale at $50, the minimum transfer price acceptable to the Fabric Division is $50.

Negotiation will result in a transfer if the maximum transfer price the Tent Division is willing to pay is greater than the minimum transfer price the Fabric Division is willing to accept. When the Fabric Division has idle capacity, a transfer at a price between $40 and $47 will occur. The exact transfer price may depend on the negotiating ability of the two division managers. However, if the Fabric Division has no idle capacity, a transfer will not occur. Therefore, the manager's decisions are congruent with the company's best interests.

What should top management of a decentralized organization do if it sees segment managers making dysfunctional decisions? As usual, the answer is, "It depends." Top management can step in and force transfers, but doing so undermines segment managers' autonomy and the overall notion of decentralization. Frequent intervention results in recentralization. Indeed, if more centralization is desired, the organization could be redesigned by combining segments.

Top managers who wish to encourage decentralization will often make sure that both producing and purchasing division managers understand all the facts and then allow the managers to negotiate a transfer price. Even when top managers suspect that a dysfunctional decision might be made, they may swallow hard and accept the segment manager's judgment as a cost of decentralization. (Of course, repeated dysfunctional decision making may be a reason to change the organizational design or to change managers.)

Well-trained and informed segment managers who understand opportunity costs and fixed and variable costs will often make better decisions than will top managers. The producing division manager knows best the various uses of its capacity, and the purchasing division manager knows best what profit can be made on the items to be transferred. In addition, negotiation allows segments to respond flexibly to changing market conditions when setting transfer prices. One transfer price may be appropriate in a time of idle capacity, and another when demand increases and operations approach full capacity.

To increase segment managers' willingness to accommodate one another's needs and benefit the organization as a whole, top managers rely on both formal and informal communications. They may informally ask segment managers to be "good company citizens" and to sacrifice results for the good of the organization. They may also formalize this communication by basing performance evaluation and rewards on companywide as well as segment results. In the case of our outdoor equipment maker, the contribution to the company as a whole, $70,000 in the idle capacity case, could be split between the Fabric and Tent Divisions, perhaps equally, perhaps in proportion to the variable costs of each, or perhaps via negotiation.

THE NEED FOR MANY TRANSFER PRICES

As you can see, there is seldom a single transfer price that will ensure the desired decisions. The "correct" transfer price depends on the economic and legal circumstances and the decision at hand. Organizations may have to make trade-offs between pricing for congruence and pricing to spur managerial effort. Furthermore, the optimal price for either may differ from that employed for tax reporting or for other external needs.

Income taxes, property taxes, and tariffs often influence the setting of transfer prices so that the firm as a whole will benefit, even though the performance of a segment may suffer. For example, to maximize tax deductions for percentage depletion allowances, which are based on revenue, a petroleum company may want to transfer crude oil to other segments at as high a price as legally possible.

Transfer pricing is also influenced in some situations by state fair-trade laws and national antitrust acts. Because of the differences in national tax structures around the world, or because of the differences in the incomes of various divisions and subsidiaries, the firm may wish to shift profits and "dump" goods, if legally possible. These considerations further illustrate the limits of decentralization where heavy interdependencies exist and explain why the same company may use different transfer prices for different purposes.

Objective 5
Identify the factors affecting multinational transfer prices.

MULTINATIONAL TRANSFER PRICING

Transfer-pricing policies of domestic companies focus on goal congruence and motivation. In multinational companies, other factors may dominate. For example, multinational companies use transfer prices to minimize worldwide income taxes, import duties, and tariffs.

Suppose a division in a high-income-tax-rate country produces a subcomponent for another division in a low-income-tax-rate country. By setting a low transfer price, most of the profit from the production can be recognized in the low-income-tax-rate country, thereby minimizing taxes. Likewise, items produced by divisions in a low-income-tax-rate country and transferred to a division in a high-income-tax-rate country should have a high transfer price to minimize taxes.

Sometimes income tax effects are offset by import duties. Usually import duties are based on the price paid for an item, whether bought from an outside company or transferred from another division. Therefore low transfer prices generally lead to low import duties.

Of course, tax authorities recognize the incentive to set transfer prices to minimize taxes and import duties. Therefore most countries have restrictions on allowable transfer prices. U.S. multinationals must follow an Internal Revenue Code rule specifying that transfers be priced at "arm's-length" market values, or at the values that would be used if the divisions were independent companies. Even with this rule, companies have some latitude in deciding an appropriate "arm's-length" price.

Consider an item produced by Division A in a country with a 25% income tax rate and transferred to Division B in a country with a 50% income tax rate. In addition, an import duty equal to 20% of the price of the item is assessed. Suppose the full unit cost of the item is $100, and the variable cost is $60. If tax authorities allow either variable- or full-cost transfer prices, which should be chosen? By transferring at $100 rather than $60, the company gains $2 per unit:

Effect of Transferring at $100 Instead of at $60	
Income of A is $40 higher; therefore A pays 25% × $40 more income taxes	$(10)
Income of B is $40 lower; therefore B pays 50% × $40 less income taxes	20
Import duty is paid by B on an additional $100 − $60 = $40; therefore B pays 20% × $40 more duty	(8)
Net savings from transferring at $100 instead of $60	$ 2

Companies may also use transfer prices to avoid financial restrictions imposed by some governments. For example, a country might restrict the amount of dividends paid to foreign owners. It may be easier for a company to get cash from a foreign division as payment for items transferred than as cash dividends.

In summary, transfer pricing is more complex in a multinational company than it is in a domestic company. Multinational companies have more objectives to be achieved through transfer-pricing policies, and some of the objectives often conflict with one another.

PERFORMANCE MEASURES AND MANAGEMENT CONTROL

Transfer pricing affects segment profit, thereby affecting the performance measures of profit centers. This section looks more generally at how performance measures affect managers' incentives.

MOTIVATION, PERFORMANCE, AND REWARDS

Exhibit 10-2 shows the criteria and choices faced by top management when designing a management control system. Using the criterion of cost-benefit and the motivational criteria of congruence and effort, top management chooses responsibility centers (for example,

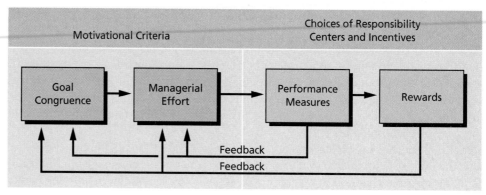

Exhibit 10-2

Criteria and Choices when Designing a Management Control System

incentives Those formal and informal performance-based rewards that enhance managerial effort toward organizational goals.

cost center versus profit center), performance measures, and rewards. **Incentives** are defined as those informal and formal performance-based rewards that enhance managerial effort toward organizational goals. For example, how the $70,000 contribution in Exhibit 10-1 is split between the Fabric and Tent Divisions affects the measures of their performance. In turn, the performance measures may affect the managers' rewards.

Numerous performance measurement choices have been described in this book, such as whether to use tight or loose standards, whether to measure divisional performance by contribution margins or operating incomes, and whether to use both financial and nonfinancial measures of performance. Research on rewards has yielded a basic principle that is simple and important: Managers tend to focus their efforts in areas where performance is measured and where performance affects rewards. Research shows that the more objective the measures of performance, the more likely the manager will provide effort. Thus accounting measures, which provide relatively objective evaluations of performance, are important. Moreover, if individuals believe there is no connection between their behavior and their measure of performance, they will not see how to alter their performance to affect their rewards.

Objective 6
Explain how the linking of rewards to responsibility center results affects incentives and risk.

The choice of rewards clearly belongs with an overall system of management control. Rewards may be both monetary and nonmonetary. Examples include pay raises, bonuses, promotion, praise, self-satisfaction, elaborate offices, and private dining rooms. However, the design of a reward system is mainly the concern of top managers, who frequently get advice from many sources besides accountants.

AGENCY THEORY, PERFORMANCE, REWARDS, AND RISK

Linking rewards to performance is desirable. But often a manager's performance cannot be measured directly. For example, responsibility center results may be measured easily, but a manager's effect on those results (that is, managerial performance) may not. Ideally, rewards should be based on managerial performance, but in practice the rewards usually depend on the financial results in the manager's responsibility center. Managerial performance and responsibility center results are certainly related, but factors beyond a manager's control also affect results. The greater the influence of noncontrollable factors on responsibility center results, the more problems there are in using the results to represent a manager's performance. For example, the profits of a regional distribution center of Airborne Express increased dramatically in 1997. Which of the following factors that contributed to the increase in profit were controllable by the regional manager?

- A lengthy strike by workers of a competitor (UPS) resulted in many former UPS customers switching to Airborne.

- The regional center implemented a new cost management system resulting in a significant reduction in the costs of handling packages.
- Overall population growth in the region has been much higher than has been the average for the entire Airborne system.
- Fuel costs in the region have not increased as much as in the system overall.
- Employee turnover is lower than is the system average. Employees cite their excellent relationship with fellow employees and management as the reason for their high level of job satisfaction.

Should the regional manager's performance be measured by profit results compared to the overall Airborne system? What other measures could be used? From the factors listed, it is likely that a significant portion of the regional center profit was due to factors not controllable by the regional manager (the UPS strike, population growth, and fuel costs). But, it is likely that the manager did a good job of refining the cost management system and creating a productive working environment for all employees.

Economists describe the formal choices of performance measures and rewards as **agency theory.** When top management hires a manager, both should agree to an employment contract that details performance measures and how they will affect rewards.[1] For example, a manager might receive a bonus of 15% of her salary if her responsibility center achieves its budgeted profit. According to agency theory, employment contracts will trade off three factors:

> **agency theory** A theory used to describe the formal choices of performance measures and rewards.

1. *Incentive:* The more a manager's reward depends on a performance measure, the more incentive the manager has to take actions that maximize that measure. Top management should define the performance measure to promote goal congruence and base enough reward on it to achieve managerial effort.
2. *Risk:* The greater the influence of uncontrollable factors on a manager's reward, the more risk the manager bears. People generally avoid risk, so managers must be paid more if they are expected to bear more risk. Creating incentive by linking rewards to responsibility center results, which is generally desirable, has the undesirable side effect of imposing risk on managers.
3. *Cost of measuring performance:* The incentive versus risk trade-off is not necessary if a manager's performance is perfectly measured. Why? Because then a manager could be paid a fixed amount if he or she performs as expected, and nothing if not. Whether to perform or not is completely controllable by the manager, and observation of the level of performance is all that is necessary to determine the compensation earned. But directly measuring a manager's performance is usually expensive and sometimes infeasible. Responsibility center results are more readily available. The cost-benefit criterion usually indicates that perfect measurement of a manager's performance is not worth its cost.

Consider a concert promoter hired by a group of investors to promote and administer an outdoor rock performance. If the investors cannot directly measure the promoter's effort and judgment, they would probably pay a bonus based on the economic success of the concert. The bonus would motivate the promoter to put his effort toward generating a profit but the promoter is taking a big risk. For example, what happens if it rains? Through no fault of the promoter, the weather might keep fans away and ruin the concert. Factors such as bad weather also could affect the concert's economic success. The promoter might do an outstanding job and still not receive a bonus. Suppose the investors offer a contract with part guaranteed pay and part bonus. A larger bonus portion compared with the guaranteed portion creates more incentive, but it also means a larger expected total payment to compensate the promoter for the added risk.

---

[1] *Often performance measures and rewards are implicit. For example, promotion is a reward, but usually the requirements for promotion are not explicit.*

SUMMARY PROBLEM FOR YOUR REVIEW

PROBLEM

Examine Exhibit 10-1 on page 372. In addition to the data there, suppose the Fabric Division has annual fixed manufacturing costs of $800,000 and expected annual production of 500,000 square yards. The "fully allocated cost" per square yard was computed as follows:

Variable costs per square yard	$8.00
Fixed costs, $800,000 ÷ 500,000 square yards	1.60
Fully allocated cost per square yard	$9.60

Therefore the "fully allocated cost" of the five square yards required for one tent is 5 × $9.60 = $48.

Required Assume that the Fabric Division has idle capacity. The Tent Division is considering whether to buy enough fabric for 10,000 tents. Each tent will be sold for $100. The additional costs shown in Exhibit 10-1 for the Tent Division would prevail. If transfers were based on fully allocated cost, would the Tent Division manager buy? Explain. Would the company as a whole benefit if the Tent Division manager decided to buy? Explain.

SOLUTION

The Tent Division manager would not buy. The resulting transfer price of $48 would make the acquisition of the fabric unattractive to the Tent Division:

Tent Division			
Sales price of final product			$100
Deduct costs			
Transfer price paid to the Fabric Division			
(fully allocated cost)		$48	
Additional costs (from Exhibit 10-1)			
Processing	$41		
Selling	12	53	
Total costs to the Tent Division			101
Contribution to profit of the Tent Division			$ −1
Contribution to company as a whole			
(from Exhibit 10-1)			$ 7

As Exhibit 10-1 shows, the company as a whole would benefit by $70,000 (10,000 tents × $7) if the fabric were transferred.

The major lesson here is that, when idle capacity exists in the supplier division, transfer prices based on fully allocated costs may induce the wrong decisions. Working in her own best interests, the Tent Division manager has no incentive to buy from the Fabric Division.

MEASURES OF PROFITABILITY

A favorite objective of top management is to maximize profitability. Segment managers in decentralized organizations are often evaluated based on their segment's profitability. The trouble is that profitability does not mean the same thing to all people. Is it net income? Income before taxes? Net income percentage based on revenue? Is it an absolute amount? A percentage? In this section we consider the strengths and weaknesses of several commonly used measures.

RETURN ON INVESTMENT

Too often, managers stress net operating income or income percentages without tying the measure into the investment associated with generating the income. To say that project A has an operating income of $200,000 and project B has an operating income of $150,000 is an insufficient statement about profitability. A better test of profitability is the rate of **return on investment (ROI),** which is income (or profit) divided by the investment required to obtain that income or profit. Given the same risks, for any given amount of resources required, the investor wants the maximum income. If project A requires an investment of $500,000 and project B requires only $250,000, all other things being equal, where would you put your money?

$$\text{ROI} = \frac{\text{income}}{\text{investment}}$$

$$\text{ROI project A} = \frac{\$200,000}{\$500,000} = 40\%$$

$$\text{ROI project B} = \frac{\$150,000}{\$250,000} = 60\%$$

ROI is a useful common denominator. It can be compared with rates inside and outside the organization, and with opportunities in other projects and industries. It is affected by two major items, **income percentage of revenue** (also called **return on sales**)—income divided by revenue—and **capital turnover**—revenue divided by invested capital.

$$\frac{\text{return on}}{\text{investment}} = \frac{\text{income}}{\text{invested capital}}$$

$$= \frac{\text{income}}{\text{revenue}} \times \frac{\text{revenue}}{\text{invested capital}}$$

$$= \text{income percentage of revenue} \times \text{capital turnover}$$

An improvement in either of these rates without changing the other will improve the rate of return on invested capital. Consider an example of these relationships:

	Rate of Return on Invested Capital (%)	=	Income / Revenue	×	Revenue / Invested Capital
Present outlook	20	=	$\frac{16}{100}$	×	$\frac{100}{80}$
Alternatives					
1. Increase income percentage by reducing expenses	25	=	$\frac{20}{100}$	×	$\frac{100}{80}$
2. Increase turnover by decreasing investment in inventories	25	=	$\frac{16}{100}$	×	$\frac{100}{64}$

Alternative 1 is a popular way to improve performance. Alert managers try to decrease expenses without reducing sales or to boost sales without increasing related expenses. Alternative 2 is less obvious, but it may be a quicker way to improve performance. Increasing the turnover of invested capital means generating higher revenue for each dollar invested in such assets as cash, receivables, inventories, or equipment. There is an optimal level of investment in these assets. Having too much is wasteful, but having too little may hurt credit standing and the ability to compete for sales. Increasing turnover is one of the advantages of implementing the JIT philosophy (see Chapters 1 and 4). Many

---

return on investment (ROI) A measure of income or profit divided by the investment required to obtain that income or profit.

Objective 7
Compute ROI, residual income, and economic value added (EVA) and contrast them as criteria for judging the performance of organization segments.

income percentage of revenue (return on sales) Income divided by revenue.

capital turnover Revenue divided by invested capital.

companies implementing JIT purchasing and production systems have realized dramatic improvements in their ROI.

RESIDUAL INCOME (RI) AND ECONOMIC VALUE ADDED (EVA)

residual income (RI) Net operating income less "imputed" interest.

cost of capital What a firm must pay to acquire more capital, whether or not it actually has to acquire more capital to take on a project.

Most managers agree that measuring return in relation to investment provides the ultimate test of profitability. ROI is one such comparison. However, some managers favor emphasizing an absolute amount of income rather than a percentage rate of return. They use **residual income (RI),** defined as net operating income less "imputed" interest. "Imputed" interest refers to the **cost of capital,** what the firm must pay to acquire more capital—whether or not it actually has to acquire more capital to take on a project. In short, RI tells you how much your company's operating income exceeds what it is paying for capital. For example, suppose a division's net operating income was $900,000, the average invested capital (total assets) in the division for the year was $10 million, and the corporate headquarters assessed an imputed interest charge of 8%:

Divisional net operating income (after taxes)	$900,000
Minus imputed interest on average invested capital (.08 × $10,000,000)	800,000
Equals residual income	$100,000

economic value added (EVA) Equals net operating income minus the after-tax weighted-average cost of capital multiplied times the sum of long-term liabilities and stockholders' equity.

There are several different ways to calculate residual income depending on how we choose to define the terms used. For example, some companies define "average invested capital" as funds provided by long-term creditors and stockholders (that is, long-term liabilities plus stockholders' equity). This variant of residual income is called economic value added (EVA), a term coined and marketed by Stern Stewart & Co. **Economic value added (EVA)** equals net operating income minus the after-tax weighted-average cost of capital multiplied times the sum of long-term liabilities and stockholders' equity.

$$\begin{array}{c} \text{Economic value} \\ \text{added (EVA)} \end{array} = \begin{array}{c} \text{Net operating} \\ \text{income} \end{array} - \left[\begin{array}{c} \text{Weighted-average} \\ \text{cost of capital} \end{array} \times \left(\begin{array}{c} \text{Long-term} \\ \text{liabilities} \end{array} + \begin{array}{c} \text{Stockholders'} \\ \text{equity} \end{array} \right) \right]$$

The weighted-average cost of capital is the cost of long-term liabilities and stockholders' equity weighted by their relative size for the company or division. RI and EVA have received much attention recently as scores of companies are adopting them as financial performance measures. AT&T, Coca-Cola, CSX, FMC, and Quaker Oats claim that using EVA-motivated managers to make decisions that increased shareholder value. All these companies are successful. Why? Because they do a better job than their competitors at allocating, managing, and redeploying scarce capital resources (fixed assets such as heavy equipment, computers, real estate, and working capital). For example, the following data compare PepsiCo and Coca-Cola:

	PepsiCo	**Coca-Cola**
1988 Sales revenue ($billions)	$12	$ 8
1997 Sales revenue ($billions)	$21	$19
Invested capital ($billions)	$20.1	$17.5

PepsiCo had revenue growth of 75% compared to 138% for Coca-Cola. But both companies are in business to create wealth for their shareholders. So, which company created more value for its shareholders? PepsiCo's market value in 1997 was $52 billion but Coca-Cola's market value was $165 billion. Thus, compared to PepsiCo, Coca-Cola created over three times as much market value for its shareholders with less invested capital. Coca-Cola began practicing EVA in the early 1980s.

ROI or Residual Income?

Why do some companies prefer residual income (or EVA) to ROI? For a division with net operating income of $900,000 and average invested capital of $10,000,000, the ROI approach shows:

Divisional net operating income after taxes	$ 900,000
Average invested capital	$10,000,000
Return on investment	9%

Under ROI, the basic message is: Go forth and maximize your rate of return, a percentage. Thus, if performance is measured by ROI, managers of divisions currently earning 20% may be reluctant to invest in projects that earn only 15% because doing so would reduce their average ROI.

However, from the viewpoint of the company as a whole, top management may want this division manager to accept projects that earn 15%. Why? Suppose the company's cost of capital is 8%. Investing in projects earning 15% will increase the company's profitability. When performance is measured by residual income, managers tend to invest in any project earning more than the imputed interest rate and thus raise the firm's profits. That is, the residual income approach fosters goal congruence and managerial effort. Its basic message is: Go forth and maximize residual income, an absolute amount.

General Electric (GE) was one of the first companies to adopt a residual income approach. Consider two divisions of GE as an example. Division A has net operating income of $200,000; Division B has $50,000. Both have average invested capital of $1 million. Suppose a project is proposed that can be undertaken by either A or B. The project will earn 15% annually on a $500,000 investment, or $75,000 a year. The cost of capital for the project is 8%. ROI and residual income with and without the project are as follows:

	Without Project		With Project	
	Division A	**Division B**	**Division A**	**Division B**
Net operating income	$ 200,000	$ 50,000	$ 275,000	$ 125,000
Invested capital	$1,000,000	$ 1,000,000	$1,500,000	$ 1,500,000
ROI (net operating income ÷ invested capital)	20%	5%	18.3%	8.3%
Capital charge (8% × invested capital)	$ 80,000	$80,000	$ 120,000	$ 120,000
Residual income (net operating income − capital charge)	$ 120,000	$(− 30,000)	$ 155,000	$ 5,000

Suppose you are the manager of Division A. If your evaluation is based on ROI, would you invest in the project? No. It would decrease your ROI from 20% to 18.3%. But suppose you are in Division B. Would you invest? Yes, because ROI increases from 5% to 8.3%. In general, in companies using ROI, the least-profitable divisions have more incentive to invest in new projects than do the most profitable divisions.

Now suppose you are evaluated using residual income. The project would be equally attractive to either division. Residual income increases by $35,000 for each division, $155,000 − $120,000 for A and $5,000 − (− $30,000) for B. Both divisions have the same incentive to invest in the project, and the incentive depends on the profitability of the project compared with the cost of the capital used by the project.

In general, use of residual income will promote goal congruence and lead to better decisions than using ROI. Still, most companies use ROI. Why? Probably because it is easier for managers to understand, and it facilitates comparison across divisions. Furthermore, combining ROI with appropriate growth and profit targets can minimize its dysfunctional motivations.

A CLOSER LOOK AT INVESTED CAPITAL

Objective 8
Compare the advantages and disadvantages of various bases for measuring the invested capital used by organization segments.

To apply either ROI or residual income, both income and invested capital must be measured. However, there are many different interpretations of these concepts. To understand what ROI or residual income figures really mean, you must first determine how invested capital and income are being defined and measured. We discussed various definitions of income in Chapter 9, pages 337–340, so we will not repeat them here. We will, however, explore various definitions of invested capital.

DEFINITION OF INVESTED CAPITAL

Consider the following balance sheet classifications:

Current assets	$ 400,000	Current liabilities	$ 200,000
Property, plant, and equipment, net	800,000	Long-term liabilities	400,000
Construction in progress	100,000	Stockholders' equity	700,000
Total assets	$1,300,000	Total liab. and stk. eq.	$1,300,000

Possible definitions of invested capital and their values on the preceding balance sheet include

1. *Total assets:* All assets are included, $1,300,000.
2. *Total assets employed:* All assets except agreed-on exclusions of vacant land or construction in progress, $1,300,000 − $100,000 = $1,200,000.
3. *Total assets less current liabilities:* All assets except that portion supplied by short-term creditors, $1,300,000 − $200,000 = $1,100,000. This is sometimes expressed as *long-term invested capital;* note that it can also be computed by adding the long-term liabilities and the stockholders' equity, $400,000 + $700,000 = $1,100,000, which is the definition used for EVA.
4. *Stockholders' equity:* Focuses on the investment of the owners of the business, $700,000.

(All the preceding should be computed as averages for the period under review. These averages may be based on simply the beginning and ending balances or on more complicated averages that weigh changes in investments through the months.)

For measuring the performance of division managers, any of the three asset definitions is recommended rather than stockholders' equity. If the division manager's mission is to put all assets to their best use without regard to their financing, then total assets is best. If top management directs the manager to carry extra assets that are not currently productive, then total assets employed is best. If the manager has direct control over obtaining short-term credit and bank loans, then total assets less current liabilities is best. A key behavioral factor in choosing an investment definition is that managers will focus attention on reducing those assets and increasing those liabilities that are included in the definition. In practice, most companies using ROI or residual income include all assets in invested capital, and about half deduct some portion of current liabilities.

A few companies allocate long-term debt to their divisions and thus have an approximation of the stockholders' equity in each division. However, this practice has doubtful merit. Division managers typically have little responsibility for the long-term financial management of their divisions, as distinguished from operating management. The investment bases of division managers from two companies could differ radically if one company has heavy long-term debt and the other is debt-free.

ASSET ALLOCATION TO DIVISIONS

Just as cost allocations affect income, asset allocations affect the invested capital of particular divisions. The aim is to allocate this capital in a manner that will be goal congruent, will spur managerial effort, and will recognize segment autonomy insofar as possible. (As long as the managers feel that they are being treated uniformly, though, they tend to be more tolerant of the imperfections of the allocation.)

A frequent criterion for asset allocation is avoidability. That is, the amount allocable to any given segment for the purpose of evaluating the division's performance is the amount that the corporation as a whole could avoid by not having that segment. Commonly used bases for allocation, when assets are not directly identifiable with a specific division, include:

Asset Class	Possible Allocation Base
Corporate cash	Budgeted cash needs
Receivables	Sales weighted by payment terms
Inventories	Budgeted sales or usage
Plant and equipment	Usage of services in terms of long-run forecasts of demand or area occupied

The allocation base should be the activity that caused the asset to be acquired. When the allocation of an asset would indeed be arbitrary (i.e., no causal activity can be identified), many managers think that it is better not to allocate.

Should cash be included in a division's investment if the cash balances are strictly controlled by corporate headquarters? Arguments can be made for both sides, but the manager is usually regarded as being responsible for the volume of business generated by the division. In turn, this volume is likely to have a direct effect on the overall cash needs of the corporation.

A popular allocation base for cash is sales dollars. However, the allocation of cash on the basis of sales dollars seldom gets at the economic rationale of cash holdings. As Chapter 7 explains, cash needs are influenced by a host of factors including payment terms of customers and creditors.

Central control of cash is usually undertaken to reduce the holdings from what would be used if each division had a separate account. Fluctuations in cash needs of each division might offset one another. For example, Division A might have a cash deficiency of $1 million in February, but Division B might have an offsetting cash excess of $1 million. Taken together for the year, Divisions A, B, C, D, and E might require a combined investment in cash of, say, $16 million if all were independent entities, but only $8 million if cash were controlled centrally. Hence, if Division C would ordinarily require a $4 million investment in cash as a separate entity, it would be allocated an investment of only $2 million as a segment of a company in which cash was controlled centrally.

VALUATION OF ASSETS

Whatever assets are included in a division's invested capital must be measured in some way. Should the assets contained in the investment base be valued at *gross book value* or *net book value*? **Gross value** is the original cost of an asset before deducting accumulated depreciation. **Net book value** is the original cost of an asset less any accumulated depreciation. Should values be based on historical cost or some version of current value? Practice is overwhelmingly in favor of using net book value based on historical cost. Very few companies use replacement cost or any other type of current value. Historical cost has been widely criticized for many years as providing a faulty basis for decision making and performance evaluation. As Chapters 5 and 6 point out, historical costs per se are irrelevant for making economic decisions. Despite these criticisms, managers have been slow to depart from historical cost.

gross book value The original cost of an asset before deducting accumulated depreciation.

net book value The original cost of an asset less any accumulated depreciation.

Why is historical cost so widely used? Some critics would say that sheer ignorance is the explanation. But a more persuasive answer comes from cost-benefit analysis. Accounting systems are costly. Historical records must be kept for many legal purposes, so they are already in place. No additional money must be spent to evaluate performance based on historical costs. Furthermore, many top managers believe that such a system provides the desired goal congruence and managerial effort and that a more sophisticated system will not radically improve collective operating decisions. Some believe, in fact, that using current values would cause confusion unless huge sums were spent educating personnel.

Historical costs may even improve some decisions because they are more objective than current costs. Moreover, managers can better predict the historical-cost effects of their decisions, so their decisions may be more influenced by the control system. Furthermore, the uncertainty involved with current-cost measures may impose undesirable risks on the managers. In short, the historical-cost system may be superior for the routine evaluation of performance. In nonroutine instances, such as replacing equipment or deleting a product line, managers should conduct special studies to gather any current valuations that seem relevant.

Finally, although historical-cost systems are common, most well-managed organizations do not use historical-cost systems alone. The alternatives available to managers are not

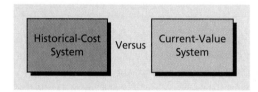

More accurately stated, the alternatives are

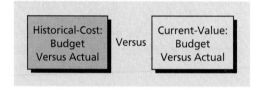

A budget system, whether based on historical cost or current value, causes managers to worry about inflation. Most managers seem to prefer to concentrate on improving their existing historical-cost budget system.

In sum, our cost-benefit approach provides no universal answers with respect to such controversial issues as historical values versus current values or return on investment versus residual income. Instead, using a cost-benefit test, each organization must judge for itself whether an alternative control system or accounting technique will improve collective decision making. The latter is the primary criterion.

Too often, the literature engages in pro-and-con discussions about which alternative is more nearly perfect or truer than another in some logical sense. The cost-benefit approach is not concerned with "truth" or "perfection" by itself. Instead it asks: Do you think your perceived "truer" or "more logical" system is worth its added cost? Or will our existing imperfect system provide about the same set of decisions if it is skillfully administered?

PLANT AND EQUIPMENT: GROSS OR NET?

In valuing assets, it is important to distinguish between net and gross book values. Most companies use net book value in calculating their investment base. However, according to a recent survey, a significant minority uses gross book value. The proponents of gross book value maintain that it facilitates comparisons between years, and between plants or divisions.

Consider an example of a $600,000 piece of equipment with a three-year life and no residual value.

	Operating Income Before Depreciation	Depreciation	Operating Income	Average Investment			
Year				Net Book Value*	Rate of Return	Gross Book Value	Rate of Return
1	$260,000	$200,000	$60,000	$500,000	12%	$600,000	10%
2	260,000	200,000	60,000	300,000	20	600,000	10
3	260,000	200,000	60,000	100,000	60	600,000	10

* ($600,000 + $400,000) ÷ 2; ($400,000 + $200,000) ÷ 2; and so on.

The rate of return on net book value goes up as the equipment ages. It could increase even if operating income gradually declined through the years. In contrast, the rate of return on gross book value is unchanged if operating income does not change. The rate would decrease if operating income gradually declined through the years.

Advocates of using net book value maintain that:

1. It is less confusing because it is consistent with the assets shown on the conventional balance sheet and with the net income computations.
2. The major criticism of net book value is not peculiar to its use for ROI purposes. It is really a criticism of using historical cost as a basis for evaluation.

The effect on motivation should be considered when choosing between net and gross book value. Managers evaluated using gross book value will tend to replace assets sooner than will those managers in firms using net book value. Consider a four-year-old machine with an original cost of $1,000 and net book value of $200. It can be replaced by a new machine that also costs $1,000. The choice of net or gross book value does not affect net income. However, the investment base increases from $200 to $1,000 in a net-book-value firm, but it remains at $1,000 in a gross-book-value firm. To maximize ROI or residual income, managers want a low-investment base. Managers in firms using net book value will tend to keep old assets with their low book value. Those in firms using gross book value will have less incentive to keep old assets. Therefore, to motivate managers to use state-of-the-art production technology, gross book value is preferred. Net asset value promotes a more conservative approach to asset replacement.

KEYS TO SUCCESSFUL MANAGEMENT CONTROL SYSTEMS

Successful management control systems have several key factors in addition to appropriate measures of profitability. We next explore some of these factors.

FOCUS ON CONTROLLABILITY

As Chapter 9 explained (see Exhibit 9-5, page 339), a distinction should be made between the performance of the division manager and the performance of the division as an investment by the corporation. Managers should be evaluated on the basis of their controllable performance (in many cases, some controllable contribution in relation to controllable investment). However, decisions such as increasing or decreasing investment in a division are based on the economic viability of the division, not the performance of its managers.

This distinction helps to clarify some vexing difficulties. For example, top management may want to use an investment base to gauge the economic performance of a retail store, but the manager may best be judged by focusing on income and forgetting about any investment allocations. If investment is assigned to the manager, the aim should be to assign only that investment the manager can control. Controllability depends on what decisions managers can make regarding the size of the investment base. In a highly decentralized company, for instance, managers can influence the size of these assets and can exercise judgment regarding the appropriate amount of short-term credit and perhaps some long-term credit.

MANAGEMENT BY OBJECTIVES

management by objectives (MBO) The joint formulation by a manager and his or her superior of a set of goals and plans for achieving the goals for a forthcoming period.

Management by objectives (MBO) describes the joint formulation by a manager and his or her superior of a set of goals and plans for achieving the goals for a forthcoming period. For our purposes here, the terms goals and objectives are synonyms. The plans often take the form of a responsibility accounting budget (together with supplementary goals such as levels of management training and safety that may not be incorporated into the accounting budget). The manager's performance is then evaluated in relation to these agreed-on budgeted objectives.

Regardless of whether it is so labeled, a management-by-objectives approach lessens the complaints about lack of controllability because of its stress on budgeted results. That is, a budget is negotiated between a particular manager and his or her superior for a particular period and a particular set of expected outside and inside influences. In this way, a manager may more readily accept an assignment to a less successful segment. This is preferable to a system that emphasizes absolute profitability for its own sake. Unless focus is placed on currently attainable results, able managers will be reluctant to accept responsibility for segments that are in economic trouble.

Thus, skillful budgeting and intelligent performance evaluation will go a long way toward overcoming the common lament: "I'm being held responsible for items beyond my control."

TAILORING BUDGETS FOR MANAGERS

Many of the troublesome motivational effects of performance evaluation systems can be minimized by the astute use of budgets. The desirability of tailoring a budget to particular managers cannot be overemphasized. For example, either an ROI or a residual income system can promote goal congruence and managerial effort if top management gets everybody to focus on what is currently attainable in the forthcoming budget period. Typically, divisional managers do not have complete freedom to make major investment decisions without checking with senior management.

SUMMARY PROBLEM FOR YOUR REVIEW

PROBLEM

A division has assets of $200,000, current liabilities of $20,000 and net operating income of $60,000.

  1. What is the division's ROI?
  2. If the weighted-average cost of capital is 14%, what is the EVA?
  3. What effects on management behavior can be expected if ROI is used to gauge performance?
  4. What effects on management behavior can be expected if EVA is used to gauge performance?

	Company		
	A	B	C
Sales	$9,000,000	$ 2,500,000	$37,500,000
Income	1,350,000	375,000	375,000
Capital	4,500,000	12,500,000	12,500,000

Required

1. Why would you desire the breakdown of return on investment into return on sales and turnover on capital?

2. Compute the return on sales, turnover on capital, and return on investment for the three companies, and comment on the relative performance of the companies as thoroughly as the data permit.

10-39 ROI by Business Segment

Rupert Services Inc. does business in three different business segments: (1) Entertainment, (2) Publishing/Information, and (3) Consumer/Commercial Finance. Results for a recent year were (in millions):

	Revenues	Operating Income	Total Assets
Entertainment	$1,272.2	$223.0	$1,120.1
Publishing/Information	705.5	120.4	1,308.7
Consumer/Commercial Finance	1,235.0	244.6	924.4

Required

1. Compute the following for each business segment:
   a. Income percentage of revenue
   b. Capital turnover
   c. ROI

2. Comment on the differences in return on investment among the business segments. Include reasons for the differences.

BUSINESS FIRST   www.prenhall.com/phlip

PHLIP

10-40 Economic Value Added at Nike.

Nike, Inc. is the largest seller of athletic footwear and athletic apparel in the world. Its financial results for the 1996 and 1997 fiscal years include (in millions):

	1997	1996
Revenues	$9,187	$6,471
Operating expenses	7,807	5,495
Interest expense	52	39
Income taxes	499	346
Capital	3,156	2,431

Required

1. Suppose that Nike's cost of capital is 12.5%. Compute the company's economic value added (EVA) for 1996 and 1997.

2. Discuss the change in EVA between 1996 and 1997. ■

10-41 Evaluation of Divisional Performance

As the chief executive officer of Tiger Shoe Company, you examined the following measures of the performance of three divisions (in thousands of dollars):

	Net Assets Based on		Operating Income Based on*	
Division	Historical Cost	Replacement Cost	Historical Cost	Replacement Cost
Shoes	$15,000	$15,000	$2,700	$2,700
Clothing	45,000	55,000	6,750	6,150
Accessories	30,000	48,000	4,800	3,900

* The differences in operating income between historical and replacement cost are attributable to the differences in depreciation revenues.

Required

1. Calculate for each division the rate of return on net assets and the residual income based on historical cost and on replacement cost. For purposes of calculating residual income, use 10% as the minimum desired rate of return.
2. Rank the performance of each division under each of the four different measures computed in requirement 1.
3. What do these measures indicate about the performance of the divisions? Of the division managers? Which measure do you prefer? Why?

10-42 Economic Value Added

The Coca-Cola Company uses economic value added (EVA) to evaluate top management performance. In 1996, Coca-Cola had net operating income of $3,915 million, income taxes of $1,104 million, and long-term debt plus stockholders' equity of $8,755 million. The company's capital is about 30% long-term debt and 70% equity. Assume that the after-tax cost of debt is 5% and the cost of equity is 12%.

Required

1. Compute Coca-Cola's economic value added (EVA).
2. Explain what EVA tells you about the performance of the top management of Coca-Cola in 1996.

10-43 Use of Gross or Net Book Value of Fixed Assets

Assume that a particular plant acquires $800,000 of fixed assets with a useful life of four years and no residual value. Straight-line depreciation will be used. The plant manager is judged on income in relation to these fixed assets. Annual net income, after deducting depreciation, is $80,000.

Assume that sales, and all expenses except depreciation, are on a cash basis. Dividends equal net income. Thus, cash in the amount of the depreciation charge will accumulate each year. The plant manager's performance is judged in relation to fixed assets because all current assets, including cash, are considered under central-company control. Assume (unrealistically) that any cash accumulated remains idle. Ignore taxes.

Required

1. Prepare a comparative tabulation of the plant's rate of return and the company's overall rate of return based on
   a. Gross (i.e., original cost) assets.
   b. Net book value of assets.
2. Evaluate the relative merits of gross assets and net book value of assets as investment bases.

10-44 Role of Economic Value and Replacement Value

(This problem requires understanding of the concept of present values. See Appendix B.) "To me, economic value is the only justifiable basis for measuring plant assets for purposes of evaluating performance. By economic value, I mean the present value of expected future services. Still, we do not even do this on acquisition of new assets—that is, we may compute a positive net present value, using discounted cash flow; but we record the asset at no more than its cost. In this way, the excess present value is not shown in the initial balance sheet. Moreover, the use of replacement costs in subsequent years is also unlikely to result in showing economic values. The replacement cost will probably be less than the economic value at any given instant of an asset's life.

"Market values are totally unappealing to me because they represent a second-best alternative value—that is, they ordinarily represent the maximum amount obtainable from an alternative that has been rejected. Obviously, if the market value exceeds the economic value of the assets in use, they should be sold. However, in most instances, the opposite is true; market values of individual assets are far below their economic value in use.

"The obtaining and recording of total present values of individual assets based on discounted-cash-flow techniques is an infeasible alternative. I, therefore, conclude that replacement cost (less accumulated depreciation) of similar assets producing similar services is the best practical approximation of the economic value of the assets in use. Of course, it is more appropriate for the evaluation of the division's performance than the division manager's performance."

Required Critically evaluate these comments. Please do not wander; concentrate on the issues described by the quotation.

10-45 Review of Major Points in Chapter

The Indiana Instruments Company uses the decentralized form of organizational structure and considers each of its divisions as an investment center. The Fort Wayne Division is currently selling 15,000 air filters annually, although it has sufficient productive capacity to produce 21,000 units per year. Variable manufacturing costs amount to $17 per unit, while the total fixed costs amount to $90,000. These 15,000 air filters are sold to outside customers at $37 per unit.

The Indianapolis Division, also a part of Indiana Instruments, has indicated that it would like to buy 1,500 air filters from the Fort Wayne Division, but at a price of $36 per unit. This is the price the Indianapolis Division is currently paying an outside supplier.

Required
1. Compute the effect on the operating income of the company as a whole if the Indianapolis Division purchases the 1,500 air filters from the Fort Wayne Division.

2. What is the minimum price that the Fort Wayne Division should be willing to accept for these 1,500 air filters?

3. What is the maximum price that the Indianapolis Division should be willing to pay for these 1,500 air filters?

4. Suppose instead that the Fort Wayne Division is currently producing and selling 21,000 air filters annually to outside customers. What is the effect on the overall Indiana Instruments Company operating income if the Fort Wayne Division is required by top management to sell 1,500 air filters to the Indianapolis Division at (a) $17 per unit and (b) $36 per unit?

5. For this question only, assume that the Fort Wayne Division is currently earning an annual operating income of $36,000, and the division's average invested capital is $300,000. The division manager has an opportunity to invest in a proposal that will require an additional investment of $20,000 and will increase annual operating income by $2,200. (a) Should the division manager accept this proposal

if the Indiana Instruments Company uses ROI in evaluating the performance of its divisional managers? (b) If the company uses residual income? (Assume an imputed interest charge of 9%.)

CASES

10-46 Management by Objectives

(CMA.) Roger Brandt is the chief executive officer of Langston Company. Brandt has a financial management background and is known throughout the organization as a "no-nonsense" executive. When Brandt became chief executive officer, he emphasized cost reduction and savings and introduced a comprehensive cost control and budget system. The company goals and budget plans were established by Brandt and given to his subordinates for implementation. Some of the company's key executives were dismissed or demoted for failing to meet projected budget plans. Under the leadership of Roger Brandt, Langston has once again become financially stable and profitable after several years of poor performance.

Recently Brandt has become concerned with the human side of the organization and has become interested in the management technique referred to as "management by objectives" (MBO). If there are enough positive benefits of MBO, he plans to implement the system throughout the company. However, he realizes that he does not fully understand MBO because he does not understand how it differs from the current system of establishing firm objectives and budget plans.

Required

1. Briefly explain what MBO entails and identify its advantages and disadvantages.
2. Does the management style of Roger Brandt incorporate the human value premises and goals of MBO? Explain your answer.

10-47 Profit Centers and Central Services

Sun Manufacturing, Inc., manufacturer of Sunlite brand small appliances, has an Engineering Consulting Department (ECD). The department's major task has been to help the production departments improve their operating methods and processes.

For several years, Sun has charged the cost of consulting services to the production departments based on a signed agreement between the managers involved. The agreement specifies the scope of the project, the predicted savings, and the number of consulting hours required. The charge to the production departments is based on the costs to the Engineering Department of the services rendered. For example, senior engineer hours cost more per hour than junior engineer hours. An overhead cost is included. The agreement is really a "fixed-price" contract. That is, the production manager knows the total cost of the project in advance. A recent survey revealed that production managers have a high level of confidence in the engineers.

The ECD department manager oversees the work of about 40 engineers and 10 technicians. She reports to the engineering manager, who reports to the vice president of manufacturing. The ECD manager has the freedom to increase or decrease the number of engineers under her supervision. The ECD manager's performance evaluation is based on many factors including the annual incremental savings to the company in excess of the costs of operating the ECD department.

The production departments are profit centers. Their goods are transferred to subsequent departments, such as a sales department or sales division, at prices that approximate market prices for similar products.

Top management is seriously considering a "no-charge" plan. That is, production departments would receive engineering services at absolutely no cost. Proponents of the new plan maintain that it would motivate the production managers to take better advantage of engineering talent. In all other respects, the new system would be unchanged from the present system.

Required

1. Compare the present and proposed plans. What are their strong and weak points? In particular, will the ECD manager tend to hire the "optimal" amount of engineering talent?

2. Which plan do you favor? Why?

COLLABORATIVE LEARNING EXERCISE

10-48   Return on Investment

Form groups of three to six students. Each student should select a company. Coordinate the selection of companies so that each group has companies from a wide variety of industries. For example, a good mix of industries for a group of five students would be a retail company, a basic manufacturing company, a computer software company, a bank, and an electric utility.

Required

1. Each student should find the latest annual report for his or her company. (The Internet is a good source. If you cannot find the company's home page, try http::/sec.gov, and search the Security and Exchange Commission's Edgar files for the company's 10-K report, which will contain its financial statements.) Compute:

   a. Income percentage of revenue (return on sales)

   b. Capital turnover

   c. Return on investment (ROI)

2. As a group, compare these performance measures for the chosen companies. Why do they differ across companies? What characteristic of the company and its industry might explain the differences in the measures?

CAPITAL BUDGETING

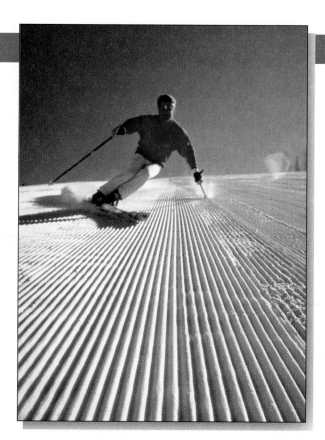

Skiers do not often realize the planning and investment that goes into preparing the slopes. Managers at Deer Valley Lodge, a ski resort in Utah's Wasatch Mountains and one of the hosts of the 2002 Winter Olympics, understand this fully. Much effort goes into their capital budgeting decisions—decisions that affect the fun, comfort, and safety of their guests.

Learning Objectives

When you have finished studying this chapter, you should be able to

1 Describe capital budgeting decisions and use the net present value (NPV) method to make such decisions.

2 Evaluate projects using sensitivity analysis.

3 Calculate the NPV difference between two projects using both the total project and differential approaches.

4 Identify relevant cash flows for NPV analyses.

5 Compute the after-tax net present values of projects.

6 Explain the after-tax effect on cash of disposing of assets.

7 Compute the impact of inflation on a capital-budgeting project.

8 Use the payback model and the accounting rate-of-return model and compare them with the NPV model.

9 Reconcile the conflict between using an NPV model for making a decision and using accounting income for evaluating the related performance.

10 **Understand how companies make long-term capital investment decisions and how such decisions can affect the companies' financial results for years to come.**

C apital investment is probably the last thing you would think of while schussing down the snow-covered slopes of the Rockies—unless you happen to be the manager of a ski resort. A resort guest might see slopes, chairlifts, and a nice warm lodge, while a resort manager will see millions of dollars worth of investments.

Consider Deer Valley Lodge, a posh ski resort in the Wasach Mountains of Utah. Deer Valley has a strong customer orientation—what Director of Finance Jim Madsen calls "the Deer Valley difference." From valets who help with skis to gourmet meals in the lodges, Deer Valley is a first-class resort. When facilities become too crowded, the resort limits sales of lift tickets to keep lift lines from getting too long. After crowding forced Deer Valley officials to close ticket sales offices early several times in 1994–95, managers started thinking it was time to expand.

Deer Valley keeps a 10-year plan for capital expansion. Currently the plans include five new lifts that will expand operations into neighboring Empire Canyon, a day lodge, and a new parking facility. By continually measuring crowding, using measures such as waiting time for lifts and length of lines at restaurants and cafeterias, Deer Valley managers decide when the next capital expansion phase is needed.

One capital expansion phase will be needed just before the year 2002, when Deer Valley will host the Olympic Winter Games. Deer Valley will feature slalom and freestyle skiing, with slalom competition on Big Stick, moguls on a ski run called Know You Don't, and aerial events on Solid Meldoon. Just as athletes hone their skills to compete in these events, Deer Valley managers must improve their facilities through additional capital investments.

CAPITAL BUDGETING FOR PROGRAMS OR PROJECTS

capital budgeting The long-term planning for making and financing investments that affect financial results over more than just the next year.

Ski resorts such as Deer Valley are not the only companies that face decisions about capital investment and expansion. At some time, every company needs to decide where and how to spend its money on major projects that will affect company financial results for years to come. This chapter concentrates on the planning and controlling decisions for programs or projects that affect financial results over more than just the next year. Such decisions require investments of large amounts of resources (capital) that are often called capital outlays. The term **capital budgeting** describes the long-term planning for making and financing such outlays.

Capital budgeting has three phases: (1) identifying potential investments, (2) choosing which investments to make (which includes gathering data to aid the decision), and (3) follow-up monitoring, or "postaudit," of the investments. Accountants usually are not involved in the first phase, but they play important roles in phases 2 and 3.

Why are accountants involved in capital budgeting decisions? They function primarily as information specialists. As you know, one of the uses of accounting information is in predicting future events, such as the outcome of capital budgeting decisions.

Accountants will gather and interpret as much information as possible to help managers make such decisions. To help organize what could be pages and pages worth of information, accountants rely on capital-budgeting models. Let's take a look at how some of these models work.

DISCOUNTED-CASH-FLOW MODELS

discounted-cash-flow (DCF) models A type of capital-budgeting model that focuses on cash inflows and outflows while taking into account the time value of money.

The most widely used capital budgeting models are **discounted-cash-flow (DCF) models.** These models focus on a project's cash inflows and outflows while taking into account time value of money. They are based on the old adage that a bird in the hand is worth two in the bush—that a dollar in the hand today is worth more than a dollar to be received (or spent) five years from today. This adage applies because the use of money has a cost (interest), just as the use of a building or an automobile may have a cost (rent). More than 85% of the large industrial firms in the United States use a DCF model.

MAJOR ASPECTS OF DCF

As the name suggests, DCF models focus on expected cash inflows and outflows rather than on net income. Companies invest cash today in order to receive cash in future periods. DCF models compare the value of today's *cash outflows* with the value of the future *cash inflows.*

DCF methods are based on the theory of compound interest which you should be familiar with from your course in financial accounting. For those of you whose knowledge of compound interest and time value of money is a little rusty, be sure to read Appendix B, pp. B1-B8. Do not try to learn about the DCF methods until you are able to use Tables 1 (p. B7) and 2 (p. B8) in Appendix B.

To illustrate how DCF models work, we will use the following example throughout the rest of this section: A buildings and grounds manager at the University of Arizona is contemplating the purchase of some lawn maintenance equipment that is expected to increase efficiency and produce cash-operating savings of $2,000 per year. The useful life of the equipment is four years, after which it will have a net disposal value of zero. The equipment will cost $6,075 now, and the minimum desired rate of return is 10% per year.

NET PRESENT VALUE (NPV)

We will focus on the most popular version of DCF, the **net-present-value (NPV) method.** The NPV method computes the present value of all expected future cash flows using a minimum desired rate of return. The minimum desired rate of return depends on the risk of a proposed project—the higher the risk, the higher the rate. Based on the cost of capital—what the firm pays to acquire more capital—this minimum rate is also called the **required rate of return, hurdle rate,** or **discount rate.** Using this required rate, managers determine the sum of the present values of all expected cash flows from the project. If this sum is positive, the project is desirable. If the sum is negative, the project is undesirable. Why? A positive NPV means that accepting the project will increase the value of the firm because the present value of the project's cash inflows exceeds the present value of its cash outflows. (An NPV of zero means that the present value of the inflows equals the present value of the outflows, and the project will exactly break even.) When choosing among several investments, managers should pick the one with the greatest net present value.

net-present-value (NPV) method A discounted-cash-flow approach to capital budgeting that computes the present value of all expected future cash flows using a minimum desired rate of return.

required rate of return (hurdle rate, discount rate) The minimum desired rate of return, based on the firm's cost of capital.

APPLYING THE NPV METHOD

To apply the NPV method, you can use the following three steps, which are shown in Exhibit 11-1:

Objective 1
Describe capital budgeting decisions and use the net present value (NPV) method to make such decisions.

1. *Prepare a diagram of relevant expected cash inflows and outflows:* The right-hand side of Exhibit 11-1 shows how these cash flows are sketched. Outflows are in parentheses. Be sure to include the outflow at time zero, the date of acquisition. You do not have to use a sketch, but sketches do help you to see costs and cost relationships.

2. *Find the present value of each expected cash inflow or outflow:* Examine Table 1 in Appendix B on page B7. Find the present-value (PV) factor for each year's cash flow from the correct row and column of the table. Multiply each expected cash inflow or outflow by the appropriate present-value factor. For example, the $2,000 cash savings that will occur two years hence is worth $2,000 × .8264 = $1,653 today.

3. *Sum the individual present values:* The sum is the project's NPV. Accept a project whose NPV is positive, and reject a project whose NPV is negative.

The value today (at time zero) of the four $2,000 cash inflows is $6,340. The manager pays only $6,075 to obtain these cash inflows. Thus the net present value is $6,340 − $6,075 = $265, so the investment is desirable.

CHOICE OF THE CORRECT TABLE

Exhibit 11-1 also shows another way to calculate the NPV, shown here as approach 2. The basic steps are the same as for approach 1. The only difference is that approach 2 uses Table 2 in Appendix B (see page B8) instead of Table 1. Table 2 is an annuity table that provides a

Exhibit 11-1
Net-Present-Value Method

Original investment, $6,075. Useful life, four years. Annual cash inflow from operations, $2,000. Minimum desired rate of return, 10%. Cash outflows are in parentheses; cash inflows are not. Total present values are rounded to the nearest dollar.

	Present Value of $1, Discounted at 10%	Total Present Value	Sketch of Cash Flows at End of Year				
			0	1	2	3	4

Approach 1: Discounting Each Year's Cash Inflow Separately*

Cash flows

Annual savings	.9091	$1,818		←———— $2,000			
	.8264	1,653		←————————— $2,000		
	.7513	1,503		←—————————————— $2,000	
	.6830	1,366		←————————————————————— $2,000

Present value of future inflows		$6,340					
Initial outlay	1.0000	(6,075)	$(6,075)				
Net present value		$ 265					

Approach 2: Using Annuity Table †

Annual savings	3.1699	$6,340		←———— $2,000	$2,000	$2,000	$2,000
Initial outlay	1.0000	(6,075)	$(6,075)				
Net present value		$ 265					

*Present values from Table 1, Appendix B, page B7.

†Present values of annuity from Table 2, Appendix B, page B8. (Incidentally, calculators or computers may give slightly different answers than tables because of rounding differences.)

shortcut to reduce hand calculations. It gives discount factors for computing the present value of a *series* of equal cash flows at equal intervals. Because the four cash flows in our example are all equal, you can use Table 2 to make one present-value computation instead of using Table 1 to make four individual computations. Table 2 merely sums up the pertinent present-value factors of Table 1. Therefore the annuity factor for four years at 10% is:[1]

$$.9091 + .8264 + .7513 + .6830 = 3.1698$$

Beware of using the wrong table. You should use Table 1 for discounting individual amounts, Table 2 for a series of equal amounts. Of course, Table 1 is the basis for Table 2 and it can be used for all present-value calculations.

You can avoid Tables 1 and 2 entirely by using the present-value function on a hand-held calculator or the present-value function on a computer spreadsheet program. However, we encourage you to use the tables when learning the NPV method. Using the tables will let you better understand the process of present-value computation. Once you are comfortable with the method, you can take advantage of the speed and convenience of calculators and computers.

EFFECT OF MINIMUM RATE

The minimum desired rate of return can have a large effect on NPVs. The higher the minimum desired rate of return, the lower the present value of each future cash inflow. Why? Because the higher the rate of return, the more it costs you to wait for the cash rather than having it available to invest today. Thus, higher required rates lead to lower project NPVs. For examle, at a rate of 16%, the NPV of the project in Exhibit 11-1 would be −$479 (that is, $2,000 × 2.7982 = $5,596, which is $479 less than the required investment of $6,075), instead of the +$265 computed with a 10% rate. (Present-value factor 2.7982 is taken from Table 2 in Appendix B on page B8.) When the desired rate of return is 16% rather than 10%, the project is undesirable at a price of $6,075.

ASSUMPTIONS OF THE NPV MODEL

We have to make two major assumptions to use the NPV model. First, we assume a world of certainty. That is, we act as if the predicted cash inflows and outflows are certain to occur at the times specified. Second, we assume perfect capital markets. That is, if we need or have extra cash at any time, we can borrow or lend money at the same interest rate. This rate is our minimum desired rate of return. If these assumptions are met, no model could possibly be better than the NPV model.

Unfortunately, the real world has neither certainty nor perfect capital markets. Nevertheless, the NPV model is usually preferred to other models because the assumptions of most other models are even less realistic. The NPV model is not perfect, but it generally meets our cost-benefit criterion. That is, the benefit of better decisions based on NPV is greater than the cost of applying it. More sophisticated models often do not improve decisions enough to be worth their cost.

DEPRECIATION AND NPV

NPV calculations do not include deductions for depreciation. Why not? Because NPV is based on inflows and outflows of cash and not on the accounting concepts of revenues and expenses.[2] Depreciation is not a cash flow. It is a way of allocating the cost of a long-

---

[1] *Rounding error causes a .0001 difference between the Table 2 factor and the summation of Table 1 factors.*

[2] *Throughout this chapter, our examples often assume that cash inflows are equivalent to revenues and that cash outflows are equivalent to expenses (except for depreciation). Of course, if the revenues and expenses are accounted for on the accrual basis of accounting, there will be leads and lags of cash inflows and cash outflows that a precise DCF model must recognize. For example, a $10,000 sale on credit may be recorded as revenue in one period, but the related cash inflow would not be recognized in a DCF model until collected, which may be in a second period. Such refinements are not made in this chapter.*

lived asset (which was usually paid for in cash upon purchase) to different periods. Because the cash outflow for the cost of the asset has already been recorded and accounted for, deducting depreciation from future cash flows would be like counting this cost twice—once at purchase and again over the asset's life.

REVIEW OF DECISION RULES

Be sure that you understand why the NPV method works, not just how to apply it. The decision maker in our example cannot directly compare an immediate outflow of $6,075 with a series of future inflows of $2,000 each because of the time value of money. The NPV model aids comparison by expressing all amounts in today's monetary units (such as dollars, francs, marks, or yen) at time zero. The required rate of return measures the cost of using money. At a rate of 12%, the comparison would be:

Outflow in today's dollars	$(6,075)
Inflow equivalent in today's dollars @ 12%	6,075
Net present value	$ 0

Therefore, at a required rate of return of 12%, the decision maker is indifferent between having $6,075 now or having a stream of four annual inflows of $2,000 each. If the interest rate were 16%, the decision maker would find the project unattractive because the net present value would be a negative $479, as shown in the following graph:

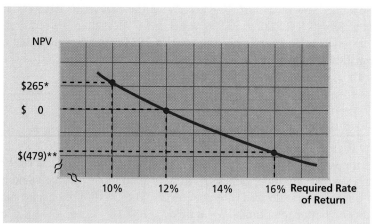

*($2,000 × 3.1699) − $6,075 = $265
**($2,000 × 2.7982) − $6,075 = $(479)

At 10%, the NPV is a positive $265, so the project is desirable. At all rates below 12%, the NPV is positive. At all rates above 12%, the NPV is negative.

SENSITIVITY ANALYSIS AND RISK ASSESSMENT IN DCF MODELS

Objective 2
Evaluate projects using sensitivity analysis.

Because the future is uncertain, actual cash inflows may differ from what was expected or predicted. To examine this uncertainty, managers often use sensitivity analysis, which shows the financial consequences that would occur if actual cash inflows and outflows differ from those expected. It can answer such "what-if" questions as: What will happen to my NPV if my predictions of useful life or cash flows change? The best way to understand sensitivity analysis is to see it in action, so let's take a look at an example.

Suppose that a manager knows that the actual cash inflows in Exhibit 11-1 could fall below the predicted level of $2,000. How far below $2,000 must the annual cash inflow drop before the NPV becomes negative? The cash inflow at the point where NPV = 0 is the "break-even" cash flow:

$$NPV = 0$$
$$(3.1699 \times \text{cash flow}) - \$6,075 = 0$$
$$\text{cash flow} = \$6,075 \div 3.1699$$
$$= \$1,916$$

If the annual cash inflow is less than $1,916, the NPV is negative, and the project should be rejected. Therefore annual cash inflows can drop only $2,000 − $1,916 = $84, or 4.2%, before the manager would change the decision.

Managers like sensitivity analysis because it can give them immediate answers about possible future events. It also shows managers how risky a given project might be by showing how sensitive it is to change. The more sensitive to change a project is (the more NPV changes as cash flows change), the riskier it is. Of course, sensitivity analysis can become complicated very quickly, and doing all of the calculations by hand can be tricky and tedious. Fortunately, there is a good deal of sensitivity analysis software available that lets managers and accountants sit back while computers do all the work.

THE NPV COMPARISON OF TWO PROJECTS

So far we have seen how to use the NPV method to evaluate a single given project. In practice, managers very rarely look at one project or option at a time. Instead, managers need to compare several options to see which is the best or most profitable. We will now see how to use NPV to compare two or more alternatives.

TOTAL PROJECT VERSUS DIFFERENTIAL APPROACH

Two common methods for comparing alternatives are (1) the total project approach and (2) the differential approach.

The **total project approach** computes the total impact on cash flows for each alternative and then converts these total cash flows to their present values. It is the most popular approach and can be used for any number of alternatives. The alternative with the largest NPV of total cash flows is best.

The **differential approach** computes the differences in cash flows between alternatives and then converts these differences to their present values. This method cannot be used to compare more than two alternatives. Often the two alternatives being compared are (1) take on a project and (2) do nothing.

Let's compare the differential and total project approaches. Suppose a company owns a packaging machine that it purchased three years ago for $56,000. The machine has a remaining useful life of five years but will require a major overhaul at the end of two more years at a cost of $10,000. Its disposal value now is $20,000. In five years, its disposal value is expected to be $8,000, assuming that the $10,000 major overhaul will be done on schedule. The cash-operating costs of this machine are expected to be $40,000 annually. A sales representative has offered a substitute machine for $51,000, or for $31,000 plus the old machine. The new machine will reduce annual cash-operating costs by $10,000, will not require any overhauls, will have a useful life of five years, and will have a disposal value of $3,000. If the minimum desired rate of return is 14%, what should the company do to minimize long run costs? (Try to solve this problem yourself before examining the solution that follows.)

Regardless of the approach used, perhaps the hardest part of making capital-budgeting decisions is predicting the relevant cash flows. Seeing which events will cause money to flow either in or out can be very tricky, especially when there are many sources of cash flows. However, you cannot compare alternatives if you do not know their costs, so the first step for either the total project or differential approach is to arrange the relevant cash flows by project. Exhibit 11-2 shows how the cash flows for each alternative are sketched. The next step depends on the approach used.

Objective 3
Calculate the NPV difference between two projects using both the total project and differential approaches.

total project approach A method for comparing alternatives that computes the total impact on cash flows for each alternative and then converts these total cash flows to their present values.

differential approach A method for comparing alternatives that computes the differences in cash flows between alternatives and then converts these differences in cash flows to their present values.

Total Project Approach: Determine the net present value of the cash flows for each individual project. Choose the project with the largest positive net present value (that is, the largest benefit) or smallest negative net present value (that is, the smallest cost).

Differential Approach: Compute the differential cash flows. In other words, subtract the cash flows for project B from the cash flows for project A for each year. Remember that cash inflows are positive numbers while cash outflows are negative. Next, calculate the present value of the differential cash flows. If this present value is positive, choose project A; if it is negative, choose project B.

Exhibit 11-2 illustrates both the total project approach and the differential approach. Note that both methods produce the same answer. As a result, these methods can be used interchangeably, as long as there are only two alternatives under consideration. Because our example had only two alternatives, we could use either method. If our example had more than two alternatives, our only choice would be to use the total project approach.

RELEVANT CASH FLOWS FOR NPV

Objective 4
Identify relevant cash flows for NPV analyses.

As we said earlier, predicting cash flows is the hardest part of capital budgeting. When you array the relevant cash flows, be sure to consider four types of inflows and outflows: (1) initial cash inflows and outflows at time zero, (2) investments in receivables and inventories, (3) future disposal values, and (4) operating cash flows.

INITIAL CASH INFLOWS AND OUTFLOWS AT TIME ZERO These cash flows include both outflows for the purchases and installation of equipment and other items required by the new project, and either inflows or outflows from disposal of any items that are replaced. In Exhibit 11-2 the $20,000 received from selling the old machine was offset against the $51,000 purchase price of the new machine, resulting in a net cash outflow of $31,000. If the old machine could not be sold, any cost incurred to dismantle and discard it would have been added to the purchase price of the new machine.

INVESTMENTS IN RECEIVABLES AND INVENTORIES Investments in receivables and inventories are initial cash outflows just like investments in plant and equipment. In the NPV model, the initial outlays are entered in the sketch of cash flows at time zero. However, receivables and inventories usually differ from plant and equipment at the end of the useful life of the project. Plant and equipment is usually used up during the life of the project, leaving little, if any, salvage value. In contrast, the entire original investments in receivables and inventories are usually recouped when the project ends. Therefore all initial investments are typically regarded as outflows at time zero, and their terminal disposal values, if any, are regarded as inflows at the end of the project's useful life.

The example in Exhibit 11-2 required no additional investment in inventory or receivables. However, the expansion of a retail store, for example, entails an additional investment in a building and fixtures plus inventories. Such investments would be shown in the format of Exhibit 11-2 as follows:

	Sketch of Cash Flows			
End of year	0	1	2...19	20
Investment in building and fixtures	(10)			1
Investment in working capital (inventories)	(6)			6

As the sketch shows, the residual value of the building and fixtures might be small. However, the entire investment in inventories would ordinarily be recouped when the venture is terminated.

Exhibit 11-2

Total Project Versus Differential Approach to Net Present Value

	Present Value Discount Factor, at 14%	Total Present Value	Sketch of After-Tax Cash Flows at End of Year					
			0	1	2	3	4	5
I. Total Project Approach								
A. Replace								
Recurring cash operating costs, using an annuity table*	3.4331	$(102,993)		($30,000)	($30,000)	($30,000)	($30,000)	($30,000)
Disposal value, end of year 5	.5194	1,558						$3,000
Initial required investment	1.0000	(31,000)	($31,000)					
Present value of net cash outflows		$(132,435)						
B. Keep								
Recurring cash operating costs, using an annuity table*	3.4331	$(137,324)		($40,000)	($40,000)	($40,000)	($40,000)	($40,000)
Overhaul, end of year 2	.7695	(7,695)			($10,000)			
Disposal value, end of year 5	.5194	4,155						$8,000
Present value of net cash outflows		$(140,864)						
Difference in favor of replacement		$ 8,429						
II. Differential Approach								
A–B. Analysis confined to differences								
Recurring cash operating savings, using an annuity table*	3.4331	$ 34,331		$10,000	$10,000	$10,000	$10,000	$10,000
Overhaul avoided, end of year 2	.7695	7,695		$10,000				
Difference in disposal values, end of year 5	.5194	(2,597)						$(5,000)
Incremental initial investment	1.0000	(31,000)	($31,000)					
Net present value of replacement		$ 8,429						

*Table 2, Appendix B.

413

The difference between the initial outlay for working capital (mostly receivables and inventories) and the present value of its recovery is the present value of the cost of using working capital in the project.

FUTURE DISPOSAL VALUES Assets other than receivables and inventories may have relevant disposal values. The disposal value at the end of a project is an increase in the cash inflow in the year of disposal. Errors in forecasting terminal disposal values are usually not crucial because the present value is usually small.

OPERATING CASH FLOWS The major purpose of most investments is to affect operating cash inflows and outflows. Many of these effects are difficult to measure, and three points deserve special mention.

First, using relevant-cost analysis, the only relevant cash flows are those that will differ among alternatives. Often fixed overhead will be the same under all the available alternatives. If so, it can be safely ignored. In practice, it is not easy to identify exactly which costs will differ among alternatives.

Second, as mentioned earlier, depreciation and book values should be ignored. The cost of assets is recognized by the initial outlay, not by depreciation as computed under accrual accounting.

Third, a reduction in a cash outflow is treated the same as a cash inflow. Both signify increases in value.

CASH FLOWS FOR INVESTMENTS IN TECHNOLOGY

Many capital-budgeting decisions compare undertaking a possible investment with doing nothing. One such decision is investment in a highly automated production system to replace a traditional system. Cash flows predicted for the automated system should be compared with those predicted for continuation of the present system into the future. The latter are not necessarily the cash flows currently being experienced. Why? Because the competitive environment is changing. If others invest in automated systems, failure to invest may cause a decline in sales and an uncompetitive cost structure. The future without an automated system might be a continual decline in cash flows.

Suppose a company has a $10,000 net cash inflow this year using a traditional system. Investing in an automated system will increase the net cash inflow to $12,000. Failure to invest will cause net cash inflows to fall to $8,000. The benefit from the investment is a cash inflow of $12,000 − $8,000 = $4,000, not $12,000 − $10,000 = $2,000.

SUMMARY PROBLEM FOR YOUR REVIEW

PROBLEM

Review the problem and solution shown in Exhibit 11-2, page 413. Conduct a sensitivity analysis as indicated below. Consider each requirement as independent of other requirements.

1. Compute the NPV if the minimum desired rate of return were 20%.
2. Compute the NPV if predicted cash operating costs were $35,000 instead of $30,000, using the 14% discount rate.
3. By how much may the cash operating savings fall short of the $30,000 predicted before the NPV of the project reaches zero, using the original discount rate of 14%?

SOLUTION

1. Either the total project approach or the differential approach could be used. The differential approach would show:

	Total Present Value
Recurring cash operating savings, using an annuity table (Table 2, p. B8): 2.9906 × $10,000 =	$29,906
Overhaul avoided: .6944 × $10,000 =	6,944
Difference in disposal values: .4019 × $5,000 =	(2,010)
Incremental initial investment	(31,000)
NPV of replacement	$ 3,840

2.

NPV value in Exhibit 11-2	$ 8,429
Present value of additional $5,000 annual operating costs 3.4331 × $5,000	(17,166)
New NPV	$ (8,737)

With $5,000 less in annual savings, the new machine has a negative NPV and therefore is not desirable.

3. Let X = annual cash operating savings and find the value of X such that NPV = 0. Then

$$0 = 3.4331(X) + \$7,695 - \$2,597 - \$31,000$$
$$3.4331X = \$25,902$$
$$X = \$7,545$$

(Note that the $7,695, $2,597, and $31,000 are at the bottom of Exhibit 11-2.)

If the annual savings fall from $10,000 to $7,545, a decrease of $2,455 or almost 25%, the NPV will hit zero.

An alternative way to obtain the same answer would be to divide the NPV of $8,429 (see bottom of Exhibit 11-2) by 3.4331, obtaining $2,455, the amount of the annual difference in savings that will eliminate the $8,429 of NPV.

INCOME TAXES AND CAPITAL BUDGETING

There is another type of cash flow that we must consider when making capital-budgeting decisions: income taxes. Income taxes paid by companies are cash outflows. Their basic role in capital budgeting is not different from that of any other cash outflow. However taxes tend to narrow the cash differences between projects. For example, if the cash savings from operations of one project over another were $1 million, a 40% tax rate would shrink the savings to $600,000. Why? Because $400,000 (40% × $1 million) of the savings would have to be paid in taxes.

Corporations in the United States must pay both federal income taxes and state income taxes. Federal taxes are based on income, with tax rates rising as income rises. The current federal tax rate on ordinary corporate taxable income below $50,000 is 15%. Rates then increase until companies with taxable income over $335,000 pay between 34% and 38% on additional income. State tax rates vary widely from state to state. Therefore, the total tax rate a company has to pay, federal rates plus state rates, also varies widely.

In capital budgeting, the relevant tax rate is the **marginal income tax rate,** that is, the tax rate paid on additional amounts of pretax income. Suppose a corporation pays income

Objective 5
Compute the after-tax net present values of projects.

marginal income tax rate
The tax rate paid on additional amounts of pretax income.

taxes of 15% on the first $50,000 of pretax income and 30% on pretax income over $50,000. What is the company's *marginal income tax rate* when it has $75,000 of pretax income? The marginal rate is 30%, because 30% of any additional income will be paid in taxes. In contrast, the company's *average income tax rate* is only 20% (that is, 15% × $50,000 + 30% × $25,000 = $15,000 of taxes on $75,000 of pretax income). When we assess tax effects of capital-budgeting decisions, we will always use the marginal tax rate because that is the rate applied to the additional cash flows generated by a proposed project.

EFFECTS OF DEPRECIATION DEDUCTIONS

accelerated depreciation A pattern of depreciation that charges a larger proportion of an asset's cost to the earlier years and less to later years.

Organizations that pay income taxes generally keep two sets of books—one for reporting to the public and one for reporting to the tax authorities. In the United States, this practice is not illegal or immoral—in fact, it is necessary. Tax reporting must follow detailed rules designed to achieve certain social goals. These rules do not usually lead to financial statements that best measure an organization's financial results and position, so it is more informative to financial statement users if a separate set of rules is used for financial reporting. In this chapter, we are concerned with measuring cash payments for taxes. Therefore we focus on the tax reporting rules, not those for public financial reporting.

One item that often differs between tax reporting and public reporting is depreciation. Recall that depreciation spreads the cost of an asset over its useful life. Income tax laws and regulations have increasingly permitted the cost to be spread over depreciable lives that are shorter than the assets' useful lives. In addition, **accelerated depreciation,** which charges a larger proportion of an asset's cost to the earlier years and less to later years, is often allowed for tax purposes. In contrast, an asset's depreciation for public reporting purposes is usually the same each year, called straight-line depreciation. For example, a $10,000 asset depreciated over a 5-year useful life would result in *straight-line depreciation* of $10,000 ÷ 5 = $2,000 each year but *accelerated depreciation* of more than $2,000 per year in the early years and less than $2,000 in the later years.

recovery period The number of years over which an asset is depreciated for tax purposes.

Exhibit 11-3 shows the interrelationship of income before taxes, income taxes, and depreciation for Martin's Printing. Assume that the company has a single fixed asset, a printing press, that was purchased for $125,000 cash. The press has a 5-year **recovery period,** which is the number of years over which an asset is depreciated for tax purposes. Using the press produces annual sales revenue of $130,000 and expenses (excluding depreciation) of $70,000. The purchase cost of the press is tax deductible in the form of yearly depreciation.

Depreciating a fixed asset such as the press creates future tax deductions. In this case, these deductions will total $125,000. The present value of this deduction depends directly on its specific yearly effects on future income tax payments. Therefore the present value is influenced by the recovery period, the depreciation method selected, the tax rates, and the discount rate.

Exhibit 11-4 analyzes the Martin's Printing data for capital budgeting, assuming straight-line depreciation. The net present value is $40,821 for the investment in this asset.

The $125,000 investment really buys two streams of cash: (1) net inflows from operations plus (2) savings of income tax outflows (which have the same effect in capital budgeting as do additions to cash inflows) because the depreciation is deductible in computing taxable income. The choice of depreciation method will not affect the cash inflows from operations. But different depreciation methods will affect the cash outflows for income taxes. That is, a straight-line method will produce one present value of tax savings, and an accelerated method will produce a different present value.

Exhibit 11-3

Martin's Printing

Basic Analysis of Income Statement, Income Taxes, and Cash Flows

Traditional Annual Income Statement		
(S)	Sales	$130,000
(E)	Less: Expenses, excluding depreciation	$ 70,000
(D)	Depreciation (straight-line)	25,000
	Total expenses	$ 95,000
	Income before taxes	$ 35,000
(T)	Income taxes @ 40%	14,000
(I)	Net income	$ 21,000

Total after-tax effect on cash is
either S − E − T = $130,000 − $70,000 − $14,000 = $46,000
or I + D = $21,000 + $25,000 = $46,000

Analysis of the Same Facts for Capital Budgeting		
	Cash effects of operations:	
(S−E)	Cash inflow from operations: $130,000 − $70,000	$ 60,000
	Income tax outflow @ 40%	24,000
	After-tax inflow from operations (excluding depreciation)	$ 36,000
	Cash effects of depreciation:	
(D)	Straight-line depreciation: $125,000 ÷ 5 = $25,000	
	Income tax savings @ 40%	10,000
	Total after-tax effect on cash	$ 46,000

TAX DEDUCTIONS, CASH EFFECTS, AND TIMING

Note that the net cash effects of operations in Exhibit 11-4 are computed by multiplying the pretax amounts by one minus the tax rate, or 1 − .40 = .60. The total effect is the cash flow itself less the tax effect. Each additional $1 of sales also adds $.40 of taxes, leaving a net cash inflow of $.60. Each additional $1 of cash expense reduces taxes by $.40, leaving a net cash outflow of $.60. Thus the after-tax effect of the $130,000 − $70,000 = $60,000 net cash inflow from operations is $130,000 × .6 − $70,000 × .6 = ($130,000 − $70,000) × .6 = $60,000 × .6 = $36,000.

In contrast, the after-tax effects of the *noncash* expenses (depreciation) are computed by multiplying the tax deduction of $25,000 by the tax rate itself, or $25,000 × .40 = $10,000. Note that this is a cash inflow because it is a decrease in the tax payment. The total cash effect of a noncash expense is only the tax-savings effect.

Throughout the illustrations in this chapter, we assume that all income tax flows occur at the same time as the related pretax cash flows. For example, we assume that both the net $60,000 pretax cash inflow and the related $24,000 tax payment occurred in year 1 and that no part of the tax payment was delayed until year 2. We also assume that the companies in question are profitable. That is, the companies will have enough taxable income from all sources to use all income tax benefits in the situations described.

ACCELERATED DEPRECIATION

Governments frequently allow accelerated depreciation to encourage investments in long-lived assets. To see why accelerated depreciation is attractive to investors, reconsider the facts in Exhibit 11-4. Suppose, as is the case in some countries, that the entire initial

Exhibit 11-4

Impact of Income Taxes on Capital-Budgeting Analysis

Assume: original cost of equipment, $125,000; 5-year life; zero terminal disposal value; pretax annual cash inflow from operations, $60,000; income tax rate, 40%; required after-tax rate of return, 12%. All items are in dollars except discount factors. The after-tax cash flows are from Exhibit 11-3.

	12% Discount Factor, from Appropriate Tables	Total Present Value at 12%	Sketch of After-Tax Cash Flows at End of Year					
			0	1	2	3	4	5
Cash effects of operations, excluding depreciation, $60,000 × (1 − .4)	3.6048	$129,773		36,000	36,000	36,000	36,000	36,000
Cash effects of straight-line depreciation: savings of income taxes, $25,000 × .4	3.6048	36,048		10,000	10,000	10,000	10,000	10,000
Total after-tax effect on cash		165,821						
Investment	1.0000	(125,000)	(125,000)					
Net present value of the investment		$ 40,821						

investment can be written off immediately for income tax reporting. We see that net present value will rise from $40,821 to $54,773:

	Present Values	
	As in Exhibit 11-4	Complete Write-Off Immediately
Cash effects of operations	$ 129,773	$ 129,773
Cash effects of depreciation	36,048	50,000*
Total after-tax effect on cash	165,821	179,773
Investment	(125,000)	(125,000)
Net present value	$ 40,821	$ 54,773

*Assumes that the tax effect occurs simultaneously with the investment at time zero: $125,000 × .40 = $50,000.

In summary, the earlier you can take the depreciation, the greater the present value of the income tax savings. The total tax savings will be the same regardless of the depreciation method. In the example, the tax savings from the depreciation deduction is either .40 × $125,000 = $50,000 immediately or .40 × $25,000 = $10,000 per year for five years, a total of $50,000. However, the time value of money makes the immediate savings worth more than future savings. The mottoes in income tax planning are: "When there is a legal choice, take the deduction sooner rather than later," and "Recognize taxable income later rather than sooner."

Managers have an obligation to stockholders to minimize and delay taxes to the extent permitted by law. For example, astute managers use accelerated depreciation instead of straight-line depreciation whenever the law permits its use. This is called tax avoidance. Careful tax planning can have large financial payoffs. In contrast, managers must not engage in tax evasion, which is illegally reducing taxes by recording fictitious deductions or failing to report income. Managers who *avoid* taxes get bonuses; those who *evade* taxes often land in jail.

MODIFIED ACCELERATED COST RECOVERY SYSTEM (MACRS)

Under U.S. income tax laws, most assets purchased since 1987 are depreciated using the Modified Accelerated Cost Recovery System (MACRS). This system specifies a recovery period and an accelerated depreciation schedule for all types of assets. Each asset is placed in one of the eight classes shown in Exhibit 11-5.

Exhibit 11-5

Examples of Assets in Modified Accelerated Cost Recovery System (MACRS) Classes

3-year	Special tools for several specific industries; tractor units for over-the-road.
5-year	Automobiles; trucks; research equipment; computers; machinery and equipment in selected industries.
7-year	Office furniture; railroad tracks; machinery and equipment in a majority of industries.
10-year	Water transportation equipment; machinery and equipment in selected industries.
15-year	Most land improvements; machinery and equipment in selected industries.
20-year	Farm buildings; electricity generation and distribution equipment.
27.5-year	Residential rental property.
31.5-year	Nonresidential real property.

Exhibit 11-6

Selected MACRS Depreciation Schedules

Tax Year	3-Year Property	5-Year Property	7-Year Property	10-Year Property
1	33.33%	20.00%	14.29%	10.00%
2	44.45	32.00	24.49	18.00
3	14.81	19.20	17.49	14.40
4	7.41	11.52	12.49	11.52
5		11.52	8.93	9.22
6		5.76	8.92	7.37
7			8.93	6.55
8			4.46	6.55
9				6.56
10				6.55
11				3.28

Exhibit 11-6 presents MACRS depreciation schedules for recovery periods of 3, 5, 7, and 10 years. Note that each schedule extends one year beyond the recovery period because MACRS assumes one half-year of depreciation in the first year and one half-year in the final year. Thus, a 3-year MACRS depreciation schedule has one half-year of depreciation in years 1 and 4 and a full year of depreciation in years 2 and 3. MACRS depreciation can be applied to the example in Exhibit 11-4 as follows, assuming that the printing press that was purchased is a 5-year MACRS asset:

Year	Tax Rate (1)	PV Factor @12% (2)	Depreciation (3)	Present Value of Tax Savings (1) × (2) × (3)
1	.40	0.8929	$125,000 × .2000 = $25,000	$ 8,929
2	.40	0.7972	125,000 × .3200 = 40,000	12,755
3	.40	0.7118	125,000 × .1920 = 24,000	6,833
4	.40	0.6355	125,000 × .1152 = 14,400	3,660
5	.40	0.5674	125,000 × .1152 = 14,400	3,268
6	.40	0.5066	125,000 × .0576 = 7,200	1,459
				$36,904

How much was gained by using MACRS instead of straight-line depreciation? The $36,904 present value of tax savings is $856 higher with MACRS than the $36,048 achieved with straight-line depreciation (see Exhibit 11-4 on p. 418).

PRESENT VALUE OF MACRS DEPRECIATION

In capital-budgeting decisions managers often want to know the present value of the tax savings from depreciation. Exhibit 11-7 provides present values for $1 to be depreciated over MACRS schedules for 3-, 5-, 7-, and 10-year recovery periods for a variety of interest rates. For example, consider a company with a 3-year asset and 10% minimum desired rate of return. The present value of $1 of MACRS depreciation is:

Year	Depreciation (1)	PV Factor (2)	PV of Depreciation (1) × (2)
1	$0.3333	0.9091	0.3030
2	0.4445	0.8264	0.3673
3	0.1481	0.7513	0.1113
4	0.0741	0.6830	0.0506
Total Depreciation	1.0000		
Present Value of $1 depreciation, shown in Exhibit 11-7			0.8322

Exhibit 11-7

Present Value of $1 of MACRS Depreciation

Discount Rate	3-year	5-year	7-year	10-year
3%	0.9439	0.9215	0.9002	0.8698
4%	0.9264	0.8975	0.8704	0.8324
5%	0.9095	0.8746	0.8422	0.7975
6%	0.8931	0.8526	0.8155	0.7649
7%	0.8772	0.8315	0.7902	0.7344
8%	0.8617	0.8113	0.7661	0.7059
9%	0.8468	0.7919	0.7432	0.6792
10%	0.8322	0.7733	0.7214	0.6541
12%	0.8044	0.7381	0.6810	0.6084
14%	0.7782	0.7055	0.6441	0.5678
15%	0.7657	0.6902	0.6270	0.5492
16%	0.7535	0.6753	0.6106	0.5317
18%	0.7300	0.6473	0.5798	0.4993
20%	0.7079	0.6211	0.5517	0.4702
22%	0.6868	0.5968	0.5257	0.4439
24%	0.6669	0.5740	0.5019	0.4201
25%	0.6573	0.5631	0.4906	0.4090
26%	0.6479	0.5526	0.4798	0.3985
28%	0.6299	0.5327	0.4594	0.3787
30%	0.6128	0.5139	0.4404	0.3606
40%	0.5381	0.4352	0.3632	0.2896

You can find the present value of tax savings in three steps:

1. Find the factor from Exhibit 11-7 for the appropriate recovery period and required rate of return.
2. Multiply the factor by the tax rate to find the tax savings per dollar of investment.
3. Multiply the result by the amount of the investment to find the total tax savings.

For example, consider our investment of $125,000 in equipment with a 5-year MACRS recovery period. A 12% after-tax required rate of return and a 40% tax rate produce a tax savings with a present value of .7381 × .40 × $125,000 = $36,905. This differs from the $36,904 above by a $1 rounding error.

GAINS OR LOSSES ON DISPOSAL

The disposal of equipment for cash can also affect income taxes. Suppose the press purchased for $125,000 in our Martin's Printing example is sold at the end of year 3 after taking three years of straight-line depreciation. If it is sold for its book value, $125,000 − (3 × $25,000) = $50,000, there is no tax effect. If Martin's Printing receives more than $50,000, there is a gain and an additional tax payment. If the company receives less than $50,000 there is a loss and a tax savings. The following table shows the effects on cash flow for sales prices of $70,000 and $20,000:

(a)	Cash proceeds of sale	$70,000	$ 20,000
	Book value: zero and [$125,000 − 3 ($25,000)]	50,000	50,000
	Gain (loss)	$20,000	$(30,000)
	Effect on income taxes at 40%:		
(b)	Tax saving, an inflow effect: .40 × loss		$ 12,000
(c)	Tax paid, an outflow: .40 × gain	$(8,000)	
	Net cash inflow from sale:		
	(a) plus (b)		$ 32,000
	(a) minus (c)	$62,000	

SUMMARY PROBLEM FOR YOUR REVIEW

PROBLEM

In the investment opportunity in Exhibit 11-4, page 418: original cost of equipment, $125,000; 5-year economic life; zero terminal salvage value; pretax annual cash inflow from operations, $60,000; income tax rate, 40%; required after-tax rate of return, 12%. Assume the equipment is a 5-year MACRS asset for tax purposes. The net present value (NPV) is:

	Present Values (PV)
Cash effects of operations,*	
$60,000 × (1 − .40) × 3.6048	$129,773
Cash effects of depreciation on income	
tax savings using MACRS,	
$125,000 × .40 × .7381†	36,905
Total after-tax effect on cash	$166,678
Investment	125,000
Net present value	$ 41,678

*See Exhibit 11-4, page 418, for details; †Factor .7381 is from Exhibit 11-7, page 421.

Consider each requirement independently. Compute the NPV of the investment for each.

Required

1. Suppose the equipment was expected to be sold for $20,000 cash immediately after the end of year 5.

2. Ignore the assumption in requirement 1. Return to the original data. Suppose the economic life of the equipment was 8 years, not 5 years. But, MACRS cost recovery over 5 years is still allowed for tax purposes.

SOLUTION

1.	Net present value as given		$41,678
	Cash proceeds of sale	$ 20,000	
	Book value	0	
	Gain	$ 20,000	
	Income taxes at 40%	8,000	
	Total after-tax effect on cash	$ 12,000	
	PV of $12,000 to be received in		
	5 years at 12%, $12,000 × .5674		6,809
	NPV of investment		$48,487
2.	Net present value as given		$41,678
	Add the present value of $36,000 per year for 8 years		
	Discount factor of 4.9676 × $36,000 =	$178,834	
	Deduct the present value of $36,000 per year for 5 years	129,773	
	Increase in present value		49,061
	Net present value		$90,739

The investment would be very attractive. Note especially that the recovery period for tax purposes and the economic useful life of the asset need not be equal. The tax law specifies lives (or recovery periods) for various types of depreciable assets. The tax life is unaffected by the economic useful life of the asset. Thus a longer useful life for an asset increases operating cash flows without decreasing the present value of the tax savings.

CONFUSION ABOUT DEPRECIATION

The meanings of *depreciation* and *book value* are widely misunderstood. Let's review their role in decisions. Suppose a bank is considering the replacement of some old copying equipment with a book value of $30,000, an expected terminal disposal value of zero, a current disposal value of $12,000, and a remaining useful life of three years. For simplicity, assume that the bank will take straight-line depreciation of $10,000 yearly. The tax rate is 40%.

These data should be examined in perspective, as Exhibit 11-8 indicates. In particular, note that the inputs to the decision model are the predicted income tax effects on cash. Book values and depreciation may be necessary for making predictions. By themselves, however, they are not inputs to DCF decision models.

CAPITAL BUDGETING AND INFLATION

In addition to taxes, capital-budgeting decision makers should consider the effects of inflation on their cash flow predictions. **Inflation** is the decline in the general purchasing power of the monetary unit. For example, a dollar today will buy only half as much as it did in the early 1980s. At a 5% annual inflation rate, average prices rise more than 60%

inflation The decline in the general purchasing power of the monetary unit.

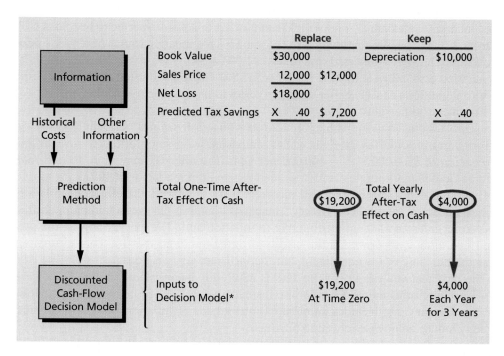

*There will, of course, be other related inputs to this decision model, for example, the cost of the new equipment and the differences in future annual cash flows from operations.

Exhibit 11-8

Perspective on Book Value and Depreciation

over 10 years. In countries such as Brazil and Argentina, triple-digit annual inflation rates (that is, average prices more than doubling each year) have been commonplace and have significantly affected business decisions. If significant inflation is expected over the life of a project, it should be specifically and consistently analyzed in a capital-budgeting model.

WATCH FOR CONSISTENCY

The key to appropriate consideration of inflation in capital budgeting is consistent treatment of the minimum desired rate of return and the predicted cash inflows and outflows. Such consistency can be achieved by including an element for inflation in both the minimum desired rate of return and in the cash-flow predictions.

nominal rate Quoted market interest rate that includes an inflation element.

Many firms base their minimum desired rate of return on market interest rates, also called **nominal rates,** that include an inflation element. For example, consider three possible components of a 15% nominal rate:

(a)	Risk-free element—the "pure" rate of interest that is paid on long-term federal bonds		6%
(b)	Business-risk element—the "risk" premium that is demanded for taking larger risks		5
(a) + (b)	Often called the "real rate"		11%
(c)	Inflation element—the premium demanded because of expected deterioration of the general purchasing power of the monetary unit		4
(a) + (b) + (c)	Often called the "nominal rate"		15%

Four percentage points out of the 15% return compensate an investor for receiving future payments in inflated dollars, that is, in dollars with less purchasing power than those invested. Therefore, basing the minimum desired rate of return on quoted market rates automatically includes an inflation element in the rate. Companies that base their minimum desired rate of return on market rates should also adjust their cash-flow predictions for anticipated inflation. For example, suppose 1,000 units of a product are expected to be sold in each of the next two years. Assume this year's price is $50, and inflation causes next year's price to be $52.50. This year's predicted cash inflow is 1,000 × $50 = $50,000 and next year's inflation adjusted cash inflow is 1,000 × $52.50 = $52,500. Inflation-adjusted cash flows are the inflows and outflows expected after adjusting prices to reflect anticipated inflation.

Consider another illustration: purchase cost of equipment, $200,000; useful life, five years; zero terminal salvage value; pretax operating cash savings per year, $83,333 (in 19X0 dollars); income tax rate, 40%. For simplicity, we assume ordinary straight-line depreciation of $200,000 ÷ 5 = $40,000 per year. The after-tax minimum desired rate, based on quoted market rates, is 25%. It includes an inflation factor of 10%.

Exhibit 11-9 displays correct and incorrect ways to analyze the effects of inflation. The key words are internal consistency. The correct analysis (1) uses a minimum desired rate that includes an element attributable to inflation and (2) explicitly adjusts the predicted operating cash flows for the effects of inflation. Note that the correct analysis favors the purchase of the equipment, but the incorrect analysis does not.

The incorrect analysis in Exhibit 11-9 is inherently inconsistent. The predicted cash inflows exclude adjustments for inflation. Instead, they are stated in 19X0 dollars. However, the discount rate includes an element attributable to inflation. Such an analytical flaw may induce an unwise refusal to purchase.

ROLE OF DEPRECIATION

The correct analysis in Exhibit 11-9 shows that the tax effects of depreciation are not adjusted for inflation. Why? Because U.S. income tax laws permit a depreciation deduction based on the original dollars invested, nothing more.

Exhibit 11-9
Inflation and Capital Budgeting

Description	At 25% PV Factor	At 25% Present Value	Sketch of Relevant Cash Flows (at End of Year) 0	1	2	3	4	5
Correct Analysis (Be sure the discount rate includes an element attributable to inflation and adjust the predicted cash flows for inflationary effects.)								
Cash operating inflows:								
Pretax inflow in 19X0 dollars $83,333								
Income tax effect at 40% 33,333								
After-tax effect on cash $50,000								
	.8000	$ 44,000		$55,000*				
	.6400	38,720			$60,500			
	.5120	34,074				$66,550		
	.4096	29,985					$73,205	
	.3277	26,388						$80,526
Subtotal		$173,167						
Annual depreciation $200,000 ÷ 5 = $40,000								
Cash effect of depreciation Savings in income taxes @ 40% = $40,000 × .40 = $16,000	2.6893	43,029		$16,000†	$16,000	$16,000	$16,000	$16,000
Investment in equipment	1.0000	(200,000)	(200,000)					
Net present value		$ 16,196						
Incorrect Analysis (A common error is to include an inflation element in the discount rate as above, but not adjust the predicted cash inflows.)								
Cash operating inflows after taxes	2.6893	$134,465		$50,000	$50,000	$50,000	$50,000	$50,000
Tax effect of depreciation	2.6893	43,029		16,000	16,000	16,000	16,000	16,000
Investment in equipment	1.0000	(200,000)	($200,000)					
Net present value		$(22,506)						

* Each year is adjusted for anticipated inflation: $50,000 × 1.10, $50,000 × 1.10^2, $50,000 × 1.10^3$, and so on.

† The annual savings in income taxes from depreciation will be unaffected by inflation. Why? Because the income tax deduction must be based on original cost of the asset in 19X0 dollars.

425

Critics of income tax laws emphasize that capital investment is discouraged by not allowing the adjusting of depreciation deductions for inflationary effects. For instance, the net present value in Exhibit 11-9 would be larger if depreciation were not confined to the $40,000 amount per year. The latter generates a $16,000 saving in 19X1 dollars, then $16,000 in 19X2 dollars, and so forth. Defenders of existing U.S. tax laws assert that capital investment is encouraged in many other ways. The most prominent example is provision for accelerated depreciation over lives that are much shorter than the economic lives of the assets.

IMPROVEMENT OF PREDICTIONS WITH FEEDBACK

The ability to forecast and cope with changing prices is a valuable management skill, especially when inflation is significant. Auditing and feedback should help evaluate management's predictive skills.

The adjustment of the operating cash flows in Exhibit 11-9 uses a *general-price-level* rate of 10%. However, where feasible, managers should use *specific* rates or tailor-made predictions for price changes in materials, labor, and other items. These predictions may have different percentage changes from year to year.

SUMMARY PROBLEMS FOR YOUR REVIEW

PROBLEM

Examine the correct analysis in Exhibit 11-9, page 425. Suppose the cash operating inflows persisted for an extra year. Compute the present value of the inflow for the sixth year. Ignore depreciation.

SOLUTION

The cash operating inflow would be $50,000 \times 1.10^6$, or $80,526 \times 1.10$, or $88,579. Its present value would be $88,579 \times .2621$, the factor from Table 1 of Appendix B (period 6 row, 25% column), or $23,217.

PROBLEM

Examine the MACRS depreciation schedule near the top of page 420. Assume an anticipated inflation rate of 7%. How would you change the present values of depreciation to accommodate the inflation rate?

SOLUTION

The computations on page 420 would not be changed. The tax effects of depreciation are unaffected by inflation. U.S. income tax laws permit a deduction based on the original dollars invested, nothing more.

OTHER MODELS FOR ANALYZING LONG-RANGE DECISIONS

Although more and more companies are using DCF models to make their capital-budgeting decisions, there are still other models in use. All of these models are simpler than is NPV, but they are also less useful. However, many companies still use these lesser models, which can provide some interesting supplemental information to DCF models. We will examine the payback and accounting-rate-of-return models.

Payback Model

Objective 8
Use the payback model and the accounting rate-of-return model and compare them with the NPV model.

Payback time or **payback period** is the time it will take to recoup, in the form of cash inflows from operations, the initial dollars invested in a project. Assume that $12,000 is spent for a machine with an estimated useful life of 8 years. Annual savings of $4,000 in cash outflows are expected from operations. Depreciation is ignored. The payback period is three years, calculated as follows:

$$\text{payback time} = \frac{\text{initial incremental amount invested}}{\text{equal annual incremental cash}}$$
$$\text{inflow from operations}$$

$$P = \frac{I}{O} = \frac{\$12,000}{\$4,000} = 3 \text{ years}$$

payback time (payback period) The time it will take to recoup, in the form of cash inflows from operations, the initial dollars invested in a project.

This formula for payback time can be used only when there are equal annual cash inflows from operations. When annual cash inflows are not equal, we must add up each year's net cash flows until the initial investment is recouped. Assume the following cash flow pattern:

End of Year	0	1	2	3
Investment	($31,000)			
Cash inflows		$10,000	$20,000	$10,000

The calculation of the payback period is:

Year	Initial Investment	Net Cash Inflows Each Year	Net Cash Inflows Accumulated
0	$31,000	—	—
1	—	$10,000	$10,000
2	—	20,000	30,000
2.1	—	1,000	31,000

In this case, the payback time is slightly beyond the second year. Interpolation within the third year reveals that an additional .1 years is needed to recoup the final $1,000, making the payback period 2.1 years:

$$2 \text{ years} + \left(\frac{\$1,000}{\$10,000} \times 1 \text{ year} \right) = 2.1 \text{ years}$$

A major weakness of the payback model is that it does not measure profitability, which is a primary goal of businesses and the basis for choosing capital investments. The payback model merely measures how quickly investment dollars may be recouped. However, a project with a shorter payback time is not necessarily preferable to one with a longer payback time. After all, a company can recoup its entire investment immediately by not investing.

Sometimes managers use the payback period as a rough estimate of the riskiness of a project. Suppose a company faces rapid technological changes. Cash flows beyond the first few years may be extremely uncertain. In such a situation, projects that recoup their investment quickly may be less risky than those that require a longer wait until the cash starts flowing in.

Accounting Rate-of-Return Model

accounting rate-of-return (ARR) model A non-DCF capital-budgeting model expressed as the increase in expected average annual operating income divided by the initial required investment.

The **accounting rate-of-return (ARR) model,** also known as the *accrual accounting rate-of-return model* (a more accurate description), the *unadjusted rate-of-return model,* and the *book-value model,* expresses a project's return as the increase in expected average annual operating income divided by the initial required investment:

$$\text{accounting rate-of-return (ARR)} = \frac{\text{increase in expected average annual operating income}}{\text{initial required investment}}$$

$$= \frac{O-D}{I} = \frac{\text{average annual incremental cash inflow from operations} - \text{incremental average annual depreciation}}{\text{initial required investment}}$$

Its computations dovetail most closely with conventional accounting models of calculating income and required investment, and they show the effect of an investment on an organization's financial statements.

To see how ARR works, assume the same facts as in Exhibit 11-1: Investment is $6,075, useful life is four years, estimated disposal value is zero, and expected annual cash inflow from operations is $2,000. Annual depreciation would be $6,075 ÷ 4 = $1,518.75, rounded to $1,519. Substitute these values in the accounting rate-of-return equation:

$$\text{ARR} = \frac{\$2,000 - \$1,519}{\$6,075} = 7.9\%$$

Some companies use the "average" investment (often assumed for equipment as being the average book value over the useful life) instead of original investment in the denominator. Therefore, the denominator becomes $6,075 ÷ 2 = $3,037.5, and the rate doubles:[3]

$$\text{ARR} = \frac{\$2,000 - \$1,519}{\$3,037.50} = 15.8\%$$

The accounting rate-of-return model is based on the familiar financial statements prepared under accrual accounting. Unlike the payback model, the accounting model at least has profitability as an objective. Nevertheless, it has a major drawback. The accounting model ignores the time value of money. Expected future dollars are erroneously regarded as equal to present dollars. DCF models explicitly allow for the force of interest and the timing of cash flows. In contrast, the accounting model is based on annual averages. It uses concepts of investment and income that were originally designed for the quite different purpose of accounting for periodic income and financial position.

PERFORMANCE EVALUATION

POTENTIAL CONFLICT

Objective 9
Reconcile the conflict between using an NPV model for making a decision and using accounting income for evaluating the related performance.

Many managers are reluctant to accept DCF models as the best way to make capital-budgeting decisions. Their reluctance stems from the wide usage of accounting income for evaluating performance. That is, managers become frustrated if they are instructed to use a DCF model for making decisions but are evaluated later using a non-DCF model, such as the typical accounting rate-of-return model.

To illustrate, consider the potential conflict that might arise in the example of Exhibit 11-1. Recall that the NPV was $265 based on a 10% required rate of return and an outlay of $6,075 that would generate cash savings of $2,000 for each of 4 years and have no terminal disposal value. Using accounting income computed with straight-line depreciation, the evaluation of performance for years one through four would be:

---

[3]*The measure of the investment recovered in the preceding example is $1,519 per year, the amount of the annual depreciation. Consequently, the average investment committed to the project would decline at a rate of $1,519 per year from $6,075 to zero; hence the average investment would be the beginning balance plus the ending balance ($6,075 + 0) divided by 2, or $3,037.50. Note that when the ending balance is not zero, the average investment will not be half the initial investment.*

	Year 1	Year 2	Year 3	Year 4
Cash-operating savings	$2,000	$2,000	$2,000	$2,000
Straight-line depreciation, $6,075 ÷ 4	1,519	1,519	1,519	1,519*
Effect on operating income	481	481	481	481
Book value at beginning of year	6,075	4,556	3,037	1,518
Accounting rate of return	7.9%	10.6%	15.8%	31.7%

* Total depreciation of 4 × $1,519 = $6,076 differs from $6,075 because of rounding error.

Many managers would be reluctant to replace equipment, despite the positive NPV, if their performance were evaluated by accounting income. They might be especially reluctant if they are likely to be transferred to new positions every year or two. Why? This accrual accounting system understates the return in early years, especially in year 1 when the return is below the required rate, and a manager might not be around to reap the benefits of the later overstatement of returns.

As Chapter 6 indicated, managerial reluctance to replace is reinforced if a heavy book loss on old equipment would appear in year 1's income statement—even though such a loss would be irrelevant in a properly constructed decision model. Thus, performance evaluation based on typical accounting measures can cause the rejection of major, long-term projects such as investments in technologically advanced production systems. This pattern may help explain why many U.S. firms seem to be excessively short-term oriented.

RECONCILIATION OF CONFLICT

The best way to reconcile any potential conflict between capital budgeting and performance evaluation is to use DCF for both capital-budgeting decisions and performance evaluation. A recent survey showed that most large companies (approximately 76%) conduct a follow-up evaluation of at least some capital-budgeting decisions, often called a **postaudit.** The purposes of postaudits include

postaudit A follow-up evaluation of capital-budgeting decisions.

1. Seeing that investment expenditures are proceeding on time and within budget.
2. Comparing actual cash flows with those originally predicted, in order to motivate careful and honest predictions.
3. Providing information for improving future predictions of cash flows.
4. Evaluating the continuation of the project.

By focusing the postaudit on actual versus predicted cash flows, the evaluation is consistent with the decision process.

However, postauditing of all capital-budgeting decisions is costly. Most accounting systems are designed to evaluate operating performances of products, departments, divisions, territories, and so on, year by year. In contrast, capital-budgeting decisions frequently deal with individual projects, not the collection of projects that are usually being managed at the same time by divisional or department managers. Therefore, usually only selected capital-budgeting decisions are audited.

The conflicts between the longstanding, pervasive accrual accounting model and various formal decision models represent one of the most serious unsolved problems in the design of management control systems. Top management cannot expect goal congruence if it favors the use of one type of model for decisions and the use of another type for performance evaluation.

Highlights to Remember

Describe capital budgeting decisions and use the net present value (NPV) method to make such decisions. Capital budgeting is long-term planning for proposed capital outlays and their financing. The net present value (NPV) model aids this process by computing the present value of all expected future cash flows using a minimum desired rate of return. Projects with an NPV greater than zero should be accepted.

Evaluate projects using sensitivity analysis. Managers use sensitivity analysis to aid risk assessment by examining the effects if actual cash flows differ from those expected.

Calculate the NPV difference between two projects using both the total project and differential approaches. The total project approach compares the NPVs of the cash flows from each project, while the differential approach computes the NPV of the difference in cash flows between two projects. Both produce the same results if there are two alternatives. The total project approach must be used with more than two alternatives.

Identify relevant cash flows for NPV analyses. Predicting cash flows is the hardest part of capital budgeting. Four categories of cash flows should be considered: initial cash inflows and outflows at time zero, investments in receivables and inventories, future disposal values, and operating cash flows.

Compute the after-tax net present values of projects. Income taxes can have a significant effect on the desirability of an investment. Additional taxes are cash outflows, and tax savings are cash inflows. Accelerated depreciation speeds up a company's tax savings. Generally, depreciation deductions should be taken as early as legally permitted.

Explain the after-tax effect on cash of disposing of assets. When assets are sold for more than their book value, the gain generates additional taxes. When assets are sold for less than their book value, the loss generates tax savings.

Compute the impact of inflation on a capital-budgeting project. Consistency is the key in adjusting capital budgeting analyses for inflation. The required rate of return should include an element attributable to anticipated inflation, and cash flow predictions should be adjusted for the effects of anticipated inflation.

Use the payback model and the accounting rate-of-return model and compare them with the NPV model. The payback model is simple to apply, but it does not measure profitability. The accounting rate-of-return model uses accounting measures of income and investment, but it ignores the time value of money. Both models are inferior to the NPV model.

Reconcile the conflict between using an NPV model for making a decision and using accounting income for evaluating the related performance. NPV is a summary measure of all the cash flows from a project. Accounting income is a one-period measure. A positive NPV project can have low (or even negative) accounting income in the first year. Managers may be reluctant to invest in such a project, despite its positive value to the company, especially if they expect to be transferred to a new position before the positive returns are recognized.

Understand how companies make long-term investment decisions and how such decisions can affect the companies' financial results for years to come. Long-term capital investments are critical to a company's financial success. Using a discounted cash flow method, such as NPV, helps managers make optimal capital budgeting decisions. Predicting cash flows, including the effects of taxes and inflation, is an important part of capital budgeting decisions.

Accounting Vocabulary

accelerated depreciation, p. 416

accounting rate-of-return (ARR) model, p. 427

capital budgeting, p. 406

differential approach, p. 411

discount rate, p. 407

discounted-cash-flow (DCF) models, p. 406

hurdle rate, p. 407

inflation, p. 423

marginal income tax rate, p. 415

net-present-value (NPV) method, p. 407

nominal rate, p. 424

payback period, p. 427

payback time, p. 427

postaudit, p. 429

recovery period, p. 416

required rate of return, p. 407

total project approach, p. 411

Fundamental Assignment Material

Special note: In all assignment material where taxes are considered, assume, unless directed otherwise, that (1) all income tax cash flows occur simultaneously with the pre-tax cash flows, and (2) the companies in question will have enough taxable income from other sources to use all income tax benefits from the situations described.

11-A1 Exercises in Compound Interest: Answers Supplied
Use the appropriate interest table from Appendix B (see pp. B7 or B8) to complete the following exercises:

The answers appear at the end of the assignment material for this chapter, p. 450.

1. It is your 55th birthday. You plan to work five more years before retiring. Then you and your spouse want to take $20,000 for a round-the-world tour. What lump sum do you have to invest now to accumulate the $20,000? Assume that your minimum desired rate of return is
   a. 4%, compounded annually
   b. 10%, compounded annually
   c. 20%, compounded annually

2. You want to spend $2,000 on a vacation at the end of each of the next five years. What lump sum do you have to invest now to take the five vacations? Assume that your minimum desired rate of return is
   a. 4%, compounded annually
   b. 10%, compounded annually
   c. 20%, compounded annually

3. At age 60, you find that your employer is moving to another location. You receive termination pay of $100,000. You have some savings and wonder whether to retire now.
   a. If you invest the $100,000 now at 4%, compounded annually, how much money can you withdraw from your account each year so that at the end of five years there will be a zero balance?
   b. Answer part a assuming that you invest it at 10%.

4. Two NBA basketball players, Johnson and Jackson, signed five-year, $30 million contracts. At 16%, compounded annually, which of the following contracts is more desirable in terms of present values? Show computations to support your answer.

	Annual Cash Inflows (000)	
Year	*Johnson*	*Jackson*
1	$10,000	$ 2,000
2	8,000	4,000
3	6,000	6,000
4	4,000	8,000
5	2,000	10,000
	$30,000	$30,000

11-A2 NPV for Investment Decisions
A manager of the Administrative Computer Center of Northern State University is contemplating acquiring 60 computers. The computers will cost $330,000 cash, have zero terminal salvage value and a useful life of three years. Annual cash savings from operations will be $150,000. The required rate of return is 16%. There are no taxes.

Required

1. Compute the net present value.
2. Should the Computer Center acquire the computers? Explain.

11-A3 Taxes, Straight-Line Depreciation, and Present Values

A manager of Quantum Software is contemplating acquiring 60 computers used for designing software. The computers will cost $330,000 cash and will have zero terminal salvage value. The recovery period and useful life are both three years. Annual pretax cash savings from operations will be $150,000. The income tax rate is 40%, and the required after-tax rate of return is 12%.

Required

1. Compute the net present value, assuming straight-line depreciation of $110,000 yearly for tax purposes. Should Quantum acquire the computers? Explain.

2. Suppose the computers will be fully depreciated at the end of year 3 but can be sold for $40,000 cash. Compute the net present value. Should Quantum acquire the computers? Explain.

3. Ignore requirement 2. Suppose the required after-tax rate of return is 8% instead of 12%. Should the computers be acquired? Show computations.

11-A4 MACRS and Present Values

The president of Southern States Power Company is considering whether to buy some equipment for its White River plant. The equipment will cost $1.5 million cash and will have a 10-year useful life and zero terminal salvage value. Annual pretax cash savings from operations will be $360,000. The income tax rate is 40%, and the required after-tax rate of return is 16%.

Required

1. Compute the net present value, using a 7-year recovery period and MACRS depreciation for tax purposes. Should the equipment be acquired?

2. Suppose the economic life of the equipment is 15 years, which means that there will be $360,000 additional annual cash savings from operations in years 11 to 15. Assume that a 7-year recovery period is used. Should the equipment be acquired? Show computations.

11-A5 Gains or Losses on Disposal

An asset with a book value of $50,000 was sold for cash on January 1, 19X6.

Required

Assume two selling prices: $65,000 and $30,000. For each selling price, prepare a tabulation of the gain or loss, the effect on income taxes, and the total after-tax effect on cash. The applicable income tax rate is 30%.

11-B1 Exercises in Compound Interest

Use the appropriate table to compute the following:

1. You have always dreamed of taking a trip to the Great Barrier Reef. What lump sum do you have to invest today to have the $12,000 needed for the trip in three years? Assume that you can invest the money at
   a. 5%, compounded annually
   b. 10%, compounded annually
   c. 18%, compounded annually

2. You are considering partial retirement. To do so you need to use part of your savings to supplement your income for the next five years. Suppose you need an extra $15,000 per year. What lump sum do you have to invest now to supplement your income for five years? Assume that your minimum desired rate of return is
   a. 5%, compounded annually
   b. 10%, compounded annually
   c. 18%, compounded annually

3. You just won a lump sum of $400,000 in a local lottery. You have decided to invest the winnings and withdraw an equal amount each year for 10 years. How much can you withdraw each year and have a zero balance left at the end of 10 years if you invest at
   a. 6%, compounded annually
   b. 10%, compounded annually

4. A professional athlete is offered the choice of two 4-year salary contracts, contract A for $1.4 million and contract B for $1.3 million:

	Contract A	Contract B
End of year 1	$ 200,000	$ 450,000
End of year 2	300,000	350,000
End of year 3	400,000	300,000
End of year 4	500,000	200,000
Total	$1,400,000	$1,300,000

Which contract has the higher present value at 14% compounded annually? Show computations to support your answer.

11-B2 NPV for Investment Decisions
The head of the Oncology Department of Lincoln County Hospital is considering the purchase of some equipment used for cancer research. The cost is $400,000, the economic life is five years, and there is no terminal disposal value. Annual cash inflows from operations would increase by $140,000 and the required rate of return is 18%. There are no taxes.

Required

1. Compute the net present value.
2. Should the equipment be acquired? Explain.

11-B3 Taxes, Straight-Line Depreciation, and NPV
The president of CellTech, Inc., a biotechnology company, is considering the purchase of some equipment used for research and development. The cost is $400,000, the economic life and the recovery period are both five years, and there is no terminal disposal value. Annual pretax cash inflows from operations would increase by $140,000, the income tax rate is 40%, and the required after-tax rate of return is 14%.

Required

1. Compute the net present value, assuming straight-line depreciation of $80,000 yearly for tax purposes. Should the equipment be acquired?
2. Suppose the asset will be fully depreciated at the end of year 5 but is sold for $25,000 cash. Should the equipment be acquired? Show computations.
3. Ignore requirement 2. Suppose the required after-tax rate of return is 10% instead of 14%. Should the equipment be acquired? Show computations.

11-B4 MACRS and Present Values
The general manager of an Alaskan fishing company has a chance to purchase a new navigation device for all its vessels at a total cost of $250,000. The recovery period is five years. Additional annual pretax cash inflow from operations is $84,000, the economic life of the equipment is five years, there is no salvage value, the income tax rate is 35%, and the after-tax required rate of return is 16%.

Required

1. Compute the net present value, assuming MACRS depreciation for tax purposes. Should the equipment be acquired?
2. Suppose the economic life of the equipment is six years, which means that there will be an $84,000 cash inflow from operations in the sixth year. The recovery period is still five years. Should the equipment be acquired? Show computations.

11-B5 Income Taxes and Disposal of Assets

Assume that income tax rates are 30%.

1. The book value of an old machine is $20,000. It is to be sold for $8,000 cash. What is the effect of this decision on cash flows, after taxes?

2. The book value of an old machine is $20,000. It is to be sold for $35,000 cash. What is the effect on cash flows, after taxes, of this decision?

Additional Assignment Material

Questions

11-1. Capital budgeting has three phases: (1) identification of potential investments, (2) selection of investments, and (3) postaudit of investments. What is the accountant's role in each phase?

11-2. Why is discounted cash flow a superior method for capital budgeting?

11-3. "The higher the minimum desired rate of return, the higher the price that a company will be willing to pay for cost-saving equipment." Do you agree? Explain.

11-4. "The DCF model assumes certainty and perfect capital markets. Thus, it is impractical to use it in most real-world situations." Do you agree? Explain.

11-5. "Double-counting of costs occurs if depreciation is separately considered in DCF analysis." Do you agree? Explain.

11-6. "We can't use sensitivity analysis because our cash-flow predictions are too inaccurate." Comment.

11-7. Why should the differential approach to alternatives always lead to the same decision as the total project approach?

11-8. "The NPV model should not be used for investment decisions about advanced technology such as computer-integrated manufacturing systems." Do you agree? Explain.

11-9. Distinguish between average and marginal tax rates.

11-10. "Congress should pass a law forbidding corporations to keep two sets of books." Do you agree? Explain.

11-11. Distinguish between tax avoidance and tax evasion.

11-12. Explain why accelerated depreciation methods are superior to straight-line methods for income tax purposes.

11-13. "An investment in equipment really buys two streams of cash." Do you agree?" Explain.

11-14. Why should tax deductions be taken sooner rather than later?

11-15. "The MACRS half-year convention causes assets to be depreciated beyond the lives specified in the MACRS recovery schedules." Do you agree? Explain.

11-16. "When there are income taxes, depreciation is a cash outlay." Do you agree? Explain.

11-17. What are the three components of market (nominal) interest rates?

11-18. Describe how internal consistency is achieved when considering inflation in a capital-budgeting model.

11-19. "Capital investments are always more profitable in inflationary times because the cash inflows from operations generally increase with inflation." Comment on this statement.

11-20. "If DCF approaches are superior to the payback and the accounting rate-of-return methods, why should we bother to learn the others? All it does is confuse things." Answer this contention.

11-21. What is the basic flaw in the payback model?

11-22. Explain how a conflict can arise between capital-budgeting decision models and performance evaluation methods.

Exercises

11-23 Exercise in Compound Interest

Rhonda Reynolds wishes to purchase a $250,000 house. She has accumulated a $50,000 down-payment, but she wishes to borrow $200,000 on a 30-year mortgage. For simplicity, assume annual mortgage payments at the end of each year and no loan fees.

1. What are Reynolds's annual payments if her interest rate is (a) 8%, (b) 10%, and (c) 12%, compounded annually?

2. Repeat requirement 1 for a 15-year mortgage.

3. Suppose Reynolds had to choose between a 30-year and a 15-year mortgage, either one at a 10% interest rate. Compute the total payments and total interest paid on (a) a 30-year mortgage and (b) a 15-year mortgage.

Required

11-24   Exercise in Compound Interest
Suppose General Electric (GE) wishes to borrow money from Bank of America. They agree on an annual rate of 12%.

Required

1. Suppose GE agrees to repay $400 million at the end of 4 years. How much will Bank of America lend GE?

2. Suppose GE agrees to repay a total of $400 million at a rate of $100 million at the end of each of the next 4 years. How much will Bank of America lend GE?

11-25   Exercise in Compound Interest
A building contractor has asked you for a loan. You are pondering various proposals for repayment:

1. Lump sum of $600,000 four years hence. How much will you lend if your desired rate of return is (a) 12%, compounded annually, and (b) 20%, compounded annually?

2. Repeat requirement 1, but assume that the interest rates are compounded semi-annually.

3. Suppose the loan is to be paid in full by equal payments of $150,000 at the end of each of the next four years. How much will you lend if your desired rate of return is (a) 12%, compounded annually, and (b) 20%, compounded annually?

11-26   Basic Relationships in Interest Tables

1. Suppose you borrow $80,000 now at 14% interest, compounded annually. The borrowed amount plus interest will be repaid in a lump sum at the end of 8 years. How much must be repaid? Use Table 1 (p. B7) and the basic equation PV = future amount × conversion factor.

2. Assume the same facts as previously except that the loan will be repaid in equal installments at the end of each of eight years. How much must be repaid each year? Use Table 2 (p. B8) and the basic equation: PV = future annual amounts × conversion factor.

11-27   Present Value and Sports Salaries
Because of a salary cap, National Basketball Association teams are not allowed to exceed a certain annual limit in total player salaries. Suppose the Chicago Bulls had scheduled salaries exactly equal to their cap of $16 million for 19X7. Michael Pippin, a star player, was scheduled to receive $3 million in 19X7. To free up money to pay a prize rookie, Pippin agreed to defer $1 million of his salary for two years, by which time the salary cap will have been increased. His contract called for salary payments of $3 million in 19X7, $3.5 million in 19X8, and $4 million in 19X9. Now he will receive $2 million in 19X7, still $3.5 million in 19X8, and $5 million in 19X9. For simplicity, assume that all salaries are paid on July 1 of the year they are scheduled. Pippin's minimum desired rate of return is 12%.

Did the deferral of salary cost Pippin anything? If so, how much? Compute the present value of the sacrifice on July 1, 19X7. Explain.

Required

11-28 Simple NPV

Fill in the blanks:

	Number of Years			
	8	18	20	28
Amount of annual cash inflow*	$10,000	$ _____	$ 9,000	$ 7,000
Required initial investment	$ _____	$ 80,000	$65,000	$29,099
Minimum desired rate of return	14%	20%	$	26%
NPV	$ 5,613	($13,835)	$ 2,225	$ _____

* To be received at the end of each year.

11-29 New Equipment

The Office Equipment Company has offered to sell some new packaging equipment to the Diaz Company. The list price is $42,000, but Office Equipment has agreed to allow a trade-in allowance of $9,000 on some old equipment. The old equipment was carried at a book value of $7,700 and could be sold outright for $6,000 cash. Cash-operating savings are expected to be $5,000 annually for the next 12 years. The minimum desired rate of return is 12%. The old equipment has a remaining useful life of 12 years. Both the old and the new equipment will have zero disposal values 12 years from now.

Required

Should Diaz buy the new equipment? Show your computations, using the NPV method. Ignore income taxes.

11-30 Present Values of Cash Inflows

Orlando Novelty Company has just been established. Operating plans indicate the following expected cash flows:

	Outflows	Inflows
Initial investment now	$210,000	$ —
End of year: 1	150,000	200,000
2	200,000	250,000
3	250,000	300,000
4	300,000	400,000
5	350,000	450,000

Required

1. Compute the NPV for all of these cash flows. This should be a single amount. Use a discount rate of 14%.

2. Suppose the minimum desired rate was 12%. Without further calculations, determine whether the NPV is positive or negative. Explain.

11-31 Sensitivity Analysis

Rocky Mountain Dental Group is considering the replacement of an old billing system with new software that should save $5,000 per year in net cash operating costs. The old system has zero disposal value, but it could be used for the next 12 years. The estimated useful life of the new software is 12 years, and it will cost $25,000. The minimum desired rate of return is 10%.

Required

1. What is the payback period?

2. Compute the net present value (NPV).

3. Management is unsure about the useful life. What would be the NPV if the useful life were (a) six years instead of 12 or (b) 20 years instead of 12?

4. Suppose the life will be 12 years, but the savings will be $3,000 per year instead of $5,000. What would be the NPV?

5. Suppose the annual savings will be $4,000 for eight years. What would be the NPV?

11-32 NPV and Sensitivity Analysis

Chippewa County Jail currently has its laundry done by a local cleaners at an annual cost of $46,000. It is considering a purchase of washers, dryers, and presses at a total installed cost of $50,000 so that inmates can do the laundry. The county expects savings of $15,000 per year, and the machines are expected to last five years. The desired rate of return is 10%.

Answer each part separately.

Required

1. Compute the NPV of the investment in laundry facilities.
2. **a.** Suppose the machines last only four years. Compute the NPV.
   b. Suppose the machines last seven years. Compute the NPV.
3. **a.** Suppose the annual savings are only $11,000. Compute the NPV.
   b. Suppose the annual savings are $18,000. Compute the NPV.
4. **a.** Compute the most optimistic estimate of NPV, combining the best outcomes in requirements 2 and 3.
   b. Compute the most pessimistic estimate of NPV, combining the worst outcomes in requirements 2 and 3.
5. Accept the expected life estimate of five years. What is the minimum annual savings that would justify the investment in the laundry facilities?

11-33 Depreciation, Income Taxes, Cash Flows

Fill in the unknowns (in thousands of dollars):

(S)	Sales	530
(E)	Expenses excluding depreciation	350
(D)	Depreciation	100
	Total expenses	450
	Income before income taxes	?
(T)	Income taxes at 40%	?
(I)	Net income	?
	Cash effects of operations	
	Cash inflow from operations	?
	Income tax outflow at 40%	?
	After-tax inflow from operations	?
	Effect of depreciation	
	Depreciation, $100	
	Income tax savings	?
	Total after-tax effect on cash	?

11-34 Depreciation, Income Taxes, Cash Flows

Fill in the unknowns (in thousands of dollars):

(S)	Sales	?
(E)	Expenses excluding depreciation	?
(D)	Depreciation	300
	Total expenses	1,350
	Income before income taxes	?
(T)	Income taxes at 40%	?
(I)	Net income	480
	Cash effects of operations	
	Cash inflow from operations	?
	Income tax outflow at 40%	?
	After-tax inflow from operations	?
	Effect of depreciation	
	Depreciation, $300	
	Income tax savings	?
	Total after-tax effect on cash	?

11-35 After-Tax Effect on Cash

The 19X6 income statement of Central Satellite TV Company included the following:

Sales	$1,200,000
Less: Expenses, excluding depreciation	$ 600,000
Depreciation	300,000
Total expenses	$ 900,000
Income before taxes	$ 300,000
Income taxes (40%)	120,000
Net income	$ 180,000

Required

Compute the total after-tax effect on cash. Use the format of the second part of Exhibit 11-3, page 417, "Analysis of the Same Facts for Capital Budgeting."

11-36 MACRS Depreciation

In 1999, Redcloud Shoe Company acquired the following assets and immediately placed them into service:

1. Special tools (a 3-year-MACRS asset) that cost $40,000 on February 1.
2. A desktop computer that cost $8,000 on December 15.
3. Special calibration equipment that was used in research and development and cost $5,000 on July 7.
4. A set of file cabinets that cost $4,000, purchased on March 1.

Required

Compute the depreciation for tax purposes, under the prescribed MACRS method, in 1999 and 2000.

11-37 Present Value of MACRS Depreciation

Compute the present value of the MACRS tax savings for each of the following five assets:

	Asset Cost	Recovery Period	Discount Rate	Tax Rate
(a)	$160,000	3-year	12%	35%
(b)	$560,000	5-year	10%	40%
(c)	$ 55,000	7-year	16%	50%
(d)	$910,000	10-year	8%	35%
(e)	$430,000	10-year	15%	25%

11-38 Inflation and Capital Budgeting

The head of the corporate tax division of a major law firm has proposed investing $300,000 in personal computers for the staff. The useful life and recovery period for the computers are both five years. MACRS depreciation is used. There is no terminal salvage value. Labor savings of $125,000 per year (in year-zero dollars) are expected from the purchase. The income tax rate is 45%, the after-tax required rate of return is 20%, which includes a 4% element attributable to inflation.

Required

1. Compute the net present value of the computers. Use the nominal required rate of return and adjust the cash flows for inflation. (For example, year 1 cash flow = 1.04 × year 0 cash flow.)
2. Compute the net present value of the computers using the nominal required rate of return without adjusting the cash flows for inflation.
3. Compare your answers in requirements 1 and 2. Which is correct? Would using the incorrect analysis generally lead to overinvestment or underinvestment? Explain.

11-39 Sensitivity of Capital Budgeting to Inflation

R. Esteban, the president of a Mexican wholesale company, is considering whether to invest 410,000 pesos in new semiautomatic loading equipment that will last five years, have zero scrap value, and generate cash operating savings in labor usage of 160,000 pesos annually, using 19X4 prices and wage rates. It is December 31, 19X4.

The minimum desired rate of return is 18% per year after taxes.

Required

1. Compute the net present value of the project. Use 160,000 pesos as the savings for each of the five years. Assume a 40% tax rate and, for simplicity, assume ordinary straight-line depreciation of 410,000 pesos ÷ 5 = 82,000 pesos annually for tax purposes.

2. Esteban is wondering if the model in requirement 1 provides a correct analysis of the effects of inflation. She maintains that the 18% rate embodies an element attributable to anticipated inflation. For purposes of this analysis, she assumes that the existing rate of inflation, 10% annually, will persist over the next five years. Repeat requirement 1, adjusting the cash operating savings upward by using the 10% inflation rate.

3. Which analysis, the one in requirement 1 or 2, is correct? Why?

11-40 NPV, ARR, and Payback

Bonnie's Burgers is considering a proposal to invest in a speaker system that would allow its employees to service drive-through customers. The cost of the system (including installation of special windows and driveway modifications) is $60,000. Bonnie Holding, manager of Bonnie's Burgers, expects the drive-through operations to increase annual sales by $50,000, with a 40% contribution margin ratio. Assume that the system has an economic life of six years, at which time it will have no disposal value. The required rate of return is 14%. Ignore taxes.

Required

1. Compute the payback period. Is this a good measure of profitability?
2. Compute the NPV. Should Holding accept the proposal? Why or why not?
3. Using the accounting rate of return model, compute the rate of return on the initial investment.

11-41 Comparison of Capital-Budgeting Techniques

Maplewood Gym is considering the purchase of a new exercise machine at a cost of $20,000. It should save $4,000 in cash operating costs per year. Its estimated useful life is 8 years, and it will have zero disposal value. Ignore taxes.

Required

1. What is the payback time?
2. Compute the net present value if the minimum rate of return desired is 8%. Should the company buy? Why?
3. Using the accounting rate-of-return model, compute the rate of return on the initial investment.

PROBLEMS

11-42 Replacement of Office Equipment

Rice University is considering replacing some Xerox copiers with faster copiers purchased from Kodak. The administration is very concerned about the rising costs of operations during the last decade.

To convert to Kodak, two operators would have to be retrained. Required training and remodeling would cost $2,000.

Rice's three Xerox machines were purchased for $10,000 each, five years ago. Their expected life was 10 years. Their resale value now is $1,000 each and will be zero in five more years. The total cost of the new Kodak equipment will be $49,000; it will have zero disposal value in five years.

The three Xerox operators are paid $8 an hour each. They usually work a 40-hour week. Machine breakdowns occur monthly on each machine, resulting in repair costs of $50 per month and overtime of four hours, at time-and-one-half, per machine per month, to complete the normal monthly workload. Toner, supplies, and so on, cost $100 a month for each Xerox copier.

The Kodak system will require only two regular operators, on a regular work week of 40 hours each, to do the same work. Rates are $10 an hour, and no overtime is expected. Toner, supplies, and so on, will cost a total of $3,300 annually. Maintenance and repairs are fully serviced by Kodak for $1,050 annually. (Assume a 52-week year.)

Required

1. Using DCF techniques, compute the present value of all relevant cash flows, under both alternatives, for the five-year period discounted at 12%. As a non-profit university, Rice does not pay income taxes.

2. Should Rice keep the Xerox copiers or replace them if the decision is based solely on the given data?

3. What other considerations might affect the decision?

11-43 Replacement Decision for Railway Equipment

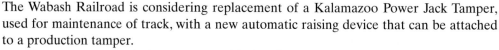

The Wabash Railroad is considering replacement of a Kalamazoo Power Jack Tamper, used for maintenance of track, with a new automatic raising device that can be attached to a production tamper.

The present power jack tamper cost $18,000 five years ago and had an estimated life of 12 years. A year from now, the machine will require a major overhaul estimated to cost $5,000. It can be disposed of now via an outright cash sale for $3,500. There will be no value at the end of another seven years.

The automatic raising attachment has a delivered selling price of $72,000 and an estimated life of 12 years. Because of anticipated future developments in combined maintenance machines, it is felt that the machine would be disposed of at the end of the seventh year to take advantage of newly developed machines. Estimated sales value at the end of seven years is $5,000.

Tests have shown that the automatic raising machine will produce a more uniform surface on the track than the power jack tamper now in use. The new equipment will eliminate one laborer whose annual compensation, including fringe benefits, is $30,000.

Track maintenance work is seasonal, and the equipment normally works from May 1 to October 31 each year. Machine operators and laborers are transferred to other work after October 31, at the same rate of pay.

The salesman claims that the annual normal maintenance of the new machine will run about $1,000 per year. Because the automatic raising machine is more complicated than the manually operated machine, it will probably require a thorough overhaul at the end of the fourth year at an estimated cost of $7,000.

Records show the annual normal maintenance of the Kalamazoo machine to be $1,200. Fuel consumption of the two machines is equal.

Required

Should the Wabash keep or replace the Kalamazoo Power Jack Tamper? A 10% rate of return is desired. Compute present values. Ignore income taxes.

11-44 Discounted Cash Flow, Uneven Revenue Stream, Relevant Costs

Anika Paar, the owner of a nine-hole golf course on the outskirts of a large city, is considering a proposal that the course be illuminated and operated at night. Ms. Paar purchased the course early last year for $90,000. Her receipts from operations during the 28-week season were $25,000. Total disbursements for the year, for all purposes, were $16,500.

The required investment in lighting this course is estimated at $20,000. The system will require 150 lamps of 1,000 watts each. Electricity costs $.032 per kilowatt-hour. The expected average hours of operation per night is five. Because of occasional bad weather and the probable curtailment of night operation at the beginning and end of the season, it is estimated that there will be only 130 nights of operation per year. Labor for keeping the course open at night will cost $15 per night. Light bulb cost is estimated at $300 per year; other maintenance and repairs, per year, will amount to 4% of the initial cost of the lighting system. Property taxes on this equipment will be about 1.7% of its initial cost. It is estimated that the average revenue, per night of operation, will be $90 for the first two years.

Considering the probability of competition from the illumination of other golf courses, Ms. Paar decides that she will not make the investment unless she can make at least 10% per annum on her investment. Because of anticipated competition, revenue is expected to drop to $60 per night for years 3 through 5. It is estimated that the lighting equipment will have a salvage value of $7,000 at the end of the five-year period.

Using DCF techniques, determine whether Ms. Paar should install the lighting system.

Required

11-45   Investment in Machine and Working Capital

The Glasgow Company has an old machine with a net disposal value of £15,000 now and £4,000 five years from now. A new Speedo machine is offered for £62,000 cash or £47,000 with a trade-in. The new machine will result in an annual operating cash outflow of £40,000 as compared with the old machine's annual outflow of £50,000. The disposal value of the new machine five years hence will be £4,000.

Because the new machine will produce output more rapidly, the average investment in inventories by using the new machine will be £160,000 instead of £200,000.

The minimum desired rate of return is 20%. The company uses DCF techniques to guide these decisions.

Should the Speedo machine be acquired? Show your calculations. Company procedures require the computing of the present value of each alternative. The most desirable alternative is the one with the least cost. Assume that the PV of £1 at 20% for five years is £.40; the present value of an annuity of £1 at 20% for five years is £3.

Required

11-46   Replacement Decision

Amtrak, a passenger train company subsidized by the U.S. government, has included a dining car on the passenger train it operates from Buffalo to Albany, New York. Yearly operations of the dining car have shown a consistent loss, which is expected to persist, as follows:

Revenue (in cash)		$200,000
Expenses for food, supplies, etc. (in cash)	$100,000	
Salaries	110,000	210,000
Net loss (ignore depreciation on the dining		
car itself)		$ 10,000

The Auto-vend Company has offered to sell automatic vending machines to Amtrak for $22,000, less a $3,000 trade-in allowance on old equipment (which is carried at $3,000 book value, and which can be sold outright for $3,000 cash) now used in the dining car operation. The useful life of the vending equipment is estimated at 10 years, with zero scrap value. Experience elsewhere has led executives to predict that the equipment will serve 50% more food than the dining car, but prices will be 50% less, so the new revenue will probably be $150,000. The variety and mix of food sold are expected to be the same as for the dining car. A catering company will completely service and supply food and beverages for the machines, paying 10% of revenue to the Amtrak company and bearing all costs of food, repairs, etc. All dining car employees will be discharged immediately.

Their termination pay will total $28,000. However, an attendant who has some general knowledge of vending machines will be needed for one shift per day. The annual cost to Amtrak for the attendant will be $13,000.

For political and other reasons, the railroad will definitely not abandon its food service. The old equipment will have zero scrap value at the end of 10 years.

Required Using the preceding data, compute the following. Label computations. Ignore income taxes.

1. Use the NPV method to analyze the incremental investment. Assume that Congress has specified that a minimum desired rate of return of 10% be used for these types of investments. For this problem, assume that the PV of $1 at 10% to be received at the end of ten years is $.400 and that the PV of an annuity of $1 at 10% for 10 years is $6.000.

2. What would be the minimum amount of annual revenue that Amtrak would have to receive from the catering company to justify making the investment? Show computations.

11-47 Minimization of Transportation Costs Without Income Taxes

The Luxor Company produces industrial and residential lighting fixtures at its manufacturing facility located in Los Angeles. Shipment of company products to an eastern warehouse is presently handled by common carriers at a rate of $.25 per pound of fixtures. The warehouse is located in Cleveland, 2,500 miles from Los Angeles.

Joanne Harris, the treasurer of Luxor, is presently considering whether to purchase a truck for transporting products to the eastern warehouse. The following data on the truck are available:

Purchase price	$35,000
Useful life	5 years
Salvage value after 5 years	0
Capacity of truck	10,000 lb
Cash costs of operating truck	$.90 per mile

Harris feels that an investment in this truck is particularly attractive because of her successful negotiation with Retro, Inc., to back-haul Retro's products from Cleveland to Los Angeles on every return trip from the warehouse. Retro has agreed to pay Luxor $2,400 per load of Retro's products hauled from Cleveland to Los Angeles up to and including 100 loads per year.

Luxor's marketing manager has estimated that 500,000 pounds of fixtures will have to be shipped to the eastern warehouse each year for the next five years. The truck will be fully loaded on each round trip.

Ignore income taxes.

Required 1. Assume that Luxor requires a minimum rate of return of 20%. Should the truck be purchased? Show computations to support your answer.

2. What is the minimum number of trips that must be guaranteed by Retro, Inc., to make the deal acceptable to Luxor, based on the foregoing numbers alone?

3. What qualitative factors might influence your decision? Be specific.

11-48 Straight-Line Depreciation, MACRS Depreciation, and Immediate Write-Off

Mr. Tamura bought a new $30,000 freezer for his grocery store on January 2, 1997. The freezer has a five-year economic life and recovery period, Mr. Tamura's minimum desired rate of return is 12%, and his tax rate is 40%.

Required 1. Suppose Mr. Tamura uses straight-line depreciation for tax purposes. Compute the present value of the tax savings from depreciation. Assume that a full year of depreciation is taken at the end of 1997.

2. Suppose Mr. Tamura uses MACRS depreciation for tax purposes. Compute the present value of the tax savings from depreciation.

3. Suppose Mr. Tamura was allowed to immediately deduct the entire cost of the freezer for tax purposes. Compute the present value of the tax savings from depreciation.

4. Which of the three methods of deducting the cost of the freezer would Mr. Tamura prefer if all three were allowable for tax purposes? Why?

11-49 MACRS, Residual Value

The Smoltz Company estimates that it can save $10,000 per year in annual operating cash costs for the next five years if it buys a special-purpose machine at a cost of $33,000. Residual value is expected to be $2,000, although no residual value is being provided for in using MACRS depreciation (five-year recovery period) for tax purposes. The equipment will be sold at the beginning of the sixth year; for purposes of this analysis assume that the proceeds are received at the end of the sixth year. The minimum desired rate of return, after taxes, is 12%. Assume the income tax rate is 45%.

1. Using the net-present-value model, show whether the investment is desirable.   **Required**

2. Suppose the equipment will produce savings for seven years instead of five. Residual value is expected to be zero at the end of the seventh year. Using the net-present-value model, show whether the investment is desirable.

11-50 Purchase of Equipment

The Key West Clinic, a for-profit medical facility, is planning to spend $45,000 for modernized x-ray equipment. It will replace equipment that has zero book value and no salvage value, although the old equipment would last another seven years.

The new equipment will save $13,500 in cash operating costs for each of the next seven years, at which time it will be sold for $4,000. A major overhaul costing $5,000 will occur at the end of the fourth year; the old equipment would require no such overhaul. The entire cost of the overhaul is deductible for tax purposes in the fourth year. The equipment has a five-year recovery period. MACRS depreciation is used for tax purposes.

The minimum desired rate of return after taxes is 12%. The applicable income tax rate is 40%.

Compute the after-tax net present value. Is the new equipment a desirable investment?   **Required**

11-51 Minimization of Transportation Costs After Taxes, Inflation

(This problem is a version of 11-47 that includes taxes and inflation elements.) The Luxor Company produces industrial and residential lighting fixtures at its manufacturing facility in Los Angeles. Shipment of company products to an eastern warehouse is presently handled by common carriers at a rate of 25¢ per pound of fixtures (expressed in year-zero dollars). The warehouse is located in Cleveland, 2,500 miles from Los Angeles.

Joanne Harris, the treasurer of Luxor, is presently considering whether to purchase a truck for transporting products to the eastern warehouse. The following data on the truck are available:

Purchase price	$35,000
Useful life	5 years
Terminal residual value	0
Capacity of truck	10,000 lb
Cash costs of operating truck (expressed in year-1 dollars)	$.90 per mile

Harris feels that an investment in this truck is particularly attractive because of her successful negotiation with Retro, Inc., to back-haul Retro's products from Cleveland to Los Angeles on every return trip from the warehouse. Retro has agreed to pay Luxor $2,400 per load of Retro's products hauled from Cleveland to Los Angeles for as many loads as Luxor can accommodate, up to and including 100 loads per year over the next five years.

Luxor's marketing manager has estimated that 500,000 pounds of fixtures will have to be shipped to the eastern warehouse each year for the next five years. The truck will be fully loaded on each round trip.

Make the following assumptions:

a. Luxor requires a minimum 20% after-tax rate of return, which includes a 10% element attributable to inflation.
b. A 40% tax rate.
c. MACRS depreciation based on five-year cost recovery period.
d. An inflation rate of 10%.

Required

1. Should the truck be purchased? Show computations to support your answer.
2. What qualitative factors might influence your decision? Be specific.

11-52 Inflation and Nonprofit Institution

The city of Biluxi is considering the purchase of a photocopying machine for $7,300 on December 31, 19X7. The machine will have a useful life of five years and no residual value. The cash operating savings are expected to be $2,000 annually, measured in 19X7 dollars.

The minimum desired rate is 14%, which includes an element attributable to anticipated inflation of 6%. (Remember that the city pays no income taxes.)

Required

Use the 14% minimum desired rate for requirements 1 and 2:

1. Compute the net present value of the project without adjusting the cash operating savings for inflation.
2. Repeat requirement 1, adjusting the cash operating savings upward in accordance with the 6% inflation rate.
3. Compare your results in requirements 1 and 2. What generalization seems applicable about the analysis of inflation in capital budgeting?

11-53 MACRS and Low-Income Housing

Hector Ramirez is a real estate developer who specializes in residential apartments. A complex of 20 run-down apartments has recently come on the market for $155,000. Ramirez predicts that after remodeling, the 12 one-bedroom units will rent for $190 per month and the 8 two-bedroom apartments for $220. He budgets 15% of the rental fees for repairs and maintenance. The apartments should last for 30 years if the remodeling is done well. Remodeling costs are $6,000 per apartment. Both purchase price and remodeling costs qualify as 27.5-year MACRS property.

Assume that the MACRS schedule assigns an equal amount of depreciation to each of the first 27 years and one-half year to the 28th year. The present value at 10% of $1 of cost recovery spread over the 28 years in this way is $.3372.

Ramirez does not believe he will keep the apartment complex for its entire 30-year life. Most likely he will sell it just after the end of the tenth year. His predicted sales price is $450,000.

Ramirez's after-tax required rate of return is 10%, and his tax rate is 38%.

Required

Should Ramirez buy the apartment complex? What is the after-tax net present value? Ignore the investment tax credit and other tax complications such as capital gains.

11-54 Present Value of After-Tax Cash Flows, Payback, and ARR

Kobe Chemicals Company, located in Kobe, Japan, is planning to buy new equipment to expand their production of a popular solvent. Estimated data are (monetary amounts are in thousands of Japanese yen):

Cash cost of new equipment now	¥400,000
Estimated life in years	10
Terminal salvage value	¥ 50,000
Incremental revenues per year	¥320,000
Incremental expenses per year other than depreciation	¥165,000

Assume a 60% flat rate for income taxes. All revenues and expenses other than depreciation will be received or paid in cash. Use a 14% discount rate. Assume that ordinary straight-line depreciation based on a 10-year recovery period is used for tax purposes. Also assume that the terminal salvage value will affect the depreciation per year.

Compute:

Required

1. Depreciation expenses per year
2. Anticipated net income per year
3. Annual net cash flow
4. Payback period
5. Accounting rate of return on initial investment
6. Net present value

11-55 Fixed and Current Assets; Evaluation of Performance

Oneida County Medical Center has been under pressure to keep costs down. Indeed, the hospital administrator has been managing various revenue-producing centers to maximize contributions to the recovery of the operating costs of the medical center as a whole. The administrator has been considering whether to buy a special-purpose X-ray machine for $193,000. Its unique characteristics would generate additional cash operating income of $50,000 per year for the medical center as a whole.

The machine is expected to have a useful life of six years and a terminal salvage value of $22,000. The machine is delicate. It requires a constant inventory of various supplies and spare parts. When these items can no longer be used, they are instantly replaced, so an investment of $15,000 must be maintained at all times. However, this investment is fully recoverable at the end of the useful life of the machine.

Required

1. Compute NPV if the required rate of return is 14%.
2. Compute the accounting rate of return on (a) the initial investment and (b) the "average" investment.
3. Why might the administrator be reluctant to base her decision on the DCF model?

BUSINESS FIRST   www.prenhall.com/phlip

11-56 Deer Valley Lodge

Deer Valley Lodge, a ski resort in the Wasach Mountains of Utah, has plans to eventually add five new chairlifts. Suppose that one of the lifts costs $2 million, and preparing the slope and installing the lift costs another $1.2 million. The lift will allow 300 additional skiers on the slopes, but there are only 40 days a year when the extra capacity will be needed. (Assume that Deer park will sell all 300 lift tickets on those 40 days.) Running the new lift will cost $500 a day for the entire 200 days the lodge is open. Assume that lift tickets at Deer Valley cost $55 a day, and added cash expenses for each skier-day are $5. The new lift has an economic life of 20 years.

1. Assume that the before-tax required rate of return for Deer Valley is 14%. Compute the before-tax NPV of the new lift and advise the managers of Deer Valley about whether adding the lift will be a profitable investment.

2. Assume that the after-tax required rate of return for Deer Valley is 8%, the income tax rate is 40%, and the MACRS recovery period is 10 years. Compute the after-tax NPV of the new lift and advise the managers of Deer Valley about whether adding the lift will be a profitable investment.

3. What subjective factors would affect the investment decision? ■

CASES

11-57 Investment in CAD/CAM

The Gustav Borg Manufacturing Company is considering the installation of a computer-aided design/computer-aided manufacturing (CAD/CAM) system. The current proposal calls for implementation of only the CAD portion of the system. Bergit Olsson, the manager in charge of production design and planning, has estimated that the CAD portion of CAD/CAM could do the work of five designers, who are each paid SKr 260,000 per year (52 weeks × 40 hours × Skr 125 per hour), where SKr is the symbol for Swedish Kroner.

The CAD/CAM system can be purchased for SKr 1.6 million. (The CAD portion cannot be purchased separately.) The annual out-of-pocket costs of running the CAD portion of the system are $900,000. The system is expected to be used for eight years. Gustov Borg's minimum desired rate of return is 12%.

1. Compute the NPV of the investment in the CAD/CAM system. Should the system be purchased? Explain.

2. Suppose Olsson was not certain about her predictions of savings and economic life. Possibly only four designers will be replaced, but if everything works out well, as many as six might be replaced. If better systems become available, the CAD/CAM system might be used only five years, but it might last as long as 10 years. Prepare pessimistic, most likely, and optimistic predictions of NPV. Would this analysis make you more confident or less confident in your decision in requirement 1? Explain.

3. What subjective factors might influence your decision?

11-58 Investment in Technology

Wisconsin Auto Parts Company is considering installation of a computer-integrated manufacturing (CIM) system as part of its implementation of a JIT philosophy. Benjamin Goldworthy, company president, is convinced that the new system is necessary, but he needs the numbers to convince the Board of Directors. This is a major move for the company, and approval at board level is required.

Leah Goldworthy, Benjamin's daughter, has been assigned the task of justifying the investment. She is a business school graduate and understands the use of NPV for capital budgeting decisions. To identify relevant costs, she developed the following information.

Wisconsin Auto Parts Company produces a variety of small automobile components and sells them to auto manufacturers. It has a 40% market share, with the following condensed results expected for 1997:

Sales		$12,000,000
Cost of goods sold		
Variable	$4,000,000	
Fixed	4,300,000	8,300,000
Selling and administrative expenses		
Variable	$2,000,000	
Fixed	400,000	2,400,000
Operating income		$ 1,300,000

Installation of the CIM system will cost $6 million, and the system is expected to have a useful life of six years with no salvage value. In 1998, the training costs for personnel will exceed any cost savings by $400,000. In years 1999 through 2003, variable cost of goods sold will decrease by 40%, an annual savings of $1.6 million. There will be no savings in fixed cost of goods sold—in fact, it will increase by the amount of the straight-line depreciation on the new system. Selling and administrative expenses will not be affected. The required rate of return is 12%. Assume that all cash flows occur at the end of the year, except the initial investment, which occurs at the beginning of 1998.

Required

1. Suppose that Leah Goldworthy assumes that production and sales would continue for the next six years as they were in 1997 in the absence of investment in the CIM. Compute the NPV of investing in the CIM.

2. Now suppose Leah predicts that it will be difficult to compete if the CIM is not installed. In fact, she has undertaken market research that estimates a drop in market share of 3 percentage points a year starting in 1998 in the absence of investment in the CIM (i.e., market share will be 37% in 2000, 34% in 1999, 31% in 2000, etc.). Her study also showed that the total market sales level will stay the same, and market prices are not expected to change. Compute the NPV of investing in the CIM.

3. Prepare a memo from Leah Goldworthy to the Board of Directors of Wisconsin Auto Parts Company. In the memo, explain why the analysis in requirement 2 is appropriate and why analyses such as that in requirement 1 cause companies to underinvest in high-technology projects. Include an explanation of qualitative factors that are not included in the NPV calculation.

11-59 Investment in Quality

The Woolongong Manufacturing Company produces a single model of a CD player that is sold to Australian manufacturers of sound systems. Each CD player is sold for $210, resulting in a contribution margin of $70 before considering any costs of inspection, correction of product defects, or refunds to customers.

In 19X0, top management at Woolongong is contemplating a change in its quality control system. Currently, $40,000 is spent annually on quality control inspections. Woolongong produces and ships 50,000 CD players a year. In producing those CD players, an average of 2,000 defective units are produced. Of these, 1,500 are identified by the inspection process, and an average of $85 is spent on each to correct the defects. The other 500 players are shipped to customers. When a customer discovers a defective CD player, Woolongong refunds the $210 purchase price.

As more and more customers change to JIT inventory systems and automated production processes, the receipt of defective goods poses greater and greater problems for them. Sometimes a defective CD player causes them to delay their whole production line while the CD player is being replaced. Companies competing with Woolongong recognize this situation, and most have already begun extensive quality control programs. If Woolongong does not improve quality, sales volume is expected to fall by 5,000 CD players a year, beginning in 19X1:

	Predicted Sales Volume in Units Without Quality Control Program	Predicted Sales Volume in Units With Quality Control Program
19X1	50,000	50,000
19X2	45,000	50,000
19X3	40,000	50,000
19X4	35,000	50,000

The proposed quality control program has two elements. First, Woolongong would spend $900,000 immediately to train workers to recognize and correct defects at the time they occur. This is expected to cut the number of defective CD players produced from 2,000 to 500 without incurring additional manufacturing costs. Second, an earlier inspection point would replace the current inspection. This would require purchase of an x-ray machine at a cost of $200,000 plus additional annual operating costs of $50,000 more than the current inspection costs. Early detection of defects would reduce the average amount spent to correct defects from $85 to $50, and only 50 defective CD players would be shipped to customers. To compete, Woolongong would refund one-and-one-half times the purchase price ($315) for defective CD players delivered to customers.

Top management at Woolongong has decided that a four-year planning period is sufficient for analyzing this decision. The minimum required rate of return is 20%. For simplicity, assume that under the current quality control system, if the volume of production decreases, the number of defective CD players produced remains at 2,000. Also assume that all annual cash flows occur at the end of the relevant year.

Required Should Woolongong Manufacturing Company undertake the new quality control program? Explain, using the NPV model. Ignore income taxes.

11-60 Make or Buy and Replacement of Equipment

Toyland Company is one of the largest producers of miniature model automobiles. An especially complex part of one of the autos needs special tools that are not useful for other products. These tools were purchased on July 1, 1993, for $200,000.

It is now July 1, 1997. The manager of the Model Auto Division, Ramona Ruiz, is contemplating three alternatives. First, she could continue to produce the auto using the current tools; they will last another five years, at which time they would have zero terminal value. Second, she could sell the tools for $30,000 and purchase the parts from an outside supplier for $1.10 each. Third, she could replace the tools with new, more efficient tools costing $180,000.

Ruiz expects to produce 80,000 units of the auto each of the next five years. Manufacturing costs for the auto have been as follows, and no change in costs is expected:

Direct material	$ .38
Direct labor	.37
Variable overhead	.17
Fixed overhead*	.45
Total unit cost	$1.37

* Depreciation accounts for two-thirds of the fixed overhead. The balance is for other fixed overhead costs of the factory that require cash outlays, 60% of which would be saved if production of the parts were eliminated.

The outside supplier offered the $1.10 price as a once-only offer. It is unlikely such a low price would be available later. Toyland would also have to guarantee to purchase at least 70,000 parts for each of the next five years.

The new tools that are available would last for five years with a disposal value of $40,000 at the end of five years. The old tools are a five-year MACRS property, the new tools are a 3-year MACRS property, and both use the current MACRS schedules. Straight-line depreciation is used for book purposes and MACRS for tax purposes. The sales representative selling the new tools stated, "The new tools will allow direct labor and variable overhead to be reduced by $.21 per unit." Ruiz thinks this estimate is accurate. However, she also knows that a higher quality of materials would be necessary with the new tools. She predicts the following costs with the new tools:

Direct material	$ .40
Direct labor	.25
Variable overhead	.08
Fixed overhead	.60*
Total unit cost	$1.33

* The increase in fixed overhead is caused by depreciation on the new tools.

The company has a 40% marginal tax rate and requires a 12% after-tax rate of return.

Required

1. Calculate the net present value of each of the three alternatives. Recognize the tax implications. Which alternative should Ruiz select?

2. What are some factors besides the net present value that should influence Ruiz's selection?

COLLABORATIVE LEARNING EXERCISE

11-61 Capital Budgeting, Sensitivity Analysis, and Ethics

James LaGrande had recently been appointed Controller of the Breakfast Cereals Division of a major food company. The Division Manager, Renee Osterland, was known as a hard-driving, intelligent, noncompromising manager. She had been very successful, and was rumored to be on the fast-track to corporate top management, maybe even in line for the company presidency. One of Jim's first assignments was to prepare the financial analysis for a new cold cereal, Krispie Krinkles. This product was especially important to Ms. Osterland because she was convinced that it would be a success and thereby a springboard for her ascent to top management.

Mr. LaGrande discussed the product with the food lab that had designed it, with the market research department that had tested it, and with the finance people who would have to fund its introduction. After putting together all the information, he developed the following optimistic and pessimistic sales projections:

	Optimistic	Pessimistic
Year 1	$ 1,600,000	$ 800,000
Year 2	3,600,000	1,200,000
Year 3	5,000,000	1,000,000
Year 4	8,000,000	800,000
Year 5	10,000,000	400,000

The optimistic predictions assume a successful introduction of a popular product. The pessimistic predictions assume that the product is introduced but does not gain wide acceptance and is terminated after 5 years. LaGrande thinks the most likely results are halfway between the optimistic and pessimistic predictions.

LaGrande learned from finance that this type of product introduction requires a predicted rate of return of 16% before top management will authorize funds for its introduction. He also determined that the contribution margin should be about 50% on the product, but could be as low as 42% or as high as 58%. Initial investment would include $3 million for production facilities, $2.5 million for advertising and other product intro-

duction expenses, and $500,000 for working capital (inventory, etc.). The production facil-
ities would have a value of $800,000 after five years.

Based on his preliminary analysis, LaGrande recommended to Osterland that the
product not be launched. Osterland was not pleased with the recommendation. She
claimed that LaGrande was much too pessimistic and asked him to redo his numbers so
that she could justify the product to top management.

LaGrande carried out further analysis, but his predictions came out no differently. In
fact, he became even more convinced that his projections were accurate. Yet, he was certain that if he returned to Osterland with numbers that did not support introduction of
the product, he would incur her wrath. And, in fact, she could be right—that is, there is so
much uncertainty in the forecasts that he could easily come up with believable numbers
that would support going forward with the product. He would not believe them, but he
thinks he could convince top management that they are accurate.

Required This role-play could be done as an entire class or in teams of three to six persons. It will
be explained here as if being done by a team.

Choose one member of the team to be James LaGrande and one to be Renee
Osterland.

1. With the help of the entire team except the person chosen to be Osterland,
   LaGrande should prepare the capital-budgeting analysis used for his first meeting with Osterland.

2. Next, LaGrande should meet again with Osterland. They should try to agree on
   the analysis to take forward to top management. As they discuss the issues and
   try to come to an agreement, the remaining team members should record all the
   ethical judgments each discussant makes.

3. After LaGrande and Osterland have completed their role-play assignment, the
   entire team should assess the ethical judgments made by each and recommend
   an appropriate position for LaGrande to take in this situation.

Solutions to Exercises in Compound Interest, Problem 11-A1

The general approach to these exercises centers on one fundamental question: Which of
the two basic tables am I dealing with? No calculations should be made until after this
question is answered with assurance. If you made any errors, it is possible that you used
the wrong table.

1. From Table 1, Appendix B, p. B7:
   a. $16,438
   b. $12,418
   c. $8,038

   The $20,000 is an amount of future worth. You want the present value of that
   amount:

   $$PV = \$20,000 \times \left[\frac{1}{(1+i)^n}\right]$$

   The conversion factor, $1/(1 + i)^n$, is on line 5 of Table 1. Substituting:

   $$PV = \$20,000(.8219) = \$16,438$$
   $$PV = \$20,000(.6209) = \$12,418$$
   $$PV = \$20,000(.4019) = \$8,038$$

   Note that the higher the interest rate, the lower the present value.

2. From Table 2, Appendix B, page B8:

   a. $8,903.60

   b. $7,581.60

   c. $5,981.20

   The $2,000 withdrawal is a uniform annual amount, an annuity. You need to find the present value of an annuity for five years:

   PV_A = annual withdrawal $\times$ F, where F is the conversion factor.

   Substituting:

   $PV_A = \$2,000(4.4518) = \$8,903.60$

   $PV_A = \$2,000(3.7908) = \$7,581.60$

   $PV_A = \$2,000(2.9906) = \$5,981.20$

3. From Table 2:

   a. $22,462.82

   b. $26,379.66

   You have $100,000, the present value of your contemplated annuity. You must find the annuity that will just exhaust the invested principal in five years:

   PVA = annual withdrawal $\times$ F

   $\$100,000$ = annual withdrawal $\times$ 4.4518

   annual withdrawal = $\$100,000 \div 4.4518$

   = $22,462.82

   $\$100,000$ = annual withdrawal $\times$ 3.7908

   annual withdrawal = $\$100,000 \div 3.7908$

   = $26,379.66

4. Amounts are in thousands. From Table 1: Johnson's contract is preferable; its present value exceeds that of Jackson's contract by $21,572 − $17,720 = $3,852. Note that the nearer dollars are more valuable than the distant dollars.

Year	Present Value @ 16% from Table 1	Present Value of Johnson's Contract	Present Value of Jackson's Contract
1	.8621	$ 8,621	$ 1,724
2	.7432	5,946	2,973
3	.6407	3,844	3,844
4	.5523	2,209	4,418
5	.4761	952	4,761
		$21,572	$17,720

12

COST ALLOCATION AND ACTIVITY-BASED COSTING

Kevin Rollins, senior vice president of Dell Americas, with a Dell Workstation 400. The workstation is the first in a line of powerful business computers used by engineers, financial traders, and others.

Learning Objectives

When you have finished studying this chapter, you should be able to

1 Explain the major purposes for allocating costs.

2 Allocate the variable and fixed costs of service departments to other organizational units.

3 Allocate the central costs of an organization.

4 Use the direct and step-down methods to allocate service department costs to user departments.

5 Describe the traditional approach to allocating costs to products or services.

6 Use activity-based costing to allocate costs in a modern manufacturing environment to products or services.

7 Use the physical-units and relative-sales-value methods to allocate joint costs to products.

8 **Understand how cost allocation is used in cost planning and control.**

W ith annual revenue of more than 12 billion, Dell Computer Corporation is a leading producer of computer systems (desktops, notebooks, and network servers for large businesses). With manufacturing facilities in Texas, Ireland, and Malaysia, Dell has earned a reputation for high quality computer products and personalized service. During 1997, the company earned the number one spot in PC Computing magazine's notebook torture test for the second year in a row. Many companies, including Boeing, have selected Dell's computers because of their quality and Dell's commitment to service and just-in-time delivery.

Like any business, Dell's managers know that some of their products are more profitable than others. They also know that some distribution methods are more costly than others. Unfortunately, until Dell's accountants redesigned the costing system, managers did not have a solid understanding of which products or channels of distribution were more or less profitable.

Why? Because Dell's old cost allocation system was not accurate enough. A simple cost accumulation system was used to collect costs into direct labor, direct materials, and indirect cost categories. The indirect costs of most value-chain functions were not allocated. Instead, an overall markup was added to production costs for the costs of value-chain functions such as research and development, design, marketing, distribution and customer service. When Dell's profitability and growth plateaued in the early 1990s, managers determined that a key to the company's long-run success was to design a costing system that accurately allocated all value-chain costs to products and distribution channels and thus would enable managers to determine product and channel profitability.

Dell's new cost system—an activity-based cost system (ABC)—has been in place for several years and is still evolving. The initial development process took a significant commitment from managers at all levels but was wholeheartedly embraced by the management team. The benefits have been clear. In fact, the results of an ABC analysis led Dell to discontinue distribution to the consumer market through retail channels. According to John Jonez, Vice President and Controller for Dell Americas Operations, "ABC has really allowed Dell to go to the next level of understanding of its profitability for each of the products it sells."

Just as in the case for Dell, cost allocation is of strategic importance to all businesses. For example, a university's computer is used for teaching and for performing government-funded research. How much of its cost should be assigned to the research projects? A city creates a special police unit to investigate a series of related assaults. What is the total cost of the effort? A company uses a machine to make two different product lines. How much of the cost of the machine belongs to each product line? These are all problems of cost allocation, the subject of this chapter.

cost accounting systems The techniques used to determine the cost of a product, service, or other cost objective by collecting and classifying costs and assigning them to cost objects.

This is the first of three chapters on **cost accounting systems**—the techniques used to determine the cost of a product, service, customer, or other cost objective. A cost accounting system collects and classifies costs and assigns them to cost objects. The goal of a cost accounting system is to measure the cost of designing, developing, producing (or purchasing), selling, distributing, and servicing particular products or services. Cost allocation is at the heart of most cost accounting systems.

COST ALLOCATION IN GENERAL

As Chapter 4 pointed out, cost allocation is fundamentally a problem of linking some cost or group of costs with one or more cost objectives, such as products, departments, customer classes, activities, and divisions. Ideally, cost allocation should assign each cost to the cost objective that caused it.

cost-allocation base A cost driver when it is used for allocating costs.

We link costs with cost objectives by selecting appropriate cost drivers. When used for allocating costs, a cost driver is often called a **cost-allocation base.** Major costs such as newsprint for a newspaper and direct professional labor for a law firm each may be allocated to departments, jobs, and projects on an item-by-item basis, using obvious cost drivers such as tons of newsprint consumed or direct-labor-hours used. Other costs, taken one at a time, are not important enough to justify being allocated individually. These costs are pooled and then allocated together. A **cost pool** is a group of individual costs that is allocated to cost objectives using a single cost driver. For example, building rent, utilities cost, and janitorial services may be in the same cost pool because all are allocated on the basis of square footage of space occupied. Or a university could pool all the operating costs of its registrar's office and allocate them to its colleges on the basis of the number of students in each college. In summary, all costs in a given cost pool should be caused by the same factor. That factor is the cost driver.

cost pool A group of individual costs that is allocated to cost objectives using a single cost driver.

Many different terms are used to describe cost allocation in practice. You may encounter terms such as *allocate, apply, absorb, attribute, reallocate, trace, assign, distribute, redistribute, load, burden, apportion,* and *reapportion* being used interchangeably to describe the allocation of costs to cost objectives.

FOUR PURPOSES OF ALLOCATION

What logic should be used for allocating costs? This question bothers many internal users and suppliers of services in all organizations. The answer depends on the principal purpose(s) of the cost allocation.

Costs are allocated for four major purposes.

Objective 1
Explain the major purposes for allocating costs.

1. *To predict the economic effects of planning and control decisions:* Managers within an organizational unit should be aware of all the consequences of their decisions, even consequences outside of their unit. Examples are the addition of a new course in a university that causes additional work in the registrar's office, the addition of a new flight or an additional passenger on an airline that requires reservation and booking services, and the addition of a new specialty in a medical clinic that produces more work for the medical records department.

2. *To obtain desired motivation:* Cost allocations are sometimes made to influence management behavior and thus promote goal congruence and managerial effort. Consequently, in some organizations, there is no cost allocation for legal or internal auditing services or internal management consulting services because top management wants to encourage their use. In other organizations, there is a cost allocation for such items to spur managers to make sure the benefits of the specified services exceed the costs.

3. *To compute income and asset valuations:* Costs are allocated to products and projects to measure inventory costs and cost of goods sold. These allocations frequently serve financial accounting purposes. However, the resulting costs also are often used by managers in planning and performance evaluation.

4. *To justify costs or obtain reimbursement:* Sometimes prices are based directly on costs. For example, government contracts often specify a price that includes reimbursement for costs plus some profit margin. In these instances, cost allocations become substitutes for the usual working of the marketplace in setting prices.

The first two purposes specify planning and control uses for allocation. Purposes 3 and 4 show how cost allocations may differ for inventory costing (and cost of goods sold) and for setting prices. Moreover, different allocations of costs to products may be made for the various purposes. Thus full costs may guide pricing decisions (purpose 1), manufacturing costs may be proper for asset valuations (purpose 3), and some "in-between" cost may be negotiated for a government contract (purpose 4).

Ideally, all four purposes would be served simultaneously by a single cost allocation. But thousands of managers and accountants will testify that for most costs this ideal is rarely achieved. Instead, cost allocations are often a major source of discontent and confusion to the affected parties. Allocating fixed costs usually causes the greatest problems. When all four purposes cannot be attained simultaneously, the manager and the accountant should start attacking a cost-allocation problem by trying to identify which of the purposes should dominate in the particular situation at hand.

Often inventory-costing purposes dominate by default because they are externally imposed. When allocated costs are used in decision making and performance evaluation,

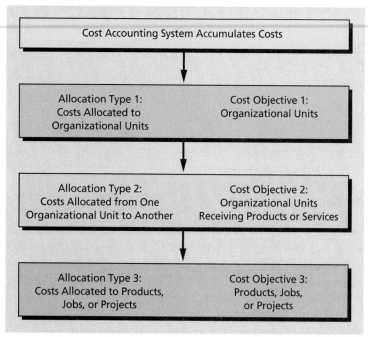

Exhibit 12-1

Three Types of Cost Allocations

managers should consider adjusting the allocations used to satisfy inventory-costing purposes. Often the added benefit of using separate allocations for planning and control and inventory-costing purposes is much greater than the added cost.

THREE TYPES OF ALLOCATIONS

As Exhibit 12-1 shows, there are three basic types of cost allocations.

1. *Allocation of costs to the appropriate organizational unit:* Direct costs are physically traced to the unit, but costs used jointly by more than one unit are allocated based on cost-driver activity in the unit. Examples are allocating rent to departments based on floor space occupied, allocating depreciation on jointly used machinery based on machine-hours, and allocating general administrative expense based on total direct cost.

2. *Reallocation of costs from one organizational unit to another:* When one unit provides products or services to another, the costs are transferred along with the products or services. Some units, called **service departments**, exist only to support other departments, and their costs are totally reallocated. Examples include personnel departments, laundry departments in hospitals, and legal departments in industrial firms.

3. *Allocation of costs of a particular organizational unit or activity to products or services:* The pediatrics department of a medical clinic allocates its costs to patient visits, the assembly activity of a manufacturing firm to units assembled, and the tax department of a CPA firm to clients served. The costs allocated to products or services include those allocated to the organizational unit in allocation types 1 and 2.

service departments
Units that exist only to support other departments.

All three types of allocations are fundamentally similar. Let us look first at how service department costs are allocated to production departments.

GENERAL GUIDELINES

The preferred guidelines for allocating service department costs are:

1. *Evaluate performance using budgets* for each service (staff) department, just as for each production or operating (line) department. The performance of a service department is evaluated by comparing actual costs with a budget, regardless of how the costs are later allocated. From the budget, variable-cost pools and fixed-cost pools can be identified for use in allocation.

2. *Allocate variable- and fixed-cost pools separately* (sometimes called the dual method of allocation). Note that one service department (such as a computer department) can contain multiple cost pools if more than one cost driver causes the department's costs. At a minimum, there should be a variable-cost pool and a fixed-cost pool.

3. *Establish part or all of the details regarding cost allocation in advance* of rendering the service rather than after the fact. This approach establishes the "rules of the game" so that all departments can plan appropriately.

Consider an example of a computer department of a university that serves two major users, the School of Business and the School of Engineering. The computer mainframe was acquired on a five-year lease that is not cancelable unless high cost penalties are paid.

> **Objective 2**
> Allocate the variable and fixed costs of service departments to other organizational units.

Suppose there are two major purposes for the allocation: (1) predicting economic effects of the use of the computer, and (2) motivating departments and individuals to use its capabilities more fully. How should the costs of the computer department (salaries, depreciation, energy, materials, and so on) be allocated to the user departments?

To apply the first of our three guidelines, we need to analyze the costs of the computer department in detail. The primary activity performed is computer processing. Resources consumed include processing time, operator time, consulting time, energy, materials, and building space. Suppose cost behavior analysis has been performed and the budget formula for the forthcoming year is $100,000 monthly fixed cost plus $200 variable cost per hour of computer time used. Applying both guidelines 2 and 3 is the topic of the next two sections.

VARIABLE-COST POOL

The cost driver for the variable-cost pool is hours of computer time used. Therefore, variable costs should be allocated as follows:

budgeted unit rate × actual hours of computer time used

The cause-and-effect relationship is clear: The heavier the usage, the higher the total costs. In this example, the rate used would be the budgeted rate of $200 per hour.

The use of *budgeted* cost rates rather than actual cost rates for allocating variable costs of service departments protects the using departments from intervening price fluctuations and also often protects them from inefficiencies in the service departments. When an organization allocates actual total service department cost, it holds user department managers responsible for costs beyond their control and provides less incentive for service departments to be efficient. Both effects are undesirable.

Consider the allocation of variable costs to a department that uses 600 hours of computer time. Suppose inefficiencies in the computer department caused the variable costs to be $140,000 instead of the 600 hours × $200, or $120,000 budgeted. A good cost-allocation scheme would allocate only the $120,000 to the consuming departments and would let the $20,000 remain as an unallocated unfavorable budget variance of the computer department. This scheme holds computer department managers responsible for the

$20,000 variance and reduces the resentment of user managers. User department managers sometimes complain more vigorously about uncertainty over allocations and the poor management of a service department than about the choice of a cost driver (such as direct-labor dollars or number of employees). Such complaints are less likely if the service department managers have budget responsibility and the user departments are protected from short-run price fluctuations and inefficiencies.

Consider an automobile repair and maintenance department for a state government. Agencies who use the department's service should receive firm prices for various services. Imagine the feelings of an agency head who had an agency automobile repaired and was told, "Normally your repair would have taken five hours. However, we had a new employee work on it, and the job took him 10 hours. Therefore, we must charge you for 10 hours of labor time."

FIXED-COST POOL

The cost driver for the fixed-cost pool is the amount of capacity required when the computer facilities were acquired. Therefore, fixed costs should be allocated as follows:

budgeted percent of capacity available for use × total budgeted fixed costs

Consider again our example of the university computer department. Suppose the deans had originally predicted the long-run average monthly usage by Business at 210 hours, and by Engineering at 490 hours, a total of 700 hours. The fixed-cost pool would be allocated as follows:

	Business	Engineering
Fixed costs per month		
210/700, or 30% of $100,000	$30,000	
490/700, or 70% of $100,000		$70,000

This predetermined lump-sum approach is based on the long-run capacity available to the user, regardless of actual usage from month to month. The reasoning is that the level of fixed costs is affected by long-range planning regarding the overall level of service and the relative expected usage, not by short-run fluctuations in service levels and relative actual usage.

A major strength of using capacity available rather than capacity used when allocating budgeted fixed costs is that short-run allocations to user departments are not affected by the actual usage of other user departments. Such a budgeted lump-sum approach is more likely to have the desired motivational effects with respect to the ordering of services in both the short run and the long run.

In practice, fixed-cost pools often are inappropriately allocated on the basis of capacity used, not capacity available. Suppose the computer department allocated the total actual costs after the fact. At the end of the month, total actual costs would be allocated in proportion to the actual hours used by the consuming departments. Compare the costs borne by the two schools when Business uses 200 hours and Engineering 400 hours:

Total costs incurred, $100,000 + (600 × $200) = $220,000	
Business: 200/600 × $220,000 =	$ 73,333
Engineering: 400/600 × $220,000 =	146,667
Total cost allocated	$220,000

What happens if Business uses only 100 hours during the following month, and Engineering still uses 400 hours?

Total costs incurred, $100,000 + (500 × $200) = $200,000

Business: 100/500 × $200,000 =	$ 40,000
Engineering: 400/500 × $200,000 =	160,000
Total cost allocated	$200,000

Engineering has done nothing differently, but it must bear an additional cost of $13,333, an increase of 9%. Its short-run costs depend on what other consumers have used, not solely on its own actions. This phenomenon is caused by a faulty allocation method for the fixed portion of total costs, a method whereby the allocations are highly sensitive to fluctuations in the actual volumes used by the various consuming departments. This weakness is avoided by using a predetermined lump-sum allocation of fixed costs, based on budgeted usage.

Consider the preceding automobile repair shop example. You would not be happy if you came to get your car and were told, "Our daily fixed overhead is $1,000. Yours was the only car in our shop today, so we are charging you the full $1,000. If we had processed 100 cars today, your charge would have been only $10."

TROUBLES WITH USING LUMP SUMS

Using lump-sum allocations can cause problems, however. If fixed costs are allocated on the basis of long-range plans, there is a natural tendency on the part of consumers to underestimate their planned usage and thus obtain a smaller fraction of the cost allocation. Top management can counteract these tendencies by monitoring predictions and by following up and using feedback to keep future predictions more honest.

In some organizations, there are even definite rewards in the form of salary increases for managers who make accurate predictions. Moreover, some cost-allocation methods provide for penalties for underpredictions. For example, suppose a manager predicts usage of 210 hours and then demands 300 hours. The manager either doesn't get the hours or pays a dear price for every hour beyond 210 in such systems.

ALLOCATION OF CENTRAL COSTS

The seeming need to allocate central costs is a manifestation of a widespread, deep-seated belief that all costs must somehow be fully allocated to the revenue-producing (operating) parts of the organization. Such allocations are neither necessary from an accounting viewpoint nor useful as management information. For this reason, central costs are not considered part of the value chain in this text. However, most managers accept them as a fact of life—as long as all managers seem to be treated alike and thus "fairly."

Whenever possible, the preferred cost driver for central services is usage, either actual or estimated. But the costs of such services as public relations, top corporate management overhead, a real estate department, and a corporate-planning department are the least likely to be allocated on the basis of usage. Data processing, advertising, and operations research are the most likely to choose usage as a cost driver.

Companies that allocate central costs by usage tend to generate less resentment. Consider the experience of JC Penney Co. as reported in *Business Week*:

> *The controller's office wanted subsidiaries such as Thrift Drug Co. and the insurance operations to base their share of corporate personnel, legal, and auditing costs on their revenues. The subsidiaries contended that they maintained their own personnel and legal departments, and should be assessed far less. . . . The subcommittee addressed the issue by asking the corporate departments to approximate the time and costs involved in servicing the subsidiaries. The final allocation plan, based on these studies, cost the divisions less than they were initially assessed but more than they had wanted to pay. Nonetheless, the plan was implemented easily.*

Objective 3
Allocate the central costs of an organization.

Usage is not always an economically viable way to allocate central costs, however. Also, many central costs, such as the president's salary and related expenses, public relations, legal services, income tax planning, companywide advertising, and basic research, are difficult to allocate on the basis of cause and effect. As a result, some companies use cost drivers such as the revenue of each division, the cost of goods sold by each division, the total assets of each division, or the total costs of each division (before allocation of the central costs) to allocate central costs.

The use of the foregoing cost drivers might provide a rough indication of cause-and-effect relationship. Basically, however, they represent an "ability to bear" philosophy of cost allocation. For example, the costs of company-wide advertising, such as the goodwill sponsorship of a program on a noncommercial television station, might be allocated to all products and divisions on the basis of the dollar sales in each. But such costs precede sales. They are discretionary costs as determined by management policies, not by sales results. Although 60% of the companies in a large survey treat sales revenue as a cost driver for cost allocation purposes, it is seldom truly a cost driver in the sense of being an activity that causes the costs.

USE OF BUDGETED SALES FOR ALLOCATION

If the costs of central services are to be allocated based on sales, even though the costs do not vary in proportion to sales, the use of budgeted sales is preferable to the use of actual sales. At least this method means that the short-run costs of a given consuming department will not be affected by the fortunes of other consuming departments.

For example, suppose $100 of fixed central advertising costs were allocated on the basis of potential sales in two territories:

| | Territories | | Total | Percent |
	A	B		
Budgeted sales	$500	$500	$1,000	100
Central advertising allocated	$ 50	$ 50	$ 100	10

Consider the possible differences in allocations when actual sales become known:

| | Territories | |
	A	B
Actual sales	$300	$600
Central advertising		
1. Allocated on basis of budgeted sales	$ 50	$ 50
or		
2. Allocated on basis of actual sales	$ 33	$ 67

Compare allocation 1 with 2. Allocation 1 is preferable. It indicates a low ratio of sales to advertising in territory A. It directs attention where it is deserved. In contrast, allocation 2 soaks territory B with more advertising cost because of the achieved results and relieves territory A despite its lower success. This is another example of the analytical confusion that can arise when cost allocations to one consuming department depend on the activity of other consuming departments.

RECIPROCAL SERVICES

Service departments often support other service departments in addition to producing departments. Consider a manufacturing company with two producing departments, molding and finishing, and two service departments, facilities management (rent, heat, light, jan-

Exhibit 12-2

Cost Drivers

	Service Departments		Production Departments	
	Facilities Management	*Personnel*	*Molding*	*Finishing*
Direct department costs	$126,000	$24,000	$100,000	$160,000
Square feet	3,000	9,000	15,000	3,000
Number of employees	20	30	80	320
Direct-labor hours			2,100	10,000
Machine-hours			30,000	5,400

itorial services, and so on) and personnel. All costs in a given service department are assumed to be caused by, and therefore vary in proportion to, a single cost driver. The company has decided that the best cost driver for facilities management costs is square footage occupied and the best cost driver for personnel is the number of employees. Exhibit 12-2 shows the direct costs, square footage occupied, and number of employees for each department. Note that facilities management provides services for the personnel department in addition to providing services for the producing departments, and that personnel aids employees in facilities management as well as those in production departments.

There are two popular methods for allocating service department costs in such cases: the direct method and the step-down method.

DIRECT METHOD As its name implies, the **direct method** ignores other service departments when any given service department's costs are allocated to the revenue-producing (operating) departments. In other words, the fact that facilities management provides services for personnel is ignored, as is the support that personnel provides to facilities management. Facilities management costs are allocated based on the relative square footage occupied by the production departments only:

- Total square footage in production departments: 15,000 + 3,000 = 18,000
- Facilities management cost allocated to molding = (15,000 ÷ 18,000) × $126,000 = $105,000
- Facilities management cost allocated to finishing = (3,000 ÷ 18,000) × $126,000 = $21,000

Likewise, personnel department costs are allocated only to the production departments on the basis of the relative number of employees in the production departments:

- Total employees in production departments = 80 + 320 = 400
- Personnel costs allocated to molding = (80 ÷ 400) × $24,000 = $4,800
- Personnel costs allocated to finishing = (320 ÷ 400) × $24,000 = $19,200

STEP-DOWN METHOD The **step-down method** recognizes that some service departments support the activities in other service departments as well as those in production departments. A sequence of allocations is chosen, usually by starting with the service department that renders the greatest service (as measured by costs) to the greatest number of other service departments. The last service department in the sequence is the one that renders the least service to the least number of other service departments. Once a department's costs are allocated to other departments, no subsequent service department costs are allocated back to it.

In our example, facilities management costs are allocated first. Why? Because facilities management renders more support to personnel than personnel provides for

Objective 4
Use the direct and step-down methods to allocate service department costs to user departments.

direct method A method for allocating service department costs that ignores other service departments when any given service department's costs are allocated to the revenue-producing (operating) departments.

step-down method A method for allocating service department costs that recognizes that some service departments support the activities in other service departments as well as those in production departments.

Exhibit 12-3

Step-Down Allocation

	Facilities Management	Personnel	Molding	Finishing	Total
Direct department costs before allocation	$ 126,000	$ 24,000	$100,000	$160,000	$410,000
Step 1					
Facilities management	$(126,000)	(9 ÷ 27) × $126,000 = $42,000	(15 ÷ 27) × $126,000 = $ 70,000	(3 ÷ 27) × $126,000 = $ 14,000	
Step 2					
Personnel		$(66,000)	(80 ÷ 400) × $66,000 = $ 13,200	(320 ÷ 400) × $66,000 = $ 52,800	
Total cost after allocation	$ 0	$ 0	$183,200	$226,800	$410,000

facilities management.[1] Examine Exhibit 12-3. After facilities management costs are allocated, no costs are allocated back to facilities management, even though personnel does provide some services for facilities management. The personnel costs to be allocated to the production departments include the amount allocated to personnel from facilities management ($42,000) in addition to the direct personnel department costs of $24,000.

Examine the last column of Exhibit 12-3. Before allocation, the four departments incurred costs of $410,000. In step 1, $126,000 was deducted from facilities management and added to the other three departments. There was no net effect on the total cost. In step 2, $66,000 was deducted from personnel and added to the remaining two departments. Again, total cost was unaffected. After allocation, all $410,000 remains, but it is all in molding and finishing. None was left in facilities management or personnel.

COMPARISON OF THE METHODS Compare the costs of the production departments under direct and step-down methods, as shown in Exhibit 12-4. Note that the method of allocation can greatly affect the costs. Molding appears to be a much more expensive operation to a manager using the direct method than it does to one using the step-down method. Conversely, finishing seems more expensive to a manager using the step-down method.

Which method is better? Generally, the step-down method.[2] Why? Because it recognizes the effects of the most significant support provided by service departments to other service departments. In our example, the direct method ignores the following possible cause-effect link: If the cost of facilities management is caused by the space used, then the space used by personnel causes $42,000 of facilities management cost. If the space used in personnel is caused by the number of production department employees supported, then the number of production department employees, not the square footage, causes $42,000 of the facilities management cost. The producing department with the most employees, not the one with the most square footage, should bear this cost.

---

[1] How should we determine which of the two service departments provides more service to the other? One way is to carry out step 1 of the step-down method with facilities management allocated first, and then repeat it assuming personnel is allocated first. With facilities management allocated first, $42,000 is allocated to personnel, as shown in Exhibit 12-3. If personnel had been allocated first, (20 ÷ 420) × $24,000 = $1,143 would have been allocated to facilities management. Because $1,143 is smaller than $42,000, facilities management is allocated first.

[2] The most defensible theoretical accuracy is generated by the reciprocal cost method, which is rarely used in practice because it is more difficult to understand. Simultaneous equations and linear algebra are used to solve for the impact of mutually interacting services.

Exhibit 12-4

Direct Versus Step-Down Method

	Molding		Finishing	
	*Direct**	*Step-down***	*Direct**	*Step-down***
Direct department costs	$100,000	$100,000	$160,000	$160,000
Allocated from facilities management	105,000	70,000	21,000	14,000
Allocated from personnel	4,800	13,200	19,200	52,800
Total costs	$209,800	$183,200	$200,200	$226,800

*From Exhibit 12-2.

**From Exhibit 12-3.

The greatest virtue of the direct method is its simplicity. If the two methods do not produce significantly different results, many companies elect to use the direct method because it is easier for managers to understand.

COSTS NOT RELATED TO COST DRIVERS

Our example illustrating direct and step-down allocation methods assumed that a single cost driver caused all costs in a given service department. For example, we assumed that square footage occupied caused all facilities management costs. Additional square footage would result in additional facilities management cost. But what if some of the costs in facilities management are independent of square footage?

Three alternative methods of allocation should be considered:

1. Identify additional cost drivers. Divide facilities management costs into two or more different cost pools and use a different cost driver to allocate the costs in each pool.

2. Divide facilities management costs into two cost pools, one with costs that vary in proportion to the square footage (variable costs) and one with costs not affected by square footage (fixed costs). Allocate the former using the direct or step-down method, but do not allocate the latter. Costs not allocated are period costs for the organization but are not regarded as a cost of a particular production department.

3. Allocate all costs by the direct or step-down method using square footage as the cost driver. This alternative implicitly assumes that, in the long run, square footage causes all facilities management costs—even if a short-term causal relationship is not easily identifiable. In other words, using more square footage may not cause an immediate increase in all facilities management costs, but eventually such costs will creep up in proportion to increases in square footage.

Suppose that most costs in a service department are caused by a single cost driver. Then alternatives 2 and 3 have much appeal. Only a small portion of costs would be unallocated (in alternative 2) or arbitrarily allocated (in alternative 3). But if large amounts of cost are not related to the single cost driver, alternative 1 should be seriously considered.

ALLOCATION OF COSTS TO FINAL COST OBJECTS

Up to this point, we have concentrated on cost allocation to divisions, departments, and similar segments of a company. Cost allocation is almost always carried one step further—to the final cost objects. Examples are *products,* such as automobiles, furniture, and newspapers, *services,* such as banking, health care, and education, and *customers.* Sometimes the allocation of total departmental costs to the revenue-producing products or services is called **cost application** or cost attribution.

cost application The allocation of total departmental costs to the revenue-producing products or services.

Costs are allocated to products for inventory valuation purposes and for decision purposes such as pricing, adding or deleting products, and promoting products. Cost allocation is also performed for cost-reimbursement purposes. As noted earlier, many defense contractors are reimbursed for the "costs" of producing products for the government.

TRADITIONAL APPROACH

Objective 5
Describe the traditional approach to allocating costs to products or services.

The traditional approach to allocating costs to products, services, or customers is the following:

1. Allocate production-related costs to the operating (line), or production or revenue-producing departments. This includes allocating service department costs to the production departments following the preceding guidelines. The production departments then contain all the costs: their direct department costs and the service department costs.

2. Select one or more cost drivers in each production department. For example, a portion of the departmental costs may be allocated on the basis of direct-labor hours, another portion on the basis of machine-hours, and the remainder on the basis of number of machine setups.

3. Allocate (apply) the total costs accumulated in step 1 to products or services that are the outputs of the operating departments using the cost drivers specified in step 2. If only one cost driver is used, two cost pools should be maintained, one for variable costs and one for fixed costs. Variable costs should be allocated on the basis of actual cost-driver activity. Fixed costs should either remain unallocated or be allocated on the basis of budgeted cost-driver activity.

Consider our manufacturing example, and assume that the step-down method was used to allocate service department costs. Exhibit 12-3 showed total costs of $183,200 accumulated in molding and $226,800 in finishing. Note that all $410,000 total manufacturing costs reside in the production departments. To allocate these costs to the products produced, cost drivers must be selected for each department. We will use a single cost driver for each department and assume that all costs are caused by that cost driver. Suppose machine-hours is the best measure of what causes costs in the molding department, and direct-labor hours drive costs in finishing. Exhibit 12-2 showed 30,000 total machine-hours used in molding and 10,000 direct-labor hours in finishing. Therefore costs are allocated to products as follows:

Molding: $183,200 ÷ 30,000 machine-hours = $6.11 per machine-hour
Finishing: $226,800 ÷ 10,000 direct-labor hours = $22.68 per direct-labor hour

A product that takes four machine-hours in molding and two direct-labor hours in finishing would have a cost of

$$(4 \times \$6.11) + (2 \times \$22.68) = \$24.44 + \$45.36 = \$69.80$$

The traditional approach to allocation of costs to the final cost objects focuses on accumulating costs within departments and then allocating departmental costs to producing departments, and finally to products, services, or customers. Many companies, seeking to improve the accuracy of product, service, or customer costing have adopted a different approach to the design of their cost allocation systems. This new approach is activity-based costing (ABC).

ACTIVITY-BASED COSTING (ABC)

The basic difference between traditional cost allocation systems and ABC systems is that ABC systems focus on accumulating costs into key activities, whereas traditional cost allocation focuses on accumulating costs into organizational units such as departments. In

ABC, we focus first on the activities required to produce the product or service. Then, we accumulate all resource costs based on their use in performing the activities.

ACTIVITY-BASED COSTING IN MANUFACTURING

Many managers in modern manufacturing firms (and automated service companies) believe it is inappropriate to allocate all costs based on measures of volume. Using direct-labor hours or cost—or even machine-hours—as the only cost driver seldom meets the cause-effect criterion desired in cost allocation. If many costs are caused by non-volume-based cost drivers, activity-based costing (ABC) should be considered. Recall from Chapter 4 that when we design an activity-based cost system, accountants identify significant overhead activities (machine processing, assembly, quality inspection, and so on). Then they allocate the costs of overhead resources used to perform these activities to the activities using cost drivers. Finally, they allocate the pooled costs of each activity to products using cost drivers (sometimes called activity drivers). In effect, the ABC system has taken one large overhead cost pool and broken it down into several pools, each associated with a key activity.

RELATIONSHIP BETWEEN ACTIVITIES, RESOURCES, COSTS, AND COST DRIVERS

Understanding the relationships between an activity, resources, resource costs, and cost drivers is the key to understanding ABC. To gain more understanding of how an ABC system actually works, we will look at one of the products produced by Woodland Park Company, a manufacturer of plastic components used in commercial trucks. Exhibit 12-5 gives

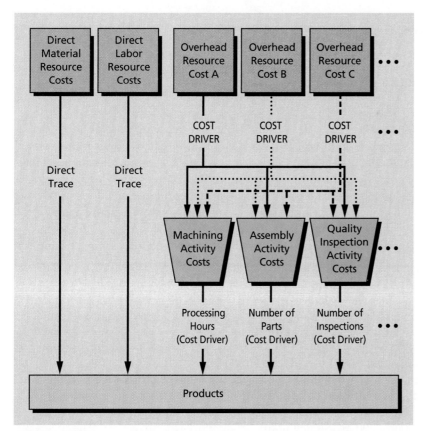

Exhibit 12-5
Woodland Park Company's ABC System

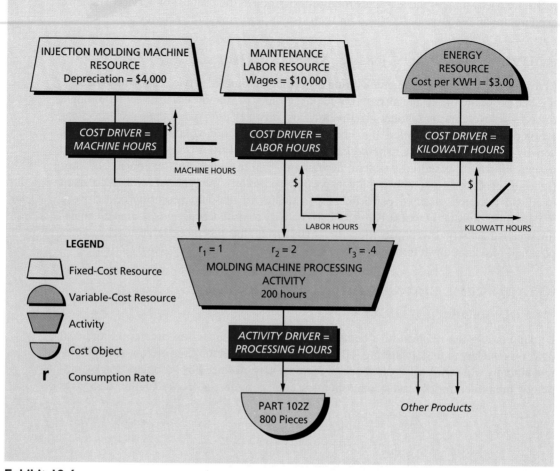

Exhibit 12-6

Relationship between an Activity, Resource Costs, and Cost Drivers

an overview of Woodland Park's ABC system. Note that there are numerous overhead-resource-cost pools (A, B, C, and so on). Each of these resource-cost pools is determined according to the guidelines discussed earlier in this chapter. For example, overhead-resource cost pool A may represent a group of machines. Several costs might be associated with these machines and thus be added together to get the overhead-resource costs for A. These costs might include machine depreciation and even replacement parts for the machines, as long as these costs have the same cost behavior with respect to the chosen cost driver. If machine hours is the cost driver chosen, we would need to make sure that both depreciation and replacement parts costs are fixed with respect to machine hours (within the relevant range). However, we would not include energy cost in resource-cost pool A (with depreciation and replacement parts costs) because energy cost is a variable-cost resource.

Product 102Z is a plastic casing for the control panel of large buses. Making 102Z requires several activities, as outlined in Exhibit 12-5. We will focus on the molding machine processing activity. The *overhead* resources required by this activity include an injection molding machine, two maintenance mechanics, and electrical energy. Exhibit 12-6 shows the relationship between the processing activity and the resources used. It takes 15 minutes to process each piece. Therefore, the current production run of 800 pieces of 102Z requires a total of 200 processing hours.

Each hour of processing activity requires (consumes) one machine hour, two labor hours (two maintenance mechanics), and 0.4 kilowatt hours. We can see that the cost drivers are a measure of the activity level (processing hours) and the amount of resources used by the processing activity. The consumption rates (the r's in Exhibit 12-6) give the rates at which resources are used in response to changes in the processing activity.

Cost drivers have been defined as *factors that affect costs*. So, how are the costs of the three resources affected by the cost drivers? Energy cost varies directly with changes in the processing activity because the power company charges Woodland Park based on the kilowatt hours used. One additional processing hour will require .4 additional kilowatt hours that will increase energy cost by $1.20 ($3.00 × .4). Thus energy is a variable-cost resource, and it is easy to see that processing hours and kilowatt hours are factors that affect energy costs.

However, the costs of the machine and labor resources are fixed with respect to changes (within the relevant range) in the cost drivers. One additional processing hour requires one additional machine hour and two labor hours, but the costs of the machine (depreciation) and labor (wages) resources do not change as long as there is available machine time and labor time to use. Have we violated our definition of cost driver? Not really. If the number of processing hours increases enough, the required machine hours or labor hours will exceed the capacities of the machine and labor. Management will then decide whether to purchase more machines or hire additional maintenance mechanics. This is why costs of fixed-cost resources do not change *automatically* when cost drivers change—it involves a management decision. So, when we say that cost drivers are "factors" that affect costs, we must keep in mind the cost behavior of resources.

SUMMARY PROBLEM FOR YOUR REVIEW

PROBLEM

Last year, TCY Company's demand for product H17 was 14,000 units. At a recent meeting, the sales manager asked the controller about the expected cost for the sales order activity for the current year. A new ABC system had been installed, and the controller had provided the sketch of the order processing activity to the sales manager (see Exhibit 12-7). The sales manager wanted to know how the order processing activity affects costs. The average sales order is for 20 units. The order processing activity shown in Exhibit 12-7 requires a computer, processing labor, and telecommunications. The computer is leased at a cost of $2,000 per period. Salaries are $7,000, and telecommunication charges are $1.60 per minute.

Required

1. How many labor hours does it take to process each order? How much telecommunication time does each order take?

2. What is the total cost formula for the order processing activity? What is the total and unit cost for demand of 14,000 units?

3. The sales manager calculated the cost per order to be $32.06, based on the expected demand of 14,000 units of H17. Because he believed that this year's demand for H17 may be only 12,000 units, he then calculated the total cost of processing 600 orders as $19,236 = 600 × $32.06. Comment on the validity of the sales manager's analysis.

SOLUTION

1. It takes .1 hours or 6 minutes of labor time and 12 minutes of telecommunications time to process an order.

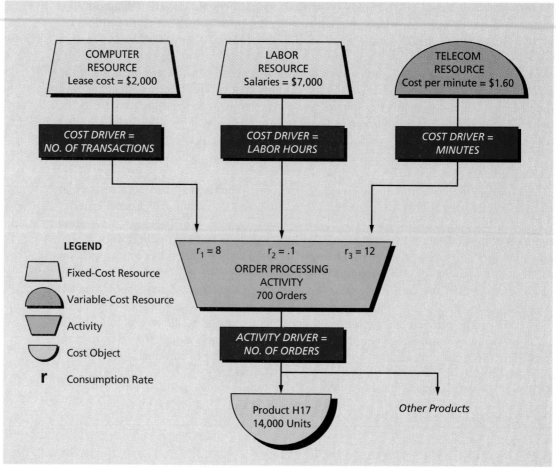

Exhibit 12-7

TCY's Order Processing Activity

2. The total cost formula for order processing activity is:

$$\text{Total cost} = \text{Fixed Costs} + \text{Variable Costs}$$
$$= \text{Lease Cost} + \text{Labor Cost} + \text{Telecommunications cost/minute} \times$$
$$\text{minutes/order} \times \text{number of orders}$$
$$= \$2,000 + \$7,000 + \$1.60 \times 12 \times \text{Number of Orders}$$
$$= \$9,000 + \$19.20 \times \text{Number of Orders}$$

For 14,000 units, there will be 700 orders processed. The total cost to process these orders is:

$$\text{Total Cost} = \$9,000 + (\$19.20 \times 700) = \$22,440$$
$$\text{and the unit cost is } \$1.60 \ (22,440 \div 14,000)$$

3. The sales manager has fallen into the trap of ignoring cost behavior. His calculation assumes that unit fixed costs will not change with changes in demand or the cost driver. The correct prediction of total cost for a demand of 12,000 units is $9,000 + $19.20 \times 600 = $20,520, and the new cost per order is $20,520 \div 600 = $34.20.

This problem illustrates why it is important to take cost behavior into consideration when using any costing system for planning purposes.

Exhibit 12-8

Product Cost Based on Former Costing System

	Product Line A	**Product Line B**	**Product Line C**
Direct material	$1,050,000	$ 575,000	$240,000
Direct labor (operators)	344,000	303,000	123,000
Factory overhead @ $27 per DLH			
Product line A (18,000 DLH)	486,000		
Product line B (16,000 DLH)		432,000	
Product line C (6,000 DLH)			162,000
Total cost	$1,880,000	$1,310,000	$525,000
Units produced	1,000,000	500,000	150,000
Unit cost	$ 1.88	$ 2.62	$ 3.50

ILLUSTRATION OF ACTIVITY-BASED COSTING IN MANUFACTURING

Chapter 4 introduced a four-step procedure for the design and implementation of activity-based-costing systems. We consider this same four-step procedure for the Molding Department of a manufacturing company that produces plastic parts using injection molding machines. The molding process produces three product lines with diverse demands on various activities and resources. Product line A consists of simple products that are produced in high volume (tape holders). Line B products are of medium volume and complexity (flashlight casings). Product line C consists of complex products that are produced in small lots (small camera casings). The former costing system allocated factory overhead costs based on the amount of direct-labor hours used to produce each product. The rate used to allocate factory overhead was $27 per direct-labor hour. This rate was calculated by dividing the total expected factory overhead ($1,080,000) by the total expected direct-labor hours (40,000). Product line C was allocated $6 \div 40 = 15\%$ of total overhead resource costs because 6,000 of the 40,000 total direct-labor hours were required to produce the 150,000 units of C. The use of this volume-based driver to allocate factory overhead (indirect) cost resulted in the unit cost for the three product lines shown in the last row of Exhibit 12-8.

Management changed to activity-based costing in this manufacturing department. Product line C is typical of complex products that require relatively more indirect resources from setup and machining activity. Management believed that the former costing system may have undercosted such products. A study was performed to determine the activity-based costs for the three product lines.

Step 1: Determine the cost objective, key activity centers, resources, and related cost drivers. The costing objective is to determine the costs of product lines A, B, and C. Direct material and direct labor (machine operators) are traced directly to each product. The remaining overhead resources are listed in Exhibit 12-9, together with the two activity centers and chosen cost drivers.

Step 2: Develop a process-based map representing the flow of activities, resources, and their interrelationships. The interrelationships between activities and resources were determined based on interviews with key personnel. Exhibit 12-10 depicts the flow of activities and resources. Note that the cost behavior for each resource is also shown. Understanding the cost behavior of resources is vital during the planning process. For example, if the volume of product line A is expected to increase (within the relevant range of activity), machine-hours and the number of setups would increase. However, the only costs that

Exhibit 12-9

Activity Centers, Cost Drivers, and Resources
Molding Department

Activity Center	Cost Driver	Resources Consumed
Setup	Number of setups	Maintenance mechanic time
		Supervisor time
		Energy (machines had to remain on during setup activity)
		Occupancy space
		Molding machine time
Molding process	Machine hours	Supplies
		Energy
		Supervisor time
		Molding machine time
		Occupancy space
		Maintenance mechanic time

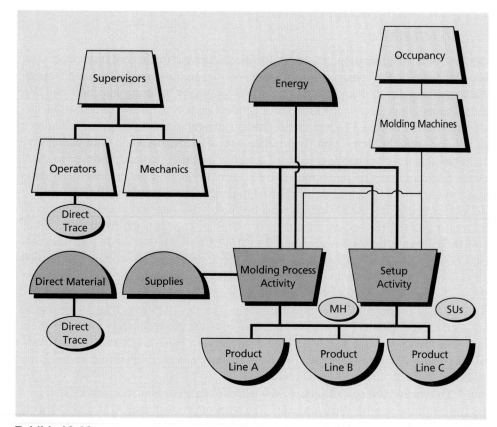

Exhibit 12-10

Process-Based Map of the Molding Department Operations

would be expected to increase are direct materials, supplies, and energy because they are variable-cost resources. Because the remaining resources are fixed-cost resources, their costs would not increase in response to increased setups or machine hours.

Step 3: Collect relevant data concerning costs and the physical flow of cost-driver units among resources and activities. Using the process map as a guide, accountants collected the required cost and operational data by further interviews with relevant personnel.

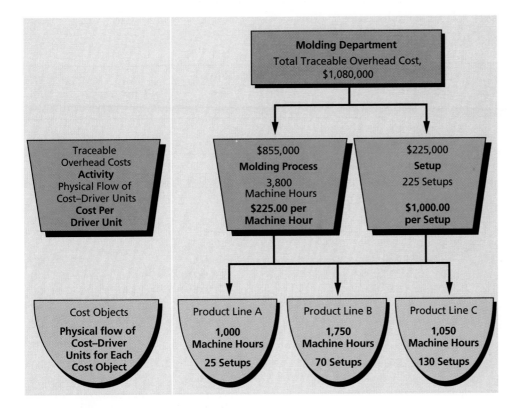

Exhibit 12-11

Activity-Based-Costing System

Exhibit 12-11 is a graphical representation and summary of the data collected for the two activity centers identified in Step 1. For each activity center, data collected included traceable overhead costs and the physical flow of cost-driver units.

Step 4: Calculate and interpret the new activity-based information. Exhibit 12-12 shows the computations to determine the cost per unit for each product line. The results of the study confirmed management's belief—product line C was being undercosted by ($4.86 − $3.50) ÷ $3.50, or 39%. Exhibit 12-13 compares the allocation of factory overhead using the former costing system with the activity-based-costing system. Product line A's allocation of overhead decreased from 45% to 23.1%, while product line C's allocation increased from 15% to 33.9%. Notice that the use of just two additional cost drivers (machine-hours and setups) can make a significant difference in product costing. Many companies use more than 20 different cost drivers to improve the accuracy of their costing system, but the costs associated with using many activity centers can be high. The benefit-cost criteria must be applied in each case.

Objective 6
Use activity-based costing to allocate costs in a modern manufacturing environment to products or services.

EFFECT OF ACTIVITY-BASED COSTING

Many companies have adopted activity-based costing in recent years. For example, consider Schrader Bellows, which increased the number of cost drivers used to allocate costs to products. Several of the new cost drivers are essentially measures of the number of transactions rather than measures of volume. The cost driver having the largest effect on unit costs is number of machine setups. The resulting changes in unit costs for the company's seven products were dramatic, as shown in Exhibit 12-14. Except for product 7, the products with low volume and a high number of setups per unit had

Exhibit 12-12

Key Results of Activity-Based-Costing Study

Activity/Resource [Driver Units]		Traceable Costs (1)		Total Physical Flow of Driver Units (2)		Cost per Driver Unit (1) ÷ (2)	
Setup [number of setups]		$225,000		225 Setups		$1,000	
Molding process [machine-hours]		$855,000		3,800 Machine Hours		$ 225	

		Product Line A		Product Line B		Product Line C	
	Cost per Driver Unit	Physical Flow of Driver Units	Cost	Physical Flow of Driver Units	Cost	Physical Flow of Driver Units	Cost
Direct material			$1,050,000		$ 575,000		$240,000
Direct labor			344,000		303,000		123,000
Setup costs	$1,000	25	25,000	70	70,000	130	130,000
Molding process	$ 225	1,000	225,000	1,750	393,750	1,050	236,250
Total			$1,644,000		$1,341,750		$729,250
Units produced			1,000,000		500,000		150,000
Cost per unit			$ 1.64		$ 2.68		$ 4.86

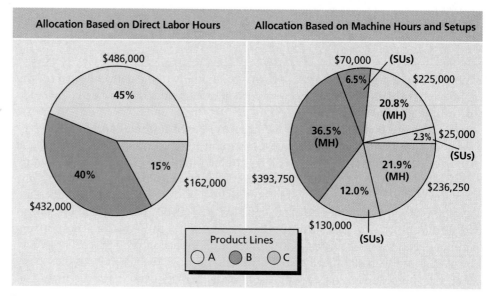

Exhibit 12-13

Comparison of Costing Systems

large increases in unit costs. The products with high volume and fewer setups per unit had decreases in unit costs. Although product 7 had low volume, its unit cost dropped because it was assembled from components used in large volumes in other products. The unit cost of the components decreased because of their high volume and relatively few setups.

Exhibit 12-14

Schrader Bellows*

Costs Before and After Activity-Based-Costing System

Product	Sales Volume	Unit Cost Old System	Unit Cost Activity-based System	Percent Change
1	43,562 units	$ 7.85	$ 7.17	(8.7)
2	500	8.74	15.45	76.8
3	53	12.15	82.49	578.9
4	2,079	13.63	24.51	79.8
5	5,670	12.40	19.99	61.2
6	11,169	8.04	7.96	(1.0)
7	423	8.47	6.93	(18.2)

*This example is from "How Cost Accounting Systematically Distorts Product Costs" by R. Cooper and R. Kaplan, in *Accounting and Management: Field Study Perspectives* by W. Bruns, Jr., and R. Kaplan (Boston, MA: Harvard Business School Press, 1987), pp. 204–28.

Activity-Based Costing at Hewlett-Packard

The Roseville Network Division (RND) of Hewlett-Packard was one of the first groups to use activity-based costing. The producer of computer-networking devices referred to its system as "cost-driver accounting." Because RND's products were increasing in number and decreasing in length of product life, the design of new products and their production processes was especially important to the division's success. But the old accounting system did not produce information helpful in comparing the production costs of different designs.

RND's new system focused on the costs of each production process—essentially, the different activities of the division. The system evolved from one with only two cost drivers—direct-labor hours and number of insertions—to one with the following nine cost drivers:

1. Number of axial insertions
2. Number of radial insertions
3. Number of DIP insertions
4. Number of manual insertions
5. Number of test hours
6. Number of solder joints
7. Number of boards
8. Number of parts
9. Number of slots

The increase in the number of cost drivers came about as accountants and managers developed a better understanding of the economics of the design and production process. By knowing the costs of the various activities, product designers could develop designs that would minimize costs for a given level of functionality and reliability.

Recognizing the average product life cycle of 24 months, RND built its cost system around its strategy to keep product lines as up-to-date as possible. RND also recognized a trade-off between accuracy and complexity. The initial two-cost-driver system was simple, but not accurate enough. But with the current nine cost drivers, concern grows that adding more cost drivers may make the system too complex—that is, make its costs greater than its benefits.

Engineering managers at RND were pleased with the activity-based-costing system. It greatly influenced the design of new products. For example, once it became clear that manual insertion was three times as expensive as automatic insertion, designs could be modified to include more automatic insertions. The system clearly had the desired effect of influencing the behavior of product designers.

Source: Adapted from R. Cooper and P. B. B. Turney, "Internally Forced Activity-Based Cost Systems," in R. S. Kaplan, ed., *Measures for Manufacturing Excellence.* Boston, MA: Harvard Business School Press, 1990.

ALLOCATION OF JOINT COSTS AND BY-PRODUCT COSTS

Joint costs and by-product costs create especially difficult cost-allocation problems. By definition, such costs relate to more than one product and cannot be separately identified with an individual product. Let's now examine these special cases, starting with joint costs.

JOINT COSTS

So far, we have assumed that cost drivers could be identified with an individual product. For example, if costs are being allocated to products or services on the basis of machine-hours, we have assumed that each machine-hour is used on a single final product or service. However, sometimes inputs are added to the production process before individual products are separately identifiable (that is, before the split-off point). Recall from Chapter 6 (page 218), that such costs are called *joint costs*. Joint costs include all inputs of material, labor, and overhead costs that are incurred before the split-off point.

Suppose a department has more than one product and some costs are joint costs. How should such joint costs be allocated to the products? As noted in Chapter 6, allocation of joint costs should not affect decisions about the individual products. Nevertheless, joint product costs are routinely allocated to products for purposes of inventory valuation and income determination.

Consider the example of joint product costs that we used in Chapter 6. A department in Dow Chemical Company produces two chemicals, X and Y. The joint cost is $100,000, and production is 1,000,000 liters of X and 500,000 liters of Y. X can be sold for $.09 per liter and Y for $.06 per liter. Ordinarily, some part of the $100,000 joint cost will be allocated to the inventory of X and the rest to the inventory of Y. Such allocations are useful for inventory purposes only. As explained in Chapter 6, joint cost allocations should be ignored for decisions such as selling a joint product or processing it further.

Objective 7
Use the physical-units and relative-sales-value methods to allocate joint costs to products.

Two conventional ways of allocating joint costs to products are widely used: physical units and relative sales values. If physical units were used, the joint costs would be allocated as follows:

	Liters	Weighting	Allocation of Joint Costs	Sales Value at Split-Off
X	1,000,000	10/15 × $100,000	$ 66,667	$ 90,000
Y	500,000	5/15 × $100,000	33,333	30,000
	1,500,000		$100,000	$120,000

This approach shows that the $33,333 joint cost of producing Y exceeds its $30,000 sales value at split-off, seemingly indicating that Y should not be produced. However, such an allocation is not helpful in making production decisions. Neither of the two products could be produced separately.

A decision to produce Y must be a decision to produce X and Y. Because total revenue of $120,000 exceeds the total joint cost of $100,000, both will be produced. The allocation was not useful for this decision.

The physical-units method requires a common physical unit for measuring the output of each product. For example, board feet is a common unit for a variety of products in the lumber industry. However, sometimes such a common denominator is lacking. Consider the production of meat and hides from butchering a steer. You might use pounds as a common denominator, but pounds is not a good measure of the output of hides. As an alternative, many companies use the *relative-sales-value method* for allocating joint costs.

The following allocation results from applying the relative-sales-value method to the Dow Chemical department:

	Relative Sales Value at Split-Off	Weighting	Allocation of Joint Costs
X	$ 90,000	90/120 × $100,000	$ 75,000
Y	30,000	30/120 × $100,000	25,000
	$120,000		$100,000

The weighting is based on the sales values of the individual products. Because the sales value of X at split-off is $90,000 and total sales value at split-off is $120,000, X is allocated 90/120 of the joint cost.

Now each product would be assigned a joint cost portion that is less than its sales value at split-off. Note how the allocation of a cost to a particular product such as Y depends not only on the sales value of Y but also on the sales value of X. For example, suppose you were the product manager for Y. You planned to sell your 500,000 liters for $30,000, achieving a profit of $30,000 − $25,000 = $5,000. Everything went as expected except that the price of X fell to $.07 per liter for revenue of $70,000 rather than $90,000. Instead of 30/120 of the joint cost, Y received 30/100 × $100,000 = $30,000 and had a profit of $0. Despite the fact that Y operations were exactly as planned, the cost-allocation method caused the profit on Y to be $5,000 below plan.

The relative-sales-value method can also be used when one or more of the joint products cannot be sold at the split-off point. To apply the method, we approximate the sales value at split-off as follows:

$$\text{Sales value at split-off} = \text{Final sales value} - \text{Separable costs}$$

For example, suppose the 500,000 liters of Y requires $20,000 of processing beyond the split-off point, after which it can be sold for $.10 per liter. The sales value at split-off would be ($.10 × 500,000) − $20,000 = $50,000 − $20,000 = $30,000.

BY-PRODUCT COSTS

By-products are similar to joint products. A **by-product** is a product that, like a joint product, is not individually identifiable until manufacturing reaches a split-off point. By-products differ from joint products because they have relatively insignificant total sales values in comparison with the other products emerging at split-off. In contrast, joint products have relatively significant total sales values at split-off in comparison with the other jointly produced items. Examples of by-products are glycerine from soap making and mill ends of cloth and carpets.

by-product A product that, like a joint product, is not individually identifiable until manufacturing reaches a split-off point, but has relatively insignificant total sales value.

If an item is accounted for as a by-product, only separable costs are allocated to it. All joint costs are allocated to the main products. Any revenues from by-products, less their separable costs, are deducted from the cost of the main products.

Consider a lumber company that sells sawdust generated in the production of lumber to companies making particle board. Suppose the company regards the sawdust as a by-product. In 19X6, sales of sawdust totaled $30,000, and the cost of loading and shipping the sawdust (that is, costs incurred beyond the split-off point) was $20,000. The inventory cost of the sawdust would consist of only the $20,000 separable cost. None of the joint cost of producing lumber and sawdust would be allocated to the sawdust. The difference between the revenue and separable cost, $30,000 − $20,000 = $10,000, would be deducted from the cost of the lumber produced.

PROBLEM

Nonmanufacturing organizations often find it useful to allocate costs to final products or services. Consider a hospital. The output of a hospital is not as easy to define as the output of a factory. Assume the following measures of output in three revenue-producing departments:

Department	Measures of Output*
Radiology	X-ray films processed
Laboratory	Tests administered
Daily Patient Services[†]	Patient-days of care (i.e., the number of patients multiplied by the number of days of each patient's stay)

* These become the "product" cost objectives, the various revenue-producing activities of a hospital.

[†]There would be many of these departments, such as obstetrics, pediatrics, and orthopedics. Moreover, there may be both inpatient and outpatient care.

Budgeted output for 19X7 is 60,000 x-ray films processed in Radiology, 50,000 tests administered in the Laboratory, and 30,000 patient-days in Daily Patient Services.

In addition to the revenue-producing departments, the hospital has three service departments: Administrative and Fiscal Services, Plant Operations and Maintenance, and Laundry. (Of course, real hospitals have more than three revenue-producing departments and more than three service departments. This problem is simplified to keep the data manageable.)

The hospital has decided that the cost driver for Administrative and Fiscal Services costs is the direct department costs of the other departments. The cost driver for Plant Operations and Maintenance is square feet occupied, and for Laundry is pounds of laundry. The pertinent budget data for 19X7 are:

	Direct Department Costs	Square Feet Occupied	Pounds of Laundry
Administrative and Fiscal Services	$1,000,000	1,000	—
Plant Operations and Maintenance	800,000	2,000	—
Laundry	200,000	5,000	—
Radiology	1,000,000	12,000	80,000
Laboratory	400,000	3,000	20,000
Daily Patient Services	1,600,000	80,000	300,000
Total	$5,000,000	103,000	400,000

Required

1. Allocate service department costs using the direct method.
2. Allocate service department costs using the step-down method. Allocate Administrative and Fiscal Services first, Plant Operations and Maintenance second, and Laundry third.
3. Compute the cost per unit of output in each of the revenue-producing departments using (a) the costs determined using the direct method for allocating service department costs (requirement 1) and (b) the costs determined using the step-down method for allocating service department costs (requirement 2).

SOLUTION

1. The solutions to all three requirements are shown in Exhibit 12-15. The direct method is presented first. Note that no service department costs are allocated to

Exhibit 12-15
Allocation of Service Department Costs: Direct and Step-Down Methods

	Administrative and Fiscal Services	Plant Operations and Maintenance	Laundry	Radiology	Laboratory	Daily Patient Services
Accumulated Base	*Accumulated Costs*	*Sq. Footage*	*Pounds*			
1. Direct Method						
Direct departmental costs before allocation	$1,000,000	$800,000	$200,000	$1,000,000	$ 400,000	$1,600,000
Administrative and Fiscal Services	(1,000,000)			333,333*	133,333	533,334
Plant Operations and Maintenance		(800,000)		101,053†	25,263	673,684
Laundry			(200,000)	40,000‡	10,000	150,000
Total costs after allocation				$1,474,386	$ 568,596	$2,957,018
Product output in films, tests, and patient-days, respectively				60,000	50,000	30,000
3a. Cost per unit of output				$24.573	$11.372	$98.567
2. Step-Down Method						
Direct departmental costs before allocation	$1,000,000	$800,000	$200,000	$1,000,000	$ 400,000	$1,600,000
Administrative and Fiscal Services	(1,000,000)	200,000§	50,000	250,000	100,000	400,000
Plant Operations and Maintenance		(1,000,000)	50,000¶	120,000	30,000	800,000
Laundry			(300,000)	60,000#	15,000	225,000
Total costs after allocation				$1,430,000	$ 545,000	$3,025,000
Product output in films, tests, and patient-days, respectively				60,000	50,000	30,000
3b. Cost per unit of output				$23.833	$10.900	$100.833

*$1,000,000 ÷ ($1,000,000 + $400,000 + $1,600,000) = 33 1/3%; 33 1/3% × $1,000,000 = $333,333; and so on.

†$800,000 ÷ (12,000 + 3,000 + 80,000) = $8.4210526; $8.4210526 × 12,000 sq. ft. = $101,053; and so on.

‡$200,000 ÷ (80,000 + 20,000 + 300,000) = $.50; $.50 × 80,000 = $40,000; and so on.

§$1,000,000 ÷ ($800,000 + $200,000 + $1,000,000 + $400,000 + $1,600,000) = 25%; 25% × $800,000 = $200,000; and so on.

¶$1,000,000 ÷ (5,000 + 12,000 + 3,000 + 80,000) = $10.00; $10.00 × 5,000 sq. ft. = $50,000; and so on.

#$300,000 ÷ (80,000 + 20,000 + 300,000) = $.75; $.75 × 80,000 = $60,000; and so on.

another service department. Therefore, allocations are based on the relative amounts of the cost driver in the revenue-producing department only. For example, in allocating Plant Operations and Maintenance, square footage occupied by the service departments is ignored. The cost driver is the 95,000 square feet occupied by the revenue-producing departments.

Note that the total cost of the revenue-producing departments after allocation, $1,474,386 + $568,596 + $2,957,018 = $5,000,000, is equal to the total of the direct department costs in all six departments before allocation.

2. The step-down method is shown in the lower half of Exhibit 12-15. The costs of Administrative and Fiscal Services are allocated to all five other departments. Because a department's own costs are not allocated to itself, the cost driver consists of the $4,000,000 direct department costs in the five departments excluding Administrative and Fiscal Services.

Plant Operations and Maintenance is allocated second on the basis of square feet occupied. No cost will be allocated to itself or back to Administrative and Fiscal Services. Therefore, the square footage used for allocation is the 100,000 square feet occupied by the other four departments.

Laundry is allocated third. No cost would be allocated back to the first two departments, even if they had used laundry services.

As in the direct method, note that the total costs of the revenue-producing departments after allocation, $1,430,000 + $545,000 + $3,025,000 = $5,000,000, equals the total of the direct department costs before allocation.

3. The solutions are labeled 3a and 3b in Exhibit 12-15. Compare the unit costs derived from the direct method with those of the step-down method. In many instances, the final product costs may not differ enough to warrant investing in a cost-allocation method that is any fancier than the direct method. But sometimes even small differences may be significant to a government agency or anybody paying for a large volume of services based on costs. For example, in Exhibit 12-15 the "cost" of an "average" laboratory test is either $11.37 or $10.90. This may be significant for the fiscal committee of the hospital's board of trustees, who must decide on hospital prices. Thus cost allocation often is a technique that helps answer the vital question, "Who should pay for what, and how much?"

Highlights to Remember

Explain the major purposes for allocating costs. The four main purposes of cost allocation are to predict the economic effects of planning and control decisions, to motivate managers and employees, to measure the costs of inventory and cost of goods sold, and to justify costs for pricing or reimbursement.

Allocate the variable and fixed costs of service departments to other organizational units. The dual method of allocation is used for service department costs. Variable costs should be allocated using budgeted cost rates times the actual cost driver level. Fixed costs should be allocated using budgeted percent of capacity available for use times the total budgeted fixed costs.

Allocate the central costs of an organization. Central costs include public relations, top corporate management overhead, legal, data processing, controller's department, and companywide planning. Often, it is best to allocate only those central costs of an organization for which measures of usage by departments are available.

Use the direct and step-down methods to allocate service department costs to user departments. When service departments support other service departments in addition to producing departments, there are two methods for allocation. The direct method ignores other service departments when allocating costs. The step-down method recognizes other service departments use of services.

Describe the traditional approach to allocating costs to products or services. The traditional approach to allocating costs to products, services, or customers is to focus first on accumulating costs by departments—service and producing (step 1). Next, cost drivers are selected for allocating service department costs to producing departments and finally from producing departments to products, services, or customers (step 2). The last step is to apply the costs accumulated in step 1 using the cost drivers selected in step 2.

Use activity-based costing to allocate costs in a modern manufacturing environment to products or services. In activity-based costing, the focus shifts from accumulating costs by department to accumulating costs by key activities performed. For each activity, supporting resources are identified. Cost drivers are used to allocate resource costs to activities and then from activities to products or services.

Use the physical-units and relative-sales-value methods to allocate joint costs to products. Joint costs are often allocated to products for inventory valuation and income determination using the physical-units or relative-sales-value method. However, such allocations should not affect decisions.

Understand how cost allocation is used in cost planning and control. Across the entire value chain, managers need accurate cost information in order to effectively plan and control operations. The proportion of total costs that are indirect has increased in most companies due to increased business complexity. As a result, the need for accurate and timely cost allocation has also increased.

Accounting Vocabulary

by-product, p. 475

cost accounting systems, p. 454

cost-allocation base, p. 454

cost application, p. 463

cost pool, p. 454

direct method, p. 461

service departments, p. 456

step-down method, p. 461

Fundamental Assignment Material

12-A1 Allocation of Central Costs

The Union Atlantic Railroad allocates all central corporate overhead costs to its divisions. Some costs, such as specified internal auditing and legal costs, are identified on the basis of time spent. However, other costs are harder to allocate, so the revenue achieved by each division is used as an allocation base. Examples of such costs were executive salaries, travel, secretarial, utilities, rent, depreciation, donations, corporate planning, and general marketing costs.

Allocations on the basis of revenue for 19X8 were (in millions):

Division	Revenue	Allocated Costs
Northeast	$120	$ 6
Mid-Atlantic	240	12
Southeast	240	12
Total	$600	$30

In 19X9, Northeast's revenue remained unchanged. However, Southeast's revenue soared to $280 million because of unusually large imports. The latter are troublesome to forecast because of variations in world markets. Mid-Atlantic had expected a sharp rise in revenue, but severe competitive conditions resulted in a decline to $200 million. The total cost allocated on the basis of revenue was again $30 million, despite rises in other costs. The president was pleased that central costs did not rise for the year.

Required

1. Compute the allocations of costs to each division for 19X9.

2. How would each division manager probably feel about the cost allocation in 19X9 as compared with 19X8? What are the weaknesses of using revenue as a basis for cost allocation?

3. Suppose the budgeted revenues for 19X9 were $120, $240, and $280, respectively, and the budgeted revenues were used as a cost driver for allocation. Compute the allocations of costs to each division for 19X9. Do you prefer this method to the one used in requirement 1? Why?

4. Many accountants and managers oppose allocating any central costs. Why?

12-A2 Direct and Step-Down Methods of Allocation

Manriques Tool and Die has three service departments:

	Budgeted Department Costs
Cafeteria, revenue of $100,000 less expenses of $250,000	$ 150,000
Engineering	2,500,000
General factory administration	950,000

Cost drivers are budgeted as follows:

Production Departments	Employees	Engineering Hours Worked for Production Departments	Total Labor Hours
Machining	120	50,000	300,000
Assembly	540	20,000	720,000
Finishing and painting	60	10,000	120,000

Required

1. Manriques allocates all service department costs directly to the production departments without allocation to other service departments. Show how much of the budgeted costs of each service department are allocated to each production department. To plan your work, examine requirement 2 before undertaking this question.

2. The company has decided to use the step-down method of cost allocation. General factory administration would be allocated first, then cafeteria, then engineering. Cafeteria employees worked 36,000 labor hours per year. There were 60 engineering employees with 120,000 total labor hours. Recompute the results in requirement 1, using the step-down method. Show your computations. Compare the results in requirements 1 and 2. Which method of allocation do you favor? Why?

12-A3 Activity-Based Costing

Yamaguchi Company makes printed circuit boards in a suburb of Kyoto. The production process is automated with computer-controlled robotic machines assembling each circuit board from a supply of parts. Yamaguchi has identified four activities:

ACTIVITY	COST DRIVER	RATE
Materials handling	Cost of direct materials	5% of materials cost
Assembly	Number of parts used	¥50 per part
Soldering	Number of circuit boards	¥1,500 per board
Quality assurance	Minutes of testing	¥400 per minute

Yamaguchi makes three types of circuit boards, models I, II, and III. Requirements for production of each circuit board are:

	Model I	Model II	Model III
Direct materials cost	¥4,000	¥6,000	¥8,000
Number of parts used	60	40	20
Minutes of testing	5	3	2

Required

1. Compute the cost of production of 100 of the three types of circuit boards and the cost per circuit board for each type.
2. Suppose the design of model I could be simplified so that it required only 30 parts (instead of 60) and took only 3 minutes of testing time (instead of 5). Compute the cost of 100 model I circuit boards and the cost per circuit board.

12-A4 Joint Products

Quebec Metals, Inc., buys raw ore on the open market and processes it into two final products, A and B. The ore costs $10 per pound, and the process separating it into A and B has a cost of $4 per pound. During 19X6, Quebec plans to produce 200,000 pounds of A and 600,000 pounds of B from 800,000 pounds of ore. A sells for $30 a pound and B for $15 a pound. The company allocated joint costs to the individual products for inventory valuation purposes.

Required

1. Allocate all the joint costs to A and B using the physical-units method.
2. Allocate all the joint costs to A and B using the relative-sales-value method.
3. Suppose B cannot be sold in the form in which it emerges from the joint process. Instead, it must be processed further at a fixed cost of $300,000 plus a variable cost of $1 per pound. Then it can be sold for $21.50 a pound. Allocate all the joint costs to A and B using the relative-sales-value method.

12-B1 Allocation of Computer Costs

Review the section "Allocation of Service Department Costs," pages 456-464, especially the example of the use of the computer by the university. Recall that the budget formula was $100,000 fixed cost monthly plus $200 per hour of computer time used. Based on long-run predicted usage, the fixed costs were allocated on a lump-sum basis, 30% to Business and 70% to Engineering.

Required

1. Show the total allocation if Business used 210 hours and Engineering used 390 hours in a given month. Assume that the actual costs coincided exactly with the budgeted amount for total usage of 600 hours.
2. Assume the same facts as in requirement 1 except that the fixed costs were allocated on the basis of actual hours of usage. Show the total allocation of costs to each school. As the dean of Business, would you prefer this method or the method in requirement 1? Explain.

12-B2 Allocation of Service Department Costs

Dallas Building Maintenance, Inc. provides cleaning services for a variety of clients. The company has two producing divisions, Residential and Commercial, and two service departments, Personnel and Administrative. The company has decided to allocate all service department costs to the producing departments—Personnel on the basis of number of employees, and Administrative on the basis of direct department costs. The budget for 19X9 shows:

	Personnel	Administrative	Residential	Commercial
Direct department costs	$70,000	$90,000	$ 240,000	$400,000
Number of employees	3	5	12	18
Direct-labor hours			24,000	36,000
Square feet cleaned			4,500,000	9,970,000

Required

1. Allocate service department costs using the direct method.
2. Allocate service department costs using the step-down method. The Personnel Department costs should be allocated first.
3. Suppose the company prices by the hour in the Residential Department and by the square foot cleaned in Commercial. Using the results of the step-down allocations in requirement 2:
   a. Compute the cost of providing one direct-labor hour of service in the Residential Department.
   b. Compute the cost of cleaning one square foot of space in the Commercial Department.

12-B3 Activity-Based Costing
The Maori Novelty company makes a variety of souvenirs for visitors to New Zealand. The Otago Division manufactures stuffed kiwi birds using a highly automated operation. A recently installed activity-based-costing system has four activity centers.

ACTIVITY CENTER	COST DRIVER	COST PER DRIVER UNIT
Materials receiving and handling	Kilograms of materials	$1.20 per kg
Production setup	Number of setups	$60 per setup
Cutting, sewing, and assembly	Number of units	$.40 per unit
Packing and shipping	Number of orders	$10 per order

Two products are called "standard kiwi" and "giant kiwi." They require .20 and .40 kg of materials, respectively, at a materials cost of $1.30 for standard kiwis and $2.20 for giant kiwis. One computer-controlled assembly line makes all products. When a production run of a different product is started, a setup procedure is required to reprogram the computers and make other changes in the process. Normally, 600 standard kiwis are produced per setup, but only 240 giant kiwis. Products are packed and shipped separately, so a request from a customer for, say, three different products is considered three different orders.

The Auckland Zoo Gift Shop just placed an order for 100 standard kiwis and 50 giant kiwis.

Required

1. Compute the cost of the products shipped to the Auckland Zoo Gift Shop.
2. Suppose the products made for the Auckland Zoo Gift Shop required "AZ" to be printed on each kiwi. Because of the automated process, printing the initials takes no extra time or materials, but it requires a special production setup for each product. Compute the cost of the products shipped to the Auckland Zoo Gift Shop.

3. Explain how the activity-based-costing system helps Maori Novelty to measure costs of individual products or orders better than a traditional system that allocates all non-materials costs based on direct labor.

12-B4 Joint Products

Des Moines Milling buys oats at $.60 per pound and produces DMM Oat Flour, DMM Oat Flakes, and DMM Oat Bran. The process of separating the oats into oat flour and oat bran costs $.30 per pound. The oat flour can be sold for $1.50 per pound, the oat bran for $2.00 per pound. Each pound of oats has .2 pounds of oat bran and .8 pounds of oat flour. A pound of oat flour can be made into oat flakes for a fixed cost of $240,000 plus a variable cost of $.60 per pound. Des Moines Milling plans to process 1 million pounds of oats in 19X9, at a purchase price of $600,000.

1. Allocate all the joint costs to oat flour and oat bran using the physical-units method. **Required**
2. Allocate all the joint costs to oat flour and oat bran using the relative-sales-value method.
3. Suppose there were no market for oat flour. Instead, it must be made into oat flakes to be sold. Oat flakes sell for $2.90 per pound. Allocate the joint cost to oat bran and oat flakes using the relative-sales-value method.

Additional Assignment Material

Questions

12-1. What is the purpose of a cost accounting system?

12-2. "A cost pool is a group of costs that is physically traced to the appropriate cost objective." Do you agree? Explain.

12-3. Give five terms that are sometimes used as substitutes for the term *allocate*.

12-4. What are the four purposes of cost allocation?

12-5. What are the three types of allocations?

12-6. Give three guidelines for the allocation of service department costs.

12-7. Why should budgeted cost rates, rather than actual cost rates, be used for allocating the variable costs of service departments?

12-8. Why do many companies allocate fixed costs separately from variable costs?

12-9. "We used a lump-sum allocation method for fixed costs a few years ago, but we gave it up because managers always predicted usage below what they actually used." Is this a common problem? How might it be prevented?

12-10. "A commonly misused basis for allocation is dollar sales." Explain.

12-11. How should national advertising costs be allocated to territories?

12-12. Briefly describe the two popular methods for allocating service department costs.

12-13. "The step-down method allocates more costs to the producing departments than does the direct method." Do you agree? Explain.

12-14. How does the term *cost application* differ from *cost allocation*?

12-15. What is a non-volume-related cost driver? Give two examples.

12-16. How are costs of various overhead resources allocated to products, services, or customers in an ABC system?

12-17. "A cost pool for a particular resource is either a variable cost pool or a fixed cost pool. There should be no mixed-cost pools." Do you agree? Explain.

12-18. Give four examples of activities and related cost drivers that can be used in an ABC system to allocate costs to products, services, or customers.

12-19. "Activity-based costing is useful for product costing, but not for planning and control." Do you agree? Explain.

12-20. Chapter 6 explained that joint costs should not be allocated to individual products for decision purposes. For what purposes are such costs allocated to products?

12-21. Briefly explain each of the two conventional ways of allocating joint costs of products.

12-22. What are by-products and how do we account for them?

12-23 Fixed- and Variable-Cost Pools

The city of Castle Rock signed a lease for a photocopy machine at $2,500 per month and $.02 per copy. Operating costs for toner, paper, operator salary, and so on are all variable at $.03 per copy. Departments had projected a need for 100,000 copies a month. The City Planning Department predicted its usage at 36,000 copies a month. It made 42,000 copies in August.

Required

1. Suppose one predetermined rate per copy was used to allocate all photocopy costs. What rate would be used and how much cost would be allocated to the City Planning Department in August?

2. Suppose fixed- and variable-cost pools were allocated separately. Specify how each pool should be allocated. Compute the cost allocated to the City Planning Department in August.

3. Which method, the one in requirement 1 or the one in requirement 2, do you prefer? Explain.

12-24 Sales-Based Allocations

Johnny's Markets has three grocery stores in the metropolitan Philadelphia area. Central costs are allocated using sales as the cost driver. Following are budgeted and actual sales during November:

	Sunnyville	Wedgewood	Independence
Budgeted sales	$600,000	$1,000,000	$400,000
Actual sales	600,000	700,000	500,000

Central costs of $200,000 are to be allocated in November.

Required

1. Compute the central costs allocated to each store with budgeted sales as the cost driver.

2. Compute the central costs allocated to each store with actual sales as the cost driver.

3. What advantages are there to using budgeted rather than actual sales for allocating the central costs?

12-25 Direct and Step-Down Allocations

Butler Home Products has two producing departments, machining and assembly, and two service departments, personnel and custodial. The company's budget for April, 19X9 is:

Service Departments	Personnel	Custodial	Production Departments Machining	Assembly
Direct department costs	$32,000	$70,000	$600,000	$ 800,000
Square feet	2,000	1,000	10,000	25,000
Number of employees	15	30	200	250

Butler allocates personnel costs on the basis of number of employees. Butler allocates custodial costs on the basis of square feet.

Required

1. Allocate personnel and custodial costs to the producing departments using the direct method.

2. Allocate personnel and custodial costs to the producing departments using the step-down method. Allocate personnel costs first.

12-26 Joint Costs

Hernandez Chemical Company's production process for two of its solvents can be diagrammed as follows:

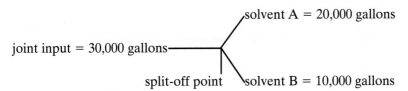

The cost of the joint input, including processing costs before the split-off point, is $400,000. Solvent A can be sold at split-off for $20 per gallon and solvent B for $60 per gallon.

Required

1. Allocate the $400,000 joint cost to solvents A and B by the physical-units method.
2. Allocate the $400,000 joint cost to solvents A and B by the relative-sales-value method.

12-27 By-Product Costing

The Wenatchee Apple Company buys apples from local orchards and presses them to produce apple juice. The pulp that remains after pressing is sold to farmers as livestock food. This livestock food is accounted for as a by-product.

During the 19X8 fiscal year, the company paid $1 million to purchase 8 million pounds of apples. After processing, 1 million pounds of pulp remained. Jones spent $35,000 to package and ship the pulp, which was sold for $50,000.

Required

1. How much of the joint cost of the apples is allocated to the pulp?
2. Compute the total inventory cost (and therefore the cost of goods sold) for the pulp.
3. Assume that $130,000 was spent to press the apples and $150,000 was spent to filter, pasteurize, and pack the apple juice. Compute the total inventory cost of the apple juice produced.

PROBLEMS

12-28 Hospital Allocation Base

Jose Ortiz, the administrator of Brooklyn Community Hospital, has become interested in obtaining more accurate cost allocations on the basis of cause and effect. The $180,000 of laundry costs had been allocated on the basis of 600,000 pounds processed for all departments, or $.30 per pound.

Ortiz is concerned that government health care officials will require weighted statistics to be used for cost allocation. He asks you, "Please develop a revised base for allocating laundry costs. It should be better than our present base, but not be overly complex either."

You study the situation and find that the laundry processes a large volume of uniforms for student nurses and physicians and for dietary, housekeeping, and other personnel. In particular, the coats or jackets worn by personnel in the radiology department take unusual handwork.

A special study of laundry for radiology revealed that 7,500 of the 15,000 pounds were jackets and coats that were five times as expensive to process as regular laundry items. Several reasons explained the difference, but it was principally because of handwork involved.

Assume that no special requirements were needed in departments other than radiology. Revise the cost-allocation base and compute the new cost-allocation rate. Compute the total cost charged to radiology using pounds and using the new base.

12-29 Cost of Passenger Traffic

Southern Pacific Railroad (SP) has a commuter operation that services passengers along a route between San Jose and San Francisco. Problems of cost allocation were highlighted in a news story about SP's application to the Public Utilities Commission (PUC) for a rate increase. The PUC staff claimed that the "avoidable annual cost" of running the operation was $700,000, in contrast to SP officials' claim of a loss of $9 million. PUC's estimate was based on what SP would be able to save if it shut down the commuter operation.

The SP loss estimate was based on a "full-allocation-of-costs" method, which allocates a share of common maintenance and overhead costs to the passenger service.

If the PUC accepted its own estimate, a 25% fare increase would have been justified, whereas SP sought a 96% fare increase.

The PUC stressed that commuter costs represent less than 1% of the system-wide costs of SP and that 57% of the commuter costs are derived from some type of allocation method—sharing the costs of other operations.

SP's representative stated that "avoidable cost" is not an appropriate way to allocate costs for calculating rates. He said that "it is not fair to include just so-called above-the-rail costs" because there are other real costs associated with commuter service. Examples are maintaining smoother connections and making more frequent track inspections.

Required

1. As public utilities commissioner, what approach toward cost allocation would you favor for making decisions regarding fares? Explain.
2. How would fluctuations in freight traffic affect commuter costs under the SP method?

12-30 Allocation of Automobile Costs

The motor pool of a major city provides automobiles for the use of various city departments. Currently, the motor pool has 50 autos. A recent study showed that it costs $3,600 of annual fixed cost per automobile plus $.10 per mile variable cost to own, operate, and maintain autos such as those provided by the motor pool.

Each month, the costs of the motor pool are allocated to the user departments on the basis of miles driven. On average, each auto is driven 24,000 miles annually, although wide month-to-month variations occur. In April 19X8, the 50 autos were driven a total of 50,000 miles. The motor pool's total costs for April were $24,000.

The chief planner for the city always seemed concerned about her auto costs. She was especially upset in April when she was charged $7,200 for the 15,000 miles driven in the department's five autos. This is the normal monthly mileage in the department. Her memo to the head of the motor pool stated, "I can certainly get autos at less than the $.48 per mile you charged in April." The response was, "I am under instructions to allocate the motor pool costs to the user departments. Your department was responsible for 30% of the April usage (15,000 miles ÷ 50,000 miles), so I allocated 30% of the motor pool's April costs to you (.30 × $24,000). That just seems fair."

Required

1. Calculate the city's average annual cost per mile for owning, maintaining, and operating an auto.
2. Explain why the allocated cost in April ($.48 per mile) exceeds the average in requirement 1.
3. Describe any undesirable behavioral effects of the cost-allocation method used.
4. How would you improve the cost-allocation method?

12-31 Allocation of Costs

The Pegasus Trucking Company has one service department and two regional operating departments. The budgeted cost behavior pattern of the service department is $750,000 monthly in fixed costs plus $.80 per 1,000 ton-miles operated in the East and West regions. (Ton-miles are the number of tons carried times the number of miles traveled.) The actual monthly costs of the service department are allocated using ton-miles operated as the cost driver.

Required

1. Pegasus processed 500 million ton-miles of traffic in April, half in each operating region. The actual costs of the service department were exactly equal to those predicted by the budget for 500 million ton-miles. Compute the costs that would be allocated to each operating region on an actual ton-miles basis.

2. Suppose the East region was plagued by strikes, so that the freight handled was much lower than originally anticipated. East moved only 150 million ton-miles of traffic. The West region handled 250 million ton-miles. The actual costs were exactly as budgeted for this lower level of activity. Compute the costs that would be allocated to East and West on an actual ton-miles basis. Note that the total costs will be lower.

3. Refer to the facts in requirement 1. Various inefficiencies caused the service department to incur total costs of $1,275,000. Compute the costs to be allocated to East and West. Are the allocations justified? If not, what improvement do you suggest?

4. Refer to the facts in requirement 2. Assume that assorted investment outlays for equipment and space in the service department were made to provide a basic maximum capacity to serve the East region at a level of 360 million ton-miles and the West region at a level of 240 million ton-miles. Suppose fixed costs are allocated on the basis of this capacity to serve. Variable costs are allocated by using a predetermined standard rate per 1,000 ton-miles. Compute the costs to be allocated to each department. What are the advantages of this method over other methods?

12-32 Hospital Equipment

Many states have a hospital commission that must approve the acquisition of specified medical equipment before the hospitals in the state can qualify for cost-based reimbursement related to that equipment. That is, hospitals cannot bill government agencies for the use of the equipment unless the commission originally authorized the acquisition.

Two hospitals in one such state proposed the acquisition and sharing of some expensive x-ray equipment to be used for unusual cases. The depreciation and related fixed costs of operating the equipment were predicted at $12,000 per month. The variable costs were predicted at $30 per patient procedure.

The commission asked each hospital to predict its usage of the equipment over its expected useful life of 5 years. University Hospital predicted an average usage of 75 x-rays per month; Children's Hospital of 50 x-rays. The commission regarded this information as critical to the size and degree of sophistication that would be justified. That is, if the number of x-rays exceeded a certain quantity per month, a different configuration of space, equipment, and personnel would be required that would mean higher fixed costs per month.

Required

1. Suppose fixed costs are allocated on the basis of the hospitals' predicted average use per month. Variable costs are allocated on the basis of $30 per x-ray, the budgeted variable-cost rate for the current fiscal year. In October, University Hospital had 50 x-rays and Children's Hospital had 50 x-rays. Compute the total costs allocated to University Hospital and to Children's Hospital.

2. Suppose the manager of the equipment had various operating inefficiencies so that the total October costs were $16,500. Would you change your answers in requirement 1? Why?

3. A traditional method of cost allocation does not use the method in requirement 1. Instead, an allocation rate depends on the actual costs and actual volume encountered. The actual costs are totaled for the month and divided by the actual

number of x-rays during the month. Suppose the actual costs agreed exactly with the budget for a total of 100 actual x-rays. Compute the total costs allocated to University Hospital and to Children's Hospital. Compare the results with those in requirement 1. What is the major weakness in this traditional method? What are some of its possible behavioral effects?

4. Describe any undesirable behavioral effects of the method described in requirement 1. How would you counteract any tendencies toward deliberate false predictions of long-run usage?

12-33 Direct Method for Service Department Allocation

Wheelock Controls Company has two producing departments, Mechanical Instruments and Electronic Instruments. In addition, there are two service departments, Building Services and Materials Receiving and Handling. The company purchases a variety of component parts from which the departments assemble instruments for sale in domestic and international markets.

The Electronic Instruments division is highly automated. The manufacturing costs depend primarily on the number of subcomponents in each instrument. In contrast, the Mechanical Instruments division relies primarily on a large labor force to hand-assemble instruments. Its costs depend on direct-labor hours.

The costs of Building Services depend primarily on the square footage occupied. The costs of Materials Receiving and Handling depend primarily on the total number of components handled.

Instruments M1 and M2 are produced in the Mechanical Instruments department, and E1 and E2 are produced in the Electronic Instruments department. Data about these products follow:

	Direct-Material Cost	Number of Components	Direct-Labor Hours
M1	$74	25	4.0
M2	86	21	8.0
E1	63	10	1.5
E2	91	15	1.0

Budget figures for 19X5 include:

	Building Services	Materials Receiving and Handling	Mechanical Instruments	Electronic Instruments
Direct department costs (excluding direct materials cost)	$150,000	$120,000	$680,000	$548,000
Square footage occupied		5,000	50,000	25,000
Number of final instruments produced			8,000	10,000
Average number of components per instrument			10	16
Direct-labor hours			30,000	8,000

Required

1. Allocate the costs of the service departments using the direct method.

2. Using the results of requirement 1, compute the cost per direct-labor hour in the Mechanical Instruments Department and the cost per component in the Electronic Instruments Department.

3. Using the results of requirement 2, compute the cost per unit of product for instruments M1, M2, E1, and E2.

12-34 Step-Down Method for Service Department Allocation

Refer to the data in Problem 12-33.

Required

1. Allocate the costs of the service departments using the step-down method.
2. Using the results of requirement 1, compute the cost per direct-labor hour in the Mechanical Instruments Department and the cost per component in the Electronic Instruments Department.
3. Using the results of requirement 2, compute the cost per unit of product for instruments M1, M2, E1, and E2.

12-35 Direct and Step-Down Methods of Allocation

General Textiles Company has prepared departmental overhead budgets for normal activity levels before reapportionments, as follows:

Building and grounds	$ 20,000
Personnel	1,200
General factory administration*	28,020
Cafeteria operating loss	1,430
Storeroom	2,750
Machining	40,100
Assembly	71,500
	$165,000

*To be reapportioned before cafeteria.

Management has decided that the most sensible product costs are achieved by using departmental overhead rates. These rates are developed after allocating appropriate service department costs to production departments.

Cost drivers for allocation are to be selected from the following data:

Department	Direct-Labor Hours	Number of Employees	Square Feet of Floor Space Occupied	Total Labor Hours	Number of Requisitions
Building and grounds	—	—	—	—	—
Personnel*	—	—	2,000	—	—
General factory administration	—	35	7,000	—	—
Cafeteria operating loss	—	10	4,000	1,200	—
Storeroom	—	5	7,000	1,200	—
Machining	6,000	50	30,000	9,600	3,000
Assembly	18,000	100	50,000	20,400	1,500
	24,000	200	100,000	32,400	4,500

*Basis used is number of employees.

Required

1. Allocate service department costs by the step-down method. Develop overhead rates per direct-labor hour for machining and assembly.
2. Same as in requirement 1, using the direct method.
3. What would be the plantwide factory-overhead application rate, assuming that direct-labor hours are used as a cost driver?

4. Using the following information about two jobs, prepare three different total overhead costs for each job, using rates developed in requirements 1, 2, and 3.

	Direct-Labor Hours	
	Machining	*Assembly*
Job K10	19	2
Job K12	3	18

12-36 Activity-Based Allocations

St. Louis Wholesale Distributors uses an activity-based costing system to determine the cost of handling its products. One important activity is receiving of shipments in the warehouse. Three resources support that activity: (1) recording and record keeping, (2) labor, and (3) inspection.

Recording and record keeping is a variable cost driven by number of shipments received. The cost per shipment is $16.50.

Labor is driven by pounds of merchandise received. Because labor is hired in shifts, it is fixed for large ranges of volume. Currently labor costs are running $23,000 per month for handling 460,000 pounds. This same cost would apply to all volumes between 300,000 pounds and 550,000 pounds.

Finally, inspection is a variable cost driven by the number of boxes received. Inspection costs are $2.75 per box.

One product distributed by St. Louis Wholesale Distributors is candy. There is a wide variety of candy, so many different shipments are handled in the warehouse. In July, the warehouse received 550 shipments, consisting of 4,000 boxes weighing a total of 80,000 pounds.

1. Compute the cost of receiving candy shipments during July.
2. Management is considering elimination of brands of candy that have small sales levels. This would reduce the warehouse volume to 220 shipments, consisting of 2,500 boxes weighing a total of 60,000 pounds. Compute the amount of savings from eliminating the small-sales-level brands.
3. Suppose receiving costs were estimated on a per pound basis. What was the total receiving cost per pound of candy received in July? If management had used this cost to estimate the effect of eliminating the 20,000 pounds of candy, what mistake might be made?

BUSINESS FIRST www.prenhall.com/phlip

12-37 Activity-Based Allocations at Dell Computer

Dell Computer Company installed an activity-based costing system to help determine its product and customer profitability. The system is quite complex and took several years to fully implement. Consider a simplified hypothetical example of one component of such a system.

Dell offers three lines of notebook computers that use Pentium processors. Consider the Latitude CP line. Suppose that there are only three activities necessary to produce one of these notebook computers: 1) receiving subcomponents, 2) assembling computers, and 3) inspecting computers. Computers are made to order, so each order has a potentially different cost. Therefore, to assess either product or customer profitability, it is important that Dell managers know how much each order costs. Assume that the cost of an order of computers is simply the cost of the subcomponents used plus the cost of the three activities needed to convert the subcomponents into final products.

Suppose that an activity analysis has revealed that the full cost of receiving subcomponents is 4% of the value of those subcomponents, the full cost of assembly is $24 per subcomponent, and the full cost of inspection is $56 per computer. The inspection cost is almost entirely variable, but only about one-half of the receiving and assembly costs is variable at current levels of operations.

Suppose Dell received an order from a CPA firm for 15 computers for its audit staff. The computers are identical, and each requires 12 subcomponents that cost Dell $1,100. The list price of the computers in the configuration required was $1,990.

Required

1. Compute the cost per computer for the 15 computers ordered by the CPA firm.
2. Suppose the customer was negotiating for a 10% discount from list price. What would be Dell's profit on the order for 15 computers if it allows the discount?
3. What role should cost play in the pricing of Dell's computers? ■

12-38 Joint Costs and Decisions

A chemical company has a batch process that takes 1,000 gallons of a raw material and transforms it into 80 pounds of X1 and 400 pounds of X2. Although the joint costs of their production are $1,200, both products are worthless at their split-off point. Additional separable costs of $350 are necessary to give X1 a sales value of $1,000 as product A. Similarly, additional separable costs of $200 are necessary to give X2 a sales value of $1,000 as product B.

You are in charge of the batch process and the marketing of both products. (Show your computations for each answer.)

Required

1. a. Assuming that you believe in assigning joint costs on a physical basis, allocate the total profit of $250 per batch to products A and B.
   b. Would you stop processing one of the products? Why?
2. a. Assuming that you believe in assigning joint costs on a net-realizable-value (relative-sales-value) basis, allocate the total operating profit of $250 per batch to products A and B. If there is no market for X1 and X2 at their split-off point, a net realizable value is usually imputed by taking the ultimate sales values at the point of sale and working backward to obtain approximated "synthetic" relative sales values at the split-off point. These synthetic values are then used as weights for allocating the joint costs to the products.
   b. You have internal product-profitability reports in which joint costs are assigned on a net-realizable-value basis. Your chief engineer says that, after seeing these reports, he has developed a method of obtaining more of product B and correspondingly less of product A from each batch, without changing the per-pound cost factors. Would you approve this new method? Why? What would the overall operating profit be if 40 pounds more of B were produced and 40 pounds less of A?

CASES

12-39 Allocation, Department Rates, and Direct-Labor Hours Versus Machine-Hours

The Manning Manufacturing Company has two producing departments, machining and assembly. Mr. Manning recently automated the machining department. The installation of a CAM system, together with robotic workstations, drastically reduced the amount of direct labor required. Meanwhile, the assembly department remained labor-intensive.

The company had always used one firmwide rate based on direct-labor hours as the cost driver for applying all costs (except direct materials) to the final products. Mr. Manning was considering two alternatives: (1) continue using direct-labor hours as the only cost driver, but use different rates in machining and assembly, and (2) using machine-hours as the cost driver in the machining department while continuing with direct-labor hours in assembly.

Budgeted data for 19X9 are:

	Machining	Assembly	Total
Total cost (except direct materials), after allocating service department costs	$630,000	$450,000	$1,080,000
Machine-hours	105,000	*	105,000
Direct-labor hours	15,000	30,000	45,000

*Not applicable.

Required

1. Suppose Manning continued to use one firmwide rate based on direct-labor hours to apply all manufacturing costs (except direct materials) to the final products. Compute the cost-application rate that would be used.

2. Suppose Manning continued to use direct-labor hours as the only cost driver but used different rates in machining and assembly:
   a. Compute the cost-application rate for machining.
   b. Compute the cost-application rate for assembly.

3. Suppose Manning changed the cost accounting system to use machine-hours as the cost driver in machining and direct-labor hours in assembly:
   a. Compute the cost-application rate for machining.
   b. Compute the cost-application rate for assembly.

4. Three products use the following machine-hours and direct-labor hours:

	Machine-Hours in Machining	Direct-Labor Hours in Machining	Direct-Labor Hours in Assembly
Product A	10.0	1.0	14.0
Product B	17.0	1.5	3.0
Product C	14.0	1.3	8.0

   a. Compute the manufacturing cost of each product (excluding direct materials) using one firmwide rate based on direct-labor hours.
   b. Compute the manufacturing cost of each product (excluding direct materials) using direct-labor hours as the cost driver, but with different cost-application rates in machining and assembly.
   c. Compute the manufacturing cost of each product (excluding direct materials) using a cost-application rate based on direct-labor hours in assembly and machine-hours in machining.
   d. Compare and explain the results in requirements 4a, 4b, and 4c.

12-40 Multiple Allocation Bases

The Glasgow Electronics Company produces three types of circuit boards; call them L, M, and N. The cost accounting system used by Glasgow until 1997 applied all costs except direct materials to the products using direct-labor hours as the only cost driver. In 1997, the company undertook a cost study. The study determined that there were six main factors causing costs to be incurred. A new system was designed with a separate cost pool for each of the six factors. The factors and the costs associated with each are as follows:

1. Direct-labor hours—direct-labor cost and related fringe benefits and payroll taxes
2. Machine-hours—depreciation and repairs and maintenance costs
3. Pounds of materials—materials receiving, handling, and storage costs
4. Number of production setups—labor used to change machinery and computer configurations for a new production batch
5. Number of production orders—costs of production scheduling and order processing
6. Number of orders shipped—all packaging and shipping expenses

The company is now preparing a budget for 1999. The budget includes the following predictions:

	Board L	Board M	Board N
Units to be produced	10,000	800	5,000
Direct-material cost	£66/unit	£88/unit	£45/unit
Direct-labor hours	4/unit	18/unit	9/unit
Machine-hours	7/unit	15/unit	7/unit
Pounds of materials	3/unit	4/unit	2/unit
Number of production setups	100	50	50
Number of production orders	300	200	70
Number of orders shipped	1,000	800	2,000

The total budgeted cost for 1999 is £3,712,250, of which £955,400 was direct-materials cost, and the amount in each of the six cost pools defined above is:

Cost Pool*	Cost
1	£1,391,600
2	936,000
3	129,600
4	160,000
5	25,650
6	114,000
Total	£2,756,850

*Identified by the cost driver used.

Required

1. Prepare a budget that shows the total budgeted cost and the unit cost for each circuit board. Use the new system with six cost pools (plus a separate direct application of direct-materials cost).

2. Compute the budgeted total and unit costs of each circuit board if the old direct-labor-hour-based system had been used.

3. How would you judge whether the new system is better than the old one?

12-41 Allocation of Data Processing Costs

The Gibralter Insurance Co. (GIC) established a Systems Department to implement and operate its own data processing systems. GIC believed that its own system would be more cost-effective than the service bureau it had been using.

GIC's three departments—Claims, Records, and Finance—have different requirements with respect to hardware and other capacity-related resources and operating resources. The system was designed to recognize these differing needs. In addition, the system was designed to meet GIC's long-term capacity needs. The excess capacity designed into the system would be sold to outside users until needed by GIC. The estimated resource requirements used to design and implement the system are shown in the following schedule:

	Hardware and Other Capacity-Related Resources	Operating Resources
Records	25%	60%
Claims	50	15
Finance	20	20
Expansion (outside use)	5	5
Total	100%	100%

GIC currently sells the equivalent of its expansion capacity to a few outside clients.

At the time the system became operational, management decided to redistribute total expenses of the Systems Department to the user departments based on actual computer time used. The actual costs for the first quarter of the current fiscal year were distributed to the user departments as follows:

Department	Percentage Utilization	Amount
Records	60%	$330,000
Claims	15	82,500
Finance	20	110,000
Outside	5	27,500
Total	100%	$550,000

The three user departments have complained about the cost distribution method since the Systems Department was established. The Records Department's monthly costs have been as much as three times the costs experienced with the service bureau. The Finance Department is concerned about the costs distributed to the outside user category because these allocated costs form the basis for the fees billed to the outside clients.

Mostafa Al Rashed, GIC's controller, decided to review the cost-allocation method. The additional information he gathered for his review is reported in Tables 1 to 3.

Table 1

Systems Department Costs and Activity Levels

| | Annual Budget | | First Quarter | | | |
| | | | Budget | | Actual | |
	Hours	Dollars	Hours	Dollars	Hours	Dollars
Hardware and other capacity-related costs	—	$ 600,000	—	$150,000	—	$155,000
Software development	18,750	562,500	4,725	141,750	4,250	130,000
Operations						
Computer related	3,750	750,000	945	189,000	920	187,000
Input/output related	30,000	300,000	7,560	75,600	7,900	78,000
		$2,212,500		$556,350		$550,000

Table 2

Historical Usage

| | Hardware and Other Capacity Needs | Software Development | | Operations | | | |
| | | | | Computer | | Input/Output | |
		Range	Average	Range	Average	Range	Average
Records	25%	0–30%	15%	55–65%	60%	10–30%	15%
Claims	50	15–60	40	10–25	15	60–80	75
Finance	20	25–75	40	10–25	20	3–10	5
Outside	5	0–25	5	3–8	5	3–10	5
	100%		100%		100%		100%

Table 3

Usage of Systems Department's Services

First Quarter (in hours)

| | Software Development | Operations | |
		Computer Related	Input/Output
Records	450	540	1,540
Claims	1,800	194	5,540
Finance	1,600	126	410
Outside	400	60	410
Total	4,250	920	7,900

Al Rashed has concluded that the method of cost allocation should be changed. He believes that the hardware and capacity-related costs should be allocated to the user departments in proportion to the planned long-term needs. Any difference between actual and budgeted hardware costs would not be allocated to the departments but remain with the Systems Department.

The costs for software development and operations would be charged to the user departments based on actual hours used. A predetermined hourly rate based on the annual budget data would be used. The hourly rates that would be used for the current fiscal year are as follows:

Function	Hourly Rate
Software development	$ 30
Operations	
Computer related	200
Input/output related	10

Al Rashed plans to use first-quarter activity and cost data to illustrate his recommendations. The recommendations will be presented to the Systems Department and the user departments for their comments and reactions. He then expects to present his recommendations to management for approval.

Required

1. Calculate the amount of data processing costs that would be included in the Claims Department's first-quarter budget according to the method Mostafa Al Rashed has recommended.

2. Prepare a schedule to show how the actual first-quarter costs of the Systems Department would be charged to the users if Al Rashed's recommended method were adopted.

3. Explain whether Al Rashed's recommended system for charging costs to the user departments will:

   a. Improve cost control in the Systems Department

   b. Improve planning and cost control in the user departments

COLLABORATIVE LEARNING EXERCISE

12-42 Library Research on ABC

Form groups of three to six students. Each student should choose a different article about activity-based costing (ABC) or activity-based management (ABM) from the current literature. The article should include evidence about at least one company's application of ABC. Such articles are available in a variety of sources. You might try bibliographic searches for "activity-based costing" or "activity-based management." Journals that will have articles on ABC and ABM include:

Management Accounting (USA)

Management Accounting (United Kingdom)

Journal of Cost Management

CMA Magazine (Canada)

Required

1. After reading the article, note the following (if given in the article) for one company:

   a. The benefits of ABC or ABM

   b. The problems encountered in implementing ABC or ABM

   c. Suggestions by the author(s) about employing ABC or ABM

2. As a group, using the collective wisdom garnered from the articles, respond to the following:

   a. What kinds of companies can benefit from ABC or ABM?

   b. What kinds of companies have little to gain from ABC or ABM?

   c. What steps should be taken to ensure successful implementation of ABC or ABM?

   d. What potential pitfalls are there to avoid in implementing ABC or ABM?

13

JOB-COSTING SYSTEMS

Dell Computer Corporation's workers assemble computers based on individual customer specifications. The assembly activity is a key part of the production process.

Learning Objectives

When you have finished studying this chapter, you should be able to

1 Distinguish between job-order costing and process costing.

2 Prepare summary journal entries for the typical transactions of a job-costing system.

3 Compute budgeted factory-overhead rates and factory overhead applied to production.

4 Use appropriate cost drivers for overhead application.

5 Identify the meaning and purpose of normalized overhead rates.

6 Use an activity-based costing system in a job order environment.

7 Show how job costing is used in service organizations.

8 **Understand how a job-order-costing system tracks the flow of costs to products.**

D ell Computer Corporation is the world's leading *direct marketer of made-to-order* computer systems. Dell does not manufacture computer components (circuit boards, hard drives), but instead assembles them into computers on a made-to-order basis.

Dell pioneered the "direct business model"—selling directly to end users instead of using a network of dealers, which avoids the dealer markup and gives Dell a competitive price advantage. Customers can design their own computer systems to specifications they desire, choosing from among a full complement of options. Before ordering, customers can receive advice and price quotes for a wide variety of computer configurations.

Once an order is taken, it is assembled in a manufacturing work cell called a mod. There is a separate mod for each of Dell's "lines of business" (Dimension Desktop PCs, OptiPlex Desktops for networked environments, Latitude and Insprion Notebooks, PowerEdge network servers, and WorkStation 400 products). Management considers rapid response to customer orders a key to gaining and maintaining a competitive edge.

Orders at Dell have traditionally been taken over the phone, but now they can be placed over the Internet. Sales from the company's Internet site are increasing rapidly and generating revenues in excess of $4 million a day. Dell currently receives more than 800,000 visits each week at www.dell.com, where the company maintains 42 country-specific sites. Customers may review, configure, and price systems within Dell's entire product line. Web sites also offer personalized system-support pages and technical services. "The Internet was tailor-made for Dell," said Michael Dell, chairman and chief executive officer. "Customers of all kinds prefer direct. They like the immediacy, convenience, savings and personal touches the Internet-direct customer experience provides." Because each computer is built to customer specifications, each order is considered a separate job for costing purposes.

Why would managers at Dell and other companies need to know product cost? Accountants compute product costs for both decision-making and financial-reporting purposes. They supply product costs to managers for evaluating pricing policy and product lines. For example, Chrysler managers need to know the cost of each kind of auto being produced to set prices, to determine marketing and production strategies for various models, and to evaluate production operations. At the same time, product costs appear as cost of goods sold in income statements and as finished-goods inventory values in balance sheets. Although it would be possible to have two product-costing systems, one for management decision making and one for financial reporting, seldom do the benefits of using two completely separate systems exceed the costs. Therefore, both decision-making and financial-reporting needs influence the design of product-costing systems.

In this chapter, we focus on one type of product-costing system—the job-order-costing system. We look at the elements of such systems and how they track the flow of costs. This system focuses on costs involved in the production of goods and services (that is, on the production phase of the value chain). Costs of activities in the other phases of the value chain (R & D, design, distribution, marketing, and customer service) are period costs, not product costs, and they are expensed immediately and excluded from the costs of product for inventory valuation and other external reporting purposes. Because this chapter draws heavily on terminology and concepts explained in Chapters 4 and 12, you might want to review those chapters before reading further.

DISTINCTION BETWEEN JOB COSTING AND PROCESS COSTING

Objective 1
Distinguish between job-order costing and process costing.

job-order costing (job costing) The method of allocating costs to products that are readily identified by individual units or batches, each of which requires varying degrees of attention and skill.

process costing The method of allocating costs to products by averaging costs over large numbers of nearly identical products.

The two most common systems of product costing are *job-order costing* and *process costing*. **Job-order costing** (or simply **job costing**) allocates costs to products that are readily identified by individual units or batches, each of which requires varying degrees of attention and skill. Industries that commonly use job-order methods include construction, printing, aircraft, furniture, special-purpose machinery, and any manufacture of tailor-made or unique goods.

Process costing averages costs over large numbers of nearly identical products. It is most often found in such industries as chemicals, oil, plastics, rubber, lumber, food processing, glass, mining, cement, and meatpacking. These industries involve mass production of like units, that usually pass in continuous fashion through a series of uniform production steps called *operations* or *processes*.

The distinction between the job-cost and the process-cost methods centers largely on how product costing is accomplished. Job costing applies costs to specific jobs, which may consist of either a single physical unit (such as a custom sofa) or a few like units (such as a dozen tables) in a distinct batch or job lot. In contrast, process costing deals with great masses of like units and broad averages of unit costs.

The most important point is that product costing is an averaging process. The unit cost used for inventory purposes is the result of taking some accumulated cost that has been allocated to production departments and dividing it by some measure of production. The basic distinction between job-order costing and process costing is the breadth of the denominator: In job-order costing, the denominator is small (e.g., one painting, 100 advertising circulars, or one special packaging machine); however, in process costing, the denominator is large (e.g., thousands of pounds, gallons, or board feet).

Job costing and process costing are extremes along a continuum of potential costing systems. Each company designs its own accounting system to fit its underlying production activities. Some companies use hybrid costing systems, which are blends of ideas from both job costing and process costing. Chapter 14 describes process costing.

ILLUSTRATION OF JOB COSTING

Job costing is best learned by example. But first we examine the basic records used in a job-cost system. The centerpiece of a job-costing system is the **job-cost record** (also called a **job-cost sheet** or **job order**), shown in Exhibit 13-1. All costs for a particular product, service, or batch of products are recorded on the job-cost record. A file of job-cost records for partially completed jobs provides supporting details for the Work-in-Process Inventory account, often simply called Work in Process (WIP). A file of completed job-cost records comprises the Finished-Goods Inventory account.

As Exhibit 13-1 shows, the job-cost record summarizes information contained on source documents such as materials requisitions and labor time tickets. **Materials requisitions** are records of materials used in particular jobs. **Labor time tickets** (or **time cards**) record the time a particular direct laborer spends on each job.

Today job-cost records and source documents are likely to be computer files, not paper records. In fact, with on-line data entry, barcoding, and optical scanning, much of the information needed for such records enters the computer without ever being written on paper. Nevertheless, whether records are on paper or in computer files, the accounting system must collect and maintain the same basic information.

As each job begins, its own job-cost record is created. As units are worked on, entries are made on the job-cost record. Three classes of costs are accumulated on the job-cost record as units pass through the departments: material requisitions are the source of direct-material costs, time tickets provide direct-labor costs, and budgeted overhead rates (a separate rate for each overhead cost pool) are used to apply factory overhead to products. (The computation of these budgeted rates will be described later in this chapter.)

job-cost record (job-cost sheet, job order) A document that shows all costs for a particular product, service, or batch of products.

materials requisitions Records of materials issued to particular jobs.

labor time tickets (time cards) The record of the time a particular direct laborer spends on each job.

BASIC RECORDS OF ENRIQUEZ MACHINE PARTS COMPANY

To illustrate the functioning of a job-order-costing system, we will use the records and journal entries of the Enriquez Machine Parts Company. On December 31, 19X7, the firm had the following inventories:

Direct materials (12 types)	$110,000
Work in process	—
Finished goods (unsold units from two jobs)	12,000

On the following page is a summary of pertinent transactions for the year 19X8:

	Machining	Assembly	Total
1. Direct materials purchased on account	—	—	$1,900,000
2. Direct materials requisitioned for manufacturing	$1,000,000	$890,000	1,890,000
3. Direct-labor costs incurred	200,000	190,000	390,000
4a. Factory overhead incurred	290,000	102,000	392,000
4b. Factory overhead applied	280,000*	95,000	375,000
5. Cost of goods completed and transferred to finished-goods inventory	—	—	2,500,000
6a. Sales on account	—	—	4,000,000
6b. Cost of goods sold	—	—	2,480,000

*We explain the nature of factory overhead applied later in this chapter.

Exhibit 13-1

Completed Job-Cost Record and Sample Source Documents

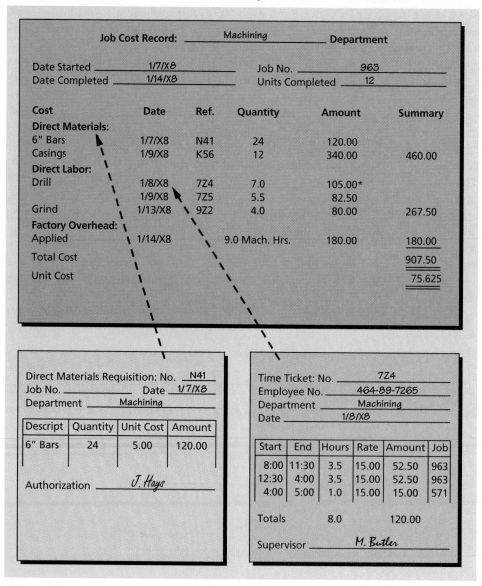

*Note that 7 of the 8 hours and $105 of the $120 in time ticket 7Z4 belong to job no. 963.

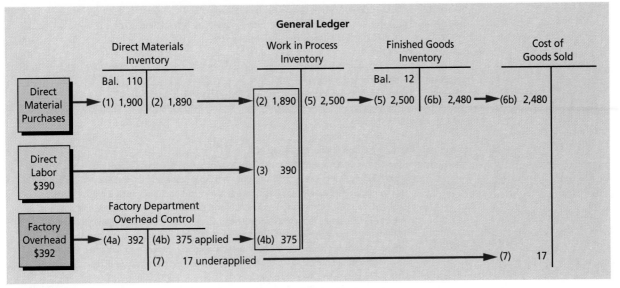

Exhibit 13-2

Job-Order Costing, General Flow of Costs (Thousands)

Exhibit 13-2 is an overview of the general flow of costs through the Enriquez Machine Parts Company's job-order-costing system.[1] The exhibit summarizes the effects of transactions on the key manufacturing accounts in the firm's books. As you proceed through the detailed explanation of transactions, keep checking each explanation against the overview in Exhibit 13-2.

EXPLANATION OF TRANSACTIONS

The following transaction-by-transaction summary analysis will explain how product costing is achieved. Entries are usually made as transactions occur. However, to obtain a sweeping overview, our illustration uses a summary for the entire year 19X8.

Objective 2
Prepare summary journal entries for the typical transactions of a job-costing system.

I. Transaction: Direct materials purchased, $1,900,000.
    Analysis: The asset Direct-Materials Inventory is increased. The liability Accounts Payable is increased.
    Journal Entry: Direct-Materials Inventory 1,900,000
                   Accounts Payable 1,900,000

---

[1] *Exhibit 13-2 and the following explanation of transactions assume knowledge of basic accounting procedures. These can be reviewed in Chapter 16, especially Appendix 16B. We will use the T-account format for a company's accounts. Entries on the left of the "T" are debits and those on the right are credits. Asset T-accounts, such as the inventory accounts, show increases on the left (debit) side and decreases on the right (credit) side of the "T":*

Inventory	
Beginning Balance	Decreases
Increases	
Ending Balance	

Transactions affecting the accounts are recorded as journal entries. Debit (left side) entries are shown flush with the left margin, and credit (right side) entries are indented, and often an explanation is included. For example, a $10,000 transfer from Direct Materials Inventory to WIP (Work in Process) Inventory would be shown as follows:

WIP Inventory 10,000
    Direct Materials Inventory 10,000
To increase WIP Inventory and decrease Direct
    Materials Inventory by $10,000.

2. Transaction: Direct materials requisitioned, $1,890,000.
   Analysis: The asset Work in Process (WIP) Inventory is increased. The asset Direct-Materials Inventory is decreased.

   Journal Entry: WIP Inventory 1,890,000
                     Direct-Materials Inventory   1,890,000

3. Transaction: Direct-labor cost incurred, $390,000.
   Analysis: The asset WIP Inventory is increased. The liability Accrued Payroll is increased.

   Journal Entry: WIP Inventory 390,000
                     Accrued Payroll   390,000

4a. Transaction: Factory overhead incurred, $392,000.
    Analysis: These actual costs are first charged to departmental overhead accounts, which may be regarded as assets until their amounts are later "cleared" or transferred to other accounts. Each department has detailed overhead accounts such as indirect labor, utilities, repairs, depreciation, insurance, and property taxes. These details support a summary Factory Department Overhead Control account. The managers are responsible for regulating these costs, item by item. As these costs are charged to the departments, the other accounts affected will be assorted assets and liabilities. Examples include cash, accounts payable, accrued payables, and accumulated depreciation.

    Journal Entry: Factory Department Overhead Control 392,000
                      Cash, Accounts Payable, and various other balance
                      sheet accounts   392,000

4b. Transaction: Factory overhead applied, $95,000 + $280,000 = $375,000.
    Analysis: The asset WIP Inventory is increased. The asset Factory Department Overhead Control is decreased. (A fuller explanation occurs later in this chapter.)

    Journal Entry: WIP Inventory 375,000
                      Factory Department Overhead Control .   375,000

5. Transaction: Cost of goods completed, $2,500,000.
   Analysis: The asset Finished Goods Inventory is increased. The asset WIP Inventory is decreased.

   Journal Entry: Finished Goods Inventory 2,500,000
                     WIP Inventory   2,500,000

6a. Transaction: Sales on account, $4,000,000.
    Analysis: The asset Accounts Receivable is increased. The revenue account Sales is increased.

    Journal Entry: Accounts Receivable 4,000,000
                      Sales   4,000,000

6b. Transaction: Cost of goods sold, $2,480,000.
    Analysis: The expense Cost of Goods Sold is increased. The asset Finished Goods Inventory is decreased.

    Journal Entry: Cost of Goods Sold 2,480,000
                      Finished Goods Inventory   2,480,000

SUMMARY OF TRANSACTIONS

Exhibit 13-2 summarizes the Enriquez transactions for the year, focusing on the inventory accounts. WIP Inventory receives central attention. The costs of direct material used, direct labor, and factory overhead applied to product are brought into WIP. In turn, the costs of completed goods are transferred from WIP to Finished Goods. As goods are sold, their costs become expense in the form of Cost of Goods Sold. The year-end accounting for the $17,000 of underapplied overhead is explained later.

ACCOUNTING FOR FACTORY OVERHEAD

In the Enriquez Machine Parts Company example, factory overhead of $375,000 was applied to the WIP account. This section describes how to determine the amount of applied factory overhead.

How Factory Overhead is Applied to Products

Managers need to know product costs in order to make ongoing decisions such as which products to emphasize or de-emphasize and the pricing of products. Ideally, all costs, including overhead, are known when these decisions must be made. Unfortunately, actual overhead costs are not available when managers need them. For this reason, budgeted (predetermined) overhead rates are used to apply overhead to jobs as they are completed.

The size of overhead costs in many manufacturing companies is large enough to motivate companies to search for ways to convert them into direct costs. Dell Computer Corporation has increased the accuracy of its product cost information by converting some of its factory-overhead costs from indirect to direct costs. How was this done? By dedicating assembly labor and factory equipment to specific product lines. Work cells (mods) do the assembly and software loading for specific product lines. This makes it easier to trace equipment costs to products. Nevertheless, significant overhead costs remain to be allocated.

Budgeted Overhead Application Rates

The following steps summarize how to account for factory overhead:

1. Select one or more cost drivers to serve as a base for applying overhead costs. Examples include direct-labor hours, direct-labor costs, machine-hours, and production setups. The cost driver should be an activity that is the common denominator for systematically relating a cost or a group of costs, such as machinery cost, set-up costs, or energy cost, with products. The cost driver(s) should be the best available measure of the cause-and-effect relationships between overhead costs and production volume.

2. Prepare a factory-overhead budget for the planning period, ordinarily a year. The two key items are (1) budgeted overhead and (2) budgeted volume of the cost driver. There will be a set of budgeted overhead costs and an associated budgeted cost-driver level for each overhead cost pool. In businesses with simple production systems, there may be just one set.

3. Compute the **budgeted factory-overhead rate(s)** by dividing the budgeted total overhead for each cost pool by the budgeted cost-driver level.

4. Obtain actual cost-driver data (such as machine-hours) as jobs are produced.

5. Apply the budgeted overhead to the jobs by multiplying the budgeted rate(s) times the actual cost-driver data.

6. At the end of the year, account for any differences between the amount of overhead actually incurred and overhead applied to products.

budgeted factory-overhead rate The budgeted total overhead for each cost pool divided by the budgeted cost-driver level.

ILLUSTRATION OF OVERHEAD APPLICATION

Now that you know the steps in accounting for factory overhead in a job-costing system, we can examine how they work in a real example. Consider the Enriquez illustration again.

This manufacturing-overhead budget has been prepared for the coming year, 19X9:

	Machining	Assembly
Indirect labor	$ 75,600	$ 36,800
Supplies	8,400	2,400
Utilities	20,000	7,000
Repairs	10,000	3,000
Factory rent	10,000	6,800
Supervision	42,600	35,400
Depreciation on equipment	104,000	9,400
Insurance, property taxes, etc.	7,200	2,400
Total	$277,800	$103,200

Objective 3
Compute budgeted
factory-overhead rates
and factory overhead
applied to production.

As products are worked on, Enriquez applies the factory overhead to the jobs. A budgeted overhead rate is used, computed as follows:

$$\text{budgeted overhead application rate} = \frac{\text{total budgeted factory overhead}}{\text{total budgeted amount of cost driver}}$$
$$\text{(such as direct-labor costs or machine-hours)}$$

Suppose machine-hours are chosen as the only cost driver in the Machining Department, and direct-labor cost is chosen in the Assembly Department. The overhead rates are as follows:

	Year 19X9	
	Machining	*Assembly*
Budgeted manufacturing overhead	$277,800	$103,200
Budgeted machine-hours	69,450	
Budgeted direct-labor cost		$206,400
Budgeted overhead rate, per machine-hour: $277,800 ÷ 69,450 =	$ 4	
Budgeted overhead rate, per direct-labor dollar: $103,200 ÷ $206,400 =		50%

Simplifying Product Costing at Harley-Davidson

When Harley-Davidson, the motorcycle manufacturer, adopted a just-in-time (JIT) philosophy, it quickly discovered that its accounting system needed revision. The main focus of the accounting system was direct labor, which not only made up a part of product cost itself, but also functioned as an all-purpose base for allocating overhead. However, direct labor was only 10% of total product cost. It certainly did not generate a majority of overhead costs. As Harley-Davidson's production process had changed, the accounting system had remained static.

The first point that became apparent with the JIT system was that detailed information on direct-labor costs was not useful to managers. It was costly to have each direct laborer record the time spent on each product or part and then enter the information from these time cards into the accounting system. For example, if each of 500 direct laborers works on 20 products per day, the system must record 10,000 entries per day, which is 200,000 entries per month. The time spent by direct laborers to record the time, by clerks to enter the data into the system, and by the accountants to check the data's accuracy is enormous—and all to produce product cost information that was used for financial reporting but was useless to managers.

The JIT system forced manufacturing managers to focus on satisfying customers and minimizing non-value-added activities. Gradually, accountants began to focus on the same objectives. Accounting's customers were the managers who used the accounting information, and effort put into activities that did not help managers was deemed counterproductive (non-value-added). Therefore, eliminating the costly, time-consuming recording of detailed labor costs became a priority. Direct labor was eliminated as a direct cost, and consequently it could not be used for overhead allocation. After considering process hours, flow-through time, material value, and individual cost per unit as possible cost drivers for allocating overhead, the company selected process hours. Direct labor and overhead were combined to form conversion costs, which were applied to products on the basis of total process hours. This did not result in costs significantly different than the old system, but the new system was much simpler and less costly. Only direct material was traced directly to the product. Conversion costs were applied at completion of production based on a simple measure of process time.

Accounting systems should generate benefits greater than their costs. More sophisticated systems are not necessarily better systems. Harley-Davidson's main objective in changing its accounting system was simplification—eliminating unnecessary tasks and streamlining others. These changes resulted in a revitalized accounting system.

Source: Adapted from W. T. Turk, "Management Accounting Revitalized: The Harley-Davidson Experience," in B. J. Brinker, ed., *Emerging Practices in Cost Management*, Warren, Gorham & Lamont, Boston, 1990, pp. 155–166.

Note that the overhead rates are budgeted; they are estimates. These rates are then used to apply overhead based on actual events. That is, the total overhead applied in our illustration is the result of multiplying *actual* machine-hours or labor cost by the *budgeted* overhead rates:

Machining: actual machine-hours of 70,000 × $4 =	$280,000	
Assembly: actual direct-labor cost of $190,000 × .50 =	95,000	
Total factory overhead applied	$375,000	

The summary journal entry for the application (entry 4b) is:

4b. WIP Inventory	375,000	
Factory Department Overhead Control		375,000

CHOICE OF COST DRIVERS

As we have noted several times in this text, no one cost driver is right for all situations. The accountant's goal is to find the driver that best links cause and effect. In the Enriquez Machining Department, use of machines causes most overhead cost, for example, depreciation and repairs. Therefore, machine-hours is the cost driver and the appropriate base for applying overhead costs. Thus, Enriquez must keep track of the machine-hours used for each job, creating an added data collection cost. That is, direct material costs, direct-labor costs, and machine-hours must be accumulated for each job.

Objective 4
Use appropriate cost drivers for overhead application.

In contrast, direct labor is a principal cost driver in the Enriquez Assembly Department because parts are assembled by hand. The workers are paid equal hourly rates. Therefore, all that is needed is to apply the 50% overhead rate to the cost of direct labor already entered on the job-cost records. No separate job records have to be kept of the labor-hours. If the hourly labor rates differ greatly for individuals performing identical tasks, the hours of labor, rather than the dollars spent for labor, might be used as a base. Otherwise, a $9-per-hour worker would cause more overhead applied than an $8-per-hour worker, even though the same time would probably be taken and the same facilities used by each employee for the same work.

Sometimes direct-labor cost is the best overhead cost driver even if wage rates vary within a department. For example, higher-skilled labor may use more costly equipment and have more indirect labor support. Moreover, many factory-overhead costs include costly labor fringe benefits such as pensions and payroll taxes. The latter are often more closely driven by direct-labor cost than by direct-labor hours.

If a department identifies more than one cost driver for overhead costs, these costs ideally should be put into as many cost pools as there are cost drivers. In practice, such a system is too costly for many organizations. Instead, these organizations select a few cost drivers (often only one) to serve as a basis for allocating overhead costs. The 80-20 rule can be used in these situations. In many cases, 80% of total overhead cost can be accounted for with just a few drivers (20% of all the drivers identified). For example, a company may identify 10 separate overhead pools with 10 different drivers. Often, approximately 80% of the total cost can be applied with only two drivers.

The selected cost drivers should be the ones that cause most of the overhead costs. For example, suppose machine-hours cause 70% of the overhead costs in a particular department, number of component parts causes 20%, and five assorted cost drivers cause the other 10%. Instead of using seven cost pools allocated on the basis of the seven cost drivers, most managers would use one cost driver, machine-hours, to allocate all overhead costs. Others would assign all cost to two cost pools, one allocated on the basis of machine-hours and one on the basis of number of component parts.

No matter which cost drivers are chosen, the overhead rates are applied day after day throughout the year to cost the various jobs worked on by each department. All overhead is applied to all jobs worked on during the year on the appropriate basis of machine-hours or direct-labor costs of each job. Suppose management predictions coincide exactly with actual amounts (an extremely unlikely situation). Then the total overhead applied to the year's jobs via these budgeted rates would be equal to the total overhead costs actually incurred.

Consider Dell Computer Company. As we said earlier, Dell has converted many of its overhead costs into direct costs. However, two important costs that cannot be directly traced (that is, indirect costs) are facilities and engineering. Facilities cost includes occupancy costs such as depreciation on the factory, insurance, and taxes. These costs are allocated using the cost driver "square footage used by each line of business (assembly line)". Product and process engineering activities are part of the design phase of the company's value chain and the associated costs incurred are significant. These costs are allocated to lines of business using a "complexity" cost driver (for example, number of distinct parts in the mother board). Server computer products, for example, require much more engineering time and effort due to the complexity of the product compared to laptops or PCs, so this would be reflected in a greater number of distinct parts in the mother board. Thus, server products receive a much greater allocation of engineering costs than laptops or PCs.

PROBLEMS OF OVERHEAD APPLICATION

NORMALIZED OVERHEAD RATES

Objective 5
Identify the meaning and purpose of normalized overhead rates.

normal costing system
The cost system in which overhead is applied on an average or normalized basis, in order to get representative or normal inventory valuations.

Basically, our illustration has demonstrated the normal costing approach. Why the term "normal"? Because an annual average overhead rate is used consistently throughout the year for product costing, without altering it from day to day and from month to month. The resultant "normal" product costs include an average or normalized chunk of overhead. As actual overhead costs are incurred by departments from month to month, they are charged to the departments. Hence, we shall label the system a **normal costing system.** The cost of the manufactured product is composed of actual direct material, actual direct labor, and normal applied overhead.

During the year and at year-end, the actual overhead amount incurred will rarely equal the amount applied. This variance between incurred and applied cost can be analyzed. The most common—and important—contributor to these variances is operating at a different level of volume than the level used as a denominator in calculating the budgeted overhead rate (for instance, using 100,000 budgeted direct-labor-hours as the denominator and then actually working only 80,000 hours). Other frequent contributory causes include: poor forecasting, inefficient use of overhead items, price changes in individual overhead items, erratic behavior of individual overhead items (for instance, repairs made only during slack time), and calendar variations (for instance, 20 workdays in one month, 22 in the next).

All these peculiarities of overhead are mingled in an annual overhead pool. Thus, an annual rate is budgeted and used regardless of the month-to-month peculiarities of specific overhead costs. Such an approach is more defensible than, say, applying the actual overhead for each month. Why? Because a normal product cost is more useful for decisions, and more representative for inventory-costing purposes, than an "actual" product cost that is distorted by month-to-month fluctuations in production volume and by the erratic behavior of many overhead costs. For example, the employees of a gypsum plant using an "actual" product cost system had the privilege of buying company-made items "at cost." Employees joked about the benefits of buying "at cost" during high-volume months, when unit costs were lower because volume was higher, as shown in the following table:

	Actual Overhead			Direct-Labor Hours	Actual Overhead Application Rate* per Direct-Labor Hour
	Variable	Fixed	Total		
Peak-volume month	$60,000	$40,000	$100,000	100,000	$1.00
Low-volume month	30,000	40,000	70,000	50,000	1.40

*Divide total overhead by direct-labor hours. Note that the presence of fixed overhead causes the fluctuation in unit overhead costs from $1.00 to $1.40. The variable component is $.60 an hour in both months, but the fixed component is $.40 in the peak-volume month ($40,000 ÷ 100,000) and $.80 in the low-volume month ($40,000 ÷ 50,000).

The overall system we have just described is sometimes called an *actual costing system* because every effort is made to trace the actual costs, as incurred, to the physical units benefited.

DISPOSITION OF UNDERAPPLIED OR OVERAPPLIED OVERHEAD

Our Enriquez illustration contained the following data:

Transaction	
4a. Factory overhead incurred	$392,000
4b. Factory overhead applied	375,000
Underapplied factory overhead	$ 17,000

Total costs of $392,000 must eventually be charged to expense in some way. The $375,000 will become part of the Cost of Goods Sold expense when the products to which it is applied are sold. The remaining $17,000 must also become expense by some method.

When budgeted rates are used, the difference between incurred and applied overhead is typically allowed to accumulate during the year. When the amount applied to product exceeds the amount incurred by the departments, the difference is called **overapplied overhead.** When the amount applied is less than incurred, the difference is called **underapplied overhead.** At year-end, the difference ($17,000 underapplied in our illustration) is disposed of through either a write-off or through proration.

overapplied overhead
The excess of overhead applied to products over actual overhead incurred.

underapplied overhead
The excess of actual overhead over the overhead applied to products.

IMMEDIATE WRITE-OFF

Under the immediate write-off method, the $17,000 is regarded as a reduction in current income by adding the underapplied overhead to the cost of goods sold. The same logic is followed for overapplied overhead except that the result would be a decrease in cost of goods sold.

The theory underlying the direct write-off is that most of the goods worked on have been sold, and a more elaborate method of disposition is not worth the extra trouble. Another justification is that the extra overhead costs represented by underapplied overhead do not qualify as part of ending inventory costs because they do not represent assets. They should be written off because they largely represent inefficiency or the underutilization of available facilities in the current period.

The immediate write-off eliminates the $17,000 difference with a simple journal entry, labeled as transaction 7 in Exhibit 13-2.

7. Cost of Goods Sold (or a separate
   charge against revenue) 17,000
       Factory Department Overhead Control 17,000
   To close ending underapplied overhead directly to Cost of
   Goods Sold.

Because of its simplicity, the immediate write-off method is most commonly used.

PRORATION AMONG INVENTORIES

prorate To assign underapplied overhead or overapplied overhead in proportion to the sizes of the ending account balances.

This method prorates over- or underapplied overhead among WIP, Finished Goods, and Cost of Goods Sold. To **prorate** underapplied overhead means to assign it in proportion to the sizes of the ending account balances. Theoretically, if the objective is to obtain as accurate a cost allocation as possible, all the overhead costs of the individual jobs worked on should be recomputed, using the actual, rather than the budgeted, rates. This approach is rarely feasible, so a practical attack is to prorate on the basis of the ending balances in · each of three accounts (WIP, $155,000; Finished Goods, $32,000; and Cost of Goods Sold, $2,480,000).

	(1) Unadjusted Balance, End of 19X8*	(2) Proration of Underapplied Overhead	(3) Adjusted Balance, End of 19X8
WIP	$ 155,000	155/2,667 × 17,000 = $ 988	$ 155,988
Finished Goods	32,000	32/2,667 × 17,000 = 204	32,204
Cost of Goods Sold	2,480,000	2,480/2,667 × 17,000 = 15,808	2,495,808
	$2,667,000	$17,000	$2,684,000

*See Exhibit 13-2 for details.

The journal entry for the proration follows:

WIP 988
Finished Goods 204
Cost of Goods Sold 15,808
    Factory Department Overhead Control 17,000
To prorate ending underapplied overhead among
    three accounts.

The amounts prorated to inventories here are not significant. In actual practice, prorating is done only when inventory valuations would be materially affected.

THE USE OF VARIABLE AND FIXED APPLICATION RATES

As we have seen, overhead application is the most troublesome aspect of product costing. The presence of fixed costs is a major reason for the costing difficulties. Most companies have made no distinction between variable- and fixed-cost behavior in the design of their accounting systems. For instance, the Machining Department at Enriquez Machine Parts Company developed the following rate:

$$\text{budgeted overhead application rate} = \frac{\text{budgeted total overhead}}{\text{budgeted machine-hours}}$$

$$= \frac{\$277,800}{69,450} = \$4 \text{ per machine-hour}$$

Some companies, though, do distinguish between variable overhead and fixed overhead for product costing as well as for control purposes. If the Machining Department at

Enriquez had made this distinction, then rent, supervision, depreciation, and insurance would have been considered the fixed portion of the total manufacturing overhead, and two rates would have been developed:

$$\text{budgeted variable-overhead application rate} = \frac{\text{budgeted total variable overhead}}{\text{budgeted machine-hours}}$$

$$= \frac{\$114,000}{69,450}$$

$$= \$1.64 \text{ per machine-hour}$$

$$\text{budgeted fixed-overhead application rate} = \frac{\text{budgeted total fixed overhead}}{\text{budgeted machine-hours}}$$

$$= \frac{\$163,800}{69,450}$$

$$= \$2.36 \text{ per machine-hour}$$

Such rates can be used for product costing. Distinctions between variable- and fixed-overhead incurrence can also be made for control purposes.

ACTIVITY-BASED COSTING/MANAGEMENT IN A JOB-COSTING ENVIRONMENT

Regardless of the nature of the company's production system, there will always be resources that are shared among different products. The costs of these resources are part of overhead and must be accounted for in the company's cost accounting system. In many cases, the magnitude of overhead is large enough to justify investing in a costing system that provides accurate cost information. Whether this cost information is being used for inventory reporting, to cost jobs, or for cost planning and control, most often the benefits of more accurate costs exceed the costs of installing and maintaining the cost system. As we have seen, activity-based costing usually increases costing accuracy because it focuses on the cause-effect relationships between work performed (activities) and the consumption of resources (costs).

ILLUSTRATION OF ACTIVITY-BASED COSTING IN A JOB ORDER ENVIRONMENT

We illustrate an activity-based costing (ABC) system in a job-order environment by again considering Dell Computer Corporation. What motivated Dell to adopt activity-based costing? Company managers cite two reasons: (1) the aggressive cost reduction targets set by top management and (2) the need to understand product-line profitability. As is the case with any business, understanding profitability means understanding the cost structure of the entire business. One of the key advantages of an ABC system is its focus on understanding how work (activity) is related to the consumption of resources (costs). So, an ABC system was a logical choice for Dell. And, of course, once Dell's managers improved their understanding of the company's cost structure, cost reduction through activity-based management was much easier.

Like most companies that implement ABC, Dell began developing its ABC system by focusing on the most critical (core) processes across the value chain. These were the design and production processes. After the initial system was in place, the remaining phases of the value chain were added. Exhibit 13-3 shows the functions (or core processes) that add value to the company's products and how the costs of these functions are assigned to an individual job under the current ABC system.

Objective 6
Use an activity-based costing system in a job order environment.

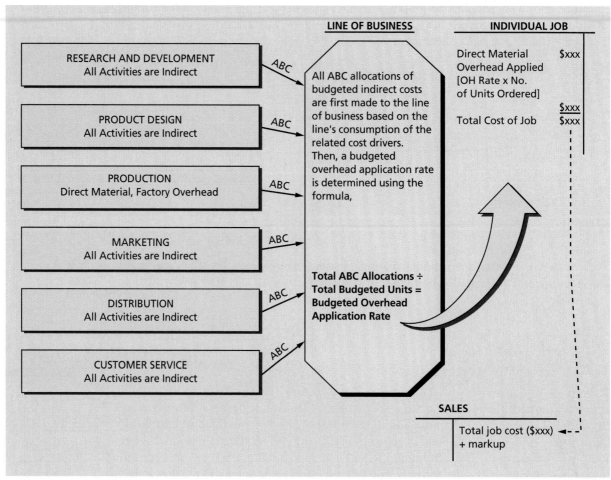

Exhibit 13-3
Dell Computer Corporation's Value Chain and ABC System

To understand product-line profitability, Dell managers identified key activities for the research and development, product design, production, distribution, marketing, and customer service phases. Then, they used appropriate cost drivers to allocate activity costs to the assembly lines (line of business) that produced product lines. While each of the phases shown in Exhibit 13-3 is important, we will focus on the product design and production phases. Product design is one of Dell's most important value-adding functions. The role of design is providing a defect-free computer product that is easy to manufacture and reliable to the customer. Engineering costs (primarily salaries and CAD equipment depreciation) account for most of the design costs. These costs are indirect and thus must be allocated to assembly lines using a cost driver.

The production costs include direct material and factory overhead. Factory overhead consists of six activity centers and related cost pools: receiving, preparation, assembly, testing, packaging, and shipping. Facility costs (plant depreciation, insurance, taxes) are considered part of the production function and are allocated to each activity center based on the square feet occupied by the center.

At Dell, there is a different assembly line for each product line. Thus, the total annual budgeted indirect cost allocated to an assembly line is divided by the total budgeted units produced to find a budgeted overhead rate. This rate, which is adjusted periodically to reflect changes in the budget, is used to cost individual jobs.

Dell is now breaking down the costs in each activity center into value added and non-value added. Non-value-added costs are targeted for cost reduction programs. An example of a non-value-added activity is the preparation activity in the production function.

PRODUCT COSTING IN SERVICE AND NONPROFIT ORGANIZATIONS

This chapter has concentrated on how to apply costs to manufactured products. However, the job-costing approach is used in nonmanufacturing situations too. For example, universities have research "projects," airlines have repair and overhaul "jobs," and public accountants have audit "engagements." In such situations, the focus shifts from the costs of products to the costs of services.

Objective 7
Show how job costing is used in service organizations.

In nonprofit organizations, the "product" is usually not called a "job order." Instead, it may be called a program or a class of service. A "program" is an identifiable group of activities that frequently produces outputs in the form of services rather than goods. Examples include a safety program, an education program, and a family counseling program. Costs or revenues may be traced to individual hospital patients, individual social welfare cases, and individual university research projects. However, departments often work simultaneously on many programs, so the "job-order" costing challenge is to "apply" the various department costs to the various programs. Only then can managers make wiser decisions regarding the allocation of limited resources among competing programs.

In service industries—such as repairing, consulting, legal, and accounting services—each customer order is a different job with a special account or order number. Sometimes only costs are traced directly to the job, sometimes only revenue is traced, and sometimes both. For example, automobile repair shops typically have a repair order for each car worked on, with space for allocating materials and labor costs. Customers are permitted to see only a copy showing the retail prices of the materials, parts, and labor billed to their orders. If the repair manager wants cost data, a system may be designed so that the "actual" parts and labor costs of each order are traced to a duplicate copy of the repair order. That is why you often see auto mechanics "punching in" and "punching out" their starting and stopping times on "time tickets" as each new order is worked on.

BUDGETS AND CONTROL OF ENGAGEMENTS

In many service organizations and some manufacturing operations, job orders are used not only for product costing, but also for planning and control purposes. For example, a public accounting firm might have a condensed budget for 19X9 as follows:

Revenue	$10,000,000	100%
Direct labor (for professional hours charged to engagements)	2,500,000	25%
Contribution to overhead and operating income	$ 7,500,000	75%
Overhead (all other costs)	6,500,000	65%
Operating income	$ 1,000,000	10%

In this illustration:

$$\text{budgeted overhead rate} = \frac{\text{budgeted overhead}}{\text{budgeted direct labor}}$$

$$= \frac{\$6,500,000}{\$2,500,000} = 260\%$$

As each engagement is budgeted, the partner in charge of the audit predicts the expected number of necessary direct-professional hours. Direct-professional hours are those worked by partners, managers, and subordinate auditors to complete the engagement. The budgeted direct-labor cost is the pertinent hourly labor costs multiplied by the budgeted hours. Partners' time is charged to the engagement at much higher rates than subordinates' time.

How is overhead applied? Accounting firms usually use either direct-labor cost or direct-labor hours as the cost driver for overhead application. In our example, the firm uses direct-labor cost. Such a practice implies that partners require proportionately more overhead support for each of their hours charged.

The budgeted total cost of an engagement is the direct-labor cost plus applied overhead (260% of direct-labor cost in this illustration) plus any other direct costs.

The engagement partner uses a budget for a specific audit that includes detailed scope and steps. For instance, the budget for auditing cash or receivables would specify the exact work to be done, the number of hours, and the necessary hours of partner time, manager time, and subordinate time. The partner monitors progress by comparing the hours logged to date with the original budget and with the estimated hours remaining on the engagement. Obviously, if a fixed audit fee has been quoted, the profitability of an engagement depends on whether the audit can be accomplished within the budgeted time limits.

ACCURACY OF COSTS OF ENGAGEMENTS

Suppose the accounting firm has costs on an auditing engagement as follows:

Direct-professional labor	$ 50,000
Applied overhead, 260% of $50,000	130,000
Total costs excluding travel costs	$180,000
Travel costs	14,000
Total costs of engagement	$194,000

Two direct costs, professional labor and travel costs, are traced to the jobs. But only direct-professional labor is a cost driver for overhead. (Note that costs reimbursed by the client—such as travel costs—do not add to overhead costs and should not be subject to any markups in the setting of fees.)

Managers of service firms, such as auditing and consulting firms, frequently use either the budgeted or "actual" costs of engagements as guides to pricing and to allocating effort among particular services or customers. Hence, the accuracy of costs of various engagements may affect decisions.

ACTIVITY-BASED COSTING IN SERVICE AND NONPROFIT ENVIRONMENTS

Our accounting firm example described a widely used, relatively simple job-costing system. Only two direct-cost items (direct-professional labor and travel costs) are used, and only a single overhead application rate is used.

In recent years, to obtain more accurate costs, many professional service firms have refined their data processing systems and adopted activity-based costing. Computers help accumulate information that is far more detailed than was feasible a few years ago. As noted in earlier chapters, firms that use activity-based costing generally shift costs from being classified as overhead to being classified as direct costs. Using our previously assumed numbers for direct labor ($50,000) and travel ($14,000), we recast the costs of our audit engagement as follows:

Direct-professional labor	$ 50,000
Direct-support labor, such as secretarial costs	10,000
Fringe benefits for all direct labor*	24,000
Telephone calls	1,000
Photocopying	2,000
Computer time	7,000
Total direct costs	94,000
Applied overhead[†]	103,400
Total costs excluding travel costs	197,400
Travel costs	14,000
Total costs of engagement	$211,400

*40% assumed rate multiplied by ($50,000 + $10,000) = $24,000.

[†]110% assumed rate multiplied by total direct costs of $94,000 = $103,400.

In an ABC system, costs such as direct-support labor, telephone calls, photocopying, and computer time are applied by directly measuring their usage on each engagement. The remaining costs to be allocated are assigned to cost pools based on their cause. The cost driver for other overhead is total direct costs.

The more detailed approach of activity-based costing will nearly always produce total costs that differ from the total costs in the general approach shown earlier: $211,400 compared with $194,000. Of course, any positive or negative difference is attributable to having more types of costs traced directly to the engagement.

EFFECTS OF CLASSIFICATIONS ON OVERHEAD RATES

The activity-based-costing approach also has a lower overhead application rate, assumed at 110% of total direct costs instead of the 260% of direct labor used in the first example, for two reasons. First, there are fewer overhead costs because more costs are traced directly. Second, the application base is broader including all direct costs rather than only direct labor.

Even with activity-based costing, some firms may prefer to continue to apply their overhead based on direct-labor costs rather than total direct costs. Why? Because the partners believe that overhead is dominantly affected by the amount of direct-labor costs rather than other direct costs such as telephone calls. But at least the activity-based-costing firm has made an explicit decision that direct-labor costs are the best cost driver.

Whether the overhead cost driver should be total direct costs, direct-professional labor costs or hours, or some other cost driver is a knotty problem for many firms, including most professional service firms. Ideally, activity analysis should uncover the principal cost drivers, and those cost drivers should all be used for overhead application. In practice, only one or two cost drivers are usually used.

SUMMARY PROBLEM FOR YOUR REVIEW

PROBLEM

Review the Enriquez illustration, especially Exhibit 13-2, page 503. Prepare an income statement for 19X8 through the gross profit line. Use the immediate write-off method for overapplied or underapplied overhead.

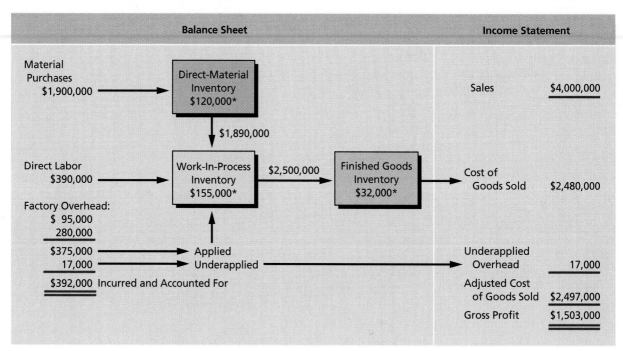

*Ending balance.

Exhibit 13-4
Relation of Costs to Financial Statements

SOLUTION

Exhibit 13-4 recapitulates the final impact of the Enriquez illustration on the financial statements. Note how the immediate write-off means that the $17,000 is added to the cost of goods sold. As you study Exhibit 13-4, trace the three major elements of cost (direct material, direct labor, and factory overhead) through the accounts.

Highlights to Remember

Distinguish between job-order costing and process costing. Product costing is an averaging process. Process costing deals with broad averages and great masses of like units. Job costing deals with narrow averages and unique units or a small batch of like units.

Prepare summary journal entries for the typical transactions of a job-costing system. The focus of journal entries in a job-order costing system is on inventory accounts. The WIP Inventory account receives central attention. Direct material used, direct labor, and factory overhead applied are accumulated in WIP. In turn, the cost of completed goods is transferred from WIP to Finished Goods.

Compute budgeted factory-overhead rates and factory overhead applied to production. Indirect manufacturing costs (factory overhead) are often applied to products using budgeted overhead rates. The rates are computed by dividing total budgeted overhead by a measure of cost-driver activity such as expected machine hours.

Use appropriate cost drivers for overhead application. There should be a strong cause-and-effect relationship between cost drivers and the overhead costs that are allocated using these drivers.

Identify the meaning and purpose of normalized overhead rates. Budgeted overhead rates are usually annual averages. The resulting product costs are normal costs, consisting of actual direct material plus actual direct labor plus applied overhead using the budgeted rates. Normal product costs are more useful for decision making and inventory-costing purposes.

Use an activity-based costing system in a job order environment. Activity-based costing can be used for any type of business that has significant levels of shared resources. In a job-order system, ABC helps managers understand the cost structure of the business on a job-by-job basis. Overhead costs are assigned to activity centers and then to jobs based on appropriate cost drivers. Activity-based management uses ABC information and the increased understanding of the organization's cost structure to control and reduce overhead costs.

Show how job costing is used in service organizations. The job-costing approach is used in nonmanufacturing as well as in manufacturing. Examples include costs of services such as auto repair, consulting, and auditing. For example, the job order is a key device for planning and controlling an audit engagement by a public accounting firm.

Understand how a job-order-costing system tracks the flow of costs to products. The basic records (source documents) used to accumulate and track costs in a job-order-costing system are materials requisitions, labor time tickets, and job-cost records. The job-cost record summarizes information on the direct materials and direct labor used as well as the factory overhead applied. Journal entries that record the basic transactions center around the three inventory accounts with particular focus on the WIP Inventory account.

Accounting Vocabulary

budgeted factory-overhead rate, p. 505	job order, p. 501	overapplied overhead, p. 509
	job-order costing, p. 500	process costing, p. 500
job costing, p. 500	labor time tickets, p. 501	prorate, p. 510
job-cost record, p. 501	materials requisitions, p. 501	time cards, p. 501
job-cost sheet, p. 501	normal costing system, p. 508	underapplied overhead, p. 509

Fundamental Assignment Material

13-A1 Basic Journal Entries

The following data (in thousands) summarize the factory operations of the Hernandez Manufacturing Co. for the year 19X8, its first year in business:

a.	Direct materials purchased for cash	$450
b.	Direct materials issued and used	420
c.	Labor used directly on production	125
d1.	Indirect labor	80
d2.	Depreciation of plant and equipment	55
d3.	Miscellaneous factory overhead (ordinarily would be detailed)	40
e.	Overhead applied: 180% of direct labor	?
f.	Cost of production completed	705
g.	Cost of goods sold	460

1. Prepare summary journal entries. Omit explanations. For purposes of this problem, combine the items in d as "overhead incurred."

2. Show the T-accounts for all inventories, Cost of Goods Sold, and Factory Department Overhead Control. Compute the ending balances of the inventories. Do not adjust for underapplied or overapplied factory overhead.

13-A2 Accounting for Overhead, Budgeted Rates

Donald Aeronautics Co. uses a budgeted overhead rate in applying overhead to individual job orders on a machine-hour basis for Department A and on a direct-labor-hour basis for Department B. At the beginning of 19X8, the company's management made the following budget predictions:

	Department A	Department B
Direct-labor cost	$1,500,000	$1,200,000
Factory overhead	$2,170,000	$1,000,000
Direct-labor hours	90,000	125,000
Machine-hours	350,000	20,000

Cost records of recent months show the following accumulations for Job Order No. M89:

	Department A	Department B
Material placed in production	$12,000	$32,000
Direct-labor cost	$10,800	$10,000
Direct-labor hours	900	1,250
Machine-hours	3,500	150

1. What is the budgeted overhead rate that should be applied in Department A? In Department B?

2. What is the total overhead cost of Job Order No. M89?

3. If Job Order No. M89 consists of 200 units of product, what is the unit cost of this job?

4. At the end of 19X8, actual results for the year's operations were as follows:

	Department A	Department B
Actual overhead costs incurred	$1,600,000	$1,200,000
Actual direct-labor hours	80,000	120,000
Actual machine-hours	300,000	25,000

Find the underapplied or overapplied overhead for each department and for the factory as a whole.

13-A3 Disposition of Overhead

Penski Precision Tooling applies factory overhead using machine-hours and number of component parts as cost drivers. In 19X8, actual factory overhead incurred was $224,000 and applied factory overhead was $216,000. Before disposition of underapplied or overapplied factory overhead, the cost of goods sold was $525,000, gross profit was $70,000, and ending inventories were:

Direct materials	$ 25,000
WIP	75,000
Finished goods	150,000
Total inventories	$250,000

1. Was factory overhead overapplied or underapplied? By how much? **Required**
2. Assume that Penski writes off overapplied or underapplied factory overhead as an adjustment to cost of goods sold. Prepare the journal entry, and compute adjusted gross profit.
3. Assume that Penski prorates overapplied or underapplied factory overhead based on end-of-the-year unadjusted balances. Prepare the journal entry, and compute adjusted gross profit.
4. Assume that actual factory overhead was $214,000 instead of $224,000, and that Penski writes off overapplied or underapplied factory overhead as an adjustment to cost of goods sold. Prepare the journal entry, and compute adjusted gross profit.

13-B1 Basic Journal Entries

Consider the following data for Oxford Printing Company (in thousands):

Inventories, December 31, 19X7	
Direct materials	£ 18
Work in process	25
Finished goods	100

Summarized transactions for 19X8:

a.	Purchases of direct materials	£112
b.	Direct materials used	98
c.	Direct labor	105
d.	Factory overhead incurred	90
e.	Factory overhead applied, 80% of direct labor	?
f.	Cost of goods completed and transferred to finished goods	280
g.	Cost of goods sold	350
h.	Sales on account	600

1. Prepare summary journal entries for 19X8 transactions. Omit explanations. **Required**
2. Show the T-accounts for all inventories, Cost of Goods Sold, and Factory Department Overhead Control. Compute the ending balances of the inventories. Do not adjust for underapplied or overapplied factory overhead.

13-B2 Disposition of Overhead

MacLachlan Mfg. Co. had overapplied overhead of $20,000 in 19X8. Before adjusting for overapplied or underapplied overhead, the ending inventories for Direct Materials, WIP, and Finished Goods were $75,000, $100,000, and $150,000, respectively. Unadjusted cost of goods sold was $250,000.

1. Assume that the $20,000 was written off solely as an adjustment to cost of goods sold. Prepare the journal entry. **Required**
2. Management has decided to prorate the $20,000 to the appropriate accounts (using the unadjusted ending balances) instead of writing it off solely as an adjustment of cost of goods sold. Prepare the journal entry. Would gross profit be higher or lower than in requirement 1? By how much?

13-B3 Application of Overhead Using Budgeted Rates

The Bellevue Clinic computes a cost of treating each patient. It allocates costs to departments and then applies departmental overhead costs to individual patients using a different budgeted overhead rate in each department. Consider the following predicted 19X7 data for two of Bellevue's departments:

	Pharmacy	Medical Records
Department overhead cost	$225,000	$300,000
Number of prescriptions filled	90,000	
Number of patient visits		60,000

The cost driver for overhead in Pharmacy is *number of prescriptions filled;* in Medical Records it is *number of patient visits.*

In June 19X7, David Li paid two visits to the clinic and had four prescriptions filled at the pharmacy.

Required

1. Compute departmental overhead rates for the two departments.
2. Compute the overhead costs applied to the patient David Li in June 19X7.
3. At the end of 19X7, actual overhead costs were:

Pharmacy	$217,000
Medical records	$325,000

The pharmacy filled 85,000 prescriptions, and the clinic had 63,000 patient visits during 19X7. Compute the overapplied or underapplied overhead in each department.

Additional Assignment Material

QUESTIONS

13-1. "There are different product costs for different purposes." Name at least two purposes.

13-2. "Job costs are accumulated for purposes of inventory valuation and income determination." State two other purposes.

13-3. Distinguish between job costing and process costing.

13-4. "The basic distinction between job-order costing and process costing is the breadth of the denominator." Explain.

13-5. How does hybrid costing relate to job costing and process costing?

13-6. Describe the supporting details for work in process in a job-cost system.

13-7. What types of source documents provide information for job-cost record?

13-8. Suppose a company uses machine-hours as a cost driver for factory overhead. How does the company compute a budgeted overhead application rate? How does it compute the amounts of factory overhead applied to a particular job?

13-9. Explain the role of the factory department overhead control account in a job-cost system.

13-10. "Each department must choose one cost driver to be used for cost application." Do you agree? Explain.

13-11. "There should be a strong relationship between the factory overhead incurred and the cost driver chosen for its application." Why?

13-12. "Sometimes direct-labor cost is the best cost driver for overhead allocation even if wage rates vary within a department." Do you agree? Explain.

13-13. Identify four cost drivers that a manufacturing company might use to apply factory overhead costs to jobs.

13-14. Is the comparison of actual overhead costs to budgeted overhead costs part of the product-costing process or part of the control process. Explain.

13-15. What are some reasons for differences between the amounts of incurred and applied overhead?

13-16. "Under actual overhead application, unit costs soar as volume increases and vice versa." Do you agree? Explain.

13-17. Define *normal costing.*

13-18. What is the best theoretical method of allocating underapplied or overapplied overhead, assuming that the objective is to obtain as accurate a cost application as possible?

13-19. State three examples of service industries that use the job-costing approach.

13-20. "Service firms trace only direct-labor costs to jobs. All other costs are applied as a percentage of direct-labor cost." Do you agree? Explain.

13-21. "As data processing becomes more economical, more costs than just direct material and direct labor will be classified as direct costs wherever feasible." Give three examples of such costs.

13-22 Direct Materials

For each of the following independent cases, fill in the blanks (in millions of dollars):

	1	2	3	4
Direct-materials inventory, Dec. 31, 19X7	8	8	5	—
Purchased	5	9	—	8
Used	7	—	7	3
Direct-materials inventory, Dec. 31, 19X8	—	6	8	7

13-23 Direct Materials

Vermont Textile Co. had an ending inventory of direct materials of $9 million. During the year the company had acquired $15 million of additional direct materials and had used $12 million. Compute the beginning inventory.

13-24 Use of WIP Inventory Account

April production resulted in the following activity in a key account of Cheung Casting Company (in thousands):

WIP Inventory	
September 1 balance	12
Direct material used	50
Direct labor charged to jobs	25
Factory overhead applied to jobs	55

Job Orders A13 and A37, with total costs of $72,000 and $56,000, respectively, were completed in April.

Required

1. Journalize the completed production for April.
2. Compute the balance in WIP Inventory, April 30, after recording the completed production.
3. Journalize the credit sale of Job A13 for $101,000.

13-25 Job-Cost Record

Western State University uses job-cost records for various research projects. A major reason for such records is to justify requests for reimbursement of costs on projects sponsored by the federal government.

Consider the following summarized data regarding a cancer research project in the Medical School:

- Jan. 5   Direct materials, various medical supplies, $925
- Jan. 7   Direct materials, various chemicals, $780
- Jan. 5–12   Direct labor, research associates, 120 hours
- Jan. 7–12   Direct labor, research assistants, 180 hours

Research associates receive $32 per hour; assistants, $19. The overhead rate is 70% of direct-labor cost.

Required

Sketch a job-cost record. Post all the data to the project-cost record. Compute the total cost of the project through January 12.

13-26 Analysis of Job-Cost Data

Job-cost records for Ganz Construction, Inc., contained the following data:

Job No.	Dates Started	Finished	Sold	Total Cost of Job at May 31
1	April 19	May 14	May 15	$3,200
2	April 26	May 22	May 25	8,800
3	May 2	June 6	June 8	6,500
4	May 9	May 29	June 5	8,100
5	May 14	June 14	June 16	3,900

Compute Ganz's (1) WIP Inventory at May 31, (2) Finished-Goods Inventory at May 31, and (3) Cost of Goods Sold for May.

13-27 Analysis of Job-Cost Data

The Cabrillo Construction Company constructs houses on speculation. That is, the houses are begun before any buyer is known. Even if the buyer agrees to purchase a house under construction, no sales are recorded until the house is completed and accepted for delivery. The job-cost records contained the following (in thousands):

Job No.	Dates Started	Finished	Sold	Total Cost of Job at Sept. 30	Total Construction Cost Added in Oct.
43	4/26	9/7	9/8	$180	
51	5/17	9/14	9/17	170	
52	5/20	9/30	10/4	150	
53	5/28	10/14	10/18	200	$50
61	6/3	10/20	11/24	115	20
62	6/9	10/21	10/27	180	25
71	7/7	11/6	11/22	118	36
81	8/7	11/24	12/24	106	48

Required

1. Compute Cabrillo's cost of (a) construction-in-process inventory at September 30 and October 31, (b) finished-houses inventory at September 30 and October 31, and (c) cost of houses sold for September and October.

2. Prepare summary journal entries for the transfer of completed houses from construction in process to finished houses for September and October.

3. Record the cash sale (price = $345,000) and cost of house sold for Job 53.

13-28 Discovery of Unknowns

DeMond Chemicals has the following balances (in millions) on December 31, 19X8.

Factory overhead applied	$200
Cost of goods sold	500
Factory overhead incurred	210
Direct-materials inventory	30
Finished-goods inventory	160
WIP inventory	120

The cost of goods completed was $420. The cost of direct materials requisitioned for production during 19X8 was $210. The cost of direct materials purchased was $225. Factory overhead was applied to production at a rate of 160% of direct-labor cost.

Compute the beginning inventory balances of direct materials, WIP, and finished goods. **Required**
Make these computations before considering any possible adjustments for overapplied or underapplied overhead.

13-29 Discovery of Unknowns

The Ramakrishnan Manufacturing Company has the following balances (in millions) as of December 31, 19X6:

WIP inventory	$ 14
Finished-goods inventory	205
Direct-materials inventory	65
Factory overhead incurred	180
Factory overhead applied at 150% of direct-labor cost	150
Cost of goods sold	350

The cost of direct materials purchased during 19X6 was $305. The cost of direct materials requisitioned for production during 19X6 was $265. The cost of goods completed was $523, all in millions.

Before considering any year-end adjustments for overapplied or underapplied overhead, **Required** compute the beginning inventory balances of direct materials, WIP, and finished goods.

13-30 Journal Entries for Overhead

Consider the following summarized data regarding 19X8:

	Budget	Actual
Indirect labor	$ 290,000	$ 305,000
Supplies	35,000	30,000
Repairs	80,000	75,000
Utilities	130,000	123,000
Factory rent	125,000	125,000
Supervision	60,000	75,000
Depreciation, equipment	220,000	220,000
Insurance, property taxes, etc.	40,000	42,000
a. Total factory overhead	$ 980,000	$ 995,000
b. Direct materials used	$1,650,000	$1,605,000
c. Direct labor	$1,225,000	$1,200,000

Omit explanations for journal entries.

1. Prepare a summary journal entry for the actual overhead incurred for 19X8. **Required**
2. Prepare summary journal entries for direct materials used and direct labor.
3. Factory overhead was applied by using a budgeted rate based on budgeted direct-labor costs. Compute the rate. Prepare a summary journal entry for the application of overhead to products.
4. Post the journal entries to the T-accounts for WIP and Factory Department Overhead Control.
5. Suppose overapplied or underapplied factory overhead is written off as an adjustment to cost of goods sold. Prepare the journal entry. Post the overhead to the overhead T-account.

13-31 Relationships Among Overhead Items

Fill in the unknowns:

	Case A	Case B	Case C
Budgeted factory overhead	$3,400,000	$?	$1,750,000
Budgeted cost drivers			
Direct-labor cost	2,000,000		
Direct-labor hours		450,000	
Machine-hours			250,000
Overhead application rate	?	$5	?

13-32 Relationship Among Overhead Items

Fill in the unknowns:

	Case 1	Case 2
a. Budgeted factory overhead	$750,000	$420,000
b. Cost driver, budgeted direct-labor cost	500,000	?
c. Budgeted factory-overhead rate	?	120%
d. Direct-labor cost incurred	570,000	?
e. Factory overhead incurred	825,000	415,000
f. Factory overhead applied	?	?
g. Underapplied (overapplied) factory overhead	?	25,000

13-33 Underapplied and Overapplied Overhead

Wosepka Welding Company applies factory overhead at a rate of $9 per direct-labor hour. Selected data for 19X6 operations are (in thousands):

	Case 1	Case 2
Direct-labor hours	30	36
Direct-labor cost	$220	$245
Indirect-labor cost	32	40
Sales commissions	20	15
Depreciation, manufac-		
turing equipment	22	32
Direct-material cost	230	250
Factory fuel costs	35	47
Depreciation, finished-		
goods warehouse	5	17
Cost of goods sold	420	510
All other factory costs	138	214

Required   Compute for both cases:

1. Factory overhead applied.
2. Total factory overhead incurred.
3. Amount of underapplied or overapplied factory overhead.

13-34 Disposition of Overhead

Assume the following at the end of 19X8 (in thousands):

Cost of goods sold	$300
Direct-materials inventory	70
WIP	50
Finished goods	150
Factory department overhead control (credit balance)	60

1. Assume that the underapplied or overapplied overhead is regarded as an adjustment to cost of goods sold. Prepare the journal entry. **Required**

2. Assume that the underapplied or overapplied overhead is prorated among the appropriate accounts in proportion to their ending unadjusted balances. Show computations and prepare the journal entry.

3. Which adjustment, the one in requirement 1 or 2, would result in the higher gross profit? Explain, indicating the amount of the difference.

13-35 Disposition of Overhead

A Paris manufacturer uses a job-order system. At the end of 19X8, the following balances existed (in millions of French francs):

Cost of goods sold	FF150
Finished goods	120
WIP	30
Factory overhead (actual)	70
Factory overhead (applied)	60

Required

1. Prepare journal entries for two different ways to dispose of the underapplied overhead.

2. Gross profit, before considering the effects in requirement 1, was FF43 million. What is the adjusted gross profit under the two methods demonstrated?

13-36 Disposition of Year-End Underapplied Overhead

Liz's Cosmetics uses a normal cost system and has the following balances at the end of its first year's operations:

WIP inventory	$200,000
Finished-goods inventory	200,000
Cost of goods sold	400,000
Actual factory overhead	409,000
Factory overhead applied	457,000

Required

Prepare journal entries for two different ways to dispose of the year-end overhead balances. By how much would gross profit differ?

BUSINESS FIRST   www.prenhall.com/phlip

PROBLEMS

13-37 Job Costing at Dell Computer

Dell Computer Company's manufacturing process at its Austin, Texas, facility consists of assembly, functional testing, and quality control of the company's computer systems. The company's build-to-order manufacturing process is designed to allow the company to quickly produce customized computer systems. For example, the company contracts with various suppliers to manufacture unconfigured base Latitude notebook computers and then custom configures these systems for shipment to customers. Quality control is maintained through the testing of components, parts, and subassemblies at various stages in the manufacturing process.

Required

Describe how Dell might set up a job-costing system to determine the costs of its computers. What is a "job" to Dell? How might the costs of components, assembly, testing, and quality control be allocated to each "job"?

13-38 Relationships of Manufacturing Costs

Selected data concerning the past fiscal year's operations of the Woodson Manufacturing Company are (in thousands):

| | Inventories | |
	Beginning	Ending
Raw materials	$55	$ 75
WIP	75	35
Finished goods	90	110

Other data:	
Raw materials used	$ 455
Total manufacturing costs charged to production during the year (includes raw materials, direct labor, and factory overhead applied at a rate of 80% of direct-labor cost)	851
Cost of goods available for sale	1,026
Selling and general expenses	50

Required

Select the best answer for each of the following items:

1. Compute the cost of raw materials purchased during the year.
2. Compute the direct-labor costs charged to production during the year.
3. Compute the cost of goods manufactured during the year.
4. Compute the cost of goods sold during the year.

13-39 Relationship of Subsidiary and General Ledgers, Journal Entries

The following summarized data are available on three job-cost records of Red Lake Manufacturing Company, a producer of packaging equipment:

| | 412 | | 413 | | 414 |
	April	May	April	May	May
Direct materials	$9,000	$2,500	$12,000	—	$13,000
Direct labor	4,000	1,500	5,000	2,500	2,000
Factory overhead applied	8,000	?	10,000	?	?

The company's fiscal year ends on May 31. Factory overhead is applied as a percentage of direct-labor costs. The balances in selected accounts on April 30 were: direct-materials inventory, $19,000; and finished-goods inventory, $18,000.

Job 412 was completed during May and transferred to finished goods. Job 413 was still in process at the end of May, as was Job 414, which had begun on May 24. These were the only jobs worked on during April and May.

Job 412 was sold, along with other finished goods, by May 30. The total cost of goods sold during May was $33,000. The balance in Cost of Goods Sold on April 30 was $450,000.

Required

1. Prepare a schedule showing the balance of the WIP Inventory, April 30. This schedule should show the total costs of each job record. Taken together, the job-cost records are the subsidiary ledger supporting the general ledger balance of work in process.
2. What is the overhead application rate?
3. Prepare summary general journal entries for all costs added to WIP during May. Also prepare entries for all costs transferred from WIP to Finished Goods and from Finished Goods to Cost of Goods Sold. Post to the appropriate T-accounts.
4. Prepare a schedule showing the balance of the WIP Inventory, May 31.

13-40 Straightforward Job Costing

The Metalcase Office Furniture Company has two departments. Data for 19X8 include the following:

Inventories, January 1, 19X8:

Direct materials (30 types)	$65,000
WIP (in assembly)	50,000
Finished goods	40,000

Manufacturing overhead budget for 19X8:

	Machining	Assembly
Indirect labor	$250,000	$410,000
Supplies	45,000	40,000
Utilities	110,000	75,000
Repairs	140,000	110,000
Supervision	130,000	215,000
Factory rent	95,000	75,000
Depreciation on equipment	160,000	105,000
Insurance, property taxes, etc.	60,000	70,000
Total	$990,000	$1,100,000

Budgeted machine-hours were 90,000; budgeted direct-labor cost in Assembly was $2,200,000. Manufacturing overhead was applied using budgeted rates on the basis of machine-hours in Machining and on the basis of direct-labor cost in Assembly.

Following is a summary of actual events for the year:

	Machining	Assembly	Total
a. Direct materials purchased			$ 1,900,000
b. Direct materials requisitioned	$1,100,000	$ 750,000	1,850,000
c. Direct-labor costs incurred	900,000	2,800,000	3,700,000
d1. Factory overhead incurred	1,100,000	1,100,000	2,200,000
d2. Factory overhead applied	880,000	?	?
e. Cost of goods completed	—	—	7,820,000
f1. Sales	—	—	13,000,000
f2. Cost of goods sold	—	—	7,800,000

The ending work in process (all in Assembly) was $60,000.

Required

1. Compute the budgeted overhead rates.
2. Compute the amount of the machine-hours actually worked.
3. Compute the amount of factory overhead applied in the Assembly Department.
4. Prepare general journal entries for transactions *a* through *f*. Work solely with the total amounts, not the details for Machining and Assembly. Explanations are not required. Show data in thousands of dollars. Present T-accounts, including ending inventory balances, for direct materials, WIP, and finished goods.
5. Prepare a partial income statement similar to the one illustrated in Exhibit 13-4, page 516. Overapplied or underapplied overhead is written off as an adjustment of current cost of goods sold.

13-41 Nonprofit Job Costing

Job-order costing is usually identified with manufacturing companies. However, service industries and nonprofit organizations also use the method. Suppose a social service agency has a cost accounting system that tracks cost by department (for example, family counseling, general welfare, and foster children) and by case. In this way, Hillary Pratt, the manager of the agency, is better able to determine how its limited resources (mostly professional social workers) should be allocated. Furthermore, the manager's interactions with superiors and various politicians are more fruitful when she can cite the costs of various types of cases.

The condensed line-item budget for the general welfare department of the agency for 19X7 showed:

Professional salaries			
Level 12	5 @ $35,000 = $175,000		
Level 10	21 @ $26,000 = 546,000		
Level 8	34 @ $18,000 = 612,000	$1,333,000	
Other costs		533,200	
Total costs		$1,866,200	

For costing various cases, the manager favored using a single overhead application rate based on the ratio of total overhead to direct labor. The latter was defined as those professional salaries assigned to specific cases.

The professional workers filled out a weekly "case time" report, which approximated the hours spent for each case.

The instructions on the report were: "Indicate how much time (in hours) you spent on each case. Unassigned time should be listed separately." About 20% of available time was unassigned to specific cases. It was used for professional development (for example, continuing education programs). "Unassigned time" became a part of "overhead," as distinguished from the direct labor.

Required

1. Compute the "overhead rate" as a percentage of direct labor (that is, the assignable professional salaries).

2. Suppose that last week a welfare case, Client No. 273, required two hours of Level 12 time, four hours of Level 10 time, and nine hours of level 8 time. How much job cost should be allocated to Client No. 273 for the week? Assume that all professional employees work a 1,800-hour year.

13-42 Job Costing in a Consulting Firm

Lubbock Engineering Consultants is a firm of professional civil engineers. It mostly does surveying jobs for the heavy construction industry throughout Texas. The firm obtains its jobs by giving fixed-price quotations, so profitability depends on the ability to predict the time required for the various subtasks on the job. (This situation is similar to that in the auditing profession, where times are budgeted for such audit steps as reconciling cash and confirming accounts receivable.)

A client may be served by various professional staff, who hold positions in the hierarchy from partners to managers to senior engineers to assistants. In addition, there are secretaries and other employees.

Lubbock Engineering has the following budget for 19X9:

Compensation of professional staff	$3,600,000
Other costs	1,449,000
Total budgeted costs	$5,049,000

Each professional staff member must submit a weekly time report, which is used for charging hours to a client job-order record. The time report has seven columns, one for each day of the week. Its rows are as follows:

- Chargeable hours
  - Client 156
  - Client 183
  - Etc.

- Nonchargeable hours
    Attending seminar on new equipment
    Unassigned time
    Etc.

In turn, these time reports are used for charging hours and costs to the client job-order records. The managing partner regards these job records as absolutely essential for measuring the profitability of various jobs and for providing an "experience base for improving predictions on future jobs."

Required

1. This firm applies overhead to jobs at a budgeted percentage of the professional compensation charged directly to the job ("direct labor"). For all categories of professional personnel, chargeable hours average 85% of available hours. Nonchargeable hours are regarded as additional overhead. What is the overhead rate as a percentage of "direct labor," the chargeable professional compensation cost?

2. A senior engineer works 48 weeks per year, 40 hours per week. His compensation is $60,000. He has worked on two jobs during the past week, devoting 10 hours to Job 156 and 30 hours to Job 183. How much cost should be charged to Job 156 because of his work there?

13-43 Choice of Cost Drivers in Accounting Firm

Brenda McCoy, the managing partner of McCoy, Brennan, and Cable, a public accounting firm, is considering the desirability of tracing more costs to jobs than just direct labor. In this way, the firm will be able to justify billings to clients.

Last year's costs were:

Direct-professional labor	$ 5,000,000
Overhead	10,000,000
Total costs	$15,000,000

The following costs were included in overhead:

Computer time	$ 750,000
Secretarial cost	700,000
Photocopying	250,000
Fringe benefits to direct labor	800,000
Phone call time with clients (estimated but not tabulated)	500,000
Total	$3,000,000

The firm's data processing techniques now make it feasible to document and trace these costs to individual jobs.

As an experiment, in December, Brenda McCoy arranged to trace these costs to six audit engagements. Two job records showed the following:

	Engagement	
	Eagledale Company	*First Valley Bank*
Direct-professional labor	$15,000	$15,000
Fringe benefits to direct labor	3,000	3,000
Phone call time with clients	1,500	500
Computer time	3,000	700
Secretarial costs	2,000	1,500
Photocopying	500	300
Total direct costs	$25,000	$21,000

1. Compute the overhead application rate based on last year's costs.
2. Suppose last year's costs were reclassified so that $3 million would be regarded as direct costs instead of overhead. Compute the overhead application rate as a percentage of direct labor and as a percentage of total direct costs.
3. Using the three rates computed in requirements 1 and 2, compute the total costs of engagements for Eagledale Company and First Valley Bank.
4. Suppose that client billing was based on a 30% markup of total job costs. Compute the billings that would be forthcoming in requirement 3.
5. Which method of job costing and overhead application do you favor? Explain.

13-44 Allocated Costs and Public Services

The Napa County (California) Grand Jury charged the city of St. Helena with overcharging customers for water and sewer services. The city allocated "administrative overhead" to the water and sewer department's budget. These charges were then added to the "jobs", that is, to the accounts of the customers of the water and sewer department. The Grand Jury called the $76,581.20 allocated to the department in 1996–97 "merely a ruse" to generate funds to cover city expenses that are unrelated to water and sewer services, resulting in "bloated water bills" for local customers.

City Finance Director explained that the overhead allocation was the way in which the city bills the water and sewer department for time that other departments spend on water and sewer issues. Mayor John Brown concluded that "it was very clear to me that they [the Grand Jury] didn't know what they were talking about."

1. Was the overhead charge to the water and sewer department a legitimate cost to be covered by water and sewer bills? Explain your reasoning to the citizens of St. Helena.
2. Assume that at least part of the overhead charge is a legitimate cost of the water and sewer department. Suggest possible changes in the accounting system that would provide a more accurate measure of the cost of services provided to the water and sewer department by other departments.

13-45 Reconstruction of Transactions

(This problem is more challenging than the others in this chapter.)

You are asked to bring the following incomplete accounts of a printing plant acquired in a merger up to date through January 31, 19X9. Also consider the data that appear after the T-accounts.

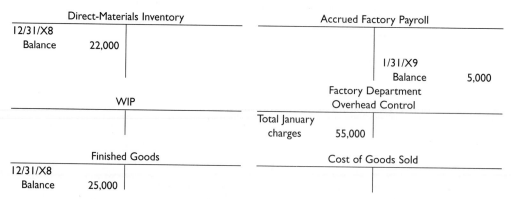

Additional information:

1. The overhead is applied using a budgeted rate that is set every December by forecasting the following year's overhead and relating it to forecasted direct-labor costs. The budget for 19X9 called for $640,000 of direct labor and $800,000 of factory overhead.

2. The only job unfinished on January 31, 19X9, was No. 419, on which total labor charges were $3,000 (200 direct-labor-hours), and total direct-material charges were $21,000.

3. Total materials placed into production during January totaled $140,000.

4. Cost of goods completed during January was $260,000.

5. January 31 balances of direct materials totaled $27,000.

6. Finished-goods inventory as of January 31 was $35,000.

7. All factory workers earn the same rate of pay. Direct-labor hours for January totaled 3,000. Indirect labor and supervision totaled $12,000.

8. The gross factory payroll paid on January paydays totaled $55,000. Ignore withholdings.

9. All "actual" factory overhead incurred during January has already been posted.

Compute the following: Required

  a. Direct materials purchased during January

  b. Cost of goods sold during January

  c. Direct-labor costs incurred during January

  d. Overhead applied during January

  e. Balance, Accrued Factory Payroll, December 31, 19X8

  f. Balance, WIP, December 31, 19X8

  g. Balance, WIP, January 31, 19X9

  h. Overapplied or underapplied overhead for January

13-46 Overhead Accounting for Control and for Product Costing

The pickle department of a major food manufacturer has an overhead rate of $4.50 per direct-labor hour, based on expected variable overhead of $125,000 per year, expected fixed overhead of $325,000 per year, and expected direct-labor hours of 100,000 per year.

Data for the year's operations follow:

	Direct-Labor Hours Used	Overhead Costs Incurred*
First six months	55,000	$236,500
Last six months	41,000	206,500

*Fixed costs incurred were exactly equal to budgeted amounts throughout the year.

1. What is the underapplied or overapplied overhead for each six-month period?   Required
   Label your answer as underapplied or overapplied.

2. Explain briefly (not more than 50 words for each part) the probable causes for the underapplied or overapplied overhead. Focus on variable and fixed costs separately. Give the exact figures attributable to the causes you cite.

CASES

13-47 Multiple Overhead Rates and Activity-Based Costing

A division of Hewlett-Packard assembles and tests printed circuit (PC) boards. The division has many different products. Some are high volume; others are low volume. For years, manufacturing overhead was applied to products using a single overhead rate based on direct-labor dollars. However, direct labor has shrunk to 6% of total manufacturing costs.

    Managers decided to refine the division's product-costing system. Abolishing the direct-labor category, they included all manufacturing labor as a part of factory overhead.

They also identified several activities and the appropriate cost driver for each. The cost driver for the first activity, the start station, was the number of raw PC boards. The application rate was computed as follows:

$$\text{application rate for start station activity} = \frac{\text{budgeted total factory overhead at the activity}}{\text{budgeted raw PC boards for the year}}$$

$$= \frac{\$150,000}{125,000} = \$1.20$$

Each time a raw PC board passes through the start station activity, $1.20 is added to the cost of the board. The product cost is the sum of costs directly traced to the board plus the indirect costs (factory overhead) accumulated at each of the manufacturing activities undergone.

Using assumed numbers, consider the following data regarding PC Board 37:

Direct materials	$55.00
Factory overhead applied	?
Total manufacturing product cost	?

The activities involved in the production of PC Board 37 and the related cost drivers were:

Activity	Cost Driver	Factory-Overhead Costs Applied for Each Activity
1. Start station	No. of raw PC boards	1 × $1.20 = $1.20
2. Axial insertion	No. of axial insertions	39 × .07 = ?
3. Dip insertion	No. of dip insertions	? × .20 = 5.60
4. Manual insertion	No. of manual insertions	15 × ? = 6.00
5. Wave solder	No. of boards soldered	1 × 3.20 = 3.20
6. Backload	No. of backload insertions	8 × .60 = 4.80
7. Test	Standard time board is in test activity	.15 × 80.00 = ?
8. Defect analysis	Standard time for defect analysis and repair	.05 × ? = 4.50
Total		$?

Required

1. Fill in the blanks.
2. How is direct labor identified with products under this product-costing system?
3. Why would managers favor this multiple-overhead rate, activity-based costing system instead of the older system?

13-48 One or Two Cost Drivers

The Matterhorn Instruments Co. in Geneva, Switzerland, has the following 19X7 budget for its two departments in Swiss francs (SF):

	Machining	Finishing	Total
Direct labor	SF 300,000	SF 800,000	SF 1,100,000
Factory overhead	SF 960,000	SF 800,000	SF 1,760,000
Machine-hours	60,000	20,000	80,000

In the past, the company has used a single plantwide overhead application rate based on direct-labor cost. However, as its product line has expanded and as competition has intensified, Hans Volkert, the company president, has questioned the accuracy of the profits or losses shown on various products.

Volkert makes custom tools on special orders from customers. To be competitive and still make a reasonable profit, it is essential that the firm measure the cost of each customer order. Mr. Volkert has focused on overhead allocation as a potential problem. He knows that changes in costs are more heavily affected by machine-hours in the machining department and by direct-labor costs in the finishing department. As company controller, you have gathered the following data regarding two typical customer orders:

	Order Number	
	K102	*K156*
Machining		
Direct materials	SF 4,000	SF 4,000
Direct labor	SF 3,000	SF 1,500
Machine-hours	1,200	100
Finishing		
Direct labor	SF 1,500	SF 3,000
Machine-hours	120	120

Required

1. Compute six factory overhead application rates, three based on direct-labor cost and three based on machine-hours for machining, finishing, and for the plant as a whole.

2. Use the application rates to compute the total costs of orders K102 and K156 as follows: (a) plantwide rate based on direct-labor cost and (b) machining based on machine-hours and finishing based on direct-labor cost.

3. Evaluate your answers in requirement 2. Which set of job costs do you prefer? Why?

COLLABORATIVE LEARNING EXERCISE

13-49 Accounting for Overhead
Form groups of four to six persons. Each group should identify a cost accountant at a local company to interview. The interviewee could be the top financial officer of a small company, but a division controller or cost analyst might be more appropriate for a large company. The essential factor is that the person understand how overhead costs are allocated to products or services in the company.

Set up an interview with the cost accountant, and explore the following issues. Be prepared with follow-up questions if your question receives a superficial answer. Your goal should be to get as much operational detail as possible about the procedures used for allocating overhead costs at the company. If the company is large, you may want to focus on one department, one product line, or some other subdivision of the company.

The issues to explore are:

a. What types of costs are included in overhead? How large is overhead compared with direct material and labor costs?

b. What types of overhead cost pools exist? Are there different pools by department? By activity? By cost driver? By fixed or variable cost? Be prepared to explain what you mean by these terms, because terminology varies widely.

c. How is overhead applied to final products or services? What cost drivers are used?

After the interview, draw a diagram of the cost allocation system in as much detail as possible. Be prepared to share this with the entire class, using it to explain the overhead cost allocation system at the company your group studied.

PROCESS-COSTING SYSTEMS

In this mine, owned and operated by Nally & Gibson Georgetown, Inc., limestone rock is loosened by carefully placing dynamite charges.

Learning Objectives

When you have finished studying this chapter, you should be able to

1 Explain the basic ideas underlying process costing and how they differ from job costing.

2 Compute output in terms of equivalent units.

3 Compute costs and prepare journal entries for the principal transactions in a process-costing system.

4 Demonstrate how the presence of beginning inventories affects the computation of unit costs under the weighted-average method.

5 Demonstrate how the presence of beginning inventories affects the computation of unit costs under the first-in, first-out method.

6 Use backflush costing with a JIT production system.

7 **Understand how a process-costing system tracks costs to products.**

Don't look now, but you are most likely surrounded by the product produced by Nally and Gibson Georgetown, Inc. In fact, if you are in a typical residence or dormitory room, there are probably about 400 tons of this product close by—in the street and driveway, the sidewalk, the walls, and maybe even your toothpaste. What is it? Limestone. Nally and Gibson is a leading producer of limestone products used for industrial and commercial purposes. Limestone is used in highways, high school track beds, concrete sidewalks, buildings, soil enhancement products, residential homes, and about a million other places (yes, even in some toothpastes).

The making of limestone products is an excellent example of a process production system. A single output—limestone rock—is subjected to several processes that result in finished limestone products. The basic production processes that convert limestone rock into usable limestone are easy to understand and are reasonably simple. Basically, the limestone rock is mined from Nally and Gibson's quarry and mine in Georgetown, Kentucky, and shipped to the processing facility. There it passes through several stages of crushing and grinding, depending on how fine the finished product needs to be. The ease and homogeneous nature of these processes might make you think that the *cost accounting system* used to track product costs should also be fairly simple and perhaps even unimportant to the success of the company. However, accurate and timely cost information is critical to both product costing and decision making at Nally and Gibson.

For example, the accurate allocation of the costs of mining and transporting limestone and then crushing the limestone to form the various products is essential to the success of the company. The company's cost accounting system accumulates the costs of these processes and then calculates an average cost per ton of product. According to company President Frank Hamilton, Jr., "If Nally and Gibson did not keep a handle on costs, we would not be here."

How does a company like Nally and Gibson assign costs to its products? After all, it is rather difficult to assign costs to individual pieces of crushed limestone. Companies that produce large quantities of a generic or homogeneous product, such as staples or sliced potato strips for french frying, in a continual process do not use the job costing techniques we have already seen. Why? First, because there are no discreet jobs. The company does not wait for a specific customer order before producing the product. The company makes a forecast of the demand for the product and produces to meet this expected demand. Second, it is amazingly difficult (and costly) to trace cost to a specific french fry or even a single truckload of limestone. And there would be no benefit in doing so in terms of increased accuracy. So the cost-benefit criterion clearly dictates that the company determine unit costs using much larger quantities—say a whole month's production.

Process costing assigns costs by measuring overall production costs and averaging them based on total production in units over a period of time—usually a month. The resulting average unit costs are then used to determine inventory cost and the cost of goods sold. This chapter will explain process costing.

PROCESS COSTING BASICS

Objective 1
Explain the basic ideas underlying process costing and how they differ from job costing.

As we noted in Chapter 13, all product costing uses averaging to determine costs per unit of production. Sometimes those averages apply to a relatively small number of units such as a particular printing job produced in a job-order production system. Other times the averages might have to be extremely broad, based on generic products from a continual-process production system, such as limestone road-fill. *Process-costing systems* apply costs to like products that are usually mass produced in continuous fashion through a series of production processes. These processes usually occur in separate departments, although a single department sometimes contains more than one process.

PROCESS COSTING COMPARED WITH JOB COSTING

It is probably easiest to understand process costing if you compare it with something you already know: job costing. Job costing and process costing are used for different types of products. Firms in industries such as printing, construction, and furniture manufacturing, in which each unit or batch (job) of product is unique and easily identifiable, use job-order costing. Process costing is used when there is mass production through a sequence of several processes, such as mixing and cooking. Examples include chemicals, flour, glass, toothpaste, and limestone.

Exhibit 14-1 shows the major differences between job-order costing and process costing. Process costing requires several work-in-process accounts, one for each process (or department). As goods move from process to process, their costs are transferred accordingly.

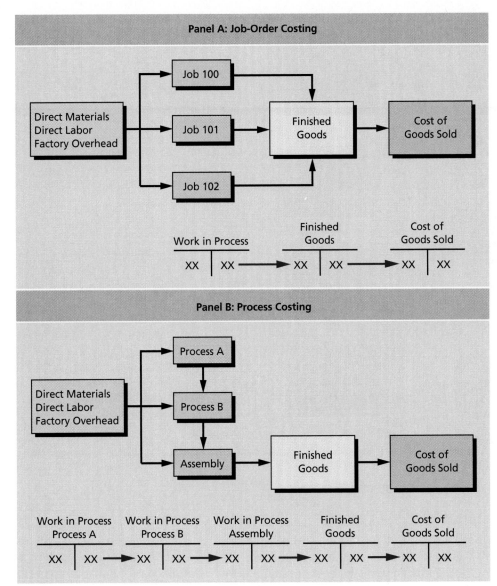

Exhibit 14-1

Comparison of Job-Order and Process Costing

Consider Nally and Gibson's process-costing system. The company's production system has four core processes as shown in Exhibit 14-2. Limestone rock is first obtained from surface quarries or from mines. The rock is then transported to the plant by rail or truck. At the plant, the rock is crushed and screened to various sizes demanded by customers. The crushed limestone is then stocked in large piles of inventory for shipment. Each process requires resources. The direct-material resource is the limestone rock that is quarried or mined. Direct-labor and overhead resources are used in all four processes.

The process-costing approach does not distinguish among individual units of product. Instead, it accumulates costs for a period and divides them by quantities produced during that period to get broad, average unit costs. Process costing can be applied to nonmanufacturing activities as well as to manufacturing activities. For example, we can divide the costs of giving state automobile driver's license tests by the number of tests given, and we can divide the cost of a post office sorting department by the number of items sorted.

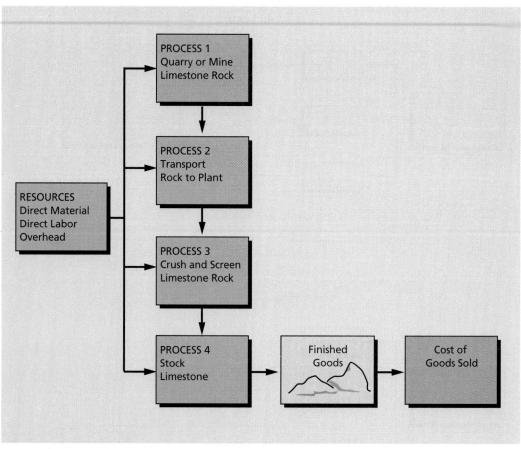

Exhibit 14-2

Process costing at Nally and Gibson

To get a rough feel for process costing, consider Magenta Midget Frozen Vegetables. It quick-cooks tiny carrots, beans, and other vegetables before freezing them. As the following T-accounts show, the costs of cooked vegetables (in millions of dollars) are transferred from the Cooking Department to the Freezing Department:

Work in Process—Cooking					Work in Process—Freezing			
Direct materials	14	Transfer cost of			Cost		Transfer cost	
		goods completed			transferred		of goods	
Direct labor	4	to next			in from		completed	
Factory overhead	8	department	24		cooking	24	to finished	
	26				Direct labor	1	goods	25
Ending inventory	2				Factory overhead	2		
						27		
					Ending inventory	2		

The amount of cost to be transferred is determined by dividing the accumulated costs in the Cooking Department by the pounds of vegetables processed. The resulting cost per pound is then multiplied by the pounds of vegetables physically transferred to the Freezing Department.

The journal entries for process-costing systems are similar to those for the job-order-costing system. That is, direct materials, direct labor, and factory overhead are accounted for as before. However, now there is more than a single work-in-process account for all units being manufactured. There is one work-in-process account for each processing department, Work in Process—Cooking and Work in Process—Freezing, in our example. The Magenta Midget data would be recorded as follows:

1. Work in Process—Cooking 14
        Direct-materials inventory 14
    To record direct materials used
2. Work in Process—Cooking 4
        Accrued payroll 4
    To record direct labor
3. Work in Process—Cooking 8
        Factory overhead 8
    To record factory overhead applied to product
4. Work in Process—Freezing 24
        Work in Process—Cooking 24
    To transfer goods from the cooking process
5. Work in Process—Freezing 1
        Accrued payroll 1
    To record direct labor
6. Work in Process—Freezing 2
        Factory overhead 2
    To record factory overhead applied to product
7. Finished goods 25
        Work in Process—Freezing 25
    To transfer goods from the freezing process

The central product-costing problem is how each department should compute the cost of goods transferred out and the cost of goods remaining in the department. If the same amount of work was done on each unit transferred and on each unit in ending inventory, the solution is easy. Total costs are simply divided by total units. Then, this unit cost is used to calculate the total cost of units transferred out and the remaining cost of unfinished units. However, if the units in the inventory are each partially completed, the product-costing system must distinguish between the costs of fully completed units transferred out and the costs of partially completed units not yet transferred.

Process manufacturing systems vary in design. The design shown in panel B of Exhibit 14-1 (as well as Exhibit 14-2) is sequential—units pass from process A to process B and so on until the product is finished. Many other designs are found in practice—each tailored to meet specific production requirements. For example, processes can be operated in parallel until final assembly. In this case, process A and process B might occur at the same time to produce different parts of the finished product. Whatever the specific layout, the basic principles of process costing are the same.

APPLICATION OF PROCESS COSTING

To help you better understand our discussion of process costing, we will use the example of Oakville Wooden Toys, Inc. The company buys wood as a direct material for its Forming Department. The department processes only one type of toy, marionettes. The marionettes are transferred to the Finishing Department, where they are hand-shaped and strings, paint, and clothing are added.

The Forming Department manufactured 25,000 identical units during April, and its costs that month were:

Direct materials		$ 70,000
Conversion costs		
Direct labor	$10,625	
Factory overhead	31,875	42,500
Costs to account for		$112,500

The unit cost of goods completed would simply be $112,500 ÷ 25,000 = $4.50. An itemization would show:

Direct materials, $70,000 \div 25,000	$2.80
Conversion costs, $42,500 \div 25,000	1.70
Unit cost of a whole completed marionette	$4.50

But what if not all 25,000 marionettes were completed during April? For example, assume that 5,000 were still in process at the end of April—only 20,000 were started and fully completed. All units—both those transferred out and those still in inventory—have received all of the necessary direct materials. However, only the transferred units have received the full amount of conversion resources. The 5,000 marionettes that remain in process have received only 25% of conversion resources. How should the Forming Department calculate the cost of goods transferred and the cost of goods remaining in the ending work-in-process inventory? The answer lies in the following five key steps:

- **Step 1:** Summarize the flow of physical units.
- **Step 2:** Calculate output in terms of equivalent units.
- **Step 3:** Summarize the total costs to account for, which are the costs applied to work in process.
- **Step 4:** Calculate unit costs.
- **Step 5:** Apply costs to units completed and to units in the ending work in process.

PHYSICAL UNITS AND EQUIVALENT UNITS (STEPS 1 AND 2)

Step 1, as the first column in Exhibit 14-3 shows, tracks the physical units of production. How should the output—the results of the department's work—be measured? This tracking tells us we have a total of 25,000 physical units to account for, but not all of these units count the same in the Forming Department's output. Why not? Because only 20,000 units were fully completed and transferred out. The remaining 5,000 units are only partially complete, and partially complete units cannot be given the same weight as the completed output. As a result, we have to state output not in terms of physical units but in terms of *equivalent units.*

equivalent units The number of completed units that could have been produced from the inputs applied.

Equivalent units are the number of completed units that could have been produced from the inputs applied. For example, four units that are each one-half completed repre-

Exhibit 14-3

Forming Department Output in Equivalent Units
Month Ended April 30, 19X9

	(Step 1)	(Step 2) Equivalent Units	
Flow of Production	**Physical Units**	*Direct Materials*	*Conversion Costs*
Started and completed	20,000	20,000	20,000
Work in process, ending inventory	5,000	5,000	1,250*
Units accounted for	25,000		
Work done to date		25,000	21,250*

*5,000 physical units × .25 degree of completion of conversion costs.

sent two equivalent units. If each unit had been one-fourth completed, the four together would have represented one equivalent unit. So, equivalent units are determined by multiplying physical units by the percent of completion.

In our example, as step 2 in Exhibit 14-3 shows, the output would be measured as 25,000 equivalent units of direct-materials cost but only 21,250 equivalent units of conversion costs. Why do we have only 21,250 equivalent units of conversion costs but 25,000 of direct-materials cost? Because direct materials had been fully added to all 25,000 units. In contrast, only 25% of the conversion costs were applied to the 5,000 partially completed units, which would have been sufficient to complete only 1,250 units in addition to the 20,000 units that were actually completed.

Of course, to compute equivalent units, you need to estimate how much of a given resource was applied to units in process, which is not always an easy task. Some estimates are easier to make than others. For example, estimating the amount of direct materials used is fairly easy. However, how do you measure how much energy, maintenance labor, or supervision was used on a given unit? Conversion costs can involve a number of these hard-to-measure resources, which leaves you estimating both how much total effort it takes to complete a unit and how much of that effort has already been put into the units in process. Coming up with accurate estimates is further complicated in industries such as textiles, where there is a great deal of work in process at all times. To simplify estimation, some companies have decided that all work in process must be deemed either one-third, one-half, or two-thirds complete. In cases where continuous processing leaves roughly the same amount in process at the end of every month, accountants ignore work in process altogether and assign all monthly production costs to units completed and transferred out.

Measures in equivalent units are not confined to manufacturing situations. Such measures are a popular way of expressing workloads in terms of a common denominator. For example, radiology departments measure their output in terms of weighted units. Various x-ray procedures are ranked in terms of the time, supplies, and related costs devoted to each. A simple chest x-ray may receive a weight of one. But a skull x-ray may receive a weight of three because it uses three times the resources (for example, technicians' time) as does a procedure with a weight of one.

Objective 2
Compute output in terms of equivalent units.

CALCULATION OF PRODUCT COSTS (STEPS 3 TO 5)

Exhibit 14-4 is a production-cost report. It shows steps 3 to 5 of process costing. Step 3 summarizes the total costs to account for (that is, the total costs in, or debits to, Work in Process—Forming). Step 4 obtains unit costs by dividing the two categories of total costs by the appropriate measures of equivalent units. The unit cost of a completed unit—material cost plus conversion costs—is $2.80 + $2.00 = $4.80.[1] Step 5 then uses these unit costs to apply costs to products. The 20,000 finished units are complete in terms of both direct materials and conversion costs. Thus, we can multiply the full unit cost times the number of completed units to determine their costs. The 5,000 physical units in process are fully completed in terms of direct materials. Therefore, the direct materials applied to work in process are 5,000 equivalent units times $2.80, or $14,000. In contrast, the 5,000 physical units are 25% completed in terms of conversion costs. Therefore, the conversion costs applied to work in process are 1,250 equivalent units (25% of 5,000 physical units) times $2.00, or $2,500.

Objective 3
Compute costs and prepare journal entries for the principal transactions in a process-costing system.

---

[1]*Why is the unit cost $4.80 instead of the $4.50 calculated earlier in this chapter? Because the $42,500 conversion cost is spread over 21,250 units instead of 25,000 units.*

Exhibit 14-4

Forming Department Production Cost Report
Month Ended April 30, 19X9

		Total Costs	Details Direct Materials	Details Conversion Costs
(Step 3)	Costs to account for	$112,500	$ 70,000	$ 42,500
(Step 4)	Divide by equivalent units		÷ 25,000	÷ 21,250
	Unit costs	$ 4.80	$ 2.80	$ 2.00
(Step 5)	Application of costs			
	To units completed and transferred to the Finishing Department, 20,000 units @$4.80	$ 96,000		
	To units not completed and still in process, April 30, 5,000 units			
	Direct materials	$ 14,000	5,000 ($2.80)	
	Conversion costs	2,500		1,250 ($2.00)
	Work in process, April 30	$ 16,500		
	Total costs accounted for	$112,500		

Journal entries for the data in our illustration would appear as:

```
1.  Work in Process—Forming......................70,000
          Direct-materials inventory........................        70,000
     Materials added to production in April
2.  Work in Process—Forming......................10,625
          Accrued payroll................................        10,625
     Direct labor in April
3.  Work in Process—Forming......................31,875
          Factory overhead..............................        31,875
     Factory overhead applied in April
4.  Work in Process—Finishing .....................96,000
          Work in Process—Forming......................        96,000
     Cost of goods completed and transferred in April from Forming to Assembly
```

The $112,500 added to the Work in Process—Forming account less the $96,000 transferred out leaves an ending balance of $16,500:

Work in Process—Forming			
1. Direct materials	$ 70,000	4. Transferred out	
2. Direct labor	10,625	to finishing	$96,000
3. Factory overhead	31,875		
Costs to account for	112,500		
Bal. April 30	$ 16,500		

SUMMARY PROBLEM FOR YOUR REVIEW

PROBLEM

Taylor Plastics makes a variety of plastic products. Its Extruding Department had the following output and costs:

Units
   Started and completed: 30,000 units
   Started and still in process: 10,000 units; 100% completed for direct materials,
      but 60% completed for conversion costs
Costs applied
   Total: $81,600; direct materials, $60,000; conversion, $21,600

Compute the cost of work completed and the cost of the ending inventory of work in process for Taylor's Extruding Department.

SOLUTION

Flow of Production	(Step 1) Physical Units	(Step 2) Equivalent Units	
		Direct Materials	Conversion
Started and completed	30,000	30,000	30,000
Ending work in process	10,000	10,000*	6,000*
Units accounted for	40,000		
Work done to date		40,000	36,000

*10,000 × 100% = 10,000; 10,000 × 60% = 6,000.

		Total Costs	Details	
			Direct Materials	Conversion Costs
(Step 3)	Costs to account for	$81,600	$60,000	$21,600
(Step 4)	Divide by equivalent units		÷40,000	÷36,000
	Unit costs	$ 2.10*	$ 1.50	$ .60
(Step 5)	Application of costs			
	To units completed and transferred,			
	30,000 units @$2.10	$63,000		
	To ending work in process, 10,000 units			
	Direct materials	$15,000	10,000 ($1.50)	
	Conversion costs	3,600		6,000 ($.60)
	Work in process, ending inventory	$18,600		
	Total costs accounted for	$81,600		

*Unit cost ($2.10) = direct materials costs ($1.50) + conversion costs ($.60).

EFFECTS OF BEGINNING INVENTORIES

So far, our example has been very straightforward because all units were started during the period. In other words, there were no units in beginning inventory. The presence of units in beginning inventory actually complicate matters a great deal.

   So how do we account for product costs now that there are units in beginning inventory? Well, we still use the same five steps as we did before, but now our results depend on which inventory system we use. The two most popular inventory systems are the *weighted-*

average method and the *first-in, first-out method.* In the next two sections, we will explore each of these methods using the following data from our Oakville example for the month of May. Recall that the ending work in process inventory for April in the Forming Department was 5,000 units. These units will be the beginning inventory for May.

Units
    Work in process, April 30: 5,000 units; 100% completed for materials,
       but only 25% completed for conversion costs
    Units started in May: 26,000
    Units completed in May: 24,000
       Work in process, May 31: 7,000 units; 100% completed for materials,
       but only 60% completed for conversion costs
Costs

Work in process, April 30		
Direct materials	$14,000	
Conversion costs	2,500	$ 16,500
Direct materials added during May		82,100
Conversion costs added during May		
($14,560 + $42,160)		56,720
Total costs to account for		$155,320*

*Note that the $155,320 total costs to account for include the $16,500 of beginning inventory in addition to the $138,820 added during May.

Objective 4
Demonstrate how the presence of beginning inventories affects the computation of unit costs under the weighted-average method.

WEIGHTED-AVERAGE METHOD

weighted-average (WA) process-costing method
A process-costing method that adds the cost of (1) all work done in the current period to (2) the work done in the preceding period on the current period's beginning inventory of work in process, and divides the total by the equivalent units of work done to date.

The **weighted-average (WA) process-costing method** determines total costs by adding the cost of (1) all work done in the current period to (2) the work done in the preceding period on the current period's beginning inventory of work in process. This total is divided by the equivalent units of work done to date, whether that work was done in the current period or previously.

Why is the term *weighted-average* used to describe this method? Primarily because the unit costs used for applying costs to products are affected by the total cost incurred to date, regardless of whether those costs were incurred during or before the current period.

Exhibit 14-5 shows the first two steps in this method, computation of physical units and equivalent units. The computation of equivalent units ignores whether all 31,000 units to account for came from beginning work in process, or all were started in May, or some combination thereof. Exhibit 14-6 presents a production-cost report, summarizing steps 3 to 5 regarding computations of product costs.

FIRST-IN, FIRST-OUT METHOD

first-in, first-out (FIFO) process-costing method
A process-costing method that sharply distinguishes the current work done from the previous work done on the beginning inventory of work in process.

The **first-in, first-out (FIFO) process-costing method** sharply distinguishes the current work done from the previous work done on the beginning inventory of work in process. The calculation of equivalent units is confined to the work done in the current period (May in this illustration).

Exhibit 14-7 presents steps 1 and 2. The easiest way to compute equivalent units under the FIFO method is, first, compute the costs associated with work done to date, as shown in Exhibit 14-7. Second, deduct the work done before the current period. The remaining costs represent the work done during the current period, which is the key to computing the unit costs by the FIFO method.

Exhibit 14–5

Forming Department Output in Equivalent Units
Weighted-Average Method
Month Ended May 31, 19X9

| Flow of Production | (Step 1) Physical Units | (Step 2) Equivalent Units | |
		Direct Materials	Conversion Costs
Work in process, April 30	5,000 (25%)*		
Started in May	26,000		
To account for	31,000		
Completed and transferred out during current period	24,000	24,000	24,000
Work in process, May 31	7,000 (60%)*	7,000	4,200†
Units accounted for	31,000		
Work done to date		31,000	28,200

*Degrees of completion for conversion costs at the dates of inventories.

†.60 × 7,000 = 4,200.

Exhibit 14-6

Forming Department Production-Cost Report
Weighted-Average Method
Month Ended May 31, 19X9

| | | Totals | Details | |
			Direct Materials	Conversion Costs
(Step 3)	Work in process, April 30	$ 16,500	$ 14,000	$ 2,500
	Costs added currently	138,820	82,100	56,720
	Total costs to account for	$155,320	$ 96,100	$59,220
(Step 4)	Divisor, equivalent units for work done to date*		31,000	28,200
	Unit costs (weighted averages)	$ 5.20	$ 3.10	$ 2.10
(Step 5)	Application of costs Completed and transferred, 24,000 units ($5.20)	$124,800		
	Work in process, May 31, 7,000 units			
	Direct materials	$ 21,700	7,000 ($3.10)	
	Conversion costs	8,820		4,200* ($2.10)
	Total work in process	$ 30,520		
	Total costs accounted for	$155,320		

Exhibit 14-8 is the production-cost report. It presents steps 3 to 5. The $16,500 beginning inventory balance is kept separate from current costs because the calculations of equivalent unit costs are confined to costs added in May only.

The bottom half of Exhibit 14-8 shows two ways to compute the costs of goods completed and transferred out. The first and faster way is to compute the $30,943 ending work in process and then deduct it from the $155,320 total costs to account for,

Objective 5
Demonstrate how the presence of beginning inventories affects the computation of unit costs under the first-in, first-out method.

Exhibit 14-7

Forming Department Output in Equivalent Units
FIFO Method
Month Ended May 31, 19X9

Same as Exhibit 14-5		(Step 2) Equivalent Units	
	(Step 1) Physical	Direct	Conversion
Flow of Production	Units	Materials	Costs
Work in process, April 30	5,000 (25%)*		
Started in May	26,000		
To account for	31,000		
Completed and transferred out during current period	24,000	24,000	24,000
Work in process, May 31	7,000 (60%)*	7,000	4,200 †
Units accounted for	31,000		
Work done to date		31,000	28,200
Less: equivalent units of work from previous periods included in beginning inventory		5,000 ‡	1,250§
Work done in current period only		26,000	26,950

*Degrees of completion for conversion costs at the dates of inventories.
† 7,000 × .60 = 4,200 equivalent units; ‡ 5,000 × 1.00 = 5,000 equivalent units; § 5,000 × .25 = 1,250 equivalent units.

Exhibit 14-8

Forming Department Production-Cost Report
FIFO Method
Month Ended May 31, 19X9

		Details	
		Direct	Conversion
	Totals	Materials	Costs
(Step 3) Work in process, April 30	$ 16,500	(work done before May)	
Costs added currently	138,820	$82,100	$56,720
Total costs to account for	$155,320		
(Step 4) Divisor, equivalent units of work done in May only		26,000 *	26,950 *
Unit costs (for FIFO basis)	$ 5.2623	$3.1577	$2.1046
(Step 5) Application of costs			
Work in process, May 31			
Direct materials	$ 22,104	7,000 ($3.1577)	
Conversion costs	8,839		4,200* ($2.1046)
Total work in process (7,000 units)	30,943		
Completed and transferred out (24,000 units), $155,320 − $30,943	124,377 †		
Total costs accounted for	$155,320		

*Equivalent units of work done. See Exhibit 14-7 for more details.
† Check:

Work in process, April 30	$ 16,500
Additional costs to complete, conversion costs of 75% of 5,000 × $2.1046 =	7,892
Started and completed, 26,000 − 7,000 = 19,000; 19,000 × $5.2623 =	99,984
Total cost transferred	$124,376 ($1 rounding error)

Unit cost transferred, $124,376 ÷ 24,000 = $5.1823

obtaining $124,377. As a check on accuracy, it is advisable to use a second way: compute the cost of goods transferred in the detailed manner displayed in the footnote in Exhibit 14-8.

DIFFERENCES BETWEEN FIFO AND WEIGHTED-AVERAGE METHODS

The key difference between the FIFO and weighted-average methods is the calculation of equivalent units:

- FIFO—Equivalent units are based on the work done in the current period only.
- Weighted-average—Equivalent units are based on the work done in the current period as well as the earlier work done on the current period's beginning inventory of work in process.

These differences in equivalent units lead to differences in unit costs, as well as differences in costs applied to goods completed and still in process. In our example, the FIFO method results in a larger work-in-process inventory on May 31 and a smaller May cost of goods transferred out:

	Weighted Average*	FIFO[†]
Cost of goods transferred out	$124,800	$124,377
Ending work in process	30,520	30,943
Total costs accounted for	$155,320	$155,320

*From Exhibit 14-6.
[†]From Exhibit 14-8.

Differences in unit costs between FIFO and weighted-average methods are ordinarily insignificant because (1) changes in material prices, labor wage rates, and other manufacturing costs from month to month tend to be small, and (2) changes in the volume of production and inventory levels also tend to be small.

You have no doubt noticed that the FIFO method involves more detailed computations than does the weighted-average method. That is why FIFO is almost never used in practice for product-costing purposes. However, the FIFO equivalent units for current work done are essential for planning and control purposes. Why? Because they isolate the output for one particular period. Consider our example. The FIFO computations of equivalent units help managers to measure the efficiency of May's performance independently from April's performance. Thus, budgets or standards for each month's departmental costs can be compared against actual results in light of the actual work done during any given month.

TRANSFERRED-IN COSTS

Many companies that use process costing have sequential production processes. For example, Oakville Wooden Toys transfers the items completed in its Forming Department to the Finishing Department. The Finishing Department would call the costs of the items it receives **transferred-in costs**—costs incurred in a previous department for items that have been received by a subsequent department. They are similar to, but not identical to, additional direct-material costs. Because transferred-in costs are a combination of all types of costs (direct-material and conversion costs) incurred in

transferred-in costs In process costing, costs incurred in a previous department for items that have been received by a subsequent department.

previous departments, they should not be called a direct-material cost in a subsequent department.

We account for transferred-in costs just as we account for direct materials, with one exception: Transferred-in costs are kept separate from the direct materials added in the department. Therefore, reports such as Exhibits 14-6 and 14-8 will include three columns of costs instead of two: transferred-in costs, direct-material costs, and conversion costs. The total unit cost will be the sum of all three types of unit costs.

SUMMARY PROBLEM FOR YOUR REVIEW

PROBLEM

Consider the Cooking Department of Middleton Foods, a British food-processing company. Compute the cost of work completed and the cost of the ending inventory of work in process, using both the (1) weighted-average (WA) method and (2) FIFO method.

Units		
Beginning work in process: 5,000 units; 100% completed for materials, 40% completed for conversion costs		
Started during month: 28,000 units		
Completed during month: 31,000 units		
Ending work in process: 2,000 units; 100% completed for materials, 50% for conversion costs		
Costs		
Beginning work in process		
Direct materials	£8,060	
Conversion costs	1,300	£ 9,360
Direct materials added in current month		41,440
Conversion costs added in current month		14,700
Total costs to account for		£65,500

SOLUTION

	(Step 1)	(Step 2) Equivalent Units	
	Physical		Conversion
Flow of Production	**Units**	*Material*	*Cost*
Completed and transferred out	31,000	31,000	31,000
Ending work in process	2,000	2,000*	1,000*
1. Equivalent units, WA	33,000	33,000	32,000
Less: beginning work in process	5,000	5,000†	2,000†
2. Equivalent units, FIFO	28,000	28,000	30,000

*2,000 × 100% = 2,000; 2,000 × 50% = 1,000.
†5,000 × 100% = 5,000; 5,000 × 40% = 2,000.

Note especially that the work done to date is the basis for computing the equivalent units under the weighted-average method. In contrast, the basis for computing the equivalent units under the FIFO method is the work done in the current period only.

1.

Weighted-Average Method	Total Cost	Direct Materials	Conversion Costs
Beginning work in process	£ 9,360	£ 8,060	£ 1,300
Costs added currently	56,140	41,440	14,700
Total costs to account for	£65,500	£49,500	£16,000
Equivalent units, weighted-average		÷33,000	÷32,000
Unit costs, weighted-average	£ 2.00	£ 1.50	£ 0.50
Transferred out, 31,000 × £2.00	£62,000		
Ending work in process			
Direct materials	£ 3,000	2,000 (£1.50)	
Conversion cost	500		1,000 (£.50)
Total work in process	£ 3,500		
Total costs accounted for	£65,500		

2.

Fifo Method	Total Cost	Direct Materials	Conversion Costs
Beginning work in process	£ 9,360	(work done before month)	
Costs added currently	56,140	£41,440	£14,700
Total costs to account for	£65,500		
Equivalent units, FIFO		÷28,000	÷30,000
Unit costs, FIFO	£ 1.97	£ 1.48	£ 0.49
Ending work in process			
Direct materials	£ 2,960	2,000 (£1.48)	
Conversion cost	490		1,000 (£.49)
Total work in process	£ 3,450		
Transferred out,			
£65,500 − £3,450	£62,050 *		
Total costs accounted for	£65,500		

*Check:

Beginning work in process	£ 9,360
Costs to complete, 60% × 5,000 × £.49	1,470
Started and completed,	
(31,000 − 5,000) (£1.48 + £.49)	51,220
Total cost transferred	£62,050

Unit cost transferred, £62,050 ÷ 31,000 = £2.00161

PROCESS COSTING IN A JIT SYSTEM: BACKFLUSH COSTING

Tracking costs through various stages of inventory—raw material, work-in-process, inventory for each process (or department), and finished goods inventory—makes accounting systems complex. If there were no inventories, all costs would be charged directly to cost of goods sold, and accounting systems would be much simpler. Organizations using JIT production systems usually have very small inventories or no inventories at all. As a result, a traditional accounting system that traces costs through several different types of inventories may be inappropriate or even useless for them. One such company is Eagle-Gypsum Products Company. The company operates in the Colorado Rockies and manufactures gypsum wallboard for commercial and residential use. Like many companies that use the JIT production system, Eagle-Gypsum has very low inventory levels and uses **backflush costing,** an accounting system that applies costs to products only when the production is complete. How does backflush costing work? As we shall see, it is a fairly simple costing system.

backflush costing An accounting system that applies costs to products only when the production is complete.

PRINCIPLES OF BACKFLUSH COSTING

Objective 6
Use backflush costing with a JIT production system.

Backflush costing has only two categories of costs: materials and conversion costs. Its unique feature is an absence of a work-in-process account. Actual material costs are entered into a materials inventory account, and actual labor and overhead costs are entered into a conversion costs account. Costs are transferred from these two temporary accounts directly into finished-goods inventories. Some backflush systems even eliminate the finished-goods inventory accounts and transfer costs directly to cost of goods sold, especially if goods are not kept in inventory but are shipped immediately on completion. Backflush systems assume that production is completed so soon after the application of conversion activities that balances in the conversion costs accounts always should remain near zero. Costs are transferred out almost immediately after being initially recorded.

EXAMPLE OF BACKFLUSH COSTING

Speaker Technology Inc. (STI) produces speakers for automobile stereo systems. STI recently introduced a JIT production system and backflush costing. Consider the July production for speaker model AX27. The standard material cost per unit of AX27 is $14, and the standard unit conversion cost is $21. During July, STI purchased materials for $5,600, incurred conversion costs of $8,400 (which included all labor costs and manufacturing overhead), and completed and sold 400 units of AX27.

Backflush costing is accomplished in three steps:

1. *Record actual materials and conversion costs.* For simplicity, we assume for now that actual materials and conversion costs were identical to the standard costs. As materials are purchased, backflush systems add their cost to the materials inventory account:

Materials inventory	5,600	
Accounts payable (or cash)		5,600
To record material purchases		

    Similarly, as direct labor and manufacturing overhead costs are incurred, they are added to the conversion-costs account:

Conversion costs	8,400	
Accrued wages and other accounts		8,400
To record conversion costs incurred		

2. *Apply costs to completed units.* When production is complete, costs from materials inventory and conversion-costs accounts are transferred directly to finished goods, based on the number of units completed and a standard cost of each unit:

Finished goods inventory (400 × $35)	14,000	
Materials inventory		5,600
Conversion costs		8,400
To record costs of completed production		

Because of short production cycle times, there is little lag between additions to the conversion-costs account and transfers to finished goods. The conversion-costs account, therefore, remains near zero.

3. *Record cost of goods sold during the period.* The standard cost of the items sold is transferred from finished goods inventory to cost of goods sold:

```
Cost of goods sold  .......................................  14,000
     Finished goods inventory  .............................          14,000
To record cost of 400 units sold @$35 per unit
```

Suppose completed units are delivered immediately to customers, so that finished goods inventories are negligible. Steps 2 and 3 can then be combined and the finished goods inventory account eliminated:

```
Cost of goods sold  .......................................  14,000
     Material inventory  ....................................          5,600
     Conversion costs  .....................................          8,400
```

What if actual costs added to the conversion-costs account do not equal the standard amounts that are transferred to finished-goods inventory? Variances are treated like overapplied or underapplied overhead. Backflush systems assume that conversion-costs account balances should be approximately zero at all times. Any remaining balance in the account at the end of an accounting period is charged to cost of goods sold. Suppose actual conversion costs for July had been $8,600 and the amount transferred to finished goods (that is, applied to the product) was $8,400. The $200 balance in the conversion-costs account at the end of the month would be written off to cost of goods sold:

```
Cost of goods sold  .......................................   200
     Conversion costs  .....................................           200
To recognize underapplied conversion costs
```

SUMMARY PROBLEM FOR YOUR REVIEW

PROBLEM

The most extreme (and simplest) version of backflush costing makes product costing entries at only one point. Suppose Speaker Technology Inc. (STI) had no materials inventory account (in addition to no work-in-process inventory account). Materials are not "purchased" until they are needed for production. Therefore, STI enters both material and conversion costs directly into its finished goods inventory account.

Prepare journal entries (without explanations) and T-accounts for July's production of | Required |
400 units. As given earlier, materials purchases totaled $5,600, and conversion costs were $8,400. Why might a company use this extreme type of backflush costing?

SOLUTION

In one step, material and conversion costs are applied to finished goods inventories:

```
Finished goods inventories  .................................  14,000
     Accounts payable  .....................................          5,600
     Wages payable and other accounts  .....................          8,400
```

	Finished Goods Inventories		Accounts Payable, Wages Payable, and Other Accounts	
Materials	5,600			5,600
Conversion costs	8,400			8,400

This example shows that backflush costing is simple and inexpensive. Backflush costing provides reasonably accurate product costs if (1) materials inventories are low (most likely because of JIT delivery schedules), and (2) production cycle times are short, so that at any time only inconsequential amounts of material costs or conversion costs have been incurred for products that are not yet complete.

Highlights to Remember

Explain the basic ideas underlying process costing and how they differ from job costing. Process costing is used for inventory costing when there is continuous mass production of like units. Process-cost systems accumulate costs by department (or process); each department has its own work-in-process account. Job-order cost systems differ because costs are accumulated and tracked by the individual job order.

Compute output in terms of equivalent units. The key concept in process costing is that of equivalent units, the number of fully completed units that could have been produced from the inputs applied.

Compute costs and prepare journal entries for the principal transactions in a process-costing system. There are five basic steps to process costing:

1. Summarize the flow of physical units.
2. Calculate output in terms of equivalent units.
3. Summarize the total costs to account for.
4. Calculate unit costs (Step 3 ÷ Step 2).
5. Apply costs to units completed and to units in the ending work in process.

Steps 3 and 5 provide the data for journal entries. These entries all involve the Work in Process accounts for the various departments (processes) producing products.

Demonstrate how the presence of beginning inventories affects the computation of unit costs under the weighted-average method. Process costing is complicated by the presence of beginning inventories. The weighted-average method includes the work done in previous periods on the current period's beginning inventory with work done in the current period to compute unit costs.

Demonstrate how the presence of beginning inventories affects the computation of unit costs under the first-in, first-out method. The FIFO method focuses on the work done only in the current period.

Use backflush costing with a JIT production system. Many companies with JIT production systems use backflush costing. Such systems have no work-in-process inventory account and apply costs to products only after the production process is complete.

Understand how a process-costing system tracks costs to products. A process-costing system tracks costs to products using broad averages. These averages represent equivalent unit costs incurred in each of several departments or processes. Unit costs from one department or process becomes the transferred-in material for downstream departments or processes until the product is finished.

Appendix 14: Hybrid Systems—Operation Costing

Job costing and process costing are actually extremes along a continuum of potential costing systems. Each company designs its own accounting system to fit its underlying production activities. Many companies use **hybrid-costing systems,** which are blends of ideas from both job costing and process costing. This appendix discusses one of many possible hybrid-costing systems, operation costing.

hybrid-costing system
An accounting system that is a blend of ideas from both job costing and process costing.

NATURE OF OPERATION COSTING

Operation costing is a hybrid-costing system often used in the batch or group manufacturing of goods that are similar but have enough individual characteristics to be distinct from one another. Such products—for example, personal computers, clothing, and semiconductors—are specifically identified by work orders and are often variations of a single design but require different operations to be completed. For instance, suits of clothes may differ, requiring various materials and hand operations. Similarly, a textile manufacturer may apply special chemical treatments (such as waterproofing) to some fabrics but not to others.

Operation costing may entail mass production, but there is sufficient product variety to have products scheduled in different batches or groups, each requiring a particular sequence of operations.

An *operation* is a standardized method or technique that is repetitively performed, regardless of the distinguishing features of the finished product. Examples include cutting, planing, sanding, painting, and chemical treating. Products proceed through the various operations in groups as specified by work orders or production orders. These work orders list the necessary direct materials and the step-by-step operations required to make the finished product.

Suppose a clothing manufacturer produces two lines of blazers. The wool blazers use better materials and undergo more operations than do the polyester blazers, as follows:

operation costing A hybrid-costing system often used in the batch or group manufacturing of goods that have some common characteristics plus some individual characteristics.

	Wool Blazers	Polyester Blazers
Direct materials	Wool Satin lining Bone buttons	Polyester Rayon lining Plastic buttons
Operations	1. Cutting cloth 2. Checking edges 3. Sewing body 4. Checking seams 5. — 6. Sewing collars and lapels by hand	1. Cutting cloth — 3. Sewing body — 5. Sewing collars and lapels by machine —

The costs of the blazers are compiled by work order. As in job costing, the direct materials—different for each work order—are specifically identified with the appropriate order. Conversion costs—direct labor plus factory overhead—are initially compiled for each operation. A cost driver, such as the number of units processed or minutes or seconds used, is identified for each operation, and a conversion cost per unit of cost driver activity is computed. Then conversion costs are applied to products in a manner similar to the application of factory overhead in a job-cost system.

EXAMPLE OF OPERATION-COSTING ENTRIES

Suppose our manufacturer has two work orders, one for 100 wool blazers and the other for 200 polyester blazers, as follows:

	Wool Blazers	Polyester Blazers
Number of blazers	100	200
Direct materials	$2,500	$3,100
Conversion costs		
1. Cutting cloth	600	1,200
2. Checking edges	300	—
3. Sewing body	500	1,000
4. Checking seams	600	—
5. Sewing collars and lapels by machine	—	800
6. Sewing collars and lapels by hand	700	—
Total manufacturing costs	$5,200	$6,100

Direct labor and factory overhead vanish as separate classifications in an operation-costing system. The sum of these costs is most frequently called conversion cost. The conversion cost is applied to products based on the company's budgeted rate for performing each operation. For example, suppose the conversion costs of operation 1, cutting cloth, are driven by machine hours and are budgeted for the year as follows:

$$\begin{array}{l}\text{budgeted rate for applying} \\ \text{conversion costs for} \\ \text{cutting cloth to product}\end{array} = \frac{\begin{array}{l}\text{budgeted conversion cost for cutting cloth} \\ \text{for the year (direct labor, power, repairs,} \\ \text{supplies, other factory overhead of this operation)}\end{array}}{\begin{array}{l}\text{budgeted machine-hours for the year for} \\ \text{cutting cloth}\end{array}}$$

$$\text{rate per machine-hours} = \frac{\$150,000 + \$450,000}{20,000 \text{ hours}} = \$30 \text{ per machine-hour}$$

As goods are manufactured, conversion costs are applied to the work orders by multiplying the $30 hourly rate times the number of machine-hours used for cutting cloth.

If 20 machine-hours are needed to cut the cloth for the 100 wool blazers, then the conversion cost involved is $600 (20 hours × $30 per hour). For the 200 polyester blazers, the conversion cost for cutting cloth is twice as much, $1,200 (40 hours × $30), because each blazer takes the same cutting time, and there are twice as many polyester blazers.

Summary journal entries for applying costs to the polyester blazers follow. (Entries for the wool blazers would be similar.)

The journal entry for the requisition of direct materials for the 200 polyester blazers is:

Work-in-process inventory (polyester blazers)	3,100	
Direct-materials inventory		3,100

Direct labor and factory overhead are subparts of a conversion-costs account in an operation-costing system. Suppose actual conversion costs of $3,150 were entered into the conversion-costs account:

Conversion costs	3,150	
Accrued payroll, accumulated depreciation,		
accounts payable, etc.		3,150

The application of conversion costs to products in operation costing is similar to the application of factory overhead in job-ordering costing. A budgeted rate per unit of cost-driver activity is used. To apply conversion costs to the 200 polyester blazers, the following summary entry is made for operations 1, 3, and 5 (cutting cloth, sewing body, and sewing collars and lapels by machine):

Work-in-process inventory (polyester blazers)	3,000	
Conversion costs, cutting cloth		1,200
Conversion costs, sewing body		1,000
Conversion costs, sewing collars		
and lapels by machine		800

After posting, work-in-process inventory has the following debit balance

Work-in-Process Inventory (polyester blazers)

Direct materials	3,100	
Conversion costs applied	3,000	
Balance	6,100	

As the blazers are completed, their cost is transferred to finished-goods inventory in the usual manner.

Any overapplication or underapplication of conversion costs is disposed of at the end of the year in the same manner as overapplied or underapplied overhead in a job-order costing system. In this case, conversion costs have been debited for actual cost of $3,150 and credited for costs applied of $3,000. The debit balance of $150 indicates that conversion costs are underapplied.

Accounting Vocabulary

backflush costing, p. 549
equivalent units, p. 540
first-in, first-out (FIFO)
  process-costing method,
  p. 545

hybrid-costing system,
  p. 553
operation costing, p. 553
transferred-in costs, p. 547

weighted-average (WA)
  process-costing method,
  p. 544

Fundamental Assignment Material

14-A1 Basic Process Costing

CellTel, Inc., produces cellular phones in large quantities. For simplicity, assume that the company has two departments, assembly and testing. The manufacturing costs in the Assembly Department during February were:

Direct materials added		$57,000
Conversion costs		
Direct labor	$50,000	
Factory overhead	40,000	90,000
Assembly costs to account for		$147,000

There was no beginning inventory of work in process. Suppose work on 19,000 phones was begun in the assembly department during February, but only 17,000 phones were fully completed. All the parts had been made or placed in process, but only half the labor had been completed for each of the phones still in process.

Required

1. Compute the equivalent units and unit costs for February.
2. Compute the costs of units completed and transferred to the Testing Department. Also compute the cost of the ending work in process. (For journal entries, see Problem 14-21.)

14-A2 Weighted-Average Process-Costing Method

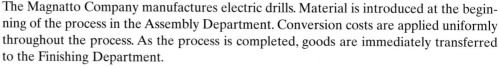

The Magnatto Company manufactures electric drills. Material is introduced at the beginning of the process in the Assembly Department. Conversion costs are applied uniformly throughout the process. As the process is completed, goods are immediately transferred to the Finishing Department.

Data for the Assembly Department for the month of July 19X8 follow:

Work in process, June 30: $175,500 (consisting of $138,000 materials and $37,500 conversion costs); 100% completed for direct materials, but only 25% completed for conversion costs	10,000 units
Units started during July	80,000 units
Units completed during July	70,000 units
Work in process, July 31: 100% completed for direct materials, but only 50% completed for conversion costs	20,000 units
Direct materials added during July	$852,000
Conversion costs added during July	$642,500

Required

1. Compute the total cost of goods transferred out of the Assembly Department during July.
2. Compute the total costs of the ending work in process. Prepare a production-cost report or a similar orderly tabulation of your work. Assume weighted-average product costing. (For the FIFO method and journal entries, see Problems 14-31 and 14-38.)

14-A3 Backflush Costing

Digital Controls, Inc., makes electronic thermostats for homes and offices. The Kansas City Division makes one product, Autotherm, which has a standard cost of $37, consisting of $22 of materials and $15 of conversion costs. In January, actual purchases of materials totaled $46,000, labor payroll costs were $11,000, and manufacturing overhead was $19,000. Completed output was 2,000 units.

The Kansas City Division uses a backflush-costing system that records costs in materials inventory and conversion costs accounts and applies costs to products at the time production is completed. There were no finished goods inventories on January 1 and 20 units on January 31.

Required

1. Prepare journal entries (without explanations) to record January's costs for the Kansas City Division. Include the purchase of materials, incurrence of labor and manufacturing overhead costs, application of product costs, and recognition of cost of goods sold.

2. Suppose January's actual manufacturing overhead costs had been $21,000 instead of $19,000. Prepare the journal entry to recognize underapplied conversion costs at the end of January.

14-B1 Basic Process Costing

Hassan Company produces digital watches in large quantities. The manufacturing costs of the Assembly Department were:

Direct materials added		$1,620,000
Conversion costs		
Direct labor	$475,000	
Factory overhead	275,000	750,000
Assembly costs to account for		$2,370,000

For simplicity, assume that this is a two-department company, assembly and finishing. There was no beginning work in process.

Suppose 900,000 units were begun in the Assembly Department. There were 600,000 units completed and transferred to the Finishing Department. The 300,000 units in ending work in process were fully completed regarding direct materials but half-completed regarding conversion costs.

Required

1. Compute the equivalent units and unit costs in the Assembly Department.

2. Compute the costs of units completed and transferred to the Finishing Department. Also compute the cost of the ending work in process in the Assembly Department.

14-B2 Weighted-Average Process-Costing Method

The Rainbow Paint Co. uses a process-costing system. Materials are added at the beginning of a particular process, and conversion costs are incurred uniformly. Work in process at the beginning of the month is 40% complete; at the end, 20%. One gallon of material makes one gallon of product. Data follow:

Beginning inventory	550 gal
Direct materials added	7,150 gal
Ending inventory	400 gal
Conversion costs incurred	$34,986
Cost of direct materials added	$65,340
Conversion costs, beginning inventory	$ 1,914
Cost of direct materials, beginning inventory	$ 3,190

Use the weighted-average method. Prepare a schedule of output in equivalent units and a schedule of application of costs to products. Show the cost of goods completed and cost of ending work in process. (For journal entries, see Problem 14-30. For the FIFO method, see Problem 14-37.)

14-B3 Backflush Costing

Audio Components, Inc. recently installed a backflush-costing system. One department makes 4-inch speakers with a standard cost as follows:

Materials	$10.00
Conversion costs	4.20
Total	$14.20

Speakers are scheduled for production only after orders are received, and products are shipped to customers immediately on completion. Therefore, no finished goods inventories are kept, and product costs are applied directly to cost of goods sold.

In October, 1,500 speakers were produced and shipped to customers. Materials were purchased at a cost of $16,000, and actual conversion costs (labor plus manufacturing overhead) of $6,300 were recorded.

1. Prepare journal entries to record October's costs for the production of 4-inch speakers.

2. Suppose October's actual conversion costs had been $5,900 instead of $6,300. Prepare a journal entry to recognize overapplied conversion costs.

Additional Assignment Material

QUESTIONS

14-1. Give three examples of industries where process-costing systems are probably used.

14-2. Give three examples of nonprofit organizations where process-costing systems are probably used.

14-3. What is the central product-costing problem in process costing?

14-4. "There are five key steps in process-cost accounting." What are they?

14-5. Identify the major distinction between the first two and the final three steps of the five major steps in accounting for process costs.

14-6. Suppose a university has 10,000 full-time students and 5,000 half-time students. Using the concept of equivalent units, compute the number of "full-time equivalent" students.

14-7. "Equivalent units are the work done to date." What method of process costing is being described?

14-8. Present an equation that describes the physical flow in process costing when there are beginning inventories in work in process.

14-9. "The beginning inventory is regarded as if it were a batch of goods separate and distinct from the goods started and completed by a process during the current period." What method of process costing is being described?

14-10. Why is "work done in the current period only" a key measurement of equivalent units?

14-11. "The total conversion costs are divided by the equivalent units for the work done to date." Does this quotation describe the weighted-average method or does it describe FIFO?

14-12. "Ordinarily, the differences in unit costs under FIFO and weighted-average methods are insignificant." Do you agree? Explain.

14-13. "FIFO process costing is helpful for planning and control even if it is not used for product costing." Do you agree? Explain.

14-14. How are transferred-in costs similar to direct costs? How are they different?

14-15. "Backflush-costing systems work only for companies using a JIT production system." Do you agree? Explain.

14-16. Explain what happens in a backflush-costing system when the amount of actual conversion cost in a period exceeds the amount applied to the products completed that period.

14-17. Give three examples of industries that probably use operation costing.

14-18. "In operation costing, average conversion costs are applied to products in a manner similar to the application of factory overhead in a job-cost system." Do you agree? Explain.

EXERCISES

14-19 Basic Process Costing

A department of Jamestown Textiles produces cotton fabric. All direct materials are introduced at the start of the process. Conversion costs are incurred uniformly throughout the process.

In April, there was no beginning inventory. Units started, completed, and transferred: 650,000. Units in process, April 30: 220,000. Each unit in ending work in process was 60% converted. Costs incurred during April: direct materials, $3,741,000; conversion costs, $860,200.

Required

1. Compute the total work done in equivalent units and the unit cost for April.
2. Compute the cost of units completed and transferred. Also compute the cost of units in ending work in process.

14-20 Uneven Flow

One department of Dallas Instruments Company manufactures basic hand-held calculators. Several materials are added at various stages of the process. The outer front shell and the carrying case, which represent 10% of the total material cost, are added at the final step of the assembly process. All other materials are considered to be "in process" by the time the calculator reaches a 50% stage of completion.

Seventy-four thousand calculators were started in production during 19X8. At year-end, 6,000 calculators were in various stages of completion, but all of them were beyond the 50% stage and, on the average, they were regarded as being 70% completed.

The following costs were incurred during the year: direct materials, $205,520; conversion costs, $397,100.

Required

1. Prepare a schedule of physical units and equivalent units.
2. Tabulate the unit costs, cost of goods completed, and cost of ending work in process.

14-21 Journal Entries

Refer to the data in Problem 14-A1. Prepare summary journal entries for the use of direct materials, direct labor, and factory overhead applied. Also prepare a journal entry for the transfer of goods completed and transferred. Show the postings to the Work-in-Process account.

14-22 Journal Entries

Refer to the data in Problem 14-B1. Prepare summary journal entries for the use of direct materials, direct labor, and factory overhead applied. Also prepare a journal entry for the transfer of goods completed and transferred. Show the posting to the Work-in-Process—Assembly Department account.

14-23 Physical Units

Fill in the unknowns in physical units:

	Case	
Flow of Production	*A*	*B*
Work in process, beginning inventory	1,500	4,000
Started	6,500	?
Completed and transferred	?	8,000
Work in process, ending inventory	2,000	3,300

14-24 Flow of Production, FIFO

Fill in the unknowns in physical or equivalent units:

	Physical	Equivalent Units	
Flow of Production	**Units**	*Direct Materials*	*Conversion Costs*
Beginning work in process	1,000 (50%)*		
Started	?		
To account for	36,000		
Completed and			
transferred out	33,000	33,000	33,000
Ending work in process	? (40%)*	?	?
Units accounted for	?		
Work done to date		?	?
Equivalent units in			
beginning inventory		?	?
Work done in current			
period only		?	?

*Degree of completion of conversion costs at dates of inventory. Assume that all materials are added at the beginning of the process.

14-25 Equivalent Units

The Preparation Department of Garcia Paints, Inc., had the following flow of latex paint production (in gallons) for the month of April:

Gallons completed	
From work in process on April 1	5,000
From April production	25,000
	30,000

Direct materials are added at the beginning of the process. Gallons of work in process at April 30 were 10,000. The work in process at April 1 was 30% complete as to conversion costs, and the work in process at April 30 was 50% complete as to conversion costs.

Required

What are the equivalent units (gallons) of production for (a) direct materials and (b) conversion costs for the month of April using the FIFO method?

14-26 Equivalent Units, FIFO

Fill in the unknowns:

Flow of Production in Units	(Step 1) Physical Units	(Step 2) Equivalent Units	
		Direct Materials	Conversion Costs
Work in process, beginning inventory	20,000 *		
Started	45,000		
To account for	65,000		
Completed and transferred out	?	?	?
Work in process, ending inventory	2,000 †	?	?
Units accounted for	65,000		
Work done to date		?	?
Less: Equivalent units of work from previous periods included in beginning inventory		?	?
Work done in current period only (FIFO method)		?	?

*Degree of completion: direct materials, 80%; conversion costs, 40%.

†Degree of completion: direct materials, 40%; conversion costs, 10%.

14-27 Compute Equivalent Units

Consider the following data for 19X8:

	Physical Units
Started in 19X8	80,000
Completed in 19X8	90,000
Ending inventory, work in process	10,000
Beginning inventory, work in process	20,000

The beginning inventory was 80% complete regarding direct materials and 40% complete regarding conversion costs. The ending inventory was 20% complete regarding direct materials and 30% complete regarding conversion costs.

Prepare a schedule of equivalent units for the work done to date and the work done during 19X8 only.

Required

14-28 FIFO and Unit Direct-Material Costs

The Fujita Company uses the FIFO process-cost method. Consider the following for July:

- Beginning inventory, 15,000 units, 70% completed regarding direct materials, which cost ¥89,250,000
- Units completed, 80,000
- Cost of materials placed in process during July, ¥580,000,000
- Ending inventory, 5,000 units, 60% completed regarding materials

Compute the direct-material cost per equivalent unit for the work done in July only.

Required

14-29 FIFO Method, Conversion Cost

Given the following information, compute the conversion cost per pound for the month of February for the Benjamin Company, using the FIFO process-costing method. Show details of your calculation.

- Pounds completed, 45,000
- Conversion cost in beginning inventory, $30,000
- Beginning inventory, 10,000 pounds with 75% of conversion cost
- Ending inventory, 15,000 pounds with 30% of conversion cost
- Conversion costs put into production in February, $222,600

14-30 Journal Entries

Refer to the data in Problem 14-B2. Prepare summary journal entries for the use of direct materials and conversion costs. Also prepare a journal entry for the transfer of goods completed, assuming that the goods are transferred to another department.

14-31 Journal Entries

Refer to the data in Problem 14-A2. Prepare summary journal entries for the use of direct materials and conversion costs. Also prepare a journal entry for the transfer of the goods completed and transferred from the Assembly Department to the Finishing Department.

PROBLEMS

BUSINESS FIRST   www.prenhall.com/phlip

14-32 Process Costing at Nally and Gibson

Nally and Gibson produces crushed limestone used in highway construction, among other products. To produce the crushed limestone, the company starts with limestone rocks from its quarry in Georgetown, Kentucky and puts the rocks through a crushing process. Suppose that on May 1, Nally and Gibson has 24 tons of rock (75% complete) in the crushing process. The cost of that beginning work-in-process inventory was $6,000. During May, the company added 288 tons of rock from its quarry, and at the end of the month, 15 tons remained in process, on average one-third complete. The cost of rocks from the quarry for the last five months has been $120 per ton. Labor and overhead cost during May in the rock crushing process were $40,670. Nally and Gibson uses weighted-average process costing.

Required

1. Compute the cost per ton of crushed rock for production in May.
2. Compute the cost of the work in process inventory at the end of May.
3. Suppose the flexible budget for labor and overhead was $16,000 plus $80 per ton. Evaluate the control of overhead and labor costs during May. ■

14-33 Process and Activity-Based Costing

Consider the potato chip production process at a company such as Frito-Lay. Frito-Lay uses a continuous flow technology that is suited for high volumes of product. At the Plano, Texas, facility, between six and seven thousand pounds of potato chips are produced each hour. The plant operates 24 hours a day. It takes 30 minutes to completely produce a bag of potato chips from the raw potato to the packed end-product.

Required

1. What product and process characteristics of potato chips dictate the cost accounting system used? Describe the costing system best suited to Frito-Lay.
2. What product and process characteristics dictate the use of an activity-based-costing system? What implications does this have for Frito-Lay?

3. When beginning inventories are present, product costing becomes more complicated. Estimate the relative magnitude of beginning inventories at Frito-Lay compared to total production. What implication does this have for the costing system?

14-34 Nonprofit Process Costing

The IRS must process millions of income tax returns yearly. When the taxpayer sends in a return, documents such as withholding statements and checks are matched against the data submitted. Then various other inspections of the data are conducted. Of course, some returns are more complicated than others, so the expected time allowed to process a return is geared to an "average" return.

Some work-measurement experts have been closely monitoring the processing at a particular branch. They are seeking ways to improve productivity.

Suppose three million returns were received on April 15. On April 22, the work-measurement teams discovered that all supplies (punched cards, inspection check-sheets, and so on) had been affixed to the returns, but 40% of the returns still had to undergo a final inspection. The other returns were fully completed.

Required

1. Suppose the final inspection represents 25% of the overall processing time in this process. Compute the total work done in terms of equivalent units.
2. The materials and supplies consumed were $600,000. For these calculations, materials and supplies are regarded just like direct materials. The conversion costs were $4,725,000. Compute the unit costs of materials and supplies and of conversion.
3. Compute the cost of the tax returns not yet completely processed.

14-35 Two Materials

The following data pertain to the Blending Department at Pennsylvania Chemicals for April:

Units	
Work in process, March 31	0
Units started	60,000
Completed and transferred	
to finishing department	40,000
Costs	
Materials	
Plastic compound	$300,000
Softening compound	$ 80,000
Conversion costs	$240,000

The plastic compound is introduced at the start of the process, while the softening compound is added when the product reaches an 80% stage of completion. Conversion costs are incurred uniformly throughout the process.

The ending work in process is 40% completed for conversion costs. None of the units in process reached the 80% stage of completion.

Required

1. Compute the equivalent units and unit costs for April.
2. Compute the total cost of units completed and transferred to finished goods. Also compute the cost of the ending work in process.

14-36 Materials and Cartons

A Birmingham, England, company manufactures and sells small portable tape recorders. Business is booming. Several materials are added at various stages in the assembly department. Costs are accounted for on a process-cost basis. The end of the process involves conducting a final inspection and adding a cardboard carton.

The final inspection requires 5% of the total processing time. All materials, besides the carton, are added by the time the recorders reach an 80% stage of completion of conversion.

There were no beginning inventories. One hundred fifty thousand recorders were started in production during 19X6. At the end of the year, which was not a busy time, 5,000 recorders were in various stages of completion. All the ending units in work in process were at the 95% stage. They awaited final inspection and being placed in cartons.

Total direct materials consumed in production, except for cartons, cost £2,250,000. Cartons used cost £290,000. Total conversion costs were £1,198,000.

Required

1. Present a schedule of physical units, equivalent units, and unit costs of direct materials, cartons, and conversion costs.

2. Present a summary of the cost of goods completed and the cost of ending work in process.

14-37 FIFO Computations

Refer to Problem 14-B2. Using FIFO, answer the same questions.

14-38 FIFO Methods

Refer to Problem 14-A2. Using FIFO costing, answer the same questions.

14-39 Backflush Costing

Adirondak Meter Company manufactures a variety of measuring instruments. One product is an altimeter used by hikers and mountain climbers. Adirondak adopted a JIT philosophy with an automated, computer-controlled, robotic production system. The company schedules production only after an order is received, materials and parts arrive just as they are needed, the production cycle time for altimeters is less than one day, and completed units are packaged and shipped as part of the production cycle.

Adirondak's backflush-costing system has only three accounts related to production of altimeters: materials and parts inventory, conversion costs, and finished goods inventory. At the beginning of April (as at the beginning of every month), each of the three accounts had a balance of zero. Following are the April transactions related to the production of altimeters:

Materials and parts purchased	$287,000
Conversion costs incurred	$ 92,000
Altimeters produced	11,500 units

The budgeted (or standard) cost for one altimeter is $24 for materials and parts and $8 for conversion costs.

Required

1. Prepare summary journal entries for the production of altimeters in April.

2. Compute the cost of goods sold for April. Explain any assumptions you make.

3. Suppose the actual conversion costs incurred during April were $94,600 instead of $92,000, and all other facts were as given. Prepare the additional journal entry that would be required at the end of April. Explain why the entry was necessary.

14-40 Basic Operation Costing

Study Appendix 14. Oak Furniture, Inc. manufactures a variety of wooden chairs. The company's manufacturing operations and costs applied to products for June were:

	Cutting	Assembly	Finishing
Direct labor	$ 60,000	$30,000	$ 96,000
Factory overhead	115,500	37,500	156,000

Three styles of chairs were produced in June. The quantities and direct-material costs were:

Style	Quantity	Direct Materials
Standard	6,000	$108,000
Deluxe	4,500	171,000
Unfinished	3,000	66,000

Each unit, regardless of style, required the same cutting and assembly operations. The unfinished chairs, as the name implies, had no finishing operations whatsoever. Standard and deluxe styles required the same finishing operations.

Required

1. Tabulate the total conversion costs of each operation, the total units produced, and the conversion cost per unit.

2. Tabulate the total costs, the units produced, and the cost per unit.

14-41 Operation Costing with Ending Work in Process

Study Appendix 14. Sonar Instruments, Inc. uses three operations in sequence to make two models of its depth finders for sport fishing. Production information for March follows:

	Production Orders	
	For 1,000 Standard Depth Finders	*For 1,000 Deluxe Depth Finders*
Direct materials (actual costs applied)	$57,000	$100,000
Conversion costs (predetermined costs applied on the basis of machine-hours used)		
Operation 1	19,000	19,000
Operation 2	?	?
Operation 3	—	15,000
Total manufacturing costs applied	$?	$?

1. Operation 2 was highly automated. Product costs depended on a budgeted application rate for conversion costs, based on machine-hours. The budgeted costs for 19X8 were $220,000 direct labor and $580,000 factory overhead. Budgeted machine-hours were 20,000. Each depth finder required six minutes of time in operation 2. Compute the costs of processing 1,000 depth finders in operation 2.

2. Compute the total manufacturing costs of 1,000 depth finders and the cost per standard depth finder and deluxe depth finder.

3. Suppose that at the end of the year, 500 standard depth finders were in process through operation 1 only and 600 deluxe depth finders were in process through operation 2 only. Compute the cost of the ending work-in-process inventory. Assume that no direct materials are applied in operation 2, but that $10,000 of the $100,000 direct-material cost of the deluxe depth finders are applied to each 1,000 depth finders processed in operation 3.

COLLABORATIVE LEARNING EXERCISE

14-42 Job, Process, and Hybrid Costing
Form groups of three to six students. For each of the following production processes, assess whether a job-cost, process-cost, or hybrid-cost system is most likely to be used to determine the cost of the product or service. Also, explain why you think that system is most logical. (This can be done by individuals, but it is a much richer experience when done as a group, because the knowledge and judgment of several students interact to produce a much better analysis than a single student can produce.)

a. Production of Cheerios by General Mills.

b. Production of a 4-Runner sport utility vehicle by Toyota.

c. Processing an application for life insurance by Prudential.

d. Production of a couch by Ethan Allan.

e. Building of a bridge by Kiewit Construction Co.

f. Production of gasoline by Chevron.

g. Production of 200 copies of a 140-page course packet by Kinkos.

h. Production of a superferry by Todd Shipyards.

15

OVERHEAD APPLICATION: VARIABLE AND ABSORPTION COSTING

LA Darling Store Fixtures designs, makes, and installs displays such as this one at Best Buy Computers.

Learning Objectives

When you have finished studying this chapter, you should be able to

1 Construct an income statement using the variable-costing approach.

2 Construct an income statement using the absorption-costing approach.

3 Compute the production-volume variance and show how it should appear in the income statement.

4 Differentiate among the three alternative cost bases of an absorption-costing system: actual, normal, and standard.

5 Explain why a company might prefer to use a variable-costing approach.

6 Identify the two methods for disposing of the standard cost variances at the end of a year and give the rationale for each.

7 **Understand how product-costing systems affect operating income.**

Recall the last time you shopped in one of the following stores—Wal Mart, JC Penney, Kmart, Dillards, Best Buy, T.J. Maxx. Do you remember anything about the store fixtures? Chances are, the answer is "no." Store fixtures such as shelving, counters, garment racks, and displays are an important part of the merchandising programs of all leading merchandise, discount, specialty, and department stores, but not many people are aware of them when shopping. One company that is an industry leader in store fixtures is L.A. Darling Store Fixtures.

L.A. Darling Store Fixtures works in partnership with major retailers such as Wal-Mart to design, manufacture, and install store fixtures. Darling is a member of the Marmon Group, an international association of more than 60 manufacturing and service companies with annual sales in excess of $6 billion.

Recently, when a major retailer undertook an aggressive growth program, it selected Darling to meet its fixturing needs. According to Ray Watson, Controller, "One of the advantages Darling offers companies is its large production capacity." But while this gives the company a competitive advantage, accounting for capacity costs, most of which are fixed manufacturing overhead, is a real challenge. How should these fixed overhead costs be treated for product costing and income determination purposes? Should Darling consider these costs when a manager's performance is evaluated? Watson explains that the absorption approach is required for external reporting, but provides little value for measuring customer profitability. As a result, the contribution approach, combined with activity-based costing, is used by Darling for decision making and performance evaluation purposes.

The evaluation of managers is often based at least partly on the income of the organizational segment they manage. Therefore, managers strive to make their performance look good by making decisions that increase income. But how should we measure income? Accountants make many judgments when measuring income, and one of the most important is choosing the appropriate method for calculating product costs. Some managers think product costing is a subject of interest only to accountants. However, when they realize that product costs affect their evaluations, they quickly begin to pay attention to the determination of product costs. Only by knowing what influences product costs will they be able to predict how their decisions will affect income and hence their evaluations.

In the preceding three chapters, we concentrated on how an accounting system accumulates costs by departments or activities and applies costs to the products or services that are produced by those departments or activities. This chapter focuses on two major variations of product costing: variable costing and absorption costing. Note that although we use a standard product-costing system here for illustrative purposes, these variations can be used in nonstandard product-costing systems too.

VARIABLE VERSUS ABSORPTION COSTING

ACCOUNTING FOR FIXED MANUFACTURING OVERHEAD

Two major methods of product costing are compared in this chapter: *variable costing* (the contribution approach) and *absorption costing* (the functional, full-costing, or traditional approach). These methods differ in only one respect: Fixed manufacturing overhead is excluded from the cost of products under variable costing but is included in the cost of products under absorption costing. In other words, variable costing signifies that fixed factory overhead is not inventoried. In contrast, absorption costing indicates that inventory values include fixed factory overhead.

As Exhibit 15-1 shows, a variable-costing system treats fixed manufacturing overhead (fixed factory overhead) as a period cost to be immediately charged against sales—not as a product unexpired cost to be counted as inventory and charged against sales as cost of goods sold when the inventory is sold. Note that the only difference between variable and absorption costing is the accounting for fixed manufacturing overhead.[1]

Absorption costing is more widely used than variable costing. Why? Because neither the public accounting profession nor the U.S. IRS approves of variable costing for external-reporting or tax purposes. Therefore, all U.S. firms use absorption costing for their reports to shareholders and tax authorities.

However, the growing use of the contribution approach in performance measurement and cost analysis has led to increasing use of variable costing for internal-reporting purposes. Over half the major firms in the United States use variable costing for some internal reporting, and nearly a quarter use it as the primary internal format. For example, the Muncie, Indiana, plant of Borg-Warner Automotive Diversified Transmission Products Corporation recently changed its product-line performance reporting from an absorption-costing approach to variable costing. Why? Because variable costing "links

---

[1] *Variable costing is sometimes called* direct costing. *However, variable costing is a more descriptive term, so we will use it exclusively in this text.*

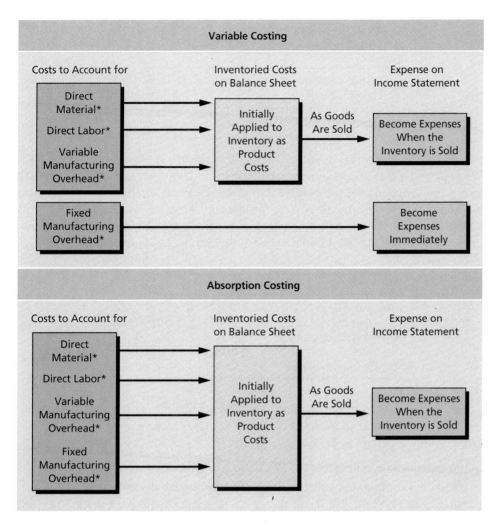

Variable Costing

Costs to Account for	Inventoried Costs on Balance Sheet		Expense on Income Statement
Direct Material* Direct Labor* Variable Manufacturing Overhead*	Initially Applied to Inventory as Product Costs	As Goods Are Sold	Become Expenses When the Inventory is Sold
Fixed Manufacturing Overhead*			Become Expenses Immediately

Absorption Costing

Costs to Account for	Inventoried Costs on Balance Sheet		Expense on Income Statement
Direct Material* Direct Labor* Variable Manufacturing Overhead* Fixed Manufacturing Overhead*	Initially Applied to Inventory as Product Costs	As Goods Are Sold	Become Expenses When the Inventory is Sold

*As goods are manufactured, the costs are "applied" to inventory, usually via the use of unit costs.

Exhibit 15-1

Comparison of Flow of Costs

manufacturing performance more closely with measures of that performance by removing the impact of changing inventory levels from financial results."

Until the last decade or two, use of variable costing for internal reporting was expensive. It requires information to be processed two ways, one for external reporting and one for internal reporting. The increasing use and decreasing cost of computers has reduced the added cost of a variable-costing system. Most managers no longer face the question of whether to invest in a separate variable-costing system. Rather, they simply choose a variable-costing or absorption-costing format for reports. Many well-designed accounting systems used today can produce either format.

FACTS FOR ILLUSTRATION

So you can see exactly how these two product costing systems work, we will use the Greenberg Company as an illustration. The Greenberg Company makes a replacement part (a plastic ring) for large plastic injection molding machines. Each machine requires four new rings a year. In 19X8 and 19X9, the company had the following standard costs for production of rings:

Direct material	$1.30
Direct labor	1.50
Variable manufacturing overhead	.20
Standard variable costs per ring	$3.00

Fixed manufacturing overhead (fixed factory overhead) is budgeted at $150,000. Expected (or budgeted) production in each year is 150,000 rings, and the sales price is $5 per ring. For simplicity, we will assume that the single cost driver for the $.20 per ring variable-manufacturing overhead is rings produced.[2] Also, we will assume that both budgeted and actual selling and administrative expenses are $65,000 yearly fixed cost plus sales commissions at 5% of dollar sales. Actual product quantities are:

	19X8	19X9
In units (rings)		
Opening inventory	—	30,000
Production	170,000	140,000
Sales	140,000	160,000
Ending inventory	30,000	10,000

There are no variances from the standard variable manufacturing costs, and the actual fixed manufacturing overhead incurred is exactly $150,000 each year.

Based on this information, we can

1. Prepare income statements for 19X8 and 19X9 under variable costing.
2. Prepare income statements for 19X8 and 19X9 under absorption costing.
3. Show a reconciliation of the difference in operating income for 19X8, 19X9, and the two years as a whole.

VARIABLE-COSTING METHOD

Objective 1

Construct an income statement using the variable-costing approach.

We begin by preparing income statements under variable costing. The variable-costing statement shown in Exhibit 15-2 has a familiar contribution-approach format, the same format introduced in Chapter 4. The only new characteristic of Exhibit 15-2 is the presence of a detailed calculation of cost of goods sold, which is affected by changes in the beginning and ending inventories. (In contrast, the income statements in Chapters 4 through 9 assumed that there were no changes in the beginning and ending inventories.)

The costs of the product are accounted for by applying all variable manufacturing costs to the goods produced, at a rate of $3 per unit (ring); thus inventories are valued at standard variable costs. In contrast, fixed manufacturing costs are not applied to any products but are regarded as expenses in the period they are incurred.

Before reading on, be sure to trace the facts from our Greenberg example to the presentation in Exhibit 15-2, step by step. Note that both variable cost of goods sold and variable selling and administrative expenses are deducted in computing the contribution margin. However, variable selling and administrative expenses are not inventoriable. They are affected only by the level of sales, not by changes in inventory.

---

[2]*Increasingly, companies are using activity analysis to identify relevant cost drivers for manufacturing overhead. The use of cost drivers other than units of production does not affect the basic principles illustrated in the examples that follow.*

Exhibit 15-2

Greenberg Company
Comparative Income Statements Using Variable Costing
Years 19X8 and 19X9 (thousands of dollars)

		19X8	19X9
Sales, 140,000 and 160,000 rings, respectively	(1)	$700	$800
Variable expenses:			
Variable manufacturing cost of goods sold			
Opening inventory, at standard variable costs of $3		$ —	$ 90
Add: variable cost of goods manufactured at standard, 170,000 and 140,000 rings, respectively		510	420
Available for sale, 170,000 rings in each year		$510	$510
Deduct: ending inventory, at standard variable cost of $3		90*	30†
Variable manufacturing cost of goods sold		$420	$480
Variable selling expenses, at 5% of dollar sales		35	40
Total variable expenses	(2)	455	520
Contribution margin	(3) = (1) − (2)	$245	$280
Fixed expenses:			
Fixed factory overhead		$150	$150
Fixed selling and administrative expenses		65	65
Total fixed expenses	(4)	215	215
Operating income, variable costing	(3) − (4)	$ 30	$ 65

*30,000 rings × $3 = $90,000.
†10,000 rings × $3 = $30,000.

ABSORPTION-COSTING METHOD

Exhibit 15-3 shows the standard absorption-costing framework. As you can see, it differs from the variable-costing format in three ways.

First, the unit product cost used for computing cost of goods sold is $4, not $3. Why? Because fixed manufacturing overhead of $1 is added to the $3 variable manufacturing cost. The $1 of fixed manufacturing overhead applied to each unit is the **fixed-overhead rate.** It is determined by dividing the budgeted fixed overhead by the expected cost-driver activity, in this case volume of production, for the budget period:

$$\text{fixed-overhead rate} = \frac{\text{budgeted fixed manufacturing overhead}}{\text{expected volume of production}} = \frac{\$150,000}{150,000 \text{ units}} = \$1$$

Second, fixed factory overhead does not appear as a separate line in an absorption-costing income statement. Instead, the fixed factory overhead is included in two places: as part of the cost of goods sold and as a production-volume variance.[3] A **production-volume variance** (which is explained further in the next section of this chapter) appears whenever actual production deviates from the expected volume of production used in computing the fixed overhead rate:

production-volume variance = (actual volume − expected volume) × fixed-overhead rate

fixed-overhead rate The amount of fixed manufacturing overhead applied to each unit of production. It is determined by dividing the budgeted fixed overhead by the expected volume of production for the budget period.

production-volume variance A variance that appears whenever actual production deviates from the expected volume of production used in computing the fixed overhead rate. It is calculated as (actual volume − expected volume) × fixed-overhead rate.

---

[3] In general, this will be a cost-driver activity variance. In our example, production volume is the only cost driver, so it can be called a production-volume variance.

Exhibit 15-3

Greenberg Company
Comparative Income Statements Using Absorption Costing
Years 19X8 and 19X9 (thousands of dollars)

	19X8		19X9	
Sales		$700		$800
Cost of goods sold:				
Opening inventory, at standard absorption cost of $4*	$ —		$120	
Cost of goods manufactured at standard of $4	680		560	
Available for sale	680		680	
Deduct: ending inventory at standard absorption cost of $4	120		40	
Cost of goods sold, at standard		560		640
Gross profit at standard		140		160
Production-volume variance†		20F		10U
Gross margin or gross profit, at "actual"		160		150
Selling and administrative expenses		100		105
Operating income		$ 60		$ 45

* Variable cost $3
   Fixed cost ($150,000 ÷ 150,000)   1
   Standard absorption cost $4
†Computation of production-volume variance based on expected volume of
   production of 150,000 rings:

19X8	$20,000 F	$(170,000 − 150,000) × 1
19X9	10,000 U	$(140,000 − 150,000) × 1
Two years together	$10,000 F	$(310,000 − 300,000) × 1

  U = Unfavorable. F = Favorable.

Objective 2
Construct an income statement using the absorption-costing approach.

Finally, the format for an absorption-costing income statement separates costs into the major categories of *manufacturing* and *nonmanufacturing*. In contrast, a variable-costing income statement separates costs into the major categories of fixed and variable. In an absorption-costing statement, revenue less *manufacturing* cost (both fixed and variable) is *gross profit* or *gross margin*. In a variable-costing statement, revenue less all *variable* costs (both manufacturing and nonmanufacturing) is the *contribution margin*. This difference is illustrated by a condensed comparison of 19X9 income statements (in thousands of dollars):

Variable Costing		**Absorption Costing**	
Revenue	$800	Revenue	$800
All variable costs	520	All manufacturing costs*	650
Contribution margin	280	Gross margin	150
All fixed costs	215	All nonmanufacturing costs	105
Operating income	$ 65	Operating income	$ 45

*Standard absorption cost of goods sold plus production-volume variance.

Despite the importance of such differences in most industries, more and more firms are not concerned with the choice between variable and absorption costing. Why? Because they have implemented just-in-time (JIT) production methods (see Chapter 4) and sharply reduced inventory levels. There is no difference between

Variable Costing at Northern Telecom

Northern Telecom, the $15 billion Canadian designer and manufacturer of telecommunications equipment, gradually came to understand that its standard absorption costing income statement did not provide the information that managers needed. The company also realized that the problem was one of format more than of substance. The information needed for a more meaningful income statement was in the accounting system, but the traditional reported income statement did not present the information in the most useful way. Therefore, Northern Telecom's accountants adopted a "variable costing" approach to the income statement.

Statutory and regulatory reporting requirements did not allow Northern Telecom to completely abandon absorption costing. The company's solution left the top line—revenue—and the bottom line—earnings before tax—unchanged. But everything in between was reported differently, in the following format:

Revenue
   Product cost
Product margin
   Manufacturing/operational costs
   Inventory provisions
   New product introduction
   Selling and marketing
Direct margin
   Administrative cost
   Other operating (income) expense
Operating profit
   Corporate assessments
   Other nonoperating (income) expense
Earnings before balance sheet adjustments
   Balance sheet adjustment
Earnings before tax

This format represents an extreme application of variable costing. Only direct-material costs are considered product costs. All other costs, including direct labor and variable overhead, are period costs that are charged to expense when incurred, not added to inventory. For example, direct labor is part of manufacturing costs. The amount charged in any period is the amount actually incurred that period, regardless of whether the labor is related to goods sold or those still in inventory. Four measures of "profit" are used by managers: product margin (to measure the value added), direct margin (to measure results of product production and sales), operating profit (to measure total results of operations), and earnings before balance sheet adjustments (to measure effect on companywide profits).

The main difference between the old absorption-costing system and the new system is that the new system expenses *all* costs except material costs, while the old system capitalized a portion of them. Reconciling the two systems was an accounting problem, unrelated to operating the business. Therefore, a final line was added to the income statement to provide a reconciliation—balance sheet adjustment. This represents the difference between the absorption and variable costing statements, as needed for statutory and regulatory reporting, but it can be ignored by managers.

Northern Telecom's efforts illustrate two important points. First, it is possible to adapt accounting methods to meet the specific needs of managers. Second, companies often do not have to choose between absorption and variable costing—either format can be produced by the same basic accounting system.

Source: From P. Sharman, "Time to Re-examine the P&L," *CMA Magazine*, September 1991, pp. 22–25.

variable-costing and absorption-costing income if the inventory level does not change, and companies with little inventory generally experience only insignificant changes in inventory.

FIXED OVERHEAD AND ABSORPTION COSTS OF PRODUCT

All three differences between variable- and absorption-costing formats arise solely because variable costing treats fixed manufacturing overhead differently from absorption costing. In this and subsequent sections, we explore how to account for factory overhead in an absorption-costing system.

VARIABLE AND FIXED UNIT COSTS

Continuing our example of the Greenberg Company, we begin by comparing (1) the manufacturing overhead costs in the flexible budget used for departmental budgeting and control purposes with (2) the manufacturing overhead costs applied to products under an absorption-costing system. To stress the basic assumptions behind absorption costing, we will also split manufacturing overhead into variable and fixed components. (Most real absorption-costing systems do not make such a split.)

Consider the following graphs of *variable-overhead costs*:

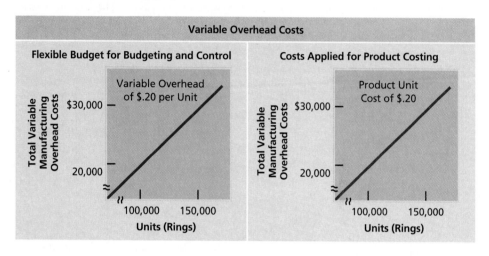

Note that the two graphs are identical. The expected variable-overhead costs from the flexible budget are the same as the variable-overhead costs applied to the products. Both budgeted and applied variable overhead are $.20 per ring. Each time 1,000 additional rings are produced, we expect to incur an additional $200 of variable overhead, and $200 of variable-overhead cost is added to the inventory account for rings. The variable costs used for budgeting and control are the same as those used for product costing.

In contrast, the graph for *applied fixed-overhead costs* differs from that for the flexible budget:

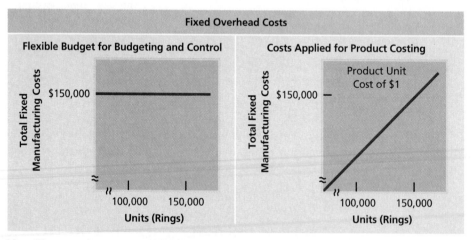

Note: These graphs are not to the same scale as the preceding graphs.

The flexible budget for fixed overhead is a lump-sum budgeted amount of $150,000. It is unaffected by volume. In contrast, the applied fixed cost depends on actual volume:

$$\text{fixed cost applied} = \text{actual volume} \times \text{fixed-overhead rate}$$
$$= \text{units produced} \times \$1$$

Suppose actual volume equals the expected volume of 150,000 rings. Applied fixed overhead would be 150,000 rings × $1 per ring = $150,000, the same as the flexible-budget amount. However, whenever actual volume differs from expected volume, the costs used for budgeting and control differ from those used for product costing. For budgeting and control purposes, managers use the actual cost behavior pattern for fixed costs. In contrast, as the graphs indicate, the absorption product-costing approach treats these fixed costs as though they had a variable-cost behavior pattern. The difference between applied and budgeted fixed overhead is the production-volume variance.

NATURE OF PRODUCTION-VOLUME VARIANCE

The *production-volume variance* can be calculated as follows:

production-volume variance = applied fixed overhead − budgeted fixed overhead
= (actual volume × fixed-overhead rate)
− (expected volume × fixed-overhead rate)

or

production-volume variance = (actual volume − expected volume)
× fixed overhead rate

Objective 3
Compute the production-volume variance and show how it should appear in the income statement.

In practice, the production-volume variance is usually called simply the **volume variance.** We use the term production-volume variance because it is a more precise description of the fundamental nature of the variance.

A production-volume variance arises when the actual production volume achieved does not coincide with the expected volume of production used as a denominator for computing the fixed-overhead rate for product-costing purposes:

volume variance A common name for production-volume variance.

1. When expected production volume and actual production volume are identical, there is no production-volume variance.

2. When actual volume is less than expected volume, the production-volume variance is unfavorable because usage of facilities is less than expected and fixed overhead is underapplied. It is measured in Exhibit 15-3 for 19X9 as follows:

   (actual volume − expected volume)
   × budgeted fixed-overhead rate = production-volume variance
   (140,000 hours − 150,000 hours) × $1 = −$10,000 or $10,000 U

   or

   budget minus applied = production-volume variance
   $150,000 − $140,000 = $10,000 U

   The $10,000 unfavorable production-volume variance increases the manufacturing costs shown on the income statement. Why? Recall that $150,000 of fixed manufacturing cost was incurred, but only $140,000 was applied to inventory. Therefore only $140,000 will be charged as expense when the inventory is sold. But all $150,000 must be charged sometime, so the extra $10,000 is an added expense in the current income statement.

3. When actual volume exceeds expected volume, as was the case in 19X8, the production-volume variance is favorable because use of facilities is better than expected, and fixed overhead is overapplied:

   production-volume variance = (170,000 units − 150,000 units) × $1 = $20,000 F

   In this case, $170,000 will be charged through inventory. Because actual costs of only $150,000 are incurred, future expenses will be overstated by $20,000. Therefore, current period expenses are reduced by the $20,000 favorable variance.

The production-volume variance is the conventional measure of the cost of departing from the level of activity originally used to set the fixed-overhead rate.[4] Most companies consider production-volume variances to be beyond immediate control, although sometimes a manager responsible for volume has to do some explaining or investigating. Sometimes, failure to reach the expected volume is caused by idleness because of disappointing total sales, poor production scheduling, unusual machine breakdowns, shortages of skilled workers, strikes, storms, and the like.

There is no production-volume variance for variable overhead. The concept of production-volume variance arises for fixed overhead because of the conflict between accounting for control (by flexible budgets) and accounting for product costing (by application rates). Note again that the fixed-overhead budget serves the control purpose, whereas the development of a product-costing rate results in the treatment of fixed overhead as if it were a variable cost.

Above all, remember that fixed costs are simply not divisible as variable costs are. Rather, they come in big chunks and are related to the provision of big chunks of production or sales capability, not to the production or sale of a single unit of product.

SELECTION OF EXPECTED ACTIVITY LEVEL FOR COMPUTING THE FIXED-OVERHEAD RATE

The fixed-overhead rate in an absorption-costing framework depends on the expected activity level chosen as the denominator in the computation. The higher the level of activity, the lower the rate.

The selection of an appropriate activity level for the denominator is a matter of judgment. Management usually wants to apply a single representative standard fixed cost for a unit of product over a period of at least one year, despite month-to-month changes in activity level. Therefore, the predicted total fixed cost and the expected activity level used in calculating the fixed-overhead rate should cover at least a one-year period. Most managers favor using the budgeted annual activity level as the expected activity level in the denominator. Others favor using some longer-run (three- to five-year) approximation of "normal" activity. Still others favor using maximum or full capacity (often called **practical capacity**).

practical capacity
Maximum or full capacity.

Although fixed-overhead rates are often important for product costing and long-run pricing, such rates have limited significance for control purposes. At the lower levels of management activity, almost no fixed costs are under direct control. Even at higher levels of management activity, many fixed costs are uncontrollable in the short run, within wide ranges of anticipated activity.

Objective 4
Differentiate among the three alternative cost bases of an absorption-costing system: actual, normal, and standard.

ACTUAL, NORMAL, AND STANDARD COSTING

Overhead variances are not restricted to standard-costing systems. Many companies apply actual direct materials and actual direct-labor costs to products or services but use budgeted rates for applying overhead. Such a procedure is called normal costing. The following chart compares normal costing with two other basic ways for applying costs by the absorption-costing method:

	Actual Costing	Normal Costing	Standard Costing
Direct materials	Actual costs	Actual costs	Standard prices or
Direct labor	Actual costs	Actual costs	rates × standard inputs
Variable factory overhead		Budgeted	allowed
Fixed factory overhead	Actual costs	rates ×	for actual
		actual inputs	output
			achieved

[4]*Do not confuse the production-volume variance described here with the sales-volume variance described in Chapter 8. Despite similar nomenclature, they are completely different concepts.*

Dropping fixed factory overhead from this chart produces a comparison of the same three basic ways of applying costs by the variable-costing method.

Both normal absorption costing and standard absorption costing generate production-volume variances. In addition, normal- and standard-costing systems produce all other overhead variances under both variable and absorption formats.

RECONCILIATION OF VARIABLE COSTING AND ABSORPTION COSTING

Exhibit 15-4 reconciles the operating incomes shown in Exhibits 15-2 and 15-3. The difference in those two earlier exhibits is quickly explained by multiplying the fixed-overhead product-costing rate by the change in the total units in the beginning and ending inventories. Consider 19X9: The change in inventory was 20,000 units, so the difference in net income would be 20,000 units $\times$ $1.00 = $20,000.

The difference in income also equals the difference in the total amount of fixed manufacturing overhead charged as an expense during a given year. (See Exhibits 15-5 and 15-6.) The $150,000 fixed manufacturing overhead incurred in 19X9 is automatically the amount recognized as an expense on a variable-costing income statement.

Under absorption costing, fixed manufacturing overhead appears in two places: cost of goods sold and production-volume variance. Note that $30,000 of these fixed costs were incurred before 19X9 and held over in the beginning inventory. During 19X9, $140,000 of fixed manufacturing overhead was added to inventory, and $10,000 was still lodged in the ending inventory of 19X9. Thus, the fixed manufacturing overhead included in cost of goods sold for 19X9 was $30,000 + $140,000 − $10,000 = $160,000. In addition, the production-volume variance is $10,000, unfavorable. The total fixed manufacturing overhead charged as 19X9 expenses under absorption costing is $170,000, or $20,000 more than the $150,000 charged under variable costing. Therefore, 19X7 variable-costing income is higher by $20,000.

Remember that it is the relationship between sales and production that determines the difference between variable-costing and absorption-costing income. Whenever sales

Exhibit 15-4

Reconciliation of Operating Income Under Variable Costing and Absorption Costing

	19X8	19X9	Together
Operating income under			
Absorption costing (see			
Exhibit 15-3)	$60,000	$ 45,000	$105,000
Variable costing (see			
Exhibit 15-2)	30,000	65,000	95,000
Difference to be explained	$30,000	$−20,000	$ 10,000
The difference can be reconciled by multiplying the fixed-overhead rate by the change in the total inventory units			
Fixed-overhead rate	$1	$1	$1
Change in inventory units			
Opening inventory	—	30,000	—
Ending inventory	30,000	10,000	10,000
Change	30,000	−20,000	10,000
Difference in operating income explained	$30,000	$−20,000	$ 10,000

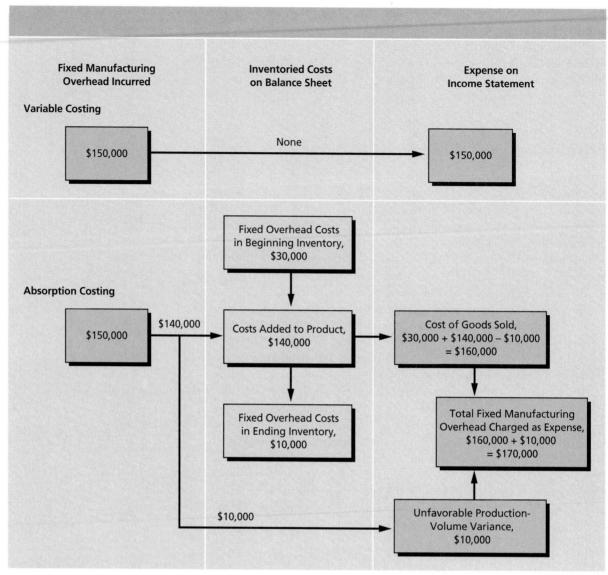

Exhibit 15-5

Flow of Fixed Manufacturing Overhead Costs during 19X9

exceed production, that is, when inventory decreases, variable-costing income is greater than absorption-costing income.

In a just-in-time inventory and production system, the inventories are minimal so sales and production are almost equal. This means that the difference between variable and absorption income in JIT systems is not significant.

WHY USE VARIABLE COSTING?

Objective 5
Explain why a company might prefer to use a variable-costing approach.

Why do many companies use variable costing for internal statements? One reason is that absorption-costing income is affected by production volume while variable-costing income is not. Consider the 19X9 absorption-costing statement in Exhibit 15-3, which shows operating income of $45,000. Suppose a manager decides to produce 10,000 additional units in December 19X9 even though they will remain unsold. Will this affect operating income? First, note that the gross profit will not change. Why?

Exhibit 15-6

Tracing Fixed Manufacturing Costs during 19X9 (data are from Exhibits 15-2 and 15-3)

	Costs	Inventory	Expense
Variable Costing			
No fixed overhead carried over from 19X8			
Fixed overhead actually incurred in 19X9	$150,000 ———————————————→		$150,000

	Costs	Units	Dollars	Expense
Absorption Costing				
Fixed overhead in beginning inventory	$ 30,000	30,000	$ 30,000	
Fixed overhead incurred in 19X9	150,000			
To account for	$180,000			
Applied to product, 140,000 @ $1		140,000	140,000	
Available for sale		170,000	$170,000	
Contained in standard cost of goods sold	$160,000	160,000	160,000 ⟶	$160,000
In ending inventory	10,000	10,000	$ 10,000	
Not applied, so becomes unfavorable production-volume variance	10,000 ———————————————→			10,000
Fixed factory overhead charged against 19X9 operations				$170,000
Accounted for, as above	$180,000			
Difference in operating income occurs because $170,000 expires rather than $150,000				$ 20,000

Because it is based on sales, not production. However, the production-volume variance will change:

$$\text{If production} = 140,000 \text{ units}$$
$$\text{Production-volume variance} = (150,000 - 140,000) \times \$1 = \$10,000 \text{ U}$$
$$\text{If production} = 150,000 \text{ units}$$
$$\text{Production-volume variance} = (150,000 - 150,000) \times \$1 = 0$$

Because there is no production-volume variance when 150,000 units are produced, the new operating income equals gross profit less selling and administrative expenses, $160,000 − $105,000 = $55,000. Therefore, increasing production by 10,000 units without any increase in sales increases absorption-costing operating income by $10,000, from $45,000 to $55,000.

How will such an increase in production affect the variable-costing statement in Exhibit 15-2? Nothing will change. Production does not affect operating income under variable costing.

Suppose the evaluation of a manager's performance is heavily based on operating income. If the company uses the absorption-costing approach, a manager might be tempted to produce unneeded units just to increase reported operating income. No such temptation exists with variable costing.

Companies also choose variable or absorption costing based on which system they believe gives a better signal about performance. A sales-oriented company may prefer variable costing because its income is affected primarily by the level of sales. In contrast, a production-oriented company, for example a company that can easily sell all the units it produces, might prefer absorption costing. Why? Because additional production increases the operating income with absorption costing but not with variable costing.

EFFECT OF OTHER VARIANCES

So far, our example has deliberately ignored the possibility of any variance except the production-volume variance, which appears only on an absorption-costing statement. All other variances appear on both variable- and absorption-costing income statements. In this section, we will consider other variances that were explained in Chapter 8.

FLEXIBLE-BUDGET VARIANCES

Returning again to the Greenberg Company, we will assume some additional facts for 19X9 (the second of the two years covered by our example):

Flexible-budget variances	
Direct material	None
Direct labor	$34,000 U
Variable factory overhead	$ 3,000 U
Fixed factory overhead	$ 7,000 U
Supporting data (used to compute the above variances as shown in Appendix 15):	
Standard direct-labor-hours allowed for 140,000 units of output produced	35,000
Standard direct-labor rate per hour	$6.00
Actual direct-labor-hours of inputs	40,000
Actual direct-labor rate per hour	$6.10
Variable manufacturing overhead actually incurred	$31,000
Fixed manufacturing overhead actually incurred	$157,000

As Chapter 8 explained, flexible-budget variances may arise for both variable overhead and fixed overhead. Consider the following:

	Actual Amounts	Flexible-Budget Amounts @ 140,000 Units	Flexible-Budget Variances
Variable factory overhead	$ 31,000	$ 28,000	$3,000 U
Fixed factory overhead	157,000	150,000	7,000 U

Exhibit 15-7 shows the relationship between the fixed-overhead flexible-budget variance and the production-volume variance. The difference between the actual fixed overhead and that applied to products is the underapplied (or overapplied) overhead. Because the actual fixed overhead of $157,000 exceeds the $140,000 applied, fixed overhead is underapplied by $17,000, which means that the variance is unfavorable. The $17,000 underapplied fixed overhead has two components: (1) a production-volume variance of $10,000 U and (2) a fixed-overhead flexible-budget variance (also called the *fixed-overhead spending variance* or simply the *fixed-overhead budget variance*) of $7,000 U.

All variances other than the production-volume variance are essentially flexible-budget variances. They measure components of the differences between actual amounts and the flexible-budget amounts for the output achieved. Flexible budgets are primarily designed to

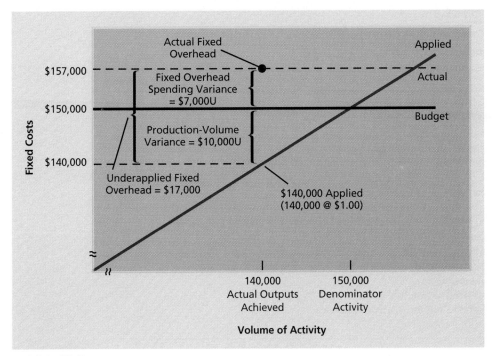

Exhibit 15-7

Fixed-Overhead Variances for 19X9 (data are from Exhibit 15-3)

assist planning and control rather than product costing. The production-volume variance is not a flexible-budget variance. It is designed to aid product costing.

Exhibit 15-8 contains the income statement under absorption costing that incorporates these new facts. These new variances hurt income by $44,000 because, like the production-volume variance, they are all unfavorable variances that are charged against income in 19X9. When cost variances are favorable, they increase operating income.

DISPOSITION OF STANDARD-COST VARIANCES

Advocates of standard costing contend that variances are generally subject to current control, especially when the standards are viewed as being currently attainable. Therefore, variances are not inventoriable and should be considered as adjustments to the income of the period instead of being added to inventories. In this way, inventory valuations will be more representative of desirable and attainable costs.

Others favor assigning the variances to the inventories and cost of goods sold related to the production during the period the variances arose. This is often called **prorating the variances.** Prorating makes inventory valuations more representative of the "actual" costs incurred to obtain the products. In practice, unless variances and inventory levels are significant, the variances are usually not prorated.

Therefore, in practice, all cost variances are typically regarded as adjustments to current income. Where variances appear on the income statement is generally unimportant. Exhibit 15-8 shows variances as a component of gross profit at "actual." But the variances could appear instead as a completely separate section elsewhere in the income statement. Such placement would help to distinguish between product costing (that is, the cost of goods sold, at standard) and loss recognition (unfavorable variances are "lost" or "expired" costs because they represent waste and inefficiency thereby not qualifying as inventoriable costs; that is, waste is not an asset). The placement of the variance does not affect operating income.

Objective 6
Identify the two methods for disposing of the standard cost variances at the end of a year and give the rationale for each.

prorating the variances
Assigning the variances to the inventories and cost of goods sold related to the production during the period the variances arose.

Exhibit 15-8

Absorption Costing Modification of Exhibit 15-3 for 19X9

(additional facts are in text)

	(in thousands)	
Sales, 160,000 at $5		$800
Opening inventory at standard, 30,000 at $4	$120	
Cost of goods manufactured at standard, 140,000 at $4	560	
Available for sale, 170,000 at $4	$680	
Deduct ending inventory at standard, 10,000 at $4	40	
Cost of goods sold at standard, 160,000 at $4		640
Gross profit at standard		$160
Flexible-budget variances, both unfavorable		
Variable manufacturing costs ($34,000 + $3,000)	$ 37	
Fixed factory overhead	7	
Production-volume variance (arises only because of		
fixed overhead), unfavorable	10	
Total variances		54
Gross profit at "actual"		$106
Selling and administrative expenses		105
Operating income		$ 1

SUMMARY PROBLEM FOR YOUR REVIEW

PROBLEM

1. Reconsider Exhibits 15-2 and 15-3 on pages 573 and 574. Suppose production in 19X9 was 145,000 units instead of 140,000 units, but sales were 160,000 units. Assume that the net variances for all variable manufacturing costs were $37,000, unfavorable. Regard these variances as adjustments to the standard cost of goods sold. Also assume that actual fixed costs were $157,000. Prepare income statements for 19X9 under variable costing and under absorption costing.

2. Explain why operating income was different under variable costing from what it was under absorption costing. Show your calculations.

3. Without regard to requirement 1, would variable costing or absorption costing give a manager more leeway in influencing short-run operating income through production-scheduling decisions? Why?

SOLUTION

1. See Exhibits 15-9 and 15-10. Note that the ending inventory will be 15,000 units instead of 10,000 units.

2. Decline in inventory levels is 30,000 − 15,000, or 15,000 units. The fixed-overhead rate per unit in absorption costing is $1. Therefore $15,000 more fixed overhead was charged against operations under absorption costing than under variable costing. The variable-costing statement shows fixed factory overhead of $157,000, whereas the absorption-costing statement includes fixed factory overhead in three places: $160,000 in cost of goods sold, $7,000 U in fixed factory overhead flexible-budget variance, and $5,000 U as a production-volume variance, for a total of $172,000. Generally, when inventories decline, absorption costing will show less income than will variable costing; when inventories rise, absorption costing will show more income than variable costing.

Exhibit 15-9

Greenberg Company

Income Statement (variable costing), Year 19X9 (thousands of dollars)

Sales			$800
Opening inventory, at variable			
standard cost of $3	$ 90		
Add: variable cost of goods manufactured	435		
Available for sale	$525		
Deduct: ending inventory, at variable			
standard cost of $3	45		
Variable cost of goods sold, at standard		$480	
Net flexible-budget variances for			
all variable costs, unfavorable		37	
Variable cost of goods sold, at actual		$517	
Variable selling expenses, at 5% of dollar sales		40	
Total variable costs charged against sales			557
Contribution margin			$243
Fixed factory overhead		$157*	
Fixed selling and administrative expenses		65	
Total fixed expenses			222
Operating income			$ 21†

*This could be shown in two lines, $150,000 budget plus $7,000 variance.

†The difference between this and the $65,000 operating income in Exhibit 15-2 occurs because of the $37,000 unfavorable variable-cost variances and the $7,000 unfavorable fixed-cost flexible-budget variance.

Exhibit 15-10

Greenberg Company

Income Statement (absorption costing), Year 19X9 (thousands of dollars)

Sales			$800
Opening inventory, at standard cost of $4		$120	
Cost of goods manufactured, at standard		580	
Available for sale		$700	
Deduct: ending inventory, at standard		60	
Cost of goods sold, at standard		$640	
Net flexible-budget variances for all variable			
manufacturing costs, unfavorable	$37		
Fixed factory overhead flexible-budget			
variance, unfavorable	7		
Production-volume variance, unfavorable	5*		
Total variances		49	
Cost of goods sold, at actual		689†	
Gross profit, at "actual"		$111	
Selling and administrative expenses			
Variable	40		
Fixed	65	105	
Operating income			$ 6‡

*Production-volume variance is $1 × (150,000 expected volume − 145,000 actual production).

†This format differs slightly from Exhibit 15-8. The difference is deliberate; it illustrates that the formats of income statements are not rigid.

‡Compare this result with the $1,000 operating income in Exhibit 15-8. The only difference is traceable to the production of 145,000 units instead of 140,000 units, resulting in an unfavorable production-volume variance of $5,000 instead of $10,000.

3. Some version of absorption costing will give a manager more leeway in influencing operating income via production scheduling. Operating income will fluctuate in harmony with changes in net sales under variable costing, but it is influenced by both production and sales under absorption costing. For example, compare the variable costing in Exhibits 15-2 and 15-9. As the second note to Exhibit 15-9 indicates, the operating income may be affected by assorted variances (but not the production-volume variance) under variable costing, but production scheduling per se will have no effect on operating income.

On the other hand, compare the operating income of Exhibits 15-8 and 15-10. As the third note to Exhibit 15-10 explains, production scheduling as well as sales influence operating income. Production was 145,000 rather than 140,000 units. So $5,000 of fixed overhead became a part of ending inventory (an asset) instead of part of the production-volume variance (an expense)—that is, the production-volume variance is $5,000 lower and the ending inventory contains $5,000 more fixed overhead in Exhibit 15-10 than in Exhibit 15-8. The manager adds $1 to 19X9 operating income with each unit of production under absorption costing, even if the unit is not sold.

Highlights to Remember

Construct an income statement using the variable-costing approach. Two major methods of product costing are variable (contribution approach) and absorption costing. The variable-costing method emphasizes the effects of cost behavior on income. This method excludes fixed manufacturing overhead from the cost of products and expenses it immediately.

Construct an income statement using the absorption-costing approach. The absorption or traditional approach ignores cost behavior distinctions. As a result, all costs incurred in the production of goods are inventoried. Thus, fixed manufacturing overhead is inventoried and appears on the income statement only when the goods are sold.

Compute the production-volume variance and show how it should appear in the income statement. Whenever the absorption method is used and the actual production volume does not equal the expected (budgeted) volume that is used for computing the fixed-overhead rate, a production volume variance arises. When the actual volume is less than budgeted, the variance is unfavorable and the amount is equal to the fixed-overhead rate times the difference between the budgeted and actual volume. The opposite is true when actual production volume exceeds budgeted production volume; that is, a favorable volume variance arises. Both types of variances are usually adjustments to the current period income. Favorable variances increase current-period income and unfavorable variances reduce current-period income.

Differentiate among the three alternative cost bases of an absorption-costing system: actual, normal, and standard. Absorption costing accumulates product costs using a variety of systems. Actual costing is based on actual costs for direct materials, direct labor, and factory overhead. Normal costing is based on actual costs for direct material and direct labor but budgeted rates for applying factory overhead. Standard costing uses budgeted prices or rates times standard inputs for actual output of production. Both normal- and standard-costing systems will generate production-volume variances.

Explain why a company might prefer to use a variable-costing approach. Variable costing is preferred by companies that use operating income to measure results. This is because variable-costing income is not affected by changes in production volume, whereas absorption income is affected. A company that wants to focus managers' energies on sales would prefer to use variable costing, since its income is primarily affected by the level of sales.

Exhibit 15-11

Comparative Income Effects

	Variable Costing	Absorption Costing	Comments
1. Fixed factory overhead inventoried?	No	Yes	Basic theoretical question of when a cost should become an expense.
2. Production-volume variance?	No	Yes	Choice of expected volume of production affects measurement of operating income under absorption costing.
3. Treatment of other variances?	Same	Same	Underscores the fact that the basic difference is the accounting for fixed factory overhead, not the accounting for variable factory overhead.
4. Classifications between variable and fixed costs are routinely made?	Yes	No	However, absorption cost can be modified to obtain subclassifications of variable and fixed costs, if desired.
5. Usual effects of changes in inventory levels on operating income			Differences are attributable to timing of the transformation of fixed factory overhead into expense.
Production = sales	Equal	Equal	
Production > sales	Lower*	Higher†	
Production < sales	Higher	Lower	
6. Cost-volume-profit relationships	Tied to sales	Tied to production *and* sales	Management control benefit: Effects of changes in volume on operating income are easier to understand under variable costing.

*That is, lower than absorption costing.

†That is, higher than variable costing.

Identify the two methods for disposing of the standard cost variances at the end of a year and give the rationale for each. Variances arising in a standard costing system may be treated two different ways. They may be prorated to cost of goods sold and ending inventories. This adjusts inventories and cost of goods sold to actual costs. Usually, however, variances are not prorated. Instead, they are treated as an adjustment to current income.

Understand how product-costing systems affect operating income. Managers' performance measures and rewards are most often based on operating income. As a result, managers are motivated to take actions that improve current operating income. Each of the topics covered in this chapter has an effect on income. Absorption- and variable-costing systems affect operating income because of their treatment of fixed factory overhead. Absorption-costing systems, both normal and standard, generate production-volume variances that also affect income. Exhibit 15-11 compares variable- and absorption-costing effects.

APPENDIX 15: COMPARISONS OF PRODUCTION-VOLUME VARIANCE WITH OTHER VARIANCES

The only new variance introduced in this chapter is the production-volume variance, which arises because fixed-overhead accounting must serve two masters: the *control-budget* purpose and the *product-costing* purpose. Let's examine this variance in perspective by using the approach originally demonstrated in Exhibit 8-9. The results of the approach appear in Exhibit 15-12, which deserves your careful study, particularly the two footnotes. Please ponder the exhibit before reading on.

Exhibit 15-12

Analysis of Variances
(Data Are from Text for 19X9)

Inputs	(A) Costs Incurred: Actual Inputs × Actual Price	(B) Flexible Budget Based On Actual Inputs × Expected Prices	(C) Flexible Budget Based on Standard Inputs Allowed for Actual Outputs Achieved × Expected Prices	(D) Product Costing: Applied to Product
Direct labor	40,000 × $6.10 = $240,000	40,000 × $6 = $240,000	(35,000 × $6) or (140,000 × $1.50) = $210,000*	(35,000 × $6) or (140,000 × $1.50) = $210,000*
	40,000 × ($6.10 − $6) = price variance, $4,000 U		5,000 × $6 = usage variance, $30,000 U	
		Flexible-budget variance, $34,000 U	Never a variance	Never a variance
Variable factory overhead	(given) $31,000	40,000 × $.80 = $32,000	(35,000 × $.80 or 140,000 × $.20) = $28,000*	$28,000*
	Spending variance, $1,000 F		5,000 × $.80 = efficiency variance, $4,000 U	
		Flexible-budget variance, $3,000 U	Never a variance	Never a variance
		Underapplied overhead, $3,000 U		
Fixed factory overhead	$157,000	Lump sum $150,000	Lump sum $150,000†	140,000 × $1.00 = $140,000
	Spending variance, $7,000 U	Never a variance	Production-volume variance, $10,000 U	Production-volume variance, $10,000 U
		Flexible-budget variance, $7,000 U		
		Underapplied overhead, $17,000 U		

U = Unfavorable. F = Favorable.

*Note especially that the flexible budget for variable costs rises and falls in direct proportion to production. Note also that the control-budget purpose and the product-costing purpose harmonize completely. The total costs in the flexible budget will always agree with the standard variable costs applied to the product because they are based on standard costs per unit multiplied by units produced.

†In contrast with variable costs, the flexible-budget total for fixed costs will always be the same regardless of the units produced. However, the control-budget purpose and the product-costing purpose conflict; whenever actual production differs from expected production, the standard costs applied to the product will differ from the flexible budget. This difference is the production-volume variance. In this case, the production-volume variance may be computed by multiplying the $1 rate times the difference between the 150,000 expected volume and the 140,000 units of output achieved.

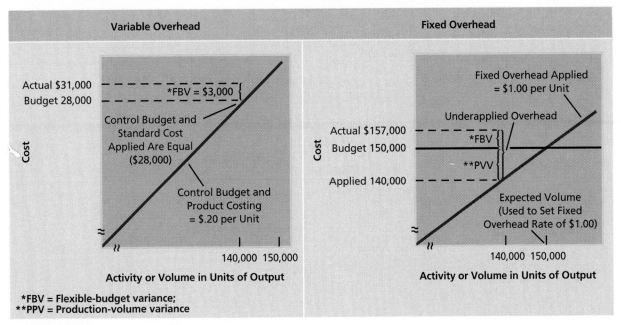

Variable Overhead

Actual $31,000
Budget 28,000
*FBV = $3,000
Control Budget and Standard Cost Applied Are Equal ($28,000)
Control Budget and Product Costing = $.20 per Unit
Cost
140,000 150,000
Activity or Volume in Units of Output

Fixed Overhead

Fixed Overhead Applied = $1.00 per Unit
Underapplied Overhead
Actual $157,000
Budget 150,000
*FBV
**PVV
Applied 140,000
Expected Volume (Used to Set Fixed Overhead Rate of $1.00)
Cost
140,000 150,000
Activity or Volume in Units of Output

*FBV = Flexible-budget variance;
**PPV = Production-volume variance

Exhibit 15-13

Comparison of Control and Product-Costing Purposes, Variable Overhead and Fixed Overhead (not to scale)

Exhibit 15-13 graphically compares the variable- and fixed-overhead costs analyzed in Exhibit 15-12. Note how the control-budget line and the product-costing line (the applied line) are superimposed in the graph for variable overhead but differ in the graph for fixed overhead.

Underapplied or overapplied overhead is always the difference between the actual overhead incurred and the overhead applied. An analysis may then be made:

$$\text{underapplied overhead} = \left(\begin{array}{c}\text{flexible-budget}\\\text{variance}\end{array}\right) + \left(\begin{array}{c}\text{production-volume}\\\text{variance}\end{array}\right)$$

for variable overhead = $3,000 + 0 = $3,000
for fixed overhead = $7,000 + $10,000 = $17,000

Accounting Vocabulary

fixed-overhead rate, p. 573
normal costing, p.578
practical capacity, p. 578

production-volume
variance, p. 573
prorating the variance, p. 583

volume variance, p. 577

Fundamental Assignment Material

15-A1   Comparison of Variable Costing and Absorption Costing
Consider the following information pertaining to a year's operation of Blair Company:

Units produced	3,000
Units sold	2,400
Direct labor	$4,500
Direct material used	3,000
Selling and administrative expenses (all fixed)	900
Fixed manufacturing overhead	4,000
Variable manufacturing overhead	2,500
All beginning inventories	0
Gross margin (gross profit)	2,400
Direct-materials inventory, end	400
Work-in-process inventory, end	0

Required

1. What is the ending finished-goods inventory cost under absorption costing?
2. What is the ending finished-goods inventory cost under variable costing?
3. Would operating income be higher or lower under variable costing? By how much? Why? (Answer: $800 lower, but explain why.)

15-A2 Comparison of Absorption and Variable Costing

Examine the Trahn Company's simplified income statement based on variable costing. Assume that the budgeted volume for absorption costing in 19X5 and 19X6 was 1,400 units and that total fixed costs were identical in 19X5 and 19X6. There is no beginning or ending work in process.

Income Statement
Year Ended December 31, 19X6

Sales, 1,280 units @ $11		$14,080
Deduct variable costs		
Beginning inventory, 110 units @ $7	$ 770	
Variable manufacturing cost of goods manufactured, 1,200 units @ $7	8,400	
Variable manufacturing cost of goods available for sale	$9,170	
Ending inventory, 30 units @ $7	210	
Variable manufacturing cost of goods sold	$8,960	
Variable selling and administrative expenses	600	
Total variable costs		9,560
Contribution margin		$ 4,520
Deduct fixed costs		
Fixed factory overhead at budget	$2,800	
Fixed selling and administrative expenses	350	
Total fixed costs		3,150
Operating income		$ 1,370

Required

1. Prepare an income statement based on absorption costing. Assume that actual fixed costs were equal to budgeted fixed costs.
2. Explain the difference in operating income between absorption costing and variable costing. Be specific.

15-B1 Comparison of Variable Costing and Absorption Costing

Consider the following information pertaining to a year's operations of Cleveland Manufacturing, Inc.:

Units sold	1,200
Units produced	1,600
Direct labor	$4,200
Direct material used	3,500
Fixed manufacturing overhead	2,200
Variable manufacturing overhead	300
Selling and administrative expenses (all fixed)	700
Beginning inventories	0
Contribution margin	5,800
Direct-material inventory, end	800

There are no work-in-process inventories.

Required

1. What is the ending finished-goods inventory cost under absorption costing?
2. What is the ending finished-goods inventory cost under variable costing?

15-B2 Extension of Chapter Illustration

Reconsider Exhibits 15-2 and 15-3, pages 573 and 574. Suppose that in 19X9 production was 155,000 rings instead of 140,000 rings, and sales were 150,000 rings. Also assume that the net variances for all variable manufacturing costs were $18,000, unfavorable. Also assume that actual fixed manufacturing costs were $156,000.

Required

1. Prepare income statements for 19X9 under variable costing and under absorption costing. Use a format similar to Exhibits 15-9 and 15-10, page 585.
2. Explain why operating income was different under variable costing and absorption costing. Show your calculations.

Additional Assignment Material

QUESTIONS

15-1. "With variable costing only direct material and direct labor are inventoried." Do you agree? Why?

15-2. "Absorption costing regards more categories of costs as product costs." Explain. Be specific.

15-3. "An increasing number of companies are using variable costing in their corporate annual reports." Do you agree? Explain.

15-4. Why is variable costing used only for internal reporting and not for external financial reporting or tax purposes?

15-5. Compare the contribution margin with the gross margin.

15-6. How is fixed overhead applied to products?

15-7. Name the three ways that an absorption-costing format differs from a variable-costing format.

15-8. "The flexible budget for budgeting and control differs from the costs applied for product costing." What type of cost is being described? Explain.

15-9. "Variable costing is consistent with cost-volume-profit analysis." Explain.

15-10. "In a standard absorption-costing system, the amount of fixed manufacturing overhead applied to the products rarely equals the budgeted fixed manufacturing overhead." Do you agree? Explain.

15-11. "The dollar amount of the production-volume variance depends on what expected volume of production was chosen to determine the fixed-overhead rate." Explain.

15-12. Why is there no production-volume variance for direct labor?

15-13. "An unfavorable production-volume variance means that fixed manufacturing costs have not been well controlled." Do you agree? Explain.

15-14. "The fixed cost per unit is directly affected by the expected volume selected as the denominator." Do you agree? Explain.

15-15. "Production-volume variances arise with normal-absorption and standard-absorption costing, but not with actual costing." Explain.

15-16. "Absorption-costing income exceeds variable-costing income when the number of units sold exceeds the number of units produced." Do you agree? Explain.

15-17. Suppose a manager is paid a bonus only if standard absorption-costing operating income exceeds the budget. If operating income through November is slightly below budget, what might the manager do in December to increase his or her chance of getting the bonus?

15-18. Why are companies with small levels of inventory generally unconcerned with the choice of variable or absorption costing?

15-19. "Overhead variances arise only with absorption-costing systems." Do you agree? Explain.

EXERCISES

15-20 Simple Comparison of Variable and Absorption Costing

Khalid Company began business on January 1, 19X6, with assets of $150,000 cash and equities of $150,000 capital stock. In 19X6, it manufactured some inventory at a cost of $60,000, including $16,000 for factory rent and other fixed factory overhead. In 19X7, it manufactured nothing and sold half of its inventory for $42,000 cash. In 19X8, it manufactured nothing and sold the remaining half for another $42,000 cash. It had no fixed expenses in 19X7 or 19X8.

There are no other transactions of any kind. Ignore income taxes.

Required   Prepare an ending balance sheet plus an income statement for 19X6, 19X7, and 19X8 under (1) absorption costing and (2) variable costing (direct costing).

15-21 Comparisons over Four Years

The Balakrishnan Corporation began business on January 1, 19X5, to produce and sell a single product. Reported operating income figures under both absorption and variable costing for the first four years of operation are:

Year	Variable Costing	Absorption Costing
19X5	$70,000	$50,000
19X6	70,000	60,000
19X7	50,000	50,000
19X8	40,000	70,000

Standard production costs per unit, sales prices, application (absorption) rates, and expected volume levels were the same in each year. There were no underapplied or over-applied overhead costs, and no variances in any year. All nonmanufacturing expenses were fixed, and there were no nonmanufacturing cost variances in any year.

Required   1. In what year(s) did "units produced" equal "units sold"?
2. In what year(s) did "units produced" exceed "units sold"?
3. What is the dollar amount of the December 31, 19X8 finished-goods inventory? (Give absorption-costing value.)

4. What is the difference between "units produced" and "units sold" in 19X8, if you know that the absorption-costing fixed-manufacturing-overhead application rate is $3 per unit? (Give answer in units.)

15-22 Variable and Absorption Costing

Chan Company data for 19X8 follow:

Sales: 12,000 units at $17 each		
Actual production	15,000 units	
Expected volume of production	18,000 units	
Manufacturing costs incurred		
Variable	$105,000	
Fixed	63,000	
Nonmanufacturing costs incurred		
Variable	$ 24,000	
Fixed	18,000	

Required

1. Determine operating income for 19X8, assuming the firm uses the variable-costing approach to product costing. (Do not prepare a statement.)

2. Assume that there is no January 1, 19X8 inventory; no variances are allocated to inventory; and the firm uses a "full absorption" approach to product costing. Compute (a) the cost assigned to December 31, 19X8, inventory; and (b) operating income for the year ended December 31, 19X8. (Do not prepare a statement.)

15-23 Computation of Production-Volume Variance

Osaka Manufacturing Company budgeted its 19X8 variable overhead at ¥14,100,000 and its fixed overhead at ¥25,620,000. Expected 19X8 volume was 6,100 units. Actual costs for production of 5,800 units during 19X8 were:

Variable overhead	¥14,160,000
Fixed overhead	25,620,000
Total overhead	¥39,780,000

Required

Compute the production-volume variance. Be sure to label it favorable or unfavorable.

15-24 Reconciliation of Variable-Costing and Absorption-Costing Operating Income

Blackstone Tools, Inc. produced 12,000 electric drills during 19X8. Expected production was only 10,500 drills. The company's fixed-overhead rate is $7 per drill. Absorption-costing operating income for the year is $18,000, based on sales of 11,000 drills.

1. Compute:
   a. Budgeted fixed overhead
   b. Production-volume variance
   c. Variable-costing operating income

2. Reconcile absorption-costing operating income and variable-costing operating income. Include the amount of the difference between the two and an explanation for the difference.

15-25 Overhead Variances

Study Appendix 15. Consider the following data for the Rivera Company:

	Factory Overhead	
	Fixed	*Variable*
Actual incurred	$14,200	$13,300
Budget for standard hours allowed		
for output achieved	12,500	11,000
Applied	11,600	11,000
Budget for actual hours of input	12,500	11,400

From the above information, fill in the blanks below. Be sure to mark your variances *F* for favorable and *U* for unfavorable.

---

a. Flexible-budget variance $_____   Fixed $_____

                                                        Variable $_____

b. Production-volume variance $_____   Fixed $_____

                                                        Variable $_____

c. Spending variance $_____   Fixed $_____

                                                        Variable $_____

d. Efficiency variance $_____   Fixed $_____

                                                        Variable $_____

15-26 Variances

Study Appendix 15. Consider the following data regarding factory overhead:

	Variable	Fixed
Budget for actual hours of input	$45,000	$70,000
Applied	41,000	64,800
Budget for standard hours allowed		
for actual output achieved	?	?
Actual incurred	48,500	68,500

Required Using the above data, fill in the following blanks with the variance amounts. Use *F* for favorable or *U* for unfavorable for each variance.

	Total Overhead	Variable	Fixed
1. Spending variance	_____	_____	_____
2. Efficiency variance	_____	_____	_____
3. Production-volume variance	_____	_____	_____
4. Flexible-budget variance	_____	_____	_____
5. Underapplied overhead	_____	_____	_____

PROBLEMS

15-27 Comparison of Variable Costing and Absorption Costing

Simple numbers are used in this problem to highlight the concepts covered in the chapter.

Assume that the Canberra Company produces one product—a bath mat—that sells for $10. Canberra uses a standard cost system. Total standard variable costs of production are $4 per mat, fixed manufacturing costs are $1,500 per year, and selling and administrative expenses are $300 per year, all fixed. Expected production volume is 500 mats per year.

1. For each of the following nine combinations of actual sales and production (in units) for 19X7, prepare condensed income statements under variable costing and under absorption costing.

Required

	(1)	(2)	(3)	(4)	(5)	(6)	(7)	(8)	(9)
Sales units	300	400	500	400	500	600	500	600	700
Production units	400	400	400	500	500	500	600	600	600

Use the following formats:

Variable Costing		Absorption Costing	
Revenue	$ aa	Revenue	$ aa
Cost of goods sold	(bb)	Cost of goods sold	(uu)
Contribution margin	$ cc	Gross profit at standard	$ vv
Fixed manufacturing costs	(dd)	Favorable (unfavorable)	
Fixed selling and		production-volume	
administrative expenses	(ee)	variance	ww
		Gross profit at "actual"	$ xx
		Selling and administrative	
		expenses	(yy)
Operating income	$ ff	Operating income	$ zz

2. **a.** In which of the nine combinations is variable-costing income greater than absorption-costing income? In which is it lower? The same?

   b. In which of the nine combinations is the production-volume variance unfavorable? Favorable?

   c. How much profit is added by selling one more unit under variable costing? Under absorption costing?

   d. How much profit is added by producing one more unit under variable costing? Under absorption costing?

   e. Suppose sales, rather than production, is the critical factor in determining the success of Canberra Company. Which format, variable costing or absorption costing, provides the better measure of performance?

15-28 All-Fixed Costs

The Marple Company has built a massive water-desalting factory next to an ocean. The factory is completely automated. It has its own source of power, light, heat, and so on. The salt water costs nothing. All producing and other operating costs are fixed; they do not vary with output because the volume is governed by adjusting a few dials on a control panel. The employees have flat annual salaries.

The desalted water is not sold to household consumers. It has a special taste that appeals to local breweries, distilleries, and soft-drink manufacturers. The price, $.50 per gallon, is expected to remain unchanged for quite some time.

The following are data regarding the first two years of operations:

| | In Gallons | | Costs (All Fixed) | |
	Sales	Production	Manufacturing	Other
19X7	1,500,000	3,000,000	$600,000	$200,000
19X8	1,500,000	0	600,000	200,000

Orders can be processed in four hours, so management decided, in early 19X8, to gear production strictly to sales.

Required

1. Prepare three-column income statements for 19X7, for 19X8, and for the two years together using (a) variable costing and (b) absorption costing.

2. What is the break-even point under (a) variable costing and (b) absorption costing?

3. What inventory costs would be carried on the balance sheets on December 31, 19X7 and 19X8, under each method?

4. Comment on your answers in requirements 1 and 2. Which costing method appears more useful?

15-29 Semifixed Costs

The Carley Company differs from the Marple Company (described in Problem 15-28) in only one respect: It has both variable and fixed manufacturing costs. Its variable costs are $.14 per gallon, and its fixed manufacturing costs are $390,000 per year.

Required

1. Using the same data as in the preceding problem, except for the change in production-cost behavior, prepare three-column income statements for 19X7, for 19X8, and for the two years together using (a) variable costing and (b) absorption costing.

2. What inventory costs would be carried on the balance sheets on December 31, 19X7 and 19X8, under each method?

15-30 Absorption and Variable Costing

The Trapani Company had the following actual data for 19X6 and 19X7:

	19X6	19X7
Units of finished goods		
Opening inventory	—	2,000
Production	15,000	13,000
Sales	13,000	14,000
Ending inventory	2,000	1,000

The basic production data at standard unit costs for the 2 years were:

Direct materials	$22
Direct labor	18
Variable factory overhead	4
Standard variable costs per unit	$44

Fixed factory overhead was budgeted at $98,000 per year. The expected volume of production was 14,000 units, so the fixed overhead rate was $98,000 ÷ 14,000 = $7 per unit.

Budgeted sales price was $75 per unit. Selling and administrative expenses were budgeted at variable, $9 per unit sold, and fixed, $80,000 per month.

Assume that there were absolutely no variances from any standard variable costs or budgeted selling prices or budgeted fixed costs in 19X6.

There were no beginning or ending inventories of work in process.

Required

1. For 19X6, prepare income statements based on standard variable (direct) costing and standard absorption costing. (The next problem deals with 19X7.)

2. Explain why operating income differs between variable costing and absorption costing. Be specific.

15-31 Absorption and Variable Costing

Assume the same facts as in the preceding problem. In addition, consider the following actual data for 19X7:

Direct materials	$ 285,000
Direct labor	174,200
Variable factory overhead	36,000
Fixed factory overhead	95,000
Selling and administrative costs	
Variable	118,400
Fixed	80,000
Sales	1,068,000

Required

1. For 19X7, prepare income statements based on standard variable (direct) costing and standard absorption costing.

2. Explain why operating income differs between variable costing and absorption costing. Be specific.

15-32 Fundamentals of Overhead Variances

The Mendoza Company is installing an absorption standard-cost system and a flexible-overhead budget. Standard costs have recently been developed for its only product and are as follows:

Direct material, 3 pounds @ $20	$60
Direct labor, 2 hours @ $14	28
Variable overhead, 2 hours @ $5	10
Fixed overhead	?
Standard cost per unit of finished product	$?

Expected production activity is expressed as 7,500 standard direct-labor-hours per month. Fixed overhead is expected to be $60,000 per month. The predetermined fixed-overhead rate for product costing is not changed from month to month.

Required

1. Calculate the proper fixed-overhead rate per standard direct-labor-hour and per unit.

2. Graph the following for activity from zero to 10,000 hours:
   a. Budgeted variable overhead
   b. Variable overhead applied to product

3. Graph the following for activity from zero to 10,000 hours:
   a. Budgeted fixed overhead
   b. Fixed overhead applied to product

4. Assume that 6,000 standard direct-labor-hours are allowed for the output achieved during a given month. Actual variable overhead of $30,600 was incurred; actual fixed overhead amounted to $62,000. Calculate the
   a. Fixed-overhead flexible-budget variance
   b. Fixed-overhead production-volume variance
   c. Variable-overhead flexible-budget variance

5. Assume that 7,800 standard direct-labor-hours are allowed for the output achieved during a given month. Actual overhead incurred amounted to $99,700, $62,200 of which was fixed. Calculate the
   a. Fixed-overhead flexible-budget variance
   b. Fixed-overhead production-volume variance
   c. Variable-overhead flexible-budget variance

BUSINESS FIRST   www.prenhall.com/phlip

15-33   Production-Volume Variance at LA Darling Store Fixtures

LA Darling Store Fixtures receives $6 billion of revenue each year from designing, manufacturing, and installing store fixtures in retail stores. Accounting for fixed manufacturing overhead is a challenge for the company. Suppose a manufacturing division of the company has the following budgeted costs for production of 700,000 shelving units in 1998:

Direct materials	$140,000,000
Direct labor	20,000,000
Other variable manufacturing costs	15,000,000
Fixed manufacturing costs	105,000,000
Total manufacturing cost	$280,000,000

During 1998, this division of LA Darling produced 750,000 of the shelving units and sold 725,000 of them for $362.5 million. Assume that LA Darling does not allocate selling or administrative costs to the individual products.

Required

1. Compute the following budgeted unit costs for 1998:

Variable manufacturing costs per unit	?
Fixed manufacturing costs per unit	?
Total manufacturing costs per unit	?

2. Compute the production-volume variance for 1998. Be sure to label it favorable or unfavorable.

3. Compute the 1998 profit from the production and sales of the shelving using absorption costing. Ignore selling and administrative costs.

4. Compute the 1998 profit from the production and sales of the shelving using variable costing. Ignore selling and administrative costs.

5. Which measure of profit, absorption-costing profit or variable-costing profit, is a better measure of performance during 1998? Explain. ■

15-34 Fixed Overhead and Practical Capacity

The expected activity of the paper-making plant of Leventhal Paper Company was 45,000 machine-hours per month. Practical capacity was 60,000 machine-hours per month. The standard machine-hours allowed for the actual output achieved in January were 54,000. The budgeted fixed-factory-overhead items were:

Depreciation, equipment	$340,000
Depreciation, factory building	64,000
Supervision	47,000
Indirect labor	234,000
Insurance	18,000
Property taxes	17,000
Total	$720,000

Because of unanticipated scheduling difficulties and the need for more indirect labor, the actual fixed factory overhead was $751,000.

Required

1. Using practical capacity as the base for applying fixed factory overhead, prepare a summary analysis of fixed-overhead variances for January.

2. Using expected activity as the base for applying fixed factory overhead, prepare a summary analysis of fixed-overhead variances for January.

3. Explain why some of your variances in requirements 1 and 2 are the same and why some differ.

15-35 Selection of Expected Volume

Reba Cash is a consultant to Oregon Paper Products Company. She is helping one of the company's divisions to install a standard cost system for 19X4. For product-costing purposes, the system must apply fixed factory costs to products manufactured. She has decided that the fixed-overhead rate should be based on machine hours, but she is uncertain about the appropriate volume to use in the denominator. Oregon Paper has grown rapidly; the division has added production capacity approximately every 4 years. The last addition was completed in early 19X4, and the total capacity is now 2,800,000 machine-hours per year. Cash predicts the following operating levels (in machine hours) through 19X8:

Year	Capacity Used
19X4	2,250,000 hours
19X5	2,500,000 hours
19X6	2,700,000 hours
19X7	2,790,000 hours
19X8	2,900,000 hours

The current plan is to add another 500,000 machine hours of capacity in 19X8. Cash has identified three alternatives for the allocation base:

a. Predicted volume for the year in question

b. Average volume over the four years of the current production setup

c. Practical (or full) capacity

Required

1. Suppose annual fixed factory overhead is expected to be $36,400,000 through 19X7. For simplicity, assume no inflation. Calculate the fixed-overhead rates (to the nearest cent) for 19X5, 19X6, and 19X7, using each of the three alternative allocation bases.

2. Provide a brief description of the effect of using each method of computing the allocation base.

3. Which method do you prefer? Why?

15-36 Extension of Appendix 15 Illustration

Study the format of the analysis of variances in Exhibit 15-12, page 588. Suppose production is 156,000 units. Also assume:

Standard direct-labor-hours allowed per unit produced	.25
Standard direct-labor-rate per hour	$6.00
Actual direct-labor hours of input	42,000
Actual direct-labor-rate per hour	$6.15
Variable manufacturing overhead actually incurred	$ 36,000
Fixed manufacturing overhead actually incurred	$154,000

Other data are as shown in Exhibit 15-12.

Required

Prepare an analysis of variances similar to that shown in Exhibit 15-12.

15-37 Analysis of Operating Results

Manchester Machining Company produces and sells a variety of machine-tooled products. The company employs a standard cost accounting system for record-keeping purposes.

At the beginning of 19X8, the president of Manchester Machining presented the budget to the company's board of directors. The board accepted a target 19X8 profit of £16,400 and agreed to pay the president a bonus if profits exceeded the target. The president has been confident that the year's profit would exceed the budget target, since the monthly sales reports that he has been receiving have shown that sales for the year will exceed budget by 10%. The president is both disturbed and confused when the controller presents an adjusted forecast as of November 30, 19X8, indicating that profit will be 14% under budget:

Manchester Machining Company
Forecasts of Operating Results

	Forecasts as of	
	1/1/X8	*11/30/X8*
Sales	£156,000	£171,600
Cost of sales at standard	108,000*	118,800
Gross margin at standard	£ 48,000	£ 52,800
Over- (under-) absorbed fixed manufacturing overhead	0	(6,000)
Actual gross margin	£ 48,000	£ 46,800
Selling expenses	£ 11,200	£ 12,320
Administrative expenses	20,400	20,400
Total operating expenses	£ 31,600	£ 32,720
Earnings before tax	£ 16,400	£ 14,080

*Includes fixed manufacturing overhead of £30,000.

There have been no sales price changes or product-mix shifts since the January 1, 19X8 forecast. The only cost variance on the income statement is the underabsorbed manufacturing overhead. This arose because the company produced only 16,000 standard machine-hours (budgeted machine-hours were 20,000) during 19X8, as a result of a shortage of raw materials while its principal supplier was closed by a strike. Fortunately, Manchester Machining's finished-goods inventory was large enough to fill all sales orders received.

Required

1. Analyze and explain why the profit has declined despite increased sales and good control over costs. Show computations.

2. What plan, if any, could Manchester Machining Company adopt during December to improve its reported profit at year-end? Explain your answer.

3. Illustrate and explain how Manchester Machining Company could adopt an alternative internal cost-reporting procedure that would avoid the confusing effect of the present procedure. Show the revised forecasts under your alternative.

4. Would the alternative procedure described in requirement 3 be acceptable to the board of directors for financial-reporting purposes? Explain.

15-38 Standard Absorption and Standard Variable Costing
DeCroix Company has the following results for a certain year. All variances are written off as additions to (or deductions from) the standard cost of goods sold. Find the unknowns, designated by letters.

Sales: 150,000 units, @ $21	$3,150,000
Net variance for standard variable manufacturing costs	$ 33,000, unfavorable
Variable standard cost of goods manufactured	$ 11 per unit
Variable selling and administrative expenses	$ 3 per unit
Fixed selling and administrative expenses	$ 650,000
Fixed manufacturing overhead	$ 165,000
Maximum capacity per year	190,000 units

(continued)

Expected production volume for year	150,000 units
Beginning inventory of finished goods	15,000 units
Ending inventory of finished goods	10,000 units
Beginning inventory: variable-costing basis	*a*
Contribution margin	*b*
Operating income: variable-costing basis	*c*
Beginning inventory: absorption-costing basis	*d*
Gross margin	*e*
Operating income: absorption-costing basis	*f*

15-39 Disposition of Variances

In January 19X8, Mattox Toy Company started a division for making "Cries-A-Lot" dolls. Management hoped that these toys would be the new fad of 19X8. During 19X8, it produced 100,000 dolls. Financial results were as follows:

- Sales: 75,000 units @ $20
- Direct labor at standard: 100,000 × $8 = $800,000
- Direct-labor variances: $34,000 U
- Direct material at standard: 100,000 × $5 = $500,000 Direct-material variances: $9,500 U
- Overhead incurred at standard: 100,000 × $4 = $400,000
- Overhead variances: $3,500 F

Mattox uses an absorption costing system and allows divisions to choose one of two methods of accounting for variances:

- **a.** Direct charge to income.
- **b.** Proration to the production of the period. Method b requires variances to be spread equally over the units produced during the period.

Required

1. Calculate the division's operating income (a) using method a and (b) using method b. Assume no selling and administrative expenses.
2. Calculate ending inventory value (a) using method a and (b) using method b. Note that there was no beginning inventory.
3. What is the major argument in support of each method?

15-40 Comparison of Performance of Two Plants

On your first day as assistant controller of Pike Place Novelties, your in-box contains the following memo:

To: Assistant Controller

From: The President

Subject: Elvis Watch Situation

This note is to bring you up to date on one of our acquisition problem areas. Market research detected the current nostalgia wave almost a year ago and concluded that PPN should acquire a position in this market. Research data showed that Elvis Watches could become profitable ($5 contribution margin on a $13 sales price) at a volume of 40,000 units per plant if they became popular. Consequently, we acquired closed-down facilities in Massachusetts and Texas, staffed them, and asked them to keep us posted on operations.

Friday, I got preliminary information from accounting that is unclear. I want you to find out why their costs of goods sold are far apart and how we should have them report in the future to avoid confusion. This is particularly important in the Elvis case, as market projections look bad and we may have to close one plant. I guess we'll close the Texas plant unless you can show otherwise.

Preliminary Accounting Report

	Massachusetts	Texas
Sales	$520,000	$520,000
Cost of goods sold	320,000	490,000
Gross margin	$200,000	$ 30,000
Administration costs (fixed)	30,000	30,000
Net income	$170,000	$ 0
Production	80,000 units	40,000 units
Variances (included in cost of goods sold)	$170,000, F	$ 85,000, U

U = Unfavorable. F = Favorable.

Reconstruct the given income statements in as much detail as possible. Then explain in detail why the income statements differ, and clarify this situation confronting the president. Assume that there are no price, efficiency, or spending variances.

Required

15-41 Straightforward Problem on Standard Cost System

Study Appendix 15. The Oak Harbor Company uses flexible budgets and a standard cost system.

- Direct-labor costs incurred, 12,000 hours, $150,000
- Variable-overhead costs incurred, $35,000
- Fixed-overhead flexible-budget variance, $1,600, favorable
- Finished units produced, 1,800
- Fixed-overhead costs incurred, $38,000
- Variable overhead applied at $3 per hour
- Standard direct-labor cost, $13 per hour
- Denominator production per month, 2,000 units
- Standard direct-labor hours per finished unit, 6

Prepare an analysis of all variances (similar to Exhibit 15-12, p. 588).

Required

15-42 Straightforward Problem on Standard Cost System

Study Appendix 15. The Newton Company uses a standard cost system. The month's data regarding its single product follow:

- Fixed-overhead costs incurred, $6,300
- Variable overhead applied at $1.10 per hour
- Standard direct-labor cost, $4.40 per hour
- Denominator production per month, 2,200 units
- Standard direct-labor hours per finished unit, 5
- Direct-labor costs incurred, 10,000 hours, $42,500

- Variable-overhead costs incurred, $10,400
- Fixed-overhead budget variance, $300, favorable
- Finished units produced, 1,800

Required Prepare an analysis of all variances (similar to Exhibit 15-12, p. 588).

CASES

15-43 Absorption Costing and Incentive to Produce

Charles Weber is manager of the Gulf Coast Division of Ziemba, Inc. His division makes a single product that is sold to industrial customers. Demand is seasonal but is readily predictable. The division's budget for 19X8 called for production and sales of 120,000 units, with production of 10,000 units each month and sales varying between 8,000 and 13,000 units a month. The division's budget for 19X8 had operating income of $780,000:

Sales (120,000 × $55)	$6,600,000
Cost of goods sold (120,000 × $45)	5,400,000
Gross margin	$1,200,000
Selling and administrative expenses (all fixed)	420,000
Operating income	$ 780,000

By the end of November, sales had lagged projections, with only 105,000 units sold. Sales of 9,000 units were originally budgeted and are still expected in December. Production through November had remained stable at 10,000 units per month, and the cost of production had been exactly as budgeted:

Direct materials, 110,000 × $14	$1,540,000
Direct labor, 110,000 × $10	1,100,000
Variable overhead, 110,000 × $8	880,000
Fixed overhead	1,430,000
Total production cost	$4,950,000

The division's operating income for the first eleven months of 19X8 was:

Sales (105,000 × $55)	$5,775,000
Cost of goods sold (105,000 × $45)	4,725,000
Gross margin	$1,050,000
Selling and administrative expenses (all fixed)	385,000
Operating income	$ 665,000

Weber receives an annual bonus only if his division's operating income exceeds the budget. He sees no way to increase sales beyond 9,000 units in December.

Required

1. From the budgeted and actual income statements shown, determine whether Ziemba used direct or absorption costing.

2. Suppose Ziemba uses a standard absorption-costing system. (a) Compute the 19X8 operating income if 10,000 units are produced and 9,000 units are sold in December. (b) How could Weber achieve his budgeted operating income for 19X8?

3. Suppose Ziemba uses a standard variable-costing system. (a) Compute the 19X8 operating income if 10,000 units are produced and 9,000 units are sold in December. (b) How could Weber achieve his budgeted operating income for 19X8?

4. Which system motivates Weber to make the decision that is in the best interests of Ziemba? Explain.

15-44 Inventory Measures, Production Scheduling, and Evaluating Divisional Performance

The Calais Company stresses competition between the heads of its various divisions, and it rewards stellar performance with year-end bonuses that vary between 5% and 10% of division net operating income (before considering the bonus or income taxes). The divisional managers have great discretion in setting production schedules.

The Brittany Division produces and sells a product for which there is a long-standing demand but which can have marked seasonal and year-to-year fluctuations. On November 30, 19X6, Veronique Giraud, the Brittany Division manager, is preparing a production schedule for December. The following data are available for January 1 through November 30 (FF means French franc):

Beginning inventory, January 1, in units	10,000
Sales price, per unit	FF400
Total fixed costs incurred for manufacturing	FF9,350,000
Total fixed costs: other (not inventoriable)	FF9,350,000
Total variable costs for manufacturing	FF18,150,000
Total other variable costs (fluctuate with units sold)	FF4,000,000
Units produced	110,000
Units sold	100,000
Variances	None

Production in October and November was 10,000 units each month. Practical capacity is 12,000 units per month. Maximum available storage space for inventory is 25,000 units. The sales outlook for December through February is 6,000 units monthly. To retain a core of key employees, monthly production cannot be scheduled at less than 4,000 units without special permission from the president. Inventory is never to be less than 10,000 units.

The denominator used for applying fixed factory overhead is regarded as 120,000 units annually. The company uses a standard absorption-costing system. All variances are disposed of at year-end as an adjustment to standard cost of goods sold.

1. Given the restrictions as stated, and assuming that Giraud wants to maximize the company's net income for 19X6:

   a. How many units should be scheduled for production in December?

   b. What net operating income will be reported in 19X6 as a whole, assuming that the implied cost behavior patterns will continue in December as they did throughout the year to date? Show your computations.

   c. If December production is scheduled at 4,000 units, what would reported net income be?

2. Assume that standard variable costing is used rather than standard absorption costing:
   a. What would net income for 19X6 be, assuming that the December production schedule is the one in requirement 1, part a?
   b. Assuming that December production was 4,000 units?
   c. Reconcile the net incomes in this requirement with those in requirement 1.

3. From the viewpoint of the long-run interests of the company as a whole, what production schedule should the division manager set? Explain fully. Include in your explanation a comparison of the motivating influence of absorption and variable costing in this situation.

4. Assume standard absorption costing. Giraud wants to maximize her after-income-tax performance over the long run. Given the data at the beginning of the problem, assume that income tax rates will be halved in 19X7. Assume also that year-end write-offs of variances are acceptable for income tax purposes. How many units should be scheduled for production in December? Why?

15-45 Performance Evaluation

A division of Midland Grains produces seed corn for farmers throughout the Midwest. Peter Einerson became president in 19X7. He is concerned with the ability of his division manager to control costs. To aid his evaluation, Einerson set up a standard cost system.

Standard costs were based on 19X7 costs in several categories. Each 19X7 cost was divided by 1,520,000 cwt, the volume of 19X7 production, to determine a standard for 19X8 (cwt means hundredweight, or 100 pounds):

	19X7 Cost (thousands)	19X8 Standard (per hundredweight)
Direct materials	$1,824	$1.20
Direct labor	836	.55
Variable overhead	1,596	1.05
Fixed overhead	2,432	1.60
Total	$6,688	$4.40

At the end of 19X8, Einerson compared actual results with the standards he established. Production was 1,360,000 cwt, and variances were as follows:

	Actual	Standard	Variance
Direct materials	$1,802	$1,632	$170 U
Direct labor	735	748	13 F
Variable overhead	1,422	1,428	6 F
Fixed overhead	2,418	2,176	242 U
Total	$6,377	$5,984	$393 U

Einerson was not surprised by the unfavorable variance in direct materials. After all, corn prices in 19X8 averaged 10% above those in 19X7. But he was disturbed by the lack of control of fixed overhead. He called in the production manager and demanded an explanation.

1. Prepare an explanation for the large unfavorable fixed-overhead variance.
2. Discuss the appropriateness of using one year's costs as the next year's standards.

COLLABORATIVE LEARNING EXERCISE

15-46 Variable and Absorption Costing

Form groups of four persons each. Each person should select one of the following four roles (if groups have between four and eight persons, two persons can play any of the roles in the exercise):

Bernard Schwartz, President

Ramona Sanchez, Controller

Leonard Swanson, Marketing Manager

Kate Cheung, Treasurer

Each of the four should prepare a justification for the type of financial statements, variable or absorption costing, that he or she favors. The setting is explained in the case, "Boylston Company," that follows.

BOYLSTON COMPANY

Bernard Schwartz took over as president of Boylston Company in mid-May, 1998. The company's operating income for May was $4,000, and Schwartz was determined that June would be a better month. But, he was shocked when he received the following income statements for May and June:

	May	June
Sales	$280,000	$340,000
Standard cost of sales	150,000	180,000
Gross margin	130,000	160,000
Variances:		
Labor	6,000 F	4,000 F
Material	5,000 U	3,000 U
Overhead:		
Volume	1,000 F	27,000 U
Spending	2,000 U	1,000 U
Selling & administrative	126,000	136,000
Operating income (loss)	$ 4,000	$ (3,000)

He called Ramona Sanchez, the company's controller, and asked, "Sales were up by $60,000 in June. How could operating income possibly have decreased by $7,000? There must be something wrong with your numbers."

Sanchez replied, "The numbers are right. I agree with you that they don't make sense, but since our production was down in June, operating income suffered." Schwartz wasn't satisfied with that explanation. "If your accounting numbers don't give a good signal about performance, what good are they?"

Sanchez had anticipated this reaction. She suggested charging the fixed manufacturing costs as a period cost instead of including them in the product cost. Her reworked income statement was as follows:

	May	June
Sales	$ 280,000	$340,000
Standard cost of sales	102,000	125,000
Gross margin	178,000	215,000
Fixed overhead	66,000	67,000
Variances:		
Labor	6,000 F	4,000 F
Material	5,000 U	3,000 U
Overhead spending	2,000 U	1,000 U
Selling & administrative	126,000	136,000
Operating income (loss)	$ (15,000)	$ 12,000

Sanchez also called on Leonard Swanson, the marketing manager, to support her new statements. He pointed out that the current accounting system did not provide the right incentives to his salesforce. For example, he pointed to two products, A and B, with the following price and costs:

Product	Price	Standard Cost	Margin	% of Sales
A	$1.90	$1.10	$.80	42.1
B	$2.30	1.30	1.00	43.5

The salesforce would be inclined to focus on Product B because of its higher margin as a percent of sales. However, he believed the following figures, based on the controller's new product costs, were a better measure of the relative profitability of the products.

Product	Price	Standard Cost	Margin	% of Sales
A	$1.90	$ .50	$1.40	73.7
B	$2.30	1.00	1.30	56.5

After some discussion, Schwartz brought in Kate Cheung, corporate treasurer, who was skeptical about the new system. She maintained that "the salesforce will start cutting prices if we leave fixed costs out of our product costs. They will try for the same margin over the reduced costs, and we will not be able to cover our fixed costs. Further, it's lack of control of long-run costs, not short-run variable costs that can destroy a company. In the short-run, things constantly change and we don't make much of a commitment. But if long-run costs get out of control, there isn't much we can do about it."

Cheung was not finished. "And what about taxes? The government won't let us use your new system. And what about the balance sheet? Inventories that we now show at about $520,000 would have to be shown at about $365,000 if the fixed costs are not considered product costs. That sure doesn't make us look better to investors."

Although Schwartz liked the June profit shown by the revised statements, he thought there was some truth in all of the comments made. He wasn't sure how to proceed.

A RECOMMENDED READINGS

The following readings will aid readers who want to pursue some topics in more depth than is possible in this book. There is a hazard in compiling a group of recommended readings. Inevitably, some worthwhile books or periodicals are omitted. Moreover, such a list cannot include books published subsequent to the compilation date. The list is not comprehensive, but it suggests many excellent readings.

PERIODICALS

PROFESSIONAL JOURNALS

The following professional journals are typically available in university libraries and include articles on the application of management accounting:

- *Accounting Horizons.* Published by the American Accounting Association; stresses current practice-oriented articles in all areas of accounting.
- *CMA: The Management Accounting Magazine.* Published by The Society of Management Accountants of Canada; includes much practice-oriented research in management accounting.
- *Financial Executive.* Published by the Financial Executives Institute; emphasizes general policy issues for accounting and finance executives.
- *GAO Journal.* Covers managerial accounting issues of interest to the General Accounting Office of the U.S. government.
- *Harvard Business Review.* Published by Harvard Business School; directed to general managers, but contains excellent articles on applications of management accounting.
- *Journal of Accountancy.* Published by the American Institute of CPAs; emphasizes financial accounting and is directed at the practicing CPA.
- *Journal of Cost Management.* Published by CAM-I; covers new developments in cost management practice and theory.
- *Journal of Strategic Performance Measurement.* Covers issues related to performance measurement.
- *Management Accounting.* Published by the Institute of Management Accountants; many articles on actual applications by individual organizations.
- *Planning Review.* Published by the Planning Executives Institute; a journal designed for business planners.
- *Business Week, Forbes, Fortune, The Economist, The Wall Street Journal.* Popular publications that cover a variety of business and economics topics; often their articles relate to management accounting.

ACADEMIC JOURNALS

The academic journal that focuses most directly on current management and cost accounting research is the *Journal of Management Accounting Research,* published by the Management Accounting section of the American Accounting Association. *The Accounting Review,* the general research publication of the American Accounting Association, and *Journal of Accounting Research,* published at the University of Chicago, and *Contemporary Accounting Research,* published by the Canadian Academic Association, cover all accounting topics at a more theoretical level. *Accounting, Organizations and Society,* a British journal, publishes much research on behavioral aspects of management accounting. *The Journal of Accounting and Economics* covers economics-based accounting research.

BOOKS IN MANAGEMENT ACCOUNTING

Most of the topics in this text are covered in more detail in the many books entitled *Cost Accounting* including *Cost Accounting: A Managerial Emphasis* by C. T. Horngren, G. Foster, and Srikant Datar (Prentice Hall, 1997). You can find more advanced coverage in *Advanced Management Accounting,* 3rd ed. by R. S. Kaplan and Anthony A. Atkinson (Prentice Hall, 1998).

The Financial Executives Institute, 10 Madison Avenue, P.O. Box 1938, Morristown, NJ 07960, and the Institute of Management Accounting, 10 Paragon Drive, P.O. Box 433, Montvale, NJ 07645-0433, have long lists of accounting research publications.

HANDBOOKS, GENERAL TEXTS, AND CASE BOOKS

The books in this list have wide application to management accounting issues. The handbooks are basic references. The textbooks are designed for classroom use but may be useful for self-study. The case books present applications from real companies.

- Bierman, H., Jr., C. Bonini, and W. Hausman, *Quantitative Methods for Management,* 9th ed. Homewood, IL: Richard D. Irwin, 1997.
- Bierman, H., Jr., and S. Smidt, *The Capital Budgeting Decision,* 8th ed. New York: Macmillan, 1992. Expands the capital budgeting discussion in Chapter 11.
- Brinker, B. ed. *Handbook of Cost Management.* New York: Warren, Gorham and Lamont, 1994.
- Cooper, D., R. Scapens, and J. Arnold, eds., *Management Accounting Research and Practice.* London: Institute of Cost and Management Accountants, 1983.
- Davidson, S., and R. Weil, eds., *Handbook of Cost Accounting.* Prentice Hall, 1989.
- Pryor, T., et al., *Activity Dictionary: A Comprehensive Reference Tool for ABM and ABC,* ICMS, Inc., 1992.
- Rotch, W., B. Allen, and C. Smith, *Cases in Management Accounting and Control Systems* 3rd ed., Upper Saddle River, NJ: Prentice Hall, 1995.
- Shank, J., *Cases in Cost Management: A Strategic Emphasis,* Cincinnati, South-Western, 1995.

STRATEGIC NATURE OF MANAGEMENT ACCOUNTING

Management accountants realize that cost and performance information is most useful to organizations when it helps define strategic alternatives and helps in the management of resources to achieve strategic objectives. The books in this list, though not necessarily accounting books, provide valuable foundation to the interaction of strategy and accounting information.

- Hronec, S., *Vital Signs.* New York: Amacom, 1993.
- Kaplan, R., and H. T. Johnson, *Relevance Lost: The Rise and Fall of Management Accounting.* Boston, MA: Harvard Business School Press, 1987.
- Porter, M., *Michael Porter's Landmark Trilogy.* New York: Free Press, 1998.
- Rappaport, A., *Creating Shareholder Value: The New Standard for Business Performance.* New York: Free Press, 1997.
- Shank, J., and V. Govidarajan, *Strategic Cost Analysis: The Evolution from Managerial to Strategic Accounting,* Homewood, IL: Irwin, 1989.

MODERN MANUFACTURING

The following books provide background on the nature of modern manufacturing.

- Chase, R., and N. Aquilano, *Production and Operation Management.* Homewood, IL: Irwin, 1997.
- Hayes, R., S. Wheelright, and K. Clark, *Dynamic Manufacturing.* New York, Free Press, 1988.
- Schonberger, R., *World Class Manufacturing: The Next Decade.* New York, Free Press, 1996.
- Teece, D., *Competitive Challenge.* Harper Business, 1987.
- Zuboff, S., *In the Age of the Smart Machine.* New York: Basic Books, 1989.

MANAGEMENT ACCOUNTING IN MODERN MANUFACTURING SETTINGS

These books present responses of management accountants to changes in manufacturing methods and practices.

- Atkinson, A., R. Banker, R. Kaplan, and S. Young, *Management Accounting,* 2nd ed., Upper Saddle River, NJ: Prentice Hall, 1997.
- Bennett, R., J. Hendricks, D. Keys, and E. Rudnicki, *Cost Accounting for Factory Automation.* Montvale, NJ: National Association of Accountants, 1987.
- Goldratt, E., and J. Cox, *The Goal.* Croton-On-Hudson, NY: North River Press, Inc., 1992. A novel illustrating the new manufacturing environment.
- Goldratt, E., *Critical Chain.* Croton-On-Hudson, NY: North River Press, Inc., 1997.
- Howell, R., J. Brown, S. Soucy, and A. Seed, *Management Accounting in the New Manufacturing Environment.* Montvale, NJ: National Association of Accountants, 1987.
- Howell, R., and S. Soucy, *Factory 2000 + .* Montvale, NJ: National Association of Accountants, 1988. A collection of five articles by the authors originally published in *Management Accounting.*
- Kaplan, R., ed., *Measures for Manufacturing Excellence,* Boston, MA: Harvard Business School Press, 1990.
- Lee, J., *Managerial Accounting Changes for the 1990s.* Artesia, CA: McKay Business Systems, 1987.

MANAGEMENT CONTROL SYSTEMS

The topics of Chapters 7 to 10 can be explored further in several books, including:

- Anthony, R. N., J. Dearden, and V. Govindarajan, *Management Control Systems,* 8th Ed. Homewood, IL: Irwin, 1994. A popular textbook that includes many cases.
- Arrow, K. J., *The Limits of Organization.* New York: Norton, 1974. A readable classic by the Nobel laureate.
- Emmanuel, C., K. Merchant, and D. Otley, *Accounting for Management Control.* Chapman & Hall, 1990.
- Kaplan, R., and D. Norton, *The Balanced Scorecard.* Boston: Harvard Business School Press, 1996.
- Maciariello, J. A. and C. Kirby, *Management Control Systems: Using Adaptive Systems to Attain Control,* Upper Saddle River, NJ: Prentice Hall, 1994.
- Solomons, D., *Divisional Performance: Measurement and Control.* New York: Markus Wiener, 1983. A reprint of a 1965 classic that is still relevant.

Many books discuss management accounting in nonprofit organizations, especially in health care. Four examples are

- Anthony, R. N., and D. W. Young, *Management Control in Nonprofit Organizations,* 5th ed. Homewood, IL: Irwin, 1994.
- Brimson, J., and J. Antos, *Activity Based Management for Service Industries, Government Entities, and Non-Profit Organizations.* New York: Wiley, 1994.
- Herzlinger, R. and D. Nitterhouse, *Financial Accounting and Managerial Control for Nonprofit Organizations.* Cincinnati, OH: Southwestern Publishing Co., 1994.
- Neumann, B., and K. Boles, *Management Accounting for Healthcare Organizations,* 5th Ed. Bonus Books, 1998.

BOOKS IN FINANCIAL ACCOUNTING

This book's companion volume, *Introduction to Financial Accounting,* provides an expansion of the financial accounting material (Chapters 16-19). A more detailed coverage of the topics can be found in books entitled *Intermediate Accounting* including that by T.R. Dyckman, R.E. Dukes, and C.J. Davis (Irwin, 1995).

Opinions of the Accounting Principles Board are available from the American Institute of CPAs, 1211 Avenue of the Americas, New York, NY 10036-8775. The institute also has a series of research studies on a variety of topics. The pronouncements of the Financial Accounting Standards Board are available from the board's offices, 401 Merritt 7, P.O. Box 5116, Norwalk, CT 06856-5116.

Financial accounting has such an extensive literature that it is impossible to provide a short list of books that adequately covers the field. However, we will mention four books that cover a wide range of issues. For a perspective on the large firms practicing accounting, see two books by M. Stevens, *The Accounting Wars* (Macmillan, 1985) and *The Big Six* (Touchstone Books, 1992). Research relating financial reporting to the capital markets is summarized in T. R. Dyckman, et al., *Efficient Capital Markets and Accounting: A Critical Analysis* (Prentice Hall, 1986). The interaction of financial reporting and management's economic incentives is covered in text and readings in R. Ball and C. Smith, *The Economics of Accounting Policy Choice,* New York: McGraw-Hill, 1992. Application of this research to financial statement analysis is provided in C. Stickney, *Financial Statement Analysis,* 3rd Ed. (Harcourt Brace, 1995).

B

FUNDAMENTALS OF COMPOUND INTEREST AND THE USE OF PRESENT-VALUE TABLES

Interest is the cost of using money. It is the rental charge for cash, just as rental charges are often made for the use of automobiles or boats.

Interest does not always entail an outlay of cash. The concept of interest applies to ownership funds as well as to borrowed funds. The reason why interest must be considered on *all* funds in use, regardless of their source, is that the selection of one alternative necessarily commits funds that could otherwise be invested in some other opportunity. The measure of the interest in such cases is the return foregone by rejecting the alternative use. For instance, a wholly owned home or business asset is not cost free. The funds so invested could alternatively be invested in government bonds or in some other venture. The measure of this opportunity cost depends on what alternative incomes are available.

Newspapers often contain advertisements of financial institutions citing interest rates that are "compounded." This appendix explains compound interest, including the use of present-value tables.

Simple interest is calculated by multiplying an interest rate by an unchanging principal amount. In contrast, *compound interest* is calculated by multiplying an interest rate by a principal amount that is increased each interest period by the previously accumulated (unpaid) interest. The accumulated interest is added to the principal to become the principal for the new period. For example, suppose you deposited $10,000 in a financial institution that promised to pay 10% interest per annum. You then let the amount accumulate for three years before withdrawing the full balance of the deposit. The *simple-interest* deposit would accumulate to $13,000 at the end of three years:

	Principal	Simple Interest	Balance, End of Year
Year 1	$10,000	$10,000 × 0.10 = $1,000	$11,000
Year 2	10,000	10,000 × 0.10 = 1,000	12,000
Year 3	10,000	10,000 × 0.10 = 1,000	13,000

Compound interest provides interest on interest. That is, the principal changes from period to period. The deposit would accumulate to $10,000 \times (1.10)^3 = \$10,000 \times 1.331 = \$13,310$:

	Principal	Compound Interest	Balance, End of Year
Year 1	$10,000	$10,000 × 0.10 = $1,000	$11,000
Year 2	11,000	11,000 × 0.10 = 1,100	12,100
Year 3	12,100	12,100 × 0.10 = 1,210	13,310

The "force" of compound interest can be staggering. For example, the same deposit would accumulate as follows:

	At End of		
	10 Years	20 Years	40 Years
Simple interest			
$10,000 + 10 ($1,000) =	$20,000		
10,000 + 20 ($1,000) =		$30,000	
10,000 + 40 ($1,000) =			$ 50,000
Compound interest			
$10,000 \times (1.10)^{10} = $10,000 \times 2.5937 =	$25,937		
$10,000 \times (1.10)^{20} = $10,000 \times 6.7275 =		$67,275	
$10,000 \times (1.10)^{40} = $10,000 \times 45.2593 =			$452,593

Hand calculations of compound interest quickly become burdensome. Therefore compound interest tables have been constructed to ease computations. (Indeed, many hand-held calculators contain programs that provide speedy answers.) Hundreds of tables are available, but we will use only the two most useful for capital budgeting.[1]

TABLE 1: PRESENT VALUE OF $1

How shall we express a future cash inflow or outflow in terms of its equivalent today (at time zero)? Table 1 provides factors that give the present value of a single, lump-sum cash flow to be received or paid at the end of a future period.[2]

Suppose you invest $1.00 today. It will grow to $1.06 in one year at six percent interest; that is, $1 \times 1.06 = 1.06. At the end of the second year its value is ($1 \times 1.06) \times 1.06 = $1 \times (1.06)^2 = 1.124, and at the end of the third year it is $1 \times (1.06)^3 = 1.191$. In general, $1.00 grows to $(1 + i)^n$ in n years at i percent interest.

To determine *the present value,* you reverse this accumulation process. If $1.00 is to be received in one year, it is worth $1 \div 1.06 = 0.9434 today at an interest rate of 6%. Suppose you invest $0.9434 today. In one year you will have $0.9434 \times 1.06 = 1.00. Thus $0.9434 is the *present value* of $1.00 a year hence at 6%. If the dollar will be received in two years, its present value is $1.00 \div (1.06)^2 = 0.8900. The general formula for the present value (*PV*) of an amount S to be received or paid in n periods at an interest rate of i% per period is

$$PV = \frac{S}{(1 + i)^n}$$

Table 1 gives factors for the present value of $1.00 at various interest rates over several different periods. Present values are also called *discounted* values, and the process of finding the present value is *discounting.* You can think of this as discounting (decreasing)

---

[1] *For additional tables, see R. Vichas,* Handbook of Financial Mathematics, Formulas and Tables *(Upper Saddle River, NJ: Prentice Hall, 1979).*

[2] *The factors are rounded to four decimal places. The examples in this text use these rounded factors. If you use tables with different rounding, or if you use a calculator or personal computer, your answers may differ from those given because of a small rounding error.*

the value of a future cash inflow or outflow. Why is the value discounted? Because the cash is to be received or paid in the future, not today.

Assume that a prominent city is issuing a 3-year non-interest-bearing note payable that promises to pay a lump sum of $1,000 exactly three years from now. You desire a rate of return of exactly 6%, compounded annually. How much would you be willing to pay now for the 3-year note? The situation is sketched as follows:

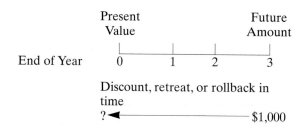

The factor in the period 3 row and 6% column of Table 1 is 0.8396. The present value of the $1,000 payment is $1,000 × 0.8396 = $839.60. You would be willing to pay $839.60 for the $1,000 to be received in three years.

Suppose interest is compounded semiannually rather than annually. How much would you be willing to pay? The three years become six interest payment periods. The rate per period is half the annual rate, or 6% ÷ 2 = 3%. The factor in the period 6 row and 3% column of Table 1 is 0.8375. You would be willing to pay $1,000 × 0.8375 or only $837.50 rather than $839.60.

As a further check on your understanding, review the earlier example of compound interest. Suppose the financial institution promised to pay $13,310 at the end of three years. How much would you be willing to deposit at time zero if you desired a 10% rate of return compounded annually? Using Table 1, the period 3 row and the 10% column show a factor of 0.7513. Multiply this factor by the future amount:

$$PV = 0.7513 \times \$13,310 = \$10,000$$

A diagram of this computation follows:

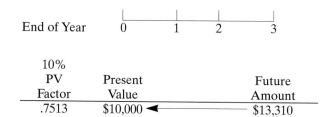

Pause for a moment. Use Table 1 to obtain the present values of

1. $1,700, at 20%, at the end of 20 years
2. $8,300, at 10%, at the end of 12 years
3. $8,000, at 4%, at the end of 4 years

Answers:

1. $1,700 (0.0261) = $44.37
2. $8,300 (0.3186) = $2,644.38
3. $8,000 (0.8548) = $6,838.40

TABLE 2: PRESENT VALUE OF AN ORDINARY ANNUITY OF $1

An ordinary annuity is a series of equal cash flows to take place at the end of successive periods of equal length. Its present value is denoted PV_A. Assume that you buy a note from a municipality that promises to pay $1,000 at the end of *each* of three years. How much should you be willing to pay if you desire a rate of return of 6%, compounded annually?

You could solve this problem using Table 1. First, find the present value of each payment, and then add the present values as in Exhibit B-1. You would be willing to pay $943.40 for the first payment, $890.00 for the second, and $839.60 for the third, a total of $2,673.00.

Since each cash payment is $1,000 with equal 1-year periods between them, the note is an ordinary annuity. Table 2 provides a shortcut method. The present value in Exhibit B-1 can be expressed as

$$PV_A = \$1,000 \times \frac{1}{1.06} + \$1,000 \times \frac{1}{(1.06)^2} + \$1,000 \times \frac{1}{(1.06)^3}$$

$$= \$1,000 \left[\frac{1}{1.06} + \frac{1}{(1.06)^2} + \frac{1}{(1.06)^3} \right]$$

The three terms in brackets are the first three numbers from the 6% column of Table 1, and their sum is in the third row of the 6% column of Table 2: .9434 + .8900 + .8396 = 2.6730. Instead of calculating three present values and adding them, you can simply multiply the PV factor from Table 2 by the cash payment: 2.6730 × $1,000 = $2,673.

This shortcut is especially valuable if the cash payments or receipts extend over many periods. Consider an annual cash payment of $1,000 for 20 years at 6%. The present value, calculated from Table 2, is $1,000 × 11.4699 = $11,469.90. To use Table 1 for this calculation, you would perform 20 multiplications and then add the twenty products.

The factors in Table 2 can be calculated using the following general formula:

$$PV_A = \left[\frac{1}{i} \left(1 - \frac{1}{(1+i)^n} \right) \right]$$

Applied to our illustration:

$$PV_A = \frac{1}{.06} \left[1 - \frac{1}{(1.06)^3} \right] = \frac{1}{.06}(1 - .8396) = \frac{.1604}{.06} = 2.6730$$

Use Table 2 to obtain the present values of the following ordinary annuities:

1. $1,600 at 20% for 20 years
2. $8,300 at 10% for 12 years
3. $8,000 at 4% for 4 years

Exhibt B-I

Payment	End of Year Table One Factor	0 Present Value	1	2	3
1	$\frac{1}{1.06} = .9434$	$ 943.40	$1,000		
2	$\frac{1}{(1.06)^2} = .8900$	890.00		1,000	
3	$\frac{1}{(1.06)^3} = .8396$	839.60			$1,000
Total		$2,673.00			

Answers:

1. $1,600 (4.8696) = $7,791.36
2. $8,300 (6.8137) = $56,553.71
3. $8,000 (3.6299) = $29,039.20

In particular, note that the higher interest rate, the lower the present value.

Table1

Present Value of $1

$$PV = \frac{1}{(1+i)^n}$$

Periods	3%	4%	5%	6%	7%	8%	10%	12%	14%	16%	18%	20%	22%	24%	25%	26%	28%	30%	40%
1	.9709	.9615	.9524	.9434	.9346	.9259	.9091	.8929	.8772	.8621	.8475	.8333	.8197	.8065	.8000	.7937	.7813	.7692	.7143
2	.9426	.9246	.9070	.8900	.8734	.8573	.8264	.7972	.7695	.7432	.7182	.6944	.6719	.6504	.6400	.6299	.6104	.5917	.5102
3	.9151	.8890	.8638	.8396	.8163	.7938	.7513	.7118	.6750	.6407	.6086	.5787	.5507	.5245	.5120	.4999	.4768	.4552	.3644
4	.8885	.8548	.8227	.7921	.7629	.7350	.6830	.6355	.5921	.5523	.5158	.4823	.4514	.4230	.4096	.3968	.3725	.3501	.2603
5	.8626	.8219	.7835	.7473	.7130	.6806	.6209	.5674	.5194	.4761	.4371	.4019	.3700	.3411	.3277	.3149	.2910	.2693	.1859
6	.8375	.7903	.7462	.7050	.6663	.6302	.5645	.5066	.4556	.4104	.3704	.3349	.3033	.2751	.2621	.2499	.2274	.2072	.1328
7	.8131	.7599	.7107	.6651	.6227	.5835	.5132	.4523	.3996	.3538	.3139	.2791	.2486	.2218	.2097	.1983	.1776	.1594	.0949
8	.7894	.7307	.6768	.6274	.5820	.5403	.4665	.4039	.3506	.3050	.2660	.2326	.2038	.1789	.1678	.1574	.1388	.1226	.0678
9	.7664	.7026	.6446	.5919	.5439	.5002	.4241	.3606	.3075	.2630	.2255	.1938	.1670	.1443	.1342	.1249	.1084	.0943	.0484
10	.7441	.6756	.6139	.5584	.5083	.4632	.3855	.3220	.2697	.2267	.1911	.1615	.1369	.1164	.1074	.0992	.0847	.0725	.0346
11	.7224	.6496	.5847	.5268	.4751	.4289	.3505	.2875	.2366	.1954	.1619	.1346	.1122	.0938	.0859	.0787	.0662	.0558	.0247
12	.7014	.6246	.5568	.4970	.4440	.3971	.3186	.2567	.2076	.1685	.1372	.1122	.0920	.0757	.0687	.0625	.0517	.0429	.0176
13	.6810	.6006	.5303	.4688	.4150	.3677	.2897	.2292	.1821	.1452	.1163	.0935	.0754	.0610	.0550	.0496	.0404	.0330	.0126
14	.6611	.5775	.5051	.4423	.3878	.3405	.2633	.2046	.1597	.1252	.0985	.0779	.0618	.0492	.0440	.0393	.0316	.0254	.0090
15	.6419	.5553	.4810	.4173	.3624	.3152	.2394	.1827	.1401	.1079	.0835	.0649	.0507	.0397	.0352	.0312	.0247	.0195	.0064
16	.6232	.5339	.4581	.3936	.3387	.2919	.2176	.1631	.1229	.0930	.0708	.0541	.0415	.0320	.0281	.0248	.0193	.0150	.0046
17	.6050	.5134	.4363	.3714	.3166	.2703	.1978	.1456	.1078	.0802	.0600	.0451	.0340	.0258	.0225	.0197	.0150	.0116	.0033
18	.5874	.4936	.4155	.3503	.2959	.2502	.1799	.1300	.0946	.0691	.0508	.0376	.0279	.0208	.0180	.0156	.0118	.0089	.0023
19	.5703	.4746	.3957	.3305	.2765	.2317	.1635	.1161	.0829	.0596	.0431	.0313	.0229	.0168	.0144	.0124	.0092	.0068	.0017
20	.5537	.4564	.3769	.3118	.2584	.2145	.1486	.1037	.0728	.0514	.0365	.0261	.0187	.0135	.0115	.0098	.0072	.0053	.0012
21	.5375	.4388	.3589	.2942	.2415	.1987	.1351	.0926	.0638	.0443	.0309	.0217	.0154	.0109	.0092	.0078	.0056	.0040	.0009
22	.5219	.4220	.3418	.2775	.2257	.1839	.1228	.0826	.0560	.0382	.0262	.0181	.0126	.0088	.0074	.0062	.0044	.0031	.0006
23	.5067	.4057	.3256	.2618	.2109	.1703	.1117	.0738	.0491	.0329	.0222	.0151	.0103	.0071	.0059	.0049	.0034	.0024	.0004
24	.4919	.3901	.3101	.2470	.1971	.1577	.1015	.0659	.0431	.0284	.0188	.0126	.0085	.0057	.0047	.0039	.0027	.0018	.0003
25	.4776	.3751	.2953	.2330	.1842	.1460	.0923	.0588	.0378	.0245	.0160	.0105	.0069	.0046	.0038	.0031	.0021	.0014	.0002
26	.4637	.3607	.2812	.2198	.1722	.1352	.0839	.0525	.0331	.0211	.0135	.0087	.0057	.0037	.0030	.0025	.0016	.0011	.0002
27	.4502	.3468	.2678	.2074	.1609	.1252	.0763	.0469	.0291	.0182	.0115	.0073	.0047	.0030	.0024	.0019	.0013	.0008	.0001
28	.4371	.3335	.2551	.1956	.1504	.1159	.0693	.0419	.0255	.0157	.0097	.0061	.0038	.0024	.0019	.0015	.0010	.0006	.0001
29	.4243	.3207	.2429	.1846	.1406	.1073	.0630	.0374	.0224	.0135	.0082	.0051	.0031	.0020	.0015	.0012	.0008	.0005	.0001
30	.4120	.3083	.2314	.1741	.1314	.0994	.0573	.0334	.0196	.0116	.0070	.0042	.0026	.0016	.0012	.0010	.0006	.0004	.0000
40	.3066	.2083	.1420	.0972	.0668	.0460	.0221	.0107	.0053	.0026	.0013	.0007	.0004	.0002	.0001	.0001	.0001	.0000	.0000

Table 2
Present Value of Ordinary Annuity of $1

$$PV_A = \frac{1}{i}\left[1 - \frac{1}{(1+i)^n}\right]$$

Periods	3%	4%	5%	6%	7%	8%	10%	12%	14%	16%	18%	20%	22%	24%	25%	26%	28%	30%	40%
1	.9709	.9615	.9524	.9434	.9346	.9259	.9091	.8929	.8772	.8621	.8475	.8333	.8197	.8065	.8000	.7937	.7813	.7692	.7143
2	1.9135	1.8861	1.8594	1.8334	1.8080	1.7833	1.7355	1.6901	1.6467	1.6052	1.5656	1.5278	1.4915	1.4568	1.4400	1.4235	1.3916	1.3609	1.2245
3	2.8286	2.7751	2.7232	2.6730	2.6243	2.5771	2.4869	2.4018	2.3216	2.2459	2.1743	2.1065	2.0422	1.9813	1.9520	1.9234	1.8684	1.8161	1.5889
4	3.7171	3.6299	3.5460	3.4651	3.3872	3.3121	3.1699	3.0373	2.9137	2.7982	2.6901	2.5887	2.4936	2.4043	2.3616	2.3202	2.2410	2.1662	1.8492
5	4.5797	4.4518	4.3295	4.2124	4.1002	3.9927	3.7908	3.6048	3.4331	3.2743	3.1272	2.9906	2.8636	2.7454	2.6893	2.6351	2.5320	2.4356	2.0352
6	5.4172	5.2421	5.0757	4.9173	4.7665	4.6229	4.3553	4.1114	3.8887	3.6847	3.4976	3.3255	3.1669	3.0205	2.9514	2.8850	2.7594	2.6427	2.1680
7	6.2303	6.0021	5.7864	5.5824	5.3893	5.2064	4.8684	4.5638	4.2883	4.0386	3.8115	3.6046	3.4155	3.2423	3.1611	3.0833	2.9370	2.8021	2.2628
8	7.0197	6.7327	6.4632	6.2098	5.9713	5.7466	5.3349	4.9676	4.6389	4.3436	4.0776	3.8372	3.6193	3.4212	3.3289	3.2407	3.0758	2.9247	2.2306
9	7.7861	7.4353	7.1078	6.8017	6.5152	6.2469	5.7590	5.3282	4.9464	4.6065	4.3030	4.0310	3.7863	3.5655	3.4631	3.3657	3.1842	3.0190	2.3790
10	8.5302	8.1109	7.7217	7.3601	7.0236	6.7101	6.1446	5.6502	5.2161	4.8332	4.4941	4.1925	3.9232	3.6819	3.5705	3.4648	3.2689	3.0915	2.4136
11	9.2526	8.7605	8.3064	7.8869	7.4987	7.1390	6.4951	5.9377	5.4527	5.0286	4.6560	4.3271	4.0354	3.7757	3.6564	3.5435	3.3351	3.1473	2.4383
12	9.9540	9.3851	8.8633	8.3838	7.9427	7.5361	6.8137	6.1944	5.6603	5.1971	4.7932	4.4392	4.1274	3.8514	3.7251	3.6059	3.3868	3.1903	2.4559
13	10.6350	9.9856	9.3936	8.8527	8.3577	7.9038	7.1034	6.4235	5.8424	5.3423	4.9095	4.5327	4.2028	3.9124	3.7801	3.6555	3.4272	3.2233	2.4685
14	11.2961	10.5631	9.8986	9.2950	8.7455	8.2442	7.3667	6.6282	6.0021	5.4675	5.0081	4.6106	4.2646	3.9616	3.8241	3.6949	3.4587	3.2487	2.4775
15	11.9379	11.1184	10.3797	9.7122	9.1079	8.5595	7.6061	6.8109	6.1422	5.5755	5.0916	4.6755	4.3152	4.0013	3.8593	3.7261	3.4834	3.2682	2.4839
16	12.5611	11.6523	10.8378	10.1059	9.4466	8.8514	7.8237	6.9740	6.2651	5.6685	5.1624	4.7296	4.3567	4.0333	3.8874	3.7509	3.5026	3.2832	2.4885
17	13.1661	12.1657	11.2741	10.4773	9.7632	9.1216	8.0216	7.1196	6.3729	5.7487	5.2223	4.7746	4.3908	4.0591	3.9099	3.7705	3.5177	3.2948	2.4918
18	13.7535	12.6593	11.6896	10.8276	10.0591	9.3719	8.2014	7.2497	6.4674	5.8178	5.2732	4.8122	4.4187	4.0799	3.9279	3.7861	3.5294	3.3037	2.4941
19	14.3238	13.1339	12.0853	11.1581	10.3356	9.6036	8.3649	7.3658	6.5504	5.8775	5.3162	4.8435	4.4415	4.0967	3.9424	3.7985	3.5386	3.3105	2.4958
20	14.8775	13.5903	12.4622	11.4699	10.5940	9.8181	8.5136	7.4694	6.6231	5.9288	5.3527	4.8696	4.4603	4.1103	3.9539	3.8083	3.5458	3.3158	2.4970
21	15.4150	14.0292	12.8212	11.7641	10.8355	10.0168	8.6487	7.5620	6.6870	5.9731	5.3837	4.8913	4.4756	4.1212	3.9631	3.8161	3.5514	3.3198	2.4979
22	15.9369	14.4511	13.1630	12.0416	11.0612	10.2007	8.7715	7.6446	6.7429	6.0113	5.4099	4.9094	4.4882	4.1300	3.9705	3.8223	3.5558	3.3230	2.4985
23	16.4436	14.8568	13.4886	12.3034	11.2722	10.3711	8.8832	7.7184	6.7921	6.0442	5.4321	4.9245	4.4985	4.1371	3.9764	3.8273	3.5592	3.3254	2.4989
24	16.9355	15.2470	13.7986	12.5504	11.4693	10.5288	8.9847	7.7843	6.8351	6.0726	5.4509	4.9371	4.5070	4.1428	3.9811	3.8312	3.5619	3.3272	2.4992
25	17.4131	15.6221	14.0939	12.7834	11.6536	10.6748	9.0770	7.8431	6.8729	6.0971	5.4669	4.9476	4.5139	4.1474	3.9849	3.8342	3.5640	3.3286	2.4994
26	17.8768	15.9828	14.3752	13.0032	11.8258	10.8100	9.1609	7.8957	6.9061	6.1182	5.4804	4.9563	4.5196	4.1511	3.9879	3.8367	3.5656	3.3297	2.4996
27	18.3270	16.3296	14.6430	13.2105	11.9867	10.9352	9.2372	7.9426	6.9352	6.1364	5.4919	4.9636	4.5243	4.1542	3.9903	3.8387	3.5669	3.3305	2.4997
28	18.7641	16.6631	14.8981	13.4062	12.1371	11.0511	9.3066	7.9844	6.9607	6.1520	5.5016	4.9697	4.5281	4.1566	3.9923	3.8402	3.5679	3.3312	2.4998
29	19.1885	16.9837	15.1411	13.5907	12.2777	11.1584	9.3696	8.0218	6.9830	6.1656	5.5098	4.9747	4.5312	4.1585	3.9938	3.8414	3.5687	3.3317	2.4999
30	19.6004	17.2920	15.3725	13.7648	12.4090	11.2578	9.4269	8.0552	7.0027	6.1772	5.5168	4.9789	4.5338	4.1601	3.9950	3.8424	3.5693	3.3321	2.4999
40	23.1148	19.7928	17.1591	15.0463	13.3317	11.9246	9.7791	8.2438	7.1050	6.2335	5.5482	4.9966	4.5439	4.1659	3.9995	3.8458	3.5712	3.3332	2.5000

GLOSSARY

absorption approach A costing approach that considers all factory overhead (both variable and fixed) to be product (inventoriable) costs that become an expense in the form of manufacturing cost of goods sold only as sales occur.

accelerated depreciation A pattern of depreciation that charges a larger proportion of an asset's cost to the earlier years and less to later years.

account analysis Selecting a volume-related cost driver and classifying each account as a variable cost or as a fixed cost.

account Each item in a financial statement.

accounting rate-of-return (ARR) model A non-DCF capital-budgeting model expressed as the increase in expected average annual operating income divided by the initial required investment.

accounting system A formal mechanism for gathering, organizing, and communicating information about an organization's activities.

accounts payable Amounts owed to vendors for purchases on open accounts.

accounts receivable Amounts due from customers for sales on open account.

accrual basis A process of accounting that recognizes the impact of transactions on the financial statements in the time periods when revenues and expenses occur instead of when cash is received or disbursed.

accrue To accumulate a receivable or payable during a given period even though no explicit transaction occurs.

activity analysis The process of identifying appropriate cost drivers and their effects on the costs of making a product or providing a service.

activity-based costing (ABC) A system that first accumulates overhead costs for each of the activities of an organization, and then assigns the costs of activities to the products, services, or other cost objects that caused that activity.

activity-based flexible budget A budget based on budgeted costs for each activity and related cost driver.

activity-based management (ABM) Using an activity-based costing system to improve the operations of an organization.

activity-level variances The differences between the master budget amounts and the amounts in the flexible budget.

adjustments Recording of implicit transactions, in contrast to the explicit transactions that trigger nearly all day-to-day routine entries.

agency theory A theory used to describe the formal choices of performance measures and rewards.

assets Economic resources that are expected to benefit future activities.

attention directing Reporting and interpreting information that helps managers to focus on operating problems, imperfections, inefficiencies, and opportunities.

audit An examination or in-depth inspection of financial statements and companies' records that is made in accordance with generally accepted auditing standards. It culminates with the accountant's testimony that management's financial statements are in conformity with generally accepted accounting principles.

available-for-sale securities Investments that the investor company has no intention to sell in the near future.

avoidable costs Costs that will not continue if an ongoing operation is changed or deleted.

backflush costing An accounting system that applies costs to products only when the production is complete.

balance sheet (statement of financial position, statement of financial condition) A snapshot of the financial status of an organization at an instant of time.

balanced scorecard A performance measurement and reporting system that strikes a balance between financial and operating measures, links performance to rewards, and gives explicit recognition to the diversity of organizational goals.

behavioral implications The accounting system's effect on the behavior (decisions) of managers.

benchmarks General rules of thumb specifying appropriate levels for financial ratios.

book value (net book value) The original cost of equipment less accumulated depreciation, which is the summation of depreciation charged to past periods.

break-even point The level of sales at which revenue equals expenses and net income is zero.

budget A quantitative expression of a plan of action, and an aid to coordinating and implementing the plan.

budgeted factory-overhead rate The budgeted total overhead for each cost pool divided by the budgeted cost-driver level.

by-product A product that, like a joint product, is not individually identifiable until manufacturing reaches a split-off point, but has relatively insignificant total sales value.

capacity costs The fixed costs of being able to achieve a desired level of production or to provide a desired level of service while maintaining product or service attributes, such as quality.

capital budget A budget that details the planned expenditures for facilities, equipment, new products, and other long-term investments.

capital budgeting The long-term planning for making and financing investments that affect financial results over more than just the next year.

capital turnover Revenue divided by invested capital.

cash basis A process of accounting where revenue and expense recognition would occur when cash is received and disbursed.

cash budget A statement of planned cash receipts and disbursements.

cash equivalents Short-term investments that can easily be converted into cash with little delay.

cash flow Usually refers to the net cash flow from operating activities.

cash flows from operating activities The first major section in the statement of cash flows.

cellular manufacturing A production system in which machines are organized in cells according to the specific requirements of a product family.

Certified Management Accountant (CMA) The management accountant's counterpart to the CPA.

Certified Public Accountant (CPA) In the United States, an accountant earns this designation by a combination of education, qualifying experience, and the passing of a two-day written national examination.

coefficient of determination (R^2) A measurement of how much of the fluctuation of a cost is explained by changes in the cost driver.

committed fixed costs Costs arising from the possession of facilities, equipment, and a basic organization: large, indivisible chunks of cost that the organization is obligated to incur or usually would not consider avoiding.

common costs Those costs of facilities and services that are shared by users.

common stock Stock that has no predetermined rate of dividends and is the last to obtain a share in the assets when the corporation is dissolved. It usually has voting power to elect the board of directors of the corporation.

common-size statements Financial statements expressed in component percentages.

component percentages Analysis and presentation of financial statements in percentage form to aid comparability, frequently used when companies differ in size.

computer-integrated manufacturing (CIM) systems Systems that use computer-aided design and computer-aided manufacturing, together with robots and computer-controlled machines.

conservatism convention Selecting the method of measurement that yields the gloomiest immediate results.

consolidated financial statements Financial statements that combine the financial statements of the parent company with those of various subsidiaries, as if they were a single entity.

constant dollars Nominal dollars that are restated in terms of current purchasing power.

continuity convention (going concern convention) The assumption that an organization will continue to exist and operate.

continuous budget (rolling budget) A common form of master budget that adds a month in the future as the month just ended is dropped.

contribution approach A method of internal (management accounting) reporting that emphasizes the distinction between variable and fixed costs for the purpose of better decision making.

contribution margin (marginal income) The sales price minus the variable cost per unit.

controllable cost Any cost that is influenced by a manager's decisions and actions.

controller (comptroller) The top accounting officer of an organization. The term comptroller is used primarily in government organizations.

conversion costs Direct labor costs plus factory overhead costs.

corporation A business organized as a separate legal entity and owned by its stockholders.

cost A sacrifice or giving up of resources for a particular purpose, frequently measured by the monetary units that must be paid for goods and services.

cost accounting systems The techniques used to determine the cost of a product, service, or other cost objective by collecting and classifying costs and assigning them to cost objects.

cost accounting That part of the accounting system that measures costs for the purposes of management decision making and financial reporting.

cost accumulation Collecting costs by some natural classification such as materials or labor.

cost allocation　Tracing and reassigning costs to one or more cost objectives such as activities, departments, customers, or products.

cost-allocation base　A cost driver when it is used for allocating costs.

cost application　The allocation of total departmental costs to the revenue-producing products or services.

cost behavior　How costs are related to and affected by the activities of an organization.

cost-benefit balance　Weighing estimated costs against probable benefits, the primary consideration in choosing among accounting systems and methods.

cost-benefit criterion　An approach that implicitly underlies the decisions about the design of accounting systems. As a system is changed, its potential benefits should exceed its additional costs.

cost center　A responsibility center in which a manager is accountable for costs only.

cost drivers　Output measures of resources and activities.

cost function　An algebraic equation used by managers to describe the relationship between a cost and its cost driver(s).

cost-management system　Identifies how management's decisions affect costs, by first measuring the resources used in performing the organization's activities and then assessing the effects on costs of changes in those activities.

cost measurement　Estimating or predicting costs as a function of appropriate cost drivers.

cost objective (cost object)　Anything for which a separate measurement of costs is desired. Examples include departments, products, activities, and territories.

cost of capital　What a firm must pay to acquire more capital, whether or not it actually has to acquire more capital to take on a project.

cost of goods sold　The cost of the merchandise that is acquired or manufactured and resold.

cost of quality report　A report that displays the financial impact of quality.

cost pool　A group of individual costs that is allocated to cost objectives using a single cost driver.

cost prediction　The application of cost measures to expected future activity levels to forecast future costs.

cost recovery　A concept in which assets such as inventories, prepayments, and equipment are carried forward as assets because their costs are expected to be recovered in the form of cash inflows (or reduced cash outflows) in future periods.

cost-volume-profit (CVP) analysis　The study of the effects of output volume on revenue (sales), expenses (costs), and net income (net profit).

credit　An entry on the right side of an account.

critical process　A series of related activities that directly affects the achievement of organizational goals.

cross-sectional comparisons　Comparisons of a company's financial ratios with ratios of other companies or with industry averages for the same period.

current assets　Cash and all other assets that are reasonably expected to be converted to cash or sold or consumed within one year or during the normal operating cycle, if longer than a year.

current cost　The cost to replace an asset, as opposed to its historical cost.

current-cost method　The measurement method that uses current costs and nominal dollars.

current liabilities　An organization's debts that fall due within the coming year or within the normal operating cycle if longer than a year.

currently attainable standards　Levels of performance that can be achieved by realistic levels of effort.

cycle time　The time taken to complete a product or service, or any of the components of a product or service.

debentures　Formal certificates of indebtedness that are accompanied by a promise to pay interest at a specified annual rate.

debit　An entry on the left side of an account.

decentralization　The delegation of freedom to make decisions. The lower in the organization that this freedom exists, the greater the decentralization.

decision making　The purposeful choice from among a set of alternative courses of action designed to achieve some objective.

decision model　Any method for making a choice, sometimes requiring elaborate quantitative procedures.

depreciation　The periodic cost of equipment which is spread over (or charged to) the future periods in which the equipment is expected to be used.

differential approach　A method for comparing alternatives that computes the differences in cash flows between alternatives and then converts these differences in cash flows to their present values.

differential cost (incremental cost)　The difference in total cost between two alternatives.

direct costs　Costs that can be identified specifically and exclusively with a given cost objective in an economically feasible way.

direct-labor costs　The wages of all labor that can be traced specifically and exclusively to the manufactured goods in an economically feasible way.

direct-material costs　The acquisition costs of all materials that are physically identified as a part of the manufactured goods and that may be traced to the manufactured goods in an economically feasible way.

direct method　A method for allocating service department costs that ignores other service departments when any given service department's costs are allocated to the revenue-producing (operating) departments.

discounted-cash-flow (DCF) models A type of capital-budgeting model that focuses on cash inflows and outflows while taking into account the time value of money.

discretionary fixed costs Costs determined by management as part of the periodic planning process in order to meet the organization's goals.

discriminatory pricing Charging different prices to different customers for the same product or service.

dividends Distributions of assets to stockholders that reduce retained income.

double-entry system A method of record keeping in which each transaction affects at least two accounts.

dysfunctional behavior Any action taken in conflict with organizational goals.

earnings per share Net income divided by the average number of common shares outstanding during the year.

economic value added (EVA) Equals net operating income minus the after-tax weighted-average cost of capital multiplied times the sum of long-term liabilities and stockholders' equity.

effectiveness The degree to which a goal, objective, or target is met.

efficiency The degree to which inputs are used in relation to a given level of outputs.

efficient capital market A market in which market prices fully reflect all information available to the public.

engineering analysis The systematic review of materials, supplies, labor, support services, and facilities needed for products and services; measuring cost behavior according to what costs should be, not by what costs have been.

equities The claims against, or interests in, an organization's assets.

equity method Accounts for the investment at the acquisition cost adjusted for dividends received and the investor's share of earnings or losses of the investee after the date of investment.

equivalent units The number of completed units that could have been produced from the inputs applied.

expected cost The cost most likely to be attained.

expenses Decreases in ownership claims arising from delivery goods or services or using up assets.

favorable expense variance A variance that occurs when actual expenses are less than budgeted expenses.

financial accounting The field of accounting that develops information for external decision makers such as stockholders, suppliers, banks, and government regulatory agencies.

Financial Accounting Standards Board (FASB) The primary regulatory body over accounting principles and practices in the U.S. Consisting of seven full-time members, it is an independent creation of the private sector.

financial budget The part of a master budget that focuses on the effects that the operating budget and other plans (such as capital budgets and repayments of debt) will have on cash.

financial capital maintenance The concept that income emerges after financial resources are recovered.

financial planning models Mathematical models of the master budget that can react to any set of assumptions about sales, costs, or product mix.

first-in, first-out (FIFO) An inventory method that assumes that the stock acquired earliest is sold (used up) first.

first-in, first-out (FIFO) process-costing method A process-costing method that sharply distinguishes the current work done from the previous work done on the beginning inventory of work in process.

fixed assets (tangible assets) Physical items that a person can see and touch, such as property, plant, and equipment.

fixed cost A cost that is not immediately affected by changes in the cost driver.

fixed-overhead rate The amount of fixed manufacturing overhead applied to each unit of production. It is determined by dividing the budgeted fixed overhead by the expected volume of production for the budget period.

flexible budget (variable budget) A budget that adjusts for changes in sales volume and other cost-driver activities.

flexible-budget variances The variances between the flexible budget and the actual results.

Foreign Corrupt Practices Act U.S. law forbidding bribery and other corrupt practices, and requiring that accounting records be maintained in reasonable detail and accuracy, and that an appropriate system of internal accounting controls be maintained.

full cost (fully allocated cost) The total of all manufacturing costs plus the total of all selling and administrative costs.

general ledger A collection of the group of accounts that supports the items shown in the major financial statements.

general price index A comparison of the average price of a group of goods and services at one date with the average price of a similar group at another date.

generally accepted accounting principles (GAAP) Broad concepts or guidelines and detailed practices, including all conventions, rules, and procedures that together make up accepted accounting practice at a given time.

goal congruence A condition where employees, working in their own personal interests, make decisions that help meet the overall goals of the organization.

goodwill The excess of the cost of an acquired company over the sum of the fair market values of its identifiable individual assets less its liabilities.

gross book value The original cost of an asset before deducting accumulated depreciation.

gross margin (gross profit) The excess of sales over the total cost of goods sold.

high-low method   A simple method for measuring a linear-cost function from past cost data, focusing on the highest-activity and lowest-activity points and fitting a line through these two points.

historical cost   The amount originally paid to acquire an asset.

holding gains (or losses)   Increases (or decreases) in the replacement costs of the assets held during the current period.

hybrid-costing system   An accounting system that is a blend of ideas from both job costing and process costing.

imperfect competition   A market in which the price a firm charges for a unit will influence the quantity of units it sells.

incentives   Those formal and informal performance-based rewards that enhance managerial effort toward organizational goals.

income percentage of revenue (return on sales)   Income divided by revenue.

income statement   A statement that measures the performance of an organization by matching its accomplishments (revenue from customers, which is usually called sales) and its efforts (cost of goods sold and other expenses).

incremental effect   The change in total results (such as revenue, expenses, or income) under a new condition in comparison with some given or known condition.

indirect costs   Costs that cannot be identified specifically and exclusively with a given cost objective in an economically feasible way.

indirect manufacturing costs (factory burden, factory overhead, manufacturing overhead)   All costs other than direct material or direct labor that are associated with the manufacturing process.

indirect method   In a statement of cash flows, the method that reconciles net income to the net cash provided by operating activities.

inflation   The decline in the general purchasing power of the monetary unit.

Institute of Management Accountants (IMA)   The largest U.S. professional organization of accountants whose major interest is management accounting.

intangible assets   Long-lived assets that are not physical in nature. Examples are goodwill, franchises, patents, trademarks, and copyrights.

International Accounting Standards Committee (IASC)   The group that establishes international GAAP.

inventory turnover   The number of times the average inventory is sold per year.

investment center   A responsibility center whose success is measured not only by its income but also by relating that income to its invested capital, as in a ratio of income to the value of the capital employed.

investments in affiliates (investments in associates)   Investments in equity securities that represent 20% to 50% ownership. They are accounted for under the equity method.

job-cost record (job-cost sheet, job order)   A document that shows all costs for a particular product, service, or batch of products.

job-order costing (job costing)   The method of allocating costs to products that are readily identified by individual units or batches, each of which requires varying degrees of attention and skill.

joint costs   The costs of manufacturing joint products prior to the split-off point.

joint products   Two or more manufactured products that (1) have relatively significant sales values and (2) are not separately identifiable as individual products until their split-off point.

just-in-time (JIT) philosophy   A philosophy to eliminate waste by reducing the time products spend in the production process and eliminating the time products spend on activities that do not add value.

just-in-time (JIT) production system   A system in which an organization purchases materials and parts and produces components just when they are needed in the production process, the goal being to have zero inventory, because holding inventory is a non-value-added activity.

kaizen costing   The Japanese word for continuous improvement during manufacturing.

key performance indicators   Measures that drive the organization to achieve its goals.

key success factor   Actions that must be done well in order to drive the organization towards its goals.

labor time tickets (time cards)   The record of the time a particular direct laborer spends on each job.

last-in, first-out (LIFO)   An inventory method that assumes that the stock acquired most recently is sold (used up) first.

least-squares regression (regression analysis)   Measuring a cost function objectively by using statistics to fit a cost function to all the data.

ledger accounts   A method of keeping track of how multitudes of transactions affect each particular asset, liability, revenue, and expense.

liabilities   The entity's economic obligations to nonowners.

LIFO layers (LIFO increments)   Separately identifiable additional layers of LIFO inventory.

limited liability   Creditors cannot seek payment from shareholders as individuals if the corporation itself cannot pay its debts.

limiting factor (scarce resource)   The item that restricts or constrains the production or sale of a product or service.

linear-cost behavior   Activity that can be graphed with a straight line because costs are assumed to be either fixed or variable.

line authority   Authority exerted downward over subordinates.

liquidation Converting assets to cash and using the cash to pay off outside claims.

long-range planning Producing forecasted financial statements for five- to ten-year periods.

lower-of-cost-or-market (LCM) An inventory method in which the current market price of inventory is compared with its cost (derived by specific identification, FIFO, LIFO, or weighted average) and the lower of the two is selected as the basis for the valuation of goods at a specific inventory date.

management accounting The process of identifying, measuring, accumulating, analyzing, preparing, interpreting, and communicating information that helps managers fulfill organizational objectives.

management audit A review to determine whether the policies and procedures specified by top management have been implemented.

management by exception Concentrating on areas that deviate from the plan and ignoring areas that are presumed to be running smoothly.

management by objectives (MBO) The joint formulation by a manager and his or her superior of a set of goals and plans for achieving the goals for a forthcoming period.

management control system A logical integration of techniques to gather and use information to make planning and control decisions, to motivate employee behavior, and to evaluate performance.

managerial effort Exertion toward a goal or objective including all conscious actions (such as supervising, planning, and thinking) that result in more efficiency and effectiveness.

margin of safety The planned unit sales less the break-even unit sales; it shows how far sales can fall below the planned level before losses occur.

marginal cost The additional cost resulting from producing and selling one additional unit.

marginal income tax rate The tax rate paid on additional amounts of pretax income.

marginal revenue The additional revenue resulting from the sale of an additional unit.

market method The method of accounting for investments in equity securities that shows the investment on the balance sheet at market value.

markup The amount by which price exceeds cost.

master budget (pro forma statement) A budget that summarizes the planned activities of all subunits of an organization.

master budget variance (static budget variance) The variance of actual results from the master budget.

matching The relating of accomplishments or revenues (as measured by the selling prices of goods and services delivered) and efforts or expenses (as measured by the cost of goods and services used) to a particular period for which a measurement of income is desired.

materiality The accounting convention that justifies the omission of insignificant information when its omission or misstatement would not mislead a user of the financial statements.

materials requisitions Records of materials issued to particular jobs.

measurement of cost behavior Understanding and quantifying how activities of an organization affect levels of costs.

minority interests An account that shows the outside stockholders' interest, as opposed to the parent's interest, in a subsidiary corporation.

mixed costs Costs that contain elements of both fixed- and variable-cost behavior.

motivation The drive for some selected goal that creates effort and action toward that goal.

net book value The original cost of an asset less an accumulated depreciation.

net income The popular "bottom line"—the residual after deducting from revenues all expenses, including income taxes.

net worth A synonym for owner's equity.

net-present-value (NPV) method A discounted-cash-flow approach to capital budgeting that computes the present value of all expected future cash flows using a minimum desired rate of return.

nominal dollars Dollar measurements that are not restated for fluctuations in the general purchasing power of the monetary unit.

nominal rate Quoted market interest rate that includes an inflation element.

non-value-added costs Costs that can be eliminated without affecting a product's value to the customer.

noncurrent liabilities (long-term liabilities) An organization's debts that fall due beyond one year.

normal costing system The cost system in which overhead is applied on an average or normalized basis, in order to get representative or normal inventory valuations.

normal costing A cost system that applies actual direct materials and actual direct-labor costs to products or services but uses budgeted rates for applying overhead.

objectivity (verifiability) Accuracy supported by a high extent of consensus among independent measures of an item.

operating budget (profit plan) A major part of a master budget that focuses on the income statement and its supporting schedules.

operating cycle The time span during which a company spends cash to acquire goods and services that it uses to produce the organization's output, which in turn it sells to customers, who in turn pay for their purchases with cash.

operating leverage A firm's ratio of fixed to variable costs.

operation costing A hybrid-costing system often used in the batch or group manufacturing of goods that have some common characteristics plus some individual characteristics.

opportunity cost The maximum available contribution to profit foregone (or passed up) by using limited resources for a particular purpose.

outlay cost A cost that requires a cash disbursement.

overapplied overhead The excess of overhead applied to products over actual overhead incurred.

owners' equity The excess of the assets over the liabilities.

paid-in capital The ownership claim arising from funds paid-in by the owners.

par value (legal value, stated value) The value that is printed on the face of the certificate.

parent company A company owning more than 50 percent of another business's stock.

participative budgeting Budgets formulated with the active participation of all affected employees.

partnership An organization that joins two or more individuals together as co-owners.

payback time (payback period) The time it will take to recoup, in the form of cash inflows from operations, the initial dollars invested in a project.

perfect competition A market in which a firm can sell as much of a product as it can produce, all at a single market price.

perfection standards (ideal standards) Expressions of the most efficient performance possible under the best conceivable conditions, using existing specifications and equipment.

performance reports Feedback provided by comparing results with plans and by highlighting variances.

period costs Costs that are deducted as expenses during the current period without going through an inventory stage.

physical capital maintenance The concept that income emerges only after recovering an amount that allows physical operating capability to be maintained.

postaudit A follow-up evaluation of capital-budgeting decisions.

practical capacity Maximum or full capacity.

predatory pricing Establishing prices so low that competitors are driven out of the market. The predatory pricer then has no significant competition and can raise prices dramatically.

preferred stock Stock that typically has some priority over other shares regarding dividends or the distribution of assets upon liquidation.

price elasticity The effect of price changes on sales volume.

price variance The difference between actual input prices and expected input prices multiplied by the actual quantity of inputs used.

prime costs Direct labor costs plus direct materials costs.

problem solving Aspect of accounting that quantifies the likely results of possible courses of action and often recommends the best course of action to follow.

process costing The method of allocating costs to products by averaging costs over large numbers of nearly identical products.

product costs Costs identified with goods produced or purchased for resale.

production cycle time The time from initiating production to delivering the goods to the customer.

production-volume variance A variance that appears whenever actual production deviates from the expected volume of production used in computing the fixed overhead rate. It is calculated as (actual volume − expected volume) × fixed-overhead rate.

productivity A measure of outputs divided by inputs.

product life cycle The various stages through which a product passes, from conception and development through introduction into the market through maturation and, finally, withdrawal from the market.

profit center A responsibility center for controlling revenues as well as costs (or expenses)—that is, profitability.

profits (earnings, income) The excess of revenues over expenses.

prorate To assign underapplied overhead or overapplied overhead in proportion to the sizes of the ending account balances.

prorating the variances Assigning the variances to the inventories and cost of goods sold related to the production during the period the variances arose.

quality control The effort to ensure that products and services perform to customer requirements.

quality-control chart The statistical plot of measures of various product dimensions or attributes.

recovery period The number of years over which an asset is depreciated for tax purposes.

relevant information The predicted future costs and revenues that will differ among alternative courses of action.

relevant range The limit of cost-driver activity within which a specific relationship between costs and the cost driver is valid.

required rate of return (hurdle rate, discount rate) The minimum desired rate of return, based on the firm's cost of capital.

residual income (RI) Net operating income less "imputed" interest.

residual value The predicted sales value of a long-lived asset at the end of its useful life.

responsibility accounting Identifying what parts of the organization have primary responsibility for each objective, developing measures and targets to achieve, and creating reports of these measures by organization subunit or responsibility center.

responsibility center A set of activities assigned to a manager, a group of managers, or other employees.

retained income (retained earnings) The ownership claim arising from the reinvestment of previous profits.

return on investment (ROI)　A measure of income or profit divided by the investment required to obtain that income or profit.

revaluation equity　A portion of stockholders' equity that shows all accumulated holding gains.

revenue　Increases in ownership claims arising from the delivery of goods or services.

sales-activity variances　Variances that measure how effective managers have been in meeting the planned sales objective, calculated as actual unit sales less master budget unit sales times the budgeted unit contribution margin.

sales budget　The result of decisions to create conditions that will generate a desired level of sales.

sales forecast　A prediction of sales under a given set of conditions.

sales mix　The relative proportions or combinations of quantities of products that constitute total sales.

scorekeeping　The accumulation and classification of data.

Securities and Exchange Commission (SEC)　By federal law, the agency with the ultimate responsibility for specifying the generally accepted accounting principles for U.S. companies whose stock is held by the general investing public.

segment autonomy　The delegation of decision-making power to managers of segments of an organization.

segments　Responsibility centers for which a separate measure of revenues and costs is obtained.

sensitivity analysis　The systematic varying of budget data input to determine the effects of each change on the budget.

separable costs　Any cost beyond the split-off point.

service departments　Units that exist only to support other departments.

sole proprietorship　A business entity with a single owner.

source documents　Explicit evidence of any transactions that occur in the entity's operation, for example, sales slips and purchase invoices.

specific identification　An inventory method that recognizes the actual cost paid for the specific item sold.

specific price index　An index used to approximate the current costs of particular assets or types of assets.

split-off point　The juncture of manufacturing where the joint products become individually identifiable.

staff authority　Authority to advise but not command. It may be exerted downward, laterally, or upward.

standard cost　A carefully determined cost per unit that should be attained.

standard cost systems　Accounting systems that value products according to standard costs only.

Standards of Ethical Conduct for Management Accountants　Codes of conduct developed by the Institute of Management

Accountants, which include competence, confidentiality, integrity, and objectivity.

statement of cash flows　A statement that reports the cash receipts and cash payments of an organization during a particular period.

statement of retained earnings (statement of retained income)　A financial statement that analyzes changes in the retained earnings or retained income account for a given period.

step costs　Costs that change abruptly at intervals of activity because the resources and their costs come in indivisible chunks.

step-down method　A method for allocating service department costs that recognizes that some service departments support the activities in other service departments as well as those in production departments.

stockholders' equity　The owners' equity of a corporation.

strategic plan　A plan that sets the overall goals and objectives of the organization.

subordinated　A creditor claim that is junior to the other creditors in exercising claims against assets.

subsidiary　A company owned by a parent company that owns more than 50 percent of its stock.

sunk cost　A cost that has already been incurred and, therefore, is irrelevant to the decision making process.

target costing　A cost management tool for making cost a key focus throughout the life of a product.

time-series comparisons　Comparison of a company's financial ratios with its own historical ratios.

total project approach　A method for comparing alternatives that computes the total impact on cash flows for each alternative and then converts these total cash flows to their present values.

total quality management (TQM)　The application of quality principles to all of the organization's endeavors to satisfy customers.

trading securities　Investments that the investor company buys only with intent to sell them shortly.

transaction　Any event that affects the financial position of an organization and requires recording.

transfer price　The amount charged by one segment of an organization for a product or service that it supplies to another segment of the same organization.

transferred-in costs　In process costing, costs incurred in a previous department for items that have been received by a subsequent department.

treasury stock　A corporation's own stock that has been issued and subsequently repurchased by the company and is being held for a specific purpose.

unavoidable costs　Costs that continue even if an operation is halted.

uncontrollable cost Any cost that cannot be affected by the management of a responsibility center within a given time span.

underapplied overhead The excess of actual overhead over the overhead applied to products.

unearned revenue (deferred revenue) Collections from customers received and recorded before they are earned.

unexpired cost Any asset that ordinarily becomes an expense in future periods, for example, inventory and prepaid rent.

unfavorable expense variance A variance that occurs when actual expenses are more than budgeted expenses.

usage variance (quantity variance, efficiency variance) The difference between the quantity of inputs actually used and the quantity of inputs that should have been used to achieve the actual quantity of output multiplied by the expected price of the input.

value-added cost The necessary cost of an activity that cannot be eliminated without affecting a product's value to the customer.

value chain The set of business functions that add value to the products or services of an organization.

value engineering A cost-reduction technique, used primarily during design, that uses information about all value-chain functions to satisfy customer needs while reducing costs.

variable cost A cost that changes in direct proportion to changes in the cost driver.

variable-cost ratio (variable-cost percentage) All variable costs divided by sales.

variable-overhead efficiency variance An overhead variance caused by actual cost-driver activity differing from the standard amount allowed for the actual output achieved.

variable-overhead spending variance The difference between the actual variable overhead and the amount of variable overhead budgeted for the actual level of cost-driver activity.

variances Deviations from plans.

visual-fit method A method in which the cost analyst visually fits a straight line through a plot of all the available data, not just between the high point and the low point, making it more reliable than the high-low method.

volume variance A common name for production-volume variance.

weighted-average cost The inventory method that assigns the same unit cost to each unit available for sale. The unit cost is computed by dividing the cost of all units available for sale by the number of units available.

weighted-average (WA) process-costing method A process-costing method that adds the cost of (1) all work done in the current period to (2) the work done in the preceding period on the current period's beginning inventory of work in process, and divides the total by the equivalent units of work done to date.

INDEX

SUBJECT INDEX

Note: A separate Index of Companies begins on page I8.

ABC. *See* Activity-based costing
ABM. *See* Activity-based management
Absorption costing, 573–75
    activity based costing *versus,* 136, 138
    advantages of, 184
    fixed overhead and, 573, 575–82
        reconciliation, 579–80
    income statement under, 133–34, 574, 583, 584
    variable costing *versus,* 570–75
Accelerated depreciation, 416, 417, 419
Account analysis, 92–93
Accountants
    certified management, 20
    certified public, 20
    code of ethics for, 23–25
    role of in organization, 16–18
Accounting
    decision making and, 4–7
    management process and, 9–15. *See also* Control; Planning
    manufacturing, 128
    merchandising, 128
    in nonprofit organizations, 9
    position of in company, 16–18
    pricing and, 179–80
    purposes of, 5–6, 7–8
    responsibility, 331–32, 337
    users of information in, 5–6
Accounting rate-of-return (ARR) model, 427–28
Accounting systems, 6–7
    behavioral implications of, 9
    cost-benefit balance and, 9
    government regulations and, 7
    internal *versus* external, 6–7
    simplicity and, 8
Accrual accounting rate-of-return model. *See* Accounting rate-of-return (ARR) model
Accumulation, cost, 124, 125
Accuracy
    of costs of engagements, 514
    relevance and, 168–69
Activity analysis, 89, 90, 93–94, 572n
Activity-based budgeting, 264

Activity-based costing (ABC), 136–43, 185, 337, 454, 464–67
    advantages of, 142–43
    contribution approach and, 137
    cost drivers and, 465–67
    effect of, 471–73
    examples of, 137–42, 465–67
    in job order environment, 511–13
    in manufacturing, 465, 469–71
    principles of, 464–65
    relevant information and, 172
    in service and nonprofit environments, 514–15
    target costing with, 188, 189
    traditional costing *versus,* 136, 138
    transfer pricing and, 370–71
Activity-based flexible budgets, 291, 292
Activity-based management (ABM), 144, 145, 188
Activity centers, activity-based costing and, 139–40, 469
Activity-level variances, 291
Actual costing, 508–9, 578
Agency theory, 376–77
AICPA. *See* American Institute of Certified Public Accountants
Akers, John, 340
American Institute of Certified Public Accountants (AICPA), 20
Applied fixed-overhead costs, 576
Appraisal, cost of, 340, 341
ARR. *See* Accounting rate-of-return (ARR) model
Aspin, Les, 223
Asset allocations, to divisions, 383
Assets valuation, 383–85
    cost allocation and, 455
Attention directing, accounting and, 5
Audit
    improvement of predications with, 426
    management, 7
Authority, line and staff, 16, 17
Auto industry, break-even point in, 46
Autonomy, segment, 368
Avoidable costs, 173–76
Azenberg, Emanuel, 242

Backflush costing, 549–51
Balanced scorecard, 334–35
Balance sheet equation, 164

Balance sheets
    budgeted, 253, 260–62
    cost accounting for
        period costs and, 128–29
        product costs and, 128–29
    current asset sections of, 130
    of manufacturers, 129–30
    of merchandisers, 120–30
    presentation of, 129–30
Baldrige Award, 332, 342
Bankruptcy, 23
Barleycorn, Inc. example, 337–39
Beginning inventories, 543–44
Behavioral implications, of accounting systems, 9
Bennet, James, 46
Berg, J., 223
Boeing, William, 39
Bohn, J., 189
Book value, 423
    gross, 383–85
    net, 383–85
    of old equipment, 221–22, 384–85
Book-value model. *See* Accounting rate-of-return (ARR) model
Brausch, J., 189
Break-even point, 45–51
    in auto industry, 46
    changes in contribution margin per unit and, 50–51
    changes in fixed expenses and, 50
    contribution-margin (marginal income) techniques for, 45–47, 48
    equation technique for, 47–48
    graphical technique for, 48–50
    lowering, 56
    margin of safety and, 45
    multiple factor change and, 52–53
    sales-mix analysis of, 49, 59–60
Budgeted balance sheet, 253, 260–62
Budgeted factory-overhead rate, 505, 506–7
Budgeted income statement, 253, 258–59
Budgeted sales, 460
Budgets, 10, 248–85. *See also* Capital budgeting; Flexible budgets; Master budget (pro forma statements)
    activity-based, 264
    advantages of, 251–52
    capital, 252, 253
    cash, 253, 259–60

continuous, 252
of engagements, 513–14
financial, 253, 254
human relations problems and, 263
illustration of, 11–12
managers and, 386
operating, 253, 254
operating expense, 253, 258
participative, 263
performance and, 251
purchases, 253, 257
sales, 253, 256–57, 262
sensitivity analysis and, 269–72
spreadsheets for, 269–72
static, 288–89
strategic plan and, 252
Business Week, 20, 56, 75, 373, 459
By-product costs, 475

CAD. *See* Computer-aided design
Call, Kevin, 165
Callan, J., 137
CAM. *See* Computer-aided manufacturing
Capacity, practical, 578
Capacity costs, 85–86
Capital
   cost of, 380
   decentralization and, 382–85
      allocation to divisions, 383
      assets valuation, 383–85
   in excess of stated value, 662
   invested
      allocation to divisions, 383
      assets valuation and, 383–85
      definition of, 382
Capital budgeting, 252, 253, 404–51
   accounting rate-of-return model of,
      427–28
   cash flows for investments in technology
      and, 414
   decisions on, 406
   discounted-cash-flow models of,
      406–15
      assumptions, 409
      choice of minimum desired rate of
         return, 409
      decision rules, 410
      depreciation, 409–10
      future disposal values, 414
      initial cash inflows and outflows at time
         zero, 412
      investments in receivables and invento-
         ries, 412, 414
      major aspects, 406–7
      net present value, 407–10, 411–14
      operating cash flows, 414
      reconciliation of conflict, 429
      sensitivity analysis and risk assessment,
         410–11
   income taxes and, 415–22
      cash effects, 417
      depreciation deductions, 416–21
      gains or losses on disposal of equip-
         ment, 421–22
   inflation and, 423–26
   payback model of, 427

performance evaluation and, 428–29
   postaudit and, 429
   program or project focus of, 406
Capital outlays, 406
Capital stock. *See* Stocks
Capital turnover, 379
Career opportunities in management
   accounting, 20
Casaverde Company example, 11–12
Cash budget, 253, 259–60
Cash collections, 257
Cash flows
   discounted-cash-flow analysis and, 412
   for investments in technology, 414
   for net present value, 412
   operating, 414
   postaudit and, 429
Cash flow statements. *See* Statement of cash
   flows
Cellular manufacturing, 146
Central costs, allocation of, 459–60
Centralization, decentralization *versus*,
   366–68
Certified Management Accountant (CMA), 20
Certified Public Accountant (CPA), 20
Change, adaptation to, 21–23
Charts, quality control, 343–46
CIM. *See* Computer-integrated manufacturing
   (CIM) systems
Classified balance sheets. *See* Balance sheets
CMA. *See* Certified Management Accountant
Coefficient of determination (R^2), 98
Collins, Don, 136
Committed fixed costs, 86
Common costs, 174
Communication, budgets and, 252
Competition
   imperfect, 178, 179
   perfect, 177–78
Competitors, pricing and, 180–81
Computer-aided design (CAD), 22
Computer-aided manufacturing (CAM), 22
Computer-integrated manufacturing (CIM)
   systems, 22
Computers. *See also* Spreadsheets
   cost-volume-profit analysis using, 53–54
   least-squares regression method and,
      101–4
Condit, Philip, 14, 40
Congruence, goal, 335–36
Conley, Mike, 15
Continuous budget, 252
Continuous improvement. *See* Kaizen costing
Contribution, by segments, 338, 339
Contribution approach. *See also* Variable
   costing
   activity-based costing and, 137
   cost-plus pricing and, 182–84
   income statement and, 134–35
   optimal use of limited resources and,
      176–77
   special sales order and, 169–73
Contribution margin, 185, 337, 339
   cost-volume profit analysis and, 45–47, 48
   gross margin *versus*, 55–56
   margin per unit, 50–51

Control. *See also* Budgets; Inventory; Management control systems
   accounting framework for, 9–10
   allocation and, 455
   of cycle time, 344
   of engagements, 513–14
   expected or standard costs and, 295–96
   financial performance and, 336–40
   performance reports and, 10–12
   for product life cycles, 12–13
   of quality, 340–44
Controllable costs, 337
Controller/comptroller, 16, 18
Conversion costs, 127
Cooking Hut Company example, 254–61,
   269–72
Cooper, R., 473
Coordination, budgets and, 252
Corbett, M. F., 219
Cost accounting, 124–25
   cost accumulation and, 124, 125
   for financial statements, 128–32
Cost accounting systems, 454, 535. *See also*
   Cost allocation
Cost accumulation, 124, 125
Cost allocation, 124, 125, 454–64
   of by-product costs, 475
   to final cost objects, 463–64
   of joint costs, 474–75
   purposes of, 455–56
   of service department costs, 457–63
      budgeted sales, 460
      central costs, 459–60
      fixed-cost pool, 457, 458–59
      lump-sum allocations, 459
      not related to cost drivers, 463
      reciprocal services, 460–62
      variable-cost pool, 457–58
   traditional approach to, 464
   transfer pricing and, 369
   types of, 456
Cost-allocation base, 454
Cost application, 463–64. *See also* Absorption
   costing
Cost attribution. *See* Cost application
Cost behavior, 40. *See also* Income statements
   cost drivers and, 40–41, 82–85
   linear, 82–83
   management and, 85–87
   mathematical expression of. *See* Cost
      functions
   measurement of, 82–85
   mixed-, 84–85
   relevant range and, 42–43, 82, 83
   step-, 83–84
   types of, 83–85
Cost-benefit balance, 9
Cost-benefit criterion, 636
Cost center, 331–32
Cost control, 40
   incentives for, 87
Cost drivers. *See also* Cost allocation
   activity analysis and, 89, 90, 93–94
   activity-based costing and, 465–67
   choice of, 89–90
   cost behavior and, 40–41, 82–85

cost prediction and, 89
health care industry, 145
for overhead, 507–8
relevant range and, 42–43
Cost functions
cost drivers and, 89–90
criteria for choosing, 88–89
linear-, 88
measuring, 82, 87–88, 91–100
account analysis, 92–93
engineering analysis, 91–92
high-low method, 94–96
least-square regression method, 94,
97–99, 101–4
visual fit method, 97
mixed-, 88
Costing system, normal, 508, 578–79
Cost-management systems, 144–46
activity-based management and, 144, 145
just-in-time production system and, 144–46
Cost measurement. See Cost functions
Cost object. See Cost objective
Cost objective, 125–26
Cost of capital, 380
Cost of goods sold, 55, 130, 615
proration and, 510
Cost-of-goods-sold budget, 253
Cost of quality report, 340–42
Cost-plus pricing. See Pricing
Cost pool, 454
Cost prediction, 89
Costs. See also Fixed costs; Unit costs; Variable
costing
activities and, 40–41
avoidable, 173–76
by-product, 475
capacity, 85–86
central, 459–60
classifications of, 44, 125–28
committed fixed, 86
common, 174
controllable, 337
conversion, 127
definition, 125–26
differential, 214
direct, 126
direct-labor, 127
direct-material, 126
discretionary fixed, 86
expected, 295, 296
fixed-overhead, 576, 589
fixed unit, 576–77
full, 182
future, 223–24
historical, 221, 383–84
on income statements, 130–31
indirect, 126
indirect manufacturing, 127
joint, 218–20, 474–75
manufacturing, 126–27, 574
marginal, 178, 179
mixed, 84–85
of new equipment, 222
non-value added, 144, 146
opportunity, 214–15, 341–42
outlay, 214

past, 220–23
period, 128–29
pricing and, 181–86
prime, 127
product, 128–29, 130
quality, 340–44
selling and administrative, 128
separable, 218
standard, 295–96
step, 83–84
sunk, 221, 223
transfer pricing at, 369
transferred-in, 547–48
unallocated, 338, 339, 340
unavoidable, 173–76
uncontrollable, 337
unit, 130, 224
value-added, 144
variable, 179, 574
variable-overhead, 576, 589
variable unit, 576–77
Cost structure, cost-volume-profit analysis for
best, 54
Cost systems, multiple and standard, 296
Cost-volume-profit (CVP) analysis, 44–56.
See also Break-even point
best cost structure and, 54
computers and, 53–54
income taxes and, 60–61
multiple factor changes and, 52–53
nonprofit organizations and, 44–45,
56–57
of operating leverage, 54–55
sales-mix analysis and, 49, 59–60
target net profit and, 51–52
CPA. See Certified Public Accountant
Critical process, 330
Critical success factors, 330
Current assets
on balance sheets, 130
Currently attainable standards, 296–97
Cycle time, control of, 344

DCF (discounted-cash-flow models). See Capital budgeting
Decentralization, 365–403. See also Capital
centralization versus, 366–68
performance measures and, 375–77
profitability measures and, 378–81
profit center versus, 368
transfer pricing, 368–75
activity-based costing and, 370–71
at cost, 369
dysfunctional behavior, 373–74
incentives, 376
market-based, 371
multinational, 374–75
need for, 374
negotiated, 372–73
purpose of, 369
variable-cost, 371–72
Decision making, 9. See also Information; Relevant information
accounting and, 4–7
performance evaluation and, 224–25
Decision model, 167, 168

Decisions. See also Production decisions
capacity, 85–86
capital-budgeting. See Capital budgeting
make-or-buy, 216–18, 219
pricing, 181–86
product and service, 85
sell or process further, 218–20
technology, 87
Deferred revenue. See Unearned revenue
Dell, Michael, 500
Deming, W. Edwards, 342
Departments, deletion or addition of, 173–76
Depreciation, 221, 222, 423
accelerated, 416, 417, 419
capital budgeting and, 424, 426
confusion about, 423
discounted-cash-flow computation and,
408–10
Modified Accelerated Cost Recovery System
(MACRS) and, 419–21
net present value and, 409–10
straight-line, 416
tax effects of, 416–17
Desheh, Eyal, 371
Determination, coefficient of (R^2), 98
Dickhaut, J., 223
Differential analysis, 214
Differential approach, to net present value,
411–12, 413
Differential cost, 214
Differential income, 214
Differential revenue, 214
Differential savings, 214
Direct costing, 570n. See also Contribution
approach; Variable costing
Direct costs, 126
Direct-labor costs, 127
Direct-material costs, 126
Direct-materials inventory, 130, 131, 132
Direct method
of service departmental cost allocation,
461, 462–63
Disbursements
operating expense, 258
for purchases, 257–58
Discounted-cash-flow models. See Capital
budgeting
Discount rate. See Required rate of return
Discretionary fixed costs, 86–87
Discriminatory pricing, 180
Disposal value
future, 414
of old equipment, 221–22, 421–22
Dominion Company example, 288, 289,
290–95, 298–99, 302–3
Drtina, R. E., 219
Dysfunctional behavior, transfer pricing and,
373–74

Earnings before interest and taxes (EBIT), 333
Eastside Manufacturing Company example,
341, 343, 344
Economic value added (EVA), 380, 381
Effectiveness, performance evaluation and,
293
Efficiency, performance evaluation and, 293

Efficiency variance. *See* Usage variance
Effort, managerial, 336
Eisenstein, Paul A., 46
Elliott, John A., 5
Ending-inventory budget, 253
Engagements
    budgets and control of, 513–14
    costs of, 514
Engineering analysis, 91–92
Engineering News Record, 749
Enriquez Machine Parts Company example,
    501–4, 505–9, 510–11
EPS. *See* Earnings per share
Equation technique, 47–48
Equipment
    book value of old, 221–26, 384–85
    disposal value of, 221–22
    income tax gains or losses on disposal of,
        421–22
Equivalent units, in process costing, 540–41
Ethics, 23–25
EVA. *See* Economic value added
Evaluation of performance. *See* Performance
    evaluation
Expected cost, 295, 296
Expenses
    fixed, 50
External failure, cost of, 341

Facilities, make-or-buy decisions and, 216–18
Factory burden. *See* Indirect manufacturing
    costs
Factory overhead. *See* Indirect manufacturing
    costs; Overhead
FAS. *See* Financial Accounting Standards
    Board (FASB)
Favorable expense variances, 289
Feedback, improvement of predications with,
    426
Feil, David, 90
FIFO. *See* First-in, first-out (FIFO) method
Financial accounting, 5, 6
Financial budget, 253, 254, 259–62
Financial capital maintenance, 746
Financial Executives Institute, 18
Financial performance, controllability and
    measurement of, 336–40
Financial planning models, 264–65
Financial statements, 6. *See also* Annual
    reports; Balance sheets; Consolidated
    financial statements; Income statements;
    Statement of cash flows
    cost accounting for, 128–32
    internal and external uses of, 6–7
Finished-goods inventory, 130, 131, 132
Finished-Goods Inventory account, 501
    proration and, 510
First-in, first-out (FIFO) method, 544–47
Fixed-cost pool, 457, 458–59
Fixed costs, 41, 42, 44
    capacity costs, 85–86
    committed, 86
    cost prediction and, 89
    discretionary, 86
    relevant range and, 43
    variable costs *versus*, 170–72

Fixed expenses, break-even point and, 50
Fixed manufacturing overhead, 570–71
Fixed overhead, 510–11
    absorption costs of product and, 575–82
Fixed-overhead budget variance. *See* Fixed-
    overhead flexible-budget variance
Fixed-overhead costs, 589
Fixed-overhead flexible-budget variance, 582,
    583
Fixed-overhead rate, 573
    computing, 578
Fixed-overhead spending variance. *See* Fixed-
    overhead flexible-budget variance
Fixed unit costs, 576–77
Flexible budgets, 287–93. *See also* Variances
    activity-based, 291, 292
    comparisons with prior period's results
        versus, 298
    financial performance evaluation using,
        291–93
    flexible-budget variances and. *See* Vari-
        ances
    formulas in, 290–91
    static budgets and, 288–89
Flexible-budget variances. *See* Variances
Forecasting
    feedback improving, 426
    sales and, 262–63
Foreign Corrupt Practices Act, 7
Fried, M., 264
Full cost, 182
Full-cost approaches, 184. *See also* Absorption
    costing
Fully allocated cost. *See* Full cost
Functional approach. *See* Absorption costing
Future costs, 223–24
Future disposal values, 414

GAAP. *See* Generally accepted accounting
    principles (GAAP)
Gains
    disposal of equipment and, 221–22,
        421–22
    holding, 748–49
Game theory, 181
General Accounting Office (GAO), 7
Generally accepted accounting principles
    (GAAP), 6–7
GIGO (garbage in, garbage out), 265
Goal congruence, 335–36
Goals, organizational, 328–30
Going concern convention. *See* Continuity
    convention
Goodmanson, Richard, 81
Gordon, M., 223
Government
    management control systems in, 347
    sales forecasting and, 263
Government contracts, sunk costs and, 223
Government regulations, management
    accounting and, 7
Grant, Charles L., 255
Graphical techniques, in cost-volume-profit
    analysis, 48–50
Greenberg Company example, 572–74,
    576–77, 582, 584–86

Gross book value, 383–85
Gross margin, 574
    contribution margin *versus*, 55–56
Gross National Product Implicit Price Defla-
    tor, 749
Gross profit. *See* Gross margin
Gross profit rate or percentage, 177

Haedicke, Jack, 90
Hamilton, Frank, Jr., 536
Hanks, G., 264
Hardy, Arlene, 100
Healy, James A., 25
Heath, Loyd, 672
High-low method, 94–96
Historical costs, 221, 383–84. *See also* Past
    costs
Hobdy, T., 140, 161
Hoffman, G., 189
Horngren, Charles T., 5
Huber, J., 264
Hurdle rate. *See* Required rate of return
Hybrid costing, 553–55

IASC. *See* International Accounting Standards
    Committee
Ideal standards. *See* Perfection standards
Idle facilities, 216–17
IMA. *See* Institute of Management Accountants
Immediate write-off method, 509–10
Imperfect competition, 178, 179
Incentives
    cost-control, 87
    motivation and, 375–76
    transfer pricing and, 376
Income. *See also* Earnings; Net income; Profits
    cost allocation and, 455
    residual, 380–81
Income measurement. *See* Net income
Income percentage of revenue, 379
Income statements
    under absorption costing, 133–34, 574,
        583, 584
    budgeted, 253, 258–59
    cost accounting for
        costs on, 130–31
        period costs and, 128–29
        product costs and, 128–29
    cost behavior and, 132–36
        absorption approach and, 113–14
        contribution approach and, 134–35
    under variable costing, 572, 573, 574
Income taxes, 664. *See also* Capital budgeting
    cost-volume profit analysis and, 60–61
    depreciation and cash flows and,
        416–17
Income tax rate, marginal, 415–16
Incremental cost. *See* Differential cost
Incremental effect, 51–52
Independent opinion, of auditors, 629–30
Indirect costs, 126
Indirect manufacturing costs, 127
Indirect method, of statement of cash flows
Inflation
    capital budgeting and, 423–26
    depreciation and, 424, 426

nominal rate of return and, 424
prediction and, 426
Information. *See also* Relevant information
internal *versus* external, 6–7
qualitative *versus* quantitative,
168–69
users of, 5–6
Institute of Management Accountants (IMA),
20, 31
Management Accounting, 25
Standards of Ethical Conduct for Management Accountants of, 23, 24
Intercorporate investments
consolidations. *See* Consolidated financial
statements
Internal auditors, 7
Internal failure, cost of, 341
Internal Revenue Service (IRS), 113
International business, 21
Inventory
beginning, 543–44
direct-materials, 130, 131, 132
discounted-cash-flow analysis of investments in, 412, 414
finished-goods, 130, 131, 132
flexible-budget variances and, 302
net present value and investments in, 412,
414
obsolete, 220–21
preparation of, 510
transactions affecting, 131–32
work-in-process, 130, 131, 132
Inventory accounting. *See* Net income
Inventory turnover, 177
Invested capital. *See* Capital
Investment centers, 332
Investments. *See also* Capital budgeting; Intercorporate investments
discounted-cash-flow analysis of, 412,
414
Izzo, T. J., 75

Jedlicka, Dan, 46
Jensen, Christopher, 46
JIT. *See* Just-in-time (JIT) systems
Job costing
activity-based costing/management and,
511–13
factory overhead and, 504–5
illustration of, 501–4
process costing compared with, 500–501,
536–39
in service and nonprofit organizations. *See*
Product costing
Job-cost record, 501, 502
Job-cost sheet. *See* Job-cost record
Job order. *See* Job-cost record
Job-order costing. *See* Job costing
Joint costs, 218, 474–75
Joint product costs, 218–20
Joint products, 218
Jones, Lou F., 296
Jonez, John, 454
Jordan, Michael, 365
Journal of Cost Management, 158

Just-in-time (JIT) systems, 22, 144–46, 297,
506, 574
process costing in, 549–51
turnover and, 379–80
variable and absorption income in, 580

Kaizen costing, 188
Kanodia, C., 223
Kaplan, Robert, 371
Key Business Ratios (Dun & Bradstreet), 715
Key performance indicators, 334–35
Key success factors, 330
Khan, U., 343
KISS, 8
Knight, Philip, 365, 366
Koehler, Robert, 137

Labor standards, 299–300
Labor time tickets, 501
Larson, Ralph, 367
Lawson, Raef A., 140
LCM. *See* Lower-of-cost-or-market method
Least-squares regression method, 94, 97–99,
101–4
Lee, J., 261
Legal value. *See* Par value
Leverage, operating, 54–55
LIFO. *See* Last-in, first-out (LIFO) method
LIFO increments. *See* LIFO layers
Limiting factor, 176
Linear-cost behavior, 82–83
Linear-cost function, 88
Line authority, 16
Long-range planning, 252
Long-term liabilities. *See* Noncurrent liabilities
Losses
disposal of equipment and, 221–22,
421–22
Lump-sum allocations, 459
Luxury Suites example, 329–30, 334–35

Machinery, 656
MACRS. *See* Modified Accelerated Cost Recovery System
Make-or-buy decisions, 216–18, 219
Management. *See also* Control; Planning
accounting and, 9–15
cost behavior and, 85–87
capacity decisions and, 85–86
committed fixed costs and, 86
cost-control incentives and, 87
discretionary fixed costs and, 86–87
technology decisions and, 87
by exception, 10–11
by objectives, 386
total quality, 342–44
training for positions in, 20
Management accounting
adaptation to change of, 21–23
career opportunities in, 20
cost-benefit and behavioral considerations
in, 9
current trends in, 21–22
definition, 5
ethical conduct and, 23–25

financial accounting differentiated from,
5, 6
government regulations and, 7
position of in organization, 16–18
in service and nonprofit organizations, 8
Management Accounting, 21, 25, 158, 161
Management audit, 7
Management by exception, 288
Management by objectives (MBO), 386
Management control systems, 327–63. *See
also* Decentralization; Performance
budgets tailored for managers in, 386
controllability in, 336–40, 385–86
designing, 331–35
cost, profit, and investment centers,
331–32
cost-benefit analysis, 335
employee motivation, 335–36
monitoring and reporting results and
balanced scorecard, 333–35
performance measures development,
332–33
responsibility centers, 331
working within organizational structure,
331
financial performance and, 336–40
future of, 348
management by objectives (MBO), 386
nonfinancial, 340–47
cycle time control, 344
productivity control, 345–47
quality control, 340–44
organizational goals and objectives and,
328–31
in service, government, and nonprofit
organizations, 347
Managerial effort, 336
Managers
budgets tailored for, 386
ethics and, 23–25
segment, 339, 368
Manufacturing
activity-based costing in, 465,
469–71
balance sheet of, 129–30
Manufacturing accounting, 128
Manufacturing costs, 574
Manufacturing overhead. *See* Overhead
Margin. *See* Contribution margin; Gross margin
Marginal cost, 178, 179
Marginal income. *See* Contribution margin
Marginal income tax rate, 415–16
Marginal revenue, 178, 179
Margin of safety, break-even point and, 45
Market-based transfer prices, 371
Marketing decisions, 164–211. *See also* Costs;
Pricing; Relevant information
optimal use of limited resources and,
176–77
product/service addition or deletion and,
173–76
Markup, 181–82
Martin's Printing example, 416–17, 421–22
Master budget (pro forma statements),
252–62

components of, 253–54
definition, 252
financial planning models and, 264–65
preparation of, 254–62
  budgeted income statement, 253, 260–62
  financial budget, 253, 254, 259–62
  operating budget, 253, 254, 256–59
  spreadsheet for, 271
  static budgets and, 288–89
Master budget variances, 288–89
Materials requisitions, 501
Material standards, 299–300
Material yield, 345
MBO. *See* Management by objectives
Measurement of cost behavior. *See* Cost functions
Merchandisers, balance sheet of, 129–30
Merchandising accounting, 128
Merz, Mike, 100
Minority interests, consolidated financial statements and, 702–3
Mission, of organizations, 16
Mixed-cost behavior, 84–85
Mixed-cost function, 88
Modified Accelerated Cost Recovery System (MACRS), 419–21
Monden, Y., 261
Money market funds, 656
Montreal Gazette, 174
Motivation
  cost allocation and, 455
  of employees, 335–36
  performance and rewards and, 375–76
Multinational transfer pricing, 374–75
Multiple cost systems, 296
Multiple regression, 97

Negotiated transfer prices, 372–73
Nersesian, Roy L., 25
Net book value, 383–85
Net present value (NPV), 407–10, 411–14
Net worth, 629. *See* Stockholders' equity
New Product development, target costing and, 187–88
Nominal dollars, 746–51
Nominal rate of return, 424
Noncash investing activities, 672
Nonfinancial performance. *See* Performance
Nonprofit organizations. *See also* Product costing
  accounting in, 9
  cost-volume-profit analysis in, 44–45, 53, 56–57
  decentralization and, 267
  management accounting in, 8
  management control systems in, 347
  product costing in, 513–15
  sales forecasting and, 263
Non-value-added cost, 144, 146
Normal costing system, 508, 578–79
Normalized overhead rates, 508–9
NPV. *See* Net-present-value

Oakville Wooden Toys, Inc. example, 539–42, 544–47
Objectives
  cost, 125–26
  management by, 386
  organizational, 330–31
Obsolete inventory, 220–21
Operating budget, 253, 254, 256–59
Operating cash flows, 414
Operating expense budget, 258
Operating expense disbursements, 258
Operating leverage, 54–55
Operating management, 664
Operation costing, 553–55
Operations, 553
  in process costing, 500
Opportunity costs, 214–15, 341–42
Orders, special sale, 169–73
Organizations, role of accounting in, 16–18. *See also* Nonprofit organizations; Service organizations
Outdoor Equipment Company, Inc. example, 371, 372, 373–74
Outlay cost, 214
Outsourcing, 219
Overapplied overhead, 509
Overhead. *See also* Absorption costing; Variable costing
  cost drivers for, 507–8
  factory
    accounting for, 504–5
    budgeted, 505, 506–7
    products and, 505
  fixed, 510–11, 573, 578
  illustration of, 505–8
  immediate write-off method and, 509–10
  manufacturing, fixed, 570–71, 575–82
  normalized rates, 508–9
  overapplied, 509, 589
  proration among inventories and, 510
  in service and nonprofit organizations, 515
  underapplied, 509, 589
  variable, 510–11
Overhead variances, 303–5

Parkview Medical Center example, 84–85, 86, 87, 91–92, 94–96, 98–99, 101–4
Participative budgeting, 263
Past costs, 220–23
Payback period. *See* Payback time
Payback time, 427
Perfect competition, 177–78
Perfection standards, 296–97
Performance
  agency theory and, 376–77
  balanced scorecard on, 334–35
  budgets and, 251
  financial, 332–33, 336–40
  measures of, 332–33
  motivation and rewards and, 375–76
  nonfinancial
    cycle time control and, 344
    productivity control and, 345–47
    quality control and, 340–44

Performance evaluation
  capital budgeting and, 428–29
  decision making and, 224–25
  effectiveness *versus* efficiency in, 293
  flexible budgets and, 291–93
  grading and, 336
Performance measures, goals and, 329–30
Performance reports, 10–12, 288
Period costs, 128–29
Phillips, A., 136
Physical units, in process costing, 540–41
Physical-units method, for allocating joint costs, 474
Planning. *See also* Budgets; Inventory
  accounting framework for, 9–10
  allocation and, 455
  budgets and formalization of, 251
  costs-volume profit model and, 53–54
  expected or standard costs and, 295–96
  formalization of, 251
  long-range, 252
  for product life cycles, 12–13
Plan, strategic, 252
P & L statement. *See* Income statements
Portland Power Company (PPC) example, 137–42, 144
Postaudit, 429
Practical capacity, 578
Predatory pricing, 180
Prediction, cost, 89
Present value
  of MACRS depreciation, 420–21
  net, 407–10, 411–14
Prevention, costs of, 340, 341
Price elasticity, 178
Prices, changing. *See* Net income
Price variance, 300–302
Pricing, 177–90
  accounting and, 179–80
  approaches to. *See* Absorption costing; Contribution approach; Variable costing
  competitors and, 180–81
  concept of, 177–79
  cost-plus, 181–86
    contribution approach to, 182–84
    cost bases for, 181–82
    full-cost approach, 184
    multiple approaches to, 184–85
    target costing *versus*, 189–90
  customer demands and, 181
  discriminatory, 180
  formats for, 185–86
  legal requirements and, 180
  markup and, 181–82
  predatory, 180
  quote sheet for, 185
  target, 181–82
  target costing and, 186–90
    activity-based costing with, 188, 189
    cost-plus pricing *versus*, 189–90
    illustration of, 188
    new product development and, 187–88
  transfer. *See* Decentralization
Prime costs, 127

Problem-solving, accounting and, 5–6
Process-based modeling approach, to activity-based costing, 140, 141
Process costing, 534–67. *See also* Product costing
  application of, 539–40
  beginning inventories and, 543–44
  equivalent units in, 540–41
  first in, first out (FIFO), 544–47
  hybrid systems and, 553–55
  job costing comparison, 500–501
  job costing *versus*, 536–39
  just-in-time (JIT) systems with, 549–51
  physical units in, 540–41
  product costs calculation in, 541–42
  transferred-in costs and, 547–48
  weighted-average (WA) method and, 544, 545, 547
Processes, in process costing, 500
Product costing. *See also* Absorption costing; Job costing; Process costing; Variable costing
  in service and nonprofit organizations, 513–15
    accuracy of costs of engagements and, 514
    activity-based, 514–15
    budgets and control of engagements and, 513–14
    effects of classification on overhead rates and, 515
  target costing and. *See* Pricing
Product costs, 128–29, 130
  calculation of in process-costing system, 541–42
Product decisions, 85
Production cycle times, just-in-time production system and, 145–46
Production decisions, 212–47
  alternatives over long run and, 222–23
  book value of old equipment and, 221–23
  differential costs and, 214
  future costs and, 223–24
  joint product costs and, 218–20
  make-or-buy decisions, 216–18, 219
  obsolete inventory and, 220–21
  opportunity costs and, 214–15
  outlay costs and, 214
  past costs and, 220–23
  unit costs and, 224
Production-volume variance. *See* Variances
Productivity control, 345–47
Product life cycles, planning and control for, 12–13
Products
  deletion or addition of, 173–76
  joint, 218–20
Profitability measures, decentralization and, 378–81
Profit centers, 332
  decentralization *versus*, 368
Profit plan. *See* Operating budget
Pro forma statements. *See* Master budget (pro forma statements)
Proration
  of overhead, 510
  of variances, 583

Purchases, disbursements for, 257–58
Purchases budget, 253, 257

Qualitative information, 168–69
Quality
  costs of, 340–44
  just-in-time production system and, 146
Quality control, 340
  performance measures with, 340–44
Quality-control charts, 343–46
Quantitative information, 168–69
Quantity variance. *See* Usage variance
Quote sheet, pricing, 185

Radigan, J., 219
Ramos Company example, 59–60
Rate of return
  accounting, 427–28
  on investments, 716–17
  minimum desired, 409
  nominal, 424
  required, 407
Receivables, discounted-cash-flow analysis and, 412, 414
Reciprocal services, 460–62
Regression analysis. *See* Least-squares regression method
Relative-sales-value method, for allocating joint costs, 474–75
Relevant information. *See also* Costs; Marketing decisions; Production decisions
  accuracy and, 168–69
  decision process and, 167, 168
  definition, 166
  deletion or addition of products or departments and, 173–76
  examples of, 167
  optimal use of limited resources and, 176–77
  special sale order and, 169–72
Relevant range, 42–43
  break-even graph and, 49
  cost behavior and, 82, 83
Reports
  cost of quality, 340–42
  performance, 288
  shareholder, 680–81
Required rate of return, 407
Residual income (RI), 380–81
Responsibility accounting, 331, 337
Responsibility centers, 331–32
  rewards and, 375–76
Retained earnings. *See* Retained income
Return on investment (ROI), 379–80, 381
Return on sales. *See* Income percentage of revenue
  differential, 214
  marginal, 178, 179
Rewards, motivation and performance and, 375–76
RI. *See* Residual income
Risk, 376–77
  discounted-cash-flow models and, 410–11
ROI. *See* Return on investment
Rolling budgets. *See* Continuous budget
Rollins, Kevin, 452

Sales
  budgeted, 460
  forecasting, 262–63
  return on. *See* Income percentage of revenue
Sales-activity variances, 294–95
Sales budget, 253, 256–57, 262
Sales forecast, 262–63
Sales-mix analysis, 49, 59–60
Samson Company example, 132–35, 169–73
Scarce resource. *See* Limiting factor
Schumacher, Michael, 366
Scorekeeping, accounting and, 5
SEC. *See* Securities and Exchange Commission
Securities and Exchange Commission (SEC), 6
Segment autonomy, 368
Segment managers, 338, 339, 368
Segments, 337
  contribution, 338, 339
Selling and administrative costs, 128
Sensitivity analysis, 269–72
  in discounted-cash-flow models, 410–11
Separable costs, 218
Service decisions, 85
Service departments, 456
  allocation of costs of. *See* Cost allocation
Service organizations, 21. *See also* Product costing
  management accounting in, 8
  management control systems in, 347
  product costing in, 513–15
Sharman, P., 140, 161, 575
Siers, Howard L., 25
Simon, Neil, 242
Simple regression, 97–98
Simplicity, 8, 52
Smith, Jim, 3, 4
Smith, Orin, 213
Smith, Roger B., 25
Speaker Technology Inc. example, 550–51
Special sales order, relevant information and, 169–73
Split-off point, 218–20
Spreadsheets
  budgeting with, 265, 269–72
  cost-volume-profit analysis using, 53
  financial planning models and, 265
  least-squares regression method and, 101–4
Staff authority, 16, 17
Standard cost, 295–96
Standard costing, 578–79
Standard cost systems, 296
Standard-cost variances, 583–84
Standards
  currently attainable, 296–97
  labor, 299–300
  material, 299–300
  perfection, 296–97
Standards of Ethical Conduct for Management Accountants, 23, 24
Stated value. *See* Par value
Statement of earnings. *See* Income statements
Statement of financial condition. *See* Balance sheets

Statement of financial position. *See* Balance sheets
Statement of profit and loss. *See* Income statements
Statement of retained income. *See* Statement of retained earnings
Static budgets, 288–89. *See also* Master budget (pro forma statements)
Static budget variances. *See* Master budget variances
Step-cost behavior, 83–84
Step-down method, of service departmental cost allocation, 461–63
Stich, Michael, 365
Straight-line depreciation, 416
Strategic plan, 252
Suh, R., 219
Sundem, Gary L., 5
Sunk costs, 221, 223. *See also* Historical costs; Past costs
Sweeney, Robert B., 25

Tangible assets. *See* Fixed assets
Target costing. *See* Pricing
Target net profit, 51–52
Target pricing, 181–82
Taxes. *See* Income taxes
Technology
    cash flows for investments in, 414
    change and, 21–22
    decisions on, 87
Thomson, J., 140, 161
Throughput time. *See* Cycle time
Time cards. *See* Labor time tickets
Top management positions, 20
Total project approach, to net present value, 411–12, 413
Total quality control (TQC), 146
Total quality management (TQM), 342–44
TQC. *See* Total quality control
TQM. *See* Total quality management
Traditional approach. *See* Absorption costing
Transaction-based accounting. *See* Activity-based costing
    inventories affected by, 131–32
Transfer pricing. *See* Decentralization
Transferred-in costs, 547–48
Treasurer, controller *versus*, 18
Tredup, W., 137
Turk, W. T., 506
Turney, P. B. B., 473
Turnover
    capital, 379
    inventory, 177

Unadjusted rate-of-return model. *See* Accounting rate-of-return (ARR) model
Unallocated costs, 338, 339, 340
Unavoidable costs, 173–76
Uncontrollable costs, 337
Underapplied overhead, 509, 589
Unfavorable expense variances, 288–89
Unit costs, 130, 224
    misuse of, 170
    variable and fixed, 576–77

Units-of-production depreciation, 657
Usage variance, 300–302

Vail, Curtis F., 343
Value-added cost, 144
Value chain, 13–15
    drivers across, 41
    management influences on cost behavior and, 85
Value engineering, 188
Value, residual, 620, 657
Vander Schaaf, Mary Beth, 46
Variable budgets. *See* Flexible budgets
Variable cost, 179
Variable costing, 41–42, 572–73, 574. *See* Contribution approach
    absorption costing *versus*, 570–75
    flexible-budget variances and, 582–83
    income statement under, 574
    Northern Telecom, 575
    reasons for using, 580–82
    reconciliation, 579–80
    relevant range and, 43
    standard-cost variance and, 583–84
Variable-cost percentage. *See* Variable-cost ratio
Variable-cost pool, 457–58
Variable-cost pricing, 371–72
Variable-cost ratio, 55
Variable costs, 44, 574
    cost prediction and, 89
    fixed costs *versus*, 170–72
Variable overhead, 510–11
Variable-overhead costs, 576, 589
Variable-overhead efficiency variance, 303
Variable-overhead spending variance, 303
Variable unit costs, 576–77
Variances, 288, 293–305
    activity-level, 291
    favorable expense, 289
    fixed-overhead flexible-budget, 582, 583
    flexible-budget, 294, 582–83, 584, 588, 589
        effects of inventories, 302
        from material and labor standards, 299–300
        price and usage variances, 300–302
    investigation of, 298
    isolating causes of, 293
    master budget, 288–89
    overhead, 303–5
    performance reports and, 10, 11
    price, 300–302
    production-volume, 573–74, 577, 582, 583
        comparisons with other variances, 587–89
    proration of, 583
    sales-activity, 294–95
    standard-cost, 583–84
    trade-offs among, 297
    unfavorable expense, 288–89
    usage, 300–302
Verifiability. *See* Objectivity
Vick, Ralph, 249
Visual-fit method, 97
Volume variance (production-volume variance). *See* Variances

WA. *See* Weighted-average (WA) process-costing method
Wald, M., 223
Wall Street Journal, 340, 740, 760
Washington Business, 76
Watson, Ray, 569
Weighted-average (WA) process-costing method, 544, 545, 547
Weiss, Dan, 371
Welch, Larry O., 223
Wissinger, R., 137
Woodland Park Company example, 465–67
Woods, Tiger, 365
Work-in-process inventory, 130, 131, 132
Work-in-Process Inventory account, 501
    proration and, 510
Write-off, immediate, 509–10

Young, D., 189

Zafar, Alahassane Diallon, 343
Zahler, R., 219

INDEX OF COMPANIES

Aetna, 366
Airborne Express, 376–77
Air France, 366
Alcoa, 28
Allen-Bradley Co., 336
Allstate, 334
American Airlines, 39, 214
America West, 80, 81, 113
Ameritech Corporation, 346–47
Amtrak, 174, 441–42
A&P, 124–25
Apple Computer, 334, 369
Arkansas Blue Cross Blue Shield (ABCBS), 145
AT&T, 122, 123–24, 146, 161–62, 219, 334, 380, 692
AT&T Universal Card Services, 332

Baldwin, 56
Best Buy Computers, 568, 569
Best Western Motel, 65
BMW, 231–32
Boeing Company, 4, 14, 32, 38, 39–40, 166, 213, 216, 351
Borg-Warner, 136, 264, 570–71
Briggs & Stratton, 732
British Airways, 39
BT North America, 219

Caterpiller, Inc., 190, 296
Champion International Corporation, 21, 334
Chevron, 219
Chrysler Corporation, 46, 56, 149, 189, 190, 214, 346, 500
Citicorp, 213, 335
Coca-Cola Company, 380, 400
ConAgra, Inc., 68, 232

Continental Airlines, Inc., 71, 203
Corning, 336
Costco, 194, 198
CSX, 380
Culp, Inc., 189

Daihatsu Motor Company, 261
Deere & Co., 60
Deer Valley Lodge, 404, 405–6, 445–46
Dell Computer Corporation, 13, 452,
    453–54, 490–91, 498, 499–500, 508,
    511–13, 525
Digital Equipment, 219
Dillards, 569
Disney, Walt, Company, 202–3
Dow Chemical Company, 218, 264, 474, 475
DuPont de Nemours, E. I., Company, 367

Eagle-Gypsum Products Company, 549
Eastman Kodak Company, 71, 219, 439,
    440
Electronic Data Systems, 219
Elgin Sweeper Company, 137
Embassy Suites Hotel, 238
Equitable, 366
Exxon, 234

FMC, 380
Ford Motor Company, 28, 85–86, 111–12,
    189, 346
Foundation Health Systems, Inc. (FHS), 326,
    327–28, 356
Frito-Lay, 562–63
Frontier Airlines, 238–39

GE Information Services, 219
General Dynamics, 220–21
General Electric (GE), 16, 28, 43, 180,
    216–17, 224, 358, 381, 435
General Mills, 65, 214, 300
General Motors Corporation (GM), 25
Georgia-Pacific, 229–30
Grace, W. R., & Co., 251
Grand Canyon Railway, The, 164, 165–66,
    181, 203–4
Gulf Oil, 373

Hambley's Toy Store, 195
Harley-Davidson, 506
Hertz, 85
Hewlett-Packard Company, 22, 75–76, 100,
    124, 473, 531–32

Honda, 28
Hughes Aircraft Company, 90

Iberia Airlines, 366
IBM, 216, 219, 340
Inland Steel, 28
Integrated Financial Management System
    (IFMS), 355
ITT Automotive, 188–90
Izzo Systems, 75

Jaguar, 46
Johnson & Johnson, 367

Kawasaki, 22
Kellog's, 4
Kmart, 177, 569
Kraft, 707

L.A. Darling Store Fixtures, 568, 569–70,
    598–99
La Brasserie, 76–77
Lands' End, 194
London Suite, 242

McDonald's Corporation, 15, 286, 287–88
Mainz Corporation, 231
Marietta Corporation, 86–87
Marks & Spencer, 32
Marmon Group, Inc., The, 3–4, 16, 34
Marriott Corporation, 236–37
MascoTech, 56
Maxx, T.J., 569
Mazda Motor Corporation, 28, 85, 111
MBNA America, 347
MCI, 219
Mercedes-Benz, 188, 190
Morgan, J. P., & Co., 219
Moscow Cable Company, 336

Nally and Gibson Georgetown, Inc., 534,
    535–36, 537–39, 562
Newsweek, 659
Nike, Inc., 33, 276, 364, 365–66, 399
Nissan, 346
Northern Telecom, 575
Northwestern Computers, 89–90

Outboard Marine Corporation, 45

Peace Corps, 347
Penney, JC, Co., 459, 569

Penril DataComm, 342
Pepsico Co., 20, 367
Perceptron, Inc., 343
Pfizer, 20
Photon Technology International, Inc., 255
Procter & Gamble, 189, 190, 337, 367
Providence Hospital, 28
Public Service Electric & Gas, 265

Quaker Oats, 380

Rice University, 439–40
Ritz-Carlton, 248, 249–50, 262, 263, 289
Rochester Instrument Systems, Inc., 2
Rockwell, 32
Rolls-Royce, 46

Saab, 46
Sabena, 366
Safeway, 166
Sam's Club, 198
Schrader Bellows, 471–73
Sony, 42
South Central Bell, 124
South China Airlines, 366
Southern Pacific Railroad (SP), 486
Sprint, 219
SStanford University, 7
Starbucks Coffee Company, 212, 213, 243
Stern Stewart & Co., 380
Sun Microsystem, 219

Target, 177
TECHNICON, 9
Teva Pharmaceutical Industries Ltd.,
    370–71
Texas Instruments, 196, 722–23
Toyota, 22

Unilever, 219
United Airlines, 39, 44, 213
United Parcel Service (UPS), 376, 377
University of Florida, 213
Upjohn, Inc., 337

Wal-Mart, 166, 177, 180, 569
Watkins Products, 41
Western Area Power Authority (WAPA),
    332
Weyerhauser Company, 91

Xerox, 22, 439–40